Vital Records of
TUFTONBORO
and
BROOKFIELD
New Hampshire

1888-2005

Richard P. Roberts

HERITAGE BOOKS
2007

HERITAGE BOOKS

AN IMPRINT OF HERITAGE BOOKS, INC.

Books, CDs, and more—Worldwide

For our listing of thousands of titles see our website
at
www.HeritageBooks.com

Published 2007 by
HERITAGE BOOKS, INC.
Publishing Division
65 East Main Street
Westminster, Maryland 21157-5026

International Standard Book Number: 978-0-7884-4328-3

TABLE OF CONTENTS

INTRODUCTION

Early vital records of many New Hampshire towns can be located either through the State's Vital Records Department or on microfilms made available through LDS Family History Centers. Some, however, have been lost or are inaccessible for various reasons. A valuable, but labor intensive, source of information for events occurring in 1887 and thereafter is the vital statistics which are provided in a section of the Annual Town Reports of many New Hampshire towns. Many of these town reports have been collected at the New Hampshire State Library in Concord, as well as more local repositories.

The amount of information published in these Annual Town Reports varies tremendously over time. Early records are far more detailed and comprehensive. Recent records are rather cursory, but issues of confidentiality and sensitivity to the privacy of those residents still living offsets the lack of information of genealogical value.

While the information provided is often very helpful, one must remember that it is not fool-proof or universally accurate, nor is it the primary source or the actual vital record itself. The fact that much of the data is self-reported suggests that it is reliable. However, errors in transcription, spelling (particularly with respect to French-Canadian and European families), and printing often are obvious. In addition, there may be, for example, two children listed as the third child of a particular couple, or the mother's maiden name, age or place of birth may differ or may be inconsistent from one entry to another. It is also important to note that a birth, marriage or death may have been reported in another town, quite likely Wolfeboro, although the subject resided in Tuftonboro or Brookfield, or the entry may not have been made in the first place.

Despite these shortcomings, the information contained in the Annual Town Reports can be a valuable tool for the genealogist. Marriage and death records from the late 1800's often identify parents who were married nearly a century before. Finally, those families that have remained in Tuftonboro, Brookfield or adjacent towns for several generations can be traced and connected to the present.

Although vital records were published in annual reports beginning in 1887, those for Tuftonboro between 1887 and 1889 and for Brookfield for 1887 have not been located

Births - To the extent the information is available, the entries in the list of births are given as follows: child's name; date of birth; place of birth (where provided); the number of children in the family; father's name, place of birth, age and occupation; and the mother's maiden name, age and place of birth. As noted above, the amount of information in earlier records is substantially greater than in more recent years.

At times, the given names of many children are missing from the early reports. In this case, the sex of the child is given and they are listed chronologically at the beginning of the surname heading. On occasion, the child's name can be determined from marriage or death records, as well as secondary sources. These names are shown in brackets where available.

Marriages - To the extent the information is available, the entries in the list of marriages follow this format: groom's name; groom's residence; bride's name; bride's residence; date of marriage; place of marriage (where provided); H, signifying husband's information, and W, signifying wife's information, each in the following order - age, occupation, number of the marriage (if other than first), father's name, father's place of birth, father's occupation, mother's name, mother's place of birth, and mother's occupation. The name of the official conducting the marriage has been omitted but is generally provided in the original document. A separate listing of brides in alphabetical order follows this section in order to allow for cross-referencing.

Deaths - To the extent available, the entries in the list of deaths contain the following information: name of decedent; place of death; date of death; age at death; cause of death; marital status; birthplace; father's name; father's place of birth; mother's name; and mother's place of birth. Most of the entries listing a cause of death are self-explanatory.

TUFTONBORO
BIRTHS

ADJUTANT,

daughter, b. 8/1/1891 in Tuftonboro; fifth; Willie W. Adjutant (farmer, 32, Tuftonboro) and Eliza J. Piper (30, Tuftonboro)

son, b. 1/4/1902 in Tuftonboro; first; Charles L. Adjutant (carpenter, 39, Tuftonboro) and Lena I. Eaton (23, Brookfield)

Cody Matthew, b. 9/4/1999 in N. Conway; Matthew Adjutant and Deana Adjutant

Elizabeth Jane, b. 5/7/1940 in Wolfeboro; second; Roscoe Varney Adjutant (sch. bus driver, 42, Tuftonboro) and Blanch Evelyn Perkins (housewife, 40, Tamworth); residence – Ctr. Tuftonboro

Emily Krystine, b. 8/9/2004 in Wolfeboro; Eric Adjutant and Katie Adjutant

Eva M., b. 5/6/1903 in Tuftonboro; fourth; Leonard C. Adjutant (carpenter, 40, Tuftonboro) and Lena L. Eaton (24, Brookfield)

Leora, b. 9/17/1902 in Tuftonboro; ninth; William W. Adjutant (farmer, 43, Tuftonboro) and Eliza J. Piper (41, Tuftonboro)

Patricia Ann, b. 12/13/1950 in Wolfeboro; second; Raymond M. Adjutant (laborer, Tuftonboro) and Helen P. Dougherty (Chester, PA); residence – Ctr. Tuftonboro

Roscoe V., b. 3/8/1898 in Tuftonboro; seventh; Willie W. Adjutant (farmer, 38, Tuftonboro) and Eliza J. Piper (36, Tuftonboro)

ALBEE,

Abigail, b. 12/5/1975 in Laconia; William L. Albee and Pamela G. Devork

ALLARD,

Lillian Faith, b. 7/7/2005 in Wolfeboro; Bert Allard and Sara Trudnak

ALLEN,

Oliver R., b. 10/7/1913; first; George W. Allen (farmer, Albany) and Etta E. Libby (Tuftonboro)

AMES,

Angel Michelle May, b. 2/1/2005 in Wolfeboro; Cory Ames and Erika Mata

Jonathan David, b. 4/1/1996 in Wolfeboro; James Ronald Ames and Laura Lee Van Tassel

ANDERSEN,
Steven William, b. 3/22/1980 in Wolfeboro; William D. Andersen and
   Anna S. Brendle

ANDERSON,
Hannah Nichole, b. 6/1/2003 in Wolfeboro; Nicholas Anderson and
   Christina Anderson
Thomas Travis, b. 5/10/1989 in Wolfeboro; Dana Mark Anderson
   and Jeri Jo Olsen

ANTONUCCI,
Thomas William, b. 8/2/1978 in Wolfeboro; William Antonucci and
   Mary Hunter
William Zachary, b. 1/25/1980 in Wolfeboro; William Antonucci and
   Mary Hunter

APPLETON,
Robin Elizabeth, b. 10/26/1970 in Wolfeboro; Paul M. Appleton (MA)
   and Carol A. Johnson (MA)
Scott Thomas, b. 12/7/1972 in Wolfeboro; Paul M. Appleton and
   Carol Ann Johnson

ARION,
Cherilynn Elizabeth, b. 4/25/2002 in Lebanon; Michael Arion and
   Lisa Arion

AUSTIN,
Dale Albert, Jr., b. 5/11/1973 in Wolfeboro; Dale Albert Austin and
   Sandra Lee Parsons
David Brian, b. 10/14/1960 in Wolfeboro; thirteenth; David B. Austin
   (laborer, VT) and Nellie MacCreighton (NH)
Stephanie Anne, b. 7/4/1982 in Wolfeboro; David B. Austin and
   Heidi Luken

AVERY,
Jade Louise, b. 12/11/1991 in Wolfeboro; William G. Avery and
   Micheline M. H. Fafard

AYERS,
son, b. 8/10/1891 in Tuftonboro; fourth; Charles Ayers (farmer, 45,
   Tuftonboro) and Sarah J. Canney (40, Tuftonboro)

daughter, b. 4/11/1904 in Tuftonboro; first; Herbert Ayers (farmer, 27, Tuftonboro) and Ina M. Adjutant (17, Tuftonboro)
daughter, b. 11/4/1906; third; Herbert Ayers (farmer, 29, Tuftonboro) and Ina M. Adjutant (19, Tuftonboro)
son, b. 5/20/1908; fourth; Herbert Ayers (farmer, 31, Tuftonboro) and Ina W. Adjutant (21, Tuftonboro)
son, b. 4/30/1913; seventh; Herbert Ayers (farmer, Tuftonboro) and Mabel Adjutant (Tuftonboro)
Florence Irene, b. 11/12/1940 in Wolfeboro; second; Levi Langdon Ayers (laborer, 48, Tuftonboro) and Ruth Evelyn Champaigne (housewife, 30, Wolfeboro)

BABALIS,
Steven John, b. 7/21/1984 in Dover; Steven R. Babalis and Sandra Ann Gunn

BAGG,
Nicholas Evan, b. 9/12/1986 in Laconia; Richard A. Bagg and Mary E. Konigsberg

BALSER,
Brandon Michael, b. 12/20/1987 in Wolfeboro; Danny Lee Balser and Diane V. Bye

BAMBERGER,
Laurie Maeve, b. 6/27/1964 in Wolfeboro; first; Craig S. Bamberger (student, Selma, AL) and Sheila L. MacDonald (San Francisco, CA); residence – Selma, AL

BANFIELD,
Rita, b. 10/4/1930 in Wolfeboro; fourth; Fred Banfield (farmer, 31, Franklin) and Meleda Desharnais (33, Sherbrooke, PQ)

BARNES,
Gertrude E., b. 10/13/1902 in Tuftonboro; first; Charles W. Barnes (farmer, 37, Hiram, ME) and Bertha M. Ayers (19, Tuftonboro)
Nikulaus James, b. 9/22/2005 in Concord; Andrew Barnes and Christina Barnes

BARTLETT,
daughter, b. 8/29/1891 in Tuftonboro; fifth; Clifton J. Bartlett (farmer, 30, Manchester) and Emma E. Fernald (32, Tuftonboro)

BATCHELDER,
Deborah Anne, b. 9/4/1956 in Wolfeboro; first; Rockwood M. Batchelder (chiropractor, Meredith) and Minnie C. Johnson (Concord)

BATEMAN,
Robert LeRoy, b. 3/13/1938 in Wolfeboro; fourth; John Newell Bateman (sawyer, 27, Pittsfield) and Helen Ruth Corliss (24, Northwood)

BATTLES,
Arthur Jason, b. 1/21/1978 in Wolfeboro; Robert M. Battles and Mary E. Nason

BAXTER,
Ann Christine, b. 6/1/1933 in Wolfeboro; second; George P. Baxter (farmer, 28, Providence, RI) and Priscilla West (housewife, 28, Ctr. Tuftonboro); residence – Ctr. Tuftonboro
Helen May, b. 2/25/1935 in Wolfeboro; third; George P. Baxter (farmer, 30, Providence, RI) and Priscilla C. West (housewife, 30, Tuftonboro); residence – Ctr. Tuftonboro

BEAN,
daughter, b. 12/29/1891 in Tuftonboro; fifth; James F. Bean (farmer, 39, Tuftonboro) and Mary F. Bean (35, Tuftonboro)
son, b. 4/29/1892 in Tuftonboro; eighth; Willie L. Bean (farmer, 31, Tuftonboro) and Ula D. Foss (30, Tuftonboro)
son, b. 9/6/1893 in Tuftonboro; first; Silas W. Bean (farmer, 38, Tuftonboro) and Cora A. Bean (32, Saco, ME)
daughter, b. 3/23/1894; ninth; Willie L. Bean (farmer, Tuftonboro) and Ula D. Foss (Tuftonboro)
son, b. 9/21/1894; James F. Bean (farmer, Tuftonboro) and Mary F. Bean (Tuftonboro)
daughter, b. 6/30/1896 in Tuftonboro; tenth; Willie F. Bean (farmer, 35, Tuftonboro) and Ula D. Foss (34, Tuftonboro)
daughter, b. 9/24/1896 in Tuftonboro; sixth; Isaiah J. Bean (farmer, 53, Tuftonboro) and Amy E. Bragg (38, Windsor, England)

daughter, b. 2/20/1897 in Tuftonboro; fifth; Silas W. Bean (farmer, 42, Tuftonboro) and Cora A. Bean (35, Saco, ME)
son, b. 11/12/1902 in Tuftonboro; tenth; Willie L. Bean (farmer, 41, Tuftonboro) and Ula Foss (41, Tuftonboro)
daughter, b. 8/14/1912; second; Arthur M. Bean (farmer, Moultonboro) and Delia Carter (Birmingham, England)
Ambrose Augustine, b. 9/4/1998 in Laconia; Daniel J. Bean and Danielle A. Augros
Delia M., b. 7/17/1899 in Tuftonboro; ninth; Willie L. Bean (farmer, 38, Tuftonboro) and Ula D. Foss (37, Tuftonboro)
Dorothy, b. 5/11/1903 in Tuftonboro; first; John W. Bean (laborer, 36, Tuftonboro) and Clara A. Horn (37, Lawrence, MA)
Frances Louise, b. 12/25/1925 in Wolfeboro; second; Ralph L. Bean (farmer, Tuftonboro) and Lura Peru Sargent (Moultonboro)
Frank John, b. 10/21/1931 in Wolfeboro; first; Frank J. Bean (laborer, 26, Tuftonboro) and Mary Bourque (21, Amesbury, MA); residence – Ctr. Tuftonboro
Gertrude, b. 3/8/1901 in Tuftonboro; third; Isaiah J. Bean (farmer, 58, Tuftonboro) and Amy E. Bragg (43, England)
James Allen, b. 8/30/1966 in Wolfeboro; second; Melvin D. Bean (electrician, Amesbury, MA) and Donna L. Auger (Lynn, MA)
Juliette Marien, b. 11/23/1999 in Concord; Daniel Bean and Danielle Bean
Laurie Ann, b. 8/15/1979 in Wolfeboro; Melvin D. Bean and Donna Lee Auger
Leon Edgar, b. 2/27/1928 in Tuftonboro; third; Ralph L. Bean (farmer, Tuftonboro) and Lura P. Sargent (housewife, Moultonboro)
Louisa C., b. 2/11/1894 in; first; Isaiah J. Bean (farmer, Tuftonboro) and Amy S. Bragg (Windsor, England)
Michael Edward, b. 12/16/1972 in Rochester; Edward A. Bean and Linda L. Biehl
Michele Lynnette, b. 11/5/1975 in Rochester; Edward A. Bean and Linda Lee Biehl
Milton L. H., b. 7/24/1906; first; Arthur M. Bean (farmer, 38, Tuftonboro) and Delia A. Carter (35, Bimington, England)
Richard Errol, b. 10/14/1943 in Wolfeboro; Leon Isaac Bean (lumberman, Henniker) and Barbara Eloise Bean (E. Jaffrey)
Robert Ellsworth, b. 9/9/1932 in Wolfeboro; second; Frank Bean (laborer, Tuftonboro) and Mary Bourque (22, Amesbury, MA)

BENNETT,
daughter, b. 10/22/1916; fifth; Maurice P. Bennett (farmer, Tuftonboro) and Annie Kidd (Fifeshire, Scotland)

Alice G., b. 11/8/1917; third; Frank S. Bennett (laborer, Tuftonboro) and Eleanor G. Dawes (Boston, MA)

Brian Dennis, b. 9/9/1972 in Wolfeboro; Paul M. Bennett and Norma Jean Emack

Donald C., b. 5/21/1911; second; Maurice P. Bennett (farmer, 27, Tuftonboro) and Annie Kidd (24, Scotland)

Dorothy F., b. 8/29/1912; first; Frank S. Bennett (carpenter, Tuftonboro) and Eleanor Dawes (Boston, MA)

James, b. 6/17/1916; second; Frank S. Bennett (farmer, Tuftonboro) and Eleanor G. Dawes (Boston, MA)

James Douglas, b. 11/18/1970 in Wolfeboro; Paul M. Bennett (NH) and Norma J. Emack (NH)

Janet E., b. 5/29/1910; first; Maurice P. Bennett (farmer, Tuftonboro) and Annie Kidd (Scotland)

John S., b. 11/1/1914; fourth; Maurice P. Bennett (farmer, Tuftonboro) and Annie Kidd (Gottotown, Scotland)

Paul Mark, b. 11/12/1946 in Wolfeboro; second; Douglass L. Bennett (carpenter, Tuftonboro) and Marjorie Louise Porter (Moultonboro)

Ralph V., b. 4/29/1895 in Tuftonboro; first; Orsino V. Bennett (farmer, 31, Tuftonboro) and Lizzie M. Gannon (21, Ireland)

Ruth F. C., b. 10/23/1891 in Tuftonboro; fifth; James A. Bennett (farmer, 44, Tuftonboro) and Frances E. Fernald (42, Tuftonboro)

Thea Anne, b. 11/28/1941 in Wolfeboro; first; Douglas Levin Bennett (laborer, 29, Tuftonboro) and Marjorie Louise Porter (housewife, 27, Moultonboro)

BENSON,
son, b. 1/25/1953 in Wolfeboro; sixth; Ronald K. Benson (carpenter, ME) and Norma E. Malloy (MA); residence – Mirror Lake

Darlene Ann, b. 5/21/1948 in Wolfeboro; fourth; Ronald K. Benson (carpenter, Newfield, ME) and Norma L. Malloy (Lynn, MA)

Robert Keith, b. 3/28/1950 in Wolfeboro; fifth; Ronald K. Benson (carpenter, Newfield, ME) and Norma E. Malloy (Lynn, MA)

Steven Charles, b. 4/13/1954 in Wolfeboro; seventh; Ronald H. Benson (sand blasting, ME) and Norma E. Malloy (MA)

BERNASCONI,
Jaran Todd, b. 10/9/1993 in Laconia; Todd R. Bernasconi and
Jennifer R. Keefe

BERNIER,
Renee Nicole, b. 1/29/1992 in Wolfeboro; Peter M. Bernier and
Renee Bender

BERRY,
Alyssa Marie, b. 10/9/1993 in Wolfeboro; Steven D. Berry and
Wendy Lynn Warren
Harold S., b. 5/23/1912; third; Nathaniel L. Berry, Jr. (physician,
Lynn, MA) and Josephine Smith (Guelph, ON)
Tanner Dean, b. 1/18/1997 in Wolfeboro; Steven Dean Berry and
Wendy Lynn Warren

BEVILACQUA,
Madison Paige, b. 10/31/2005 in Wolfeboro; Ralph Bevilacqua and
Nichole Bevilacqua

BICKERTON,
Ann, b. 1/31/1998 in Wolfeboro; Jason J. Bickerton and Heidi Ann
Holand
Fisher John, b. 3/16/2000 in Wolfeboro; Jason Bickerton and Heidi
Bickerton

BICKFORD,
Elizabeth Anne, b. 12/22/1959 in Wolfeboro; Jackson S. Bickford
(cabin manager, MA) and Grace M. Hanscom (MA)
June Ellen, b. 4/2/1946 in Wolfeboro; first; Jackson Sam Bickford
(photography, Salem, MA) and Grace Hanscom (Worcester,
MA)
Ronald Charles, b. 8/18/1948 in Wolfeboro; second; Jackson S.
Bickford (manager, Salem, MA) and Grace M. Hanscom
(Worcester, MA)

BISBEE,
son, b. 3/20/1900 in Tuftonboro; first; Archer C. Bisbee (farmer, 25,
Effingham) and Addie M. Libby (22, Tuftonboro)
daughter, b. 6/1/1901 in Tuftonboro; second; Arthur Bisbie (farmer,
25, Effingham) and Addie M. Libbie (23, Tuftonboro)

daughter, b. 7/31/1910; third; Harrie E. Bisbee (blacksmith) and
Ethel M. Rand (Randolph)
Clyde Emery, b. 5/13/1926; first; Arthur H. Bisbee (farmer, 26,
Tuftonboro) and Maud E. Emery (41, Tuftonboro)
Lillian F., b. 9/22/1925 in Tuftonboro; first; Wilbur Bisbee (mail
carrier, Wolfeboro) and Beula Abbott (Ossipee)

BLACK,
Carey Jean, b. 8/14/1985 in Rochester; Wayne A. Black and Marilyn
J. Ott
Jason Daniel, b. 10/25/1978 in Rochester; Wayne A. Black and
Marilyn J. Ott

BLAIR-TERRIBLE,
Tyler Avery, b. 8/8/1995 in Wolfeboro; Christopher G. Terrible and
Sally Blair

BLAKE,
Tyler Jon, b. 1/3/1974 in Wolfeboro; Norman T. Blake and Janet E.
Ramsbotham

BLANCHETTE,
Andrea Maralee, b. 5/15/1991 in Wolfeboro; Timothy P. Blanchette
and Barbara G. Frampton
Erin Frances, b. 3/11/1994 in Tuftonboro; Timothy Paul Blanchette
and Barbara Garold Frampton

BOARDMAN,
Evelyn M., b. 6/7/1921; first; Forest E. Boardman (farmer, Camden,
ME) and Ada M. Wentworth (Tuftonboro)

BODGE,
daughter, b. 1/4/1912; second; Walter C. Bodge (farmer, Tuftonboro)
and Maud Hanson (Ossipee)
daughter, b. 1/4/1912; third; Walter C. Bodge (farmer, Tuftonboro)
and Maud Hanson (Ossipee)

BOLTON,
Linda Joyce, b. 8/1/1943 in Wolfeboro; second; Richard Elliot Bolton
(lumberman, Concord) and Joyce Gertrude Brown (Concord)

BONENFANT,
Abigail Bridget, b. 1/25/2002 in Rochester; Andrew Bonenfant and Patricia Bonenfant

BORELLI,
Anthony Carmen, b. 8/20/1998 in Wolfeboro; Philip A. Borelli and Catherine J. Kiah
Gianna Catherine, b. 4/26/2005 in Wolfeboro; Philip Borelli and Catherine Borelli
Kiah Marie, b. 7/20/2002 in Wolfeboro; Philip Borelli and Catherine Borelli
Philip Anthony, b. 5/9/2000 in Wolfeboro; Philip Borelli and Catherine Borelli

BOUTCHER,
Jamie Scott, b. 8/30/1969 in Wolfeboro; James W. Boutcher (MA) and Patricia A. Conrad (MA)

BOWER,
Megan Lynn, b. 7/1/1983 in Concord; Richard H. Bower, Jr. and Elizabeth A. Bobbette

BRADEAU,
daughter, b. 6/15/1921; second; Joseph S. Bradeau (farmer, NB) and Mary M. Emery (Tuftonboro)

BREWER,
Pamela Joan, b. 1/27/1947 in Wolfeboro; second; Winfield G. Brewer (store manager, Grand Rapids, MI) and Natalie Anna Brookes (Boston, MA)

BRITTON,
William Harry, b. 2/2/1960 in Wolfeboro; first; Harry V. Britton (lumberman, NH) and Carrie Taylor (NH)

BROOKS,
daughter, b. 10/11/1913; fifth; Walter E. Brooks (clergyman, England) and Alice E. Harding (England)
daughter, b. 1/25/1920; first; A. A. Brooks (brakeman, Boston, MA) and Cecile F. Burk (Boston, MA); residence – Lawrence, MA

BROUSSEAU,

Matthew Foster, b. 10/16/1997 in Lebanon; Andrew Alan Brousseau and Andrea Lee Picard

BROWN,

daughter, b. 2/15/1892 in Tuftonboro; first; Charles H. Brown (farmer, Tuftonboro) and Katie E. Abbott (Ossipee)

daughter, b. 2/15/1892 in Tuftonboro; second; Charles H. Brown (farmer, Tuftonboro) and Katie E. Abbott (Ossipee)

son, b. 6/1/1905 in Tuftonboro; Charles H. Brown (farmer, 44, Tuftonboro) and Katie E. Abbott (32, Ossipee)

Ashley Anne, b. 9/12/1990 in Wolfeboro; Michael A. Brown and Lesa M. Cozzie

Bernard N., b. 9/5/1895 in Tuftonboro; third; Charles H. Brown (farmer, 32, Tuftonboro) and Katie C. Abbott (22, Ossipee)

Marjorie Ann, b. 12/10/1934 in Wolfeboro; third; George H. Brown (farmer, 33, Campton) and Nellie Morris (housewife, 32, England); residence – Ctr. Tuftonboro

Matthew M., b. 4/17/1992 in Wolfeboro; Michael A. Brown and Lesa M. Cozzie

BROWNELL,

Linden Carter, b. 1/3/1941 in Wolfeboro; second; Harold Parker Brownell (helper, sawmill, 25, Effingham) and Evelyn Rose Banfill (housewife, 19, S. Berwick, ME)

Patricia Anne, b. 8/21/1943 in Wolfeboro; fourth; Harold Parker Brownell (farmer, Effingham) and Evelyn Rose Banfill (S. Berwick, ME)

Ralph Wayne, b. 9/25/1942 in Wolfeboro; second; Harold Parker Brownell (farmer, Effingham) and Evelyn Rose Banfill (S. Berwick, ME)

BULLIS,

Russell Hathaway, Jr., b. 7/26/1972 in Wolfeboro; Russell H. Bullis and Marcia A. Parker

BUNCE,

son, b. 10/30/1914; fourth; Charles E. Bunce (laborer, Dover) and Catherine Winters (Ireland)

BURBANK,
Abaigeal Ciar, b. 8/7/1983 in Tuftonboro; Paul H. Burbank and Diane
    M. Mucher
Brie Hope, b. 8/6/1981 in Tuftonboro; Paul H. Burbank and Diane M.
    Mucher

BURKE,
Jared Russell, b. 9/27/1978 in Laconia; Frank W. Burke and Virginia
    A. Chesley
Jeremiah Chesley, b. 4/10/1976 in Laconia; Frank W. Burke and
    Virginia A. Chesley
Joshua Weston, b. 12/28/1973 in Wolfeboro; Frank W. Burke and
    Virginia A. Chesley

BURLEIGH,
Wilma R., b. 8/23/1916; third; William C. Burleigh (farmer, Portland,
    ME) and Jane E. McRae (ON)

BUSH,
Jonathan William, b. 11/12/1986 in Wolfeboro; Steven S. Bush and
    Carol Ann Moody
Polly Cecilia, b. 8/30/1984 in Wolfeboro; Steven S. Bush and Carol
    Moody

BUSHEY,
Kyle Jeffrey, b. 2/21/1991 in Plymouth; Jeffrey A. Bushey and
    Christine L. Boyd
Megan Lynn, b. 11/30/1992 in Plymouth; James D. Bushey and
    Denise E. Martin

BUSHMAN,
Alison Valeria, b. 2/22/1966 in Wolfeboro; fourth; Richard J.
    Bushman (carpenter, Wolfeboro) and Olivia A. Ridnour (Detroit,
    MI)
Barbara Marie, b. 1/30/1945 in Wolfeboro; third; Robert John
    Bushman (US Army, Lynn, MA) and Faye Lillian Eldridge
    (Rochester); residence – Ctr. Tuftonboro
Richard John, b. 7/14/1940 in Wolfeboro; second; Robert John
    Bushman (gardener, 30, Lynn, MA) and Faye Lillian Eldridge
    (private estate, 22, Rochester)

Robert Joseph, b. 2/17/1963 in Wolfeboro; second; Richard J. Bushman (tree surgeon, Wolfeboro) and Olivia A. Ridnour (Detroit, MI)

Thomas Orville, b. 5/20/1964 in Wolfeboro; third; Richard J. Bushman (carpenter, Wolfeboro) and Olivia A. Ridnour (Detroit, MI)

BUSSIERE,
Thomas Jeffrey, b. 11/25/2002 in Wolfeboro; Thomas Bussiere and April Bussiere

BUTTRICK,
Ami Lynn, b. 11/5/1991 in Conway; Daniel C. Buttrick and Stephanie A. Chandler

CAIL,
Haley Elizabeth, b. 9/15/1992 in Tuftonboro; Joseph J. Cail and Lynda Ann Seaman

CANNIFF,
Justin Arthur, b. 8/6/1982 in Wolfeboro; William F. Canniff, Jr. and Darlene J. Libby

CANTWELL,
Glenn Cameron, b. 9/16/1956 in Wolfeboro; first; Bruce D. Cantwell (tire & rubber co., Lowell, MA) and Ramona A. Stevens (Wolfeboro); residence – OH

CARLETON,
Michael William, b. 6/4/1970 in Wolfeboro; Robert H. Carleton (MA) and Cheryl A. Joubert (MA)

CARPENTER,
Jane Louise, b. 6/1/1931 in Wolfeboro; third; Louis J. Carpenter (mechanic, 42, MA) and Beatrice McKean (25, MA); residence – Mirror Lake

Kyle Robert, b. 4/17/1994 in Dover; Ralph Allen Carpenter and Paula Jean Buckley

Leo Alfred, b. 5/18/1930 in Wolfeboro; second; Louis Joseph Carpenter (caretaker & repairman, 42, Marlboro, MA) and Beatrice McKean (housewife, 24, Easton, MA)

Samantha Marie, b. 8/30/1998 in Dover; Ralph Carpenter and Paula Buckley

CARTER,
Davlyn Brooke, b. 10/28/1983 in Wolfeboro; David F. Carter and Kelly L. Fogg

CASH,
Braden Alexander, b. 7/14/2005 in Wolfeboro; Matthew Cash and Carrie Bunnell

CASS,
Rodney Frank, b. 8/1/1932 in Laconia; first; Henry Woodmancy (laborer, 28) and Pearl Eleanor Cass (waitress, 21, Weirs); residence of father – Mirror Lake; residence of mother – Weirs

CATALANO,
Daniel James, b. 7/13/1992 in rx; Bart A. Catalano and Kathryn Anne Catalano

CAVERLY,
Beatrice L., b. 7/1/1908; first; Arthur L. Caverly (merchant, 25, Moultonboro) and Emma L. Lamprey (22, Moultonboro)
Gardner A., b. 8/2/1910; second; Arthur L. Caverly (merchant, Moultonboro) and Emma L. Lamprey (Moultonboro)

CHAMBERLAIN,
Mathew Scott, b. 12/26/1968 in Rochester; James E. Chamberlain (NH) and Charlotte E. Glidden (NH)

CHASE,
Daniel Owen, b. 8/30/1977 in Wolfeboro; David O. Chase and Arlene G. Nesbitt

CHELLMAN,
Isaac Christopher, b. 2/11/1980 in Wolfeboro; Chester E. Chellman III and Jerildine M. Rines
Joseph James, b. 5/3/1977 in Wolfeboro; Chester E. Chellman III and Jerildine M. Rines

CHENEY,
daughter, b. 4/2/1913; second; Wyatt D. Cheney (farmer, Dickinson Ctr., NY) and Mattie L. Stokes (Tuftonboro)
daughter, b. 5/16/1913; fourth; George M. Cheney (clergyman, Dickinson Ctr., NY) and Ella F. Stevens (Hopkinton, NY)
son, b. 5/1/1915; fifth; George M. Cheney (Dickinson Ctr., NY) and Ella F. Stevens (Hampton, RI)
daughter, b. 5/12/1918; fifth; Wyatt D. Cheney (farmer, Dickenson Ctr., NY) and Mattie L. Stokes (Tuftonboro)
son, b. 11/7/1921; seventh; Wyatt D. Cheney (laborer, Dickinson Ctr., NY) and Mattie L. Stokes (Tuftonboro)
daughter, b. 5/7/1938 in Wolfeboro; second; Earl Lorenzo Cheney (roller-sawmill, 23, Tuftonboro) and Isabelle Louise Moore (19, Skowhegan, ME)
Benzie Frederick, b. 10/30/1946 in Wolfeboro; first; Raymond E. Cheney (woodsman, Tuftonboro) and Hattie Wade Jones (Tamworth)
Brenda Susan, b. 12/13/1944 in Wolfeboro; second; John Gordon Cheney (farmer, Ellensburg D., NY) and Edna Susan Young (Watertown, MA)
Cindy June, b. 8/25/1961 in Wolfeboro; second; Gilbert F. Cheney (machinist, Tuftonboro) and Sandra June Ridlon (Wolfeboro)
Darlene Patricia, b. 2/12/1963 in Wolfeboro; first; Warren D. Cheney (machinist, Wolfeboro) and Evelyn I. Hlushuk (Wolfeboro)
Donald James, b. 7/2/1968 in Wolfeboro; Wayne E. Cheney (NH) and Alta L. Lawn (NH)
Earl, b. 4/3/1914; third; Wyatt D. Cheney (laborer, Dickinson Ctr., NY) and Mattie L. Stokes (Tuftonboro)
Gary Benjamin, b. 7/11/1947 in Wolfeboro; first; Ralph Benjamin Cheney (garage mech., Tuftonboro) and Pearl E. Dodge (Exeter)
George W., b. 8/9/1910; third; George M. Cheney (clergyman, Dickinson Ctr., NY) and Ella F. Stevens (Hopkinton, RI)
Gilbert Frederick, b. 7/5/1940 in Wolfeboro; second; Gordon Warren Cheney (carpenter, 29, Tuftonboro) and Violet Pember Bowen (housewife, 26, Randolph, VT)
Gordon W., b. 6/27/1911; first; Wyatt D. Cheney (laborer, 19, Dickinson Ctr., NY) and Mattie L. Stokes (23, Tuftonboro)
Jennifer Marie, b. 3/23/1978 in Wolfeboro; Sidney E. Cheney and Vicki L. Johnson

Leslie Adele, b. 8/28/1938 in Wolfeboro; first; Lillian May Cheney
(30, Ellenburg Depot, NY)
Linda May, b. 5/11/1948 in Wolfeboro; fourth; Earl L. Cheney
(sawyer, Tuftonboro) and Isabelle L. Moore (Skowhegan, ME)
Melinda, b. 10/17/1962 in Wolfeboro; third; Gilbert F. Cheney
(machinist, Wolfeboro) and Sandra J. Ridlon (Wolfeboro)
Michael David, b. 2/4/1991 in Wolfeboro; Michael G. Cheney and
Lynn Ann Roome
Norma Ann, b. 3/3/1940 in Wolfeboro; third; Earl Lorenzo Cheney
(roller, sawmill, 25, Tuftonboro) and Isabelle Louise Moore
(housekeeper, 20, Skowhegan, ME)
Randy Gordon, b. 4/26/1964 in Wolfeboro; fourth; Gilbert F. Cheney
(Tuftonboro) and Sandra J. Ridlon (Wolfeboro)
Ray Ellsworth, b. 2/27/1926; eighth; Wyatt D. Cheney (laborer, 34,
Dickinson Ctr., NY) and Mattie L. Stokes (37, Tuftonboro)
Richard Eugene, b. 6/25/1928 in Tuftonboro; ninth; Wyatt Cheney
(farmer, Dickinson Ctr., NY) and Mattie Stokes (Tuftonboro)
Richard Gordon, b. 7/19/1944 in Wolfeboro; third; Gordon Warren
Cheney (laborer, Tuftonboro) and Violet Pember Bowen
(Braintree, VT)
Ronald Wyatt, b. 3/10/1946 in Wolfeboro; first; Ralph Benjamin
Cheney (War Vet., II, Tuftonboro) and Pearl Elizabeth Dodge
(Exeter); residence – Ctr. Tuftonboro
Steven Douglas, b. 12/30/1953 in Wolfeboro; second; Raymond E.
Cheney (woodsman, NH) and Hattie W. Jones (NH); residence
– Melvin Village
Warren Dale, b. 7/7/1938 in Wolfeboro; first; Gordon Warren Cheney
(gardner, 27, Tuftonboro) and Mildred Frances Whiting (24,
Braintree, VT); residence – Melvin Village

CLIFFORD,
Walter, Jr., b. 8/23/1922; sixth; Walter H. Clifford (teamster,
Pamfrey, VT) and Edith M. Glidden (Alton)

CLINTON,
Beth Susan, b. 6/2/1972 in Laconia; Stuart K. Clinton and Judith G.
Ambrose

CLOUGH,
Barbara, b. 5/22/1930 in Tuftonboro; first; Simon T. Thompson (farmer, 45, Tuftonboro) and Alice Clough (housewife, 21, Wolfeboro)
Brittany Dawn, b. 7/1/1992 in Wolfeboro; Harold W. Clough and Tina Marie Craigue
Jennifer Lynn, b. 12/27/1973 in Wolfeboro; Russell E. Clough and Mazy Anne Rowe

COBURN-AMADIO,
Galen Ray, b. 4/4/1998 in Tuftonboro; Paul R. Amadio and Donita G. Coburn

COLBY,
son, b. 6/9/1908; first; Ralph M. Colby (mechanic, 29, Ossipee) and Ida M. Bean (24, Tuftonboro); residence – Wolfeboro
Anita Barbara, b. 2/25/1964 in Wolfeboro; third; Reginald C. Colby (construction, Wolfeboro) and Marylin E. Smith (Wolfeboro)
Penny Lee, b. 8/8/1961 in Wolfeboro; second; Reginald C. Colby (shovel operator, Wolfeboro) and Marylin Ellen Smith (Wolfeboro)
Reginald Clyde, b. 10/3/1930 in Wolfeboro; first; Howard C. Colby (truck driver, 21, Wolfeboro) and Thelma E. Drucker (23, Nashua); residence – Melvin Village
Terry June, b. 10/14/1958 in Wolfeboro; first; Reginald C. Colby (shovel operator, Wolfeboro) and Marylin E. Smith (Wolfeboro); residence – Melvin Village

COLE,
daughter, b. 8/28/1896 in Tuftonboro; first; Irvin Cole (farmer, 23, Charlestown, MA) and Evelyn Wiggin (18, Tuftonboro)
Arthur L., b. 9/2/1898 in Tuftonboro; second; Irving C. Cole (blacksmith, 25, Charlestown, MA) and Evelyn M. Wiggin (21, Tuftonboro)

COLLINS,
daughter, b. 5/20/1905 in Tuftonboro; Fred W. Collins (carpenter, 32, Laconia) and Ella M. Blaisdell (31, Tuftonboro)

CONANT,
son, b. 8/4/1914; second; Edmund B. Conant (manufacturer, Boston, MA) and Eleanor H. Worth (Orange, NJ); residence – Orange, NJ

CONLEY,
Kristen Rose, b. 5/6/1986 in Rochester; Christopher E. Conley and Lois A. DiGiuseppe

CONNOR,
stillborn daughter, b. 4/28/1894; first; Joseph H. Connor (teacher, Ossipee) and Lydia O. Wingate (Tuftonboro); residence – Ossipee

CONNORS,
John Stickney, b. 12/16/1938 in Wolfeboro; John William Connors (dairy worker, 23, New York, NY) and Nathalie Loring True (23, Georgetown, MA)

COOK,
daughter, b. 6/12/1918; first; Walter Cook (laborer) and Margaret Emery (Tuftonboro)

COOMBS-QUILL,
Eliza Jeannette, b. 7/24/1994 in Tuftonboro; Bruce L. Quill and Mary Susan Coombs

COPPLESTONE,
Katherine Jean, b. 5/4/1987 in Wolfeboro; Steven A. Copplestone and Sarah Jane Wingate
Rosalind Turner, b. 8/3/1984 in Wolfeboro; Steven Allen Copplestone and Sarah Jane Wingate

CORNWELL,
Andrew Denton, b. 5/18/1974 in Concord; Ralph W. Cornwell and Jerilyn L. Baker

CORSON,
son, b. 12/1/1904 in Tuftonboro; first; R. Corson (laborer, 30) and Lula Horn (23, Newfield, ME); residence – Wolfeboro

COULTER,
Abigail Porter, b. 10/14/1999 in Laconia; Christian Coulter and
  Jennifer Coulter
Hannah Miles, b. 10/3/1997 in Laconia; Christian Warren Coulter
  and Jennifer Ann Miles

COURTNEY,
Eric, III, b. 2/9/1948 in Wolfeboro; first; Eric Courtney, Jr. (carpenter,
  Newton Ctr., MA) and Gladys G. Pasco (W. Ossipee)
William Keith, b. 5/16/1950 in Wolfeboro; second; Eric Courtney, Jr.
  (state trooper, Newton, MA) and Gladys G. Pascoe (Ossipee)

CRAIGUE,
Anthony Scott, b. 1/20/1988 in Wolfeboro; Scott B. Craigue and
  Bonnie Lynn Atwood
Brian Scott, b. 6/15/1981 in Wolfeboro; Scott B. Craigue and
  Michelle Y. Wood
Carole Ann, b. 2/5/1952 in Wolfeboro; second; Kenneth E. Craigue
  (carpenter, NH) and Mary L. Bense (NH)
Cynthia Mary, b. 10/9/1950 in Wolfeboro; first; Kenneth E. Craigue
  (carpenter, Wolfeboro) and Mary L. Bense (Meredith);
  residence – Mirror Lake
Jacob Hayes, b. 5/20/1998 in Dover; James E. Craigue and Carolyn
  L. Toms
James Edwin, b. 3/13/1964 in Wolfeboro; fourth; Kenneth E. Craigue
  (carpenter, Wolfeboro) and Mary L. Bense (Meredith)
Kenneth, Jr., b. 6/13/1962 in Wolfeboro; third; Kenneth E. Craigue
  (builder, Wolfeboro) and Mary L. Bense (Meredith)

CRANE,
Hannah Penhallow, b. 9/16/2002 in Laconia; Nathaniel Crane and
  Lara Crane

CROSSMAN,
son, b. 11/21/1902 in Tuftonboro; third; John S. Crossman
  (carpenter, 34, NB) and Mary A. Whyte (30, Boston, MA)

CROTEAU,
Hannah Laurel, b. 6/20/1984 in Tuftonboro; Richard G. Croteau and
  Janet Lynn Helling

Maggie Blue, b. 7/15/1980 in Tuftonboro; Richard G. Croteau and
  Janet L. Helling

CULLEN,
Elaine, b. 10/10/1899 in Tuftonboro; third; Charles E. Cullen
  (laborer, 27, Worcester, MA) and Aace E. Ash (25, Passaic, NJ)

CURRIER,
son, b. 3/1/1900 in Tuftonboro; third; John P. Currier (laborer, 28,
  Wentworth) and Alace W. Sharp (25, Boston, MA)
Josephine, b. 3/29/1901 in Tuftonboro; fourth; John P. Currier
  (lumberman, 29, Wentworth) and Alace W. Sharp (26, S.
  Boston, MA)
Lorenzo G., b. 4/3/1899 in Tuftonboro; second; John P. Currier
  (laborer, 27, Wentworth) and Alace W. Sharp (24, Boston, MA)

CURRY,
Adrien John, b. 7/17/1947 in Wolfeboro; second; John Richard Curry
  (head waiter, Winthrop, MA) and Elaine R. Haley (Wolfeboro)
Rebecca Ann, b. 4/13/1951 in Wolfeboro; third; John R. Curry (hotel
  waiter, Winthrop, MA) and Elaine R. Haley (Melvin Village)

CURTIS,
Heather Myra, b. 2/1/1970 in Kittery, ME; Kenneth G. Curtis (MA)
  and Janice M. Lassett (MA)

CUSHING,
Felecia Niccole, b. 10/11/1988 in Wolfeboro; Dennis Lee Cushing
  and Twila Sue Arey
Stephanie LaVonne, b. 5/16/1983 in Wolfeboro; Dennis L. Cushing
  and Twila Sue Arey

DALEY,
Liam Miles, b. 4/19/2002 in N. Conway; Jon Daley and Maegan
  Daley
Shannon Michelle, b. 2/20/2005 in Wolfeboro; Jon Daley and Megan
  Daley

DAMON,
Sarah Marie, b. 8/20/1977 in Wolfeboro; Christopher S. Damon and
  Dorcas A. Margeson

DANFORTH,

son, b. 2/5/1921; third; James Danforth (teamster, E. Concord) and Ida Whittier (Wolfeboro)

daughter, b. 4/13/1922; fourth; James Danforth (teamster, E. Concord) and Ida Whittier (Wolfeboro)

Helen E., b. 4/29/1917; first; James B. Danforth (laborer, E. Concord) and Ida M. Whitten (Wolfeboro)

DAVEY,

Isabel May, b. 12/23/1926; second; Ernest Davey (laborer, 35, Canada) and Eva Daigneault (31, Southbridge, MA)

DAVIS,

son, b. 12/23/1897 in Tuftonboro; third; Harry Davis (farmer, 24, Franklin) and Sadie Gilman (19, Tuftonboro)

daughter, b. 2/13/1907; fourth; Harry A. Davis (farmer, 33, Gilmanton) and Sadie B. Gilman (29, Tuftonboro)

son, b. 11/11/1916; fourth; Harry L. Davis (carpenter, Moultonboro) and Flora B. McDonald (Moultonboro)

son, b. 11/2/1918; first; Harry L. Davis (farmer, Moultonboro) and Flora B. McDonald (Moultonboro)

daughter, b. 3/13/1921; sixth; Harry L. Davis (carpenter, Moultonboro) and Flora B. McDonald (Tuftonboro)

Alan Leroy, b. 2/7/1958 in Wolfeboro; second; Paul W. Davis (route salesman, Wolfeboro) and Rhoda L. Ham (Tuftonboro); residence – Ctr. Tuftonboro

Albert E., b. 4/15/1895 in Tuftonboro; first; Harry A. Davis (farmer, 22, Franklin) and Sadie Gilman (17, Tuftonboro)

Andrew Tolar, b. 11/24/1980 in Concord; Stephen M. Davis and Joyce M. Narushef

Beatrice E., b. 4/15/1895 in Tuftonboro; second; Harry A. Davis (farmer, 22, Franklin) and Sadie Gilman (17, Tuftonboro)

Betsy Ellen, b. 6/14/1976 in Laconia; Foster Lee Davis II and Diane G. Saunders

Cori Elizabeth, b. 9/1/1987 in Rochester; John R. Davis and Mary C. Yates

Donald G., b. 2/20/1923; seventh; Harry L. Davis (carpenter, Moultonboro) and Flora B. McDonald (Tuftonboro)

Duane Willard, b. 10/24/1966 in Wolfeboro; second; Foster L. Davis (construction, Wolfeboro) and Diane G. Saunders (Laconia)

Eleanor M., b. 3/19/1914; fifth; Harry A. Davis (farmer, Gilmanton)
and Sadie Gilman (Tuftonboro)
Elizabeth Page, b. 9/25/1936 in Wolfeboro; second; Willis Page
Davis (laborer, 19, Melvin Village) and Eleanor May Thompson
(19, Melvin Village)
Kristen Leigh, b. 10/8/1985 in Wolfeboro; Craig A. Davis and Susan
Ann Ellison
Paul W., b. 6/20/1930 in Wolfeboro; first; Albert Davis (laborer, 25,
Tuftonboro) and Eda M. Wallace (housewife, 30, Ossipee)
Paul Wallace, Jr., b. 1/22/1955 in Wolfeboro; first; Paul W. Davis
(truck operator, NH) and Rhoda L. Ham (NH)
Rebecca Lynn, b. 8/30/1968 in Wolfeboro; Foster Lee Davis (NH)
and Diane G. Saunders (NH)
Ruth Harriet, b. 2/17/1918; sixth; Harry A. Davis (farmer, Gilmanton)
and Sadie B. Gilman (Tuftonboro)
Sandra, b. 12/19/1941 in Wolfeboro; second; Willis Paige Davis
(auto mechanic, 25, Tuftonboro) and Eleanor Thompson
(housewife, 24, Tuftonboro); residence – Melvin Village

DAWSON,
James Williams, b. 3/6/1985 in Wolfeboro; John W. Dawson, Jr. and
Linda Marie Starke

DEARBORN,
Annie Bella, b. 6/1/1990 in Plymouth; Mark E. Dearborn and Zita
Bodonyi

DELEMUS,
Erica Rose, b. 7/7/2003 in Wolfeboro; Kristopher Delemus and
Adrienne Delemus

DEMASI,
Brody Burke, b. 5/30/2003 in Wolfeboro; Paul Demasi and Mary
Demasi

DEVORK,
Dwight Allen, b. 3/16/1953 in Wolfeboro; third; Anthony Devork
(mechanic, OH) and Grace M. Dale (England)
Pamela Dale, b. 8/7/1948 in Wolfeboro; second; Anthony Devork
(mechanic, Steubenville, OH) and Grace M. Dale (Sheffield,
England); residence – Ctr. Tuftonboro

DEWITT,

Hannah Mary, b. 1/23/1999 in Wolfeboro; Kirk Dewitt and Carole (Sullivan) Dewitt

Nicholas Hanson, b. 12/6/2000 in Wolfeboro; Kirk Dewitt and Carole Dewitt

DILL,

Jason Lee, b. 5/28/2004 in Wolfeboro; Jeremy Dill and Wendeline Dill

DILTZ,

Melvin Frank, b. 12/8/1954 in Wolfeboro; first; Melvin A. Diltz (woodsman, CA) and Thelma L. Reed (NH)

DOE,

Harry, b. 8/3/1895 in Tuftonboro; third; Frank A. Doe (farmer, 37, Tuftonboro) and C. Belle McKinzie (31, Picton, NS)

DONAHUE,

Madeleine Joan, b. 5/5/1996 in Laconia; Brendan Thomas Donahue and Maura Ann Hogan

DONOVAN,

Carly Rose, b. 6/5/1995 in Wolfeboro; William J. Donovan III and Amy Elyse Salmon

James Liam, b. 1/9/2002 in Wolfeboro; William Donovan and Amy Donovan

Kathleen Maura, b. 11/5/1973 in Wolfeboro; John F. Donovan and Kathleen M. Brennick

William James, IV, b. 6/17/1991 in Wolfeboro; William J. Donovan III and Amy Elyse Salmon

DORE,

Christopher Michael, b. 2/6/1983 in Wolfeboro; Larry Lee Dore and Sheila A. Fontaine

Eunice May, b. 10/11/1932 in Tuftonboro; third; Leon E. Dore (laborer, 37, Ossipee) and Mildred E. Davis (25, Tuftonboro)

Larry Lee, b. 8/8/1957 in Wolfeboro; Richard L. Dore (woodsman, Wolfeboro) and Barbara L. Hlushuk (Tuftonboro)

Linda May, b. 5/25/1955 in Wolfeboro; first; Richard L. Dore (lumberjack, NH) and Barbara L. Hlushuck (NH)

Michael, b. 12/12/1961 in Wolfeboro; second; Ivan E. Dore (N. E., Milton) and Carolyn E. Haley (Wolfeboro)

Richard Leon, b. 10/2/1934 in Wolfeboro; fourth; Leon E. Dore (farmer, 39, Ossipee) and Mildred F. Davis (housewife, 27, Tuftonboro); residence – Ctr. Tuftonboro

Roy Elwin, b. 7/24/1931 in Tuftonboro; second; Leon E. Dore (laborer, 35, Ossipee) and Mildred F. Davis (housewife, 24, Tuftonboro)

Ruby Frances, b. 9/6/1926; first; Leon E. Dore (farmer, 31, Ossipee) and Mildred F. Davis (19, Tuftonboro)

DOW,

son, b. 5/14/1891 in Tuftonboro; third; Alvah E. Dow (farmer, 41, Coventry, VT) and Anna M. Nutter (36, Tuftonboro)

daughter, b. 10/1/1895 in Tuftonboro; fourth; Alvah Dow (farmer, Coventry, VT) and Annie M. Nutter (Tuftonboro)

Adam Wayne, b. 11/1/1973 in Wolfeboro; Wayne A. Dow and Marilyn L. McGloin

Albert Henry, III, b. 8/18/1953 in Wolfeboro; second; Albert Henry Dow, Jr. (cabinet maker, MA) and Marjorie E. Holmes (MA)

Aubri Lisa, b. 2/3/1977 in Laconia; Wayne A. Dow and Marilyn L. McGloin

Caryl Holmes, b. 4/16/1958 in Wolfeboro; third; Albert H. Dow, Jr. (cabinet maker, MA) and Marjorie E. Holmes (MA)

Richard Vernon, b. 7/12/1947 in Wolfeboro; second; Vernon Robert Dow (carpenter, Moultonboro) and Dorothy E. Kenney (Dorchester, MA)

Rodney Nutter, b. 4/10/1949 in Rochester; third; Roland D. Dow (sawyer, NH) and Greta E. May (VT)

Stephen Roland, b. 3/2/1951 in Rochester; fifth; Roland D. Dow (sawyer, NH) and Greta E. May (Canaan, VT)

Susan Elizabeth, b. 5/27/1952 in Wolfeboro; first; Albert H. Dow, Jr. (antiques, MA) and Marjorie B. Holmes (MA)

DOWNING,

Brian Geoffrey, b. 9/27/1989 in Rochester; Geoffrey A. Downing and Karen Cross

Scott Alan, b. 11/1/1993 in Wolfeboro; Geoffrey A. Downing and Karen K. Cross

DREW,
daughter, b. 7/20/1902 in Tuftonboro; second; Charles H. Drew (painter, 34, Wolfeboro) and Ida M. Waldron (20, Wolfeboro)

DUBRINO,
Brittany Leigh, b. 11/19/1990 in Laconia; Francis A. J. Dubrino and Caryn J. Collamore
Chelsea Anne, b. 11/19/1990 in Laconia; Francis A. J. Dubrino and Caryn J. Collamore
Elizabeth Joy, b. 3/1/1988 in Laconia; Francis A. J. DuBrino and Caryn Joy Collamore

DUFAULT,
Mark Alan, b. 1/8/1964 in Wolfeboro; fifth; Wilfred Dufault (construction, Laconia) and Geraldine Paige (Wolfeboro)

DUNCAN,
Jameson Shannon, b. 8/1/1971 in Wolfeboro; James H. S. Duncan and Penelope A. Shannon

DUNN,
Tammy A., b. 4/1/1958 in Wolfeboro; third; Kenneth G. Dunn (salesman, MA) and Elsie W. Willard (MA); residence – Melvin Village

DUPRE,
Deborah Ann, b. 4/14/1955 in Wolfeboro; first; William P. Dupre (boat yard worker, MA) and Helen M. Baxter (NH)

DURFEE,
Amie Austad, b. 9/15/1980 in Wolfeboro; John W. Durfee and Wendy Lou Austad
Hyrum Cy, b. 11/20/1982 in Wolfeboro; John W. Durfee and Wendy Lou Austad
Joseph Quincy, b. 5/13/1985 in Wolfeboro; John W. Durfee and Wendy Lou Austad

DURHAM,
Deanna Jennifer, b. 8/24/1970 in Wolfeboro; David L. Durham (MA) and Dianne P. Bean (NH)

EATON,
Mikayla Colette, b. 8/26/2005 in Wolfeboro; Brian Eaton and Sandra Eaton

EDGERLY,
Gyme Lynn, b. 1/18/1947 in Wolfeboro; second; John Irving Edgerly (hotel manager, Tuftonboro) and Alice Gertrude Bennett (Tuftonboro)

John I., b. 7/27/1914; first; Edwin B. Edgerly (hotel manager, Tuftonboro) and Caroline Crossman (Providence, RI)

John Irving, Jr., b. 2/13/1944 in Wolfeboro; first; John Irving Edgerly (caretaker, Tuftonboro) and Alice Gertrude Bennett (Tuftonboro)

ELDRIDGE,
son, b. 4/2/1905; Dana Eldridge (laborer, 24, Ossipee) and Susie Wiggin (26, Tuftonboro)

Avis Lorraine, b. 11/9/1930 in Tuftonboro; fourth; Carlton S. Eldridge (laborer, 28, Ossipee) and Esther M. Haley (25, Tuftonboro)

Barbara Jeanne, b. 10/19/1934 in Tuftonboro; sixth; Carlton S. Eldridge (farmer, 32, Ossipee) and Esther M. Haley (housewife, 29, Tuftonboro)

David Dwight, b. 6/2/1953 in Wolfeboro; third; Carlton O. Eldridge (lumbering, MA) and Martha M. Hayes (MA)

Janice Marie, b. 5/8/1949 in Wolfeboro; second; Carlton O. Eldridge (lumberman, Milton) and Martha M. Hayes (Boston, MA)

John Carroll, b. 5/8/1949 in Wolfeboro; first; Carlton O. Eldridge (lumberman, Milton) and Martha M. Hayes (Boston, MA)

Madison Rose, b. 10/19/1997 in Dover; Ronald Robert Eldridge and Tracy Leigh Michaud

Mark Allan, b. 7/18/1967 in Wolfeboro; second; Charles P. Eldridge (mill work, Wolfeboro) and Leola J. Downing (Wolfeboro)

ELLIOTT,
son, b. 1/2/1907; eighth; Willie W. Elliott (laborer, 31, Rumney) and Etta L. Plummer (31, Groton)

EMERT,
Wyatt James, b. 11/1/2005 in Wolfeboro; Jason Emert and Christine Metcalfe

EMERY,
daughter, b. 6/13/1905 in Tuftonboro; Dana Emery (farmer, 36, Bartlett) and Ina Drew (22, Wolfeboro)
Lillian Blanche, b. 3/24/1899 in Tuftonboro; first; Howard E. Emery (laborer, 25, Tuftonboro) and Emma S. Swasey (34, Ossipee)
Mary Margaret, b. 4/3/1903 in Tuftonboro; first; Cheston R. Emery (farmer, 35, Bartlett) and Carrie A. Hersey (34, Tuftonboro)

ENNIS,
Margaret Grace, b. 5/30/1992 in N. Conway; Barry T. Ennis and Jane Anne Marshall
Sean Michael, b. 11/7/1989 in N. Conway; Barry Thomas Ennis and Jane Anne Marshall

EVANS,
Jacob Brian, b. 9/18/1991 in Laconia; Lane W. Evans and Dawn S. Moody
Tyler Moody, b. 2/6/1994 in Wolfeboro; Lane Wilson Evans and Dawn Sherry Evans

FAHLMAN,
Betsy Lee, b. 7/18/1951 in Wolfeboro; first; Richard B. Fahlman (chicken farm, Stoneham, MA) and Lucille W. Davis (Dover)

FAIR,
Alicia Nicole, b. 2/28/1991 in Concord; Steven J. Fair and Anita L. Lemieux
Kayla Michele, b. 10/14/1987 in Concord; Steven J. Fair and Anita L. Lemieux

FALL,
daughter, b. 4/4/1907; first; Vergil Fall (carpenter, 28, Ossipee0 and Leva Piper (16, Effingham)
stillborn son, b. 7/31/1924 in Tuftonboro; second; Ausbrey C. Fall (farmer, Ossipee) and Mertie B. Thompson (Tuftonboro)
Helen T., b. 6/6/1911; first; Ausbrey C. Fall (painter, 26, Ossipee) and Myrtle B. Thompson (27, Tuftonboro)

FALLMAN,
Pamela Ann, b. 8/31/1963 in Wolfeboro; first; Harry T. Fallman (warehouseman, Methuen, MA) and Claire E. Cate (Wolfeboro)

FAUCETTE,
John, Jr., b. 11/19/1962 in Wolfeboro; first; John H. Faucette (gas
sta. attendant, Minominee, MI) and Marcia A. Parker (Exeter)
John Henry, b. 1/8/1985 in Wolfeboro; John H. Faucette, Jr. and
Rose-Marie Emerson
Michelle Anne, b. 3/20/1968 in Wolfeboro; John Henry Faucette (MI)
and Marcia Ann Parker (NH)

FERNALD,
Nancy Jane, b. 4/27/1940 in Wolfeboro; first; Chester Campbell
Fernald (hotel mgr., 25, Wolfeboro) and Marion Ardell Hobbs
(housewife, 25, Laconia); residence – Melvin Village

FINNERON,
Nicholas John, b. 6/29/2004 in Wolfeboro; Robert Finneron and
Jacqueline Finneron

FISKE,
Christopher William, b. 9/30/1978 in Concord; Charles W. Fiske and
Sally I. Rosell
Elizabeth Lynne, b. 6/22/1988 in Rochester; Stephen F. Fiske and
Pamela J. Donaldson

FOLSOM,
Amy Corinne, b. 10/17/1973 in Wolfeboro; James E. Folsom and
Elizabeth A. Madden
Timothy Allen, b. 7/9/1995 in Dover; Shane P. Folsom and Kim
Jeanne Wilson

FORSYTHE,
Frank Faulkner, Jr., b. 7/21/1935 in Wolfeboro; third; Frank F.
Forsythe (farmer, 31, Lynn, MA) and Gladys V. Spidell
(housewife, 27, Lexington, MA); residence – Ctr. Tuftonboro
Janet Marie, b. 5/11/1944 in Wolfeboro; first; Frank Faulkner
Forsythe (janitor, Tuftonboro S., Lynn, MA) and Nettie Belle
Bean (Tuftonboro)
Joan Marilyn, b. 4/13/1934 in Wolfeboro; second; Frank F. Forsyth,
Jr. (farming, 31, Lynn, MA) and Gladys Viola Spidell
(housewife, 26, Lexington, MA); residence – Ctr. Tuftonboro

Shirley Arlene, b. 12/13/1932 in Wolfeboro; first; Frank E. Forsyth, Jr. (farmer, 30, Lynn, MA) and Gladys Spidel (24, Lexington, MA)

FOSS,
son, b. 6/15/1916; first; Charles E. Foss (farmer, Tuftonboro) and Florence B. Bean (Tuftonboro)

FRASER,
Douglas Samuel, b. 5/3/1950 in Wolfeboro; first; Harold A. Fraser (carpenter, Wentworth) and Hazel E. Hart (Malden, MA)

FRAWLEY,
Kathleen, b. 1/21/1972 in Wolfeboro; Frederic L. Frawley and Sharon R. Kennedy

FRENCH,
Vickie, b. 10/14/1962 in Wolfeboro; third; Donald R. French (carpenter, Boston, MA) and Nancy L. Smith (Ossipee)

FRYE,
son, b. 9/1/1904 in Tuftonboro; first; Louis Frye (hostler, 22, Moultonboro) and Jennie Hoyt (18, Tuftonboro)

FURBER,
Tyler James, b. 7/3/2003 in Wolfeboro; John Furber and Angela Furber

GAGNE,
Vanessa Mae, b. 8/13/1981 in Wolfeboro; Ernest A. Gagne and Bonnie L. Ridlon

GALLAGHER,
April Alexis, b. 10/10/1976 in Laconia; Robert M. Gallagher and Randi S. Kerr
Robert David, b. 10/31/1990 in Wolfeboro; Bryan D. Gallagher and Denise D. Leger

GARREPY,
Patricia Ann, b. 9/30/1958 in Wolfeboro; second; William W. Garrepy (therapist, MA) and Elsa L. Rosenband (MA); residence – Tuftonboro Cor.

GARRETT,
Keith Justin, b. 9/21/1977 in Wolfeboro; Edwin R. Garrett and Penelope Stevens
Kevin James, b. 6/4/1979 in Wolfeboro; Edwin Ray Garrett and Penelope Stevens

GAUTHIER,
Charlotte Ruth, b. 10/29/2004 in Wolfeboro; Aaron Gauthier and Liese Gauthier
Cyrus Alexander, b. 5/4/2002 in Wolfeboro; Aaron Gauthier and Liese Gauthier

GEORGE,
Eleanor P., b. 10/2/1911; fourth; Charles E. George (boatman, 33, Lisbon) and Hannah E. Willand (27, Center Harbor)

GIBSON,
Adelaide E., b. 12/26/1895 in Tuftonboro; first; Albert E. Gibson (farmer, 35, Chelsea) and Mary Bickford (33, Tuftonboro)
Michael Joseph, b. 4/9/1991 in Laconia; William H. Gibson III and Jill Ann Daley-Gibson
Peter William, b. 9/22/1994 in Laconia; William Henry Gibson and Jill Daley

GILMAN,
Charles H., b. 11/6/1895 in Tuftonboro; third; Charles Gilman (farmer, 29, Moultonboro) and Georgia A. Buzzell (27, Meredith)
Lillian F., b. 8/9/1898 in Tuftonboro; fourth; Charles L. Gilman (laborer, 32, Moultonboro) and Georgie A. Buzzell (30, Meredith)
Louise B., b. 1/8/1916; first; Chester H. Gilman (farmer, Tuftonboro) and Edith B. Fernald (Chelsea, MA)
Mildred A., b. 4/14/1894; second; Charles L. Gilman (farmer, Moultonboro) and Georgia A. Buzzell (Meredith)

GIROUX,
daughter, b. 9/18/1923; second; Archibald R. Giroux (lumber mill, Somerville, MA) and Audrey McDugal (Mt. Vernon, NY); residence – Fullerton, LA

GLAZIER,
Austin David, b. 3/4/1990 in Tuftonboro; David L. Glazier and Deborah L. Elder
Brittanymay, b. 7/19/1985 in Wolfeboro; David L. Glazier and Deborah L. Elder
Gabrielle Lee, b. 9/2/1987 in Rochester; David L. Glazier and Debbie Lee Elder

GLEASON,
Eric Thane, b. 8/27/1972 in Kittery, ME; George W. Gleason and Phyllis A. Kroeger
Kristen Ashley, b. 10/9/1994 in Wolfeboro; John Westley Gleason and Tabitha Renee Boyle

GLIDDEN,
Gordon Hall, b. 5/9/1955 in Wolfeboro; fifth; Gordon E. Glidden (lineman, elec. co., MA) and Ruth M. Osgood (NH)

GOLDEN,
Elizabeth Ann, b. 9/23/1933 in Wolfeboro; second; Andrew Golden (golf professional, 32, Tuxedo, NY) and Elizabeth Jacob (housewife, 27, Elizabeth, NJ); residence – Melvin Village
Robert Clyde, b. 10/30/1931 in Wolfeboro; first; Andrew Golden (golf professional, 30, Tuxedo, NY) and Elizabeth Jacob (25, Elizabeth, NJ); residence – Melvin Village

GORDON,
Jesse Cooper, b. 3/25/1972 in Wolfeboro; Bart J. Gordon and Sarah M. Cooper-Ellis
Matthew Loring, b. 12/16/1972 in Wolfeboro; Peter N. Gordon and Gail S. Loring

GOUIN,
Barbara Dawn, b. 12/9/1939 in Wolfeboro; second; Thornton Xavier Gouin (carpenter, 28, Wolfeboro) and Leona Lucille Libbey (26, Ossipee)

Christina, b. 12/29/1970 in Wolfeboro; Thornton L. Gouin and
  Deborah Bean
David Thornton, b. 4/12/1961 in Wolfeboro; first; Thornton F. Gouin
  (odd jobs, Wolfeboro) and Judith Ann Hamlin (Wolfeboro)
Thornton Franklin, b. 2/16/1943 in Wolfeboro; third; Thornton Xavia
  Gouin (lumber foreman, Wolfeboro) and Leonia Lucille Libby
  (Ossipee)

GOULD,
Lebias Richardson, b. 12/29/1950 in Wolfeboro; sixth; Lebias R.
  Gould (wool carder, NB) and Barbara J. Sharp (New Hampton);
  residence – Ctr. Tuftonboro
Timothy James, b. 10/19/1954 in Wolfeboro; seventh; Lebias R.
  Gould (asbestos plant, Canada) and Barbara J. Sharp (NH)

GOVE,
Winnifred L., b. 12/5/1893 in Tuftonboro; first; Hubert F. Gove
  (laborer, 27, U. Stillwater, ME) and Lottie M. Chick (20, Lake
  Village)

GRAHAM,
Linda Marie, b. 11/14/1978 in Wolfeboro; William E. Graham and
  Dorothy A. Carroll

GRAY,
James Arthur, b. 5/12/1975 in Wolfeboro; Arthur M. Gray and Linda
  J. Woodbury

GREENE,
Ian Thomas, b. 1/2/1995 in Wolfeboro; Francois R. Greene and
  Muriel J. Nicol

GREENWOOD,
Aaron James, b. 4/23/1989 in Tuftonboro; Kenneth A. Greenwood
  and Lisa M. Potenza
Justin Daniel, b. 5/23/1991 in Tuftonboro; Kenneth A. Greenwood
  and Lisa Marie Potenza
Traci Lee, b. 2/18/1977 in Wolfeboro; Lionel J. Greenwood and
  Elinore Lindell Allen

GROOM,
Gregory Robert, b. 4/11/2003 in Laconia; Sean Groom and Heather Groom

GRUPP,
Adam Christopher, b. 12/16/1979 in Laconia; Arthur Curt Grupp and Sarah Ann Harrington

GUILBAULT,
Alayna Nicole, b. 9/24/2003 in N. Conway; Anthony Guilbault and Alyssa Guilbault

HAEGER,
Brendan Michael, b. 8/17/1994 in Wolfeboro; Michael David Haeger and Karen Anne Lampron

HALE,
Jesse Robert, b. 8/16/1977 in Tuftonboro; Stephen R. Hale and Leslie F. Carr
Rachel Sarah, b. 12/5/1974 in Wolfeboro; Stephen R. Hale and Leslie F. Carr
Tristian Scott, b. 9/7/2003 in Wolfeboro; Scott Hale and Billie Sue Hale

HALEPIS,
Harriette Beatrice, b. 9/7/1979 in Laconia; Andrew Manuel Halepis and Cheryl Adeline Riley
James Michael, b. 12/13/1977 in Laconia; Andrew M. Halepis and Cheryl A. Riley

HALEY,
son, b. 11/24/1896 in Tuftonboro; third; George Haley (farmer, 36, Moultonboro) and Edith C. Ayers (23, Tuftonboro)
daughter, b. 7/30/1901 in Tuftonboro; fourth; George H. Haley (farmer, 41, Moultonboro) and Edith C. Ayers (28, Tuftonboro)
son, b. 8/24/1902 in Tuftonboro; fifth; George H. Haley (farmer, 42, Moultonboro) and Edith C. Ayers (29, Tuftonboro)
daughter, b. 6/23/1905 in Tuftonboro; George H. Haley (farmer, 45, Moultonboro) and Edith Ayers (31, Tuftonboro)
son, b. 6/10/1908; second; Willie I. Haley (carpenter, 21, Tuftonboro) and Bernice E. Dow (20, Moultonboro)

daughter, b. 1/25/1910; third; Willie I. Haley (laborer, Tuftonboro) and Bernice Dow (Moultonboro)

daughter, b. 3/17/1912; ninth; George H. Haley (farmer, Moultonboro) and Edith C. Ayers (Tuftonboro)

son, b. 5/4/1916; sixth; Willis L. Haley (laborer, Tuftonboro) and Bernice E. Dow (Moultonboro)

daughter, b. 5/25/1921; sixth; Charles E. Haley (laborer, Tuftonboro) and Dora E. Bragg (Moultonboro)

Caroline Ethel, b. 5/10/1940 in Wolfeboro; second; Lawrence Erwin Haley (electrician, 34, Tuftonboro) and Frances Addie Thibedeau (housewife, 22, New Durham); residence – Melvin Village

Delbert Clarence, b. 5/12/1933 in Wolfeboro; first; Delbert C. Haley (green keeper, 24, Melvin Village) and Muriel C. Robarge (housewife, 18, Tamworth); residence – Melvin Village

Delbert Clarence, III, b. 10/7/1957 in Wolfeboro; first; Delbert C. Haley, Jr. (carpenter, Wolfeboro) and Geraldine E. Estes (Wolfeboro)

Evelyn A., b. 7/17/1919; second; Charles E. Haley (farmer, Tuftonboro) and Dora Bragg (Moultonboro)

Frank E., b. 11/2/1895 in Tuftonboro; second; George H. Haley (farmer, Moultonboro) and Edith C. Ayers (Tuftonboro)

James E., b. 12/24/1893 in Tuftonboro; first; George H. Haley (laborer, 30, Tuftonboro) and Edith C. Ayers (20, Tuftonboro)

James Russell, b. 1/12/1938 in Wolfeboro; second; Howard Russell Haley (carpenter, 21, Tuftonboro) and Helen Louise Ferris (20, Boston, MA)

Janet Louise, b. 6/27/1936 in Wolfeboro; first; Howard Haley (laborer, 20, Tuftonboro) and Helen Ferris (18, Boston, MA)

Jo-Ann Helen, b. 7/28/1940 in Wolfeboro; third; Howard Russell Haley (painter, 24, Tuftonboro) and Helen Louise Ferris (housewife, 22, Boston, MA)

Joyce Annette, b. 3/17/1935 in Wolfeboro; second; Delbert C. Haley (green keeper, 26, Melvin Village) and Muriel Robarge (housewife, 20, Somersworth); residence – Melvin Village

Kenneth E., b. 9/14/1917; first; Charles E. Haley (farmer, Tuftonboro) and Dora Bragg (Moultonboro)

Leroy Willis, b. 8/8/1936 in Wolfeboro; third; Delbert Clarence Haley (greenskeeper, 28, Tuftonboro) and Muriel C. Roberge (22, Tamworth); residence – Melvin Village

Richard Allen, b. 6/12/1961 in Wolfeboro; second; Delbert C. Haley, Jr. (carpenter, Wolfeboro) and Geraldine E. Estes (Wolfeboro)

Rosalyn Mae, b. 11/26/1938 in Wolfeboro; first; Lawrence Ervin Haley (carpenter, 32, Tuftonboro) and Frances Addie Thibedeau (20, New Durham)

HALLAM,

Carin Elizabeth, b. 8/26/1983 in Tuftonboro; Timothy D. Hallam, Sr. and Janice S. Sciarpelletti

Joshua Zachary, b. 6/28/2000 in Wolfeboro; Timothy Hallam and Kelli Hallam

Kathryn Grace, b. 12/25/2003 in Lebanon; Michael Westrich and Cheryle Westrich (?)

Nathan James, b. 10/25/2001 in Lebanon; Timothy Hallam and Kelli Hallam

Robert Anthony, b. 7/6/1981 in Wolfeboro; Timothy D. Hallam, Sr. and Janice S. Sciarpelletti

HAM,

Nancy Jane, b. 3/26/1939 in Laconia; third; Leroy Ellsworth Ham (truck driver, 44, Acton, ME) and Florence Louise Haley (27, Tuftonboro)

Rhoda Louise, b. 10/4/1935 in Tuftonboro; first; Leroy E. Ham (truck driver, 42, Acton, ME) and Florence L. Haley (housewife, 23, Tuftonboro)

Sylvia Grace, b. 3/27/1937 in Laconia; second; Leroy Ellsworth Ham (truck driver, 42, Acton, ME) and Florence L. Haley (25, Tuftonboro)

HANSEN,

Christine Mary, b. 3/22/1940 in Wolfeboro; second; Harold Edward Hansen (merchant, 31, Newark, NJ) and Irene Alice St. Laurent (postmaster, 29, Florence, MA); residence – Ctr. Tuftonboro

Mark Allen, b. 10/28/1961 in Wolfeboro; fourth; Carl Irving Hansen (resort owner, Lynn, MA) and Pearl A. Gulliford (Lynn, MA)

Michelle Lynne, b. 4/28/1976 in Wolfeboro; Carl I. Hansen, Jr. and Marsha C. Madden

Scott Taylor, b. 3/6/1978 in Wolfeboro; Carl I. Hansen, Jr. and Marsha C. Madden

Vicki, b. 5/30/1953 in Wolfeboro; third; Carl I. Hansen (resort owner, MA) and Pearl A. Gulliford (MA); residence – Melvin Village

HARRINGTON,
Patrick Shawn, b. 8/5/1984 in Wolfeboro; Daniel F. Harrington and
 Diane J. Charles
Ryan David, b. 6/16/2003 in Wolfeboro; James Harrington and
 Susan Harrington
Susan Elizabeth, b. 7/28/1980 in Wolfeboro; Daniel F. Harrington
 and Diane J. Charles

HARRIS,
Jessica Victoria, b. 6/2/1985 in Wolfeboro; William O. Harris and
 Carlene L. Contois

HARTLEY,
William Wesley, b. 12/2/1963 in Wolfeboro; fourth; John W. Hartley
 (resort owner, Melrose, MA) and Vera M. Ashton (Long Beach,
 CA)

HASTINGS,
Ani Sky, b. 3/2/2000 in N. Conway; Brian Hastings and Anika
 Hastings
Brian Elias, b. 11/19/2002 in N. Conway; Brian Hastings and Anika
 Hastings

HATCH,
daughter, b. 4/10/1891 in Tuftonboro; second; Albert Hatch (farmer,
 Tuftonboro) and Georgia A. Wendell (Tuftonboro)
daughter, b. 9/8/1897 in Tuftonboro; fourth; Albert C. Hatch (farmer,
 31, Wolfeboro) and Georgia A. Wendall (29, Tuftonboro)
Lottie E., b. 11/5/1894; third; Albert C. Hatch (laborer, Wolfeboro)
 and Georgia A. Wendell (Tuftonboro)

HAUNGS,
Misty, b. 12/15/1980 in Wolfeboro; Charles F. Haungs and Vicki
 Hansen
Toria, b. 11/19/1982 in Wolfeboro; Charles F. Haungs and Vicki
 Hansen

HAWKES,
Robert Bruce, Jr., b. 8/2/1933 in Wolfeboro; first; Robert Bruce
 Hawkes (hotel room clerk, 27, Washburn, WI) and Mildred
 Capen (housewife, 27, Boston, MA); residence – Melvin Village

HAWKINS,
Pamela Ann, b. 6/18/1948 in Wolfeboro; first; Richard O. Hawkins (civil engineer, Holderness) and Elfrieda A. Vetter (Hamburg, Germany); residence – Melvin Village

HAYES,
daughter, b. 4/9/1908; second; Henry F. Hayes (chauffeur, 27, Moultonboro) and Mabelle Welch (23, Meredith)

HEALD,
Brianna Marie, b. 6/29/2000 in Wolfeboro; Gerald Heald and Justina Heald
Cody James, b. 10/31/1998 in Wolfeboro; Gerald M. Heald, Jr. and Justina L. Goble

HEATH,
Kimberly Alice, b. 1/8/1974 in Wolfeboro; Richard H. Heath and Nancy J. Moulton

HEBERT,
Jamie Alan, b. 12/8/1975 in Wolfeboro; Michael A. Hebert and Holly Faulkner
Mary Anne, b. 9/23/1950 in Wolfeboro; third; Omer A. Hebert (laborer, Canaan) and Ruth Eldridge (Ctr. Ossipee); residence – Mirror Lake
Michael Eric, b. 12/2/2002; Eric Hebert and Victoria   Hebert
Philip Leon, b. 8/31/1949 in Wolfeboro; Omer A. Hebert (laborer, Canaan) and Ruth Eldridge (Ctr. Ossipee); residence – Mirror Lake
Reuben H., b. 12/24/1979 in Tuftonboro; Michael Alan Hebert and Holly Frances Faulkner
Sharon Kay, b. 5/10/1948 in Wolfeboro; first; Omer A. Jebert (truck driver, Grafton) and Ruth Eldridge (Ctr. Ossipee)
Timothy Lewis, b. 7/28/1952 in Wolfeboro; fourth; Omer A. Hebert (labor, Canaan) and Ruth Eldridge (Ctr. Ossipee)
Zachary Scott, b. 4/28/2004; Eric Hebert and Victoria   Hebert

HEINE,
M. A. [female], b. 10/21/1894; fourth; Roscoe Heine (clergyman, Apohaqui, NB) and Margaret Hanson (Bradford, England)

HENDERSON,
Jeffrey Bruce, b. 6/27/1960 in Wolfeboro; second; Roy A. Henderson (teacher, WV) and Julie Slade (MA)

HENSLEY,
Ruth Alice, b. 6/25/1943 in Wolfeboro; first; Francis Willis Hensley (clergyman, Middleton, TN) and Mary Allen Wright (Montgomery, VT)

HERRICK,
Donald Arthur, Jr., b. 9/20/1955 in Wolfeboro; first; Donald A. Herrick (laborer, ME) and Ginger M. Britton (NH)
Raymond Edwin, b. 10/21/1956 in Wolfeboro; second; Donald A. Herrick (laborer, Saco, ME) and Ginger M. Britton (Wolfeboro); residence – Melvin Village

HERSEY,
daughter, b. 2/9/1891 in Tuftonboro; second; George W. Hersey (farmer, 36, Tuftonboro) and Mary L. Hodgdon (24, Tuftonboro)
son, b. 5/26/1907; fourth; George W. Hersey (farmer, 52, Tuftonboro) and Lizzie M. Hodgdon (41, Tuftonboro)
daughter, b. 5/10/1909; first; Edwin C. Hersey (farmer, Tuftonboro) and Hattie B. Springer (Marshfield, VT)
daughter, b. 8/18/1911; second; Edwin C. Hersey (farmer, 34, Tuftonboro) and Hattie B. Springer (26, Marshfield, VT)
daughter, b. 1/19/1915; third; Edwin C. Hersey (Tuftonboro) and Hattie B. Springer (Marshfield, VT)
Angie M., b. 5/5/1894; third; George W. Hersey (farmer, Tuftonboro) and Mary L. Hodgdon (Tuftonboro)
Beatrice E., b. 9/3/1898 in Tuftonboro; fourth; George W. Hersey (farmer, 43, Tuftonboro) and Mary E. Hodgdon (31, Tuftonboro)
Brian James, b. 5/2/1984 in Wolfeboro; James L. Hersey and Madge J. Hodgdon
John Bowen, b. 7/4/1965 in Wolfeboro; second; John L. Hersey (farmer, Wolfeboro) and Elizabeth J. Adjutant (Wolfeboro)

HIGGINS,
Connor Wayne, b. 3/10/2005 in Wolfeboro; John Higgins and Leslie Lahti

HILL,

Ronald Stephen, b. 9/9/1955 in Wolfeboro; sixth; Raymond E. Hill (woodsman, ME) and Madeline Sprague (ME)

Susan Joy, b. 9/24/1947 in Wolfeboro; first; Frank Vincent Hill (highway dept., Boston, MA) and Agnes J. Haley (Wolfeboro)

HILLIARD,

Kathleen, b. 11/26/1941 in Wolfeboro; first; Louis Everett Hilliard (machinist, 30, Waterville, ME) and Dorothea Esther Hanson (housewife, 25, Lancaster); residence – Laconia

HINCKLEY,

Alexandra Erskine, b. 11/17/1999 in Wolfeboro; Benjamin Hinckley and Heather Hinckley

HIRD,

John Zachary, b. 2/15/1994 in Portsmouth; Bruce John Hird and Agnes Lengyel

HITCHCOCK,

Elizabeth Louise, b. 8/3/1961 in Wolfeboro; first; Martin Allen Hitchcock (bus. exec. manuf., Bridgeport, CT) and Patricia Louise Page (New York City)

HLUSHUK,

daughter, b. 4/25/1928 in Tuftonboro; fourth; Jack Hlushuk (laborer, Russia) and Leora E. Adjutant (housewife, Tuftonboro)

Evelyn Irene, b. 8/16/1941 in Wolfeboro; ninth; Jack Hlushuk (laborer, 46, Moscow, Russia) and Leora Elizabeth Adjutant (housewife, 38, Tuftonboro); residence – Ctr. Tuftonboro

Harold, b. 1/16/1927 in Tuftonboro; first; Jack Hlushuk (laborer, Russia) and Leora Adjutant (Tuftonboro)

Kenneth Willie, b. 6/21/1932 in Tuftonboro; sixth; Jack Hlushuk (laborer, 37, Moscow, Russia) and Leora E. Adjutant (29, Tuftonboro)

Michael Sargent, b. 3/18/1991 in Laconia; Wade A. Hlushuk and Theresa L. Sargent

HOCKWALD,

Judith, b. 7/29/1941 in Wolfeboro; first; Earle Charles Hockwald (minister, 29, Philadelphia, PA) and Virginia Gertrude Egger (housewife, 22, Middleboro, MA); residence – Melvin Village

HODGDON,

son, b. 7/28/1907; second; Franklin H. Hodgdon (farmer, 39, Tuftonboro) and Nora L. Burk (33, Ireland)

daughter, b. 4/1/1909; first; Forrest E. Hodgdon (painter, Tuftonboro) and Mary E. Haley (Tuftonboro)

daughter, b. 11/15/1910; third; Franklin H. Hodgdon (farmer, Tuftonboro)

daughter, b. 2/17/1912; first; Forrest E. Hodgdon (painter, Tuftonboro) and Hattie E. May (Providence, RI)

son, b. 8/3/1922; third; Forest E. Hodgdon (farmer, Tuftonboro) and Hattie E. May (Providence, RI)

Bruce Freeman, b. 12/18/1953 in Wolfeboro; second; Glenn F. Hodgdon (own business, Tuftonboro) and Eunice M. Dore (Tuftonboro); residence – Melvin Village

David Glenn, b. 8/6/1951 in Wolfeboro; first; Glenn F. Hodgdon (truck driver, NH) and Eunice M. Dore (NH)

Glenn Freeman, b. 5/29/1926; first; Forrest W. Hodgdon (farmer, 25, Cambridge, MA) and Velma A. Merrifield (27, Tuftonboro)

Greydon Herbert, b. 6/23/1934 in Wolfeboro; second; Forrest W. Hodgdon (asst. foreman, 33, Cambridge, MA) and Frances Canning (housewife, 28, Stowe, VT)

Jeffry Gordon, b. 5/23/1955 in Wolfeboro; first; Raeburn W. Hodgdon (electrician, st. hy, NH) and M. Patricia Williams (NH)

Jeremy Graydon, b. 8/2/1959 in Wolfeboro; second; Raeburn W. Hodgdon (carpenter, NH) and M. Patricia Williams (NH)

Jessika Haley, b. 12/3/1991 in Wolfeboro; Jeffrey G. Hodgdon and Tina MacDonald

Joshua Jeremy, b. 2/8/1983 in Wolfeboro; Jeffrey G. Hodgdon and Tina MacDonald

Judy Lynn, b. 5/24/1958 in Wolfeboro; stillborn; third; Glenn F. Hodgdon (caretaker, NH) and Eunice M. Dore (Wolfeboro)

Lillian M., b. 3/18/1919; second; Forrest E. Hodgdon (painter, Tuftonboro) and Hattie E. May (Providence, RI)

Raeburn Winfield, b. 1/2/1930 in Wolfeboro; first; Forrest W. Hodgdon (farmer, 29, Cambridge, MA) and Frances Canning (housewife, 22, Stowe, VT)

HODGES,
Anne Bernhardt, b. 2/14/1985 in Tuftonboro; Burgess G. Hodges III
and Joan White Hamilton
Burgess Gardner, IV, b. 11/14/1991 in Tuftonboro; Burgess G.
Hodges III and Joan W. Hamilton
Clara Ayers, b. 7/27/1994 in Laconia; Burgess Gardner Hodges III
and Joan White Hamilton
Frances Gregg, b. 4/18/1982 in Tuftonboro; Burgess G. Hodges III
and Joan W. Hamilton
Julia Marden, b. 8/20/1979 in Tuftonboro; Burgess G. Hodges III and
Joan White Hamilton
Mahera Gray, b. 11/9/1976 in Tuftonboro; Burgess G. Hodges III
and Joan W. Hamilton
Sara Elizabeth, b. 1/22/1989 in Laconia; Burgess G. Hodges and
Joan White Hamilton

HOLBROOKS,
Cynthia Farwell, b. 1/16/1952 in Wolfeboro; second; Wayne E.
Holbrooks (US Navy, NC) and Velma J. Bullock (MA)

HOLMES,
Bruce Edmund, b. 10/11/1954 in Laconia; second; Sumner M.
Holmes (machinist, MA) and Jeanne W. Parker (MA)
Christine Elizabeth, b. 7/29/1987 in Rochester; Bruce E. Holmes and
Linda Noyes
Edwin Sumner, b. 4/21/1952 in Laconia; first; Sumner M. Holmes
(machinist, MA) and Jeanne W. Parker (MA)
Patricia Lynne, b. 8/8/1990 in Rochester; Bruce E. Holmes and
Linda Noyes

HOOPER,
Charles Fraser, b. 9/19/1987 in Wolfeboro; Ronald G. Hooper and
Barbara Fraser
David Russell, b. 9/11/1961 in Wolfeboro; fifth; Ellsworth W. Hooper
(carpenter, Wolfeboro) and Muriel V. Lucas (Leicester, MA)
Debra Ann, b. 8/26/1955 in Wolfeboro; third; Ellsworth W. Hooper
(truck driver, NH) and Muriel V. Lucas (MA)
Katherine Lindsey, b. 7/13/1982 in Wolfeboro; Ronald G. Hooper
and Barbara T. Fraser
Nancy Lee, b. 8/1/1951 in Wolfeboro; first; Ellsworth W. Hooper (mill
worker, NH) and Muriel V. Lucas (Lester, MA)

Pamela Jean, b. 2/12/1959 in Wolfeboro; fourth; Ellsworth W.
Hooper (truck driver, NH) and Muriel V. Lucas (MA)
Sandra Louise, b. 3/21/1953 in Wolfeboro; second; Ellsworth W.
Hooper (truck driver, NH) and Muriel V. Lucas (MA); residence
– Ctr. Tuftonboro

HOOVER,
Lisa Rose, b. 5/5/1985 in Concord; Keith Hoover and Cheryl Anne
Nelson

HOPKINSON,
stillborn son, b. 3/31/1923; seventh; Thomas Hopkinson (laborer,
England) and Sarah E. Jose (Saco, ME)
Richard H., b. 7/18/1925 in Tuftonboro; Thomas Hopkinson (laborer,
England) and Sara E. Jose (Saco, ME)
Virginia May, b. 4/27/1934 in Wolfeboro; tenth; Thomas Hopkinson
(farmer, 50, England) and Sarah E. Jose (housewife, 38, Saco,
ME); residence – Mirror Lake

HORNER,
Marion L., b. 4/30/1898 in Tuftonboro; first; George S. Horner
(merchant, 36, Tuftonboro) and Grace A. Hodgdon (36,
Tuftonboro)

HOWE,
daughter, b. 11/15/1908; third; Carlton L. Howe (carpenter, 25,
Southboro, MA) and Ina M. Cordeau (26, Marlboro, MA)
Linda Sue, b. 4/3/1953 in Wolfeboro; second; Robert D. Howe
(contractor, MA) and Dorothy R. Hull (RI)
Nancy Ruth, b. 7/23/1948 in Wolfeboro; first; Robert D. Howe
(contractor, Southboro, MA) and Dorothy R. Hull (Pawtucket,
RI); residence – Melvin Village

HOYT,
son, b. 4/17/1895 in Tuftonboro; first; Charles S. Hoyt (farmer, 25,
Tuftonboro) and Katie M. Sawyer (20, Tuftonboro)
child, b. 5/--/1897 in Tuftonboro; second; Kate Hoyt
daughter, b. 11/18/1900 in Tuftonboro; fourth; Herbert C. Hoyt
(farmer, 28, Tuftonboro) and Nora M. Donahue (29, Ireland)
son, b. 7/15/1905 in Tuftonboro; Herbert C. Hoyt (blacksmith, 33,
Tuftonboro) and Mary Donahue (34, Ireland)

son, b. 3/30/1907; seventh; Herbert C. Hoyt (blacksmith, 35,
Tuftonboro) and Mary M. Donahue (36, Ireland)
son, b. 3/30/1907; eighth; Herbert C. Hoyt (blacksmith, 35,
Tuftonboro) and Mary M. Donahue (36, Ireland)
Archibald D., b. 11/8/1908; ninth; Herbert C. Hoyt (blacksmith,
Tuftonboro) and Nora M. Donahue (Ireland)
Lillie H., b. 11/7/1897 in Tuftonboro; third; Herbert C. Hoyt (farmer,
25, Tuftonboro) and Nora M. Donahue (26, Cork, Ireland)

HUFF,
Vanessa Mary, b. 1/26/1982 in Wolfeboro; Stephen G. Huff and Lisa
Ann Lessing

HUNT,
daughter, b. 8/2/1893 in Tuftonboro; first; Christopher R. Hunt
(carpenter, 34) and Eva N. Bean (27, Tuftonboro)
son, b. 3/25/1896 in Tuftonboro; second; Christopher Hunt (farmer,
36, Newport, England) and Eva M. Bean (29, Tuftonboro)
son, b. 4/3/1899 in Tuftonboro; third; Christopher R. Hunt (laborer,
39, Newport, England) and Eva M. Bean (32, Tuftonboro)
son, b. 10/3/1907; fourth; Christopher R. Hunt (carpenter, 47,
Newport, England) and Eva Bean (41, Tuftonboro)
Eva F., b. 12/8/1908; fifth; Christopher R. Hunt (carpenter, 50,
Newport, England) and Eva Bean (42, Tuftonboro)

HUNTER,
Annette, b. 2/24/1960 in Wolfeboro; seventh; Thomas W. Hunter
(self employed, NY) and Phyllis H. Bean (NH)
Asa Jacob, b. 1/24/1987 in Concord; Stephen W. Hunter and Robin
Emerson
Benjamin Adam, b. 2/27/1953 in Wolfeboro; third; Bradbury E.
Hunter (sawmill operator, Boston, MA) and Barbara Wood
(Boston, MA); residence – Melvin Village
Bonnie Day, b. 9/25/1949 in Wolfeboro; first; Bradbury E. Hunter
(farmer, Melrose, MA) and Barbara Wood (Boston, MA);
residence – Melvin Village
Bradbury Ellis, b. 7/15/1920; first; Ernest M. Hunter (farmer,
Chelsea, MA) and Margaret Ellis (Melrose, MA)
Bradbury Ellis, Jr., b. 4/4/1952 in Wolfeboro; second; Bradbury E.
Hunter (saw mill oper., MA) and Barbara Wood (MA)

Cory Melville, b. 1/25/1977 in Wolfeboro; Bradbury E. Hunter, Jr. and Marsha J. Belknap

Jacqueline, b. 3/8/1946 in Wolfeboro; first; Thomas Walter Hunter (farmer, Ticonderoga, NY) and Phyllis Audrey Bean (Jaffrey); residence – Melvin Village

Jeffrey Thomas, b. 6/7/1947 in Wolfeboro; second; Thomas Walter Hunter (farmer, Ticonderoga, NY) and Phyllis A. Bean (E. Jaffrey)

Kristie, b. 5/5/1971 in Wolfeboro; Jeffrey L. Hunter and Jane M. Smith

Kyle Nelson, b. 4/21/1987 in Rochester; Philip N. Hunter and Desira L. Syvinski

Larcie, b. 7/20/1973 in Wolfeboro; Tad A. Hunter and Kathryn E. Rupnow

Mac Andrew, b. 8/16/1976 in Wolfeboro; Tad A. Hunter and Kathryn E. Rupnow

Mary, b. 8/20/1951 in Wolfeboro; fifth; Thomas W. Hunter (farmer, NY) and Phyllis A. Bean (NH)

Nickie, b. 5/5/1971 in Wolfeboro; Jeffrey L. Hunter and Jane M. Smith

Paul Christopher, b. 4/15/1969 in Wolfeboro; Thomas W. Hunter (NY) and Phyllis A. Bean (NH)

Philip Nelson, b. 8/9/1961 in Wolfeboro; eighth; Thomas W. Hunter (farmer, Tyconderoga, NY) and Phyllis Audrey Bean (Jaffrey)

Stacey Lee, b. 9/1/1975 in Wolfeboro; Bradbury E. Hunter, Jr. and Marsha J. Belknap

Stephanie May, b. 5/14/1979 in Wolfeboro; Bradbury Ellis Hunter, Jr. and Marsha Jean Belknap

Stephen Walter, b. 8/13/1954 in Wolfeboro; sixth; Thomas W. Hunter (self employed, NY) and Phyllis A. Bean (NH)

Susan, b. 2/5/1949 in Wolfeboro; third; Thomas W. Hunter (farmer, Ticonderoga, NY) and Phyllis A. Bean (Jaffrey)

Tad Alan, b. 4/15/1950 in Wolfeboro; fourth; Thomas W. Hunter (self employed, Ticonderoga, NY) and Phyllis A. Bean (W. Jaffrey)

HUOT,

Ashley Renee, b. 7/20/1989 in Wolfeboro; Richard Allen Huot and Janet Marie Quaiotto

HURT,

Lucas Cody, b. 2/21/1984 in Tuftonboro; Raymond E. Hurt and
Robin Abigail Lawrence

Randall Clinton, b. 6/16/1988 in Tuftonboro; Raymond Edgar Hurt
and Robin A. Lawrence

Travis James, b. 11/28/1990 in Tuftonboro; Raymond E. Hurt III and
Robin Abigail Lawrence

IMHOOF,

Nicholas Raymond, b. 11/7/1998 in Wolfeboro; John W. Imhoof, Jr.
and Jody B. Syvinski

INGHAM,

Christian William, b. 1/20/1995 in Wolfeboro; Brett William Ingham
and Patricia C. Venable

JACKSON,

Celia M., b. 10/23/1893 in Tuftonboro; first; George Jackson
(shoemaker, 42, Rochester) and Adelia Burleigh (26,
Tuftonboro)

JAMIESON,

Christina Lee, b. 8/4/1987 in Wolfeboro; Ronald S. Jamieson and
Donna A. Donahue

Christopher Robert, b. 8/15/1983 in Wolfeboro; Robert F. Jamieson
and Linda J. Todesco

Jill Ann, b. 4/21/1986 in Wolfeboro; Robert F. Jamieson and Linda J.
Todesco

Megan Marie, b. 6/10/1989 in Wolfeboro; Robert F. Jamieson and
Linda Jean Todesco

JENKINS,

Jesse Allan, b. 6/16/2004 in Concord; Mark Jenkins and Paula
Jenkins

Kate Elizabeth, b. 8/8/2005 in Concord; Mark Jenkins and Paula
Jenkins

JOHNSON,

daughter, b. 12/20/1899 in Tuftonboro; third; Charles E. Johnson
(stage driver, 43, Tuftonboro) and Lizzie L. Wiggin (39,
Tuftonboro)

Alan Weston, b. 7/10/1966 in Wolfeboro; fifth; Arthur W. Johnson
(maintenance, N. Conway) and Judith O. Austin (Grafton)
Ariana C., b. 3/16/1977 in Laconia; Donald S. Johnson and Gail S.
Enwright
Arthur Westly, b. 5/9/1965 in Wolfeboro; fourth; Arthur W. Johnson
(maintenance, Conway) and Judith Ona Austin (Grafton)
Bobbi, b. 7/16/1962 in Wolfeboro; third; Arthur W. Johnson
(maintenance, Conway) and Judtith O. Austin (Grafton)
Craig Robert, b. 11/8/1975 in Wolfeboro; Bruce A. Johnson and
Linda Ann Farmer
Laura Diane, b. 9/23/1977 in Wolfeboro; Bruce A. Johnson and
Linda A. Farmer
Lucas Stevenson, b. 9/26/1994 in Wolfeboro; Andrew Alan Johnson
and Sally Frances G. Muir
Owen Thomas, b. 11/13/1996 in Wolfeboro; Andrew Alan Johnson
and Sally F. G. Muir

JONES,
son, b. 8/8/1921; first; J. Perley Jones (carpenter, ME) and Leora
Adjutant (Tuftonboro)
Michael Jeffrey, b. 5/20/1985 in Laconia; Michael F. Jones and
Laurie R. Hawes
Michelle Rea, b. 10/8/1986 in Laconia; Michael F. Jones and Laurie
R. Hawes
Mindy Louise, b. 3/17/1966 in Wolfeboro; first; Kenneth D. Jones
(chef, Wolfeboro) and Susan Hunter (Wolfeboro)

JORDAN,
Adam Gilbert, b. 7/1/1989 in Dover; Mark Wetre Jordan and Diane
Eileen Bell
Peter Delvin, b. 11/23/1948 in Wolfeboro; fourth; Robert C. Jordan
(school teacher, Mexico, ME) and Priscilla D. Roberts (Sanford,
ME); residence – Melvin Village

JOSEPH,
Ashley Jane, b. 5/14/1986 in Wolfeboro; Irving F. Joseph, Jr. and
Cynthia J. McLean

KANE,
Robert, b. 8/17/1931 in Wolfeboro; third; Edward Kane (painter, 42,
Boston, MA) and Angie Hersey (37, Tuftonboro)

KATWICK,

James Sidney, b. 7/13/1999 in Rochester; James Katwick and Shelley Katwick

KELLY,

Owen Alexander, b. 9/8/2004 in Concord; Robert Kelly and Jessica Kelly

KENDAL,

Herbert George, b. 6/8/1950 in Wolfeboro; second; Herbert B. Kendall (factory worker, Lynn, MA) and Charlotte L. Gouin (Ossipee); residence – Ctr. Tuftonboro

Robert Thornton, b. 4/9/1952 in Wolfeboro; third; Herbert B. Kendal (steel press oper., MA) and Charlotte L. Gouin (NH)

Stacy Elizabeth, b. 12/15/1977 in Wolfeboro; Herbert G. Kendal and Linda M. Dore

KENISON-MARVIN,

Leah Mary, b. 8/17/1993 in Concord; Ernest W. Marvin and Kristine F. Kenison

KENNEDY,

Brian Thomas, b. 9/16/1977 in Wolfeboro; Thomas F. Kennedy and Eileen M. Conway

KENT,

Johanna Zepherinee, b. 11/30/1983 in Wolfeboro; Roger J. Kent and Marlene M. Thibault

KEYES,

Amanda Jane, b. 12/19/1982 in Laconia; William C. Keyes and Rebecca L. Knapp

Brian William, b. 6/25/1980 in Laconia; William C. Keyes and Rebecca L. Knapp

Kimberly Anne, b. 7/13/1964 in Wolfeboro; first; William C. Keyes (carpenter, Marblehead, MA) and Cynthia Ellison (Salem, MA)

Todd Allen, b. 12/2/1981 in Laconia; William C. Keyes and Rebecca L. Knapp

KIMBALL,
Alston E., b. 11/29/1894; first; Amos W. Kimball (farmer, Tuftonboro) and Fanny Kimball (Wolfeboro)

KNEELAND,
Frederick J., Jr., b. 12/30/1917; first; Frederick J. Kneeland (farmer, Cambridgeport, MA) and Marguerite E. Ferguson (Orient Heights, MA)

KNISLEY,
Laurie Jean, b. 10/28/1984 in Wolfeboro; Reuben E. Knisley and Peggy E. Adjutant

LAASE,
Christian Frederick, b. 12/19/1969 in Wolfeboro; Francis W. Laase (NH) and Ellen P. Hickey (NY)
Patrick William, b. 9/19/1973 in Wolfeboro; Francis W. Laase and Ellen P. Hickey
William Ernest, b. 12/5/1976 in Wolfeboro; Francis W. Laase and Ellen P. Hickey

LADD,
Ashton Charles, b. 4/1/1997 in Wolfeboro; Ian Charles Ladd and Jamie Leigh Glidden
Darrin Harvey, b. 10/13/1974 in Laconia; David C. Ladd and Gail M. Krippendorf
Ella May, b. 5/31/1897 in Tuftonboro; second; Harvey Ladd (farmer, 30, Tuftonboro) and May Hopper (33, Broughton, PQ)
Elsie Eliza, b. 3/29/1899 in Tuftonboro; sixth; George M. Ladd (farmer, 43, Tuftonboro) and Juliet Bickford (42, Tamworth)
Eunice M., b. 6/15/1893 in Tuftonboro; fifth; George M. Ladd (farmer, 37, Tuftonboro) and Juliette Bickford (26, Tamworth)
Kendra Aaron, b. 4/9/1999 in Tuftonboro; Ian Ladd and Jamie (Glidden) Ladd
Phebe Ruth, b. 1/15/1903 in Tuftonboro; third; Harvey A. Ladd (carpenter, 45, Tuftonboro) and Mary Hopper (39, Broughton, PQ)

LAFRANCE,
Tara Lise, b. 7/23/1980 in Wolfeboro; Marc P. LaFrance and Susan G. Wallace

LAGRAM,
Noah Storm, b. 1/19/2004 in Plymouth; Robert Lagram and Valerie Lagram

LAIDLAW,
Alvin Robert, b. 4/6/1968 in Wolfeboro; John E. Laidlaw (MA) and Jeannette H. Libby (MA)

LAMPREY,
son, b. 2/14/1897 in Tuftonboro; fourth; Arthur H. Lamprey (boatman, 38, Moultonboro) and Carrie F. Day (33, Boston, MA)
son, b. 5/10/1924 in Tuftonboro; first; Wilbur H. Lamprey (farmer, Moultonboro) and Frances L. Harriman (Sandwich)
Carroll, b. 1/30/1899 in Tuftonboro; first; Robert Lamprey (farmer, 53, Long Island) and Mary F. McKenna (31, E. Boston, MA)
Theodore Brackett, b. 6/3/1903 in Tuftonboro; first; Wilbur Lamprey (farmer, 31, Moultonboro) and Fannie Thompson (26, Tuftonboro)
Wilbur H., b. 8/27/1925 in Tuftonboro; second; Wilbur H. Lamprey (farmer, Moultonboro) and Frances L. Harriman (Sandwich)

LANE,
Robert Bruce, b. 1/23/1970 in Wolfeboro; Robert O. Lane (NH) and Marianne Severance (NH)

LANGEVIN,
Keith Avery, b.10/26/1968 in Wolfeboro; Frank J. Langevin (NH) and Sandra A. Snape (MA)

LANGLOIS,
Gage Oliver, b. 7/4/2004 in Wolfeboro; Gregg Langlois and Michelle Langlois

LAPAR,
Amanda Zdenka, b. 2/17/2002 in Wolfeboro; William Lapar and Sonya Lapar
Jessica Lynn Frances, b. 7/26/1994 in Laconia; Daniel Mila Lapar and Kimi Lynn Hauser

LAPLANTE,
Danielle Jean, b. 9/27/1980 in Laconia; Raymond E. LaPlante and
Jane M. Calkins
Jeremy Alex, b. 8/27/1977 in Wolfeboro; Raymond E. LaPlante and
Jane M. Calkins

LAWRENCE-HURT,
Angela Rachel, b. 6/30/1995 in Laconia; Raymond E. Hurt and
Robin Abigail Lawrence

LAZARAS,
Gail Ellen, b. 3/26/1970 in Wolfeboro; Paul V. Lazaras (CT) and
Mildred G. Bedeau (NY)

LEACH,
Connor Morgan, b. 6/1/1999 in Laconia; Stephen Leach and Tracy
Leach
Madison Healy, b. 7/31/1997 in Laconia; Stephen Morgan Leach
and Tracy Lynn Caron
Olivia Margaret, b. 7/10/2002 in Laconia; Stephen Leach and Tracy
Leach

LESSARD,
Joshua Ross, b. 10/2/1976 in Wolfeboro; William D. Lessard and
Linda L. Wakefield
Katherine, b. 3/27/2002 in Wolfeboro; Bill Lessard and Regina
Lessard

LESTER,
John Gregory, b. 2/2/1955 in Wolfeboro; first; Richard H. Lester
(salesman, MA) and Marjorie Wood (MA)
Merry Noel, b. 12/24/1956 in Wolfeboro; fourth; Richard H. Lester
(salesman, Ware, MA) and Marjorie Wood (Boston, MA)

LEVESQUE,
Ethan Winslow, b. 3/27/1990 in Wolfeboro; John A. Levesque and
Susan Ellison

LEVIN,
Amy Marie, b. 6/22/1990 in Wolfeboro; Robert E. Levin, Jr. and
Diane L. Fournier

LEWIS,
son, b. 2/20/1909; first; Rainsford W. Lewis (farmer, Albert Co., NB)
and Lena Wendell (Tuftonboro)
Bruce Elliot, b. 5/4/1947 in Wolfeboro; second; Reid Elliot Lewis (US
Army, Halifax, NS) and Priscilla H. Brookes (Boston, MA)

LIBB[E]Y,
son, b. 11/28/1892 in Tuftonboro; sixth; Frank Libby (farmer, 43,
Ossipee) and Lucy Haley (Tuftonboro)
Alvin Donald, b. 5/11/1941 in Wolfeboro; second; Robert Carleton
Libby (state laborer, 19, Milton) and Hazel McKanney
(housewife, 24, Milford, CT); residence – Ctr. Tuftonboro
Andrew Paul, b. 9/4/1986 in Laconia; Alan D. Libby and Joyce M.
Lindquist
Angelea Iris, b. 2/21/2000 in Wolfeboro; Alan Libby and Sherry Libby
Dale Robert, b. 6/6/1959 in Wolfeboro; first; Robert C. Libby (tree
surgeon, NH) and Carol J. Smith (NH)
Ethelda, b. 3/9/1925 in Tuftonboro; stillborn; second; Frank Libby
(laborer, Tuftonboro) and Bernice Canney (Ossipee)
Kay Rosalind Neath, b. 12/5/1988 in Laconia; Daniel F. Libby Sr.
and Sandra N. Larson
Keith Walter, b. 11/30/1960 in Wolfeboro; second; Robert C. Libby,
Jr. (dish washer, NH) and Carol Jean Smith (NH)
Mary A., b. 3/17/1923; fifth; Robert M. Libby (lumberman,
Tuftonboro) and Helen S. Eldridge (Ossipee)
Meghan Sarah, b. 6/15/1991 in Laconia; Daniel F. Libby and Sandra
N. Larson
Melissa Carrol Jean, b. 8/16/1987 in Wolfeboro; Joseph C. Libby
and Cyrene E. Gaudlap
Molly Marie, b. 2/12/1998 in Wolfeboro; Joseph C. Libby and Cyrene
E. Gaudlap
Robert C., b. 4/17/1921; Robert M. Libby (farmer, Tuftonboro) and
Helen S. Eldridge (Ossipee)
Robert Carleton, Jr., b. 9/4/1939 in Wolfeboro; first; Robert Carleton
Libbey (laborer on state road, 18, Milton) and Hazel Verna
McKenney (22, Milford, MA)
Robert M., b. 5/1/1895 in Tuftonboro; second; Frank Libbey (farmer,
45, Tuftonboro) and Lucy Haley (40, Tuftonboro)
Ronald John, b. 4/13/1947 in Wolfeboro; fourth; Robert C. Libby
(woodsman, Milton) and Hazel Verna McKenny (Milford, CT);
residence – Ctr. Tuftonboro

LILLIS,
stillborn son, b. 9/22/1946 in Wolfeboro; first; John Paul Lillis (asst. manager, Malden, MA) and Glenna MacSchofield (Rock Springs, WY)

LONG,
Jeffrey Alan, b. 5/4/1968 in Wolfeboro; Richard W. Long (NY) and Patricia J. Hatch (ME)

LONGPHEE,
Alyssa Joy, b. 5/18/2000 in Manchester; Kenneth Longphee and Jamie Longphee

LOPES,
Davian Jeremy, b. 8/3/2005 in Wolfeboro; Michael Lopes and Jennifer Souza

LORD,
son, b. 9/20/1905 in Tuftonboro; Charles S. Lord (laborer, 22, Effingham) and Gertrude M. Hoyt (28, Malden, MA)
son, b. 2/6/1907; third; Charles S. Lord (laborer, 24, Effingham) and Gertrude E. Hoyt (29, Malden, MA)
daughter, b. 3/25/1910; third; Milton A. Lord (machinist, Conway) and Lizzie B. Morrison (Tuftonboro)
daughter, b. 10/2/1912; fourth; Milton A. Lord (farmer, Conway) and Lizzie B. Morrison (Tuftonboro)
son, b. 4/3/1917; seventh; Harry J. Lord (Acton, ME) and Clara A. Nichols (Ossipee)
Esther B., b. 10/26/1907; second; Milton A. Lord (machinist, 29, Conway) and Lizzie B. Morrison (31, Tuftonboro)
John Morrison, b. 9/21/1905 in Tuftonboro; Milton A. Lord (machinist, 28, Conway) and Lizzie B. Morrison (32, Tuftonboro)

LOWRIE,
Richard Hartwell, b. 2/3/1970 in Wolfeboro; Arthur F. Lowrie (VT) and Natalie A. Hartwell (MA)

LUDWICK,
Amanda May, b. 9/18/1983 in Laconia; Stanley R. Ludwick and Donna M. McIntyre

LYON,

Pamela Byrd, b. 4/19/1954 in Wolfeboro; third; Peter B. Lyon (conservatrion officer, NY) and Nellie E. Bartelt (NY)

Patricia Blair, b. 5/19/1952 in Wolfeboro; second; Peter B. Lyon (technician, NY) and Nellie C. Bartelt (NY)

Peter Byrd, II, b. 6/24/1955 in Wolfeboro; fourth; Peter B. Lyon (conservation officer, NY) and Nellie E. Bartlett (NY)

MACK,

son, b. 1/28/1936 in Wolfeboro; second; Maurice Jewell Mack (laborer, 24, Laconia) and Christine May Elliott (25, Alton); residence – Melvin Village

Janet Arlene, b. 1/5/1937 in Wolfeboro; third; Maurice Jewell Mack (laborer, 25, Laconia) and Christine M. Elliott (26, Alton); residence – Melvin Village

Robert Maurice, b. 11/24/1934 in Wolfeboro; first; Maurice J. Mack (laborer, 23, Laconia) and Christine Elliott (housewife, 24, Alton); residence – Ctr. Tuftonboro

MACLEAN,

Jane Ayer, b. 12/8/1947 in Wolfeboro; second; Forrest Edward MacLean (salesman, Waltham, MA) and Helen M. Hodges (Somerville, MA)

MACMARTIN,

Steven Clow, b. 9/11/1993 in Wolfeboro; Jeffrey W. MacMartin and Sandra Lee Hower

William Lee, b. 10/23/1991 in Wolfeboro; Jeffrey W. MacMartin and Sandra Lee Hower

MACPHEE,

Lauren Casey, b. 3/2/2005 in Wolfeboro; Brian MacPhee and Jenna MacPhee

MADDEN,

Emily Elizabeth, b. 11/15/2001 in Laconia; Douglas Madden and Kimberly Madden

Erik Bailey, b. 1/9/2000 in Wolfeboro; Russell Madden and Kristen Madden

Joshua Douglas, b. 11/15/1993 in Laconia; Douglas T. Madden and Kimberly Ann Todesco

Nicholas William, b. 8/3/1998 in Laconia; Douglas T. Madden and
   Kimberly A. Todesco

MANLEY,
Elizabeth Mae, b. 11/26/1936 in Tuftonboro; first; Leroy A. Manley
   (gardner, 29, Wakefield, MA) and Dorothy E. Huckins (teacher,
   29, Freedom)
Nancy, b. 2/7/1939 in Wolfeboro; second; Leroy Augustus Manley
   (gardner, 31, Wakefield, MA) and Dorothy Edna Huckins
   (housewife, 31, Freedom)

MARTIN,
Austin Douglas, b. 6/5/1996 in Wolfeboro; Douglas Arthur Martin and
   Paula Marie Engheben
Emily Marie, b. 9/25/1993 in Plymouth; Douglas A. Martin and Paula
   Engheben

MAURA,
Autumn Rafaela, b. 1/1/1980 in Tuftonboro; Edward L. Maura and
   Lorraine Angela Malone

McCARTHY,
Katherine Anne, b. 6/23/1995 in Dover; Michael A. McCarthy and
   Suzannah E. Bohannon
Mary Elizabeth, b. 5/15/2002 in Dover; Michael McCarthy and
   Suzannah McCarthy

McDUFFEE,
Donald, b. 3/15/1916; third; Irving McDuffee (farmer, Tuftonboro)
   and Minnie Templeton (Ossipee)
Velma A., b. 9/3/1913; second; Irving McDuffee (farmer, Tuftonboro)
   and Minnie Templeton (Ossipee)

McFARLANE,
Joshua Andrew, b. 3/6/1976 in Laconia; Peter A. McFarlane and
   Nancy D. Mitchell

McINTIRE,
daughter, b. 4/14/1891 in Tuftonboro; first; Lewis McIntire
   (carpenter, 23, Tuftonboro) and Nettie C. Libbey (21,
   Tuftonboro)

son, b. 4/4/1892 in Tuftonboro; second; Lewis McIntire (carpenter, 24, Tuftonboro) and Nettie C. Libby (22, Tuftonboro)

son, b. 4/27/1905; Lewis McIntire (carpenter, 38, Tuftonboro) and Sadie Doe (19, Tuftonboro)

daughter, b. 8/22/1909; second; Lewis McIntire (carpenter, Tuftonboro) and Sadie Doe (Tuftonboro)

stillborn son, b. 1/19/1930 in Tuftonboro; first; Delma McIntire (laborer, 23, Tuftonboro) and Eunice Frye (housewife, 23, Plymouth)

Debra Ellen, b. 1/17/1958 in Wolfeboro; first; Delma L. McIntire, Jr. (laborer, Wolfeboro) and Elsie L. Smith (Wolfeboro)

Delma Louis, b. 12/24/1935 in Wolfeboro; second; Delma L. McIntire (trucking, 30, Tuftonboro) and Eunice E. Frye (housewife, 29, Plymouth); residence – Melvin Village

McLEAN,
Jane Ayer, b. 2/11/1944 in Wolfeboro; first; Forrest Edward McLean (US Marines, Waltham, MA) and Helen Marion Hodges (Somerville, MA); residence – Boston, MA

McNAMARA,
Elizabeth Corby, b. 1/7/2000 in Boston, MA; John McNamara and Anne McNamara

William Sullivan, b. 10/5/2001 in Manchester; John McNamara and Anne McNamara

McVANEY,
Ethan Michael, b. 4/26/1981 in Laconia; Thomas L. McVaney and Candace M. Shelton

Garrett Ressie, b. 7/27/1979 in Laconia; Thomas Lee McVaney and Candace Mary Shelton

McWHIRTER,
Michael James, b. 10/18/2001 in Wolfeboro; Donald McWhirter and Stephanie McWhirter

MEEHAN,
Kyleah Anne, b. 3/27/2001 in Laconia; Robert Meehan and Calista Meehan

Shayla Leigh, b. 8/3/1999 in Laconia; Robert Meehan and Calista Meehan

Teagan Patrick, b. 12/18/1997 in Laconia; Robert Michael Meehan and Calista Ann McGlaflin

MELANSON,
Lena M., b. 7/7/1917; second; Napoleon Melanson (teaming, Canaan) and Alice Elliott (Grafton)

MENDENHALL,
Jesse Roberts, b. 7/10/1979 in Wolfeboro; John Dean Mendenhall and Mary Kathryn Stepp

MERRELL,
Caroline Place, b. 3/11/1991 in Hanover; Thomas F. Merrell and Susan Place
Hannah Stopford, b. 7/14/1989 in Hanover; Thomas F. Merrell and Susan Place

MERRIFIELD,
son, b. 6/14/1895 in Tuftonboro; first; Everett Merryfield (farmer, 20, ME) and Emma I. Nichols (20, Boston, MA)
daughter, b. 7/27/1895 in Tuftonboro; first; Perley Merryfield (farmer, 16, Porter, ME) and Nellie M. Thompson (18, Tuftonboro)
daughter, b. 4/28/1897 in Tuftonboro; second; Perley Merrifield (farmer, 18, Porter, ME) and Nellie M. Thompson (21, Tuftonboro)
daughter, b. 3/8/1899 in Tuftonboro; third; Perley Merrifield (farmer, 20, Porter, ME) and Nellie M. Thompson (22, Tuftonboro)
daughter, b. 9/21/1900 in Tuftonboro; fourth; Perley Merryfield (farmer, 21, Porter, ME) and Nellie M. Thompson (24, Tuftonboro)
son, b. 4/22/1902 in Tuftonboro; fifth; Perley Merryfield (farmer, 24, Porter, ME) and Nellie M. Thompson (26, Tuftonboro)
son, b. 10/9/1904 in Tuftonboro; sixth; Perley Merrifield (farmer, 26, Porter, ME) and Nellie M. Thompson (28, Tuftonboro)
son, b. 6/13/1906; seventh; Perley Merrifield (farmer, 28, Porter, ME) and Nellie M. Thompson (20, Tuftonboro)

MERRILL,
Nathan Philip, b. 5/26/1976 in Tuftonboro; David A. Merrill and Elizabeth A. Vickers

METZ,

Gretchen Elizabeth, b. 7/18/1975 in Wolfeboro; Steven E. Metz and
  Norma F. Grant

Rebecca Lynn, b. 10/4/1972 in Wolfeboro; Steven E. Metz and
  Norma F. Grant

MEZQUITA,

Bradlee, b. 6/25/1968 in Wolfeboro; Richard B. Mezquita (MA) and
  Mary F. Hatch (NH)

Carrie Ann, b. 1/18/1967 in Wolfeboro; third; Richard B. Mesquita
  (teacher, Marblehead, MA) and Mary F. Hatch (N. Conway)

MICHAUD,

Nicholas Daniel, b. 1/21/1992 in Tuftonboro; Mark R. Michaud and
  Lauren Lynn Munroe

MILLER,

Donald Gilman, b. 6/24/1944 in Wolfeboro; stillborn; first; Roy Gilbert
  Miller (US Army, E. L. Mead., MA) and Louise Gilman
  (Tuftonboro)

MILLS,

Caroline Gail, b. 1/12/2000 in Wolfeboro; Michael Mills and Ellen
  Mills

MISOUD,

Susanna, b. 2/27/1958 in Wolfeboro; third; Fletcher A. Misoud
  (merchant seaman, MA) and Constance G. Connery (MA);
  residence - Ctr. Tuftonboro

MISSUD,

Emilie, b. 3/15/1953 in Wolfeboro; first; Fletcher A. Missud
  (merchant seaman, MA) and Constance G. Canney (MA);
  residence – Ctr. Tuftonboro

Fletcher Abbott, Jr., b. 10/23/1954 in Wolfeboro; second; Fletcher A.
  Missud (merchant seaman, MA) and Constance G. Canney
  (MA)

Laurienne Gould, b. 6/24/1960 in Wolfeboro; fourth; Fletcher A.
  Missud (merchant seaman, MA) and Constance Canney (MA)

MITCHELL,

Alison Marie, b. 12/14/1988 in Concord; Daniel R. Mitchell and Sandra E. Sherman

Amanda Eleanor, b. 1/28/1986 in Concord; Daniel R. Mitchell and Sandra E. Sherman

Beverly June, b. 3/17/1940 in Wolfeboro; first; Thomas Osborne Mitchell (caretaker, 29, NS) and Marion Edna Hersey (housewife, 28, Tuftonboro); residence – Ctr. Tuftonboro

Jane Elizabeth, b. 12/15/1967 in Wolfeboro; first; Thomas Mitchell, Jr. (caretaker, Forest Hills, MA) and Susie Williams (Wolfeboro)

Kenneth Lee, b. 11/3/1941 in Wolfeboro; second; Thomas Osborn Mitchell (landscape gardener, 31, NS) and Marion Edna Hersey (housewife, 30, Tuftonboro); residence – Ctr. Tuftonboro

Nancy Diane, b. 3/1/1950 in Wolfeboro; fifth; Thomas O. Mitchell (landscape, Glasgow, NS) and Marion E. Hersey (Ctr. Tuftonboro)

Rachel Michelle, b. 9/4/1975 in Laconia; Rodney K. Mitchell and Deborah S. Loveless

Richard Dennis, b. 4/30/1947 in Wolfeboro; first; John C. Mitchell (student, Boston, MA) and Nancy Bell Stordock (Fergus Falls, MN)

Robert Malcolm, b. 2/8/1947 in Wolfeboro; fourth; Thomas O. Mitchell (greenskeeper, New Glasco, NS) and Marion Edna Hersey (Ctr. Tuftonboro); residence – Ctr. Tuftonboro

Tyler Anthony, b. 12/31/2005 in Rochester; Brian Clark and Amanda Mitchell

Tyler James, b. 8/3/2005 in Wolfeboro; Steven Mitchell and Alicia Mitchell

Valerie Mae, b. 9/5/2000 in Wolfeboro; Steven Mitchell and Alicia Mitchell

MIXER,

Jessica Katherine, b. 1/16/1973 in Wolfeboro; Douglas M. Mixer and Norma Kate Deyak

Mardy Gale, b. 8/16/1951 in Wolfeboro; second; John M. Mixer (real est. & ins., MA) and Orilla M. McLean (MA)

MOLEA,

Maureen Julia, b. 4/5/1986 in Wolfeboro; Nicholas J. Molea and Rosemarie Crowley

MONROE,
Hunter Dean, b. 3/17/2005 in Laconia; Nathan Monroe and
Cassandra Reppucci

MONTGOMERY,
David Lee, Jr., b. 9/15/1983 in Wolfeboro; David L. Montgomery and
Jane C. Rowe
Nancy Anne, b. 8/26/1981 in Wolfeboro; David L. Montgomery and
Jane C. Rowe

MOODY,
Amanda Kathleen, b. 10/11/1988 in Laconia; Jeffrey M. Moody and
Terry June Colby
Ethel L., b. 6/3/1919; third; Aldo Moody (mill man, Effingham) and
Lillian Horne (Newfield, ME)
Natasha Marylin, b. 12/25/1989 in Laconia; Jeffrey M. Moody and
Terry June Colby
Reginald Robert, b. 11/19/1991 in Laconia; Jeffrey M. Moody and
Terry June Colby

MOORE,
Chelsea Faye, b. 6/18/1991 in Wolfeboro; Daron R. Moore and
Cindy Lee Valade
Shawna Ashley, b. 10/4/1993 in Wolfeboro; Daron R. Moore and
Cincy Lee Valade
Thomas James, b. 12/28/1989 in Laconia; Paul A. Moore, Jr. and
Susan E. York

MORAN,
Ryan Mackenzie, b. 5/18/1996 in Wolfeboro; Eric George Moran and
Patricia May Bartoswicz

MORGAN,
daughter, b. 6/4/1923; third; Charles D. Morgan (chauffeur,
Wolfeboro) and Doris E. Ayers (Wolfeboro); residence –
Wolfeboro
Jeffrey Laurence, b. 12/15/1976 in Wolfeboro; Lloyd C. Morgan, Jr.
and Laura A. Gerrity
Judith Patricia, b. 9/12/1953 in Wolfeboro; third; Lloyd C. Morgan
(truck business, ME) and Eleanor B. Lucas (MA); residence –
Ctr. Tuftonboro

Lloyd Clinton, Jr., b. 7/3/1946 in Wolfeboro; first; Lloyd Clinton
Morgan (store clerk, Sanford, ME) and Blanche Eleanor Lucas
(Brookfield, MA)
Rianna Julia, b. 10/12/1978 in Laconia; Lloyd Clinton Morgan and
Cynthia J. Cheney
Ricky Melvin, b. 6/11/1948 in Wolfeboro; second; Lloyd C. Morgan
(truck driver, Sanford, ME) and Eleanor B. Lucas (Brookfield)

MORRILL,
Seth Willey, b. 1/13/1980 in Wolfeboro; Rodney B. Morrill and
Patricia Janet Willey

MORRIS,
son, b. 7/12/1899 in Tuftonboro; first; Alfred Morris (farmer, 34,
Biddeford, ME) and Hattie J. Buzzell (32, Meredith)
stillborn daughter, b. 6/26/1901 in Tuftonboro; second; Alfred Morris
(farmer, 35, Biddeford, ME) and Hattie J. Buzzell (34, Meredith)
daughter, b. 10/13/1904 in Tuftonboro; sixth; Alfred Morris (farmer,
38, Biddeford, ME) and Hattie Buzzell (38, Meredith)
son, b. 7/2/1907; sixth; Alfred Morris (farmer, 41, Biddeford, ME) and
Hattie J. Buzzel (40, Meredith)
daughter, b. 12/9/1909; seventh; Alfred Morris (laborer, Biddeford,
ME) and Hattie J. Buzzell (Meredith)
daughter, b. 2/3/1911; Alfred Morris (laborer, 44, Biddeford, ME) and
Hattie J. Buzzell (44, Meredith)

MORSE,
Granville, b. 9/2/1898 in Tuftonboro; second; Victor M. Morse
(clergyman, 28, Andover, ME) and Mary E. French (28, Quincy,
MA)

MOULTON,
James Enrique, b. 11/17/1992 in Laconia; Darwin Moulton and Alcira
D. C. Gracia
Jillian, b. 2/6/1984 in Wolfeboro; Robert C. Moulton, Jr. and Nancy
Jane Stockman
Ora E., b. 6/9/1918; first; James Moulton (laborer, Parsonsfield, ME)
and Gladys Haley (Tuftonboro)

MURDOCK,
Jeremy Steven, b. 4/6/2000 in Wolfeboro; Mark Murdock and Louise
  Murdock

NEWCOMB,
Brett Everett, b. 7/15/1984 in Concord; Nelson E. Newcomb, Jr. and
  Betsey Gay Broderick
Dick Thomas, Jr., b. 3/7/1977 in Wolfeboro; Dick Thomas Newcomb
  and Marcia L. Patriquin
Heather Dawn, b. 8/17/1978 in Wolfeboro; Dick T. Newcomb and
  Marcia L. Patriquin
Sarah Amber, b. 6/3/1986 in Concord; Nelson F. Newcomb, Jr. and
  Betsey G. Brodrick

NICKERSON,
Esther Ruth, b. 3/21/1946 in Tuftonboro; fourth; Nelson E.
  Nickerson, Jr. (chopping timber, Spring'en, NS) and Barbara J.
  Sharp (NH)

NICOLAY,
Madeline Rose, b. 5/11/2001 in Laconia; Michael Nicolay and
  Jennifer Nicolay
Myles Thomas, b. 5/11/2001 in Laconia; Michael Nicolay and
  Jennifer Nicolay

NORRIS,
Andria Patrick, b. 3/23/2001 in Dover; Patrick Norris and Panagiota
  Norris

O'BRIEN,
Kayla Erin, b. 3/3/2005 in Rochester; James O'Brien and Cindy
  O'Brien

O'DONNELL,
Oceanna Jeanne, b. 8/22/1977 in Tuftonboro; Michael T. O'Donnell
  and Linda J. Brinkman; residence – Medway, MA

OSBORNE,
son, b. 7/21/1900 in Tuftonboro; second; Fred L. Osborn
  (shoemaker, 28, Dover) and Lena G. Shannon (18, Tuftonboro)

Ethelena, b. 10/22/1898 in Tuftonboro; first; Fred L. Osborne (shoemaker, 23) and Lena G. Shannon (16, Tuftonboro)

OVERALL,
Aubrey Lynn, b. 5/7/2004 in Rochester; David Overall and Amanda Overall

PAGE,
Milton Lord, b. 6/8/1942 in Wolfeboro; second; Lincoln Ridler Page (geologist, Lisbon) and Esther Belinda Lord (Tuftonboro); residence – Washington, DC

PAIGE,
Geraldine, b. 6/25/1930 in Wolfeboro; first; Robert Paige (electrician, 25, White River Jct., VT) and Eva Howe (housewife, 21, Tuftonboro)
Robert, b. 5/8/1962 in Wolfeboro; first; Thomas H. Paige (carpenter, Wolfeboro) and Martha E. Letteney (Dover)
Thomas Howe, b. 1/19/1940 in Wolfeboro; second; Robert Paige (electrician, 34, White River Jct., VT) and Eva May Howe (housewife, 31, Tuftonboro)

PANNO,
Wayne Frederick, b. 1/18/1966 in Wolfeboro; first; Harry F. Panno (construction, N. Conway) and Estelle Sheaff (Portsmouth)

PARADIS,
Merideth Katherine, b. 8/28/1989 in Wolfeboro; Scott F. Paradis and Lisa Newcombe

PAVLINETZ,
Michael Quinn, b. 1/19/2002 in Concord; Michael Pavlinetz and Teresa Pavlinetz

PENNELL,
Mindy Lynn, b. 7/16/1980 in Wolfeboro; Dwight W. Pennell and Carolyn C. Phelps

PERKINS,

Cheryl, b. 11/25/1938 in Wolfeboro; third; Bert Austin Perkins (fireman, 45, Ctr. Ossipee) and Mildred Edna Bruce (25, Saranac Lake, NY)

Marshall Lloyd, b. 8/7/1937 in Wolfeboro; second; Bert Perkins (laborer, 43, Ctr. Ossipee) and Mildred Bruce (24, Saranac, NY)

PERSON,

Cynthia Ann, b. 9/17/1944 in Wolfeboro; first; Herbert George Person (chemical eng., Groton, VT) and Beverly Annette Bean (E. Jaffrey)

PETERSON,

Gabriel Kaesy, b. 6/6/1986 in Franklin; Dale C. Peterson and Kathy Osinski

Joy, b. 2/1/1995 in Wolfeboro; Dale C. Peterson and Kathy Osinski

PHILBRICK,

daughter, b. 5/17/1902 in Tuftonboro; first; Delia Philbrick (Tuftonboro)

daughter, b. 5/19/1904 in Tuftonboro; fourth; Alfred Philbrick (farmer, 31, Bartlett) and Elsie Brown (22, Waterboro, ME)

stillborn daughter, b. 4/17/1913; seventh; Alfred Philbrick (farmer, Bartlett) and Elsie Drown (Waterboro, ME)

Florence J., b. 7/3/1909; seventh; Alfred Philbrick (laborer, Bartlett) and Elsie C. Drowns (Waterboro, ME)

PHILBROOK,

son, b. 8/17/1907; sixth; Alfred Philbrook (laborer, 34, Ossipee) and Elsie C. Drowns (25, Waterboro, ME)

PIGOTT,

Francis Arthur, b. 11/15/1965 in Wolfeboro; third; Robert A. Pigott (clerk, Winthrop, MA) and Florence I. Ayers (Wolfeboro)

Martha Anne, b. 8/16/1964 in Wolfeboro; second; Robert A. Pigott (asst. postmaster, Winthrop, MA) and Florence I. Ayers (Wolfeboro)

Robert Thomas, b. 7/1/1961 in Wolfeboro; first; Robert A. Pigott (clerk, Winthrop, MA) and Florence I. Ayers (Wolfeboro)

PIKE,
Alaric Tuedisson, b. 4/17/1974 in Wolfeboro; Guy Arthur Pike II and
Judith M. Dearborn
Guy Arthur, II, b. 7/21/1954 in Wolfeboro; first; Chester H. Pike (boat
yard worker, NH) and Marion C. Reed (NH)
Mary Ellen, b. 4/4/1957 in Wolfeboro; second; Chester H. Pike
(boatyard worker, Wolfeboro) and Marion C. Reed (Ossipee)

PINEO,
Nadine Roberta, b. 1/11/1967 in Wolfeboro; second; Robert B. Pineo
(truck driver, Brockton, MA) and Cheryl R. Carter (Attleboro,
MA)

PIPER,
daughter, b. 2/21/1892 in Tuftonboro; third; Frank E. Piper (farmer,
26, Tuftonboro) and Carrie Low (27, Tuftonboro)
son, b. 2/5/1896 in Tuftonboro; fourth; Frank E. Piper (farmer, 30,
Tuftonboro) and Carry Lon (31, Tuftonboro)
son, b. 9/25/1902 in Tuftonboro; fifth; Frank E. Piper (farmer,
Tuftonboro) and Carrie Low (Tuftonboro)
daughter, b. 11/2/1906; third; John F. Piper (farmer, 25, Tuftonboro)
and Nellie Staples (21, Parsonsfield, ME)
son, b. 3/10/1908; fourth; John F. Piper (farmer, 27, Tuftonboro) and
Nellie F. Staples (22, Parsonsfield, ME)
son, b. 7/30/1910; fifth; John F. Piper (farmer, Tuftonboro) and Nellie
F. Staples (Parsonsfield, ME)
son, b. 5/8/1913; sixth; Thomas F. Piper (farmer, Tuftonboro) and
Belle Dunn (Halifax, NS)
stillborn son, b. 10/19/1916; seventh; John F. Piper (farmer,
Tuftonboro) and Nellie Staples (Parsonsfield, ME)
daughter, b. 8/10/1920; first; Ralph G. Piper (carpenter, Tuftonboro)
and Emma Hersey (Tuftonboro)
Brandi Anne, b. 4/7/1973 in Wolfeboro; Richard P. Piper and Shirley
F. Ridlon
Carl R., b. 7/8/1914; sixth; John F. Piper (laborer, Tuftonboro) and
Nellie F. Staples (Parsonsfield, ME)
Doris E., b. 2/18/1919; eighth; John F. Piper (farmer, Tuftonboro)
and Nellie Staples (Parsonsfield, ME)
Emily Lane, b. 5/8/1981 in Wolfeboro; John H. Piper and Nancy
Lane

Richard Arnold, b. 12/11/1970 in Wolfeboro; Richard P. Piper (ME) and Shirley F. Ridlon (NH)

Stanley William, b. 5/10/1926; eleventh; John F. Piper (farmer, 45, Tuftonboro) and Nellie F. Staples (40, N. Parsonsfield, ME)

Travis Chase, b. 7/31/1978 in Wolfeboro; John H. Piper and Nancy Lane

PODSEN,

Laurel Anne, b. 7/19/1981 in Concord; Kenneth E. Podsen and Jane E. Krasnoff

POLLINI,

Jillian Clair, b. 3/26/2003 in Wolfeboro; Todd Pollini and Celeste Pollini

William Todd, b. 6/13/2001 in Wolfeboro; Todd Polini and Celeste Polini

PORTER,

Howard H., b. 11/30/1908; first; Orville F. Porter (plumber, 29, Orford) and Nannie M. Horn (35, Wolfeboro)

POTENZA,

Nicholas Frank, b. 3/4/2003 in Laconia; Michael Potenza and Sara Potenza

PRESCOTT,

Andrew Philip, b. 5/1/1995 in Wolfeboro; William S. Prescott and Bethanie Lynn Alger

William Aaron, b. 7/13/1993 in Wolfeboro; William S. Prescott and Bethanie L. Alger

PROUTY,

Kyle, b. 9/9/1951 in Wolfeboro; first; Gardner W. Prouty (owner & oper., MA) and Ralphina Dan Tresco (MA)

RAMSBOTHAM,

Joy, b. 6/2/1977 in Wolfeboro; Robert W. Ramsbotham and Susan Hunter

RASPANTE,
Stephan Frank, b. 1/29/1987 in Wolfeboro; Frank Raspante and Lisa
G. Tupeck
Thomas Russell, b. 1/29/1987 in Wolfeboro; Frank Raspante and
Lisa G. Tupeck

RAY,
stillborn daughter, b. 3/12/1902 in Tuftonboro; second; Edward C.
Ray (painter, 26, Boston, MA) and Catherine L. Hudson (27,
Boston, MA)

REED,
James Michael, b. 5/19/1949 in Wolfeboro; fourth; Norman E. Reed
(laborer, Wakefield) and Marjorie F. Chick (Wakefield);
residence – Melvin Village
Joyce Lorraine, b. 8/2/1938 in Wolfeboro; fifth; Frank Eugene Reed
(works on road, 38, Houlton, ME) and Mildred Frances Whiting
(28, Tuftonboro)
Norman Edward, b. 11/23/1946 in Wolfeboro; second; Norman
Elsmore Reed (arborist, Wakefield) and Marjorie F. Chick
(Wakefield)
Wayne Austin, b. 3/4/1948 in Wolfeboro; third; Norman E. Reed
(laborer, Wakefield) and Marjorie F. Chick (Wakefield);
residence – Melvin Village

REPPUCCI,
Cassandra Ruth, b. 9/16/1987 in Laconia; Ronald J. Reppucci, Jr.
and Angela R. Daignault
Greggory Ronald, b. 4/27/1989 in Laconia; Ronald J. Reppucci, Jr.
and Angela R. Daignault

REYNOLDS,
Richard Francis, b. 12/3/1979 in Concord; Richard Coltart Reynolds
III and Kathleen Ann Metterville

RHODA,
Joel Thomas, b. 3/9/2002 in Laconia; Daniel Rhoda and Jeannette
Rhoda
Julie Lynn, b. 10/26/1998 in Laconia; Daniel Rhoda and Jeannette
Rhoda

Tyler Gordon, b. 2/4/1997 in Laconia; Daniel John Rhoda and
Jeannette Louise Glidden

RICE,
Dale Matthew, b. 10/19/1988 in Tuftonboro; Richard D. Rice and
Debbo M. Dow

RICH,
Albert Clark, b. 2/8/1950 in Wolfeboro; third; Nelson B. Rich
(engineer, Boston, MA) and Alberta L. Pigon (Somerville, MA);
residence – Ctr. Tuftonboro
Rebecca Ann, b. 11/13/1973 in Wolfeboro; David N. Rich and Merrill
I. Adickes

RICHARDSON,
Alice May, b. 4/18/1891 in Tuftonboro; first; M. D. Richardson
(farmer, 38, Moultonboro) and Claribel Ladd (31, Tuftonboro)
Allen S., b. 7/8/1918; first; Walter M. Richardson (clergyman,
Ashmont, MA) and Ruth Barbour (Roxbury, MA)

RICO,
Paul Arthur, b. 8/11/1929 in Tuftonboro; third; Peter A. Rico (hauling
contractor, 34, Russia) and Helen Glidden (housewife, 22, NH);
residence – Wolfeboro

RIDER,
Joseph William, b. 5/31/1985 in Laconia; William T. Rider and Gail
B. Harmon
Molly Mary, b. 8/21/1983 in Laconia; William T. Rider and Gail B.
Harmon

RIDLON,
Ronald LeRoy, b. 11/10/1938 in Wolfeboro; first; Filbert Elton Ridlon
(caretaker, 19, Springvale, ME) and Delia May Hill (18,
Colebrook)

RILEY,
John Thomas Robert, b. 8/16/2002 in N. Conway; Thomas Riley and
Heather Riley

RINES,
son, b. 8/24/1916; second; George N. Rines (laborer, Alton) and
Lottie E. Adjutant (Tuftonboro)
daughter, b. 10/27/1919; third; Nelson Rines (farmer, Alton) and
Lottie Adjutant (Tuftonboro)

ROBARGE,
daughter, b. 12/12/1901 in Tuftonboro; first; Lewis E. Robarge
(laborer, 27, Peabody, MA) and Bessie Elliott (18, Plymouth)
daughter, b. 8/25/1905 in Tuftonboro; Lewis E. Robarge (laborer, 29,
Peabody, MA) and Bessie Elliott (Plymouth)
daughter, b. 3/14/1908; fourth; Lewis E. Robarge (farmer, 30,
Peabody, MA) and Bessie Elliott (23, Plymouth)
son, b. 3/14/1908; fifth; Lewis E. Robarge (farmer, 30, Peabody, MA)
and Bessie Elliott (23, Plymouth)
daughter, b. 9/23/1912; seventh; Louis E. Robarge (farmer,
Peabody, MA) and Bessie A. Elliott (Plymouth)

ROBIE,
Paul Bernard, b. 9/24/1935 in Gilford; third; Bernard H. Robie
(minister, 26, E. Andover) and Emma W. Sawyer (housewife,
26, Gilford); residence – Ctr. Tuftonboro

ROBINSON,
daughter, b. 10/28/1912; second; Walter B. Robinson (farmer,
Ossipee) and Ora B. Staples (Parsonsfield, ME)
daughter, b. 7/26/1922; third; Walter B. Robinson (laborer, Ossipee)
and Eva Drew (Tuftonboro)

ROCKWELL,
Becky Ann, b. 6/25/1954 in Wolfeboro; second; Everett O. Rockwell
(el. school principal, MA) and Miriam L. Tobin (ME)
John Tobin, b. 10/22/1950 in Wolfeboro; first; Everett O. Rockwell
(teacher, Boston, MA) and Miriam L. Tobin (Belgrade, ME);
residence – Melvin Village

ROGERS,
Ruth Bernice, b. 9/19/1920; third; Lucius Rogers (teamster, 29) and
Edith Elliott (26); residence – West Alton
Tucker Bruce, b. 6/1/2004 in Laconia; Keith Rogers and Susan
Rogers

ROLLINS,

Matthew Adam, b. 8/26/1972 in Wolfeboro; William R. Rollins and Jacquelyn Hunter

ROSEEN,

Cynthia Elizabeth, b. 10/18/1988 in Laconia; Eric A. Roseen and Kathleen Cole

Mary Theresa, b. 7/19/1986 in Hanover; Eric A. Roseen and Kathleen M. Cole

Shawn Eric, b. 2/15/1996 in Laconia; Eric Albert Roseen and Kathleen Marie Cole

Thomas Paul, b. 3/31/1991 in Laconia; Eric A. Roseen and Kathleen M. Cole

ROSELL,

Nicole Aimee, b. 12/24/1982 in Winchester, MA; Thomas A. Rosell and Elizabeth R. Dulong

Sally Irene, b. 3/19/1952 in Wolfeboro; second; Charles F. Rosell (boat building, CT) and Grace L. Sundbye (CT)

Thomas Arn, b. 7/27/1949 in Wolfeboro; first; Charles F. Rosell (carpenter, Strafford) and Grace I. Sundye (Bridgeport, CT); residence – Mirror Lake

RUDOLPH,

Alison, b. 12/22/1972 in Wolfeboro; Blair D. Rudolph and Nancy Croteau

Blair David, b. 8/20/1950 in Wolfeboro; second; Gerald F. Rudolph (grocery clerk, Somerville, MA) and Mary A. Libby (Milton); residence – Melvin Village

Caleb Blair, b. 9/19/1976 in Wolfeboro; Blair D. Rudolph and Nancy Croteau

Forrest Creighton, b. 10/9/1934 in Tuftonboro; third; Roy Rudolph (farmer, 36, Canada) and Julia May Roghaar (housewife, 32, Lynn, MA)

Lisa Jane, b. 11/18/1960 in Wolfeboro; third; Gerald F. Rudolph (painter, MA) and Mary A. Libby (NH)

RUEL,

Burke Mahoney, b. 10/12/1999 in Lebanon; Christopher Ruel and Lynda Ruel

RUNNALS,
Tyler James, b. 8/26/1998 in Wolfeboro; Christopher Runnals and Nancy Burke

SANBORN,
daughter, b. 6/23/1897 in Tuftonboro; first; James H. Sanborn (farmer, 37, Sandwich) and Eliza M. Sherman (27, Bethlehem)

SANDS,
Heather Marie, b. 3/10/1978 in Wolfeboro; Dennis A. Sands and Dianne M. Sargent

SARGENT,
Anne Marie, b. 4/9/1963 in Wolfeboro; second; Fred E. Sargent (truck driver, Rockland, MA) and Eunice E. English (Brockton, MA)
Fred Elwin, b. 4/3/1935 in Wolfeboro; first; C. Harold Sargent (farmer, 30, Moultonboro) and Doris Hazel Mack (housewife, 20, New Hampton)
Harold James, b. 6/28/1902 in Tuftonboro; John R. Sargent (Lynn, MA) and Ellie M. Southard (Bath, MA); residence – Lynn, MA
Mary Jane, b. 4/29/1964 in Wolfeboro; third; Fred E. Sargnet (truck driver, Wolfeboro) and Eunice E. English (Brockton, MA)
Marylin Ellen, b. 9/9/1938 in Wolfeboro; second; Clarence Harold Sargent (farmer, 30, Moultonboro) and Doris Hazel Mack (24, N. Hampton)
Richard, b. 8/8/1939 in Wolfeboro; third; Clarence Harold Sargent (farmer, 35, Moultonboro) and Doris Hazel Mack (25, New Hampton, MA)
Theresa, b. 1/31/1962 in Wolfeboro; first; Fred E. Sargent (truck driver, Wolfeboro) and Eunice E. English (Brockton, MA)

SAUNDERS,
Stacy-Jo, b. 12/25/1969 in Wolfeboro; Willard O. Saunders (NH) and Laura L. Dow (NH)

SAWYER,
Hannah Barrett-Brown, b. 3/20/1996 in Laconia; Michael Patrick Sawyer and Chris Alice Barrett
Molly Ann, b. 9/24/1998 in Laconia; Michael P. Sawyer and Chris Barrett

Sarah Ann, b. 11/11/1956 in Wolfeboro; third; Richard B. Sawyer (poultry farmer, Winthrop, MA) and Barbara I. Braley (Franklin)

Shelby Marie, b. 7/8/1994 in Laconia; Michael Patrick Sawyer and Chris Barrett

SCHROEDER,
Marques Ethan, b. 5/25/1989 in Laconia; Larry Tod Schroeder and Cynthia El. Ervin

SEVERANCE,
Marianne, b. 10/11/1948 in Wolfeboro; third; Roland T. Severance (salesman, Stoneham, MA) and Mary K. Mackey (Stockbridge, MA); residence – Melvin Village

SEYMOUR,
Marie Claire, b. 2/11/1999 in Wolfeboro; Scott Seymour and Lynn (Gordon) Seymour

SHANNON,
daughter, b. 12/11/1920; first; Edwin Shannon (lumberman, 40, Alton) and Marion Haley (14, Tuftonboro)

daughter, b. 5/8/1923; second; Edward A. Shannon (laborer, Alton) and Marion H. Haley (Tuftonboro)

Caroline Elizabeth, b. 9/4/2004 in Portsmouth; Todd Shannon and Kara Shannon

Cathryn Elizabeth, b. 10/18/2002 in Portsmouth; Todd Shannon and Kara Shannon

Guy Edward, b. 1/24/1926; third; Edward A. Shannon (laborer, 47, Alton) and Marion H. Haley (19, Tuftonboro)

SHAW,
Herbert E., b. 5/30/1899 in Tuftonboro; first; Daniel Shaw (farmer) and Margaret Philbrick

SHELTON,
Erin Alyssa, b. 3/17/1980 in Laconia; Timothy C. Shelton and Marie L. Tyburski

Jordan Timothy, b. 5/9/1983 in Wolfeboro; Timothy C. Shelton and Marie L. Tyburski

SIMMONS,
Anna Marie, b. 8/28/1997 in Wolfeboro; Scott David Simmons and
Linda Anne Carroll
Jessica Lynn, b. 9/23/1992 in Wolfeboro; Scott D. Simmons and
Linda Anne Carroll

SMITH,
Beverly June, b. 6/19/1945 in Wolfeboro; fifth; Arthur Burton Smith
(mechanic, Effingham) and Ora Elizabeth Moulton (Tuftonboro)
Carol Jean, b. 7/3/1941 in Wolfeboro; fourth; Walter Roy Smith
(caretaker estate, 33, Farmington) and Doris Hazel Mack
(housewife, 27, New Hampton)
Delaney Orlando, b. 8/20/2002 in Concord; Donald Smith and
Suzanne Smith
Elsie Louise, b. 2/22/1940 in Wolfeboro; third; Arthur Burton Smith
(caretaker, 27, Effingham) and Ora Elizabeth Moulton
(housewife, 21, Tuftonboro)
Gracie Marie, b. 7/5/2005 in Laconia; Mark Smith and Susan
Matheson
James Franklin, b. 7/21/1946 in Wolfeboro; seventh; Clifton Edward
Smith (mechanic, Cliftondale, MA) and Bertha May Riley
(Poland, ME)
James Warren, b. 8/25/1989 in Wolfeboro; Richard Leroy Smith and
Connie Renee Watson
Lorraine Evelyn, b. 3/9/1941 in Wolfeboro; first; Carleton Osborn
Smith (farmer, 30, Tuftonboro) and Ruth Evelyn Adjutant
(housewife, 21, Tuftonboro); residence – Ctr. Tuftonboro
Peggy Joan, b. 12/3/1944 in Wolfeboro; sixth; Clifton Edward Smith
(mechanic, garage, Cliftondale, MA) and Bertha May Riley
(Poland, ME)
Rachel May, b. 4/23/1945 in Wolfeboro; second; Carleton Osborn
Smith (US Army, Gilmanton) and Ruth Evelyn Adjutant
(Tamworth); residence – Ctr. Tuftonboro
Richard William, b. 12/23/1986 in N. Conway; Richard L. Smith and
Connie R. Watson
Robert Earl, b. 11/15/1938 in Wolfeboro; fifth; Edward Clifton Smith
(caretaker, 28, Cliftonvale, MA) and Bertha Riley (24, Poland,
ME)
Sandra Emily, b. 1/24/1951 in Wolfeboro; fifth; Arthur B. Smith (auto
mech., NH) and Ora E. Moulton (Ossipee)

SNOW,
Bayard Daniel, b. 11/24/1987 in Concord; Stephen D. Snow and Ann Robinson
Seth Robinson, b. 5/29/1986 in Concord; Stephen D. Snow and Ann Robinson

SNYDER,
Ralph Edward, b. 9/3/1958 in Wolfeboro; first; Ralph E. Snyder, Jr. (mechanic, MA) and Emily M. Hotchkiss (Washington, DC); residence – Ctr. Tuftonboro

SOLOMON,
Melinda, b. 8/7/1962 in Wolfeboro; first; Arthur F. Solomon (gas sta. attendant, Laconia) and Patricia C. Devork (Wolfeboro)

SONCRANT,
Douglas James, b. 6/22/1967 in Wolfeboro; first; David L. Soncrant (US Navy, Wyandotte, MI) and Judy W. Buchanan (Manhattan, NY)

SPENCER,
Heidi Lynne, b. 9/8/1955 in Wolfeboro; third; Thomas D. Spencer (cabin owner, MA) and Lorraine L. Burstead (MA)
William Austin, b. 12/24/1969 in Wolfeboro; Thomas A. Spencer (IN) and Carolyn J. Hutshison (MA)

STANARD,
Aaron Nicholas, b. 10/13/2001 in Wolfeboro; Peter Stanard and Sandra Stanard
Mark Douglas, b. 6/5/2003 in Wolfeboro; Peter Stanard and Sandra Stanard
Peter, b. 7/16/1962 in Wolfeboro; first; Peter J. Stanard (gas sta. attendant, Providence, RI) and Joyce Goodwin (Wolfeboro)

STANLEY,
Bryan Knight, b. 6/29/1964 in Wolfeboro; second; Donald C. Stanley (self-employed, New York, NY) and Roxanna Haven (Winchester, MA)
Jeanine, b. 3/9/1962 in Wolfeboro; first; Donald C. Stanley, Jr. (self employed, Elizabeth, NJ) and Roxanna Haven (Winchester, MA)

STAPLES,
son, b. 2/1/1901 in Tuftonboro; first; Frank Staples (farmer, 35) and Ina F. Piper (17, Tuftonboro)
son, b. 7/17/1907; second; John Staples (blacksmith) and Lizzie A. Nichols
Barbara Lorraine, b. 9/5/1931 in Tuftonboro; second; Charles Staples (laborer, 28, Wolfeboro) and Doris Willard (21, Alton)
Clarence Virgil, b. 9/13/1906; third; Frank Staples (farmer, 38, Ossipee) and Ina Piper (23, Tuftonboro)
Howard Virgle, b. 12/16/1929 in Tuftonboro; second; Clarence V. Staples (laborer, 23, Tuftonboro) and Elsie A. Robarge (housewife, 19, Tuftonboro)
Roland Ormand, b. 12/16/1929 in Tuftonboro; third; Clarence V. Staples (laborer, 23, Tuftonboro) and Elsie A. Robarge (housewife, 19, Tuftonboro)
Virginia Bernice, b. 8/3/1929 in Tuftonboro; first; Charles F. Staples (laborer, 25, NH) and Doris Willard (housewife, 19, Alton)

STEAD,
Joan May, b. 7/2/1934 in Tuftonboro; second; Harold L. Stead (farmer, 21, Boston, MA) and Thelma May Shannon (housewife, 20, S. Wolfeboro); residence – Mirror Lake

STEADMAN,
Steven Eugene, b. 6/1/1965 in Wolfeboro; third; K. E. Steadman, Jr. (clerk, Everett, MA) and Loretta A. Bilodeau (Wolfeboro)

STEWART,
William Arthur, b. 8/19/1988 in Laconia; Wilson W. Stewart and Sally Anne Joyce

STILL,
Harold T., b. 4/7/1896 in Tuftonboro; second; Albert Still (farmer, 30, Boston, MA) and Winnie M. McIntire (19, Tuftonboro)

STILLINGS,
son, b. 8/31/1907; first; Charles Stillings (farmer, 53, Ossipee) and Lula E. Moody (24, Wolfeboro)
son, b. 10/11/1909; second; Charles H. Stillings (farmer, Ossipee) and Lula E. Moody (Wolfeboro)

STITT,
Raymond J., b. 5/19/1894; first; Albert T. Stitt (farmer, Boston, MA) and Winnie M. McIntire (Tuftonboro)

STOCKMAN,
Adam Frank, b. 2/24/1976 in Wolfeboro; John L. Stockman and Patricia A. Rico

Ali Jo, b. 9/30/1984 in Wolfeboro; Gary P. Stockman and Jennifer M. Kalled

Amy, b. 2/24/1975 in Wolfeboro; Philip A. Stockman and Nancy Ann Wilson

Benjamin John, b. 1/6/1984 in Wolfeboro; John L. Stockman and Melody Lynn Hatton

Brian Allen, b. 3/13/1960 in Wolfeboro; fourth; Philip A. Stockman (poultry, MA) and Clare J. Peaslee (NH)

Donald Lucas, b. 2/16/1961 in Wolfeboro; fourth; Frank L. Stockman (agriculture, Newton, MA) and Muriel Mae Williams (Melvin Village)

Gary Philip, b. 3/6/1952 in Wolfeboro; second; Philip A. Stockman (poultry, MA) and Clare J. Peaslee (NH)

James Arnold, b. 11/20/1955 in Wolfeboro; third; Philip A. Stockman (poultry, MA) and Clare J. Peaslee (NH)

John Lawrence, b. 1/25/1952 in Wolfeboro; second; Frank L. Stockman, Jr. (cattle – poultry, MA) and Muriel M. Williams (NH)

Katie Lynn, b. 4/3/1982 in Wolfeboro; John L. Stockman and Melody L. Hatton

Mary Ann, b. 2/3/1950 in Wolfeboro; first; Philip A. Stockman (farming, Newton, MA) and Clare J. Peaslee (Sandwich)

Nancy Jane, b. 10/8/1954 in Wolfeboro; third; Frank L. Stockman, Jr. (farmer, MA) and Muriel M. Williams (NH)

Payde Kalled, b. 6/13/1981 in Wolfeboro; Gary P. Stockman and Jennifer M. Kalled

William Leland, b. 3/5/1950 in Wolfeboro; first; Frank L. Stockman (electrician, Newton, MA) and Muriel M. Williams (Melvin Village)

William Leland, Jr., b. 9/25/1985 in Wolfeboro; William L. Stockman and Kathleen Ann Foy

STOCKTON,
Asa Richard Andrew, b. 12/25/1994 in Wolfeboro; Andrew Philip
Stockton and Faye Lee Massey

STRAW,
son, b. 2/21/1912; first; Harry E. Straw (farmer, Tuftonboro) and
Hattie Bean (Tuftonboro)
Carroll W., b. 8/12/1908; second; George D. Straw (teamster, 33,
Tuftonboro) and Minnie E. Abbott (30, Sandwich)
David Gale, b. 12/6/1974 in Wolfeboro; David Gale Straw, Jr. and
Sandra E. Smith
Edith Natalie, b. 3/2/1924 in Tuftonboro; first; Francis G. Straw
(electrician, Tuftonboro) and Lois Ada Hart (Manchester, NS)
Elizabeth June, b. 3/14/1949 in Wolfeboro; first; Robert William
Straw (carpenter, Tuftonboro) and Barbara E. Drucker
(Londonderry); residence – Mirror Lake
Francis George, b. 11/2/1903 in Tuftonboro; first; George D. Straw
(farmer, 30, Tuftonboro) and Minnie E. Abbott (26, Sandwich)
Gail Irene, b. 9/4/1967 in Wolfeboro; first; David G. Straw, Jr.
(laborer, Manchester) and Sandra E. Smith (Wolfeboro)
Mary Ann, b. 9/19/1939 in Wolfeboro; first; Carroll Wilton Straw
(caretaker private estate, 31, Tuftonboro) and Charlotte
Gertrude Howe (34, Attleboro, MA)

SUTHERLAND,
Lee Darlene, b. 7/3/1990 in Wolfeboro; Glenn D. Sutherland and
Kathleen M. Tessier

SWIFT,
Branden William, b. 1/1/1992 in Wolfeboro; Bruce W. Swift and
Sheryl Lynne Burnett

TARBELL,
Sarah Marie, b. 10/7/1982 in Wolfeboro; Andrew G. Tarbell and
Cindy Lee White

TAYLOR,
Cassie Lynn, b. 3/6/1982 in Laconia; Bradley L. Taylor and Mary
Ann Berry
Christyn Lee, b. 2/28/1985 in Laconia; Bradley L. Taylor and Mary
Ann Berry

Jessica Mae, b. 8/17/1978 in Wolfeboro; Bradley L. Taylor and Mary
Ann Berry

Matthew Richard, b. 12/23/1976 in Laconia; James A. Taylor and
Marcella J. Reiff

TEMPLE,
Simeon James, b. 6/4/1998 in Laconia; Jeremy C. Temple and
Suzanne N. Augros

TENNEY,
Michael Warren, Jr., b. 1/20/1993 in Wolfeboro; Michael W. Tenney
and Heather M. Curtis

TERWILLEGER,
Catherine Ryan, b. 5/31/1988 in Concord; John H. Terwilleger and
Cheryl Taylor

TETREAULT,
Joel Armand, b. 6/2/1954 in Wolfeboro; first; Armand A. Tetreault
(salesman, VT) and Carol J. Bennett (NH)

THIBEAULT,
Kathleen Anne, b. 10/13/1968 in Wolfeboro; Donald G. Thibeault
(NH) and Beatrice L. Lehneman (NH)

THOMAS,
son, b. 2/10/1891 in Tuftonboro; second; Ira A. Thomas (farmer, 24,
Tuftonboro) and M. E. McCormick (25, Ireland)

daughter, b. 4/21/1891 in Tuftonboro; first; E. M. Thomas (farmer,
27, Tuftonboro) and Myra G. Welch (21, Springvale, ME)

daughter, b. 11/14/1895 in Tuftonboro; third; Ira A. Thomas (farmer,
Tuftonboro) and Maggie A. McCormic (Ireland)

son, b. 4/22/1896 in Tuftonboro; second; Willie W. Thomas (farmer,
34, Tuftonboro) and Sillian McIntire (25, Tuftonboro)

Alexander Rhys, b. 4/8/1960 in Newton, MA; Lloyd H. Thomas, Jr.
(teacher, CA) and Elizabeth Knauss (PA)

Della M., b. 3/28/1899 in Tuftonboro; fourth; Ira Thomas (farmer, 33,
Tuftonboro) and Margaret E. McCormack (35, Ireland)

Donald Edwin, b. 3/18/1963 in Wolfeboro; first; Edwin D. Thomas
(mechanic, Wolfeboro) and June Y. Meyer (Boston, MA)

Edwin Donald, b. 9/17/1964 in Wolfeboro; second; Edwin D. Thomas (mechanic, Boston, MA) and June Y. Meyer (Boston, MA)
Jade Lindsey, b. 10/18/1989 in Tuftonboro; James David Thomas and Janet Louise Conrad
James Donald, b. 9/29/1966 in Wolfeboro; third; Edwin D. Thomas (mechanic, Stoneham, MA) and June Y. Meyer (Boston, MA)
Kelly June, b. 3/25/1971 in Wolfeboro; Edwin D. Thomas and June Meyer

THOMPSON,
daughter, b. 8/11/1891 in Tuftonboro; second; Charles Thompson (farmer, 34, Tamworth) and Jennie Thompson (23, Bartlett)
son, b. 4/7/1907; first; Simon T. Thompson (farmer, 22, Tuftonboro) and Evelyn Bean (17, Tuftonboro)
daughter, b. 3/7/1908; second; Simon T. Thompson (farmer, 22, Tuftonboro) and Evelyn Bean (18, Tuftonboro)
daughter, b. 11/18/1909; third; Simon T. Thompson (farmer, Tuftonboro) and Evelyn Bean (Tuftonboro)
daughter, b. 11/17/1910; fourth; Simon T. Thompson (farmer, Tuftonboro) and Evelyn Bean (Tuftonboro)
son, b. 6/9/1912; fifth; Simon T. Thompson (farmer, Tuftonboro) and Evelyn Bean (Tuftonboro)
son, b. 7/4/1914; sixth; Simon Thompson (farmer, Tuftonboro) and Evelyn L. Bean (Tuftonboro)
Dayna Elizabeth, b. 2/10/2000 in Laconia; Ronald Thompson and Khristine Thompson
Dolly Mae, b. 9/16/1952 in Wolfeboro; third; Lester W. Thompson (bus driver, Melvin Village) and Edna M. Judd (Ctr. Sandwich)
Eleanor M., b. 6/11/1917; seventh; Simon T. Thompson (farmer, Tuftonboro) and Evelyn L. Bean (Tuftonboro)
Jack Simon, b. 2/5/2003 in Laconia; Ronald Thompson and Khristine Thompson
Linda Jeanne, b. 4/21/1949 in Wolfeboro; second; Lester W. Thompson (farmer, Melvin Village) and Edna M. Nudd (Ctr. Sandwich); residence – Melvin Village
Madeline Audrey, b. 7/30/1927 in Tuftonboro; first; Simon T. Thompson (farmer, Tuftonboro) and Cecil Morris (Tuftonboro)
Richard Bradford, b. 6/3/1942 in Wolfeboro; first; Lester Willie Thompson (farmer, Tuftonboro) and Edna Mae Nudd (Ctr. Sandwich)

Tyler Willie, b. 5/27/1998 in Wolfeboro; Richard B. Thompson, II and Kimberly A. Cochran

TIDD,
Elliot Jeffrey, b. 7/5/1999 in Laconia; Jeffrey Tidd and Monique Tidd
Emmaline Olivia, b. 5/10/1996 in Laconia; Jeffrey Kimball Tidd and Monique Alice Landry

TOEWS,
Cassidy Alexandria, b. 7/4/1999 in Wolfeboro; Michael Toews and Deborah Toews
Marah Elizabeth, b. 8/1/1996 in Wolfeboro; Michael David Toews and Deborah Denise Trocki

TORREY,
son, b. 9/18/1914; fifth; Roy Torrey (laborer, Ferrisburg, NY) and Olive B. Carr (Waybridge, VT)

TOWNSEND,
Abbey Chase, b. 2/17/1981 in Laconia; James H. Townsend and Kathy D. Chase

TREAT,
daughter, b. 1/28/1909; first; Arthur W. Treat (farmer, Watertown, MA) and Elsie Treat (Boston, MA)
daughter, b. 3/22/1912; second; Arthur W. Treat (farmer, Watertown, MA) and Elsie Treat (Boston, MA)

TRIPPETTI,
Guilia, b. 1/25/1960 in Manchester; second; Joseph V. Trippetti (craftsman, PA) and Corinne Williams (DE)

TRUDNAK,
Steven George, b. 7/2/1984 in Wolfeboro; Ronald A. Trudnak and Cindy Lou Hargraves

TUCKER,
Frank A., b. 9/9/1893 in Tuftonboro; first; Daniel R. Tucker (physician, 66, Holderness) and Malora A. Blaisdell (38, Campton)

TUPECK,
son, b. 8/11/1924 in Tuftonboro; first; Steve Tupeck (laborer, Russia) and Bernice E. Ayers (Tuftonboro)
Jason Elliot, b. 6/15/1978 in Wolfeboro; Russell G. Tupeck and Bernadette M. Johnson
Leslie, b. 6/10/1936 in Wolfeboro; stillborn; third; Steve Tupeck (laborer, 41, Russia) and Bernice Estella Ayers (29, Tuftonboro); residence – Ctr. Tuftonboro
Russell Everett, b. 11/11/1932 in Tuftonboro; second; Steve Tupeck (laborer, 38, Russia) and Bernice E. Ayers (26, Tuftonboro)
Stephen Cyrus, b. 8/1/1955 in Wolfeboro; first; Russell E. Tupeck (clerk, NH) and Joan I. Bunney (MA)

VALLE,
Michael Peter, b. 9/15/1956 in Wolfeboro; first; Peter C. Valle (laborer, Brockton, MA) and Carlina Magridge (Wolfeboro)

VAN DYKE,
Heather Elizabeth, b. 12/14/1972 in Wolfeboro; William W. Van Dyke and Barbara H. Leschin

VARNEY,
Benjamin Shawn, b. 7/28/2003 in Wolfeboro; Shawn Varney and Amy Varney
Rhonda Lee, b. 4/24/1968 in Wolfeboro; Ronald E. Varney (NH) and Gaye E. Curry (NH)
Samuel James, b. 10/24/2001 in Dover; Shawn Varney and Amy Varney

VEDO,
Kristen Hans, b. 10/18/1990 in Wolfeboro; Karl Hans Vedo and Delores Whipple

VILDERS,
Ari James, b. 3/22/1987 in Rochester; Neil R. Vilders and Anne C. Swanick
Carissa Rose, b. 9/15/1985 in Rochester; Neil R. Vilders and Anne C. Swanick

VINTINNIER,
Donna Louise, b. 7/21/1940 in Wolfeboro; second; William Harold
   Vintinnier (waiter, 26, Lisbon) and Dorothy Helen Perrot
   (housewife, 23, S. Hero, VT); residence – Ctr. Tuftonboro

VITTUM,
Cade Joseph, b. 1/4/1993 in Wolfeboro; James M. Vittum and Jamie
   Lynn Lampron
Erinn Shannon, b. 4/8/1995 in Wolfeboro; James M. Vittum and
   Jamie Lynn Lampron
James Merton, b. 1/7/1959 in Wolfeboro; third; Norman E. Vittum
   (machinist, NH) and Nancy DeWitt (MA)
Lewis Marshall, III, b. 9/6/1972 in Laconia; Lewis M. Vittum, Jr. and
   Sharon R. Oxner
Norman Earle, II, b. 11/18/1957 in Wolfeboro; second; Norman E.
   Vittum (machinist, S. Tamworth) and Nancy DeWitt (Melrose,
   MA)

WAKEFIELD,
stillborn son, b. 9/2/1919; first; George Wakefield (laborer,
   Moultonboro) and May Drew (Wolfeboro)
Charlotte, b. 5/24/1905; William Wakefield (blacksmith, 26,
   Moultonboro) and Bessie Corning (26, Laconia)

WALKER,
Abby Fraser, b. 11/28/1995 in Wolfeboro; Jeffrey H. Walker and
   Jennifer S. Fraser
Marlee Fraser, b. 2/16/1993 in Wolfeboro; Jeffrey H. Walker and
   Jennifer S. Fraser

WALSH,
Jackson Charles, b. 11/21/2001 in Wolfeboro; William Walsh and
   Camilla Walsh

WARD,
Laura Caroline, b. 10/18/1935 in Wolfeboro; second; Francis S.
   Ward (farmer, 35, Lynn, MA) and Laura J. Howe (housewife,
   37, Morrisonville, NY); residence – Ctr. Tuftonboro

WATSON,
daughter, b. 5/11/1908; first; Alfred O. Watson (farmer, 21,
Tuftonboro) and Edna Kenney (18, Ossipee)
Reginald M., b. 11/12/1903 in Tuftonboro; fourth; Russell R.
Watson (farmer, 39, Center Harbor) and Gertrude Watson (33,
Tuftonboro)

WATTERSON,
Ernest Alfred, b. 2/14/1929 in Tuftonboro; second; Ernest Watterson
(laborer, 37, NH) and Viola Moore (housewife, 20, NH)

WEEKS,
daughter, b. 9/8/1897 in Tuftonboro; first; F. S. Weeks (physician,
26, Porter, ME) and Minnie L. Alby (22, Porter, ME)
Margaret Christina, b. 11/13/1987 in Wolfeboro; Charles E. Weeks
and Susan Hunter
Terry Lorraine, b. 12/12/1951 in Wolfeboro; second; Kenneth W.
Weeks (lumberman, NH) and Ruby M. Eldridge (NH)

WEIR,
Sierra Suzanne, b. 5/19/1996 in Wolfeboro; Daniel Kenneth Weir
and Laurie Ann Mroczka
Zared Dekker, b. 8/24/1998 in Wolfeboro; Daniel K. Weir and Laurie
Ann Mroczka

WEISS,
Ella Karin, b. 9/19/2002 in Wolfeboro; Oliver Weiss and Rita Weiss

WELCH,
son, b. 11/15/1898 in Tuftonboro; fourth; George Welch (farmer, 37,
Tuftonboro) and Ellen A. Horne (32, Moultonboro)
John Joseph, Jr., b. 7/26/1973 in Wolfeboro; John Joseph Welch
and Sharon R. Giles
Lisa Anne, b. 6/29/1970 in Wolfeboro; John J. Welch (ME) and
Sharon R. Giles (ME)
Lisle Roger, b. 2/2/1926; first; Maurice Welch (farmer, 23, Ossipee)
and Blanche Emery (26, Tuftonboro)
Melody Lynn, b. 10/6/1971 in Wolfeboro; John J. Welch and Sharon
R. Giles
Orren Plummer, b. 10/20/1951 in Wolfeboro; first; Lisle R. Welch
(laborer, NH) and Norma D. Colby (NH)

WENTWORTH,
daughter, b. 11/27/1896 in Tuftonboro; first; Frank I. Wentworth
(farmer, 35, Farmington) and Annie J. Peany (45, Tuftonboro)
Tucker Arnold, b. 10/26/1996 in Wolfeboro; Dave L. Wentworth, Jr.
and Carolyn Red Andersen

WEST,
Harold P., b. 5/15/1902 in Tuftonboro; first; Charles W. West
(farmer, 27, London, England) and Addie A. Pinkham (29,
Moultonboro)
Lawrence P., b. 5/20/1908; third; Charles W. West (farmer, 33,
London, England) and Addie A. Pinkham (35, Tuftonboro)
Marjorie Elizabeth, b. 5/13/1930 in Wolfeboro; first; Laurence P.
West (clerk, 22, Tuftonboro) and Irene A. Brooks (housewife,
22, Boston, MA)
Priscilla, b. 7/24/1904 in Tuftonboro; second; Charles W. West
(farmer, 29, London, England) and Addie Pinkham (31,
Tuftonboro)

WESTON,
Sharon May, b. 8/1/1952 in Boston, MA; first; Andrew W. Weston
(student, Nashua) and Barbara MacQueen (Canada); residence
– Mirror Lake

WHILTER,
son, b. 9/9/1896 in Tuftonboro; second; Edmond Whilter (farmer, 32,
Winchester, MA) and ----- Robinson (28, England)

WHITE,
Ryan Duane, b. 10/17/1988 in Rochester; Duane R. White and Jeri-
Lynn Southard
Zaccarie Willis, b. 12/20/1984 in Tuftonboro; Ronald E. White and
Lisa Marie Potenza

WHITING,
daughter, b. 5/20/1910; second; Leon Whiting (farmer, Laconia) and
Mary R. Francis (Cambridge, MA)
son, b. 12/3/1911; third; Leon Whiting (laborer, 36, Laconia) and
Mary R. Francis (25, Cambridge, MA)

WHITTEN,

Barbara Frances, b. 6/8/1932 in Wolfeboro; first; Walter Francis
Whitten (garage mechanic, 26, Tuftonboro) and Beatrice
Boyden Watson (24, Tuftonboro)

John Rice, b. 6/12/1898 in Tuftonboro; third; Edmund Whitton
(farmer, 34, Winchester, MA) and Teresa Robinson (30,
England)

Oscar Leroy, b. 5/27/1903 in Tuftonboro; second; David Whitten
(farmer, 54, Moultonboro) and Nellie J. Whitten (34, Wolfeboro)

Phoebe C., b. 6/30/1915; first; Joseph W. Whitten (Wolfeboro) and
Mamie G. Whitten (Tuftonboro)

Steven Evans, b. 6/9/1957 in Wolfeboro; first; Edward R. Whitten
(inn keeper, Wolfeboro) and Maryetta J. Pratt (Pine Plains, NY)

Walter Frank, b. 9/28/1905 in Tuftonboro; David V. Whitten (farmer,
54, Moultonboro) and Nellie Hoyt (Wolfeboro)

WIGGIN,

son, b. 6/21/1892 in Tuftonboro; ninth; John W. Wiggin (farmer, 37,
Acton, ME) and Mary A. Elliott (39, Tuftonboro)

stillborn child, b. 3/3/1894; eleventh; John W. Wiggin (farmer, Acton,
ME) and Mary A. Elliot (Tuftonboro)

son, b. 3/3/1894; twelfth; John W. Wiggin (farmer, Acton, ME) and
Mary A. Elliot (Tuftonboro)

child, b. 6/8/1895 in Tuftonboro; John W. Wiggin (farmer, Acton, ME)
and Mary A. Elliott (Tuftonboro)

son, b. 1/9/1910; seventh; Lewis C. Wiggin (laborer, Tamworth) and
Ella M. Clark (Stoneham, MA)

son, b. 8/8/1921; twelfth; Harry L. Wiggin (laborer, Tuftonboro) and
Mabel Drowns (Ossipee)

WILHOUSKY,

Lauren Anne, b. 11/17/1987 in Concord; Vladimir Wilhousky and
Lynn T. Perrin

Peter Vladimir, b. 9/28/1991 in Concord; Vladimir Wilhousky and
Lynn T. Perrin

WILLARD,

Cheryl Ann, b. 11/7/1947 in Wolfeboro; first; Emery Durgin Willard
(motor mach., Swampscott, MA) and Dorothy G. Harris
(Franklin, MA)

Wendy, b. 10/4/1952 in Tuftonboro; third; Emery D. Willard (foreman machine shop, Lynn, MA) and Dorothy G. Harris (Franklin, MA); residence - Melvin Village

WILLIAMS,
son, b. 9/12/1891 in Tuftonboro; fourth; John F. Williams (farmer, 48, Ossipee) and Hattie S. Williams (45, Tuftonboro)

Ann Celeste, b. 3/11/1937 in Wolfeboro; seventh; Roger Lester Williams (forester, 34, Brockton, MA) and Berenece Wesley Lawrence (35, Lynn, MA)

Beth Linda, b. 3/3/1957 in Wolfeboro; first; Roger Lawrence Williams (farmer, Lowell, MA) and Barbara H. Davis (Melrose, MA)

Brenda Ellen, b. 11/18/1959 in Wolfeboro; second; Roger L. Williams (dryer operator, MA) and Barbara H. Davis (MA)

Bruce Alan, b. 9/14/1941 in Wolfeboro; eighth; Roger Lester Williams (nurseryman, 39, Brockton, MA) and Berenice Wellsley Lawrence (housewife, 39, Lynn, MA); residence – Ctr. Tuftonboro

Coleman Alan, b. 5/27/1999 in Rochester; Coleman Williams and Tavia Williams

Deborah Lee, b. 11/4/1964 in Wolfeboro; first; Ward B. Williams (draftsman, Rangeley, ME) and Judith E. Nickerson (Wolfeboro)

Frank V., b. 8/6/1908; second; George V. Williams (mechanic, 55, Taunton, MA) and Nellie M. Haley (32, Tuftonboro)

Heidi Ann, b. 9/20/1973 in Wolfeboro; Bruce A. Williams and Cheryl A. McLaughlin

Holly, b. 11/30/1983 in Wolfeboro; Frederick J. Williams and Denise D. Pray

Lance Alan, b. 4/18/1970 in Wolfeboro; Bruce A. Williams (NH) and Cheryl A. McLaughlin (MA)

Muriel May, b. 3/25/1927 in Tuftonboro; first; Roger Williams (timber surveyor, Brockton, MA) and Bernice Lawrence (Lynn, MA)

Richard Bessom, b. 3/9/1937 in Wolfeboro; fifth; Roger Lester Williams (forester, 33, Brockton, MA) and Berenece Welsley Lawrence (34, Lynn, MA)

Richmond Bessom, b. 3/9/1937 in Wolfeboro; sixth; Roger Lester Williams (forester, 33, Brockton, MA) and Berenece Welsley Lawrence (34, Lynn, MA)

Roger Lester, b. 7/7/1977 in Rochester; Bruce A. Williams and Cheryl A. McLaughlin

Ward Timothy, b. 9/29/1968 in Wolfeboro; Ward B. Williams (ME) and Judith E. Nickerson (NH)

WILSON,
Ashley Michaela, b. 11/1/1997 in Dover; Steve Michael Wilson and Shanyn Loree Truitt
Emma Rebekah, b. 9/14/1989 in Laconia; Glenn W. Wilson and Barbara Neville
Jaiden Tyler, b. 10/29/1999 in Dover; Steven Wilson and Shanyn Wilson
Taylor Anne, b. 5/17/1992 in Laconia; Glenn W. Wilson and Barbara E. Neville

WINGATE,
Audrey Burroughs, b. 5/8/1984 in Laconia; Jeffrey A. Wingate and Janice J. Kauer
Hadley Klees, b. 4/11/1989 in Laconia; Jeffrey A. Wingate and Janice Kauer

WIXSON,
Joel Nathan, b. 8/16/1963 in Wolfeboro; second; Raymond C. Wixson (clergyman, Wolfeboro) and Georgetta R. Couch (Brackenridge, PA)
Jonathan, b. 1/22/1962 in Wolfeboro; first; Raymond C. Wixson (clergyman, Rockland, ME) and Georgetta R. Couch (Brackenridge, PA)

WOOD,
Barbara Jane, b. 11/30/1957 in Wolfeboro; fifth; William Harry Wood, Jr. (ind. contractor, Boston, MA) and Carolyn J. Phillips (Claremont)
John, b. 3/6/1950 in Wolfeboro; fourth; William H. Wood, Jr. (farmer, Boston, MA) and Carolyn J. Phillips (Claremont)
Lloyd Patterson, b. 1/14/1948 in Wolfeboro; first; William Harry Wood, Jr. (salesman, Boston, MA) and Carolyn Jean Phillips (Claremont)
Robert Phillips, b. 6/6/1952 in Wolfeboro; fourth; William H. Wood, Jr. (salesman, MA) and Carolyn T. Phillips (NH)
William Harry, III, b. b. 3/6/1950 in Wolfeboro; fifth; William H. Wood, Jr. (farmer, Boston, MA) and Carolyn J. Phillips (Claremont)

WOODBURY,
Eric Manton, b. 8/30/1972 in Wolfeboro; David W. Woodbury and
Linda S. Howe

WOODMANCY,
daughter, b. 12/12/1909; fourth; Henry A. Woodmancy (Boston, MA)
and Florence I. Evans (Boston, MA)

WOODSWORTH,
R. E. [male], b. 6/21/1892 in Tuftonboro; first; C. E. Woodsworth
(shoemaker, 23, Greenland) and Mary E. Hovey (22, St.
James, NB)

WORTHINGTON,
Brooks Anthony, b. 5/25/1980 in Wolfeboro; Arthur L. Worthington
and Kathleen L. Redmond
Wesley Arthur, b. 11/29/1984 in Rochester; Arthur L. Worthington,
Jr. and Kathleen L. Redmond

WRIGHT,
Donald Southern, b. 9/8/1959 in Wolfeboro; fourth; Donald C. Wright
(Hansel & Greta Shop, MA) and Kathleen S. McKeany (NY)

YATES,
Olivia Ann, b. 1/31/1992 in N. Conway; Charles S. Yates and
Melissa Ann Yates

YOUNG,
daughter, b. 6/28/1911; first; Charles H. Young (photographer, 24,
Tuftonboro) and Florence I. Canfield (20, Boston, MA)
daughter, b. 8/17/1912; second; Charles H. Young (photographer,
Tuftonboro) and Florence I. Canfield (S. Boston, MA)
Natalie Lorraine, b. 10/13/1998 in Wolfeboro; Richard J. Young and
Noelle M. Powers

ZIEGLER,
Richard Duncan, b. 7/19/1967 in Wolfeboro; second; Richard D.
Ziegler (guidance director, New Rochelle, NY) and Catherine J.
Duncan (Washburn, ME)

UNKNOWN,
David Alan, b. 10/6/1966 in Wolfeboro; first; Ronald A. ----- (cook,
   Rochester) and Linda M. Pennell (Wolfeboro)
Donna Lou, b. 10/12/1966 in Wolfeboro; second; Richard L. -----
   (construction, Wolfeboro) and Linda LeRoux (Laconia)
Elaine Camilla, b. 10/7/1966 in Dover; first; Denis A. ------
   (horticulturist, NY, NY) and Marybell C. Keeler (Canterbury)
Holly Linn, b. 2/26/1966 in Portsmouth; first; Kenneth G. ----- (USN –
   Ret., MA) and Janice M. Lassell (MA)

TUFTONBORO MARRIAGES

ADJUTANT,
Charles L. of Tuftonboro m. Lena E. **Perry** of Brookfield 10/31/1901
in Wolfeboro; H – 39, carpenter, b. Tuftonboro, s/o Parkman D.
Adjutant and Priscilla Thompson; W – 23, housekeeper, 2nd,
divorced, b. Brookfield, d/o Samuel Eaton and Mary E. Berry
Forest E. of Tuftonboro m. Ethel J. **Frisbee** of Wolfeboro 2/18/1922
in Portsmouth; H – 38, carpenter, b. Tuftonboro, s/o Willie W.
Adjutant (Tuftonboro) and Eliza J. Piper (Tuftonboro); W – 33,
dressmaker, b. Tuftonboro, d/o Lewis N. Frisbee (Kittery, ME)
and Addie Morrison (Tuftonboro)

AIKEN,
Aubrey W. of Waltham, MA m. Ruth M. **Jones** of ME 7/11/1950 in
Moultonboro; H – 41, ship'g, rec., b. MA, s/o Roy C. Aiken (NH)
and Gertrude S. MacManus (England); W – 29, at home, b. NH,
d/o Frank P. Jones (MA) and Lillian G. Pippy (Newfoundland)

AKINS,
Michael C. of Wareham, MA m. Erin Marie **Brown** of Wareham, MA
9/25/1988

ALBEE,
William L. m. Pamela D. **Devork** 8/25/1974 in Moultonboro

ALEXANDER,
Kenneth D. m. Nancy L. **Kelliher** 3/24/1973 in Tuftonboro

ALLEN,
Frank R. of Wolfeboro m. Josephine C. **Hall** of Tuftonboro
10/28/1979
George H. m. Kate **Duseck** 8/29/1925 in Tuftonboro; H – 53,
laborer, 2nd, b. Moultonboro, s/o Mehitable Whitten (Moulton);
W – 63, housewife, 2nd, b. NS, d/o John Allen (NS) and Abigail
Forbes (NS)
George W. of Tuftonboro m. Etta A. **Libbey** of Tuftonboro
10/31/1896 in Tuftonboro; H – 28, farmer, b. Albany, s/o Smith
Allen (farmer) and Louisa Allen (housekeeper); W – 21,
housekeeper, b. Tuftonboro, d/o Levi W. Libby (Tuftonboro,
farmer) and Laura J. Libby (Parsonsfield, ME, housewife)
James W. of Tuftonboro m. Lisa-Anne **Herbst** of Tuftonboro
5/20/2000

Newton J. of W. Lebanon, ME m. Ruth E. **Oulton** of Tuftonboro
11/20/1966 in E. Wakefield; H – 61, retired, 3rd, widower, b.
Wells, ME, s/o Henry P. Allen (ME) and Francena Allen (ME);
W – 60, 3rd, widow, b. Saugus, MA, d/o James A. Dunn (MA)
and Josephine W. Bryant (MA)
Wilfred Joseph of Tuftonboro m. Dorothy **Lucia** of Tuftonboro
2/14/1962 in Tuftonboro; H – 44, merchant, 2nd, divorced, b.
Biddeford, ME, s/o Alfred Allen (England) and Mary Sheppard
(RI); W – 29, supervisor, 2nd, divorced, b. Worcester, MA, d/o
John J. Lucia (NY) and Ida A. Perreault (ME)

AMES,
Arthur Alan of Tuftonboro m. Apryl Marie **Leighton** of Moultonboro
6/17/1995
James Ronald of Tuftonboro m. LauraLee **Van Tassel** of Ossipee
12/21/1991
John R. of Tuftonboro m. Stacey Lynn **Moran** of Tuftonboro
7/20/1991
Richard Wayne of Tamworth m. Barbara Marie **Bushman** of
Tuftonboro 3/3/1964 in Conway; H – 22, woodsman, b.
Laconia, s/o James R. Ames (NH) and Ada E. Eldredge (NH);
W – 19, at home, b. Wolfeboro, d/o Robert J. Bushman (MA)
and Faye L. Eldredge (NH)
Rolland D. of Moultonboro m. Shirley A. **Reed** of Tuftonboro
7/23/1950 in Ossipee; H – 20, student, b. NH, s/o Harold B.
Ames (NH) and Charlotte E. Wakefield (NH); W – 17, at home,
b. NH, d/o Frank E. Reed (ME) and Mildred F. Whiting (NH)
Rolland D. m. Peggy Joan **Smith** 3/18/1977 in Tuftonboro

ANTHONY,
William John, Jr. of Rochester m. Sheila Marie **Jones** of Tuftonboro
6/6/1979

ANTONUCCI,
William m. Mary **Antonucci** 9/2/1977 in Tuftonboro
William of Tuftonboro m. Tina L. **Keniston** of Tuftonboro 9/1/2001

APPLETON,
Paul M. of Tuftonboro m. Carol Ann **Johnson** of Tuftonboro
4/20/1968 in Wolfeboro; H – b. MA, s/o Thomas E. Appleton

(Canada) and Greta Melville (Canada); W – b. MA, d/o Carl B.
Johnson (MA) and Louise Maichle (MA)

ARCOUETTE,
Ronald James, III of Tuftonboro m. Vicky Marie **Wilber** of Tuftonboro
9/28/2002

ARION,
Michael A. of Tuftonboro m. Lisa J. **Carlton** of Tuftonboro 8/5/2000

ARROYO,
Elvis of New York City, NY m. Kerrieanne **Hawes** of Tuftonboro
7/25/1998

ARSENAULT,
Marshall of Tuftonboro m. Grace H. **Poleman** of Wolfeboro 6/9/1946
in Wolfeboro; H – 24, mechanic, b. Sanford, ME, s/o Frank
Arsenault (Chatham) and Ethelyn Osborn (Tuftonboro); W – 25,
at home, b. Berwick, ME, d/o Theo. J. Poelman (Holland, MI)
and Helen Guptil (Berwick, ME)

ARTMAN,
Floyd R. of Sarasota, FL m. Elaine M. **Jette** of Tuftonboro 7/4/1981

ASPINWALL,
John Francis of Norwood, MA m. Valerie Linn **Post** of Norwood, MA
6/27/1992

ATWOOD,
Hubert Loring of Sandwich m. Carol Jean **Libby** of Tuftonboro
9/3/1966 in Ctr. Sandwich; H – 32, truck driver, 2nd - divorced,
b. Wolfeboro, s/o Gerald W. Atwood (NH) and Virginia Moody
(NH); W – 25, machine op., 2nd – divorced, b. Wolfeboro, d/o
Walter R. Smith (NH) and Doris H. Mack (NH)

AUSTIN,
Dale A. m. Sandra L. **Parsons** 3/25/1972 in Alton

AYERS,
Charles H. of Tuftonboro m. Josephine M. **Nudd** of Ctr. Sandwich
9/4/1949 in Tuftonboro; H – 21, laborer, b. Wolfeboro, s/o Levi

L. Ayers (Tuftonboro) and Ruth Champaigne (Wolfeboro); W –
25, housework, b. NH, d/o Wallace Nudd (NH) and Blanche
LeClare (VT)

Herbert of Tuftonboro m. Ida May **Adjutant** of Tuftonboro 4/15/1903
in Wolfeboro; H – 26, farmer, b. Tuftonboro, d/o Edmond L.
Ayers and Ella Ayers; W – 16, housekeeper, b. Tuftonboro, d/o
Willie W. Adjutant and Eliza J. Adjutant

John of Tuftonboro m. Carrie L. **Burleigh** of Tuftonboro 9/11/1891 in
Tuftonboro; H – 22, farmer, b. Tuftonboro, s/o James Ayers
(Tuftonboro, farming) and Hannah Ayers (Ossipee); W – 15,
housewife, b. Deering, ME, d/o J. J. Burleigh (Tuftonboro,
farming) and Sarah H. Burleigh (Tuftonboro)

Raymond H. of Wakefield m. Barbara **Jones** of Tuftonboro
12/22/1991

BAILEY,

Clarence L. of Lynn, MA m. Dorothy R. **Merrifield** of Tuftonboro
12/25/1919 in Tuftonboro; H – 28, leather worker, b. Biddeford,
ME, s/o Thomas Bailey (Biddeford, ME) and Emerline Harmon
(Hollis, ME); W – 19, housekeeper, b. Tuftonboro, d/o Perley
Merrifield (Porter, ME) and Nellie M. Thompson (Tuftonboro)

BAIN,

Frederick William of Tamworth m. Luella B. **McIntyre** of C.
Tuftonboro 4/8/1944 in Ctr. Harbor; H – 46, woodsman, 2nd, b.
NS, s/o James D. Bain (NS, retired) and Anna Ball (NS,
deceased); W – 34, housework, 2nd, b. C. Tuftonboro, d/o Lewis
McIntyre (C. Tuftonboro, retired) and Sadie Doe (C. Tuftonboro,
housewife)

BAKER,

Harold H. of PA m. Beth **Whitehead** of Tuftonboro 8/31/1957 in
Melvin Village; H – 24, personnel, b. PA, s/o William R. Baker
(PA) and Isabel Hayes (PA); W – 18, at home, b. MA, d/o Ross
Whitehead (RI) and Alice M. Nordmark (MA)

BANYAS,

James Richard, Jr. of Tyngsboro, MA m. Bonnie Ann **Girard** of
Haverhill, MA 10/7/1989

BARNARD,
David Fletcher, Jr. of Tuftonboro m. Cynthia Pond **Barnard** of Tuftonboro 7/20/1996

BARNETT,
Richard G. of NY m. Elizabeth **Pratt** of NY 8/22/1949 in Tuftonboro; H – 24, writer, b. Detroit, MI, s/o Guy D. Barnett (Albion, MI) and Esther I. Rask (Norwood, MA); W – 24, actress, b. Hackensack, NJ, d/o Chester J. Pratt (NY) and Lizette D. Droge (NY)

BARNHILL,
Paul M. of Cambridge, MA m. Andrea **Musacchio** of Cambridge, MA 2/2/4/1990

BARRATT,
Stephen D. m. Carol Ann **Sayce** 8/19/1978

BARRETT,
Warren Edward of N. Hampton m. Francesca **LaGuardia** of Tuftonboro 8/31/1968 in Wolfeboro; H – b. NH, s/o Warren F. Barrett (MA) and Louise Batchelder (NH); W – b. NH, d/o Lionel G. LaGuardia (NY) and Mary Janvrin (MA)

BARTLETT,
William S., Jr. m. Karen L. **Cross** 6/17/1972 in Wolfeboro

BATLEY,
Bruce E. of Gardner, MA m. Janice E. **DeFelice** of Gardner, MA 8/13/1983

BATTERSBY,
Cowan Brenton of Tuftonboro m. Cecelia **Baverstock** of Manchester 6/4/1955 in Melvin Village; H – 31, teacher, b. MA, s/o Cowan W. Battersby (PEI) and Amelia A. Umland (NY); W – 20, teacher, b. Canal Zone, d/o Clinton Baverstock (Washington) and Ellen M. Pinborg (Denmark)

BAXTER,
George P. m. Priscilla **West** 9/15/1928 in Tuftonboro; H – 24, knitter, b. Providence, RI, s/o Harry T. Baxter (Preston, England) and

Christina Pringle (Glasgow, Scotland); W – 24, nurse, b.
Tuftonboro, d/o Charles W. West (London, England) and Addie
A. Pinkham (Tuftonboro)
Harry W. of Tuftonboro m. Martha J. White of Tuftonboro 11/9/1952
in Wolfeboro; H – 23, US Army, b. NY, s/o George P. Baxter
(RI) and Priscilla C. West (NH); W – 18, at home, b. NH, d/o
Joseph W. White (MA) and Rena V. Bowering (St. Johns, NF)

BEAN,
Arthur M. of Tuftonboro m. Delia A. **Carter** of Tuftonboro 4/2/1895 in
Tuftonboro; H – 27, farmer, 2nd, b. Moultonboro, s/o Augustine
Bean and Lucy A. Bean; W – 24, housework, 2nd, b.
Birmingham, England
Benjamin A. of Tuftonboro m. Michelle Y. **Wood** of Tuftonboro
8/18/1984
Benjamin A. of Tuftonboro m. Katherine M. **Antoniadis** of
Tuftonboro 9/5/1992
Clyde Leroy, Jr. of Ctr. Ossipee m. Joyce Lorraine **Reed** of
Tuftonboro 11/10/1956 in Melvin Village; H – 21, machinist, b.
NH, s/o Clyde Leroy Bean (NH) and Hazel L. Downing (ME); W
– 18, at home, b. NH, d/o Frank E. Reed (ME) and Mildred F.
Whiting (NH)
Frank John of Tuftonboro m. Mary Fredaline **Bourque** of Haverhill,
MA 7/26/1930 in Newton; H – 25, laborer, b. Tuftonboro, s/o
John W. Bean (Tuftonboro) and Clara A. Horne (Lawrence,
MA); W – 20, shoe worker, b. Amesbury, MA, d/o William
Bourque (Digby, NS) and Caroline J. Lemerise (Newton)
Horace W. of Tuftonboro m. Ida **Bean** of Ossipee 12/25/1894 in
Ossipee; H – 22, farmer, b. Tuftonboro, s/o George F. Bean
(Tuftonboro, blacksmith) and Sarah F. Bean (Tuftonboro,
housewife); W – 23, housewife, 2nd, b. Ossipee, d/o Wentworth
Nichols (Ossipee, farmer) and Betsy Nichols (Ossipee,
housewife)
Howard E. of Tuftonboro m. Grace M. **Dewey** of Boston, MA
9/21/1910 in Tuftonboro; H – 23, farmer, b. Tuftonboro, s/o
Willie L. Bean and Ula D. Foss; W – 24, housewife, b.
Worcester, MA, d/o George A. Dewey and Helen M. Ryan
John W. of Tuftonboro m. Clara A. **Horne** of Tuftonboro 10/15/1902
in Moultonboro; H – 36, farmer, b. Tuftonboro, s/o Simon B.
Bean and Achsah M. Chace; W – 36, dressmaker, b.
Somersworth, d/o Isaac Horne and Clarinda S. Neal

Leon E. of Wolfeboro m. Arlene H. **Crosby** of Wolfeboro 4/23/1949 in Tuftonboro; H – 21, laborer, b. Tuftonboro, s/o Ralph L. Bean (Tuftonboro) and Lura P. Sargent (Moultonboro); W – 22, laundry, b. Lynn, MA, d/o Harry R. Henry (PEI) and Gertrude Richmond (Roxbury, MA)

Milton L. H. of Tuftonboro m. Constance **Sargent** of Dorchester, MA 12/6/1947 in Wolfeboro Falls; H – 41, farmer, b. Tuftonboro, s/o Arthur M. Bean (Moultonboro) and Cordelia A. Carter (Birmingham, England); W – 41, secretary, b. Brooklyn, NY, d/o Jesse Sargent (Somerville, MA) and Lenora Potter (Yarmouth, NS)

Ralph L. of Tuftonboro m. Lura P. **Sargent** of Tuftonboro 1/31/1923 in Tuftonboro; H – 40, farmer, b. Tuftonboro, s/o Willie L. Bean (Moultonboro) and Ula D. Foss (Tuftonboro); W – 21, housewife, b. Moultonboro, d/o Jesse Sargent and Ida E. Rogers (Moultonboro)

BEARSE,
Lawrence Thomas of Hyannis Port, MA m. Cynthia Ann **McNamara** of Hyannis, MA 9/7/1968 in Wolfeboro; H – b. MA, s/o Harold L. Bearse (MA) and Madeline Bourget (MA); W – b. MA, d/o Lawrence McNamara (MA) and Helen Hendrickson (MA)

BELMONT,
Micheal E. m. Helene **Bernard** 8/21/1971 in Tuftonboro

BENNETT,
David Lister of Tuftonboro m. Gloria Elaine **Moore** of Wolfeboro 6/3/1951 in Wolfeboro; H – 31, laborer, b. NH, s/o Maurice Bennett (NH) and Annie Kidd (Scotland); W – 23, reg. nurse, b. NH, d/o Eldred E. Moore (NH) and Addie F. Curtis (ME)

Donald Chase m. Dorothy Mae **Tutt** 7/18/1937 in Melvin Village; H – 26, painter, b. Tuftonboro, s/o Maurice P. Bennett (Tuftonboro, painter) and Annie Kidd (Scotland, deceased); W – 30, registered nurse, b. Boston, MA, d/o Bernard D. Tutt (Floyd, IA, RR carpenter) and Celia Beatrice Estes (Wolfeboro, deceased)

Douglas L. of Tuftonboro m. Ruth Mildred **Walton** of Wolfeboro 10/7/1966 in Wolfeboro; H – 54, carpenter, 2nd, divorced, b. Tuftonboro, s/o Maurice P. Bennett (NH) and Annie Kidd (Scotland); W – 53, at home, 4th, widow, b. Swampscott, d/o Erik G. Ostmark (Sweden) and Bertha Segelstrom (Sweden)

Frank S. of Tuftonboro m. Eleanor E. **Dawes** of Tuftonboro
 12/24/1908 in Tuftonboro; H – 25, carpenter, b. Tuftonboro, s/o
 James A. Bennett and Frances E. Fernald; W – 18, housewife,
 b. Boston, MA, d/o Alfred J. Dawes and Nellie Collins
George E. of Concord m. Georgie A. **Gilman** of Tuftonboro
 10/26/1901 in Laconia; H – 38, carpenter, b. Concord, s/o
 George Bennett and Annah S. Carroll; W – 33, housekeeper,
 2nd, divorced, b. Meredith, d/o James Buzzell and Mary A.
 Whitten
James William of Tuftonboro m. Hazel Bernice **Perry** of Wakefield
 5/4/1943 in Sanbornville; H – 26, carpenter, b. Tuftonboro, s/o
 Frank S. Bennett (Tuftonboro, carpenter) and Eleanor G.
 Dawes (Boston, MA, housewife); W – 22, hairdresser, b.
 Wolfeboro, d/o Arthur H. Perry (Brookfield, farmer) and Alice E.
 Fogg (Ossipee, housewife)
Maurice P. of Tuftonboro m. Annie **Kidd** of Tuftonboro 3/18/1909 in
 Tuftonboro; H – 25, farmer, b. Tuftonboro, s/o John S. Bennett
 and Emma E. Piper; W – 22, house, b. Scotland, d/o David
 Kidd and Janet McKay
Maurice P. of Tuftonboro m. Grace Maud **Bean** of Wolfeboro
 5/1/1943 in Tuftonboro; H – 59, farmer, 2nd, b. Tuftonboro, s/o
 John S. Bennett (Moultonboro, deceased) and Emma Piper
 (Tuftonboro, deceased); W – 56, housewife, 2nd, b. Worcester,
 MA, d/o George A. Dewey (Hanover, deceased) and Nellie M.
 Ryan (W. Boylston, MA, deceased)
Orsino V. of Tuftonboro m. Lizzie M. **Gannon** of Tuftonboro
 10/8/1893 in Wolfeboro; H – 29, farmer, b. Tuftonboro, s/oJohn
 E. Bennett (Wolfeboro, farmer) and Hannah Bennett
 (Tuftonboro, housewife); W – 19, housekeeper, b. Croghan,
 Ireland, d/o Joseph Gannon (Scotland, engineer) and Mary
 Gannon (Groghan, Ireland, housewife)
Paul Mark of Tuftonboro m. Deborah **Bean** of Wolfeboro 8/28/1965
 in Wolfeboro; H – 18, maintenance, b. Wolfeboro, s/o Douglas
 L. Bennett (NH) and Marjorie Porter (NH); W – 16, at home, b.
 Wolfeboro, d/o Leon E. Bean (NH) and Arlene E. Henry (MA)
Ralph V. of Tuftonboro m. Helen K. **Garrison** of Tuftonboro
 10/14/1944 in Wolfeboro; H – 49, farmer, 2nd, b. Tuftonboro, s/o
 Orsino V. Bennett (Tuftonboro, farmer) and Elizabeth M.
 Gannon (housewife); W – 37, secretary, 2nd, b. Morris, IL, d/o
 Isadore Klocker (France, deceased) and Marie Gerber (France,
 deceased)

Ralph V. of Tuftonboro m. Dorothy E. **Dow** of Tuftonboro 12/17/1952
   in Tuftonboro; H – 57, carpenter, b. NH, s/o Orsino V. Bennett
   (NH) and Elizabeth M. Gannon (NY); W – 40, at home, b. MA,
   d/o Albert A. Dow (NH) and Bessie Pierson (MA)
Ralph Vaughn m. Maud Evelyn **Towle** 9/3/1927 in Lebanon, ME; H
   – 32, carpenter & farmer, b. Tuftonboro, s/o Orsino V. Bennett
   (Tuftonboro) and Elizabeth M. Gannon (Tuftonboro); W – 26,
   school teacher, b. Chichester, d/o Charles A. Towle
   (Chichester) and Florence Batchelder (Chichester)
Ralph Vaughn of Tuftonboro m. Arlene Gertrude **Wiggin** of
   Tuftonboro 11/11/1956 in N. Wakefield; H – 61, carpenter,
   divorced, b. NH, s/o Orsino V. Bennett (NH) and Elizabeth W.
   Gannon (NY); W – 62, attendant nurse, widow, b. NH, d/o
   Frank D. Stillings (NH)

BENSE,
Theodore Charles of Tuftonboro m. Carol Ann **Wetherbee** of
   Nashua 7/14/1960 in Tuftonboro; H – 27, technician, b. NH, s/o
   Theodore A. Bense (MA) and Ella L. Roberts (MA); W – 20,
   student, b. NH, d/o Charles H. Wetherbee (NH) and Mabel M.
   Dwire (NH)

BENTLEY,
James A. m. Cecily T. **Crowe** 2/23/1975 in Tuftonboro

BENTON,
Richard D. of Chester m. Susan L. **Kohtz** of Tuftonboro 6/30/1968 in
   Wolfeboro; H – b. NY, s/o Richardson D. Benton (Texas) and
   Bette Howell (NY); W – b. NY, d/o Walter C. Kohtz (NY) and
   Marion J. Quimby (NY)

BERGHAUS,
William C. B. of Chatham, NY m. Joyce Louise **Anderson** of
   Tuftonboro 10/14/1967 in Tuftonboro; H – 23, b. Orange, NJ,
   s/o Paul C. Berghaus (Texas) and Katherine Gleason (NY); W
   – 25, b. Boston, MA, d/o Earle E. Anderson (MA) and Olive
   Jenks (OH)

BERNARD,
Paul L. of Tuftonboro m. Joan H. **Cline** of Tuftonboro 7/20/1980
Paul L., Jr. m. Winnifred L. **Lauder** 8/1/1971 in Manchester

BERNIER,
Michael T. of Wolfeboro m. Dana L. **Shure** of Tuftonboro 10/9/1982

BERRY,
Steven Dean of Tuftonboro m. Wendy Lynn **Warren** of Wolfeboro 10/15/1988

Steven Douglas of Wolfeboro m. Gyme Lynn **Edgerly** of Tuftonboro 4/23/1966 in Wolfeboro; H – 18, student, b. Wolfeboro, s/o Clarence G. Berry (NH) and Lois B. Colby (MA); W – 19, student, b. Wolfeboro, d/o John I. Edgerly (NH) and Alice G. Bennett (NH)

BEVILAQUA,
Ralph J. of Tuftonboro m. Nichole M. **Plamondon** of Tuftonboro 7/9/2004

BICKERTON,
Jason J. of Tuftonboro m. Heidi A. **Holland** of Tuftonboro 9/21/1996

BICKFORD,
John H., Jr. of Tuftonboro m. Frances Arnold **Wager** of Greenville, MI 11/11/1964 in Sanbornville; H – 61, resort oper., 2nd, widower, b. Salem, MA, s/o John H. Bickford (NH) and Isabella May French (NH); W – 48, secretary, 3rd, widow, d/o Berkeley, CA, d/o Julian Arnold (CA) and Gertrude Davis (IN)

BISBEE,
Arthur H. m. Maud E. **Emery** 12/24/1925 in Tuftonboro; H – 25, farmer, b. Tuftonboro, s/o Archer C. Busbee (Parsonsfield, ME) and Addie Libby (Tuftonboro); W – 39, housewife, b. Tuftonboro, d/o Charles E. Emery (Tuftonboro) and Lucy E. Haley (Tuftonboro)

BISHOP,
Richard A. m. Sarah Elizabeth **Howard** 8/9/1925 in Tuftonboro; H – 30, engineer, b. Chelsea, MA, s/o Reuben Bishop (Cornwallis, NS) and Anna Benson (Gottenberg, Sweden); W – 34, laundress, 2nd, b. Pembroke, MA, d/o Thomas Lemings (Dublin, Ireland) and Margaret E. Christy (Clinton, MA)

BISSON,
Daniel J. of Tuftonboro m. Lisa B. **Conant** of Tuftonboro 2/14/1993

BLAISDELL,
Robert P. of Tuftonboro m. Doreen C. **Kuell** of Tuftonboro 6/3/2000
Thomas H. of Tuftonboro m. Una M. **Dore** of Wolfeboro 11/25/1915
   in Tuftonboro; H – 49, farming, b. Tuftonboro, s/o Richard C.
   Blaisdell (Tuftonboro) and Ruth M. Brown (Center Harbor); W –
   37, housewife, 2nd, divorced, b. Tuftonboro, d/o Alonzo A.
   Moody and Viola Canney

BLAKE,
Joseph C. of Tuftonboro m. Nellie M. **Smith** of Wolfeboro 6/5/1901
   in Wolfeboro; H – 41, farmer, 2nd, widower, b. Tuftonboro, s/o
   Charles Blake and Sarah Welch; W – 36, housekeeper, b.
   Wolfeboro, d/o Harry A. Smith and Hannah M. Johnson
Joseph C. of Tuftonboro m. Mary Jane **O'Neil** of Boston, MA
   10/9/1912 in Tuftonboro; H – 52, farmer, 3rd, b. Tuftonboro, s/o
   Charles Blake and Sarah Welch; W – 35, dressmaker, b. Co.
   Down, Ireland, d/o James O'Neil and Sarah Balmer
Norman T. m. Janet R. **Hurt** 11/24/1972 in Madison

BLANCHETTE,
Timothy P. of Tuftonboro m. Kirsten **Deyak** of Tuftonboro 7/30/2000

BLOCK,
Andrew R. m. Deborah A. **Waldie** 6/20/1974 in Tuftonboro

BOGAR,
John D. m. Mardy Gale **Mixer** 4/10/1971 in Tuftonboro

BONACCORSO,
Robert Francis of Tuftonboro m. Jane **Lawson** of Moultonboro
   8/31/1998

BOTTOMLEY,
Bruce MacL. of RI m. Doris Louise **Thomas** of Melvin Village
   9/30/1951 in Melvin Village; H – 24, maintenance, b. MA, s/o
   Frank Bottomley (England) and Helen M. MacLaren (MA); W –
   22, student, b. IA, d/o Donald E. Thomas (IA) and Dorothy J.
   Botts (IN)

BOWLES,
Francis D. of Tuftonboro m. Madeline N. **Brooks** of Tuftonboro
1/19/1946 in Wolfeboro; H – 22, student, b. Boston, MA, s/o
Calvin C. Bowles (Chicago, IL) and Cassandra A. Hayes
(Moultonboro); W – 18, clerical, b. Westwood, MA, d/o Norman
K. Brookes (Birkenhead, England) and Madeleine H. Luce
(Dorchester, MA)

BRADEAU,
Joseph S. of NB m. Doris E. **Ayers** of Tuftonboro 4/11/1920 in
Tuftonboro; H – 23, laborer, b. NB, s/o Ben Bradeau (NB) and
Mary Savoy (NB); W – 16, at home, b. Tuftonboro, d/o Herbert
Ayers (Tuftonboro) and Ina M. Adjutant (Tuftonboro)
Joseph S. of Tuftonboro m. Mary M. **Emery** of Tuftonboro 3/19/1921
in Tuftonboro; H – 23, farmer, 2nd, b. NB, s/o Ben Bradeau (NB)
and Mary Savoy (NB); W – 17, housewife, b. Tuftonboro, d/o
Cheston R. Emery (Bartlett) and Cora A. Hersey (Tuftonboro)

BRENNICK,
Steven L. of Alton m. Lise Anne **Holmberg** of Tuftonboro
10/22/1988

BREUNINGER,
Lewis Talmage of Wolfeboro m. Judith C. **Davis** of Wolfeboro
7/21/1980

BRIGGEMAN,
Russell Matthew of Wolfeboro m. Lynda Ann **Cail** of Tuftonboro
11/11/1995

BRITTON,
Harry of Tuftonboro m. Carrie **Taylor** of Ctr. Sandwich 5/23/1959 in
Ctr. Sandwich; H – 21, mechanic, b. NH, s/o Fred I. Britton
(NH) and Ruth Simms (NH); W – 16, at home, b. NH, d/o Paul
A. Taylor (NH) and Marion E. Gray

BROADBENT,
Kenneth A. of Alexandria, VA m. Kathryn L. **Cole** of Alexandria, VA
6/28/1986

BRODERICK,
Glenn T. of Tuftonboro m. Jolene A. **Doran** of Tuftonboro 8/15/1987

BROOKS,
Donald K. of Tuftonboro m. Lillian C. **Osgood** of Wolfeboro
3/23/1946 in Wolfeboro; H – 26, plumber, b. Boston, MA, s/o
Norman K. Brookes (Birkenhead, England) and Madeleine H.
Luce (Dorchester, MA); W – 25, secretary, b. Wolfeboro, d/o
Howard E. Osgood (Moultonboro) and Mildred L. French
(Wolfeboro)

BROUSSEAU,
Andrew A. of Tuftonboro m. Andrea Lee **Picard** of Tuftonboro
6/4/1988

BROWN,
Arthur A. of Manchester, CT m. Edith D. **Conant** of Lexington, KY
7/28/1945 in Mirror Lake; H – 30, engineer, b. Cleveland, OH,
s/o Carroll W. Brown (Rye Beach) and Harriet A. Hoskins
(Moravia, NY); W – 21, at home, b. Lexington, KY, d/o William
M. Conant (Boston, MA) and Dinsmore Patrick (Lexington, KY)
Charles H. of Tuftonboro m. Hattie E. **Abbott** of Ossipee 8/30/1891
in Tuftonboro; H – 28, farmer, b. Tuftonboro, s/o Andrew J.
Brown (Wolfeboro, farming) and Martha A. Brown (Tuftonboro);
W – 18, housewife, b. Ossipee, d/o Jacob Abbott (Ossipee,
farming) and Harriett Abbott (Ossipee)
Edmond M., Jr. m. Katherine L. **Worthley** 10/22/1971 in Tuftonboro
Harold Floyd m. Ethelyn Mildred **Hersey** 5/12/1935 in Ctr.
Tuftonboro; H – 29, clerk, b. Tuftonboro, s/o Charles H. Brown
(Tuftonboro, farmer) and Kate E. Abbott (Moultonboro,
housewife); W – 25, bookkeeper, b. Tuftonboro, d/o Edwin C.
Hersey (Tuftonboro, farmer) and Hattie B. Springer (Marshfield,
VT, housewife)
John M. m. Patricia **Sawyer** 10/29/1972 in Wolfeboro
Lloyd Robert of Wolfeboro m. Margaret Hannum **Peake** of
Tuftonboro 9/6/1980
Morrill Howard m. Elva Lillian **Hersey** 7/13/1935 in Wolfeboro; H –
31, grocer, b. Exeter, s/o George C. Brown (Brentwood,
contractor) and May Lee (AR, housewife); W – 20, at home, b.
Tuftonboro, d/o Edwin C. Hersey (Tuftonboro, farmer) and
Hattie B. Springer (Marshfield, VT, housewife)

Philip K., III of Wolfeboro m. Sarah Harlan **Kingsford** of Tuftonboro
5/25/1991
Wallace Chadwick of Bradford m. Nola Gail **Britton** of Tuftonboro
8/14/1959 in New London; H – 21, carpenter, b. NH, s/o
George E. Brown (MA) and Beatrice Rhodenheizer (NS); W –
20, waitress, b. NH, d/o Fred J. Britton (NH) and Ruth I. Simms
(ME)

BROWNELL,
Harold Parker of Effingham m. Evelyn Rose **Banfill** of Tuftonboro
2/14/1939 in Effingham; H – 23, truck driver, b. Effingham, s/o
David Theo. Brownell (Ossipee, laborer) and Clara Lydia
Parker (Sherbrooke, PQ, housewife); W – 18, at home, b. S.
Berwick, ME, d/o Fred Robert Banfill (Franklin, bus driver) and
Meleda A. Desharnais (Victoriaville, PQ, housewife)

BRYANT,
Daniel m. Cynthia J. **Hodges** 9/14/2005 in Sandwich

BUEL,
Anthony S. of Tuftonboro m. Melanie E. **Sweetman** of Tuftonboro
10/25/2003

BULLIS,
Russell H. m. Marcia A. **Faucette** 8/21/1971 in Tuftonboro
Russell H., Jr. of Tuftonboro m. Yvonne **Fischer** of Pforzheim,
Germany 10/22/1993
Russell Hathaway, Jr. of Tuftonboro m. Cynthia Diane **Signoretti** of
Litchfield 2/17/1996

BULLOCK,
Charles Edwin, II of Tuftonboro m. Gloria Spaulding **Morton** of ME
12/27/1955 in Mirror Lake; H – 31, TV announcer, b. MA, s/o
Charles E. Bullock (MA) and Phyllis Conley (MA); W – 24, TV
salesperson, divorced, b. ME, d/o Leon F. Spaulding (ME) and
Effie M. Furo (ME)

BUNTING,
Bainbridge of Kansas City, MO m. Dorelen **Feise** of Baltimore, MD
8/21/1948 in Tuftonboro; H – 34, teacher, b. Kansas City, MO,
s/o William M. Bunting (International, TN) and E. Bainbridge

(Meridan, MS); W – 26, social worker, b. Mexico City, Mexico, d/o Ernest Feise (Braunschoveig, Germany) and Dorothy Findlay (Madison, WI)

BURBANK,
Paul H. of Moultonboro m. Diana M. **Sheahan** of Tuftonboro
2/14/1981

BURLEIGH,
Will C. of Tuftonboro m. Mina F. **Wiggin** of Tuftonboro 3/20/1894 in Tuftonboro; H – 22, clerk, b. Deering, ME, s/o Joseph J. Burleigh (Tuftonboro, farmer) and Sarah H. Burleigh (Barnstead); W – 22, housekeeper, b. Tuftonboro, d/o Augutus Wiggin (Tuftonboro, farmer) and Martha Wiggin (Tuftonboro)

BURSAW,
Burton Bechard of S. Acton, MA m. Gretchen Whitney **Senior** of Medway, MA 9/3/1932 in Melvin Village; H – 24, oil merchant, b. Dorchester, MA, s/o Henry William Bursaw (Paincourt, ON, oil merchant) and Rose Helen Bechard (Paincourt, ON, at home); W – 19, at home, b. Medway, MA, d/o Walter Mann. Senior (Mannington, WV, hat mfgr.) and Helen Gertrude Ayer (Winchester, MA, at home)

BURTON,
Bruce J. m. Debra A. **Ames** 8/26/1972 in Center Harbor

BUSHMAN,
Richard J. m. Patricia A. **Stockman** 10/25/1978 in Tuftonboro
Richard J. of Tuftonboro m. Hester M. **O'Neil-Lord** of Wolfeboro
9/3/1988
Richard John of Tuftonboro m. Olivia Alice **Ridnour** of Albuquerque, NM 12/19/1961 in Wolfeboro; H – 21, laborer, b. Wolfeboro, s/o Robert J. Bushman (MA); W – 18, at home, b. Detroit, MI, d/o Orville Ridnour (MT)
Robert J. of Tuftonboro m. Janet L. **Sloane** of Tuftonboro
11/14/1987

BUSSIERE,
Ralph Edward, III of Tuftonboro m. Tracey L. **Fortier** of Tuftonboro
7/4/1997

Thomas Jeffrey of Tuftonboro m. April Lynn **Smith** of Tuftonboro
  5/16/1998

BUTLER,
Wendell R. m. Yvonne H. **Young** 8/10/1974 in Tuftonboro

BUTTRICK,
Daniel C. of Tuftonboro m. Stephanie Ann **Chandler** of Tuftonboro
  5/21/1988

CALLENDER,
Donald E., II of Cedar Rapids, IA m. Vicki A. **McAllister** of Cedar
  Rapids, IA 6/15/1987
John MacPherson of Racine, WI m. Patricia Alexandra **Grzyb** of
  Racine, WI 9/12/1998

CAMIRE,
Robert R. of Tuftonboro m. Linda L. **Misiaszek** of Tuftonboro
  8/4/2001

CAMPBELL,
Donald Eugene m. Marilyn C. **Garrett** 12/26/1970 in Tuftonboro; H –
  b. 6/13/1931 in OH, s/o Earl E. Campbell and Martha Brown; W
  – b. 4/9/1935 in NH, d/o Edwin R. Craigue and Ellen Hayes
Potter B. of Tuftonboro m. Susan E. **Fuller** of Tuftonboro 2/8/1986

CAMPION,
James W., Jr. of Hanover m. Carlie H. **Kaemmerer** of Tuftonboro
  5/12/1967 in Hanover; H – 61, merchant, widower, b. Amherst,
  MA, s/o James Campion (England) and Anna B. Walsh (MA);
  W – 54, widow, b. Austria, d/o Alfred Deutsch (Austria) and
  Margaret Lanfer (Austria)

CANNIFF,
William F. of Tuftonboro m. Darlene J. **Barton** of Tuftonboro
  10/17/1981

CANTWELL,
Bruce David of Tuftonboro m. Ramona Averill **Stevens** of Wolfeboro
  7/10/1954 in Melvin Village; H – 23, US Navy, b. MA, s/o
  Edward W. Cantwell (NH) and Erma Langmaid (NH); W – 18, at

home, b. NH, d/o Philip L. Stevens (ME) and Olive D. Averill (MA)

William J., Jr. of Center Harbor m. Noel Stuart **Wright** of Tuftonboro 8/28/1965 in Wolfeboro; H – 22, salesman, b. Springfield, MA, s/o William J. Cantwell (MA) and Virginia Camp (MA); W – 21, saleswoman, b. Salem, MA, d/o Donald Chester Wright (MA) and Kathleen S. McKinney (NY)

CAO,
Ramiro of Jackson Heights, NY m. Wendy **Wright** of New York City, NY 7/11/1987

CAPOZZI,
Edmund F., Jr. of Providence, RI m. Christine Putney **Hostelley** of Tuftonboro 8/8/1998

CAPRON,
David A. of Ossipee m. Andrea **Rollins** of Tuftonboro 8/17/1991

CARLSON,
Ronald E. m. Joan W. **Marlatt** 7/10/1976 in Tuftonboro

CELLARIUS,
Kenneth of Tuftonboro m. Mary E. **Berry** of Manchester 9/30/1940 in Manchester; H – 28, caretaker, 2nd, b. Boston, MA, s/o Theodore Cellarius (Boston, MA, gardener) and Edna Hersey (Boston, MA, housewife); W – 23, reg. nurse, b. Dover, d/o Harry O. Berry (Barrington, millwright) and Mary A. Meserve (Rochester, housewife)

CHAMBERLAIN,
John Adams of Wolfeboro m. Edith Frances **Littlefield** of Tuftonboro 6/1/1963 in Tuftonboro; H – 53, carpenter, b. Wolfeboro, s/o Lester A. Chamberlain (NH) and Sadie Belle Hutchins (ME); W – 42, reg. nurse, b. Barnstead, d/o Stilson W. Littlefield (MA) and Agnes L. Holmes (MA)

CHANDLER,
Norman P. of Hill m. Jean C. **Wilkin** of Tuftonboro 7/30/1949 in Melvin Village; H – 25, US Army, b. MA, s/o Norman B. Chandler (MA) and Mary Palmer (NY); W – 24, artist, b.

Pittsburgh, PA, d/o Hugh Wilkin (Suffolk, England) and
Elizabeth K. Crawford (PA)
Perry R. m. Edith R. **Sutherland** 9/5/1926 in Tuftonboro; H – 22, ill.
engineer, b. Boston, MA, s/o Pliny C. Chandler (Woburn, MA)
and Clarabelle Kean (Mooers, NY); W – 20, saleslady, b.
Revere, MA, d/o George M. Sutherland (Scotland) and Lilla E.
Ronaldine (England)

CHAPMAN,
Walter F. of Melrose, MA m. Esther L. **Murphy** of Melrose, MA
8/23/1923 in Tuftonboro; H – 34, insurance, b. Boston, MA, s/o
George W. Chapman (Woburn, MA) and Jennie I. Leggett
(Melrose, MA); W – 28, clerk, b. Melrose, MA, d/o Thomas
Murphy (Halifax, NS) and Julia McAskill (Melrose, MA)

CHARLES,
Richard H., Jr. m. Katharine L. **Warner** 7/27/1974 in Wolfeboro

CHELLMAN,
Chester Eric, III of Tuftonboro m. Carol Ann **Yerden** of Tuftonboro
8/30/1997

CHENEY,
Earl L. m. Ruth C. **Wakefield** 1/18/1975 in Tuftonboro
Gilbert Frederick of Tuftonboro m. Sandra June **Ridlon** of Wolfeboro
8/2/1959 in Wolfeboro; H – 19, carpenter, b. NH, s/o Gordon W.
Cheney (NH) and Violet Bowen (VT); W – 17, at home, b. NH,
d/o Filburt E. Ridlon (ME) and Delia M. Hill (NH)
Gordon Warren m. Violet Pember **Bowen** 7/7/1935 in Randolph, VT;
H – 27, farmer, b. Melvin Village, s/o Wyatt D. Cheney (Melvin
Village) and Mattie Lillian Stokes (Melvin Village); W – 22, b.
Braintree, VT, d/o Azro B. Bowen (Bethel, VT) and Verna
Pember (Rochester, VT)
John G. m. Edna S. **Young** 8/21/1941 in Ossipee; H – 34, farmer, b.
Ellensburg, NY, s/o John M. Cheney (NY, deceased) and Ella
F. Stevens (Hopkinton, RI, clergyman); W – 32, teacher, b.
Watertown, MA, d/o Howard E. Young (Ossipee, farmer) and
Minnie M. Andrews (Westfield, NB, housewife)
Lyle G. of Tuftonboro m. Mary Jane **Curdo** of Alton 6/2/1988
Ralph B. of Tuftonboro m. Pearl E. **Dodge** of Tuftonboro 9/23/1945
in Tamworth; H – 23, machinist, b. Tuftonboro, s/o Wyatt D.

Cheney (Dickerson Ctr., NY) and Martha L. Stokes
(Tuftonboro); W – 18, at home, b. Exeter, d/o William H. Dodge
(Charlotte, VT) and Gladys Locke (Pittsfield)
Raymond E. of Tuftonboro m. Hattie W. **Jones** of 2/2/1946 in
Tamworth; H – 19, US Army, b. Tuftonboro, s/o Wyatt D.
Cheney (Dickerson Ctr., NY) and Martha L. Stokes
(Tuftonboro); W – 17, at home, b. Tamworth, d/o Frederick W.
Jones (Haverhill, MA) and Effie J. Brown (Tamworth)
Richard Gordon of Tuftonboro m. Donna Lee **Cilley** of N. Shapleigh,
ME 11/2/1962 in Wolfeboro; H – 18, carpenter, b. Wolfeboro,
s/o Gordon W. Cheney (NH) and Violet B. Piper (VT); W – 18,
none, b. Lewiston, ME, d/o William W. Cilley (MA) and Jennie
M. Bennett (ME)
Sidney E. m. Vicki L. **Johnson** 11/11/1977 in Tuftonboro
Warren Dale of Tuftonboro m. Evelyn Irene **Hlushuk** of Tuftonboro
8/23/1959 in Tuftonboro; H – 21, machinist, b. NH, s/o Gordon
W. Cheney (NH) and Violet F. Bowen (VT); W – 18, knit. mach.,
b. NH, d/o Jack S. Hlushuk (Russia) and Leora E. Adjutant
(NH)
William Joseph m. Alice **Philippe** 3/30/1935 in Wolfeboro; H – 19,
laborer, b. Tuftonboro, s/o George M. Cheney (Dickenson Ctr.,
NY, retired) and Ella F. Stevens (Hopkinton, RI, housewife); W
– 25, demonstrator, 2nd, b. New Glasgow, NS, d/o John Charles
Mitchell (Wakefield, MA, carpenter) and Minnie Louise Green
(PEI, housewife)
Wyatt D. of Tuftonboro m. Mattie L. **Stokes** of Tuftonboro
11/27/1910 in Tuftonboro; H – 19, farmer, b. Dickinson Ctr., NY,
s/o George M. Cheney and Lottie Haskell; W – 22, housewife,
b. Tuftonboro, d/o Benjamin F. Stokes and Lydia B. Remick

CHERRY,
Christopher D. of Southbridge, MA m. Maribeth **Cunniff** of
Southbridge, MA 9/18/1993

CHIAPETTA,
Michael L. m. Catharine W. **Unander-Scharin** 6/29/1973 in
Wolfeboro

CHILD,
Charles L. of Charleston m. Nancy Ruth **Howe** of Tuftonboro
8/14/1968 in Tuftonboro; H – b. VT, s/o James H. Child (NH)

and Lorraine Comstock (VT); W – b. NH, d/o Robert D. Howe (MA) and Dorothy Hull (RI)

CHISHOLM,
Scott Weaver of Tuftonboro m. Maureen Susan **Butler** of Manchester 9/24/1994

CHITTENDEN,
Wentworth A. of Tuftonboro m. Wilda E. **Jackson** of Tuftonboro 6/30/1983

CHRISTIAN,
William H. of Tuftonboro m. Diana L. **Haley** of Tuftonboro 2/7/1995
William H., Jr. m. Gertrude E. **O'Neil** 9/3/1977 in Tuftonboro

CLARK,
Alexander R. of Tuftonboro m. Mercy **Grant** of Tuftonboro 8/8/1921 in Laconia; H – 49, carpenter, b. NS, s/o Robert Clark (NS) and Isabel Holiday (NS); W – 38, housewife, 2nd, b. Berwick, ME, d/o Joseph B. Joy (S. Berwick, ME) and Almira Fitzjerold (S. Berwick, ME)

CLARKE,
Dennis J. of New Durham m. Holly L. **Curtis** of Tuftonboro 8/16/1987

CLIFFORD,
Bruce E. m. Wanda L. **Edwards** 6/24/1972 in Wolfeboro

CLINTON,
Stuart K. m. Judith G. **Ambrose** 6/7/1969 in Meredith; H – b. 7/19/1943 in OH, s/o Wills H. Clinton and Edith King; W – b. 10/14/1946 in NH, d/o Paul L. Ambrose and Jane Langer
Stuart K. of Tuftonboro m. Susan Mae **Evans** of Laconia 5/22/1988

CLOUGH,
Fred Wayne m. Cynthia Mary **Craigue** 9/5/1970 in Tuftonboro; H – b. 5/4/1949 in NH, s/o Fred Clough and Mary Skaltsis; W – b. 10/9/1950 in NH, d/o Kenneth E. Craigue and Mary L. Bense
Harold W. of Wolfeboro m. Annabelle Theresa **Foss** of Tuftonboro 10/5/1956 in Melvin Village; H – 20, US Army, b. NH, s/o Harold

Clough (NH) and Doris York (NH); W – 18, at home, b. NY, d/o
Gilbert Foss (ME) and Anna Crockett (ME)
Harold W. of Tuftonboro m. Tina M. **Craigue** of Tuftonboro
7/27/1985
Harold W. of Tuftonboro m. Donna M. **Hilow** of Wolfeboro Falls
7/29/2000
Randy A. of Tuftonboro m. Ruth M. **Dore** of Tuftonboro 12/31/1992
Robert William of Tuftonboro m. Evelyn Rebecca **Reed** of Wolfeboro
9/24/1966 in Wolfeboro; H – 23, ins. agent, b. Malden, MA, s/o
William L. Clough (MA) and Evelyn R. Burke (MA); W – 18, at
home, b. Wolfeboro, d/o Basil L. Reed (NH) and Dorothy J.
Warren (NH)

COGGESHALL,
Robert M. of Tuftonboro m. Susan A. **Pouliot** of Tuftonboro
7/24/1987

COLBERT,
Eugene T. m. Dorothy S. **Paterno** 6/12/1976 in Wolfeboro

COLBURN,
Everett E. of Waterville Valley m. Deborah F. **Merritt** of Tuftonboro
8/14/2005

COLBY,
Howard C. of Tuftonboro m. Thelma E. **Drucker** of Tuftonboro
4/5/1930 in Wolfeboro; H – 20, truck driver, b. Wolfeboro, s/o
Ralph M. Colby (Ossipee) and Ida Bean (Tuftonboro); W – 22,
school teacher, b. Nashua, d/o Ralph W. Drucker
(Londonderry) and Lela M. Staniels (Hillsboro Bridge)
Reginald C. of Tuftonboro m. Marylin E. **Smith** of Tuftonboro
5/18/1957 in Plainfield; H – 26, shovel oper., b. Wolfeboro, s/o
Howard C. Colby (NH) and Thelma E. Drucker (NH); W – 18, at
home, b. NH, d/o Walter R. Smith (NH) and Doris H. Mack (NH)

COLE,
Frederick Arthur, Jr. of Newtonville m. Letitia Ebbs **Doten** of
Newtonville 7/28/1963 in Tuftonboro; H – 39, tool rental, b.
Newton, MA, s/o Fredrick A. Cole (MA) and Grace E. Perry
(MA); W – 38, reg. nurse, b. Waltham, MA, d/o Clarence A.
Doten (MA) and Letitia Ebbs (MA)

Irving C. of Tuftonboro m. Evelyn M. **Wiggin** of Tuftonboro 2/9/1896
in Wolfeboro; H – 23, engineer, b. Charlestown, MA, s/o Dudley
P. Cole (Salem, MA, salesman) and Etta M. Cole
(Moultonboro); W – 18, housekeeper, b. Tuftonboro, d/o
Leander F. Wiggin (Tuftonboro, farmer) and Nancy Wiggin
(Tuftonboro, housewife)
Roger Ronald of Meriden, CT m. Joan C. **Juke** of Tuftonboro
2/14/1980

COMEAU,
James of Tuftonboro m. Michelle L. **Eldridge** of Tuftonboro
9/11/1999

COMTOIS,
Gerard J., Jr. of Tuftonboro m. Pamela **Stetson** of Tuftonboro
10/4/1997

CONRAD,
Everett G. of Tuftonboro m. Denise D. **Cole** of Tuftonboro 10/3/1983
Thomas M. m. Virginia **Richardson** 6/17/1978 in Tuftonboro

COOK,
James Herbert of MA m. Jessie Ella **Pearson** of MA 8/12/1951 in
Tuftonboro; H – 60, salesman, b. PEI, s/o James Cook
(Canada) and Flora McQuarrie (Canada); W – 58, ins. super.,
b. MA, d/o Jacob Pearson (NS)
John B. of Tuftonboro m. Abigail **Albee** of Tuftonboro 8/5/2000

COOLEY,
William U. of Huntington Beach, CA m. Cynthia D. **Boyd** of
Huntington Beach, CA 10/6/1990

COOPER,
David W. of Tuftonboro m. Susan M. **Dickinson** of Tuftonboro
6/9/1984
George William of Washington, DC m. Eleanor **Dow** of Tuftonboro
5/4/1959 in Tuftonboro; H – 41, foreign cor., divorced, b. IA, s/o
Emerson E. Cooper (IA) and Lillian Hanchett (IA); W – 31,
analyst, b. MA, d/o Kenneth C. Dow (MA) and Kathryn Beck
(MA)

COPP,
Stuart O., Jr. m. Candace A. **Yablonka** 7/26/1969 in Tuftonboro; H –
b. 3/24/1941 in MA, s/o Stuart O. Copp, Sr. and Mary Varney;
W – b. 7/27/1945 in MA, d/o Robert W. Hull and Ruth Lovely

COPPLESTONE,
Steven A. of Tuftonboro m. Sarah J. **Wingate** of Tuftonboro
9/11/1982

CORDEAU,
Peter m. Addie **Piper** 12/31/1927 in Tuftonboro; H – 68, farmer, 2nd,
s/o Prudent Cordeau and Edwige Cordeau; W – 52, at home,
2nd, d/o Lewis Geto and Hattie Parsons

CORNWELL,
Ralph W. of Tuftonboro m. Christine L. **Christiansen** of Tuftonboro
7/14/2001

CORROW,
Eric Daniel of Tuftonboro m. Blanche J. **LaPoint** of Tuftonboro
1/5/1943 in Freedom; H – 44, trucking, b. Coventry, VT, s/o
Everington Corrow (Coventry, VT, deceased) and Mabel Page
(W. Derby, VT, deceased); W – 43, housekeeper, 2nd, b. St.
Johnsbury, VT, d/o Ezra Goss (deceased) and Amelia Goss
(deceased)

CORSON,
Woodbury of Tuftonboro m. Vina **Simpson** of Boston, MA 9/25/1909
in Tuftonboro; H – 37, farmer, b. Middleton, s/o Eben Corson
and Perlina Ellis; W – 33, house, b. Boston, MA, d/o Robert
Simpson and Charlotte Huggs

COSTA,
Peter D. of Charlotte, NC m. Suzanne D. **Fish** of Concord, MA
6/21/1986

COSTONIS,
Anthony F. of Winthrop, MA m. Dorothy G. **Lind** of Chelsea, MA
7/9/1993

COULTER,

Leslie John of Chicopee, MA m. Shirley Ann **Brown** of Chicopee, MA 7/4/1964 in Melvin Village; H – 52, packer, b. Chicopee, MA, s/o James H. Coulter (Ireland) and Edith G. Jenkinson (Ireland); W – 28, teacher, b. Wolfeboro, d/o Morrill H. Brown (NH) and Elva Lillian Hersey (NH)

COVERT,

Charles W. of Tuftonboro m. Suzanne E. **Heth** of Tuftonboro 2/14/1998

CRAIGUE,

Harley P. of Wolfeboro m. Jeanne **Bushman** of Tuftonboro 7/18/1959 in Wolfeboro; H – 25, prof. soldier, divorced, b. NH, s/o Edwin R. Craigue (NH) and Ellen Hayes (NH); W – 20, at home, b. NH, d/o Robert Bushman (NH) and Faye Eldridge (NH)

James E. of Tuftonboro m. Carolyn L. **Toms** of Wolfeboro 9/8/1990

John E. m. Carol L. **Baxter** 9/24/1977 in Tuftonboro

Kenneth E. of Tuftonboro m. Mary L. **Bense** of Tuftonboro 7/2/1949 in Tuftonboro; H – 19, carpenter, b. Wolfeboro, s/o Edwin R. Craigue (Concord) and Ellen M. Hayes (Tuftonboro); W – 18, at home, b. Meredith, d/o Theodore A. Bense (S. Boston, MA) and Ella L. Roberts (Allston, MA)

Scott B. of Tuftonboro m. Michelle Y. **Wood** of Tuftonboro 8/1/1981

Scott B. of Tuftonboro m. Kimberly A. **Bolobanic** of Rochester 4/9/2001

CRANE,

Nathaniel S. of Tuftonboro m. Lara C. **McMullin** of Tuftonboro 9/25/1999

Theodore A. of Newark, NJ m. Vena Annie **Foss** of Newark, NJ 8/16/1915 in Tuftonboro; H – 27, accountant, b. Newark, NJ, s/o Andrew L. Crane (Newark, NJ) and Emma L. Gerry (New York, NY); W – 30, school teacher, b. Wolfeboro, d/o Herbert W. Frost (Wolfeboro) and Annie E. Burleigh (Tuftonboro)

CRECRAFT,

Harrison R. of Salt Lake City, UT m. Anne **Detwiler** of Tuftonboro 9/22/1979

CREILSON,
John Leo Joseph of MA m. Joann May **Ivester** of MA 7/29/1960 in
Tuftonboro; H – 20, student, b. MA, s/o John J. Creilson (MA)
and Anna Marines (MA); W – 20, secretary, b. MA, d/o Kenneth
R. Ivester (MA) and Irene F. Atkinson (MA)

CROMBIE,
Richard Louis of Lynn, MA m. Zelda **Gilliatt** of Somerville, MA
9/4/1951 in Melvin Village; H – 23, US Army, b. MA, s/o Harold
R. Crombie (MA) and Marie C. Gagnon (NH); W – 24, office
clerk, b. MA, d/o Reg. W. Gilliatt (MA) and Marion A. Eldridge
(NH)

CROOK,
Charles Henry George of Melvin Village m. Edna Frances **Gourley**
of Newton, MA 1/16/1932 in Cambridge, MA; H – 44, caretaker,
2nd, b. Winchester, England, s/o George Crook; W – 30, maid,
b. South Branch, NS, d/o Louis Gourley and Ada Bonnell

CROTEAU,
Arthur J., III of Yarmouth, ME m. Susan Anne **Sullivan** of Yarmouth,
ME 8/25/1984
Richard G. m. Jan L. **Helling** 4/25/1976 in Tuftonboro

CUBEDDU,
James John of Tuftonboro m. Heather Lynn **Kinmond** of Tuftonboro
5/24/1997

CURDO,
George Howard of Danvers, MA m. Mary Jane **Breakell** of W.
Newton, MA 12/15/1968 in Tuftonboro; H – widower, b. MA, s/o
Alexander Curdo (NS) and Delvina Gosslin (Canada); W –
divorced, b. MA, d/o W. Lloyd Allen (MA) and Muriel Wingate
(MA)

CURRELL,
James B., Jr. of Moorestown, NJ m. Sara M. **Fonseca** of Cherry Hill,
NJ 9/22/1990

CURRY,
James Joseph of Cohasset, MA m. Marie Adele **Eames** of
Tuftonboro 8/19/1943 in Tuftonboro; H – 59, pres. Waldorf, 3rd,
b. Ireland, s/o Thomas Curry (Ireland, deceased) and Mary
McMahan (Ireland, deceased); W – 42, at home, 2nd, b. Lynn,
MA, d/o William W. Hyde (VT, deceased) and Flora M. Valiquet
(PQ, at home)

CURTIS,
William B. m. Gloria J. **Elliott** 6/12/1970 in Wakefield; H – b.
1/1/1948 in MA, s/o Kenneth G. Curtis and Jacqueline Lassell;
W – b. 11/2/1950 in NH, d/o Charles H. Elliott, Sr. and Edith L.
Bodwell

DAIGNAULT,
Wilfred R. m. Joan D. **Frye** 12/16/1977 in Wolfeboro

DALEY,
Jon Peter of Tuftonboro m. Meagan Joy **Murray** of Chester 8/2/1997

DALTON,
Robert L., Sr. of Tuftonboro m. Linda May **Kendal** of Tuftonboro
11/1/1991

DALY,
Michael J. m. Elizabeth L. **Senecal** 8/11/1976 in Tuftonboro

DAMON,
Christopher S. m. Dorcas A. **Margeson** 3/12/1977 in Wolfeboro

DAN,
Julian R. A. of Houston, Texas m. Pamela Ellen **Krey** of Tuftonboro
5/24/1980

DANIELS,
Lewis S. m. Lillian J. **Hartley** 8/18/1926 in Tuftonboro; H – 23,
salesman, b. Waltham, MA, s/o Jonathan Daniels (Pittston, PA)
and Minnie Sutter (St. Clair, PA); W – 21, at home, b. Waltham,
MA, d/o Samuel Hartley (England) and Sophia Denton
(England)

DANIELSON,
Paul S. m. Cathy Marie **Spencer** 6/14/1969 in Wolfeboro; H – b. 5/14/1947 in NJ, s/o Ray F. Davidson and Betty J. Meinschein; W – b. 9/29/1947 in MA, d/o Thomas D. Spencer and Lorraine Burchstead

DARLING,
Kenneth B. of Providence, RI m. S. Frances **Davis** of Providence, RI 8/16/1915 in Tuftonboro; H – 21, clerk, b. Providence, RI, s/o Walter A. Darling (Attleboro, MA) and Mary T. Booth (Pawtucket, RI); W – 21, housewife, b. Pawtucket, RI, d/o Walter S. Davis (Dickson, IL) and Grace A. Reid (Pawtucket, RI)

DAVIS,
Albert E. of Tuftonboro m. Eda M. **Wallace** of Ossipee 9/24/1919 in Ossipee; H – 24, farmer, b. Tuftonboro, s/o Harry A. Davis and Sadie B. Gilman (Tuftonboro); W – 19, at home, b. Ossipee, d/o Charles P. Wallace (Ossipee) and Harriet L. Hurd (Boston, MA)
Charles A. of Tuftonboro m. Etta M. **Ladd** of Tuftonboro 9/25/1891 in Tuftonboro; H – 33, merchant, b. Moultonboro, s/o William H. Davis (Tuftonboro, merchant) and Elizabeth Davis (Tuftonboro); W – 28, teacher, b. Maysville, ME, d/o Levi W. Ladd (Tuftonboro, farming) and Miranda Ladd (Hudson, MA)
Eli of Tuftonboro m. Hazel B. **Elliott** of Alton 7/3/1919 in Tuftonboro; H – 25, teamster, b. Ossipee, s/o Eli N. Davis (Jackson) and Georgie Williams (Ossipee); W – 16, housekeeper, b. Alton, d/o Henry A. Elliott (Rumney) and Lizzie B. Elliott (Rumney)
Foster E. m. Mary A. **Sullivan** 5/19/1940 in Wolfeboro; H – 24, clerk, b. Tuftonboro, s/o Harry L. Davis (Tuftonboro, carpenter) and Flora B. McDonald (Moultonboro, housewife); W – 24, clerk, b. Brighton, MA, d/o John A. Sullivan (Somerville, MA, merchant) and Mary E. McKenna (Scotland, housewife)
Foster Lee m. Diane G. **Davis** 3/21/1975 in Laconia
Foster Lee of Tuftonboro m. Elizabeth Ann **Carter** of Tuftonboro 11/27/1979
Foster Lee of Tuftonboro m. Audrey May **Jackson** of Wolfeboro 6/20/1992
Harry A. of Tuftonboro m. Sadie B. **Gilman** of Tuftonboro 7/4/1894 in Tuftonboro; H – 21, laborer, b. Gilmanton, s/o Jefferson T. Davis (Lemster, clergyman) and Annie L. Davis (Franklin,

housewife); W – 17, housework, b. Tuftonboro, d/o Aaron W. Gilman (Sandwich, farmer) and Emma F. Gilman (Moultonboro, housewife)

John McQuiston of Denver, CO m. Elizabeth Anderson **Seaman** of Denver, CO 9/16/1995

Paul Wallace of Tuftonboro m. Rhoda Louise **Ham** of Tuftonboro 11/8/1953 in Tuftonboro; H – 23, lumber worker, b. Wolfeboro, s/o Albert E. Davis (Tuftonboro) and Eda M. Wallace (Ossipee); W – 18, at home, b. Tuftonboro, d/o Leroy E. Ham (Acton, ME) and Florence L. Haley (Tuftonboro)

Roger Valentine m. Doris Elizabeth **Thompson** 12/24/1936 in Laconia; H – 25, auto mechanic, b. Manchester, s/o Harry L. Davis (Moultonboro, carpenter) and Flora B. McDonald (Moultonboro, housewife); W – 26, waitress, b. Tuftonboro, d/o Simon T. Thompson (Tuftonboro, laborer) and Evelyn L. Bean (Tuftonboro, deceased)

Willis Paige m. Eleanor May **Thompson** 8/20/1936 in Meredith; H – 19, laborer, b. Tuftonboro, s/o Harry L. Davis (Moultonboro, carpenter) and Flora B. McDonald (Moultonboro, housewife); W – 19, waitress, 2nd, b. Tuftonboro, d/o Simon T. Thompson (Tuftonboro, laborer) and Evelyn L. Bean (Tuftonboro, deceased)

DAY,
Robert M. of Tuftonboro m. Darlene A. **Lynn** of Tuftonboro 7/9/2000

DEAL,
Edward L. of Rochester, NY m. Nellie N. **Southworth** of Whitman, MA 11/26/1914 in Tuftonboro; H – 28, blacksmith, 2nd, b. Halifax, NS, s/o Richard Deal and Mary Langdon; W – 28, domestic, 2nd, b. Hanson, MA, d/o L. I. Lane and Augusta Bourne

DEARBORN,
Charles Philip of Dover m. Thelma Grace **Hlushuk** of Tuftonboro 2/11/1951 in Tuftonboro; H – 22, bookbinder, b. Hiram, ME, s/o L. W. Dearborn (Hiram, ME) and Lulu J. Douglas (Hiram, ME); W – 20, office clerk, b. Tuftonboro, d/o Jack S. Hlushuk (Russia) and Leora E. Adjutant (NH)

Howard of Tuftonboro m. Pauline E. **Hlushuk** of Tuftonboro 9/25/1948 in Wolfeboro; H – 23, mechanic, b. E. Hiram, ME, s/o

Louie W. Dearborn (E. Hiram, ME) and Lulu J. Douglas
(Sebago, ME); W – 20, factory work, b. Tuftonboro, d/o Jack S.
Hlushuk (Moscow, Russia) and Leora E. Adjutant (Tuftonboro)
James D. m. Deborah M. **Antonucci** 7/26/1969 in Wolfeboro; H – b.
4/22/1945 in NH, s/o Louie W. Dearborn and Lulu J. Douglas;
W – b. 7/10/1949 in NH, d/o Silvil J. Antonucci and Irma M.
Craigue
L. W., Jr. of Tuftonboro m. Jean E. **Harrington** of Tuftonboro
10/19/1947 in Mirror Lake; H – 22, handyman, b. Hiram, ME,
s/o Louie W. Dearborn (Hiram, ME) and Lulu J. Douglas
(Sebago, ME); W – 21, at home, b. Medford, MA, d/o A. W.
Harrington (E. Boston, MA) and Annie B. MacConnell (E.
Boston, MA)
Mark Edward of Tuftonboro m. Zita **Bodonyi** of Budapest, Hungary
8/12/1989

DENEE,
Robert Craig of Landing, NJ m. Nicole Therese **Beaudoin** of
Landing, NJ 8/27/1994

DELUCA,
Vincent J. of Lynn, MA m. Ruth A. **Magrath** of N. Reading, MA
7/11/1981

DERAMER,
Frank Jacob of Tuftonboro m. Pauline Mary **Bradley-Smith** of
Tuftonboro 2/3/1996

DEROSE,
Joseph L. of Tuftonboro m. Laurie K. **Burnett** of Mashpee, MA
6/16/1990

DESMARAIS,
Brian David of Boxborough, MA m. Hilary Beth **Davey** of
Boxborough, MA 7/13/1996

DETERLING,
John S. of Bath, ME m. Susan E. **Grill** of Bath, ME 6/11/1988

DEWITT,
William Collins of Mansfield, MA m. Mary Grace **Maddock** of
Seekonk, MA 9/18/1993

DICKEY,
Robert Ellsworth of Haverhill, MA m. Inamae **Emery** of Haverhill, MA
7/29/1939 in Melvin Village; H – 26, carpenter, b. Haverhill, MA,
s/o Everett Ells. Dickey (Peterboro, real estate oper.) and Lillian
May Trulle (Merrimac, MA, housewife); W – 24, hairdresser, b.
Brockton, MA, d/o William Henry Emery (Lawrence, MA, AAA
manager) and Caroline Ida Carter (Waterford, VT, housewife)

DIETZEL,
William H., Jr. m. Jean **Cheney** 7/24/1971 in Meredith

DILLARD,
Charles A., Jr. of Mineral Bluff, GA m. Darlene T. **Johns** of Mineral
Bluff, GA 8/11/1991

DILTZ,
Melvin Arthur of CA m. Thelma Louise **Reed** of Tuftonboro 4/6/1954
in Meredith; H – 25, comm. fisherman, b. CA, s/o Melvin C.
Diltz (CA) and Erma K. Scgmerical (CA); W – 18, student, b.
Ossipee, d/o Frank E. Reed (ME) and Mildred F. Whiting
(Ossipee)

DOLLOFF,
Frederick J. m. Donna E. **Phelps** 12/28/1977 in Wolfeboro

DONOVAN,
John F., Jr. m. Kathleen M. **Brennick** 12/5/1971 in Tuftonboro

DORAIS,
Philip E. of Meredith m. Mary Ellen **Pike** of Tuftonboro 6/12/1982

DORE,
Ivan E. of Milton m. Carolyn E. **Haley** of Tuftonboro 12/13/1959 in
Wolfeboro; H – 23, mechanic, b. NH, s/o Charles E. Dore (NH)
and Blanche E. Nickerson (NH); W – 19, at home, b. NH, d/o
Lawrence Haley (NH) and Frances Tibbedeau

Jesse James of Tuftonboro m. Phoebe Carrie **Whitten** of Tuftonboro 5/29/1939 in Wolfeboro; H – 26, laborer, b. Wolfeboro, s/o Walter Grover Dore (Wolfeboro, laborer) and A. Alta Adjutant (Wolfeboro, housewife); W – 23, housework, b. Tuftonboro, d/o Joseph W. Whitten (Wolfeboro, farmer) and Mamie Gert. Whitten (Tuftonboro, housewife)

Richard Leon of Tuftonboro m. Barbara Louise **Hlushuk** of Tuftonboro 10/30/1954 in Ctr. Tuftonboro; H – 20, wood chooper, b. Wolfeboro, s/o Leon E. Dore (NH) and Mildred F. Davis (NH); W – 17, at home, b. NH, d/o Jack S. Hlushuk (Russia) and Leora E. Adjutant (NH)

Roy Elwin of Tuftonboro m. Sylvia Edith **Knights** of E. Rochester 11/27/1954 in E. Rochester; H – 23, woodsman, b. NH, s/o Leon E. Dore (NH) and Mildred F. Davis (NH); W – 18, Woolworths, b. NH, d/o Lawrence D. Knights (NH) and Rita S. Bickford (NH)

DORN,
John Z. of Tuftonboro m. Victoria **Harris** of Erwina, PA 12/13/2003

DOUGLASS,
Oliver S. m. Lillian M. **Prouty** 7/25/1942 in Bridgton, ME; H – 30, board sawyer, 2nd, b. Bridgton, ME, s/o Warren L. Douglass (Bridgton, ME, farmer) and Nellie Roes (Bridgton, ME, housewife); W – 28, housewife, 2nd, b. Fryeburg, ME, d/o Harold Wentworth (Haverhill, MA, millwright) and Estelle M. Thorne (Brownfield, ME, housewife)

DOW,
Ausbrey N. of Tuftonboro m. Bernice H. **Emerson** of Ossipee 9/9/1922 in Ossipee; H – 31, farmer, b. Tuftonboro, s/o Alvah E. Dow and Anna M. Nutter (Tuftonboro); W – 26, housewife, 2nd, b. Ossipee, d/o A. Judson Ham (Ossipee) and Etta Wentworth (Wakefield)

Ernest H. m. Alice Greanor **Dow** 9/14/1942 in Laconia; H – 44, supt., 3rd, b. Moultonboro, s/o James B. Dow (Moultonboro, deceased) and Elizabeth Garland (Moultonboro, deceased); W – 38, housekeeper, 2nd, b. Wolfeboro, d/o Frank Adjutant (Brookfield, deceased) and Adra Plummer (Wolfeboro, housekeeper)

Roland D. of Tuftonboro m. Greta E. **May** of Ossipee 8/5/1945 in
Ossipee; H – 26, farmer, b. Ossipee, s/o Ausbrey N. Dow
(Tuftonboro) and Bernice F. Hamm (Ossipee); W – 22, price
clerk, b. Canaan, VT, d/o William H. May (Eden, VT) and Nellie
M. Potter (Belvidere, VT)
Vernon Robert of Tuftonboro m. Dorothy E. **Kenny** of Long Island,
NY 3/12/1944 in Melvin Village; H – 20, US Navy, b.
Moultonboro, s/o Ernest H. Dow (Moultonboro, supt. of club)
and Alice G. Adjutant (Wolfeboro, housewife); W – 21, tel.
oper., b. Dorchester, MA, d/o Charles H. Kenny (Framingham,
MA, interior des.) and Evelyn Chapman (ME, housewife)
Wayne A. m. Marilyn L. **McGloin** 5/20/1972 in Wolfeboro

DOWNING,
Daniel Frederick of Alton m. Victoria Davis **Lyon** of Tuftonboro
9/21/2002
Geoffrey A. of Tuftonboro m. Karen C. **Cross** of Tuftonboro
6/25/1988

DROUIN,
Wilfred E. of Tuftonboro m. Marion A. **Sampson** of Tuftonboro
12/14/1979

DUBAY,
Alan R. of Tuftonboro m. Elinor C. **Biehl** of Wolfeboro 9/24/2000

DUDLEY,
Ronald A. of Littleton, MA m. Arline M. **Atlee** of Littleton, MA
8/16/1986

DUFFY,
Daniel J. of Tuftonboro m. Louise M. **Gauvreau** of Tuftonboro
4/11/1991

DUFTON,
William M. of Tuftonboro m. Liana M. **Marcotte** of Tuftonboro
12/22/1990

DUMONT,
Paul R. m. Lisa A. **Dahill** 6/10/1978 in Tuftonboro

DUNCAN,
James H. S. of Tuftonboro m. Barbara E. **Novotny** of Shaftsbury, VT
6/22/1981

DUNN,
Kenneth G. of Arlington, MA m. Elsie M. **Willard** of Tuftonboro
8/3/1947 in Melvin Village; H – 27, maintenance, b. Arlington,
MA, s/o Edward R. Dunn (Arlington, MA) and Rachael G. Call
(Alberton, PEI); W – 30, clerk, b. Swampscott, MA, d/o Arthur
E. Willard (Boston, MA) and Iva M. Durgin (Lynn, MA)
Kenneth G. m. Joanne M. **Shure** 5/20/1972 in Tuftonboro
Robert Joseph, Jr. of Wolfeboro m. Virginia Margaret **Sleeper** of
Tuftonboro 5/17/1980

DUPRE,
William Prosch of Washington, DC m. Helen May **Baxter** of
Tuftonboro 8/23/1954 in Tuftonboro; H – 19, student, b. MA, s/o
William J. Dupre (MA) and Gertrude Prosch (Germany); W –
19, at home, b. NH, d/o George P. Baxter (RI) and Priscilla C.
West (NH)

DURGIN,
Willard of Brownfield, ME m. Bernice **Hersey** of Tuftonboro 8/2/1916
in Sanbornville; H – 23, teamster, b. Porter, ME, s/o Joseph
Durgin and Mary Wormwood; W – 17, housewife, b.
Tuftonboro, d/o George W. Hersey and Elizabeth Hodgdon

DUSO,
David A. of St. Lawrence, NY m. Lugene M. **Sheen** of St. Lawrence,
NY 6/2/1984

DUSSAULT,
Mark J. of San Diego, CA m. Margaret E. **Halloran** of San Diego,
CA 1/3/1987

DWYER,
Richard Paul of San Francisco, CA m. Monica Soonie **White** of San
Francisco, CA 8/12/2000

EASTMAN,
John Allen, Jr. m. Kathryn Anne **Curtis** 6/20/1970 in Tuftonboro; H –
b. 8/28/1951 in NH, s/o John A. Eastman, Sr. and Lucille
Charles; W – b. 8/18/1951 in NH, d/o Kenneth G. Curtis and
Jacqueline Lassell

EATON,
Brian N. of Tuftonboro m. Sandra N. **Locke** of Wolfeboro 6/19/2004

EDGAR,
Arthur R. m. Carol L. **Dunn** 11/9/1968 in Tuftonboro; H – b.
8/16/1941 in NY, s/o Russell Edgar and Jeannette Village; W –
b. 10/30/1948 in MA, d/o Kenneth G. Dunn and Elsie M. Willard

EDGERLY,
Albert L. of Tuftonboro m. Ann G. **Sleeper** of Canaan, ME
12/13/1892 in Tuftonboro; H – 64, carpenter, 2nd, b. Farmington,
s/o John Edgerly (Newmarket, carpenter) and Nancy Edgerly
(Farmington, housewife); W – 50, housewife, 2nd, b. Canaan,
ME, d/o Ezekiel Hayes (Canaan, ME, carpenter)
Edwin B. of Tuftonboro m. Caroline L. **Crossman** of Providence, RI
10/14/1913 in Tuftonboro; H – 29, farmer, b. Tuftonboro, s/o
John A. Edgerly and Mary C. Blake; W – 29, teacher, b.
Providence, RI, d/o George P. Crossman and Grace A. White
John I., Jr. of Tuftonboro m. Theresa A. **Goraum** of Dover 9/1/1990
John Irving m. Alice Gertrude **Bennett** 9/18/1938 in Melvin Village;
H – 24, greens' caretaker, b. Tuftonboro, s/o Edwin Blake
Edgerly (Tuftonboro, hotel owner) and Caroline Crossman
(Providence, RI, deceased); W – 20, waitress, b. Tuftonboro,
d/o Frank Samuel Bennett (Tuftonboro, carpenter) and Eleanor
Gertrude Dawes (Boston, MA, housewife)

EDWARDS,
Judson F. of Tuftonboro m. Frances E. **Spaulding** of Tuftonboro
11/14/1982
Robert A. of Tuftonboro m. Andrea Lee **Picard** of Tuftonboro
6/4/1988

ELDRIDGE,
Bradley W. of Ossipee m. Deborah L. **Williams** of Tuftonboro
9/26/1987

Carlton O. of Tuftonboro m. Martha M. **Hayes** of Ossipee 5/16/1948
in Ctr. Ossipee; H – 23, lumberman, b. Milton, s/o Carlton S.
Eldridge (Ossipee) and Esther M. Haley (Tuftonboro); W – 19,
at home, b. Boston, MA, d/o Arthur M. Hayes (Bath, ME) and
Martha M. Tebbetts (Ossipee)
Jeremy Clyde of Ossipee m. Dorothy Cora **Brewer** of Tuftonboro
8/20/1994
John C. of Tuftonboro m. Glenda M. **Severance** of Tuftonboro
5/17/1986
Ronald Robert of Tuftonboro m. Tracy Leigh **Michaud** of Tuftonboro
7/8/1995

ELKINS,
George William of Rydal, PA m. Katherine **Laing** of Milton, MA
8/31/1968 in Tuftonboro; H – b. PA, s/o George W. Elkins, Jr.
(PA) and Elizabeth Downes (PA); W – b. MA, d/o George Laing
(Scotland) and Katherine Flint (NJ)

ELLIOT,
Eugene Waldo of Alton m. Mona Ellen **Smith** of Tuftonboro 1/8/1955
in Ctr. Ossipee; H – 26, truck driver, divorced, b. NH, s/o Walter
E. Elliott (NH) and Ella F. Gilman (NH); W – 17, at home, b. NH,
d/o Clifton E. Smith (MA) and Bertha M. Riley (ME)

ELLIOTT,
George W. of Alton m. Ethel **Welch** of Tuftonboro 12/4/1905 in
Melvin Village; H – 22, teamster, b. Rumney, s/o D. W. Elliott
and Lucy Willoughby; W – 22, housewife, b. Tuftonboro, d/o
George Welch and Bertie Horne
Richard D. of Portland, ME m. Ann M. **Ireland** of Portland, ME
10/14/1990

EMERT,
Jason E. of Tuftonboro m. Christine M. **Metcalfe** of Tuftonboro
10/23/2004

EMERY,
Howard E. of Tuftonboro m. Emma S. **Hodgdon** of Tuftonboro
6/15/1897 in Tuftonboro; H – 22, farmer, b. Tuftonboro, s/o
Charles E. Emery and Lucy A. Haley; W – 28, housekeeper,
2nd, widow, b. Ossipee, d/o Allen Swazey and Sarah Swazey

Wendall C. m. Nellie F. B. **Emery** 3/2/1941 in Tuftonboro; H – 60, farmer, b. Tuftonboro, s/o Charles Edwin Emery (Tuftonboro, farmer) and Lucy Ann Haley (Moultonboro, deceased); W – 49, housewife, 2nd, b. Somersworth, d/o John F. Brown (deceased) and Emma Jones (deceased)

ENGALICHEV,
Constantine Nicholas of Kittery Point, ME m. Judith Hastings **Berry** of Tuftonboro 9/28/1996

ENNIS,
Barry T. of Tuftonboro m. Jane A. **Marshall** of Tuftonboro 5/21/1983

ERICKSON,
Robert E. of Storrs, CT m. Joy G. **Parker** of Stafford Spring, CT 9/5/1982

EVANS,
Kenneth G. of Tuftonboro m. Annette W. **Lampron** of Wolfeboro 10/29/1955 in Wolfeboro; H – 22, laborer, b. NH, s/o Frank Evans (OH) and Evelyn Dow (NH); W – 20, at home, b. NH, d/o Wilfred Lampron (NH) and Yvonne Lacasse (Canada)
Lane W. of Tuftonboro m. Dawn S. **Moody** of Wolfeboro 5/23/1987

EVITTS,
Nathaniel Thomas of Tuftonboro m. Heather Jean **Cowper** of Tuftonboro 8/30/1997

FALK,
George M. m. Marjorie A. **Metz** 7/25/1977 in Tuftonboro

FAVRO,
Earl T. of Tuftonboro m. Elva M. **Flanders** of New Hampton 7/27/1914 in New Hampton; H – 24, clergyman, b. Providence, RI, s.o William Favro and Emma White; W – 18, student, b. New Hampton, d/o Harry Flanders

FERGUSON,
Levi D. m. Florence D. **Sprague** 9/2/1928 in Tuftonboro; H – 73, clergyman, 3rd, b. NS, s/o Alex. Ferguson (NS) and Mary McKenzie (NS); W – 48, stitcher, 2nd, b. Islesboro, ME, d/o

Simon D. Sprague (Islesboro, ME) and Elizabeth Pendleton (Islesboro, ME)

FERLAND,
Andrew M. of Tuftonboro m. Kathaleen M. **Thompson** of Tuftonboro 10/29/2005

FERNALD,
Bruce C. of Somerville, MA m. Patricia Ann **Boyd** of Somerville, MA 6/13/1982
Chester Campbell m. Marion Ardell **Dodds** 11/1/1938 in Sanbornville; H – 23, hotel manager, b. Wolfeboro, s/o Walter Edward Fernald (Tuftonboro, hotel manager) and Emily Campbell (Providence, RI, at home); W – 23, registered nurse, b. Laconia, d/o Percy Henry Dodds (Whitefield, NJ, carpenter) and Laurie Catherine Bisson (Sherbrook, Canada, housewife)
Hollis E. m. Emma J. **Hickey** 10/29/1924 in Tuftonboro; H – 69, blacksmith, 2nd, b. Tuftonboro, s/o Stephen Fernald (Berwick, ME) and Elizabeth A. Hodgdon (Tuftonboro); W – 53, nurse, 2nd, b. Manchester, England, d/o John Young (Manchester, England) and Catherine Crawford (Manchester, England)

FERNANDEZ,
Scott K. of Alton m. Amanda A. **Delaney** of Tuftonboro 4/29/2000

FERRY,
Edw. M. of Melrose, MA m. Dorothy M. **Beck** of Melrose, MA 6/22/1940 in Tuftonboro; H – 34, teacher, b. E. Hampton, MA, s/o Winthrop Ferry (E. Hampton, MA, deceased) and Catherine Morrison (E. Hampton, MA, housewife); W – 29, teacher, b. Chicago, IL, d/o Frank J. Beck (Lockport, IL, deceased) and Maud MacKesson (WI, housewife)

FISKE,
Charles W., Jr. m. Sally I. **Rosell** 4/6/1974 in Tuftonboro

FLINT,
Harley A. of Tuftonboro m. Ruth B. **Davis** of Tuftonboro 12/1/1979
Stanley Reed of Crownsville, MD m. Mary Ann **Simick** of Baltimore, MD 7/28/1989

FOGLE,
Clair M., Jr. of Rindge m. Donna H. **Hemphill** of Rindge 10/15/1982

FORBES,
Frederick William, Jr. of PA m. Alice Hubbert **Brice** of PA 8/27/1955 in Mirror Lake; H – 29, air lines official, divorced, b. PA, s/o Frederick W. Forbes (PA) and Ella C. Hilton (PA); W – 27, clerk, divorced, b. PA, d/o Roger L. Hubbert (TN) and Helen M. Goodall (NY)

FORSYTHE,
Frank Faulkner m. Nettie Bell **Bean** 11/16/1938 in Melvin Village; H – 36, farmer, 3rd, b. Lynn, MA, s/o Frank Faulkner Forsyth (Avonport, NS, deceased) and Nellie May Rouse (NS, organist); W – 26, housekeeper, b. Tuftonboro, d/o Arthur Milton Bean (Moultonboro, farmer) and Cordelia Agnes Carter (Birmingham, England, deceased)

FOSS,
Albert M. of Tuftonboro m. Elizabeth A. **Beagin** of Boston, MA 4/18/1894 in Wakefield; H – 49, farmer, 2nd, b. Moultonboro, s/o John S. Foss (Strafford, farmer) and Sarah Foss (Tuftonboro); W – 32, housewife, b. Boston, MA, d/o Owen Beagin (Ireland, clerk) and Julia Beagin (Boston, MA, housewife)

Charles E. of Tuftonboro m. Florence B. **Bean** of Tuftonboro 1/13/1915 in Ossipee; H – 24, farmer, b. Tuftonboro, s/o Fred S. Foss (Wolfeboro) and Anna R. Bean (Tuftonboro); W – 18, housewife, b. Tuftonboro, d/o Willie L. Bean (Tuftonboro) and Ula D. Foss (Tuftonboro)

Guy Leslie m. Mary Grace **Senior** 12/23/1938 in Melvin Village; H – 22, truck driver, b. Tuftonboro, s/o Charles Foss (Tuftonboro, truck driver) and Florence Bean (Tuftonboro, housewife); W – 19, at home, b. Framingham, MA, d/o Walter Manning Senior (Mannington, WV, retired) and Helen Ayer (Winchester, MA, housewife)

FOSTER,
John Hopkins of Shelburne, VT m. Claudia Marie Reznor **Bender** of Shelburne, VT 6/28/1997

FOUST,
Howard W. of Tuftonboro m. Patricia J. **Sherwood** of Tuftonboro
7/5/1990

FREDERICK,
C. Leslie of Arlington, MA m. Barbara Jane **Reed** of Damariscotta,
MA 6/27/1992

FREESE,
George C. of Tuftonboro m. Perlina **Nutter** of Middleton 10/17/1901
in Tuftonboro; H – 74, farmer, 3rd, widower, b. Moultonboro, s/o
William C. Freese and Irene Brown; W – 73, housekeeper, 3rd,
widow, b. Middleton, d/o Robert Ellis and Hannah Wentworth

FREIBERGER,
Christopher A. of Providence, RI m. Mary A. **Farwell** of Providence,
RI 6/13/1982

FRENCH,
Donald R. of Wolfeboro m. Nancy L. **Smith** of Tuftonboro 2/23/1957
in Ctr. Ossipee; H – 20, armed forces, b. MA, s/o Raymond A.
French (NH) and Dorothy L. Booth (MA); W – 21, clerk, b. NH,
d/o Clifton E. Smith (MA) and Bertha M. Riley (ME)
Norman A. of Wolfeboro m. Carlina **Mugridge** of Tuftonboro
7/15/1960 in Wolfeboro; H – 21, garage, b. MA, s/o Raymond
French (NH) and Dorothy L. Booth (MA); W – 25, beautician, b.
NH, d/o Donald J. Mugridge (Canada) and Eleanor P. Hoyve
(MA)

FRISBEE,
Ernest E. of Tuftonboro m. Carrie E. **Hepworth** of Wolfeboro
6/25/1902 in Wolfeboro; H – 22, painter, b. Tuftonboro, s/o
Lewis N. Frisbie and Addie A. Morrison; W – 22, housekeeper,
b. Wolfeboro, d/o Mark G. Wentworth and Ida E. Willey

FULGINITI,
Dominick m. Kathleen **Olsen** 8/28/1971 in Tuftonboro

FULLER,
James A. of Haverhill, MA m. Sheila A. **Dore** of Haverhill, MA
5/31/1986

William Pressley, III of Greenwich, CT m. Kathryn Ann **Keller** of New York, NY 9/8/1996

FULLERTON,
John F. m. Linda J. **Cross** 10/21/1972 in Wolfeboro

GAFNEY,
Richard C. m. Joan H. **Haslett** 7/16/1972 in Tuftonboro

GAGNE,
Ernest A. m. Bonnie L. **Ridlon** 4/6/1974 in Wolfeboro

GALLAGHER,
Robert M. m. Randi S. **Kerr** 10/2/1971 in Tuftonboro

GARABEDIAN,
Martin Sarkis of Salem m. Barbara Jane **Wood** of Tuftonboro 6/7/1980

GARLAND,
Chester A. m. Inez Evelyn **Page** 6/13/1937 in Derry; H – 56, mechanic, 2nd, b. Brookfield, s/o Fred J. Garland (Bartlett, unknown) and Mary J. Cook (Porter, ME, deceased); W – 25, stenographer, b. Halifax, NS, d/o Arthur Page (Halifax, NS, baker) and Susanne Leydon (Halifax, NS, housewife)

GARRETT,
Edwin R. m. Penelope **Stevens** 3/11/1977 in Wolfeboro

GATES,
Charles Patterson, Jr. of Martinsville, NJ m. Rosalie Elaine **Lawless** of Tuftonboro 12/15/1951 in Wolfeboro; H – 23, US Army, b. NJ, s/o Charles P. Gates (NJ) and Carolyn Randolph (NJ); W – 20, at home, b. MA, d/o Frank J. Lawless (NJ) and Mabel V. Gilmartin (NY)
Kenneth F., Jr. of Tuftonboro m. Judith M. **Pike** of Tuftonboro 5/23/1982

GAUVIN,
Daniel L. of Tuftonboro m. Paula L. **Gauvin** of Tuftonboro 2/14/1993

GENDRO,
Clement of Tuftonboro m. Amelia **Grover** of Tuftonboro 9/14/1916 in
Tuftonboro; H – 62, farmer, b. Montreal, Canada, s/o Nelson
Gendro; W – 62, housewife, b. Rumney, d/o Abraham Downing
and Permelia Innis
Clement m. Emma **Ellison** 1/13/1927 in Tuftonboro; H – 72, farmer,
3rd, b. Montreal, Canada, s/o Nelson Gendro (Montreal,
Canada); W – 63, housewife, 2nd, b. Holland, VT, d/o Frank
Cushing (Canada) and Louise Cushing

GEORGE,
Jeffrey L. of Manchester m. Lisa A. **Letoile** of Manchester 5/26/1980
Richard W. of Tuftonboro m. Elizabeth A. **Santoro** of Cambridge,
MA 2/14/1987

GERSTL,
Ernest of Norwalk, CT m. Pearle Mae **Lewis** of Norwalk, CT
10/14/1939 in Melvin Village; H – 43, pharmacist, b. Hybbe,
Hungary, s/o Samuel Gerstl (Hungary, deceased) and Julia
Stein (Hungary, deceased); W – 29, registered nurse, b.
Coxheath, Cape Breton, d/o Peter Singleston Lewis (Coxheath,
Cape Breton, deceased) and Margaret Petrie (Gardner Mines,
Cape Breton, deceased)

GILLESPIE,
Roger B. of Kingston, ON m. Sara E. **Fernald** of Tuftonboro
9/8/1979

GILMAN,
Charles L. of Tuftonboro m. Georgie **Buzzell** of Tuftonboro
8/24/1892 in Tuftonboro; H – 26, mechanic, b. Moultonboro, s/o
Charles Gilman (Wolfeboro, expressman) and Laura E. Gilman
(Tuftonboro, housewife); W – 24, housewife, b. Meredith, d/o
Jonas Buzzell (lumberman) and Mary Buzzell (Moultonboro,
housewife)
Chester H. of Tuftonboro m. Edith B. **Fernald** of Tuftonboro
1/3/1914 in Tuftonboro; H – 25, fireman, 2nd, b. Tuftonboro, s/o
Aaron W. Gilman and Emma F. Quimby; W – 31, dressmaker,
b. Chelsea, MA, d/o James F. Fernald and Sarah B. Merrill

GLIDDEN,
Edgar H. m. Nancy J. **Kelley** 9/2/1976 in Wolfeboro
Nelson R. m. Alice **Schmidt** 11/20/1977 inTamworth
Troy S. of Tuftonboro m. Julia M. **Shaheen** of Wolfeboro 6/22/2002

GOLDSCHMIDT,
Steven O. m. Anne T. **Vinnicombe** 10/11/1975 in Tuftonboro

GOLLEDGE,
Robert W., Jr. of Dartmouth, MA m. Susan Gail **Jessup** of
    Dartmouth, MA 8/27/1988

GORDON,
Bart J. m. Sarah M. **Cooper-Ellis** 9/12/1971 in Tuftonboro

GORMLEY,
Matthew M. of Roanoke, VA m. Sandra J. **Merrifield** of Tuftonboro
    10/24/1981

GOUIN,
Thornton F. of Tuftonboro m. Judy A. **Hamlin** of Wolfeboro
    10/2/1960 in Wolfeboro Falls; H – 17, unemployed, b. NH, s/o
    Thornton F. Gouin (NH) and Leona L. Libby; W – 14, at home,
    b. NH, d/o Carl W. Hamlin (NH) and Helen G. Lawton

GOULD,
Lebias R. of Ctr. Tuftonboro m. Barbara **Nickerson** of Ctr. Ossipee
    12/31/1949 in Wolfeboro; H – 59, wool carder, b. Canada, s/o
    James W. Gould (Canada) and Sarah E. Huntley (Canada); W
    – 31, housewife, b. NH, d/o John C. Sharp and Katherine
    Sanborn (NH)

GRAHAM,
John E. of Tuftonboro m. Ora B. **Staples** of Tuftonboro 10/27/1915
    in Tuftonboro; H – 29, teaming, 2nd, widower, b. Brookfield, s/o
    George H. Graham (NS) and Melvina Rhyan (NS); W – 21,
    housewife, 2nd, divorced, b. Parsonsfield, ME, d/o John E.
    Staples (Ossipee) and Ellen F. Edwards (Parsonsfield, ME)
John E. of Tuftonboro m. Lisa Christine **Wistedt** of Tuftonboro
    8/9/1953 in Melvin Village; H – 67, teamster, widower, b. NH,
    s/o George H. Graham (NS) and Melvina Ryan (NS); W – 63,

housekeeper, widow, b. MA, d/o John Nelson (Sweden) and
Emma Johnson (Sweden)

GRANT,
Leland H. of Meredith m. Edith S. **Caverly** of Tuftonboro 6/4/1947 in
Melvin Village; H – 61, wood finisher, b. Moultonboro, s/o Frank
H. Grant (Sandwich) and Hattie B. Abbott (Sandwich); W – 61,
at home, b. Moultonboro, d/o Charles Caverly (Tuftonboro) and
Mary E. Sanborn (Tuftonboro)

GRAY,
Burton R. of Harrisville, NY m. Irene C. **Shaw** of Harrisville, NY
11/22/1979

GREENBANK,
Benjamin M. of Boston, MA m. Florence M. **Gould** of Boston, MA
7/21/1948 in Tuftonboro; H – 66, salesman, b. Danville, VT, s/o
Matt. B. Greenbank (Danville, VT) and Gertrude F. Clifford
(Danville, VT); W – 64, bookkeeper, b. Salem, MA, d/o W.
Henry H. Gould (Baltimore, MD) and Sarah E. Walker (Salem,
MA)

GREENE,
Francois Robert of Tuftonboro m. Muriel Jocelyn **Nicol** of Tuftonboro
1/1/1994

GREENWOOD,
John C. of Tuftonboro m. Jody **Hoague** of Peabody, MA 6/14/1980
Kenneth A. m. Janice **Martins** 7/4/1978 in Tuftonboro
Kenneth A. of Tuftonboro m. Bernadette M. **Tupeck** of Tuftonboro
6/29/1985
Kenneth A. of Tuftonboro m. Lisa M. **Potenza** of Tuftonboro
6/11/1988

GREZATTI,
Stephen A. of Tuftonboro m. Molly **Severance** of Tuftonboro
9/28/1991

GRIFFITHS,
William Harry of Watertown, MA m. Marcia Eleanor **Clausen** of
Natick, MA 9/19/1964 in Tuftonboro; H – 23, artist, b. Baltimore,

MD, s/o William D. Griffiths (MD) and Virginia Stinchcum (MD); W – 26, Navy nurse, b. Boston, MA, d/o Paul Edward Clausen (MA) and Eleanor M. Stots (MA)

GUBERSTEIN,
Harold A. of Cambridge, MA m. Susie L. **Bennett** of Tuftonboro 6/28/1919 in Cambridge; H – 28, statistician, Cambridge, MA, s/o Edward W. Guberstein and Victoria Gray (Stark, ME); W – 30, school principal, b. Wolfeboro, d/o Charles H. Bennett (Wolfeboro) and Emma E. Piper (Tuftonboro)

GUNN,
B. Christopher of Tuftonboro m. Jennifer Leigh **Clark** of Northport, NY 10/8/1994

HAARTZ,
Luther W. m. Elizabeth J. **Straw** 5/1/1971 in Wolfeboro

HADDOCK,
Andrew Robert of Tuftonboro m. Lisa Marie **Elliott** of Tuftonboro 7/20/1996

HADLEY,
Thomas L. of Tuftonboro m. Michelle E. **Gregoire** of Tuftonboro 5/15/1982

HAEGER,
Michael D. of Tuftonboro m. Karen A. **Lampron** of Wolfeboro 5/12/1990

HAGGETT,
George E. of Portland, ME m. Bertha **Horne** of Tuftonboro 12/25/1897 in Tuftonboro; H – 22, hatter, b. Portland, ME, s/o William Haggett and Mary Guptill; W – 18, housekeeper, b. Exeter, d/o Charles Horne and Elizabeth Horne

HALE,
Scott Joseph of Tuftonboro m. Billie-Sue **Witham** of Tuftonboro 10/5/2002

HALEPIS,
Andrew M. m. Cheryl A. **Riley** 5/1/1976 in Ossipee

HALEY,
Charles E. of Tuftonboro m. Dora E. **Mack** of Tuftonboro 12/20/1916
in Tuftonboro; H – 33, farmer, b. Tuftonboro, s/o Samuel R.
Haley and Hattie J. Buzzell; W – 21, housewife, b. Moultonboro,
d/o Elmer R. Bragg and Sarah A. Parott
Delbert C., III of Tuftonboro m. Barbara J. **Seegar** of Rochester, PA
2/24/1979
Delbert C., III of Tuftonboro m. Deborah L. **Sparks** of Clovis, NM
8/1/1989
Delbert Clarence m. Muriel Cecil **Roebarge** 6/27/1931 in Sandwich;
H – 23, laborer, b. Tuftonboro, s/o Willis Irving Haley
(Tuftonboro) and Bernece Eliz. Dow (Moultonboro); W – 17, at
home, b. Tamworth, d/o Louis Roebarge (Peabody, MA) and
Bessie Elliott (Plymouth)
Delbert Clarence, Jr. of Tuftonboro m. Geraldine Elizabeth **Cates** of
Wolfeboro 7/8/1956 in Melvin Village; H – 23, carpenter, b. NH,
s/o Delbert C. Haley (NH) and Muriel C. Robarge (NH); W – 18,
employed by A&P, b. NH, d/o Richard A. Estes (NH) and
Dorothy Brown (NH)
George H. of Tuftonboro m. Edith C. **Ayers** of Tuftonboro 5/16/1893
in Tuftonboro; H – 33, farmer, b. Moultonboro, s/o Samuel R.
Haley (Lee, farmer) and Nancy M. Haley (Tuftonboro,
housewife); W – 19, housekeeper, b. Tuftonboro, d/o james
Ayers (Tuftonboro, farmer) and Hannah Ayers (Tuftonboro,
housewife)
Howard Russell m. Helen Louise **Ferris** 11/10/1935 in Wolfeboro; H
– 19, laborer, b. Melvin Village, s/o Willis I. Haley (Tuftonboro,
laborer) and Bernece Ethel Dow (Moultonboro, housewife); W –
17, at home, b. Boston, MA, d/o Edmund Ferris (NY, auto
foreman) and Florence Button (housewife)
Kenneth Edward of Tuftonboro m. Mildred Velma **Bean** of
Tuftonboro 1/21/1939 in Melvin Village; H – 21, laborer, b.
Wolfeboro, s/o Charles Edw. Haley (Tuftonboro, carpenter) and
Dora Ellen Bragg (Moultonboro, housewife); W – 16, at home,
b. Wolfeboro, d/o Ralph Leon Bean (Tuftonboro, farmer) and
Lura Pearl Bean (Moultonboro, housewife)
Lawrence Ervin m. Frances **Thibedeau** 10/23/1937 in Wolfeboro; H
– 31, electrician, b. Melvin Village, s/o Willis I. Haley

(Tuftonboro, deceased) and Bernece Ethel Dow (Moultonboro, housewife); W – 19, waitress, b. New Durham, d/o Maurice Thibedeau (unknown, deceased) and Ada Elliott (W. Rumney, shoe worker)

Myron Henry m. Lucile Mary **Herbert** 3/16/1935 in Wolfeboro; H – 31, laborer, b. Tuftonboro, s/o George H. Haley (Moultonboro, laborer) and Edith C. Ayers (Tuftonboro, housewife); W – 25, stenographer, b. Wolfeboro, d/o William B. Herbert (Oldtown, ME, bus driver) and Margaret A. Grant (S. Wolfeboro, housewife)

Ralph S. of Tuftonboro m. Gladys A. **Doying** of Dover 3/28/1920 in Wolfeboro; H – 23, laborer, b. Tuftonboro, s/o George H. Haley (Moultonboro) and Edith C. Ayers (Tuftonboro); W – 28, teacher, b. Nashua, d/o Charles E. Doying (Warwick, Canada) and Alice Bradley (Epping)

Richard A. of Tuftonboro m. Kimberly B. **Page** of Concord 2/14/1987

Willis I. of Tuftonboro m. Bernice E. **Dow** of Moultonboro 8/3/1905 in Melvin Village; H – 19, laborer, b. Tuftonboro, s/o Samuel Haley and Hattie Buzzell; W – 17, housewife, b. Moultonboro, d/o James B. Dow and Lizzie Garland

HALL,

Lindley H. of Wellesley, MA m. Judith **Yanez** of Norwood, MA 10/6/1979

Roy Michael of Tuftonboro m. Lee Ellen **Marzerka** of Tuftonboro 5/21/1997

Thomas B. of Princeton, NJ m. Ellen C. **Reynolds** of Princeton, NJ 9/1/1979

HALLAM,

Timothy Driesner, Jr. of Wolfeboro m. Kelli Jean **Sheridan** of Tuftonboro 6/7/1996

HAM,

Jeffrey W. of Arlington, MA m. Deborah L. **Foote** of Tuftonboro 8/4/1984

Leroy Ellsworth m. Florence Louise **Haley** 2/14/1935 in Wolfeboro; H – 40, truck driver, 2nd, b. Acton, ME, s/o Porter L. Ham (Shapleigh, ME, farmer) and Nancy Pillsbury (Shapleigh, ME, housekeeper); W – 22, at home, b. Tuftonboro, d/o George H.

Haley (Moultonboro, laborer) and Edith C. Ayers (Tuftonboro, housewife)

HANEY,
Keith D. m. Eva M. **O'Grady** 6/18/1977 in Wolfeboro

HANSEN,
Carl I. m. Marsha **Bilodeau** 3/22/1975 in Tuftonboro
Scott T. of Tuftonboro m. A. A. **Gallagher** of Tuftonboro 8/29/1999

HANSON,
Jon S. of Tuftonboro m. Lorraine F. **Emme** of Tuftonboro 7/29/2003
Jon S. B. C. of Tuftonboro m. Laura W. **Dodge** of Tuftonboro
    12/31/1992
Michael D. C. of N. Berwick, ME m. Laurie Ann **Kimball** of N.
    Berwick, ME 8/19/2000

HARDIE,
John W., Jr. of Tuftonboro m. Jane M. **Morris** of Haverhill 9/7/1946
    in Haverhill; H – 31, mechanic, b. NY City, NY, s/o John W.
    Hardie (NY City, NY) and Irene B. Stagg (NY City, NY); W – 25,
    teacher, b. Haverhill, d/o Walter P. Morris (Haverhill, MA) and
    Mary L. Blake (Haverhill, MA)
John W., III m. Glenda E. **Parizo** 10/30/1971 in Gilford

HARDING,
Archibald B. of Tuftonboro m. Edith T. **Bergeron** of Keene
    11/30/1985

HARDY,
Warren R. of Tuftonboro m. Anne B. **Roome** of Tuftonboro
    4/13/1985

HARPER,
Peter John of Nashville, TN m. Leslie Ann **Haase** of Nashville, TN
    6/11/1994

HARRISON,
Kevin Kreutzer of Lexington, MA m. Lynn Anne **McLaughlin** of
    Lexington, MA 10/9/1993

HASKIN,
John F. of Alton m. Ann Marie **Craigue** of Tuftonboro 12/28/1978

HASTINGS,
Brian Charles of Tuftonboro m. Anika Pauline **Brand** of Tuftonboro
8/7/1999

HAUNGS,
Charles F. m. Vicki **Hansen** 6/8/1974 in Tuftonboro

HAYES,
Carl Dewey of Tuftonboro m. Dorothea B. **Parkhurst** of Wolfeboro
11/21/1965 in Wolfeboro; H – 67, club chauff., 2nd, widower, b.
Wolfeboro, s/o Chester A. Hayes (NH) and Carrie Abbott (NH);
W – 63, at home, 2nd, widow, b. Wolfeboro, d/o Sherman
Brummitt (MA) and Harriett F. Brewster (NH)
Douglass F. m. Susanne D. **Buckley** 6/21/1975 in Tuftonboro
Henry F. of Tuftonboro m. Mabel P. **Welch** of Tuftonboro 11/24/1904
in Tuftonboro; H – 24, chauffeur, b. Center Harbor, s/o Joshua
Hayes and Ida J. Hayes; W – 20, housekeeper, b. Tuftonboro,
d/o George Welch and Albertha Welch
William H. m. Suzanne E. **Kish** 2/26/1977 in Tuftonboro

HAZELTINE,
Nathan L. of Moultonboro m. June E. **Bickford** of Tuftonboro
6/1/1968 in Wolfeboro; H – b. NH, s/o Malcolm Hazeltine (NH)
and Myrtle Stacy (NH); W – b. NH, d/o Jackson Bickford (MA)
and Grace Hanscom (MA)

HEATH,
Richard H. m. Nancy J. **Moulton** 10/5/1969 in Tuftonboro; H – b.
6/6/1946 in NH, s/o Everett M. Heath and Madeline S. White; W
– b. 12/26/1947 in NH, d/o Robert C. Moulton and Priscilla
Nettle

HEDDEN,
Robison W. of Rochester m. Debbo M. **Dow** of Tuftonboro
12/19/1992

HEINTZE,
Larry E. of Ft. Lauderdale, FL m. Susan J. **Webber** of Suffolk, VA
9/18/1982

HENNESSY,
Robert B. of Westboro, MA m. Abigail **Adams** of Worcester, MA
4/16/1983

HENSLEY,
Francis W. m. Mary A. **Wright** 9/1/1942 in Tuftonboro; H – 24,
minister, b. Middletown, TN, s/o Willis Hensley (Middletown,
TN, undertakers sup.) and Frances R. Sasser (Middletown, TN,
housewife); W – 31, reg. nurse, b. Montgomery, VT, d/o William
J. Wright (Montgomery, VT, merchant) and Alice L. Orton
(Fairfax, VT, deceased)

HERRICK,
Donald Arthur of ME m. Ginger Mae **Britton** of Tuftonboro 1/9/1955
in Melvin Village; H – 18, laborer, b. ME, s/o Edwin E. Herrick
(ME) and Rita R. Boution (ME); W – 19, at home, b. NH, d/o
Fred J. Britton (NH) and Ruth Simmons (NH)

HERSEY,
Edwin C. of Tuftonboro m. Hattie B. **Springer** of Newport, VT
7/28/1908 in Newport, VT; H – 31, farmer, b. Tuftonboro, s/o
John L. Hersey and Orianna Flanders; W – 23, housewife, b.
Newport, VT, d/o Levi C. Springer and Hatty W. Farrar
Ethan m. Lillian **Burke** 2/7/1934 in Bartlett; H – 21, laborer, b. Burke,
ME, s/o Forrest Hersey (Ctr. Tuftonboro, farmer) and Elizabeth
Hurd (Berwick, ME, housewife); W – 19, at home, b. Bartlett,
d/o Joseph Burke (Bartlett, RR S. man) and Alice Ward
(Bartlett, housewife)
Forrest W. of Tuftonboro m. Mary E. **Hurd** of Berwick, ME
12/25/1907 in Berwick, ME; H – 20, farmer, b. Tuftonboro, s/o
Charles E. Hersey and Ada A. Blaisdell; W – 18, housewife, b.
Berwick, ME, d/o Daniel N. Hurd and Eunice I. Plummer
John Leander of Tuftonboro m. Elizabeth Jane **Adjutant** of
Tuftonboro 2/8/1965 in Rochester; H – 47, farmer, b.
Wolfeboro, s/o Otis A. Hersey (NH) and Margaret E. Bishop
(MA); W – 24, domestic, b. Wolfeboro, d/o Roscoe V. Adjutant
(NH) and Blanche E. Perkins (NH)

Robert Sylvester m. Ruth Harriett **Davis** 11/19/1933 in Tuftonboro; H
– 23, farmer, b. Dover, s/o Forrest W. Hersey (Ctr. Tuftonboro,
farmer) and Mary Elizabeth Hurd (Berwick, ME, housewife); W
– 15, at home, b. Tuftonboro, d/o Harry A. Davis (Gilmanton,
carpenter) and Sadie B. Gilman (Tuftonboro, housewife)

HERTZWIG,
Kevin S. of Tarrytown, NY m. Suzanne L. **Packard** of Tarrytown, NY
6/12/1982

HEYL,
John K., Jr. of Wolfeboro m. Lydia W. **Heyl** of Tuftonboro 9/4/1984

HILL,
Frank Vincent of Winthrop, MA m. Agnes June **Haley** of Tuftonboro
11/23/1947 in Ossipee; H – 39, truck driver, b. Boston, MA, s/o
Frank Hill (Roanoke, VA) and Stella M. Dean (Taunton, MA); W
– 25, at home, b. Wolfeboro, d/o Charles E. Haley (Tuftonboro)
and Dora E. Bragg (Moultonboro)

HILLIARD,
Louis, Jr. of Melvin Village m. Dorothea **Hanson** of Melvin Village
7/28/1940 in Ctr. Harbor; H – 29, machinist, b. Waterville, ME,
s/o Louis E. Hilliard (Boston, MA, finance) and Margaret Brown
(NB, housewife); W – 23, secretary, b. Lancaster, d/o Harry O.
Hanson (MN, mechanic) and Alice A. Bonney (PQ, housewife)

HILTON,
Maynard Webster of Tuftonboro m. Nora Florence **Drew** of Madison
8/9/1930 in Ossipee; H – 24, farmer, b. Ossipee, s/o Newell C.
Hilton (Ossipee) and Elizabeth M. Webster (Tamworth); W –
18, waitress, b. Madison, d/o Herbert E. Drew (Madison) and
Florence Stuart (Eaton)

HLIDEK,
Brian Drake of Boston, MA m. Rebecca Lacy **Stevenson** of Boston,
MA 9/10/1994

HLUSHUK,
Jack m. Leora E. **Adjutant** 4/29/1925 in Tuftonboro; H – 29, laborer,
2nd, b. Moscow, Russia, s/o Steve Hlushuk (Moscow, Russia)

and Katie Deout (Moscow, Russia); W – 22, housewife, b.
Tuftonboro, d/o Willie W. Adjutant (Tuftonboro) and Eliza J.
Piper (Tuftonboro)
Kenneth Wilkie of Tuftonboro m. Claire Virginia **Glidden** of
Wolfeboro 1/4/1953 in Melvin Village; H – 20, lumberman, b.
NH, s/o Jack Hlushuk (Russia) and Leona Adjutant (NH); W –
19, knitting factory, b. NH, d/o Gordon H. Glidden (NH) and
Abbie V. Hall (NH)
Wade A. of Tuftonboro m. Theresa L. **Sargent** of Tuftonboro
9/12/1981

HOCHWALD,
Earle Chas. of Tuftonboro m. Virginia Gertrude **Egger** of Middleboro,
MA 12/8/1939 in Manchester; H – 28, clergyman, 2nd, b.
Philadelphia, PA, s/o Harry Christian Hochwald (Philadelphia,
PA, deceased) and Anna Elizabeth Rosewall (Shennandoah,
PA, deceased); W – 20, at home, b. Middleboro, MA, d/o
William Eggar (Sagamore, MA, housefurnisher and undertaker)
and Blanche Merriam (Somerville, MA, housewife)

HODGDON,
Charles H. of Tuftonboro m. Lizzie E. **Ladd** of Tuftonboro 11/8/1892
in Tuftonboro; H – 21, printer, b. Tuftonboro, s/o Nathaniel D.
Hodsdon (Tuftonboro, mechanic) and Martha Hodsdon
(Tuftonboro, housewife); W – 22, dressmaker, b. Aroostook,
ME, d/o Levi W. Ladd (Tuftonboro, carpenter) and Miranda
Ladd (MA, housewife)
Edwin Joseph m. Viola Gladys **Haley** 6/15/1935 in Sanbornville; H –
23, carpenter, b. Tuftonboro, s/o Franklin H. Hodgdon
(Tuftonboro, farmer) and Nora K. Burke (Ireland, housewife); W
– 21, nurse maid, b. Moultonboro, d/o Willis Irving Haley
(Tuftonboro, laborer) and Bernece Ethel Dow (Moultonboro,
housewife)
Forrest W. m. Velma A. **Merrifield** 7/8/1925 in Wolfeboro Falls; H –
24, farmer, b. Cambridge, MA, s/o Nat. W. Hodgdon
(Tuftonboro) and Anna Nicholson (Cambridge, MA); W – 26, at
home, b. Tuftonboro, d/o Perley Merrifield (Porter, ME) and
Nellie M. Thompson (Tuftonboro)
Forrest W. m. Frances G. **Canning** 6/19/1928 in Moultonville; H –
27, farmer, 2nd, b. Cambridge, MA, s/o Nat. W. Hodgdon
(Tuftonboro) and Annie Nicholson; W – 21, school teacher, b.

Stowe, VT, d/o Hinman G. Canning (Westmore, VT) and Fannie McKay

Franklin H. of Tuftonboro m. May F. **Geto** of Tuftonboro 11/9/1894 in Tuftonboro; H – 26, farmer, b. Tuftonboro, s/o Nathaniel D. Hodgdon (Tuftonboro, farmer) and Martha A. Hodgdon (Tuftonboro, housewife); W – 21, housewife, b. Tuftonboro, d/o Lewis Geto (France, laborer) and Hattie Geto (Wolfeboro, housewife)

Glenn F. of Tuftonboro m. Eunice M. **Dore** of Tuftonboro 8/18/1950 in Ctr. Ossipee; H – 24, truck driver, b. NH, s/o Forrest W. Hodgdon (MA) and Velma A. Merrifield (NH); W – 17, housework, b. NH, d/o Leon E. Dore (NH) and Mildred F. Davis (NH)

Graydon Herbert of Tuftonboro m. Gaye E. **Berry** of Ossipee 6/23/1996

Nathaniel W. of Tuftonboro m. Ann Mary **Matthews** of Tuftonboro 6/26/1943 in Melvin Village; H – 62, general store, 4th, b. Tuftonboro, s/o William O. Hodgdon (deceased) and Ella F. Whitehouse (Tuftonboro, deceased); W – 47, housekeeper, 2nd, b. Somerville, MA, d/o John Jarites (Lithuania, deceased) and Alice Romanus (Lithuania, deceased)

Raeburn W. of Tuftonboro m. Mary Patricia **Williams** of Tuftonboro 6/30/1953 in Concord; H – 23, USAF, b. Wolfeboro, s/o Forrest W. Hodgdon (NH) and Frances Canning (NH); W – 25, secretary, b. NH, d/o Roger L. Williams (MA) and Bernice W. Lawrence (MA)

HODGES,
Burgess G., III m. Jean W. **Hamilton** 11/29/1975 in Tuftonboro
Milton E. m. Pauline M. **Alfers** 5/24/1971 in Wolfeboro

HODSDON,
John Raymond of Tuftonboro m. Judith Nancy **Allen** 2/20/1960 in Somersworth; H – 24, teacher, b. NH, s/o John R. Hodsdon (NH) and Dorcas M. Kinsman (NH); W – 19, student, b. NH, d/o Steven E. Allen (NH) and Loretta F. Bean (MA)

HOFFER,
Frederic S., III m. Katherine E. **Williams** 8/21/1976 in Tuftonboro

HOLDEN,
Jerome C. of Moultonboro m. Lisa J. **Carleton** of Tuftonboro
6/11/1988

HOLLIS,
Bruce William of Acton, MA m. Kelly Ann **Ryan** of Tuftonboro
6/24/1989

HOLMES,
Bruce E. of Tuftonboro m. Linda R. **Noyes** of Tuftonboro 8/24/1985

HOOPER,
Ellsworth W. of Wolfeboro m. Muriel V. **Lucas** of Tuftonboro
7/16/1950 in Tuftonboro; H – 21, farmer, b. NH, s/o Ray R.
Hooper (NH) and Florence E. Adjutant (NH); W – 20, stitcher, b.
MA, d/o Carroll E. Lucas (NH) and Flora E. Charon (MA)
Ernest L. of Wolfeboro m. Frances **Williamson** of Tuftonboro
3/17/1945 in Wolfeboro; H – 20, farmer, b. Wolfeboro, s/o Ray
Hooper (Wakefield) and Florence Adjutant (Wolfeboro); W – 19,
at home, b. Ossipee, d/o Ausbrey N. Drew (Tuftonboro) and
Bernice F. Ham (Ossipee)
Ronald G. m. Barbara T. **Fraser** 10/14/1978 in Tuftonboro

HOOVER,
Scott B. of Tuftonboro m. Cheryl A. **Nelson** of Wolfeboro 8/1/1981

HORLE,
Richard G. of Tuftonboro m. Helen E. **Hixon** of Braintree, MA
11/21/1980

HORMELL,
Robert S. of Tuftonboro m. Jean A. **Perkins** of Tuftonboro 8/23/1986

HORNE,
Everett E. of Tuftonboro m. Rose **Allen** of Freedom 10/1/1898 in
Tuftonboro; H – 54, farmer, b. Tuftonboro, s/o Jeremiah P.
Horne and Annie Canney; W – 54, housekeeper, 3rd, b.
Wakefield, d/o James Perkins and Phebe Nute

HORNER,

George S. of Tuftonboro m. Grace A. **Hodgdon** of Tuftonboro
12/18/1895 in Tuftonboro; H – 33, merchant, b. Tuftonboro, s/o
Daniel Horner and Lizzie A. Horner; W – 33, housework, b.
Tuftonboro, d/o Jacob Hodgdon and Maria Hodgdon

HOWARD,

James John, Jr. of MA m. Kathryn Kingsbury **Davis** of MA 9/21/2002
William A. of Saugus, MA m. Lynda Marie **Aldred** of Saugus, MA
7/6/1991

HOWE,

George F. of Tuftonboro m. Emma **Johnson** of Brockton, MA
7/10/1922 in Lakeport; H – 30, auto mechanic, b. Southboro,
MA, s/o David F. Howe (Southboro, MA) and Sarah D. Davis
(Troy, NY); W – 33, cook, b. Stockholm, Sweden, d/o Sven
Johnson (Stockholm, Sweden) and Lotta K. Swenson
Robert D. of Tuftonboro m. Elsie **Maine** of Tuftonboro 3/26/1917 in
Wolfeboro; H – 21, carpenter, b. Southboro, MA, s/o David F.
Howe and Sarah D. Davis; W – 26, dressmaker, b. Stonington,
CT, d/o William J. Main and Annie Bentley
Robert Davis of Tuftonboro m. Dorothy Ruggles **Hull** of Pawtucket,
RI 6/18/1944 in Melvin Village; H – 47, contractor, 2nd, b.
Southboro, MA, s/o David F. Howe (Southboro, MA, deceased)
and Sarah D. Davis (Troy, NY, deceased); W – 34, teacher, b.
Pawtucket, RI, d/o Manton R. Hull (Providence, RI, retired) and
Laura Anderton (Pawtucket, RI, housewife)

HOWGATE,

Nathan J. of Springvale, ME m. Diane I. **Irester** of N. Reading, MA
5/11/1968 in Tuftonboro; H – b. ME, s/o John Howgate (ME)
and Muriel Grant (ME); W – b. MA, d/o Kenneth Irester (MA)
and Irene Atkinson (MA)

HOYT,

Charles S. of Tuftonboro m. Kate M. **Sawyer** of Tuftonboro
6/11/1894 in Tuftonboro; H – 24, farmer, b. Tuftonboro, s/o
Calvin Hoyt (Meredith, farmer) and Sarah Hoyt (Alton,
housewife); W – 20, housewife, b. Tuftonboro, d/o George W.
Sawyer (Porter, ME, carpenter) and Christie Sawyer
(Brookfield, housewife)

HUBBARD,
Eugene F. of Tuftonboro m. Ada G. **Bennett** of Tuftonboro 11/12/1899 in Laconia; H – 33, lumberman, 3rd, b. Methuen, MA, s/o Joshua O. Hubbard and Cloe E. Farrington; W – 21, milliner, b. Wolfeboro, d/o Charles H. Bennett and Emma F. Piper

HUDSON,
Harmon Paul of Tuftonboro m. Cheryl Ann **Marsh** of Tuftonboro 10/9/1993

HUEDEPOHL,
Frank of Hamm, Germany m. Ann F. **Hitchcock** of Hamm, Germany 8/7/1993

HULL,
Christopher E. of Tuftonboro m. Barbara Ann **Faherty** of Reading, MA 4/5/1986

HUNT,
Alexander C. of Rochester m. Kerry L. **Librandi** of Tuftonboro 10/15/2005

HUNTER,
Bradbury E. of Tuftonboro m. Barbara **Wood** of Tuftonboro 5/3/1947 in Melvin Village; H – 26, farmer, b. Melrose, MA, s/o Ernest M. Hunter (Chelsea, MA) and Margaret Ellis (Melrose, MA); W – 27, at home, b. Boston, MA, d/o William H. Wood (Boston, MA) and Inez Patterson (Boston, MA)
Bradbury E., Jr. m. Marsha J. **Belknap** 4/6/1974 in Tuftonboro
Ernest M. of Tuftonboro m. Margaret **Ellis** of Melrose, MA 10/24/1917 in Melrose, MA; H – 26, farmer, b. Chelsea, MA, s/o Arthur C. Hunter and Cora A. Hodgdon; W – 24, b. Melrose, MA, d/o Fred Ellis and Eleanor G. Furber
Philip N. of Tuftonboro m. Desira Lee **Taylor** of Tuftonboro 8/3/1985
Stephen W. m. Robin **Emerson** 6/18/1977 in Wolfeboro
Thomas W. of Tuftonboro m. Phyllis A. **Bean** of Tuftonboro 5/19/1945 in Melvin Village; H – 22, farmer, b. Ticonderoga, NY, s/o Ernest M. Hunter (Chelsea, MA) and Margaret Ellis (Melrose, MA); W – 22, at home, b. E. Jaffrey, d/o Philip N. Bean (Rindge) and Aldora M. Gelinas (Athol, MA)

HUOT,
Jean-Paul M. of Tuftonboro m. Brandie L. **Porter** of W. Swanzey
    11/14/1998

HUTCHINS,
Alpheus F., Jr. of Ctr. Harbor m. Ann Christine **Baxter** of Tuftonboro
    6/10/1951 in Rochester; H – 21, lineman, b. NH, s/o Alpheus F.
    Hutchins (NH) and Lura B. Wheeler (NH); W – 18, student, b.
    NH, d/o George P. Baxter (RI) and Priscilla C. West (NH)

HUYLER,
Mark T. of Charlotte, VT m. Joanne E. **Hennessy** of Charlotte, VT
    8/7/1982

INGRAM,
James Andrew of Portland, ME m. Wendy Fox **Thomas** of
    Huntingdon Valley, PA 8/26/1989

IRVINE,
Michael Francis of Laguna Niguel, CA m. Lisa Ann **Warner** of
    Laguna Niguel, CA 9/12/1989

IVESTER,
Kenneth R., Jr. m. Susan **Martino** 6/3/1972 in Tuftonboro

JACKSON,
John L., Jr. of Portland, ME m. Barbara R. **Farr**, Jr. of Portland, ME
    6/8/1985
Joshua B. of Wollaston, MA m. Cynthia **Davis** of Wollaston, MA
    9/19/1992
Luther Worley m. Kathleen C. **Davison** 9/11/1936 in Woodsville; H –
    25, clerk, b. Carrollton, GA, s/o John Henry Jackson (GA,
    merchant) and Virginia R. Worley (GA, retired); W – 28,
    teacher, b. Woodsville, d/o Lewis E. Davison (Sutton, PQ,
    station agt.) and Ella Gert. Chadwich (VT, housewife)

JALBERT,
Roland M. m. Marla **Levy** 3/5/1972 in Tuftonboro

JAMIESON,
Robert F. of Tuftonboro m. Linda J. **Todesco** of Wolfeboro
12/31/1982

JANES,
Clarence W., Jr. m. Doris **Zenk** 12/11/1976 in Tuftonboro

JENKINS,
Mark S. of Tuftonboro m. Melissa L. **Rogers** of Tuftonboro 6/6/1987
Mark S. of Tuftonboro m. Paula J. **Fitzmorris** of Concord
11/21/1998

JEROME,
Frank F. m. Naomi F. **Brown** 3/12/1941 in Wolfeboro; H – 65,
caretaker, 2nd, b. Malden, MA, s/o Edward Jerome (Buffalo, NY,
deceased) and Delia Morey (Three Rivers, deceased); W – 41,
prac. nurse, 2nd, b. Center Harbor, d/o John F. Bean (Strong,
ME, deceased) and Mary L. Manville (Rumney, housewife)

JEWELL,
Edmund A. of Wolfeboro m. Mildred I. **Hardie** of Tuftonboro
6/23/1940 in Concord; H – 26, mortician, b. Ashland, s/o
Raymond Jewell (Ashland, mortician) and Belle I. Wilkie
(Barton, VT, housewife); W – 23, nurse, b. NY, d/o John W.
Hardie (NY, farmer) and Irene B. Stagg (NY, housewife)

JEWETT,
Jameson H. of Tuftonboro m. Angela M. **Nunez** of Allston, MA
10/4/1980

JOHNSON,
Andrew A. of Tuftonboro m. Sally F. G. **Muir** of Tuftonboro 1/1/1992
Arthur Westly of Tamworth m. Judith O. **Austin** of Tuftonboro
9/10/1960 in Tamworth; H – 20, mainten., b. NH, s/o Forrest W.
Johnson (NH) and Pauline Bean (NH); W – 20, secretary, b.
NH, d/o Jasper Austin and Nelle MacCreighton
Burton L. of Deep River, CT m. Sharon L. **Matson** of Tuftonboro
10/31/1982
Charles M. m. Susan-Elizabeth **Dow** 11/24/1973 in Tuftonboro
Charles W. of Tuftonboro m. Bertha M. **Doe** of Tuftonboro 2/27/1900
in Wolfeboro; H – 18, farmer, b. Tuftonboro, s/o Charles E.

Johnson and Lizzie Wiggin; W – 19, housekeeper, b.
Tuftonboro, d/o James A. Doe and Jennie B. Fernald
Craig Robert of Tuftonboro m. Jodi Lynn **Morrison** of Portage, MI
10/21/2000
Donald S. m. Gail S. **Enwright** 9/11/1976 in Eaton
Edwin of Tuftonboro m. Grace S. **Hodgdon** of Tuftonboro 1/13/1906
in Tuftonboro; H – 20, farmer, b. Tuftonboro, s/o Charles
Johnson and Lizzie Wiggin; W – 21, housewife, b. Ossipee, d/o
Charles Hodgdon and Emma Swazey
Warren A. of Attleboro, MA m. Regina M. **Swanson** of Attleboro, MA
1/3/1968 in Tuftonboro; H – divorced, b. MA, s/o Carl H.
Johnson (Sweden) and Hattie Bunker (NY); W – widow, b. NY,
d/o Arthur H. Larmay (VT) and Mildred Charron (VT)

JONES,
Jeffrey M. of Tuftonboro m. Rebecca Ann **Branin** of Wolfeboro
9/26/1992
Kenneth Duane of Wolfeboro m. Susan **Hunter** of Tuftonboro
1/30/1966 in Wolfeboro; H – 18, cook, b. Wolfeboro, s/o
Kenneth G. Jones (NH) and Miriam L. Foster (NH); W – 16,
student, b. Wolfeboro, d/o Thomas W. Hunter (NY) and Phyllis
A. Bean (NH)
Ryan B. of Tuftonboro m. Dana E. Perez **Cruz** of Tuftonboro
7/14/2001
William McPheeters m. Helen Louise **Betchley** 9/15/1932 in Melvin
Village; H – 22, accountant, b. Charlotte, NC, s/o Joseph A.
Jones (Petersburg, VA, accountant) and Blandina Springs
(Charlotte, NC, housewife); W – 21, at home, b. New York City,
d/o Harold H. Betchley (New York City, auto dealer) and
Gertrude Gardner (New York City, housewife)
William Richardson of Lexington, MA m. Jean Ellaine **Teger** of
Wayland, MA 12/25/1965 in Tuftonboro; H – 41, executive, b.
Nashville, TN, s/o Henry Eugene Jones (GA) and Martha
Stokes Buford (TN); W – 35, at home, 2nd, widow, b.
Weymouth, MA, d/o Fred. Nelson Oliver (ME) and Thelma
Esther Niles (ME)

JORDAN,
Mark W. of Tuftonboro m. Diane E. **Erwin** of Tuftonboro 12/31/1988

KAPLAN,
Matthew Edmond of Cranston, RI m. Katherine Elizabeth **Carlsten** of Cranston, RI 5/24/1997

KATWICK,
James Peter of Tuftonboro m. Shelley Lee **White** of Tuftonboro 8/15/1998

KEENAN,
Henry E. of Wolfeboro m. Amy M. **Merrifield** of Tuftonboro 6/3/1917 in Wolfeboro; H – 25, blacksmith, b. Conway, s/o Henry F. Keenan and Elizabeth Jacobs; W – 20, housewife, b. Tuftonboro, d/o Perly Merrifield and Nellie M. Thompson

KEITH,
Rowland D. H. of Gilford m. Judith A. **Packard** of Tuftonboro 2/11/1967 in Gilford; H – 38, auto dealer, divorced, b. New Haven, CT, s/o Elmer D. Keith (CT) and Susan Bacon (NY); W – 27, housewife, divorced, b. Beverly, MA, d/o Harry Austin (MA) and Shirley M. Burnham (MA)

KELLOWAY,
Wayne J. m. Natalie M. **Walton** 9/11/1976 in Tuftonboro

KENDAL,
Herbert G. m. Patricia A. **Hutchins** 7/20/1969 in Wolfeboro; H – b. 6/8/1950 in NH, s/o Herbert B. Kendal and Charlotte Gouin; W – b. 9/6/1950 in NH, d/o Walter A. Hutchins and Frances Burleigh
Herbert G. m. Linda M. **Dore** 3/20/1976 in Tuftonboro

KENDALL,
Luke Jonathan of Meredith m. Joleen May **Mitchell** of Tuftonboro 10/8/2002

KENISTON,
Ephraim m. Edna L. **Drew** 11/25/1928 in Lebanon, ME; H – 21, chauffeur, b. Barrington, s/o S. G. Keniston (Effingham) and Martha LaCrillis (Rochester); W – 19, at home, b. Wolfeboro, d/o Ernest Drew (New Durham) and Lena Towle (Madison)

KENNEALLY,
Thomas G. of Revere, MA m. Darilyn D. **Murray** of Biemont, MA
9/1/1984

KENNELL,
James S. of Washington, DC m. Heidi Margrit **Thomas** of
Washington, DC 8/27/1994

KENNEY,
Elijah B. of Tuftonboro m. Anna P. **Adjutant** of Wolfeboro 2/18/1905
in Wolfeboro; H – 50, farmer, 2nd, b. Wolfeboro, s/o Hiram
Kenney and Clara Dore; W – 24, housewife, b. Wolfeboro, d/o
Mart. Adjutant and Ella Rollins

KENNY,
Thomas P. of Tuftonboro m. Nancy L. **Gordon** of Tuftonboro
5/30/1987

KENT,
Roger m. Marlene M. **Thibault** 9/22/1977 in Madison

KEYES,
William C. of Tuftonboro m. Rebecca **Knapp** of Ossipee 3/24/1979

KILKELLY,
Philip J. of Tuftonboro m. Michelle L. **Gillum** of Tuftonboro
6/30/2001

KILLIAN,
Jonathan D. of Narragansett, RI m. Catherine A. **Bateman** of
Narragansett, RI 7/7/1990

KING,
Peter L. of Acton, MA m. Jean M. **Bilafer** of Tuftonboro 9/19/1998

KIRBY,
Stephen H. of N. Dartmouth, MA m. Dorothea A. **Allen** of N.
Dartmouth, MA 6/21/1980
William John, Jr. of Portland, OR m. Anne Winslow **Crane** of
Portland, OR 8/29/1998

KLIPPEL,
Warren H. of North East, NY m. Louise F. **Copp** of Tuftonboro
8/31/1946 in Melvin Village; H – 21, engineer, b. Lynbrook, NY,
s/o Herbert Klippel (NY City, NY) and Emily Thies (NY City,
NY); W – 20, at home, b. Cleveland, OH, d/o Charles K. Copp
(Akron, OH) and Lucille B. Corrigan (Cleveland, OH)

KNAPP,
Richard Charles, Jr. of Westford, MA m. Pamela Ann **Purtell** of
Westford, MA 2/25/1989

KNEELAND,
Frederick J. of Tuftonboro m. Marguerite E. **Ferguson** of Tuftonboro
1/10/1917 in Wolfeboro; H – 24, farmer, b. Cambridgeport, MA,
s/o Daniel J. Kneeland and Harriet Sleeper; W – 22, b. Orient
Heights, MA, d/o John T. Ferguson and Olive Bailey

KNIGHT,
Frank C. of MA m. Joanne **DeWitt** of Tuftonboro 2/23/1957 in Melvin
Village; H – 28, salesman, b. MA, s/o George A. Knight (MA)
and Lillian R. Chapman (MA); W – 25, adv., b. MA, d/o Walter
A. DeWitt (MA) and Lillian R. Chapman (MA)

KNIGHTS,
John Franklin m. Eleanor May **Davis** 6/24/1933 in Moultonville; H –
22, mechanic, b. Limerick, ME, s/o Frank F. Knights (Limerick,
ME, laborer) and Edith A. Kimball (S. Wolfeboro, housewife); W
– 19, at home, b. Tuftonboro, d/o Harry A. Davis (Gilmanton,
carpenter) and Sadie B. Gilman (Tuftonboro, housewife)

KNISLEY,
Reuben K. of Sanbornville m. Peggy E. **Eldridge** of Tuftonboro
1/13/1984

KOHL,
Waldemar Roy of Middleboro, MA m. Ann Ruth **Runey** of Tuftonboro
6/25/1997

KOLENDA,
Stephen J. m. Janet M. **Blanchette** 10/14/1978 in Wolfeboro

KRUEGER,
William E. of Plattsburgh, NY m. Suzy L. **Johnson** of Plattsburgh, NY 2/12/1983

KULPA,
John J. of Hartford, CT m. Louise M. **Kaeser** of Hartford, CT 7/8/1950 in Tuftonboro; H – 35, ind. photog., b. CT, s/o Joseph J. Kulpa (Poland) and Lucy E. Liss (Poland); W – 25, secretary, b. CT, d/o Albert G. Kaeser (CT) and Margaret Smith (CT)

KUNKEL,
Gerald D. of Tuftonboro m. Marjorie R. **Conlon** of Tuftonboro 10/3/2001

KUNST,
Larry T. of Natick, MA m. Karen Lynn **Horvath** of Natick, MA 6/11/1988

KURTH,
John Edward m. Marguerite Bertha **Rouleau** 3/2/1935 in Providence, RI; H – 44, musician, b. Somerville, MA, s/o Richard Kurth (Germany) and Jane T. McKenna (Chelsea, MA); W – 38, secretary, b. Boston, MA, d/o Albert J. Rouleau (Canada) and Margaret Kiernan (Boston, MA)

KUZEL,
Norman E., II of Taftville, CT m. Alisa Diane **Carlson** of Norwich, CT 7/23/1989

LABRANCHE,
Ronald E. of Wakefield m. Judith N. **Williams** of Tuftonboro 9/23/1983

LACOMBE,
Henry Euclide of Concord, MA m. Elizabeth Ann **Divinell** of S. Acton, MA 5/13/1961 in Tuftonboro; H – 25, press operator for IBM, b. Arlington, MA, s/o Euclide J. LaCombe (Canada) and Elra M. LeGault (Canada); W – 22, nurse, b. Maynard, MA, d/o Philip E. Divinell (LA) and Mary E. O'Brien (MA)

LADD,
David C. of Tuftonboro m. Irene H. **Goulet** of Tuftonboro 11/2/1985
Harvey F. of Tuftonboro m. Patricia W. **Ladd** of Tuftonboro
10/17/1949 in Conway; H – 31, engineer, b. ME, s/o Byron A.
Ladd (MA) and Ruth Sargent (MA); W – 30, housewife, b. NY,
d/o Charles A. Wood (MA) and Emma Seward (China)
Ian Charles of Tuftonboro m. Jamie Leigh **Glidden** of Tuftonboro
9/28/1996
John A. of Tuftonboro m. Annie P. **Thurley** of Tuftonboro 9/3/1899 in
Tuftonboro; H – 67, farmer, 2nd, b. Tuftonboro, s/o Samuel Ladd
and Nancy Young; W – 46, housekeeper, 2nd, b. Ossipee, d/o
Erastus Hanson and Nancy Nute

LAFLEUR,
Vincent Albert of Boston, MA m. Anne Thresher **Ehlert** of Boston,
MA 4/29/1995

LAGRAM,
Robert M. of Melvin Village m. Valerie A. **Konkonen** of Melvin
Village 4/22/2003

LAIRMORE,
Mitchell R. of Rochester, NY m. Anne **Friedrichs** of Rochester, NY
9/13/1986

LAMB,
William Herbert m. Sarah Cecelia **Lord** 3/21/1936 in Melvin Village;
H – 25, radio engineer, b. Middletown, CT, s/o Herbert Allen
Lamb (Middletown, CT, mason) and Hattie Mann (Germany,
housewife); W – 25, registered nurse, b. Tuftonboro, d/o Milton
Lord (Conway, retired) and Elizabeth B. Morrison (Tuftonboro,
housewife)

LAMPREY,
Carroll A. of Tuftonboro m. Kathie M. **Stacey** of Kezar Falls, ME
1/28/1922 in Wolfeboro; H – 22, farmer, b. Tuftonboro, s/o
Robert Lamprey (Moultonboro) and Mary F. McKenna (Boston,
MA); W – 24, school teacher, b. Kezar Falls, ME, d/o Charles
O. Stacey (Kezar Falls, ME) and C. Maud Watson
Carroll A. of Tuftonboro m. Phylis Stacey **Weller** of Boston, MA
10/9/1961 in Wolfeboro; H – 62, retired, 2nd, widower, b.

Tuftonboro, s/o Robert Lamprey (Moultonboro) and Mary F.
McKenna (Chelsea, MA); W – 45, reg. nurse, 2nd, divorced, b.
Kezar Falls, ME, d/o Karl C. Stacey (Kezar Falls, ME) and
Mildred H. Philbrick (Kezar Falls, ME)
Wilbur of Tuftonboro m. Bertha E. **Kenney** of Tuftonboro 4/18/1897
in Tuftonboro; H – 25, farmer, b. Moultonboro, s/o George R.
Lamprey and Emma G. Lamprey; W – 21, housekeeper, b.
Dover, d/o Elijah F. Kenney and Clara B. Kenney
Wilbur of Tuftonboro m. Fannie E. **Thompson** of Tuftonboro
10/15/1902 in Wolfeboro; H – 30, boatman, 2nd, divorced, b.
Moultonboro, s/o George R. Lamprey and Emma Gowen; W –
25, housekeeper, b. Tuftonboro, d/o Theodore Thompson and
Rosa Tibbetts
Wilbur H. m. Frances **Palmer** 8/10/1925 in Tuftonboro; H – 53,
farmer, 2nd, b. Moultonboro, s/o George R. Lamprey
(Moultonboro) and Emma Going (Moultonboro); W – 25,
housewife, 2nd, b. Sandwich, d/o Hiram Harriman (Meredith)
and Lottie Carr (Sandwich)

LAPAR,
Daniel M. of Tuftonboro m. Kimi Lynn **Hauser** of Tuftonboro
11/9/1991
William H. R. of Tuftonboro m. Sonya R. **Maddock** of Ossipee
2/20/1988

LAPOLLA,
John C. of Tuftonboro m. Jennifer A. **Glidden** of Tuftonboro
10/13/2001

LASSELL,
Francis M. of Tuftonboro m. Blanche V. **Lord** of Wolfeboro
10/20/1946 in Wolfeboro; H – 59, truck driver, b. Greenwood,
MA, s/o Bernard Lassell (Thomaston, MA) and Harriet C.
Hughes (Lynnfield, MA); W – 39, housewife, b. Alton, d/o
George D. Elliot (Rumney) and Ethel A. Welch (Tuftonboro)
Francis M., Jr. of Portsmouth m. Julie Ann **Henderson** of Tuftonboro
8/22/1964 in Tuftonboro; H – 42, electrical insp., 2nd, divorced,
b. Lee, s/o Francis N. Lassell (MA) and Mary Helen Bessem
(MA); W – 28, housewife, 2nd, divorced, b. Natick, MA, d/o
Frank Slade (Denmark) and Helmi M. Malmberg (NH)

LAWSON,
Duward A. m. Joanne E. **Redding** 7/3/1976 in Tuftonboro

LAWTON,
Lewis C., Jr. of Tuftonboro m. Cynthia M. **Jennings** of Tuftonboro
8/15/1987

LEADER,
Charles Robert of Waterbury, CT m. Mildred C. **Hunt** of Hartford, CT
6/1/1930 in Ctr. Harbor; H – 24, dir. physical education, b.
Marlboro, MA, s/o Harry Leader (Plymouth, England) and
Agnes Saunders (Glasgow, Scotland); W – 23, stenographer, b.
Watertown, MA, d/o William A. Hunt (Abington, MA) and Lydia
T. Schwartz (Trollhatten, Sweden)

LEARY,
Richard Michael of Tuftonboro m. Susan Marie **Markell** of
Tuftonboro 10/14/1995

LEAVITT,
Harold John of Tuftonboro m. Louise Bianca **Gilman** of Tuftonboro
6/29/1963 in Melvin Village; H – 49, electrician, 2nd, divorced, b.
Lynn, MA, s/o Fred H. Leavitt (MA) and Elsie C. Wahlen (MA);
W – 47, nurse, 2nd, divorced, b. Tuftonboro, d/o Chester H.
Gilman (NH) and Edith B. Fernald (MA)
Scott M. of Ossipee m. Cynthia M. **Cochrane** of Tuftonboro
2/14/1983
Seth Francis of Tuftonboro m. Ivy Anne **Carlson** of Tuftonboro
9/28/2002

LEBLANC,
Douglas P. of Tuftonboro m. Linda G. **Steadman** of Tuftonboro
5/23/1981

LEE,
Harry S. of Dorchester, MA m. Lillian V. **Bannon** of Brighton, MA
9/5/1918 in Tuftonboro; H – 44, merchant, 2nd, b. Springfield,
MA, s/o Horace C. Lee and Fannie Shephard; W – 27, at home,
b. Brighton, MA, d/o John J. Bannon and Margaret Bradley
William Joseph of Tuftonboro m. Sharon L. **Hoitt** of Tuftonboro
8/21/1993

LEHNER,

Eugene Frederick m. Rena Christine **Brown** 3/15/1931 in Wolfeboro Falls; H – 27, clerk, b. Boston, MA, s/o Eugene W. Lehner (Germany) and Wilhelmina Dorr (Boston, MA); W – 23, clerk, b. Farmington, d/o Albert Brown (Waltham, MA) and Nellie E. Mitchell (New Durham)

LESLIE,

Raymond C. of Tuftonboro m. Carol A. **Fortin** of New Bedford, MA 7/5/1980

LESNIK,

Roger H. of Framingham, MA m. Cheryl A. **Saulnier** of Wilmington, MA 7/14/1984

LESSARD,

Bill of Tuftonboro m. Regina **Berg** of Tuftonboro 10/13/2001
William D. m. Linda L. **Wakefield** 4/5/1975 in Tuftonboro

LESTER,

Richard H. of Tuftonboro m. Marjorie **Wood** of Tuftonboro 4/7/1945 in Melvin Village; H – 24, Coast Guard, b. Ware, s/o Thomas J. Lester (Co. Arma., N. Ireland) and Leora H. Bacon (Hardwick, MA); W – 23, secretary, b. Boston, MA, d/o William Harry Wood (Boston, MA) and Ethel I. Patterson (Boston, MA)
Richard H. m. Alice E. **Kerr** 11/22/1969 in Brookfield; H – b. 3/11/1920 in MA, s/o Thomas J. Lester and Leora M. Bacon; W – b. 5/11/1924 in NC, d/o Ellsworth C. Eddy and Alice M. Crosby
Richard H. of Tuftonboro m. Lora E. **Hersey** of Portsmouth 10/13/1979

LEVESQUE,

John A. of Tuftonboro m. Susan E. **Davis** of Tuftonboro 12/31/1988

LEVITCH,

Alexander of Portland, ME m. Emily J. **Edgerly** of Tuftonboro 12/21/1946 in Melvin Village; H – 75, cabinet maker, b. Poland, s/o Vincent Levitch (Poland) and Victoria Skowish (Poland); W – 50, at home, b. NY City, NY, d/o Charles C. Asselin (NY City, NY) and Sarah L. Humphrey (NY City, NY)

LEWIS,
Harold Drury of Tuftonboro m. Claudia Ann **Pinard** of Concord
   4/16/1966 in Wolfeboro; H – 22, route man, b. Stoneham, MA,
   s/o Daniel B. Lewis (MA) and Dorothy Drury (NH); W – 20,
   hairdresser, b. Claremont, d/o Robert D. Pinard (NH) and Iola
   Tarrien (NH)
John E. of Tuftonboro m. Elinore L. **Greenwood** of Tuftonboro
   9/5/2003
Mark J. of New York City, NY m. Nancy J. **Colburn** of Cambridge,
   MA 8/13/1983
Rainsford W. of Tuftonboro m. Lenora A. **Wendell** of Tuftonboro
   4/25/1906 in Tuftonboro; H – 27, farmer, b. NB, s/o Lemuel
   Lewis and Lois Lyman; W – 26, housewife, b. Tuftonboro, d/o
   Isaiah Wendall and Alma Holmes

LIBBEY,
Frank of Tuftonboro m. Lucy A. **Emery** of Tuftonboro 5/21/1891 in
   Ossipee; H – 41, farmer, 2nd, divorced, b. Ossipee, s/o James
   C. Libbey (Ossipee, farming) and Susan Libbey (Tuftonboro);
   W – 38, housekeeper, 2nd, widow, b. Tuftonboro, d/o Samuel R.
   Haley (Lee, farming) and Nancy Haley (Tuftonboro)

LIBBY,
Alan B. of Tuftonboro m. Joyce M. **Lindquist** of Tuftonboro 3/8/1986
Alan D. of Tuftonboro m. Sherry L. **Hyslop** of Tuftonboro 8/21/1999
Jeffrey A. of Effingham m. Shannon M. **Scudder** of Tuftonboro
   5/21/2005
Joseph C. of Tuftonboro m. Cyrene E. **Gaudlap** of Tuftonboro
   2/14/1987
Robert C. of Tuftonboro m. Sharon L. **Libby** of Tuftonboro 4/21/1984
Robert Carleton, Jr. of Ctr. Tuftonboro m. Carol Jean **Smith** of
   Tuftonboro Corner 12/21/1958 in Wolfeboro; H – 19, laborer, b.
   NH, s/o Robert C. Libby (NH) and Hazel McKenney (MA); W –
   17, at home, b. NH, d/o Walter R. Smith (NH) and Doris H.
   Mack (NH)
Robert M. of Tuftonboro m. Helen S. **Eldridge** of Ossipee
   12/28/1913 in Tuftonboro; H – 18, farmer, b. Tuftonboro, s/o
   Frank Libby and Lucy Haley; W – 18, housewife, b. Ossipee,
   d/o Oridon J. Eldridge and Lucy C. Welch
Scott B. m. Vanessa **Vittum** 8/6/1971 in Tuftonboro

LITWHILER,
Karl R. of Edgewater, NJ m. Joanne F. **D'Auria** of Edgewater, NJ
8/19/1993

LOCHHEAD,
Thomas John m. Kathleen Stuart **Wright** 11/14/1970 in Wolfeboro;
H – b. 6/17/1948 in NH, s/o William C. Lochhead and Leona
Comire; W – b. 7/2/1948 in NH, d/o Donald C. Wright and
Kathleen S. McKinney

LOCKITT,
James Douglas of Sherborn, MA m. Alison Bartlett **Beckett** of
Dover, MA 6/29/1996

LOHMAN,
Andrew Davies of Peekskill, NY m. Pamela Jean **Southard** of
Tuftonboro 5/16/1992

LORD,
Charles S. of Tuftonboro m. Gertrude **Hoyt** of Moultonboro
11/15/1903 in Moultonboro; H – 22, farmer, b. Tuftonboro, s/o
Andrew A. Lord and Ada Lord; W – 26, housekeeper, b.
Moultonboro, d/o H. C. Hoyt and Harriet Hoyt
Milton A. of Tuftonboro m. Lizzie B. **Morrison** of Tuftonboro
12/7/1904 in Tuftonboro; H – 27, machinist, b. Conway, s/o
Andrew A. Lord and Ida Richardson; W – 31, school teacher, b.
Tuftonboro, d/o John D. Morrison and Sarah Morrison

LOVEREN,
John F. m. Elizabeth **Hopkinson** 12/5/1937 in Melvin Village; H –
27, farmer, 2nd, b. Deering, s/o John Frank Loveren (Deering,
farmer) and Mabel R. Davis (Lynn, MA, housewife); W – 18, at
home, b. Saco, ME, d/o Thomas Hopkinson (England, laborer)
and Sarah Jose (Saco, ME, housewife)

LOVERING,
Jefferson S. of Tuftonboro m. Karin L. **Swain** of Tuftonboro
6/28/2003

LOWRY,
Walter J. of Canton, MA m. Doris A. **Brookes** of Tuftonboro
2/5/1950 in Wolfeboro; H – 30, caretaker, b. MA, s/o Albert E.
Lowry (MA) and Ruth C. Hastedt (MA); W – 31, tel. op., b. MA,
d/o Norman K. Brookes (England) and Madeline H. Luce (MA)

LUCAS,
Carroll L. of Tuftonboro m. Lotte J. **Kelly** of Waltham, MA
10/11/1949 in Tuftonboro; H – 24, student, b. MA, s/o Carroll F.
Lucas (Wolfeboro) and Flora E. Charron (MA); W – 18, at
home, b. MA, d/o Louis M. Kelly (NH) and Lotte L. Mack
(Germany)

LUNDQUIST,
Barry E. of Needham, MA m. Nancy J. **Graham** of Needham, MA
9/25/1982
Courtney J. m. Brenda J. **Stacey** 1/17/1978 in Tuftonboro

LUPO,
Franklin Roosevelt of FL m. Patricia Ann **Skinner** of Tuftonboro
4/7/1956 in Mirror Lake; H – 21, US Army, b. FL, s/o George F.
Lupo (FL) and Ordelia Laremore (FL); W – 21, secretary, b. NH,
d/o Herbert I. Skinner (MA) and Marion P. Eldridge (NH)

LYNCH,
Andrew P. of NY m. Viola M. **Long** of NY 4/10/1949 in Tuftonboro; H
– 35, bank clerk, b. NY, s/o Andrew P. Lynch (Scotland) and
Emily Thompson (NY); W – 22, secretary, b. NY, d/o Ernest W.
Long (ME) and Annie Huttenlocker (NY)

MABBETT,
George of Hyannis, MA m. Helen J. **McNamara** of Hyannis, MA
1/22/1967 in Tuftonboro; H – 52, salesman, divorced, b.
Plymouth, MA, d/o George E. Mabbett (MA) and May D. Hill
(MA); W – 46, motel owner, widow, b. Somerville, MA, d/o
Alexander Hendrickson (NS) and Mildred Davis (RI)

MACDONALD,
Ernest Ellsworth, Jr. of Ctr. Sandwich m. Joyce Annette **Haley** of
Tuftonboro 5/16/1954 in Melvin Village; H – 20, laborer, b. NH,
s/o Ernest E. MacDonald (NH) and Ethel B. Diack (NH); W –

19, at home, b. NH, d/o Delbert C. Haley (NH) and Muriel C. Roberge (NH)

MACK,
Maurice Jewell m. Christie Mae **Elliott** 9/30/1933 in Wolfeboro; H – 22, laborer, b. Laconia, s/o George Freeman Mack (Sandwich, laborer) and Dora L. Bragg (Moultonboro, housewife); W – 22, at home, b. Alton, d/o Henry Almond Elliott (Rumney, laborer) and Lizzie Belle Elliott (Rumney, housewife)

MACMILLAN,
Duncan J., Jr. of Los Altos, CA m. Pamela J. **Chung** of Los Altos, CA 6/22/1985

MACROSTIE,
William G. of Washington, DC m. Carol O. **Blitzer** of Washington, DC 7/26/1986

MACLEAN,
Forrest E. m. Helen M. **Hodges** 6/29/1941 in Tuftonboro; H – 28, salesman, b. Waltham, MA, s/o Charles J. MacLean (NS, sales mgr.) and Harriet I. Phillips (Portage, PEI, housewife); W – 30, teacher, b. Somerville, MA, d/o Burgess G. Hodges (Yonkers, NY, deceased) and Julia A. Marden (Somerville, MA, housewife)

MADDEN,
Leonard D. of Tuftonboro m. Eva J. **O'Grady** of Tuftonboro 7/14/1981

MAHONEY,
Donald E. of Manchester m. Geraldine **Paige** of Tuftonboro 8/1/1950 in Manchester; H – 21, student, b. NH, s/o James F. Mahoney (NH) and Kathryn V. McDonald (NH); W – 20, at home, b. NH, d/o Robert K. Paige (VT) and Eva M. Howe (NH)

MALETTE,
Brian T. of Tuftonboro m. Nancy M. **Swan** of Tuftonboro 9/11/1982

MANLEY,
LeRoy A. m. Dorothy E. **Huckins** 7/1/1936 in Standish, ME; H – 29, laborer, b. Wakefield, MA, s/o Elmer E. Manley (Chelsea, MA, PWA director) and Edith M. Stonehouse (NS, deceased); W – 29, school teacher, b. Freedom, d/o Edwin L. Huckins (Freedom, deceased) and Mary E. Harmon (Freedom, housewife)

MANN,
Charles E. of Rowley, MA m. Sally Anne **Bezanson** of Rowley, MA 5/27/1989

MARCH,
Donald M. m. Eva H. **Paige** 9/15/1974 in Meredith

MARDEN,
Philip S. m. Mary Elizabeth **Hodgins** 7/4/1931 in Ashland; H – 64, carpenter, b. Wolfeboro, s/o Jonas P. Marden (Wolfeboro) and Lucinda Warren (Brookfield); W – 50, housewife, 2nd, b. Boston, MA, d/o Henry Floyd (Ossipee) and Mary E. Tracy (Bangor, ME)

MARTIN,
Ronald L. of Joliet, IL m. Eliza G. **Stowe** of Tuftonboro 12/20/1987
Steven Wayne of Moultonboro m. Brenda Susan **Cheney** of Tuftonboro 10/2/1965 in Tuftonboro; H – 21, carpenter, b. Jackson, MS. s/o Harold Edward Martin (NH) and Eileen Prey (NH); W – 20, clerical, b. Wolfeboro, d/o John Gordon Cheney (NY) and Edna Susan Young (MA)

MARVIN,
Ernest William of Tuftonboro m. Kristine F. **Kenison** of Tuftonboro 10/27/1989

MASSI,
Ildo F. of Somerville, MA m. Nancy M. **Shaffer** of Somerville, MA 7/1/1982

MASTERTON,
Kenneth R. of Bolinas, CA m. Sarah E. **Wright** of Bolinas, CA 8/16/1986

MATHER,
Bruce D. of Durham m. Priscilla **Allen** of Tuftonboro 5/19/1950 in
Rochester; H – 25, student, b. MA, s/o John A. A. Mather
(Scotland) and Helen L. Laird (MA); W – 19, student, b. NJ, d/o
Leroy V. Allen (NJ) and Edith M. White (NJ)

MATTHEWS,
C. Dixon m. Patricia C. **Fairbank** 10/6/1973 in Tuftonboro

MAULDEN,
Robert G. of Chelsea, MA m. Robin L. **Berry** of Chelsea, MA
8/4/1990

MAY,
Daniel Otto of Vernon, CT m. Elizabeth Jane **Beatter** of Rockville,
CT 4/7/1958 in Tuftonboro; H – 22, engigeer, b. CT, s/o Otis F.
May (CT) and Katherine M. Bobala (Poland); W – 23, teacher,
b. CT, d/o Walter H. Beatter (CT) and Elizabeth W. James (CT)

MAZZOCCA,
Augustus Daniel of W. Hartford, CT m. Jennifer Lee **Easdon** of W.
Hartford, CT 6/21/1997

McCALLISTER,
Kenneth V. of Del Norte, CO m. Sharon Lynn **Cantwell** of
Tuftonboro 2/27/1988

McCLEAN,
Richard E. of Woburn, MA m. Ellen Marie **Haley** of Woburn, MA
5/27/2000

McDONALD,
Christopher N. of Moultonboro m. Lorraine M. **Beauchene** of
Tuftonboro 1/20/1990

McDOUGAL,
C. B. m. Winnifred **Turner** 8/23/1941 in Tuftonboro; H – 34, lawyer,
b. Chicago, IL, s/o Robert McDougal (Peoria, IL, ret. broker)
and Mary P. Bouton (Chicago, IL, housewife); W – 29, teacher,
b. Quincy, MA, d/o A. Lincoln Turner (Quebec, ME, deceased)
and Cora A. Harthorne (Thomaston, ME, deceased)

McDUFFEE,
Gerald m. Martha **Boyden** 12/28/1928 in Londonderry; H – 18,
  farmer, b. Tuftonboro, s/o Irving McDuffee (Tuftonboro) and
  Minnie Templeton (Ossipee); W – 22, school teacher, b.
  Foxboro, MA, d/o Elmer N. Boyden (Sharon, MA) and Esther
  Butler (NS)

McGORTY,
Peter F., Jr. m. Marjorie M. **Sullivan** 5/18/1974 in Moultonboro

McGOVERN,
Michael Patrick of Ridgewood, NJ m. Deborah Ann **Albert** of
  Ridgewood, NJ 10/19/1996

McINTIRE,
Delma L. m. Eunice E. **Frye** 12/25/1926 in Tuftonboro; H – 21,
  carpenter, b. Tuftonboro, s/o Lewis McIntyre (Tuftonboro) and
  Sadie B. Doe (Tuftonboro); W – 20, at home, b. Plymouth, d/o
  John Frye (Sandwich) and Alice Leach (Moultonboro)
Delma L., Jr. of Tuftonboro m. Elsie L. **Smith** of Tuftonboro
  6/16/1957 in Ctr. Ossipee; H – 21, laborer, b. NH, s/o Delma L.
  McIntire (NH) and Eunice E. Frye (NH); W – 17, at home, b.
  NH, d/o Arthur B. Smith (NH) and Orra E. Moulton (NH)
James Arthur of Tuftonboro m. Debora Jane **Tallman** of Tuftonboro
  6/17/1989
Louis of Tuftonboro m. Sadie B. **Doe** of Tuftonboro 9/1/1904 in
  Tuftonboro; H – 36, carpenter, 2nd, b. Tuftonboro, s/o C. A.
  McIntire and Emily M. McIntire; W – 18, housekeeper, b.
  Tuftonboro, d/o James A. Doe and Jennie B. Doe

McKINLEY,
Mark C. of Wolfeboro m. Jerildine R. **Chellman** of Tuftonboro
  3/8/1998

McLELLAN,
Jacob M. of Tuftonboro m. Heather R. **Pitt** of Miami, FL 10/11/2003

McLEMAN,
Scott D. of Tuftonboro m. Virginia M. **Sleeper** of Tuftonboro
  12/9/1989

McNEIL,
John P. of Tuftonboro m. Mabel A. **Bennett** of Tuftonboro 11/7/1897
in Moultonboro; H – 23, farmer, b. Margree Harbor, NS, s/o
John N. McNeil and Isabell Thompson; W – 18, housemaid, b.
Tuftonboro, d/o James A. Bennett and Frances E. Fernald

McPHAIL,
Jeffrey Alan of Tuftonboro m. Bonnie Jean **Craigue** of Tuftonboro
10/6/1979

McWHIRTER,
Donald J. of Tuftonboro m. Leslie Ann **Johnson** of Tuftonboro
6/25/1983

MEADER,
Charles of Tuftonboro m. Mary E. **Wendell** of Tuftonboro 11/27/1893
in Gilmanton; H – 41, carpenter, 2nd, b. S. Berwick, ME, s/o
Daniel Meader (Tamworth, stone mason) and Jane Meader (S.
Berwick, ME, housewife); W – 45, housewife, 2nd, d/o Joseph P.
Lougee (Gilmanton, farmer) and Mary H. Lougee (Loudon,
housewife)

MEEHAN,
Mark L. of New Durham m. Martha Jean **Croteau** of Tuftonboro
5/1/1982
Robert Michael of Tuftonboro m. Calista Anne **McGlaflin** of
Wolfeboro 8/3/1996

MENDENHALL,
John Dean m. Mary Kathryn **Schou** 6/20/1976 in Alton

MENLOVE,
Mark Leo of Park City, UT m. Diane N. **McLeod** of Park City, UT
8/24/1991

MERRIFIELD,
Perley of Tuftonboro m. Nellie M. **Thompson** of Tuftonboro 1/2/1895
in Tuftonboro; H – 16, farmer, b. Porter, ME, s/o C. H. Merrifield
and Martha Merrifield; W – 18, housework, b. Tuftonboro, d/o
Washington Thompson and Mary E. Thompson

MERROW,
Dana Howard of Ctr. Ossipee m. Norma Ann **Cheney** of Tuftonboro 9/17/1960 in Melvin Village; H – 27, driller, b. NH, s/o Howard W. Merrow (NH) and Gertrude Bickford (ME); W – 20, secretary, b. NH, d/o Earl L. Cheney (NH) and Isabel Moore (ME)

MESERVE,
Norman A. of Wolfeboro m. Theresa **Berg** of Tuftonboro 6/6/1988

MILES,
Robert K., Jr. m. Natalie T. **Miles** 6/6/1978 in Durham

MILLS,
Darold W. of Farmington m. Tanya L. **Adjutant** of Tuftonboro 5/19/2001

MINOT,
Arthur F. of E. Braintree, MA m. Patricia L. **Emery** of Tuftonboro 1/7/1967 in Wolfeboro; H – 47, mechanic, widower, b. Charlestown, MA, s/o John Minot (MA) and Mary (MA); W – 37, at home, b. Toledo, OH, d/o George H. Emery (NH) and Nellie F. Brown (NH)

MITCHELL,
Bernard W. m. Judith A. **Johnson** 9/3/1971 in Wolfeboro
Kenneth L. m. Joy S. **Whempner** 12/26/1971 in Tuftonboro
Kevin Maurice of Tuftonboro m. Shannon Lee **Sullivan** of Tuftonboro 7/7/1997
Rodney K. m. Deborah S. **Balance** 7/4/1975 in Moultonboro
Terry M. of Tuftonboro m. Debbie **Davis** of Tuftonboro 4/9/2001
Thomas O., Jr. of Tuftonboro m. Susie C. **Williams** of Moultonboro 6/17/1967 in N. Sanbornton; H – 23, caretaker, b. NH, s/o Thomas A. Mitchell, Sr. (Canada) and Marion Hersey (NH); W – 18, student, b. MA, d/o Kenneth K. Williams (MA) and Ethel E. Cotter (MA)
Thomas Osborne m. Marion Edna **Hersey** 9/18/1938 in Tuftonboro; H – 27, gardener, b. NS, s/o John Charles Mitchell (Wakefield, MA, carpenter) and Minnie Louise Green (PEI, housewife); W – 27, teacher, b. Tuftonboro, d/o Edwin Charles Hersey

(Tuftonboro, farmer) and Hattie Belle Springer (Marshfield, VT, housewife)

MIXER,
Douglas Maxwell m. Norma Kate **Deyak** 9/20/1970 in Tuftonboro; H – b. 5/4/1949 in NH, s/o John M. Mixer and Orilla M. MacLean; W – b. 11/6/1949 in NH, d/o Robert M. Deyak and Mary W. Hall
John M. of Tuftonboro m. Jean D. **Nickerson** of Tuftonboro 9/16/1982

MOLBURG,
John D. m. Nancy Lee **Hooper** 6/26/1971 in Wolfeboro

MONROE,
Richard B. of N. Reading, MA m. Beverly I. **Colburn** of Wakefield, MA 8/9/1968 in Tuftonboro; H – widower, b. MA, s/o Lawrence C. Monroe (MA) and Lillian Giles (MA); W – widow, b. MA, d/o Robert W. Ivester (MA) and Grace H. Glover (England)

MONTROSE,
Joseph F. of Tuftonboro m. Cheryl L. **Noble** of Tuftonboro 4/27/2002

MOODY,
George A. of Tuftonboro m. Sadie F. **Strickland** of Wolfeboro 11/23/1904 in Ossipee; H – 59, farmer, 2nd, b. Ossipee, d/o Amasa B. Moody and Mary A. Moody; W – 57, housekeeper, 3rd, b. Lowell, MA, d/o Thomas Horne and Sallie Horne
Jeffrey M. of Tuftonboro m. Terry J. **Colby** of Tuftonboro 10/10/1982
Scot Macdonald of Tuftonboro m. Lisa Robin **Reed** of Tuftonboro 7/4/1997

MOORE,
Todd A. of Ctr. Tuftonboro m. Irene G. **Garvey** of Ctr. Tuftonboro 7/31/2004
Walter of Tuftonboro m. Maude Betts **Richardson** of Tuftonboro 1/30/1956 in Melvin Village; H – 68, retired, widower, b. MA, s/o Louis E. Moore (MA) and Addie S. Howard (MA); W – 55, secretary, widow, b. MA, d/o Frederick Betts (England) and Mary Ann Guild (England)

MOREAU,
Ronald A. of Tuftonboro m. Sharon R. **Welch** of Ossipee 4/19/1985

MORGAN,
Daniel S. of Tuftonboro m. Judith P. **Morgan** of Tuftonboro
    6/25/1988
Jeffrey Thomas of Tuftonboro m. Jennifer G. **Beattie** of Tuftonboro
    8/29/1992
Kenneth A. of Tuftonboro m. Kathleen L. **Brennan** of Tuftonboro
    12/5/1981
Lloyd C., Jr. m. Cynthia J. **Cheney** 4/14/1978 in Tuftonboro
Ricky M. m. Rebecca A. **Vappi** 6/1/1974 in Moultonboro

MORRIS,
Robert Graydon m. Dorothy Frances **Bennett** 7/4/1936 in
    Tuftonboro; H – 28, guide, b. Tuftonboro, s/o Alfred Morris
    (Biddeford, ME, retired) and Hattie J. Buzzell (Meredith,
    housewife); W – 23, registered nurse, b. Tuftonboro, d/o Frank
    S. Bennett (Tuftonboro, carpenter) and Eleanor Dawes (Boston,
    MA, housewife)

MORRISON,
James E. of Tuftonboro m. Jennifer A. **Bernier** of Tuftonboro
    9/22/1990

MORWAY,
Richard N. of Dorchester, MA m. Fern O. **Blair** of E. Dedham, MA
    5/19/1945 in Tuftonboro; H – 31, expediter, b. Montgomery, VT,
    s/o Walter R. Morway (Albany, VT) and Mabel F. Lumbra
    (Montgomery, VT); W – 30, asst. mgr., b. Ellsworth, IL, d/o
    Joseph Blair (Ellsworth, IL) and Goldie M. Bean (LeRoy, IL)

MOTLEY,
Harry G. of Tuftonboro m. Louise W. **Snyder** of Tuftonboro
    8/29/1948 in Tuftonboro; H – 70, station agent, b. Saco, ME,
    s/o John B. Motley (Saco, ME) and Sarah Armstrong
    (Hampden, ME); W – 42, housekeeper, b. Lynn, MA, d/o C. W.
    Thompson (Union) and Winnie M. Hatch (Madison)

MOULTON,
Darwin of Tuftonboro m. Alcira **Gracia** of Tuftonboro 2/14/1991

James L. of Tuftonboro m. Gladys E. **Haley** of Tuftonboro 8/18/1917 in Tuftonboro; H – 27, laborer, b. Parsonsfield, ME, s/o Fred Moulton and Ora Hamilton; W – 16, housewife, b. Tuftonboro, d/o George H. Haley and Edith C. Ayers

James W. of Newmarket m. Emma E. **Waldron** of Tuftonboro 9/13/1897 in Tuftonboro; H – 29, hostler, 2nd, widower, b. Effingham, s/o Lewis Moulton and Martha W. Moulton; W – 22, housekeeper, b. Wolfeboro, d/o John B. Waldron and Jennie Stevens

John S. of Tuftonboro m. Arvilla **Copp** of Tuftonboro 7/1/1892 in Tuftonboro; H – 73, cabinet maker, widower, b. Albany, s/o Joseph G. Moulton (Gilford, farmer) and Phoebe C. Moulton (Albany, housewife); W – 66, housewife, widow, b. Tuftonboro, d/o Daniel Fernald (N. Berwick, ME, blacksmith) and Lydia Fernald (housewife)

Robert C. of Tuftonboro m. Jeannette Marie **Parris** of Tuftonboro 8/15/1998

Robert C., Jr. m. Nancy J. **Stockman** 6/19/1976 in Tuftonboro

MUGRIDGE,
Donald Joseph m. Eleanor Pearl **Howe** 9/6/1934 in Wolfeboro; H – 28, mechanic, b. PEI, s/o Thomas J. Mugridge (PEI, carpenter) and Annie Gillis (PEI, at home); W – 19, waitress, b. Attleboro, MA, d/o Carlton L. Howe (Southboro, MA, carpenter) and Ina Maud Cordeau (Marlboro, MA, housewife)

MURCOTT,
Andrew W. of Omara m. Martha G. **Copplestone** of Melvin Village 6/28/2003

MUISE,
Darrell James of Tuftonboro m. Laura Ann **Gray** of Tuftonboro 9/7/1996

MULLIN,
Robert S. of Chicago, IL m. Lisa Ann **Foote** of Chicago, IL 6/22/1991

MURLEY,
Samuel m. Gertrude **Breitenbucher** 12/23/1931 in Wolfeboro; H – 53, carpenter, 3rd, b. Creston, NF, s/o James Murley (Creston, NF) and Isabella A. West (Creston, NF); W – 50, milliner, 3rd, b.

Bangor, ME, d/o Fred Cross (Bangor, ME) and Grace Mayhew (Bangor, ME)

MURNER,
Lawrence of Nashua m. Doreen M. **Lawless** of Tuftonboro
9/22/1984

MURRAY,
Harrison Slade of Maplewood, NJ m. Anna Laurie **Welch** of
Maplewood, NJ 6/28/1997

MYERS,
Robert D. of Tuftonboro m. Theresa L. **Rabzak** of Tuftonboro
4/17/2004

MYSHRALL,
Winston C. m. Nancy J. **Heath** 3/19/1978 in Tuftonboro

NARAMORE,
John C. of Tuftonboro m. Donnamarie T. **Hewitt** of Wolfeboro
12/30/1984

NEAL,
Isaac N. of Tuftonboro m. Anna R. **Foss** of Tuftonboro 2/2/1909 in
Tuftonboro; H – 42, farmer, b. Tuftonboro, s/o James H. Neal
and Adelisa Copp; W – 42, house, 2nd, b. Tuftonboro, d/o
George F. Bean and Sarah F. Abbott

NELSON,
Harry C. H. of Tuftonboro m. Cora A. **Smith** of Tuftonboro
10/25/1949 in Tuftonboro; H – 38, resort owner, b. NH, s/o
Louis Nelson (Denmark) and Anna Hansen (Denmark); W – 45,
resort owner, b. Malden, MA, d/o Leo F. Beaulieu (MA) and
Winona B. Green (NH)
Mark K. of Pottstown, PA m. Ellen M. **O'Shaughnessy** of Pottstown,
PA 6/22/1985
Paul Willard of MA m. Lorraine Bertwell **Moulton** of MA 7/2/1960 in
Tuftonboro; H – 48, broker, widower, b. MA, s/o Elmer A.
Nelson (Sweden) and Anna C. Swanson (Sweden); W – 37, at
home, divorced, b. MA, d/o Howard F. Andrews (MA) and
Eleanore F. Smith (MA)

NEWBURY,
Christopher Bernard of MA m. Jennifer **Davis** of MA 10/19/2002

NEWCOMB,
Nelson Faulks, Jr. of Tuftonboro m. Betsey Gay **Brodrick** of
Wolfeboro 10/13/1979

NEWMAN,
Theodore C., Jr. of Shelter Island, NY m. Sandra Lee **Rudolph** of
Tuftonboro 8/26/1967 in Wolfeboro; H – 26, teacher, b.
Brooklyn, NY, s/o Theodore C. Newman (NY) and Kathryn Ball
(NY); W – 21, teacher, b. Wolfeboro, d/o Gerald F. Rudolph
(MA) and Mary A. Libby (NH)

NICHOLLA,
Steven John of Sanbornton m. Susan Audrey **Dow** of Tuftonboro
10/1/1994

NICHOLLS,
William Hord m. Elizabeth Banfield **Burwell** 9/5/1936 in Tuftonboro;
H – 23, agricultural econ., b. Lexington, KY, s/o William D.
Nicholls (Springfield, KY, professor) and Mary Elizabeth Hord
(Manchester, OH, housewife); W – 26, private secretary, b.
Medford, MA, d/o Elliot Noel Burwell (Montreal, Canada, naval
arch.) and Mary E. Banfield (Wolfeboro, housewife)

NICHOLSON,
John J. G., III of Huntington, CT m. Deborah **Dennis** of Trumbull, CT
7/25/1982

NICKERSON,
Jonathan N. of Tuftonboro m. Pauline B. **Iveson** of Manchester
1/2/1982
Jonathan Nelson of Tuftonboro m. Jean Debora **Knowles** of Bangor,
ME 6/16/1962 in E. Wolfeboro; H – 19, laborer, b. Ossipee, s/o
Nelson E. Nickerson (Canada) and Barbara J. Sharp (NH); W –
19, student, b. Bangor, ME, d/o Maurice F. Knowles (ME) and
Florence B. Peacock (ME)

NINE,
John Arthur of Branford, CT m. Rosa Paige **Hayes** of Branford, CT
    8/19/1989

NOBLE,
Leslie C. m. Marion Jerusha **Raymond** 7/1/1936 in Tuftonboro; H –
    34, salesman, b. Bay City, MI, s/o Horace G. Noble (OH,
    shipwright) and Frances B. Copeland (IN, housewife); W – 24,
    at home, b. Marshfield, MA, d/o Henry T. Raymond (Boston,
    MA, farmer) and Marion J. Hatch (Wollaston, MA, housewife)

NOCKLES,
William Arthur of Lynn, MA m. Diane **Furber** of Arlington, MA
    8/21/1965 in Tuftonboro; H – 38, teacher, b. Lynn, MA, s/o John
    Austin Nockles (MA) and Mary Alice Perkins (MA); W – 32,
    teacher, b. Boston, MA, d/o Gordon May Furber (MA) and
    Katherine E. Brock (MA)

NOYES,
Charles Willard of Lowell, MA m. Violet Bowen **Cheney** of
    Tuftonboro 8/17/1962 in Wolfeboro; H – 56, painter, 2nd,
    widower, b. Boston, MA, s/o Charles W. Noyes (MA) and
    Emma Mitchell (MA); W – 49, maid, 2nd, widow, b. Braintree,
    VT, d/o Azro Bowen (VT) and Brena Pember (VT)

O'BRIEN,
Gordon A. m. Verna **Peterson** 10/4/1974 in Tuftonboro
James R. of Tuftonboro m. Cindy P. **Veilleux** of Tuftonboro
    10/12/2002
Mark of Tuftonboro m. Shirley A. **Allen** of Tuftonboro 10/3/1987
Mark J. of Mirror Lake m. Samantha J. **Meiklejohn** of Tuftonboro
    11/1/2003

O'CONNELL,
Richard P. m. Kathryn I. **Waddell** 12/30/1973 in Tuftonboro

O'GRADY,
John P. m. Barbara L. **Schaefer** 4/8/1978 in Wolfeboro

O'REILLY,
Patrick M. of Tuftonboro m. Margaret Mary **Cea** of Darien, CT
    4/23/1997

O'SHAUGHNESSY,
Timothy E. m. Leilani K. **Parker** 6/19/1976 in Tuftonboro

OLDHAM,
Nile Michael m. Laura K. **Rodgers** 9/3/1972 in Tuftonboro

OSBORN,
Frank J. m. Hilda J. **Dana** 8/22/1942 in Tuftonboro; H – 56, health
    officer, 2nd, b. Silver Creek, NY, s/o Elmer E. Osborn (Hanover
    C., NY, deceased) and Aurelia E. Lincoln (Silver Creek, NY,
    housewife); W – 47, newspaper, 2nd, b. NY City, d/o Harry
    Jackson (Russia, deceased) and Emma Goldbaar (Russia,
    deceased)

OSWALT,
Edmund D. of Tuftonboro m. Cynthia L. **Kimball** of Tuftonboro
    4/6/2005
Edmund Darrell of Tuftonboro m. Susan Brayton **Hammond** of
    Tuftonboro 8/10/1996

OULTON,
Fred R. of Tuftonboro m. Ruth C. **Stacy** of Tuftonboro 7/31/1949 in
    Tuftonboro; H – 61, metal worker, b. Cambridge, MA, s/o
    James W. Oulton (NB) and Cordelia C. Cole (Dorchester, NB);
    W – 43, stitcher, b. Saugus, MA, d/o James A. Dunn (MA) and
    Josephine Bryant (MA)

OWEN,
Derek of Hopkinton m. Patricia Ruth **Nisbet** of Tuftonboro 9/15/1962
    in Hopkinton; H – 30, student, b. Concord, s/o Harold H. Owen
    (NH) and Louise P. Guyot (NH); W – 23, student, b. Mexico,
    ME, d/o Gerrald Nisbet (ME) and Reba E. Gallop (ME)

PAGE,
Lincoln A. of Menlo Park, CA m. Donna L. **Smith** of Tuftonboro
    9/3/1983
Lincoln R. m. Shirley G. **Tarbell** 5/7/1977 in Tuftonboro

Lincoln Ridler m. Esther Belinda **Lord** 7/29/1933 in Melvin Village; H – 22, instr. of geology, b. Lisbon, s/o Norman J. Page (Benton, supt. of schools) and Helen Ridler White (Diamond Hill, RI, housewife); W – 25, teacher, b. Tuftonboro, d/o Milton A. Lord (Conway, farmer) and Elizabeth Belinda Morrison (Tuftonboro, housewife)

Norman J. of Tuftonboro m. Ann **McNair** of Hanover 6/12/1961 in Hanover; H – 22, student, b. Boulder, CO, s/o Lincoln R. Page (NH) and Esther B. Lord (NH); W – 20, student, b. Hanover, d/o Andrew H. McNair (MT) and Hattie E. Lyford (VT)

PAIGE,
Robert m. Eva May **Howe** 9/21/1929 in Tuftonboro; H – 24, electrician, b. White River Jct., VT, s/o Harry E. Paige (Sherbrook, PQ) and Nellie O'Hara (England); W – 20, at home, b. Tuftonboro, d/o Carlton L. Howe (Southboro, MA) and Ina M. Cordeau (Marlboro, MA)

Robert K. of Tuftonboro m. Eva H. **Paige** of Tuftonboro 7/12/1946 in Wolfeboro; H – 41, electrician, b. Tuftonboro, s/o Harry Paige (Canada) and Nellie Watson (England); W – 37, at home, b. Tuftonboro, d/o Carleton L. Howe (Southboro, MA) and Ina M. Cordeau (Southboro, MA)

Thomas H. m. Carla J. **Meyer** 11/16/1973 in Tuftonboro

Thomas Howe of Tuftonboro m. Sandra **Davis** of Tuftonboro 7/2/1960 in Wolfeboro; H – 20, mechanic, b. NH, s/o Robert K. Paige (VT) and Eva May Howe (NH); W – 18, nurses aide, b. NH, d/o Willis P. Davis (NH) and Eleanor M. Thompson (NH)

Thomas Howe of Tuftonboro m. Martha Elaine **Letteney** of Wolfeboro 9/3/1961 in Wolfeboro; H – 21, carpenter, 2nd, divorced, b. Wolfeboro, s/o Robert K. Paige (Hartford, VT) and Eva May Howe (NH); W – 18, clerk, b. Dover, d/o Frank G. Letteney and Esther M. Beach (Foxboro, MA)

PALATULLI,
Donald M. m. Blanid T. **Keller** 9/8/1973 in Tuftonboro

PANNO,
Harry Frederick of N. Conway m. Madalyn May **Smith** of Tuftonboro 2/12/1955 in Ctr. Ossipee; H – 25, mill worker, divorced, b. NH, s/o Harry L. Panno (ME) and Louise C. Eastman (NH); W – 20,

at home, b. NH, d/o Clifton E. Smith (MA) and Bertha M. Riley
(ME)
Harry Frederick of Tuftonboro m. Estelle **Sheaff** of Conway
1/13/1962 in Conway; H – 32, truck driver, 3rd, divorced, b. N.
Conway, s/o Harry Panno (ME) and Louise C. Eastman (NH);
W – 24, bookkeeper, b. Portsmouth, d/o Arthur R. Sheaff (ME)
and Myrtis L. Remick (ME)

PARIS,
Robert M. of Londonderry m. Laura L. **Emilson** of Maynard, MA
7/14/1979

PARKHURST,
Walter R. of Wolfeboro m. Lisa Ann **Welch** of Tuftonboro 2/14/1998

PARSONS,
Douglas B. of Lexington, MA m. Suzanne **Allen** of Tuftonboro
7/1/1950 in Tuftonboro; H – 22, salesman, b. MA, s/o Philip B.
Parsons (MA) and Bernice P. Boutwell (MA); W – 21, at home,
b. NJ, d/o Leroy V. Allen (NJ) and Edith M. White (NJ)
Douglas B. m. Grace M. **Bickford** 6/28/1978 in Wakefield
Douglas B. of Tuftonboro m. Barbara L. **Lomas** of Tuftonboro
9/10/2005

PARTIN,
Charles Fred of Meridian, MS m. Carlien Smith **Crews** of Meridian,
MS 8/6/1939 in Melvin Village; H – 22, student, b. Meridian,
MS, s/o Charles Fred Partin (Decatur, MS, deceased) and Ada
Elizabeth Edgar (Newton, MS, housewife); W – 21, student, b.
Union, MS, d/o Carl Crews (Bradford, TN, RR supt.) and Mary
Ann Jones (Oakland, TN, housewife)

PATTERSON,
Robert J. of Tuftonboro m. Marion G. **Burleigh** of Tuftonboro
7/29/1923 in Wolfeboro; H – 33, painter, b. Somerville, MA, s/o
George A. Patterson (Ireland) and Bella Ray (Ireland); W – 22,
housewife, b. Dover, d/o William C. Burleigh (Tuftonboro) and
Mina Wiggin (Tuftonboro)
Robert J. of Fitchburg, MA m. Michele A. **Tervo** of Fitchburg, MA
6/22/1980

PAUL,
Brian D. of Danvers, PA m. Julie S. **Michaud** of Salem, MA
10/7/1990

PEARE,
Arthur Gordon of Ctr. Ossipee m. Evelyn Maud **Eldridge** of
Tuftonboro 4/24/1954 in Tuftonboro; H – 29, millhand, b. NH,
s/o Ernest A. Peare (ME) and Lillian A. Wade (ME); W – 21, at
home, b. Tuftonboro, d/o Carleton S. Eldridge (NH) and Esther
M. Baker (NH)

PEDONE,
William Anton of Santa Monica, CA m. Kristina Kay **Purcell** of Santa
Monica, CA 10/21/1995

PENNELL,
Dwight W. m. Carolyn **Phelps** 9/17/1977 in Tuftonboro
Dwight Wayne of Tuftonboro m. Bonnie Mae **French** of Tuftonboro
11/4/2000

PERKINS,
Bert A. m. Mildred Edna **Bruce** 4/21/1935 in Wolfeboro; H – 40,
laborer, 3ʳᵈ, b. Ctr. Ossipee, s/o Hiram L. Perkins (Meredith,
engineer) and Etta Clough (Effingham, housewife); W – 24,
housekeeper, b. Saranac Lake, NY, d/o Harry Lloyd Bruce
(farmer) and Emma Jane McLain (housewife)
Ernest R., Jr. of Tuftonboro m. Sherri A. **Champagne** of Wolfeboro
9/3/1983
Maurice L. m. Linda H. **Woodbury** 10/6/1973 in Tuftonboro
Wayne E. of Tuftonboro m. Joy E. **Hanington** of Tuftonboro
5/23/1998

PERRY,
Stanley A. of Ctr. Ossipee m. Barbara D. **Gouin** of Tuftonboro
1/26/1957 in Ctr. Ossipee; H – 22, mill worker, b. NH, s/o
Erneta Perry (NH) and Violet M. Colbroth (NH); W – 17, at
home, b. NH, d/o Thornton Y. Gouin (NH) and Leona L. Libby
(NH)
Stephen H. of Cotuit, MA m. Andrea L. **Haynes** of Wellesley, MA
6/27/1987

PETERSON,
Ernest S. m. Eleanor F. **King** 3/3/1973 in Wolfeboro
Lawrence B. of Cambridge, MA m. Doris **Wood** of Tuftonboro
4/8/1950 in Tuftonboro; H – 62, watchman, b. MA, s/o
Theodore L. Peterson (MA) and Isabelle Burritt (NY); W – 32, at
home, b. MA, d/o William H. Wood (MA) and Inez Patterson
(MA)

PETTIT,
Russell W. m. Kathy **Buttrick** 7/22/1973 in Tuftonboro

PHILBRICK,
Alfred of Tuftonboro m. Elsie C. **Drowns** of Waterboro, ME 8/6/1896
in Tuftonboro; H – 23, farmer, b. Bartlett, s/o Hiram Philbrick
(Roxbury, farmer) and Betsy Philbrick (Limerick, ME,
housekeeper); W – 15, housekeeper, b. Waterboro, ME, d/o
Calvin Drowns (Waterboro, ME, farmer) and Caroline Drowns
(Waterboro, ME, housekeeper)
Willie W. of Tuftonboro m. Mary A. **Goldsmith** of Tuftonboro
10/28/1893 in Ossipee; H – 26, farmer, b. Fryeburg, ME, s/o
Jesse Watson (Fryeburg, ME, farmer) and Betsy Philbrook
(Conway, housewife); W – 29, housewife, 2nd, b. Tuftonboro,
d/o George F. Bean (farmer) and Sarah A. Bean (housewife)

PHINNEY,
Charles H. of MA m. Cora E. **Bangs** of MA 7/9/1952 in Tuftonboro;
H – 73, tool maker, b. MA, s/o Walter R. Phinney (MA) and
Carrie J. Jennison (MA); W – 74, at home, b. Marlboro, d/o
Francis W. Plates (Fitzwilliam) and Martha A. Emerson
(Northfield, VT)

PIERCE,
Donald H. of Tuftonboro m. Jamie L. **Martin** of Tuftonboro 4/28/1984

PIGOTT,
Robert Allison of Winthrop, MA m. Florence Irene **Ayers** of
Tuftonboro 10/17/1959 in Mirror Lake; H – 35, clerk, b. MA, s/o
Thomas E. Pigott (MA) and Eva M. Dam (MA); W – 18, rec. lib.,
b. NH, d/o Levi L. Ayers (NH) and Ruth E. Champaigne (NH)

PIKE,
Caleb Everett of Wolfeboro m. Kristen Ellen **Svenson** of Tuftonboro
10/8/1994
Chester H. of Wolfeboro m. Marion Claire **Reed** of Tuftonboro
8/29/1953 in Melvin Village; H – 22, general labor, divorced, b.
NH, s/o Guy A. Pike (NH) and Edna B. Rogers (NH); W – 24,
waitress, b. NH, d/o Frank E. Reed (NH) and Mildred F. Whiting
(Acton, ME)
Curt R. of Wolfeboro m. Susan J. **Buttrick** of Tuftonboro 11/16/1985
Curtis A. of Wolfeboro m. Ann Celeste **Williams** of Tuftonboro
7/15/1960 in Tuftonboro; H – 31, carpenter, divorced, b. NH, s/o
Guy A. Pike (NH) and Edna B. Rogers (NH); W – 23, waitress,
b. NH, d/o Roger L. Williams (MA) and Berenice W. Lawrence
(MA)
Guy A., II m. Judith M. **Dearborn** 11/17/1973 in Tuftonboro

PINKNEY,
John E. of Rowayton, CT m. Elizabeth **Higgins** of Tuftonboro
7/31/1948 in Melvin Village; H – 22, student, b. Greenwich, CT,
s/o William Pickney, Jr. (Rowayton, CT) and Dorothy E. Cowles
(New Rochelle, NY); W – 23, dental asst., b. Middleboro, MA,
d/o Darragh L. Higgins (Middleboro, MA) and Maud G.
Churbuck (Middleboro, MA)

PIPER,
Carl Raymond of Tuftonboro m. Barbara Sharp **Gould** of Tuftonboro
10/13/1961 in Tuftonboro; H – 47, construction, b. Tuftonboro,
s/o John F. Piper (NH) and Nellie F. Staples (ME); W – 43,
housewife, 3rd, widow, b. NH, d/o John E. Sharp (NH) and
Katherine E. Sanborn (NH)
Charles G. of Tuftonboro m. Addie **Geto** of Tuftonboro 11/14/1896 in
Tuftonboro; H – 40, farmer, b. Tuftonboro, s/o Richard Piper
(Tuftonboro, farmer) and Sarah J. Piper (Roxbury, MA,
housewife); W – 21, housekeeper, b. Tuftonboro, d/o Lewis
Geto (farmer) and Hattie Geto (housewife)
Frank F. m. Yvonne **LaBonte** 9/8/1978 in Tuftonboro
Ivan Charles m. Eleanor Josephine **Morris** 10/3/1934 in Wolfeboro;
H – 23, farmer, b. Wolfeboro, s/o Ivan J. Piper (Wolfeboro,
farmer) and Winnifred Allard (Eaton, housewife); W – 22,
waitress, b. Melvin Village, d/o Frederick J. Morris (Biddeford,
ME, retired) and Hattie J. Buzzell (Meredith, housewife)

John F. of Tuftonboro m. Nellie F. **Staples** of Tuftonboro 1/24/1903
in Parsonsfield, ME; H – 22, farmer, b. Tuftonboro, s/o David E.
Piper and Elizabeth Piper; W – 17, housekeeper, b. Tuftonboro,
d/o John Staples and Ellen Edwards
Norman H. of Tuftonboro m. June B. **Worster** of E. Wolfeboro
10/24/1948 in Wolfeboro; H – 24, truck driver, b. Tuftonboro,
s/o John F. Piper (Tuftonboro) and Nellie F. Staples
(Parsonsfield, ME); W – 19, housewife, b. Akron, NY, d/o Earl
H. Kenneson (Rumney) and Beatrice C. Downing (Rumney)
Ralph G. of Tuftonboro m. Emma E. **Hersey** of Tuftonboro
11/6/1906 in Tuftonboro; H – 20, farmer, b. Tuftonboro, s/o
Frank E. Piper and Carrie S. Low; W – 20, housewife, b.
Tuftonboro, d/o John L. Hersey and Vian Flanders
Richard Arnold of Tuftonboro m. Suzanne Marie **Dubuc** of
Tuftonboro 9/27/1997
Stanley W. of Tuftonboro m. Irene **Cotton** of Wolfeboro 12/18/1948
in Wolfeboro; H – 22, truck driver, b. Tuftonboro, s/o John F.
Piper (Tuftonboro) and Nellie F. Staples (Parsonsfield, ME); W
– 23, waitress, b. Wolfeboro, d/o Theo. Champaigne
(Rochester)

PLODZIK,
Benjamin J. of Tuftonboro m. Rachel M. **Smith** of Tuftonboro
4/24/1987

POALETTI,
Chester of Needham, MA m. Natalie A. **Brewer** of Tuftonboro
11/26/1950 in Wolfeboro; H – 30, bricklayer, b. Italy, s/o Paul
Poalette (Italy) and Rose Arra (Italy); W – 27, at home, b. MA,
d/o Norman K. Brookes (England) and Madeleine H. Luce (MA)

POLINI,
Todd Emery of Tuftonboro m. Celeste Mae **Askew** of Tuftonboro
12/15/2000

POLLINI,
William Sherm of Wolfeboro m. Cynthia Ann **Person** of Tuftonboro
11/18/1961 in Tuftonboro; H – 21, truck driver, b. Wolfeboro,
s/o Samuel Pollini (Italy) and Bertha Beals (NY); W – 17, at
home, b. Wolfeboro, d/o Herbert G. Peson (VT) and Beverley
A. Bean (NH)

POND,
Jonathan D. of Cambridge, MA m. Lois Ann **Zaborowski** of
  Cambridge, MA 9/2/1984

PORTER,
David R. m. Irene A. **Marion** 8/26/1972 in Tuftonboro
Graham C. m. Lottie May **Bose** 8/24/1925 in Tuftonboro; H – 39,
  Purina Mills, b. Japan, s/o Sarah K. Cummings (PA); W – 29,
  dir. of women, b. Columbia, TN, d/o John Bose (Jeffersonville,
  IN) and Susie N. Phillips (Clocksville, TN)
Scott A. of Wolfeboro m. Anita M. **D'Onofrio** of Tuftonboro
  8/22/1985
Scott W. of Tuftonboro m. Dianne M. **McKenzie** of Tuftonboro
  7/23/2005

POTTER,
Wilmer M. of Tuftonboro m. Mary A. **Thornburg** of Brattleboro, VT
  5/9/1984

PRAUSE,
Michael C. of Tucson, AZ m. Kimberly Ann **Blake** of Tucson, AZ
  6/11/1997

PROVAN,
Walter Fairfield of Boston, MA m. Hazel Lillian **Lawrence** of Boston,
  MA 10/12/1939 in Melvin Village; H – 57, dentist, 2nd, b. S.
  Boston, s/o Walter Scott Provan (Gagetown, NB, deceased)
  and Harriet May Fairfield (S. Boston, MA, deceased); W – 38,
  secretary, b. Haverhill, MA, d/o William Menediel Lawrence
  (Lawrence, MA, deceased) and Amelia Marie Beauvais
  (Haverhill, MA, housewife)

PROVERB,
Leon Gladstone of Mirror Lake m. Gladys Marion **Patterson** of
  Allston, MA 7/12/1958 in Wolfeboro; H – 60, plumber, 2nd, b.
  MA, s/o Alex T. Proverb (West Indies) and Rosa Henry (West
  Indies); W – 47, clerk, 2nd, b. NS, d/o Arthur J. Page (NS) and
  Susanna Leydon (NS)

PUCHACZ,
David M. of Tuftonboro m. Cynthia L. **Boyce** of Nashua 4/21/2001

QUILLIAM,
Francis P. of Tuftonboro m. Leonora P. **Rice** of Tuftonboro
12/31/1997

QUINBY,
Kenneth A. of Tuftonboro m. Brenda C. **Lorenz** of Philadelphia, PA
5/25/1985

RAMEY,
Shon C. of Granite Falls, WA m. Wendy J. **Forbes** of Federal Way,
WA 9/17/1983

RAMSBOTHAM,
Robert W., Jr. m. Susan H. **Jones** 9/7/1974 in Tuftonboro

RAN,
Albert C. m. Dorothy E. **Ward** 9/8/1926 in Tuftonboro; H – 37, asst.
manager, 2nd, b. Boston, MA, s/o Christopher Ran (Germany)
and Bertha Martin (New York City); W – 26, teacher, b.
England, d/o Alfred J. Ward (England) and Annie M. Smith
(England)

RAND,
Leroy D. of Lewiston, ME m. Mary E. **Haley** of Tuftonboro
12/31/1910 in Tuftonboro; H – 28, laborer, 2nd, b. Randolph, s/o
Stephen D. Rand and Carrie I. Leighton; W – 22, housewife, b.
Tuftonboro, d/o Samuel R. Haley and Hattie J. Buzzell

RANDALL,
Raymond A. of Wakefield m. Barbara J. **Eldridge** of Tuftonboro
9/2/1950 in Ctr. Ossipee; H – 22, teamster, b. NH, s/o Earle F.
Randall (NH) and Mabel A. Weeks (NH); W – 15, at home, b.
NH, d/o Carleton S. Eldridge (NH) and Esther M. Haley (NH)

RASMUSSEN,
Stephen Karl of Cranston, RI m. Deborah Lee **Cole** of N. Kingston,
RI 6/10/1995

RAULINS,
John D. m. Rita V. **O'Neill** 5/9/1970 in Tuftonboro; H – b. 9/30/1909
in MA, s/o John J. Raulins and Estelle Bradlee; W – b. 3/1/1914
in MA, d/o William Enos and Ellen Shiner

RAYMOND,
Robert A. of Jamaica Plain, MA m. Marilyn A. **Arsem** of Jamaica
Plain, MA 6/21/1990

REDMOND,
Edward P. of Scottsdale, AZ m. Lori Beth **Olson** of Scottsdale, AZ
8/18/1984

REED,
David Thomas of Tuftonboro m. Eleanor Ann **Flanagan** of Ctr.
Sandwich 7/2/1961 in Tuftonboro; H – 21, shoe maker, b. NH,
s/o Frank E. Reed (ME) and Mildred F. Whiting (NH); W – 18,
at home, b. Wolfeboro, d/o Paul Flanagan (MA) and Hilda
Colby (Ossipee)
Frank Eugene m. Mildred Francis **Whiting** 11/3/1928 in Moultonville;
H – 28, chauffeur, b. Houlton, ME, s/o Addison E. Reed
(Houlton, ME) and Florence J. Hanson (NB); W – 18, at home,
b. Tuftonboro, d/o Leon L. Whiting (Tamworth) and Mary Rose
Francis (Cambridge, MA)
James Michael of Tuftonboro m. Judy **Leroux** of Meredith
11/19/1968 in Moultonboro; H – b. NH, s/o Norman E. Reed,
Sr. (NH) and Mildred Chick (NH); W – b. NH, d/o Armand
Leroux (NH) and Harriet Harvey (NH)
Norman E., Jr. of Tuftonboro m. Gloria L. **Herbert** of Weirs 8/2/1968
in Lakeport; H – b. NH, s/o Norman E. Reed, Sr. (NH); W – b.
NH, d/o Archie Herbert (NH) and Irene Girouard (NH)
Norman Elsmore of Tuftonboro m. Roberta Ellen **Drew** of Wolfeboro
5/11/1963 in Melvin Village; H – 42, laborer, 4th, widower, b.
Woodman, s/o Austin P. Reed (NH) and Rosamond R. Leavitt
(ME); W – 35, inspector, b. Alton, d/o Harold C. Drew (NH) and
Marion F. Ransom (NH)
Robert Arnold of Tuftonboro m. Muriel Agnes **Springer** of Medford,
MA 11/14/1953 in Wolfeboro; H – 22, USMC, b. Tuftonboro, s/o
Robert E. Reed (Acton, ME) and Mildred Whiting (NH); W – 19,
secretary, b. MA, d/o Charles William Springer (VT) and Agnes
Ford (MA)

Wayne Austin of Tuftonboro m. Donna Jean **Durkee** of New Durham
7/17/1966 in Melvin Village; H – 18, laborer, b. Wolfeboro, s/o
Norman E. Reed (NH) and Marjorie F. Chick (NH); W – 18, at
home, b. Rochester, d/o Donald P. Durkee (NH) and Lorraine
M. Benton (NH)

REMMERS,
Timothy Robert of Waterville, ME m. Denise Jean **Grover** of
Rockland, ME 6/1/1989

REPPUCCI,
Ronald J., Jr. of Moultonboro m. Angela R. **Daignault** of Tuftonboro
2/13/1987

REYNOLDS,
Mark Morgan of Milford, MA m. Christina L. **Todaro** of Milford, MA
9/5/1992

RICHARD,
James A. of Tuftonboro m. Alice I. **Ward** of Tuftonboro 4/4/1987

RICHARDSON,
Bruce D. m. Virginia D. **Reed** 10/23/1976 in Tuftonboro
Frank A. of Tuftonboro m. Lillian L. **Carlson** of FL 9/17/1950 in
Wolfeboro; H – 52, real estate, b. MA, s/o Frank A. Richardson
(RI) and Caroline M. Benton (RI); W – 37, cosmetician, b. IN,
d/o Albert Nichols (IN) and Ethel Goodman (IN)
Harold E., Jr. of Moultonboro m. Deanna L. **White** of Tuftonboro
5/3/1980
Marshall D. of Tuftonboro m. Evelyn C. **Carpenter** of Tuftonboro
4/2/1899 in Tuftonboro; H – 46, farmer, 3rd, b. Moultonboro, s/o
Lucern Richardson and Joanna F. Doe; W – 29, housekeeper,
2nd, b. Farmington, d/o Stephen D. Avery and Ann M. Allen
Verne Leslie of Moultonboro m. Elizabeth Paige **Davis** of Tuftonboro
6/3/1961 in Moultonboro; H – 26, garage proprietor, 2nd,
divorced, b. NH, s/o Horace L. Richardson (NH) and Ernestine
E. Berry (NH); W – 24, reg. nurse, b. Wolfeboro, d/o Willis P.
Davis (NH) and Eleanor M. Thompson (NH)

RIDDLE,
Hollis L. m. Emma C. **Riddle** 10/20/1972 in Tuftonboro

RIDLON,
Arnold L. of Tuftonboro m. Hazel L. **Beale** of Wakefield 10/24/1945
in Rochester; H – 30, carpenter, b. Wolfeboro, s/o Arthur Ridlon
(Quincy, MA) and Lena Shannon (Tuftonboro); W – 22, at
home, b. W. Newfield, ME, d/o Roscoe Beale (N. Shapleigh,
ME) and Rose Abbott (W. Newfield, ME)
Arnold LeRoy m. Anna Estelle **Powers** 6/30/1934 in Tuftonboro; H –
20, shoe worker, b. Wolfeboro, s/o Arthur LeRoy Ridlon
(Quincy, MA, carpenter) and Lena G. Shannon (Tuftonboro,
housewife); W – 18, at home, b. Gloucester, MA, d/o William
Charles Powers (Gloucester, MA, laborer) and Alice Margaret
Meuse (Yarmouth, NS, laundry w.)
Filbert E. m. Delia M. **Hill** 6/10/1938 in Union; H – 19, shoemaker, b.
Springvale, ME, s/o Arthur L. Ridlon (Quincy, MA, carpenter)
and Lena Shannon (Tuftonboro, housewife); W – 18, domestic,
b. Colebrook, d/o John Hill (Holland, VT, lumberman) and
Florence A. Buger (Caribou, ME, housewife)

RILEY,
Adam Tracy of Ossipee m. Carolyn Anderson **Wentworth** of
Tuftonboro 12/28/2002
Ernest Granville m. Beatrice Adeline **Banfill** 9/24/1938 in Wakefield;
H – 22, laborer, b. Standish, ME, s/o Henry Franklin Riley
(Bridgton, ME, laborer) and Abbie Louise Brown (Poland, ME,
housewife); W – 16, at home, b. Sanford, ME, d/o Fred Robert
Banfill (Franklin, bus driver) and Meleda Anna Descharnais
(Victoriaville, PQ, housewife)
Franklin R. m. Cheryl A. **Cross** 8/16/1969 in Wolfeboro; H – b.
4/16/1949 in NH, s/o Ernest G. Riley, Sr. and Beatrice Banfill;
W – b. 9/2/1948 in NY, d/o Charles E. Cross and Jean
Wormood

ROBBINS,
Winthrop Sutton m. Marion Winifred **Flanagan** 10/22/1933 in
Wolfeboro; H – 24, wrestling, b. Boston, MA, s/o Frederick S. H.
Robbins (Roxbury, MA, musician) and Jennie Agnes Sutton
(Charlestown, MA, housewife); W – 25, file clerk, b. Boston,
MA, d/o Thomas E. Flanagan (Roxbury, MA, fireman) and
Margaret Anna McNeil (Soldiers Cove, Cape Breton, NS,
housewife)

ROBBLEE,
William H. of Tuftonboro m. Ruth E. **Ayers** of Tuftonboro 5/13/1967
   in Tuftonboro; H – 43, shipper, b. Dorchester, MA, s/o Louing J.
   Robblee (MA) and Margaret L. Kidd (MA); W – 57, housewife,
   widow, b. Wolfeboro, d/o Herbert Champaigne (NH) and Gladys
   Adjutant (NH)

ROBERGE,
Ernest Leroy, Jr. of Wolfeboro m. Nancy Jane **Ham** of Tuftonboro
   5/2/1959 in Dover; H – 22, laborer, b. Wolfeboro, s/o Ernest L.
   Roberge, Sr. (Tuftonboro) and Cleora Clough (Wolfeboro); W –
   20, at home, b. Laconia, d/o Leroy E. Ham (Acton, ME) and
   Florence L. Haley (Tuftonboro)

ROBERTS,
Jeffrey Scott of Tuftonboro m. Lisa Ann **Doucette** of Tuftonboro
   8/15/1992

ROBIE,
George W. of Melvin Village m. Marion L. **Horner** of Melvin Village
   4/21/1940 in Melvin Village; H – 60, retired, b. Londonderry, s/o
   Samuel P. Robie (Chester, deceased) and Adeline K. Rowell
   (Derry, deceased); W – 41, merchant, b. Tuftonboro, d/o
   George S. Horner (Tuftonboro, deceased) and Grace A.
   Hodgdon (Tuftonboro, deceased)
Kenneth Ernest of Plymouth m. Elaine Rachel **Haley** of Tuftonboro
   7/5/1954 in Melvin Village; H – 26, farmer, b. NH, s/o Ernest S.
   Robie (NH) and Alice M. Matthews (NH); W – 30, at home, b.
   NH, d/o Charles E. Haley (NH) and Dora E. Bragg (NH)

ROBINSON,
Walter B. of Tuftonboro m. Ora B. **Staples** of Tuftonboro 7/17/1909
   in Tuftonboro; H – 34, farmer, b. Ossipee, s/o John F. Robinson
   and Aace M. Thompson; W – 18, house, b. Parsonsfield, ME,
   d/o John E. Staples and Ellen F. Edwards

ROGERS,
Keith Tryon of Tuftonboro m. Susan Elizabeth **Morrison** of
   Tuftonboro 9/21/2002

ROLLINS,
Richard A. of Tuftonboro m. Sylvia **Reade-Howell** of Tuftonboro
9/10/2005
William Robert of Wolfeboro m. Jacquelyn **Hunter** of Tuftonboro
7/2/1967 in Tuftonboro; H – 20, US Army, b. Wolfeboro, s/o
Robert E. Rollins (NH) and Christine O. Rollins (NH); W – 21,
waitress, b. Wolfeboro, d/o Thomas W. Hunter (NY) and Phyllis
A. Bean (NH)

RUDOLPH,
Blair D. m. Nancy J. **Croteau** 7/10/1971 in Wolfeboro

RUGGIERO,
Michael J. of Ossipee m. Vanessa **Vittum** of Tuftonboro 10/5/1996

RUNNALS,
Christopher Mark of Tuftonboro m. Nancy Marie **Burke** of
Tuftonboro 5/31/1997

RYAN,
Dennis J. m. Kristin E. **Jones** 8/6/1977 in Wolfeboro

SABALLA,
David Lineses of Phoenix, AZ m. Pamela Byrd **Lyon** of Phoenix, AZ
9/30/1994

SALVO,
Kirk Anthony of Kingsville, MD m. Kristine C. **Carlsten** of Baltimore,
MD 5/30/1992

SANBORN,
Richard Willis of Wolfeboro m. Jane Elizabeth **Piper** of Wolfeboro
2/5/1979

SANTULLI,
Jeremy Lucas of Tuftonboro m. Andrena Lynn **Dore** of Alton
7/15/2000
Nicholas P. m. Debra A. **Hooper** 6/23/1973 in Wolfeboro
Peter M. of Tuftonboro m. Michelle L. **Gelinas** of New Durham
7/24/1999

SARGENT,

Clarence Harold of Tuftonboro m. Doris Hazel **Mack** of Tuftonboro 6/22/1932 in Ctr. Sandwich; H – 27, farmer, b. Moultonboro, s/o Jesse Sargent (Kezar Falls, ME, farmer) and Ida E. Rogers (Moultonboro, housewife); W – 18, at home, b. New Hampton, d/o George Free. Mack (Sandwich, laborer) and Dora L. Bragg (Moultonboro, housewife)

David W. of Tuftonboro m. Margaret B. **Wiesner** of Tamworth 10/27/2001

Fred Elwin of Tuftonboro m. Joan **Baker** of Wolfeboro 7/30/1955 in Wolfeboro; H – 20, truck driver, b. NH, s/o Harold C. Sargent (NH) and Doris Mack (NH); W – 20, presser, b. NH, d/o Howard P. Baker (NH) and Hazel E. Adjutant (NH)

John F. of Tuftonboro m. Etta M. **Davis** of Tuftonboro 3/24/1907 in Tuftonboro; H – 24, farmer, b. Somerville, MA, s/o John C. Sargent and Mary Keating; W – 38, housekeeper, 2nd, b. Maysville, ME, d/o Levi W. Ladd and Miranda A. Mills

SAUNDERS,

Howard N. m. Priscilla **Hodges** 2/14/1978 in Moultonboro

SAUTER,

Scott T. of Fairbanks, AK m. Cheryl J. **Beane** of Fairbanks, AK 6/19/1983

SAWYER,

George W. of Tuftonboro m. Nellie V. **Moore** of Salem, MA 5/8/1913 in Tuftonboro; H – 75, farmer, 2nd, b. Porter, ME, s/o Lemuel Sawyer and Mary Berry; W – 56, nurse, 2nd, b. Marblehead, MA, d/o John H. Shattuck and Sarah A. Wilford

Michael Patrick of Tuftonboro m. Chris Alice **Barrett** of Tuftonboro 2/7/1992

Richard Bangs of Tuftonboro m. Clara Ellen **Brown** of Wolfeboro 10/18/1996

SCHAFER,

Dennis R. m. Natalie A. **Hebden** 9/29/1973 in Tuftonboro

SCHAIT,

Harold P. m. Evelyn M. **Metzger** 7/15/1978 in Tuftonboro

SCHOU,
George Dewey of Tuftonboro m. Virginia M. **Muldoon** of Tuftonboro
    4/14/1979
Thomas Kirk of Reading, MA m. Valdirene **De Almeida** of Reading,
    MA 3/22/1997

SCOTT,
John R. of Boxford, MA m. Jean W. **Spencer** of Tuftonboro 5/1/1982
Richard C. of Manchester, MA m. Deborah M. **Russell** of
    Manchester, MA 8/27/1988

SEDLER,
Philip D. of Haverhill, MA m. Elizabeth S. **Corning** of Haverhill, MA
    9/22/1990

SENIOR,
Walter, Jr. of Melvin Village m. Mavis A. **Keith** of Ossipee 2/24/1940
    in Ctr. Ossipee; H – 21, at school, b. Medway, MA, s/o Walter
    M. Senior (WV, mfgr.) and Helen G. Ayers (Winchester, MA,
    housewife); W – 21, at home, b. Needham, MA, d/o Malcolm
    Keith (Needham, MA, salesman) and Alleyne Jennings
    (Brighton, MA)

SEVERANCE,
Brian of Tuftonboro m. Marcia J. **Richardson** of Northwood
    6/17/1967 in Northwood; H – 24, USA, b. Brookline, MA, s/o
    Roland Severance (MA) and Katherine M. Mackey (MA); W –
    22, secretary, b. Concord, d/o John P. Richardson (ME) and
    Evelyn A. Smith (NH)

SEYMOUR,
Scott Arvid of Tuftonboro m. Lynn Marie **Gordon** of Tuftonboro
    8/14/1993

SHAFFER,
Aaron K. of York, PA m. Jessica Y. **Locke** of Tuftonboro 7/28/2001

SHAFTO,
Donald B. m. Barbara H. **Neilson** 6/30/1974 in Tuftonboro

SHANNON,

Carl F. m. Corrine J. **Dubel** 7/3/1969 in Wolfeboro; H – b. 8/6/1946 in MA, s/o Carl H. Shannon and Nellie Piper; W – b. 10/19/1950 in CT, d/o Charles P. Dubel and Marian Savage

Carroll Lee of Tuftonboro m. Madeline Elizabeth **Whittemore** of Wolfeboro 10/1/1954 in Wolfeboro; H – 24, poultry, b. NH, s/o Edward Shannon (NH) and Marion Haley (NH); W – 28, office, 2nd, divorced, b. NH, d/o Roy Foster (MA) and Florence Rollins (NH)

Edward A. of Tuftonboro m. Marion H. **Haley** of Tuftonboro 5/28/1921 in Tuftonboro; H – 40, lumberman, 2nd, b. Alton, s/o Stephen Shannon (Alton) and Sarah Rollins (Wolfeboro); W – 15, at home, b. Tuftonboro, d/o George H. Haley (Moultonboro) and Edith C. Ayers (Tuftonboro)

Guy E. of Tuftonboro m. Marie L. **Wiggin** of Ossipee 11/18/1950 in Moultonville; H – 24, state emp., b. NH, s/o Edward Shannon (NH) and Marion Haley (NH); W – 18, at home, b. NH, d/o Shirley W. Wiggin (NH) and Ethel Harmon (NH)

Guy E. m. Elaine M. **Thompson** 5/11/1974 in Conway

Richard S. of Wolfeboro m. Pern S. **Bean** of Tuftonboro 8/24/1946 in Wolfeboro; H – 35, caretaker, b. S. Wolfeboro, s/o Elando Shannon and Gladys M. Kimball; W – 45, cook, b. Moultonboro, d/o Jesse Sargent (Porter, ME) and Ida E. Rogers (Moultonboro)

SHAPIRO,

Peter C. of Wickford, RI m. Sandra D. **Edwards** of Wickford, RI 8/25/1984

SHARPLES,

William Waln of Tuftonboro m. Coren Veronica **Denningham** of New York City, NY 8/19/1995

SHEPARD,

James T. of Tuftonboro m. Lillian N. **Bergeron** of Tuftonboro 5/29/1998

Robert Lane of Cleveland, OH m. Phyllis **Allen** of MA 6/16/1951 in Melvin Village; H – 24, student, b. OH, s/o Robert O. Shepard (OH) and Marjorie Lane; W – 22, at home, b. RI, d/o Horace R. Allen (MA) and Lena Holman (MA)

SHERMAN,
Steven M. of Harwich Port, MA m. Tina L. **Palmieri** of Harwich Port,
MA 8/3/1990

SHURE,
Donald D. m. Fae Anne **Engel** 9/17/1978 in Tuftonboro

SIMMONS,
Scott D. of Tuftonboro m. Linda A. **Carroll** of Wolfeboro 9/20/1990

SINGER,
Arthur L., Jr. of NY m. Joan **Cristal** of WI 7/26/1952 in Tuftonboro; H
– 23, US Navy, b. PA, s/o Arthur L. Singer (NY) and Isabel
Cocoran (NY); W – serv. represent., b. OH, d/o Philip N. Cristal
(KY) and Romalo E. Johnson (IL)

SINGLETON,
Randall G. of Tuftonboro m. Norma C. **Cabezas** of Tuftonboro
3/29/1980

SKEY,
Joseph Edward of Haddonfield, NJ m. Carrie Ann **Johnston** of
Haddonfield, NJ 7/9/1997

SKINNER,
Herbert I. of Tuftonboro m. Marion P. **Eldridge** of Tuftonboro
6/30/1920 in Tuftonboro; H – 20, chauffeur, b. Brighton, MA, s/o
Walter W. Skinner (Biddeford, ME) and Cora I. Thomas
(Quincy, MA); W – 15, scholar, b. Tuftonboro, d/o Dana
Eldridge (Ossipee) and Susie A. Wiggin (Tuftonboro)
William L. m. Marion T. **Gough** 8/20/1942 in Tamworth; H – 26, US
Army, b. Boston, MA, s/o Walter W. Skinner (Biddeford, ME,
caretaker) and Cora I. Thomas (Quincy, MA, housewife); W –
24, school teacher, b. Cranston, RI, d/o Donald A. Gough
(Newfoundland, clerk) and Theresa Main (Stonington, CT,
housewife)

SKORUPSKI,
Frank Baltas of MA m. Marion Frances **Lawless** of Tuftonboro
10/6/1956 in Wolfeboro; H – 30, salesman, b. MA, s/o Baltas
Skorupski (Poland) and Rose C. Kozacyka (Poland); W – 31,

secretary, b. MA, d/o Frank J. Lawless (NJ) and Mabel V. Gilmartin (NY)

SMITH,
Brett Allen of N. Reading, MA m. Christina Theresa **Myers** of N. Reading, MA 9/20/1997
Clifton Edward of Tuftonboro m. Bertha May **Riley** of Ossipee 7/14/1932 in Ctr. Ossipee; H – 22, laborer, b. Cliftondale, MA, s/o James William Smith (Lowell, MA, laborer) and Abbie L. Smith (NS, housekeeper); W – 18, at home, b. Poland, ME, d/o Henry Franklin Riley (Bridgeton, ME, laborer) and Abbie Louise Brown (Poland, ME, housewife)
Edward Leroy of Tuftonboro m. Madaline Delorus **Bean** of Tuftonboro 3/22/1958 in Plainfield; H – 21, Air Force, b. NH, s/o Arthur B. Smith (NH) and Orra E. Smith (NH); W – 21, at home, b. MA, d/o Frank J. Bean, Sr. (NH) and Mary F. Bourque (MA)
Richard James of Tuftonboro m. Anita Ruth **Pinard** of Ossipee 9/19/1959 in Tamworth; H – 21, laborer, b. NH, s/o Arthur B. Smith (NH) and Orra E. Moulton (NH); W – 33, stitcher, divorced, b. MA, d/o Maurice A. Osgood (NH) and Frances E. Zimmer (MA)
Richard L. of Tuftonboro m. Jo-Ann E. **Hill** of Ossipee 9/3/1960 in Ossipee; H – 21, construction, b. NH, s/o Walter R. Smith (NH) and Doris H. Mack (NH); W – 17, waitress, b. NH, d/o Waldo L. Hill (NH) and Ann B. Eastman (NH)
Richard Leroy of Tuftonboro m. June Patricia **Fortin** of Belmont 3/15/1997
Walter C. of Rochester m. Shirley A. **Bean** of Tuftonboro 7/14/1945 in Melvin Village; H – 20, US Navy, b. Waterboro, ME, s/o Walter C. Smith (Waterboro, ME) and Addie M. Johnson (Waterboro, ME); W – 17, at home, b. Peterboro, d/o Philip N. Bean (Rindge) and Aldora M. Gelinas (Athol, MA)
Walter R. of Tuftonboro m. Doris H. **Sargent** of Tuftonboro 8/14/1940 in Moultonville; H – 32, caretaker, 2nd, b. Farmington, s/o James W. Smith (Lowell, MA, deceased) and Abby L. Smith (NS, housekeeper); W – 26, housekeeper, 2nd, b. N. Hampton, d/o George F. Mack (Sandwich, deceased) and Dora E. Bragg (Moultonboro, housewife)
Walter Roy m. Cora Emma **Stillings** 2/23/1934 in Brookline, MA; H – 26, laborer, b. Farmington, s/o James W. Smith (Lowell, MA, laborer) and Abbie L. Smith (Barrington, NS, housekeeper); W

– 25, at home, b. Ossipee, d/o Frank O. Stillings (Alton, farmer) and Kate M. Stillings (Tuftonboro, housewife)

SNOW,
Stephen D. of Tuftonboro m. Ann **Robinson** of Tuftonboro 9/5/1981

SNYDER,
Robert D. m. Nancy L. **Brenner** 8/17/1973 in Tuftonboro

SOLOMON,
Arthur F., Jr. of Manchester m. Patricia C. **Devork** of Tuftonboro 6/19/1962 in Wolfeboro; H – 17, student, b. Laconia, s/o Arthur F. Solomon (NH) and Beatrix Honeyman (NY); W – 15, student, b. Wolfeboro, d/o Anthony Devork (OH) and Grace Dale (England)

SONCRANT,
David Lucien of Trenton, NJ m. Judith W. **Buchanan** of Tuftonboro 5/9/1964 in Wolfeboro; H – 22, Navy, b. Wyandotte, MI, s/o James M. Soncrant, Sr. (MI) and Eugenia T. Johann (NJ); W – 21, student, b. Manhattan, NY, d/o Robert W. Buchanan (NY) and Margaret Lockwood (NJ)

SOUTHARD,
Gary S. of Tuftonboro m. Heidi L. **Gruner** of Moultonborough 12/29/1984

SPENCER,
DeForest of MN m. Jean Wilkin **Chandler** of MN 10/12/1951 in Melvin Village; H – 29, lawyer, b. MN, s/o DeForest Spencer (MN) and Cornell B. Patterson (MN); W – 26, artist, b. PA, d/o Hugh Wilkin (England) and Elizabeth K. Crawford (PA)
Philip K. of Wolfeboro m. Karen A. **Chase** of Tuftonboro 10/9/1982

STACK,
Arthur Edward of Silver Spring, MD m. Dorothy Currell **Tucker** of Wolfeboro 8/30/1980

STACY,
Martin Hartly of Huntsville, AL m. Barbara Joan **Linnell** of Tuftonboro 8/26/1967 in Wolfeboro; H – 23, mec. eng., b. York

Beach, ME, s/o Francis M. Stacy (ME) and Arlene Littlefield
(ME); W – 22, dress designer, b. Winchester, MA, d/o Donald J.
Linnell (CT) and Virginia Taylor (MA)

STANDYCK,
James P. of Tuftonboro m. Charlene E. **Haggerty** of Tuftonboro
9/20/2003

STANLEY,
Donald C., Jr. of Tuftonboro m. Roxanna **Haven** of MA 11/26/1960
in MA; H – 28, mar. const., b. NJ, s/o Donald C. Stanley, Sr.
and Sara Hixson; W – 25, at home, b. MA, d/o Franklin K.
Haven and Elizabeth Carpenter
Donald Carleton of Mirror Lake m. Mary Benedict **King** of Darien,
CT 7/1/1958 in CT; H – 61, retired, 3rd, b. Portland, ME, s/o
James M. Stanley and Caroline W. Zelie; W – 53, housewife,
2nd, b. Glendale, OH, d/o Charles C. Benedict and Ella C. Bell

STANTON,
Michael John of W. Newton, MA m. Jessica Elsa **D'Ercole** of W.
Newton, MA 9/9/1995

STAPLES,
Charles F. m. Virginia D. **Willard** 4/8/1929 in Wolfeboro; H – 25,
farmer, 2nd, b. Wolfeboro, s/o Frank G. Staples (Ossipee) and
Ina F. Piper (Tuftonboro); W – 18, at home, b. Alton, d/o Smith
A. Willard (Alton) and Sadie E. Lamper (Alton)
Christopher W. m. Ada F. **Keniston** 11/29/1928 in Wolfeboro; H –
27, laborer, b. Tuftonboro, s/o Frank G. Staples (Ossipee) and
Ina F. Piper (Tuftonboro); W – 26, housekeeper, b.
Sanbornville, d/o Cyrus Keniston (Effingham) and Rosabelle
Taylor (Canada)
Frank of Tuftonboro m. Ina F. **Piper** of Tuftonboro 9/13/1898 in
Melvin Village; H – 32, farmer, b. Ossipee, s/o Christopher
Staples and Julia A. Templeton; W – 15, housekeeper, b.
Tuftonboro, d/o George G. Piper and Etta A. Piper
Frank of Tuftonboro m. Annie **Conley** of Boston, MA 10/25/1911 in
Wakefield; H – 41, farmer, 2nd, b. Ossipee, s/o Christopher
Staples and Julia A. Templeton; W – 41, housewife, b. Galway,
Ireland, d/o Matthias Conley and Mary Rixley

STARRETT,
Raymond Eugene of Tuftonboro m. Nancy Nelson **Rich** of
Tuftonboro 11/8/1959 in Wolfeboro; H – 24, elec. tech., b. MA,
s/o Clarence H. Starrett (MA) and France Hawes (MA); W – 18,
student, b. NH, d/o Nelson B. Rich (MA) and Alberta L. Pigon
(MA)

STAVE,
Richard James of Hamden, CT m. Jeanne Elizabeth **Drowne** of
Tuftonboro 2/20/1965 in Plymouth; H – 23, cook, b. Hamden,
CT, s/o Edward A. Stave (NJ) and Edna May Zulauf (NJ); W –
19, b. Newport, RI, d/o Vernon Eaton Drowne (MA) and Doris
Elizabeth Thayer (MA)

STEADMAN,
Kenton E., Jr. of Tuftonboro m. Loretta A. **Bilodeau** of Wolfeboro
9/19/1959 in Wolfeboro; H – 22, electrician, b. MA, s/o Kenton
E. Steadman (MA) and Ethelyn L. MacFaddzean (Canada); W
– 19, secretary, b. NH, d/o Joseph Bilodeau (Canada) and
Dorothy Valley (NH)

STEIN,
Alfred H. of New York City m. Flor. **Dinkelmeyer** of Jamaica, NY
5/31/1940 in Tuftonboro; H – 37, teacher, b. New York City, s/o
Harry J. Stein (New York City, piano maker) and Martha
Perkatinat (New York City, housewife); W – 28, teacher, b. New
York City, d/o John Dinkelmeyer (New York City, lithographer)
and Amelia Jansen (New York City, housewife)

STEINBACH,
Gary T. of Tuftonboro m. Kerry L. **McGrath** of Tuftonboro 7/5/2002

STETSON,
Frederick W., II m. Mary Esther C. **Treat** 9/21/1974 in Tuftonboro

STEVENS,
Raymond L. m. Mary E. **Upjohn** 8/8/1976 in Tuftonboro

STICKLE,

William W. m. Marjorie **Lester** 6/6/1970 in Wolfeboro; H – b. 1/4/1909 in OH, s/o Ralph Stickle and Flora G. Whittier; W – b. 6/14/1921 in MA, d/o William H. Wood and Inez Patterson

STILLINGS,

Charles H. of Tuftonboro m. Lula **Moody** of Wolfeboro 1/15/1905 in Ossipee; H – 50, carpenter, b. Ossipee, s/o Ivory Stillings and Lydia Wentworth; W – 22, housewife, b. Wolfeboro, d/o Charles Moody and Bell Berry

George E. m. Beatrice M. **Sleeper** 5/9/1929 in Moultonville; H – 21, truck driver, b. Tuftonboro, s/o Charles H. Stillings (Ossipee) and Luella Moody (Wolfeboro); W – 23, at home, b. Milton, d/o Fred Sleeper (Milton) and Stella Dacy (Union)

STITT,

Albert T. of Tuftonboro m. Winnie M. **McIntire** of Tuftonboro 4/20/1892 in Tuftonboro; H – 25, farming, b. Boston, s/o James Stitt (England, baker) and Ellen H. Stitt (Portland, ME, housewife); W – 15, housework, b. Tuftonboro, d/o Orrin D. McIntire (Tuftonboro, farmer) and Emma McIntire (Tuftonboro, housewife)

STOCK,

James S. of Wolfeboro m. Hazel F. **Tupeck** of Tuftonboro 6/24/1961 in Wolfeboro; H – 21, laborer, b. MO, s/o Albert P. Stock (MO) and Elizabeth Sargent (MO); W – 18, at home, b. Ossipee, d/o Henry Tupeck (NH) and Caroline Nudd (NH)

STOCKMAN,

Brian A. of Tuftonboro m. Judy M. **Mixer** of Tuftonboro 9/28/1985

Brian A. of Tuftonboro m. Mary B. **Grasse** of Tuftonboro 10/27/2001

Frank, Jr. of Tuftonboro m. Muriel **MacWilliams** of Tuftonboro 10/3/1948 in Tuftonboro; H – 27, agriculturist, b. Newton, MA, s/o Frank L. Stockman (Newton, MA) and Doris R. Lucas (Newton, MA); W – 21, at home, b. Tuftonboro, d/o Roger L. Williams (Brockton, MA) and Berenice Lawrence (Lynn, MA)

Gary P. m. Jennifer M. **Kalled** 9/30/1978 in Tuftonboro

Gary P. of Tuftonboro m. Tracy A. **Kelley** of Tuftonboro 2/14/2005

James A. m. Patricia A. **Fogarty** 7/17/1976 in Tuftonboro

John L. m. Patricia A. **Rico** 6/21/1969 in Tuftonboro; H – b.
1/25/1952 in NH, s/o Frank L. Stockman, Jr. and Muriel
Williams; W – b. 1/3/195 2in NH, d/o Peter A. Rico and Thelma
Holmes
John L. of Tuftonboro m. Melody Lynn **Hatton** of Moultonboro
9/27/1980
Philip A. of Tuftonboro m. Jean C. **Peaslee** of N. Sandwich
10/23/1949 in Tuftonboro; H – 23, farmer, b. MA, s/o Frank L.
Stockman (MA) and Doris R. Lucas (MA); W – 16, at home, b.
NH, d/o Ralph Q. Peaslee (NH) and Mary E. Moody (NH)
Philip A. m. Nancy A. **Wilson** 5/20/1972 in Tuftonboro
William L. of Tuftonboro m. Kathleen A. **Smith** of Tuftonboro
7/7/1984

STOKES,
Frank W. of Tuftonboro m. Ellen C. **Fox** of Wolfeboro 6/12/1907 in
Wolfeboro; H – 28, carpenter, b. Tuftonboro, s/o Benjamin F.
Stokes and Lydia B. Remick; W – 26, housekeeper, b.
Wolfeboro, d/o William C. Fox and Elizabeth A. Burbank

STRAW,
Carroll Wilton m. Charlotte Gertrude **Howe** 11/30/1933 in Wolfeboro;
H – 25, truck driver, b. Tuftonboro, s/o George D. Straw
(Tuftonboro, mail carrier) and Minnie E. Abbott (Sandwich,
housekeeper); W – 28, at home, b. Attleboro, MA, d/o Carlton
L. Howe (Southboro, MA, carpenter) and Ina Maud Cordeau
(Marlboro, MA, housewife)
David G., Jr. of Moultonboro m. Sandra E. **Smith** of Tuftonboro
2/18/1967 in Tuftonboro; H – 18, laborer, b. Manchester, s/o
David G. Straw, Sr. (NH) and Hazel M. Berry (NH); W – 16, at
home, b. Wolfeboro, d/o Arthur B. Smith (NH) and Ora E.
Moulton (NH)
Francis G. of Tuftonboro m. Lois H. **Conrad** of Waverly, MA
11/9/1923 in Meredith; H – 20, electrical engineer, b.
Tuftonboro, s/o George D. Straw (Tuftonboro) and Minnie E.
Abbott (Sandwich); W – 26, nurse, 2nd, b. Manchester, NS, d/o
John H. Hart (Manchester, NS) and Maud Roberts (Canso, NS)
George D. of Tuftonboro m. Minnie E. **Abbott** of Sandwich
10/15/1900 in Tuftonboro; H – 25, laborer, b. Tuftonboro, s/o
Francis Straw and Lizzie Hoyt; W – 22, housekeeper, b.
Sandwich, d/o Reuben F. Abbott and Abbie Tappan

Harry S. of Tuftonboro m. Hattie F. **Bean** of Tuftonboro 12/31/1902 in Tuftonboro; H – 30, laborer, b. Tuftonboro, s/o Francis Straw and Mary E. Hoyt; W – 26, housekeeper, b. Tuftonboro, d/o James F. Bean and Mary F. Bean

Robert William m. Barbara Edith **Drucker** 10/17/1936 in Melvin Village; H – 25, caretaker, b. Mirror Lake, s/o Harry E. Straw (Tuftonboro, caretaker) and Hattie F. Bean (Ctr. Tuftonboro, housekeeper); W – 21, at home, b. Derry, d/o Ralph W. Drucker (Londonderry, electrician) and Lela M. Staniels (Hillsboro Bridge, t. room prop.)

STROBRIDGE,
Edward P. m. Edna I. **Ordway** 7/1/1931 in Laconia; H – 23, student, b. Woodsville, s/o Fred H. Strobridge (Cookshire, PQ) and Annie Parks (Sherbrook, PQ); W – 27, teacher, b. Dover, d/o John L. Ordway (Castine, ME) and Margaret Sprague (Skowhegan, ME)

STURGEON,
Christopher J. of Tuftonboro m. Leslie A. **Davis** of Moultonborough 5/23/1987

SWAIN,
Robert W. of Norwalk, CT m. Barbara J. **Smith** of Norwalk, CT 8/2/1986

SWEENEY,
Thomas W., Jr. m. Janet J. **Senecal** 6/15/1974 in Tuftonboro

SWENDSON,
Guy Lindsey of Tampa, FL m. Donna Mary **Case** of NJ 7/27/1960 in Tuftonboro; H – 20, US Navy, b. FL, s/o August Swendson (Denmark) and Guilda L. Cadden (FL); W – 21, at home, b. CA, d/o Donald Case (England) and Marie Austin

SWIFT,
Thomas R. of Tuftonboro m. Mary E. **D'Eri** of Tuftonboro 11/20/2005

TAYLOR,
Louis A. of Tuftonboro m. Nancy A. **McLaughlin** of Tuftonboro 12/2/1990

Timothy A. of Savannah, GA m. Patricia A. **Milligan** of Tuftonboro
11/24/1984

TENNEY,
Michael W. of Ossipee m. Heather M. **Curtis** of Tuftonboro
6/25/1988

TEPE,
Gary Joseph of Tuftonboro m. Diane Kaye **Herter** of Tuftonboro
7/18/1992

TERRY,
Robert W. of Tuftonboro m. Lois **Dyer** of Palm Springs, FL
7/19/1980

THAYER,
Bruce Campbell m. Pamela Rae **Jenness** 8/1/1970 in Rochester; H
– b. 1/22/1947 in MA, s/o Gordon Thayer and Ann Campbell; W
– b. 9/16/1948 in NH, d/o Raymond Jenness and Pauline
Bellemeur

THERIAULT,
David A. of Tuftonboro m. Janet L. **Thomas** of Tuftonboro 5/24/1997

THOMAS,
Chester I. m. Effie A. **Thomas** 10/27/1926 in Cambridge, MA; H –
30, farmer, s/o Willie W. Thomas (Tuftonboro) and Lillian E.
McIntyre (Tuftonboro); W – 19, stenographer, d/o Frederic I.
Thomas (Medford, MA) and Eliza A. Young (Cambridge, MA)
Lloyd H., III of Atlanta, GA m. Carol Ann **Graham** of Marietta, GA
8/15/1992
Willie W. of Tuftonboro m. Mabel L. **Hodgdon** of Tuftonboro
6/1/1905 in Ctr. Tuftonboro; H – 43, farmer, b. Tuftonboro, s/o
William Thomas and Nancy Libby; W – 22, housewife, b. Ctr.
Ossipee, d/o Charles Hodgdon and Eunice Swazey

THOMPSON,
Adam L. of Tuftonboro m. Rhonda Lynn **Mandigo** of Tuftonboro
5/7/1994
Asa B. of Tuftonboro m. Carrie A. **Frost** of Wolfeboro 9/3/1922 in
Wolfeboro; H – 70, farmer, b. Tuftonboro, s/o Washington

Thompson (Tuftonboro) and Joanna Beacham (Ossipee); W –
42, school teacher, b. Wolfeboro, d/o Herbert Frost (Wolfeboro)
and Annie E. Burleigh (Tuftonboro)
Douglas R. of Azores, Portugal m. Ana Rosa T. **Vieira** of Azores,
Portugal 6/26/1984
John T. of Tuftonboro m. Margaret M. **Foote** of Lowell, MA
6/19/1904 in Ossipee; H – 28, farmer, b. Tuftonboro, s/o
Theodore Thompson and Rosa Tibbetts; W – 28, housekeeper,
2nd, b. Lowell, MA, d/o Warren S. Foote and Mattie Swaine
Lester of Melvin Village m. Edna M. **Nudd** of Ctr. Sandwich
5/18/1940 in Ctr. Harbor; H – 27, truck driver, b. Tuftonboro, s/o
Simon Thompson (Tuftonboro, caretaker) and Evelyn Bean
(Tuftonboro, deceased); W – 20, housework, b. Ctr. Sandwich,
d/o Wallace Nudd (Ctr. Sandwich, painter) and Blanche LeClair
(Northfield, VT, housewife)
Moses of Tuftonboro m. Ella E. **Plummer** of Tuftonboro 12/1/1894 in
Tuftonboro; H – 67, farmer, 2nd, b. Tuftonboro, s/o Theodore
Thompson (York, ME, farmer) and Mary Thompson (Kittery,
ME, housewife); W – 36, housewife, b. Tuftonboro, d/o Joseph
F. Plummer (farmer) and Rosetta Plummer (housewife)
Richard B. of Tuftonboro m. JoAnn E. **Smith** of Ossipee 7/12/1964
in Melvin Village; H – 22, lumberman, b. NH, s/o Lester
Thompson (NH) and Edna Nudd (NH); W – 21, card operator,
2nd, divorced, b. NH, d/o Waldo L. Hill (NH) and Anna Eastman
(NH)
Ronald S. of Tuftonboro m. Khristine A. **Guilfoyle** of Tuftonboro
9/29/1990
Simon T. of Tuftonboro m. Evelyn L. **Bean** of Tuftonboro 1/2/1907 in
Tuftonboro; H – 21, farmer, b. Tuftonboro, s/o Simon B.
Thompson and Lizzie Browning; W – 17, housewife, b.
Tuftonboro, d/o Willie L. Bean and Ula D. Foss
Simon T. m. Cecil **Morris** 4/26/1927 in Wolfeboro; H – 41, farmer,
2nd, b. Tuftonboro, s/o Simon B. Thompson (Tuftonboro) and
Lizzie Browning (NS); W – 26, at home, b. Tuftonboro, d/o
Alfred Morris (Canada) and Hattie J. Buzzell (Meredith)

THURSTON,
Scott M. of Wolfeboro m. Barbara J. **Anderson** of Tuftonboro
8/25/1990

TILTON,
Clifford Howard, Jr. of Ctr. Ossipee m. Marylynn Janet **Bean** of
Tuftonboro 2/9/1956 in Melvin Village; H – 23, florist, b. NH, s/o
Clifford H. Tilton (NH) and Leora A. Thurston (NH); W – 20,
nurses' aide, b. MA, d/o Frank John Bean (NH) and Mary F.
Bourque (MA)

TIMMERMAN,
Micheal A. of Brookline, MA m. Anita **Belt** of Brookline, MA
9/12/1987

TOMB,
William C. m. Mrilyn L. **Stowe** 10/7/1978 in Tuftonboro

TOWLE,
Francis S. of Wakefield m. Marjorie L. **Lincoln** of Tuftonboro
6/14/1986

TOWNSEND,
James H. m. Kathy D. **Chase** 6/17/1978 in Tuftonboro
Paul H. of Waltham, MA m. Lori Jean **Harriman** of Waltham, MA
10/8/1988

TRAVERS,
Peter G. of Wolfeboro m. Cheryl M. **Bonus** of Tuftonboro 7/27/2001

TROY,
William Joseph, III of New York, NY m. Laura Marie **Barnhill** of New
York, NY 9/2/1989

TRYDER,
William M. B., III m. Julie S. **Hobart** 5/27/1972 in Tuftonboro

TUCKER,
Carroll W. m. Ethelyn S. **Arsenault** 7/11/1928 in Wolfeboro; H – 23,
clerk, b. Alexandria, s/o Everett Tucker (Alexandria) and Lizzie
M. Ferrin (Alexandria); W – 29, housekeeper, 2nd, b.
Tuftonboro, d/o Fred Osborne and Lena Shannon (Tuftonboro)

TUOHIG,
Barry A. m. Gail M. **Meadows** 1/26/1974 in Manchester

TUPECK,
Henry Steven of Tuftonboro m. Caroline T. **Grolas** of Tuftonboro
  8/11/1944 in Melvin Village; H – 20, farmer, b. Ossipee, s/o
  Steve Tupeck (Russia, timberjack) and Bernice Ayers
  (Tuftonboro, housewife); W – 26, cook, 2nd, b. Ctr. Sandwich,
  d/o Wallace Nudd (Ctr. Sandwich, painter) and Blanche
  LeClaire (Ctr. Sandwich, housewife)
Russell Everett of Tuftonboro m. Joan Isabelle **Bunny** of Medford,
  MA 6/7/1953 in Medford, MA; H – 20, construction worker, b.
  Tuftonboro, s/o Steve Tupeck and Bernice Ayers; W – 17, at
  home, b. Medford, MA, d/o Cyrus Bunny and Isabelle Nadeau
Russell G. m. Bernadette M. **Johnson** 12/3/1977 in Wolfeboro
Stephen C. m. Stephanie **Tripp** 6/29/1975 in Wolfeboro

URQUHART,
Kenneth N. m. Mary Ann **Stockman** 1/12/1975 in Moultonboro
Roderick m. Helen **Bottomley** 5/15/1977 in Brookfield

VALLIER,
Myron Durgin m. Muriel Helen **Downing** 10/26/1935 in Laconia; H –
  23, oil field worker, b. Swampscott, MA, s/o Myron Vallier and
  Amy C. Durgin (Lynn, MA, ant. dealer); W – 20, waitress, b.
  Meredith, d/o James S. Downing (Gilmanton, laborer) and Lela
  B. Avery (Campton, at home)

VAN ROOY,
Frank of Sacramento, CA m. Sharlene Ann **Rice** of Tuftonboro
  10/27/1979

VARNEY,
Fenton W. of Tuftonboro m. Ivena F. M. **Bushman** of Tuftonboro
  6/18/1988

VELD,
Richard P. of Tuftonboro m. Valerie A. **Taylor** of Tuftonboro
  9/24/2005

VINCENTI,
Edward Charles of Tuftonboro m. Ellen **Reynolds** of Tuftonboro
  12/15/2000

VILDERS,
Neil R. of Tuftonboro m. Anne C. **Swanick** of Tuftonboro 1/5/1985

VITTUM,
James M. of Tuftonboro m. Jamie Lynn **Lampron** of Wolfeboro
    2/22/1991

WAHLE,
Thomas G. of Florissant, MO m. Lynn M. **Bolling** of Tuftonboro
    10/3/1987

WAITE,
James E. of Tuftonboro m. Estella A. **Croft** of Tuftonboro 12/4/1913
    in Tuftonboro; H – 28, laborer, b. PEI, s/o Charles H. Waite and
    Julia A. Bets; W – 24, housewife, 2nd, b. PEI, d/o Thomas Silliter
    and Annie M. Frost

WAKEFIELD,
George H. of Wolfeboro m. Ruth E. **Smith** of Tuftonboro 12/18/1957
    in Wolfeboro; H – 37, construction, 2nd, divorced, b. NH, s/o
    William H. Wakefield (Canada) and Bessie Canning (NS); W –
    58, housewife, 2nd, divorced, b. NH, d/o Roscoe Adjutant (NH)
    and Blanche Perkins (NH)
Leonard R. m. Terry **Keniston** 10/18/1975 in Wolfeboro

WALKER,
Horace A. of Tuftonboro m. Carrie L. **Wentworth** of Moultonboro
    11/24/1894 in Tuftonboro; H – 24, hotel keeper, b. Richmond,
    ME, s/o Albert H. Walker (Tuftonboro, mechanic) and Arabine
    W. Walker (Durham, ME, housewife); W – 25, teacher, b.
    Moultonboro, d/o Clark Wentworth (Tuftonboro, mechanic) and
    Elizabeth C. Wentworth (VT, housewife)
Horace Albert of Tuftonboro m. Ada Lela **Johnson** of Nashua
    6/11/1918 in Manchester; H – 48, laborer, 2nd, b. Richmond,
    ME, s/o Albert H. Walker and Arabine Wright; W – 31,
    bookkeeper, b. Alfred, ME, d/o Parker S. Johnson and Ada F.
    Brown
Jeffrey H. of Tuftonboro m. Jennifer S. **Fraser** of Tuftonboro
    7/12/1992
Jeffrey H. of Tuftonboro m. Julie R. **Labbe** of Tuftonboro 9/10/2005

WARD,
Britton Nash of Medway, MA m. Elizabeth Anne **Fiore** of Medway, MA 8/3/1997

WASSON,
Andrew m. Mildred Elizabeth **Haley** 2/10/1937 in Farmington; H – 20, clerk, b. Ossipee, s/o Joseph S. Wasson (NB, mill man) and Josephine Colby (Ossipee, deceased); W – 18, student, b. Wolfeboro, d/o Willis Irving Haley (Tuftonboro, deceased) and Bernece Ethel Dow (Moultonboro, housewife)

Harry A. of Wolfeboro m. Margueritt A. **Campbell** of Wolfeboro 8/23/1900 in Tuftonboro; H – 23, school teacher, b. Quincy, MA, s/o T. Henry Wasson and Anna W. Alexander; W – 24, b. Brooklyn, NY, d/o Michael Campbell

WATSON,
Alfred O. of Tuftonboro m. Edna **Kenney** of Tuftonboro 12/25/1907 in Tuftonboro; H – 21, farmer, b. Tuftonboro, s/o George G. Watson and Armina G. Elliott; W – 17, housewife, d/o James Kenney

Reginald M. of Tuftonboro m. Grace E. **Lord** of Newbury, VT 1/25/1923 in Wolfeboro; H – 19, laborer, b. Tuftonboro, s/o Nathaniel P. Watson (Meredith) and Gertrude E. Elliott (Tuftonboro); W – 20, school teacher, b. Groton, VT, d/o P. A. Lund (Barton, VT) and Eliza Emery (Groton, VT)

WAY,
John Richard of Rochester, NY m. Jean Marie **Lampert** of Bethesda, MD 7/30/1966 in Melvin Village; H – 24, student, b. Chicago, IL, s/o John S. Way (IL) and Elva Donnell (IA); W – 22, student, b. Washington, DC, d/o Chester G. Lampert (IL) and Emily F. Schuback (IL)

WEBSTER,
Steven W. m. Marjorie M. **Tweedell** 12/18/1976 in Tuftonboro

WEEKS,
Charles E. of Tuftonboro m. Susan H. **Ramsbotham** of Tuftonboro 8/24/1985

Colin E. m. Bonnie Day **Hunter** 8/28/1971 in Tuftonboro

WELCH,
George of Tuftonboro m. Annice C. **Melloon** of Moultonboro
11/14/1923 in Tuftonboro; H – 63, farmer, 2nd, b.
Tuftonboro, s/o Andrew Welch (Tuftonboro) and Jane Thompson
(Tuftonboro); W – 61, housewife, 3rd, b. Moultonboro, d/o
William H. Horne (Moultonboro) and Julia A. Wallace
(Sandwich)
Lisle R. of Tuftonboro m. Norma **Colby** of Ctr. Ossipee 7/15/1950 in
Moultonville; H – 24, lumber, b. NH, s/o Maurice P. Welch (NH)
and Blanche L. Emery (NH); W – 18, nursemaid, b. NH, d/o
Plummer A. Colby (NH) and Etta Bean (NH)

WENCK,
James H. of Cocoanut Grove, FL m. Mary J. **Button** of Newtown,
CT 8/21/1982

WENDALL,
John R. of Tuftonboro m. Sarah Jane **Ayers** of Tuftonboro 6/4/1905
in Wakefield; H – 60, farmer, 3rd, b. Tuftonboro, s/o George
Wendall and Sally Horne; W – 55, housewife, 2nd, b.
Tuftonboro, d/o John L. Canney and Beulah Mains

WENDELL,
George W. of Tuftonboro m. Jennie H. **Beaton** of Pembroke
6/27/1895 in Tuftonboro; H – 50, farmer, b. Tuftonboro, s/o
George Wendell and Sally Wendell; W – 39, housework, b.
Pembroke, d/o John Drew and Lucinda Drew
John R. of Tuftonboro m. Lydia J. **Cole** of Madbury 1/8/1893 in
Tuftonboro; H – 47, farmer, 2nd, b. Tuftonboro, s/o George
Wendell (New Hampton, farmer) and Sally Wendell (Wolfeboro,
housekeeper); W – 26, housekeeper, b. Madbury, d/o John W.
Cole (Dover, farmer) and Rachel A. Cole (Sandwich,
housekeeper)

WENGRAF,
Richard John of NY m. Alice Catherine **Chandler** of Tuftonboro
7/10/1954 in Melvin Village; H – 29, planner, b. Austria, s/o
Paul Wengraf (Austria) and Eugenia Illner (Austria); W – 23,
student, b. MA, d/o Henry P. Chandler (MA) and Florence E.
McArdle (SC)

WENTWORTH,
John L. m. Marion E. **Ferris** 7/17/1941 in Wolfeboro; H – 28, painter,
  b. Newfield, ME, s/o John Wentworth (Acton, ME, janitor) and
  Marion Leighton (Salem, MA, housewife); W – 21, waitress, b.
  Boston, MA, d/o Edmund Ferris (NY City, deceased) and
  Florence Button (S. Paris, ME, deceased)

WER-GARCIA,
Jose of San Francisco, CA m. Phyllis Marie **Adjutant** of Tuftonboro
  11/28/1964 in Tuftonboro; H – 24, US Army, b. Guatemala City,
  CA, s/o Robert Wer (Guatemala, CA) and Josefina Garcia
  (Guatemala, CA); W – 18, secretary, b. Atlantic City, NJ, d/o
  Raymond M. Adjutant (Tuftonboro) and Helene P. Dougherty
  (PA)

WEST,
Charles W. of Providence, RI m. Addie A. **Pinkham** of Tuftonboro
  7/3/1900 in Tuftonboro; H – 26, laborer, b. London, England,
  s/o Charles West and Charlotte J. Smith; W – 27, dressmaker,
  b. Moultonboro, d/o Charles W. Pinkham and Sarah E. Moulton
Lawrence P. m. Irene A. **Brooks** 6/15/1928 in Wolfeboro; H – 20,
  merchant, b. Tuftonboro, s/o Charles W. West (London,
  England) and Addie A. Pinkham (Tuftonboro); W – 20, school
  teacher, b. Boston, MA, d/o Charles A. Brooks (Davehill, CT)
  and Elizabeth J. Copp (Nottingham)

WHEDON,
Oscar A. of Tuftonboro m. Annie S. **Butler** of Tuftonboro 10/12/1916
  in Sandwich; H – 47, laborer, b. Saugate, VT, s/o John M.
  Whedon and Mary E. Parker; W – 36, housewife, b. Tuftonboro,
  d/o George E. Hersey and Velzora V. Tate

WHITE,
Duane R. of New Durham m. Jeri Lynn **Southard** of Tuftonboro
  9/26/1987
Lewis B. of Tuftonboro m. Joan D. **Martin** of Boston, MA 12/4/1948
  in Moultonboro; H – 43, salesman, b. Danvers, MA, s/o Lewis
  B. White (Danvers, MA) and Anna Bird (Manchester, MA); W –
  25, at home, b. N. Attleboro, MA, d/o Thomas L. Martin and
  Anna E. McCusker (Everett, MA)
Ronald E. of Tuftonboro m. Lisa M. **Potenza** of Tuftonboro 6/9/1984

Ronald Ernest of Tuftonboro m. Angela Ruth **Repucci** of Tuftonboro 4/14/1996

WHITEHOUSE,
Maurice French m. Luella **Smith** 4/2/1933 in Melvin Village; H – 33, farmer, b. Moultonboro, s/o Charles C. Whitehouse (Ossipee, farmer) and Cora Belle Canney (Ossipee, at home); W – 28, teacher, b. Brattleboro, VT, d/o George Houghton Smith (Wilmington, VT, farmer) and Villa E. Titus (Wilmington, VT, housewife)

WHITING,
Leon L. of Tuftonboro m. Mary R. **Francis** of Tuftonboro 7/31/1909 in Tuftonboro; H – 33, farmer, b. Tamworth, s/o George L. Whiting and Nettie W. Swain; W – 23, house, b. Cambridge, MA, d/o Joseph J. Francis and Rose F. Gomez
Raymond Charles of Ossipee m. Carolyn Ethel **Dore** of Tuftonboro 10/26/1964 in Lakeport; H – 29, factory wkr., b. Wolfeboro, s/o Charles Whiting (NH) and Addie Dore (NH); W – 24, factory wkr., 2nd, divorced, b. Wolfeboro, d/o Lawrence E. Haley (NH) and Francis A. Thibodeau (NH)
Robert C. m. Judith P. **Morgan** 2/26/1977 in Tuftonboro

WHITNEY,
Donald Allen of Tuftonboro m. Michelle Denise **Lambert** of Tuftonboro 1/21/1989

WHITTEMORE,
Kevin Dean of Bethany, OK m. Mona Jean **Chase** of Tuftonboro 1/13/1979
Leon C. m. Elsie A. **Garfield** 7/4/1941 in Tuftonboro; H – 37, salesman, 2nd, b. Freeport, ME, s/o Ernest Whittemore (Wilton, ME, barber); W – 38, hairdresser, 2nd, b. Quebec, d/o Allen H. Perkins (Quebec) and Minnie M. Hodge (Quebec, deceased)

WHITTEN,
Charles F. m. C. Jean **Stockman** 7/21/1972 in Wolfeboro
Edward Russell of Tuftonboro m. Marietta Joy **Pratt** of Tuftonboro 6/18/1956 in Sanbornville; H – 33, inn operator, b. NH, s/o John R. Whitten (NH) and Theodora E. Hayes (NH); W – 21, nursery

school teacher, b. NY, d/o Chester J. Pratt (NY) and Lizotte D. Dodge (NY)

Joseph B. of Tuftonboro m. Martha M. **Hersey** of Tuftonboro 10/25/1893 in Tuftonboro; H – 60, farmer, 2nd, b. Tamworth, s/o Samuel Whitten (Tamworth, farmer) and Sally Whitten (Conway, housewife); W – 68, housekeeper, 2nd, b. Tuftonboro, d/o Aaron Wiggin (Wolfeboro, farmer) and Mary Wiggin (housewife)

Robert D., II of Tuftonboro m. Brenda G. **Kirk** of Tuftonboro 6/23/2001

Walter Francis m. Beatrice Boyden **Watson** 12/23/1931 in Ctr. Ossipee; H – 26, mechanic, b. Tuftonboro, s/o David Whitten (Moultonboro) and Nellie J. Hoyt (Tuftonboro); W – 23, at home, b. Tuftonboro, d/o Alfred O. Watson (Moultonboro) and Edna Kenney (Wolfeboro)

WHITTIER,

Randall A., Jr. of Tuftonboro m. Alida Alma **O'Connell** of MA 1/7/1956 in Wolfeboro; H – 44, salesman, b. MA, s/o Randall A. Whittier (MA) and Jane Blakeney (ME); W – 43, at home, widow, b. MA, d/o Thomas J. DuPont (NH) and Victoria Chapdelaine (Canada) (see following entry)

Randall A., Jr. of Tuftonboro m. Alida Alma **O'Connell** of MA 1/7/1956 in Melvin Village; H – 44, salesman, b. MA, s/o Randall A. Whittier (MA) and Jane Blakeney (ME); W – 43, at home, widow, b. MA, d/o Thomas J. DuPont (NH) and Victoria Chapdelaine (Canada) (see preceding entry)

Scott W. m. Frances J. **Haley** 12/15/1941 in Ctr. Harbor; H – 22, mechanic, b. Dedham, MA, s/o Scott W. Whittier (Wolfeboro, deceased) and Ellen W. Sceggle (Brookfield, housewife); W – at home, b. Tuftonboro, d/o Charles Haley (Tuftonboro, carpenter) and Dora Bragg (Moultonboro, housewife)

WHITTON,

John R. of Tuftonboro m. Theodora E. **Hayes** of Wolfeboro 6/4/1921 in Rochester; H – 22, farmer, b. Tuftonboro, s/o Edward R. Whitten (Winchester, MA) and Teresa Robinson (Yorkshire, England); W – 22, housewife, b. Rochester, d/o Frank R. Hayes (Rochester) and Alice Z. Martin (Rochester)

Joseph W. of Tuftonboro m. Mamie G. **Whitton** of Tuftonboro 4/7/1914 in Tuftonboro; H – 24, farmer, b. Wolfeboro, s/o

Joseph W. Whitton and Katie Gove; W – 25, housewife, b. Tuftonboro, d/o Frank E. Whitton and Carrie G. Wiggin

WIGGIN,
Everett D. of Tuftonboro m. Lizzie A. **Libby** of Dell Rap., Dak. 11/7/1892 in Wolfeboro; H – 28, machine agent, b. Tuftonboro, s/o Isaiah S. Wiggin (Tuftonboro, farmer) and Maria Wiggin (Tuftonboro, housewife); W – 22, housekeeper, b. Manchester, IA, d/o Charles Libby (Tuftonboro, farmer) and Evelyn Libby (Tuftonboro, housewife)

Fred A. of Tuftonboro m. Ethel P. **Hunting** of Somerville, MA 1/12/1920 in Wolfeboro; H – 61, clergyman, 3rd, b. Tuftonboro, s/o William H. Wiggin (Tuftonboro) and Ann Wiggin (Tuftonboro); W – 43, instructor, b. Charlestown, MA, d/o Ebenezer Hunting (Boston, MA) and Georgianna Bradford (Portland, ME)

Harold I. of Tuftonboro m. Blanch H. **Bickford** of Center Harbor 10/28/1922 in Center Harbor; H – 20, clerk, b. Dorchester, MA, s/o Lewis C. Wiggin (Tamworth) and Ella M. Clark (Woburn, MA); W – 19, clerk, b. Center Harbor, d/o Minot W. Bickford (Moultonboro) and Etta M. Dow (Moultonboro)

Merle Delmone of Tuftonboro m. Patricia Ruth **Hollis** of Wolfeboro 5/29/1979

WILEY,
David C. of Melvin Village m. Karen A. **Milligan** of Melvin Village 3/23/2003

WILKINS,
Elmer L. m. Allura **Wakefield** 6/29/1929 in Moultonville; H – 23, laborer, b. Ossipee, s/o Erlin Wilkins (Ossipee) and Dora Sawyer (Saco, ME); W – 23, housework, 3rd, b. Milton, d/o Will Burrows (Milton) and Emma Knowles (Middleton)

WILKINSON,
Melvin R. of Tuftonboro m. Alice R. **Morris** of FL 2/23/1957 in Hooksett; H – 64, mechanic, 4th, divorced, b. IN, s/o Edward Wilkinson (NC) and Mary J. Adams (IN); W – 48, at home, 3rd, divorced, b. FL, d/o Ly-C-A-Morris (VA) and Emma E. Glissan (FL)

WILLAND,
Charles Aaron m. Rena Bernice Grant **Kramer** 11/26/1938 in Milan;
    H – 48, farmer, b. Wolfeboro, s/o Arthur J. Willand (Wolfeboro,
    deceased) and Etta Maria Blake (Wolfeboro, deceased); W –
    52, dietician, 2nd, b. Milton, d/o Walter Bryant Grant
    (Minneapolis, MN, deceased) and Gertrude Gray Howard
    (Milford, MA, housewife)

WILLARD,
Emery Durgin of Melvin Village m. Beverly Annette **Person** of
    Moultonboro 6/10/1960 in Moultonboro; H – 41, shovel opr.,
    divorced, b. MA, s/o Arthur E. Willard (MA) and Iva May Durgin
    (MA); W – 39, home mkr., widow, b. NH, d/o Philip Nelson
    Bean (NH) and Aldora M. Gelinas (MA)
Robert L. of Tuftonboro m. Janet L. **Leach** of Swampscott, MA
    10/10/1949 in Wakefield; H – 20, truck driver, b. Lynn, MA, s/o
    Arthur E. Willard (MA) and Iva M. Durgin (MA); W – 18, office
    work, b. MA, d/o Roy F. Leach (ME) and Murrill E. Leach (ME)

WILLIAMS,
Bruce A. m. Cheryl A. **McLaughlin** 10/14/1969 in Tuftonboro; H – b.
    9/14/1941 in NH, s/o Roger L. Williams and Berenice Bisson; W
    – b. 2/26/1945 in MA, d/o James V. McLaughlin and Virginia
    Goldthwait
Lance A. of Tuftonboro m. Susan E. **Morrison** of Tuftonboro
    3/25/1991
Roger Lawrence of Tuftonboro m. Barbara Haines **Davis** of Grafton
    11/12/1955 in Grafton Ctr.; H – 25, dozer operator, b. MA, d/o
    Roger L. Williams (MA) and Berneice L. Lawrence (MA); W –
    24, decorator, b. MA, d/o Clifton D. Davis (MA) and Dorothy L.
    Haines (MA)
Roger Lester m. Bernice Wellesly **Lawrence** 5/16/1926 in Durham;
    H – 23, forester, b. Brockton, MA, s/o George V. Williams
    (Taunton, MA) and Nellie M. Haley (Melvin Village); W – 24, at
    home, b. Lynn, MA, d/o Welles. H. Lawrence (Lynn, MA) and
    Muriel R. Besson (Lynn, MA)
Ward B. of Tuftonboro m. Judith A. **Downs** of Tamworth 4/27/1957
    in S. Tamworth; H – 24, draftsman, b. ME, s/o Roger L.
    Williams (MA) and Berneice L. Lawrence (MA); W – 18, at
    home, b. NH, d/o Clifford F. Downs (NH) and Winifred W.
    Weeks (NH)

Ward B. of Tuftonboro m. Judith E. **Nickerson** of Ctr. Ossipee
5/9/1964 in Ctr. Ossipee; H – 31, draftsman, 2nd, divorced, b.
ME, s/o Roger Williams (MA) and Berenice Lawrence (MA); W
– 21, secretary, b. NH, d/o Wendell Nickerson (NH) and
Blanche Templeton (NH)
Ward Bessom of Tuftonboro m. Bette Ann **Davis** of Sandwich
12/13/1956 in Wolfeboro; H – 22, draftsman, b. ME, s/o Roger
L. Williams (MA) and Berneice W. Lawrence (MA); W – 17, at
home, b. NH, d/o Forrest E. Davis (NH) and Charlotte Hoag
(NH)

WILSON,
Gale Sevey of Anson, ME m. Barbara H. **Seymour** of Anson, ME
6/25/1995
Philip C. of Tuftonboro m. Isabel W. **Leach** of Marblehead, MA
7/12/1947 in Tuftonboro; H – 41, auto dealer, b. Nahant, MA,
s/o Fred A. Wilson (Nahant, MA) and Alice P. Campbell (Mt.
Vernon); W – 40, housewife, b. Paisely, Scotland, d/o William
A. Walker (Scotland) and Janet Stevenson (Scotland)
Philip Clark of Tuftonboro m. Lillian May **Richardson** of Derry
7/9/1954 in Tuftonboro; H – 48, auto dealer, 2nd, divorced, b.
MA, s/o Fred A. Wilson (MA) and Alice C. Perkins (MA); W –
39, housewife, 2nd, divorced, b. MA, d/o William O. Brien (MA)
and Hannah Hayes (MA)

WINGATE,
Jeffrey A. m. Janice J. **Kauer** 6/4/1977 in Tuftonboro

WOLCOTT,
Wallace Henry of NY m. Dorothy Clement **Kirby** of NY 9/5/1954 in
Tuftonboro; H – 60, architect, 2nd, widower, b. NY, s/o David C.
Wolcott (NY) and Marion D. Benedict (NY); W – 57, real estate,
2nd, widow, b. MN, d/o Charles B. Clement (IN) and Ella
Barrows (MN)

WOLF,
Lewis A. m. Barbara **Flint** 8/30/1941 in Tuftonboro; H – 26, clerk, b.
N. Haven, CT, s/o Frank E. Wolf (N. Haven, CT, furrier) and
Sybil G. Grant (N. Haven, CT, housewife); W – 22, clerk, b.
Bridgeport, CT, d/o Harley A. Flint (Middleton, MA, chemist)
and Maud S. Fay (Boston, MA, housewife)

WOOD,
Jeffrey D. of Tuftonboro m. Rhonda E. **Bishop** of S. Burlington, VT
7/24/1982
William H., III of Tuftonboro m. Anne-Marie J. **Lemoyne** of
Wolfeboro 8/18/1984

WOODMANCY,
Charles Wesley m. Eleanor May **Thompson** 12/6/1934 in Ctr.
Ossipee; H – 26, laborer, b. Boston, MA, s/o Henry A.
Woodmancy (Roslindale, MA, retired) and Florence I. Evans
(Boston, MA, housewife); W – 17, b. Tuftonboro, d/o Simon T.
Thompson (Tuftonboro, farmer) and Evelyn L. Bean
(Tuftonboro, housewife)

YOUNG,
Charles H. of Tuftonboro m. Florence I. **Caulfield** of Boston, MA
9/8/1910 in Tuftonboro; H – 23, farmer, b. Tuftonboro, s/o
George F. Young and Josephine E. Neal; W – 20, housewife, b.
Boston, MA, d/o Albert J. Caulfield and Mary E. Evans
Royal P. m. Lura M. **Hilton** 9/22/1928 in Tuftonboro; H – 55,
photographer, b. Wolfeboro, s/o George F. Young (Tuftonboro)
and Emma Nutter (Tuftonboro); W – 58, at home, b.
Tuftonboro, d/o George A. Hilton (Ossipee) and Susan C.
Nutter (Ossipee)

ZELKO,
Darrell Patrick of Hampton, VA m. Lauren Kristen **Sheahan** of
Tuftonboro 10/8/1995

ZWICKER,
Richard J. m. Cynthia A. **Crombie** 11/4/1978 in Tuftonboro

Abbott, Minnie E. – Straw, George D.
Abbott, Hattie E. – Brown, Charles H.
Adams, Abigail – Hennessy, Robert B.
Adjutant, Tanya L. – Mills, Darold W.
Adjutant, Leora E. – Hlushuk, Jack
Adjutant, Elizabeth Jane – Hersey, John Leander
Adjutant, Phyllis Marie – Wer-Garcia, Jose
Adjutant, Ida May – Ayers, Herbert
Adjutant, Anna P. – Kenney, Elijah B.
Albee, Abigail – Cook, John B.
Albert, Deborah Ann – McGovern, Michael Patrick
Aldred, Lynda Marie – Howard, William A,
Alfres, Pauline M. – Hodges, Milton E.
Allen, Shirley A. – O'Brien, Mark
Allen, Suzanne – Parsons, Douglas B.
Allen, Dorothea A. – Kirby, Stephen H.
Allen, Judith Nancy – Hodsdon, John Raymond
Allen, Phyllis – Shepard, Robert Lane
Allen, Priscilla – Mather, Bruce D.
Allen, Rose (Perkins) – Horne, Everett E.
Ambrose, Judith G. – Clinton, Stuart King
Ames, Debra A. – Burton, Bruce J.
Anderson, Joyce Louise – Berghaus, William C. B.
Anderson, Barbara J. – Thurston, Scott M.
Antoniadis, Katherine M. – Bean, Benjamin A,
Antonucci, Deborah M. – Dearborn, James D.
Antonucci, Mary – Antonucci, William
Arsem, Marilyn A. – Raymond, Robert A.
Arsenault, Ethelyn S. (Osborne) – Tucker, Carroll W.
Askew, Celeste Mae – Pollini, Todd Emery
Atlee, Arline M. – Dudley, Ronald A.
Austin, Judith O. – Johnson, Arthur Westly
Ayers, Florence Irene – Pigott, Robert Allison
Ayers, Edith C. – Haley, George H.
Ayers, Sarah Jane (Canney) – Wendall, John R.
Ayers, Ruth E. (Champaigne) – Robblee, William H.
Ayers, Doris E. – Bradeau, Joseph S.

Baker, Joan – Sargent, Fred Elwin
Balance, Deborah S. – Mitchell, Rodney K.
Banfill, Evelyn Rose – Brownell, Harold Parker

Banfill, Beatrice Adeline – Riley, Ernest Granville
Bangs, Cora E. (Plates) – Phinney, Charles H.
Bannon, Lillian V. – Lee, Harry S.
Barnard, Cynthia Pond – Barnard, David Francis, Jr.
Barnhill, Laura Marie – Troy, William Joseph, III
Barrett, Chris Alice – Sawyer, Michael Patrick
Barton, Darlene J. – Canniff, William F.
Bateman, Catherine A. – Killian, Jonathan D.
Baverstock, Cecelia – Battersby, Cowan Brenton
Baxter, Carol L. – Craigue, John E.
Baxter, Helen May – Dupre, William Prosch
Baxter, Ann Christine – Hutchins, Alpheus F., Jr.
Beagin, Elizabeth A. – Foss, Albert M.
Beale, Hazel L. – Ridlon, Arnold L.
Bean, Mildred Velma – Haley, Kenneth Edward
Bean, Shirley A. – Smith, Walter C.
Bean, Madaline Delorus – Smith, Edward Leroy
Bean, Hattie F. – Straw, Harry E.
Bean, Grace Maud (Dewey) – Bennett, Maurice P.
Bean, Deborah – Bennett, Paul Mark
Bean, Florence B. – Foss, Charles E.
Bean, Pern S. (Sargent) – Shannon, Richard S.
Bean, Marylynn Janet – Tilton, Clifford Howard, Jr.
Bean, Ida (Nichols) – Bean, Horace W.
Bean, Nettie Bell – Forsythe, Frank Faulkner
Bean, Evelyn L. – Thompson, Simon T.
Bean, Phyllis A. – Hunter, Thomas W.
Beane, Cheryl J. – Sauter, Scott T.
Beaton, Jennie H. – Wendell, George W.
Beatter, Elizabeth Jane – May, Daniel Otto
Beattie, Jennifer G. – Morgan, Jeffrey Thomas
Beauchene, Lorraine M. – McDonald, Christopher N.
Beaudoin, Nicole Therese – Denee, Robert Craig
Beck, Dorothy M. – Ferry, Edw. M.
Beckett, Alison Bartlett – Lockitt, James Douglas
Belknap, Marsha J. - Hunter, Bradbury E., Jr.
Belt, Anita – Timmerman, Micheal A.
Bender, Claudia Marie Reznor – Foster, John Hopkins
Bennett, Mabel A. – McNeil, John P.
Bennett, Susie L. – Guberstein, Harold A.
Bennett, Alice Gertrude – Edgerly, John Irving

Bennett, Dorothy Frances – Morris, Robert Graydon
Bennett, Ada G. – Hubbard, Eugene F.
Bense, Mary L. – Craigue, Kenneth E.
Berg, Regina – Lessard, Bill
Berg, Theresa – Meserve, Norman A.
Bergeron, Edith T. – Harding, Archibald B.
Bergeron, Lillian N. – Shepard, James T.
Bernard, Helene – Belmont, Micheal E.
Bernier, Jennifer A. – Morrison, James E.
Berry, Mary E. – Cellarius, Kenneth
Berry, Gaye E. – Hodgdon, Graydon Herbert
Berry, Judith Hastings – Engalichev, Constantine Nicholas
Berry, Robin L. – Maulden, Robert G.
Betchley, Helen Louise – Jones, William McPheeters
Bezanson, Sally Anne – Mann, Charles E.
Bickford, June E. – Hazeltine, Nathan L.
Bickford, Blanch H. – Wiggin, Harold I.
Bickford, Grace M. – Parsons, Douglas B.
Biehl, Elinor C. – Dubay, Alan R.
Bilafer, Jean M. – King, Peter L.
Bilodeau, Marsha – Hansen, Carl I.
Bilodeau, Loretta A. – Steadman, Kenton E., Jr.
Bishop, Rhonda E. – Wood, Jeffrey D.
Blair, Fern O. – Morway, Richard N.
Blake, Kimberly Ann – Prause, Michael C.
Blanchette, Janet M. – Kolenda, Stephen J.
Blitzer, Carol O. – MacRostie, William G.
Bodonyi, Zita – Dearborn, Mark Edward
Bolling, Lynn M. – Wahle, Thomas G.
Bolobanic, Kimberly A. – Craigue, Scott B.
Bonus, Cheryl M. – Travers, Peter G.
Bose, Lottie May – Porter, Graham C.
Bottomley, Helen – Urquhart, Roderick
Bourque, Mary Fredaline – Bean, Frank John
Bowen, Violet Pember – Cheney, Gordon Warren
Boyce, Cynthia L. – Puchacz, David M.
Boyd, Patricia Ann – Fernald, Bruce C.
Boyd, Cynthia D. – Cooley, William U.
Boyden, Martha – McDuffee, Gerald
Bradley-Smith, Pauline Mary – DeRamer, Frank Jacob
Brand, Anika Pauline – Hastings, Brian Charles

Branin, Rebecca Ann – Jones, Jeffrey B.
Breakell, Mary Jane (Allen) – Curdo, George Howard
Breitenbucher, Gertrude (Cross) – Murley, Samuel
Brennan, Kathleen L. – Morgan, Kenneth A.
Brenner, Nancy L. – Snyder, Robert D.
Brennick, Kathleen M. – Donovan, John F., Jr.
Brewer, Dorothy Cora – Eldridge, Jeremy Clyde
Brewer, Natalie A. (Brookes) – Poaletti, Chester
Brice, Alice (Hubbert) – Forbes, Frederick William, Jr.
Briggs, Jeannette H. – Edwards, Robert A.
Britton, Nola Gail – Brown, Wallace Chadwick
Britton, Ginger Mae – Herrick, Donald Arthur
Brodrick, Betsey Gay – Newcomb, Nelson Faulks, Jr.
Brookes, Doris A. – Lowry, Walter J.
Brooks, Irene A. – West, Lawrence P.
Brooks, Madeline N. – Bowles, Francis D.
Brown, Clara Ellen – Sawyer, Richard Bangs
Brown, Naomi F. (Bean) – Jerome, Frank J.
Brown, Rena Christine – Lehner, Eugene Frederick
Brown, Erin Marie – Akins, Michael C.
Brown, Shirley Ann – Coulter, Leslie John
Bruce, Mildred Edna – Perkins, Bert A.
Buchanan, Judith W. – Soncrant, David Lucien
Buckley, Susanne D. – Hayes, Douglass F.
Bunny, Joan Isabelle – Tupeck, Russell Everett
Burke, Nancy Marie – Runnals, Christopher Mark
Burke, Lillian – Hersey, Ethan
Burleigh, Carrie L. – Ayers, John
Burleigh, Marion G. – Patterson, Robert J.
Burnett, Laurie K. – DeRose, Joseph L.
Burwell, Elizabeth Banfield – Nicholls, William Hord
Bushman, Barbara Marie – Ames, Richard Wayne
Bushman, Ivena F. M. – Varney, Fenton W.
Bushman, Jeanne – Craigue, Harley P.
Butler, Maureen Susan – Chisholm, Scott Weaver
Butler, Annie S. (Hersey) – Whedon, Oscar A.
Button, Mary J. – Wenck, James H.
Buttrick, Kathy – Pettit, Russell W.
Buttrick, Susan J. – Pike, Curt R.
Buzzell, Georgie – Gilman, Charles L.

Cabezas, Norma C. – Singleton, Randall G.
Call, Lynda Ann – Briggeman, Russell Matthew
Campbell, Margueritt A. – Wasson, Harry A.
Canning, Frances G. – Hodgdon, Forrest W.
Cantwell, Sharon Lynn – McCallister, Kenneth V.
Carleton, Lisa H. – Holden, Jerome C.
Carlson, Alisa Diane – Kuzel, Norman E., II
Carlson, Ivy Anne – Leavitt, Seth Francis
Carlsten, Kristine C. – Salvo, Kirk Anthony
Carlsten, Katherine Elizabeth – Kaplan, Matthew Edmond
Carlton, Lisa J. – Arion, Michael A.
Carpenter, Evelyn C. (Avery) – Richardson, Marshall D.
Carroll, Linda A. – Simmons, Scott D.
Carson, Lillian L. (Nichols) – Richardson, Frank A.
Carter, Della A. – Bean, Arthur M.
Carter, Elizabeth Ann – Davis, Foster Lee
Case, Donna Mary – Swendson, Gary Lindsey
Cates, Geraldine Elizabeth – Haley, Delbert Clarence, Jr.
Caulfield, Florence I. – Young, Charles H.
Caverly, Edith S. – Grant, Leland H.
Cea, Margaret Mary – O'Reilly, Patrick M.
Champagne, Sherri A. – Perkins, Ernest R., Jr.
Chandler, Alice Catherine – Wengraf, Richard John
Chandler, Stephanie Ann – Buttrick, Daniel C.
Chandler, Jean (Wilkin) – Spencer, DeForest
Chase, Karen A. – Spencer, Philip K.
Chase, Kathy D. – Townsend, James H.
Chase, Mona Jean – Whittemore, Kevin Dean
Chellman, Jerildine R. – McKinley, Mark C.
Cheney, Norma Ann – Merrow, Dana Howard
Cheney, Violet (Bowen) – Noyes, Charles Willard
Cheney, Brenda Susan – Martin, Steven Wayne
Cheney, Cynthia J. – Morgan, Lloyd C., Jr.
Cheney, Jean – Dietzel, William H., Jr.
Christiansen, Christine L. – Cornwell, Ralph W.
Chung, Pamela J. – MacMillan, Duncan J., Jr.
Cilley, Donna Lee – Cheney, Richard Gordon
Clark, Jennifer Leigh – Gunn, B. Christopher
Clausen, Marcia Eleanor –Griffiths, William Harry
Cline, Joan H. – Bernard, Paul L.
Cochrane, Cynthia M. – Leavitt, Scott M.

Colburn, Nancy J. – Lewis, Mark J.
Colburn, Beverly I. (Ivester) – Monroe, Richard B.
Colby, Terry J. – Moody, Jeffrey M.
Colby, Norma – Welch, Lisle R.
Cole, Kathryn L. – Broadbent, Kenneth A.
Cole, Denise D. – Conrad, Everett G.
Cole, Deborah Lee – Rasmussen, Stephen Karl
Cole, Lydia J. – Wendell, John R.
Conant, Edith D. – Brown, Arthur A.
Conant, Lisa B. – Bisson, Daniel J.
Conley, Annie – Staples, Frank
Conlon, Marjorie R. – Kunkel, Gerald D.
Conrad, Lois H. (Hart) – Straw, Francis G.
Cooper-Ellis, Sarah M. – Gordon, Bart J.
Copp, Louise F. – Klippel, Warren H.
Copp, Arvilla (Fernald) – Moulton, John S.
Copplestone, Martha G. – Murcott, Andrew W.
Corning, Elizabeth S. – Sedler, Philip D.
Cotton, Irene (Champaigne) – Piper, Stanley W.
Cowper, Heather Jean – Evitts, Nathaniel Thomas
Craigue, Cynthia Mary – Clough, Fred Wayne
Craigue, Tina M. – Clough, Harold W.
Craigue, Ann Marie – Haskin, John F.
Craigue, Bonnie Jean – McPhail, Jeffrey Alan
Crane, Anne Winslow – Kirby, William John, Jr.
Crews, Carlien Smith – Partin, Charles Fred
Cristal, Joan – Singer, Arthur L., Jr.
Croft, Estella A. (Silliter) – Waite, James E.
Crombie, Cynthia A. – Zwicker, Richard J.
Crosby, Arlene H. (Henry) – Bean, Leon E.
Cross, Cheryl A. – Riley, Franklin R.
Cross, Karen L. – Bartlett, William S., Jr.
Cross, Karen C. – Downing, Geoffrey A.
Cross, Linda J. – Fullerton, John F.
Crossman, Caroline L. – Edgerly, Edwin B.
Croteau, Nancy J. – Rudolph, Blair D.
Croteau, Martha Jean – Meehan, Mark L.
Crowe, Cecily T. – Bentley, James A.
Cruz, Dania E. Perez – Jones, Ryan B.
Cunniff, Maribeth – Cherry, Christopher D.
Curdo, Mary Jane – Cheney, Lyle G.

Curtis, Heather M. – Tenney, Michael W.
Curtis, Holly L. – Clarke, Dennis J.
Curtis, Kathryn Anne – Eastman, John Allen, Jr.

D'Auria, Joanne F. – Litwhiler, Karl R.
D'Ercole, Jessica Elsa – Stanton, Michael John
D'Eri, Mary E. - Swift, Thomas R.
D'Onofrio, Anita M. – Porter, Scott A.
Dahill, Lisa A. – Dumont, Paul R.
Daignault, Angela R. – Reppucci, Ronald J., Jr.
Dana, Hilda J. (Jackson) – Osborn, Frank J.
Davey, Hilary Beth – DesMarais, Brian David
Davis, Cynthia – Jackson, Joshua B.
Davis, Diane G. – Davis, Foster Lee
Davis, Kathryn Kingsbury – Howard, James John, Jr.
Davis, Susan E. – Levesque, John A.
Davis, Sandra – Paige, Thomas Howe
Davis, Ruth Harriett – Hersey, Robert Sylvester
Davis, Eleanor May – Knights, John Franklin
Davis, Leslie A. – Sturgeon, Christopher J.
Davis, Jennifer – Newbury, Christopher Bernard
Davis, Etta M. (Ladd) – Sargent, John F.
Davis, S. Frances – Darling, Kenneth B.
Davis, Debbie – Mitchell, Terry M.
Davis, Barbara Haines – Williams, Roger Lawrence
Davis, Judith C. – Brueninger, Lewis Talmage
Davis, Elizabeth Paige – Richardson, Verne Leslie
Davis, Ruth B. – Flint, Harley A.
Davis, Bette Ann – Williams, Ward Bessom
Davison, Kathleen C. – Jackson, Luther Worley
Dawes, Eleanor E. – Bennett, Frank S.
De Almeida, Valdirene – Schou, Timothy Kirk
Dearborn, Judith M. – Pike, Guy A., II
DeFelice, Janice E. – Batley, Bruce E.
Delaney, Amanda A. – Fernandez, Scott K.
Denningham, Coren Veronica – Sharples, William Waln
Dennis, Deborah – Nicholson, John J. G., III
Detwiler, Anne – Crecraft, Harrison R.
Devork, Patricia C. – Solomon, Arthur F., Jr.
Devork, Pamela D. - Albee, William L.
Dewey, Grace M. – Bean, Howard E.

DeWitt, Joanne – Knight, Frank C.
Deyak, Kirsten – Blanchette, Timothy P.
Deyak, Norma Kate – Mixer, Douglas Maxwell
Dickinson, Susan M. – Cooper, David W.
Dinkelmeyer, Flor. – Stein, Alfred H.
Divinell, Elizabeth Ann – LaCombe, Henry Euclide
Dodds, Marion Ardell – Fernald, Chester Charles
Dodge, Laura W. – Hanson, Jon S. B. C.
Dodge, Pearl E. – Cheney, Ralph B.
Doe, Bertha M. – Johnson, Charles W.
Doe, Sadie B. – McIntire, Louis
Doran, Jolene A. – Broderick, Glenn T.
Dore, Linda M. – Kendal, Herbert G.
Dore, Ruth M. – Clough, Randy A.
Dore, Sheila A. – Fuller, James A.
Dore, Andrena Lynn – Santulli, Jeremy Lucas
Dore, Carolyn Ethel (Haley) – Whiting, Raymond Charles
Dore, Eunice M. – Hodgdon, Glenn F.
Dore, Una M. (Moody) – Blaisdell, Thomas H.
Doten, Letitia Ebbs – Cole, Frederick Arthur, Jr.
Doucette, Lisa Ann – Roberts, Jeffrey Scott
Dow, Debbo M. – Hedden, Robison W.
Dow, Eleanor – Cooper, George William
Dow, Bernice E. – Haley, Willis I.
Dow, Dorothy E. – Bennett, Ralph V.
Dow, Alice Gleanor (Adjutant) – Dow, Ernest H.
Dow, Susan Audrey – Nicholla, Steven John
Dow, Susan-Elizabeth – Johnson, Charles M.
Downing, Muriel Helen – Vallier, Myron Durgin
Downs, Judith A. – Williams, Ward B.
Doying, Gladys A. – Haley, Ralph S.
Drew, Edna L. – Keniston, Ephraim
Drew, Nora Florence – Hilton, Maynard Webster
Drew, Roberta Ellen – Reed, Norman Elsmore
Drowne, Jeanne Elizabeth – Stave, Richard James
Drowns, Elsie C. – Philbrick, Alfred
Drucker, Thelma E. – Colby, Howard C.
Drucker, Barbara Edith – Straw, Robert William
Dubel, Corrine J. – Shannon, Carl F.
Dubuc, Suzanne Marie – Piper, Richard Arnold
Dunn, Carol L. – Edgar, Arthur R.

Durkee, Donna Jean – Reed, Wayne Austin
Duseck, Kate (Allen) – Allen, George H.
Dyer, Lois – Terry, Robert W.

Eames, Marie Adele (Hyde) – Curry, James Joseph
Easdon, Jennifer Lee – Mazzocca, Augustus Daniel
Edgerly, Gyme Lynn – Berry, Steven Douglas
Edgerly, Emily L. (Asselin) – Levitch, Alexander
Edwards, Sandra D. – Shapiro, Peter C.
Edwards, Wanda L. – Clifford, Bruce E.
Egger, Virginia Gertrude – Hochwald, Earle Chas.
Ehlert, Anne Thresher – LaFleur, Vincent Albert
Eldridge, Barbara J. – Randall, Raymond A.
Eldridge, Helen S. – Libby, Robert M.
Eldridge, Peggy E. – Knisley, Reuben K.
Eldridge, Marion P. – Skinner, Herbert I.
Eldridge, Evelyn Maud – Peare, Arthur Gordon
Eldridge, Michelle L. – Comeau, James
Elliott, Gloria J. – Curtis, William B.
Elliott, Lisa Marie – Haddock, Andrew Robert
Elliott, Hazel B. – Davis, Eli
Elliott, Christie Mae – Mack, Maurice Jewell
Ellis, Margaret – Hunter, Ernest M.
Ellison, Emma (Cushing) – Gendro, Clement
Emerson, Bernice H. (Ham) – Dow, Ausbrey N.
Emerson, Robin – Hunter, Stephen W.
Emery, Nettie F. B. (Brown) – Emery, Wendall C.
Emery, Inamae – Dickey, Robert Ellsworth
Emery, Lucy A. (Haley) – Libbey, Frank
Emery, Patricia L. – Minot, Albert F.
Emery, Maud E. – Bisbee, Arthur H.
Emery, Mary M. – Bradeau, Joseph S.
Emilson, Laura L. – Paris, Robert M.
Emme, Lorraine F. – Hanson, Jon S.
Engel, Fae Anne – Shure, Donald D.
Enwright, Gail S. – Johnson, Donald S.
Erwin, Diane E. – Jordan, Mark W.
Evans, Susan Mae – Clinton, Stuart K.

Faherty, Barbara Ann – Hull, Christopher E.
Fairbank, Patricia C. – Matthews, C. Dixon

Farr, Barbara R., Jr. – Jackson, John L., Jr.
Farwell, Mary A. – Freiberger, Christopher A.
Faucette, Marcia A. – Bullis, Russell H.
Feise, Dorelen – Bunting, Bainbridge
Ferguson, Marguerite E. – Kneeland, Frederick J.
Fernald, Edith B. – Gilman, Chester H.
Fernald, Sara E. – Gillespie, Roger B.
Ferris, Marion E. – Wentworth, John L.
Ferris, Helen Louise – Haley, Howard Russell
Fiore, Elizabeth Anne – Ward, Britton Nash
Fischer, Yvonne – Bullis, Russell H., Jr.
Fish, Suzanne D. – Costa, Peter D.
Fitzmorris, Paula J. – Jenkins, Mark S.
Flanagan, Eleanor Ann – Reed, David Thomas
Flanagan, Marion Winifred – Robbins, Winthrop Sutton
Flanders, Elva M. – Favro, Earl T.
Flint, Barbara – Wolf, Lewis A.
Fogarty, Patricia A. – Stockman, James A.
Fonseca, Sara M. – Currell, James B., Jr.
Foote, Deborah L. – Ham, Jeffrey W.
Foote, Lisa Ann – Mullin, Robert S.
Foote, Margaret M. – Thompson, John T.
Forbes, Wendy J. – Ramey, Shon C.
Fortier, Tracey L. – Bussiere, Ralph Edward, III
Fortin, June Patricia – Smith, Richard Leroy
Fortin, Carol A. – Leslie, Raymond C.
Foss, Annabelle Theresa – Clough, Harold W.
Foss, Anna R. (Bean) – Neal, Isaac N.
Fox, Ellen C. – Stokes, Frank W.
Francis, Mary R. – Whiting, Leon L.
Fraser, Jennifer S. – Walker, Jeffrey H.
Fraser, Barbara T. – Hooper, Ronald G.
French, Bonnie Mae – Pennell, Dwight Wayne
Friedrichs, Anne – Lairmore, Mitchell R.
Frisbee, Ethel J. – Adjutant, Forest E.
Frost, Carrie A. – Thompson, Asa B.
Frost, Vena Annie – Crane, Theodore A.
Frye, Eunice E. – McIntire, Delma L.
Frye, Joan D. – Daignault, Wilfred R.
Fuller, Susan E. – Campbell, Potter B.
Furber, Diane – Nockles, William Arthur

Gallagher, A. A. – Hansen, Scott T.
Gannon, Lizzie M. – Bennett, Orsino V.
Garfield, Elsie A. (Perkins) – Whittemore, Leon C.
Garrett, Marilyn C. (Craigue) – Campbell, Donald Eugene
Garrison, Helen K. (Klocker) – Bennett, Ralph V.
Garvey, Irene M. – Moore, Todd A.
Gaudlap, Cyrene E. – Libby, Joseph C.
Gauvin, Paula L. – Gauvin, Daniel L.
Gauvreau, Louise M. – Duffy, Daniel J.
Gelinas, Michelle L. – Santulli, Peter M.
Geto, May F. – Hodgdon, Franklin H.
Geto, Addie – Piper, Charles G.
Gilliatt, Zelda – Crombie, Richard Louis
Gillum, Michelle L. – Kilkelly, Philip J.
Gilman, Louise Bianca – Leavitt, Harold John
Gilman, Sadie B. – Davis, Harry A.
Gilman, Georgie A. (Buzzell) – Bennett, George E.
Girard, Bonnie Ann – Banyas, James Richard, Jr.
Glidden, Jamie Leigh – Ladd, Ian Charles
Glidden, Jennifer A. – Lapolla, John C.
Glidden, Claire Virginia – Hlushuk, Kenneth Wilkie
Goldsmith, Mary A. (Bean) – Philbrick, Willie W.
Goraum, Theresa A. – Edgerly, John I., Jr.
Gordon, Nancy L. – Kenny, Thomas P.
Gordon, Lynn Marie – Seymour, Scott Arvid
Gough, Marion T. – Skinner, William L.
Gouin, Barbara D. – Perry, Stanley A.
Gould, Florence M. – Greenbank, Benjamin M.
Gould, Barbara (Sharp) – Piper, Carl Raymond
Goulet, Irene H. – Ladd, David C.
Gourley, Edna Frances – Cook, Charles Henry George
Gracia, Alcira – Moulton, Darwin
Graham, Carol Ann – Thomas, Lloyd H., III
Graham, Nancy J. – Lindquist, Barry E.
Grant, Mercy (Joy) – Clark, Alexander R.
Grasse, Mary B. – Stockman, Brian A.
Gray, Laura Ann – Muise, Darrell James
Greenwood, Elinore L. – Lewis, John E.
Gregoire, Michelle E. – Hadley, Thomas L.
Grill, Susan E. – Deterling, John S.
Grolas, Caroline T. (Nudd) – Tupeck, Henry Steven

Grover, Denise Jean – Remmers, Timothy Robert
Grover, Amelia (Downing) – Gendro, Clement
Gruner, Heidi L. – Southard, Gary S.
Grzyb, Patricia Alexandra – Callender, John MacPherson
Guilfoyle, Khristine A. – Thompson, Ronald S.

Haase, Leslie Ann – Harper, Peter John
Haggerty, Charlene E. – Standyck, James P.
Haley, Carolyn E. – Dore, Ivan E.
Haley, Diana L. – Christian, William H.
Haley, Mildred Elizabeth – Wasson, Andrew
Haley, Marion H. – Shannon, Edward A.
Haley, Joyce Annette – MacDonald, Ernest Ellsworth, Jr.
Haley, Viola Gladys – Hodgdon, Edwin Joseph
Haley, Florence Louise – Ham, Leroy Ellsworth
Haley, Frances J. – Whittier, Scott W.
Haley, Agnes June – Hill, Frank Vincent
Haley, Gladys E. – Moulton, James L.
Haley, Mary E. – Rand, Leroy D.
Haley, Ellen Marie – McClean, Richard E.
Hall, Josephine C. – Allen, Frank R.
Halloran, Margaret E. – Dussault, Mark J.
Ham, Rhoda Louise – Davis, Paul Wallace
Ham, Nancy Jane – Roberge, Ernest Leroy, Jr.
Hamilton, Jean W. – Hodges, Burgess G., III
Hamlin, Judy A. – Gouin, Thornton F.
Hammond, Susan Brayton – Oswalt, Edmund Darrell
Hanington, Joy E. – Perkins, Wayne E.
Hansen, Vicki - Haungs, Charles F.
Hanson, Dorothea – Hilliard, Louis, Jr.
Hardie, Mildred I. – Jewell, Edmund A.
Harriman, Lori Jean – Townsend, Paul H.
Harrington, Jean E. – Dearborn, L. W., Jr.
Harris, Victoria – Dorn, John Z.
Hartley, Lillian J. – Daniels, Lewis S.
Haslett, Joan H. – Gafney, Richard C.
Hatton, Melody Lynne – Stockman, John L.
Hauser, Kimi Lynn – Lapar, Daniel M.
Haven, Roxanna – Stanley, Donald C., Jr.
Hawes, Kerrieanne – Arroyo, Elvis
Hayes, Martha M. – Eldridge, Carlton O.

Hayes, Rosa Paige – Nine, John Arthur
Hayes, Theodora E. – Whitton, John R.
Haynes, Andrea L. – Perry, Stephen H.
Heath, Nancy J. – Myrshall, Winston C.
Hebden, Natalie A. – Schafer, Dennis R.
Helling, Jan L. – Croteau, Richard G.
Hemphill, Donna H. – Fogle, Clair M., Jr.
Henderson, Julie Ann (Slade) – Lassell, Francis M., Jr.
Hennessy, Joanne E. – Huyler, Mark T.
Hepworth, Carrie E. – Frisbee, Ernest E.
Herbert, Lucile Mary – Haley, Myron Henry
Herbert, Gloria I. – Reed, Norman E., Jr.
Herbst, Lisa-Anne – Allen, James W.
Hersey, Bernice – Durgin, Willard
Hersey, Elva Lillian – Brown, Morrill Howard
Hersey, Martha M. (Wiggin) – Whitten, Joseph B.
Hersey, Lora E. – Lester, Richard H.
Hersey, Marion Edna – Mitchell, Thomas Osborne
Hersey, Ethelyn Mildred – Brown, Harold Floyd
Hersey, Emma E. – Piper, Ralph G.
Herter, Diane Kaye – Tepe, Gary Joseph
Heth, Suzanne E. – Covert, Charles W.
Hewitt, Donnamarie T. – Naramore, John C.
Heyl, Lydia W. – Heyl, John K., Jr.
Hickey, Emma J. (Young) – Fernald, Hollis E.
Higgins, Elizabeth – Gould, Florence M.
Hill, Delia M. – Ridlon, Filbert E.
Hill, Jo-Ann E. – Smith, Richard L.
Hilow, Donna M. – Clough, Harold W.
Hilton, Lura M. – Young, Royal P.
Hitchcock, Ann F. – Huedepohl, Frank
Hixon, Helen E. – Horle, Richard G.
Hlushuk, Thelma Grace – Dearborn, Charles Philip
Hlushuk, Evelyn Irene – Cheney, Warren Dale
Hlushuk, Pauline E. – Dearborn, Howard
Hlushuk, Barbara Louise – Dore, Richard Leon
Hoague, Jody – Greenwood, John C.
Hobart, Julie S. – Tryder, William M. B., III
Hodgdon, Grace A. – Horner, George S.
Hodgdon, Mabel L. – Thomas, Willie W.
Hodgdon, Grace S. – Johnson, Edwin

Hodgdon, Emma S. (Swazey) – Emery, Howard F.
Hodges, Priscilla – Saunders, Howard N.
Hodges, Helen M. – MacLean, Forrest E.
Hodges, Cynthia J. - Bryant, Daniel
Hodgins, Mary Elizabeth (Floyd) – Marden, Philip S.
Hoitt, Sharon L. – Lee, William Joseph
Holland, Heidi A. – Bickerton, Jason J.
Hollis, Patricia Ruth – Wiggin, Merle Delmone
Holmberg, Lise Anne – Brennick, Steven L.
Hooper, Debra A. – Santulli, Nicholas P.
Hooper, Nancy Lee – Molburg, John D.
Hopkinson, Elizabeth – Loveren, John F.
Horne, Clara A. – Bean, John W.
Horne, Bertha – Haggett, George E.
Horner, Marion L. – Robie, George W.
Hostelley, Christine Putney – Capozzi, Edmund F., Jr.
Howard, Sarah Elizabeth (Lemings) – Bishop, Richard A.
Howe, Eva May – Paige, Robert
Howe, Nancy Ruth – Child, Charles L.
Howe, Eleanor Pearl – Mugridge, Donald Joseph
Howe, Charlotte Gertrude – Straw, Carroll Wilton
Hoyt, Gertrude – Lord, Charles S.
Huckins, Dorothy E. – Manley, LeRoy A.
Hull, Dorothy Ruggles – Howe, Robert Davis
Hunt, Mildred C. – Leader, Charles Robert
Hunter, Susan – Jones, Kenneth Duane
Hunter, Jacquelyn – Rollins, William Robert
Hunter, Bonnie Day – Weeks, Colin E.
Hunting, Ethel P. – Wiggin, Fred A.
Hurd, Mary E. – Hersey, Forrest W.
Hurt, Janet R. – Blake, Norman T.
Hutchins, Patricia A. – Kendal, Herbert G.
Hyslop, Sherry L. – Libby, Alan D.

Ireland, Ann M. – Elliott, Richard D.
Irester, Diane I. – Howgate, Nathan J.
Iveson, Pauline B. – Nickerson, Jonathan N.
Ivester, Joann May – Creilson, John Leo Joseph

Jackson, Wilda E. – Chittenden, Wentworth A.
Jackson, Audrey May – Davis, Foster Lee

Jenness, Pamela Rae – Thayer, Bruce Campbell
Jennings, Cynthia M. – Lawton, Lewis C., Jr.
Jessup, Susan Gail – Golledge, Robert W., Jr.
Jette, Elaine M. – Artman, Floyd R.
Johns, Darlene T. – Dillard, Charles A., Jr.
Johnson, Leslie Ann – McWhirter, Donald J.
Johnson, Judith A. – Mitchell, Bernard W.
Johnson, Emma – Howe, George F.
Johnson, Bernadette M. – Tupeck, Russell G.
Johnson, Suzy L. – Krueger, William E.
Johnson, Carol Ann – Appleton, Paul M.
Johnson, Vicki L. – Cheney, Sidney E.
Johnson, Ada Lela – Walker, Horace Albert
Johnston, Carrie Ann – Skey, Joseph Edward
Jones, Barbara – Ayers, Raymond H.
Jones, Sheila Marie – Anthony, William John, Jr.
Jones, Hattie W. – Cheney, Raymond E.
Jones, Ruth M. – Aiken, Aubrey W.
Jones, Kristin E. – Ryan, Dennis J.
Jones, Susan H. - Ramsbotham, Robert W., Jr.
Juke, Joan C. – Cole, Roger Ronald

Kaemmerer, Carlie H. (Deutsch) – Campion, James W., Jr.
Kaeser, Louise M. – Kulpa, John J.
Kalled, Jennifer M. – Stockman, Gary P.
Kauer, Janice J. – Wingate, Jeffrey A.
Keith, Mavis A. – Senior, Walter, Jr.
Keller, Blanid T. – Palatulli, Donald M.
Keller, Kathryn Ann – Fuller, William Pressley, III
Kelley, Tracy A. - Stockman, Gary P.
Kelley, Nancy J. – Glidden, Edgar H.
Kelliher, Nancy L. – Alexander, Kenneth D.
Kelly, Lotte J. – Lucas, Carroll L.
Kendal, Linda May – Dalton, Robert L., Jr.
Kenison, Kristine F. – Marvin, Ernest William
Keniston, Terry – Wakefield, Leonard R.
Keniston, Tina L. – Antonucci, William
Keniston, Ada F. – Staples, Christopher W.
Kenney, Edna – Watson, Alfred O.
Kenney, Bertha E. – Lamprey, Wilbur
Kenny, Dorothy E. – Dow, Vernon Robert

Kerr, Alice E. (Eddy) – Lester, Richard H.
Kerr, Randi S. – Gallagher, Robert M.
Kidd, Annie – Bennett, Maurice P.
Kimball, Cynthia L. - Oswalt, Edmund D.
Kimball, Laurie Ann – Hanson, Michael D. C.
King, Eleanor F. – Peterson, Ernest S.
King, Mary (Benedict) – Stanley, Donald Carleton
Kingsford, Sarah Harlan – Brown, Philip K., III
Kinmond, Heather Lynn – Cubeddu, James John
Kirby, Dorothy (Clement) – Wolcott, Wallace Henry
Kirk, Brenda G. – Whitten, Robert D., II
Kish, Suzanne E. – Hayes, William H.
Knapp, Rebecca – Keyes, William C.
Knights, Sylvia Edith – Dore, Roy Elwin
Knowles, Jean Debora – Nickerson, Jonathan Nelson
Kohtz, Susan L. – Benton, Richard D.
Konkonen, Valerie A. – Lagram, Robert M.
Kramer, Rena Bernice (Grant) – Willand, Charles Aaron
Krey, Pamela Ellen – Dan, Julian R. A.
Kuell, Doreen C. – Blaisdell, Robert P.

Labbe, Julie R. - Walker, Jeffrey H.
LaBonte, Yvonne – Piper, Frank F.
Ladd, Patricia W. (Wood) – Ladd, Harvey F.
Ladd, Lizzie E. – Hodgdon, Charles H.
Ladd, Etta M. – Davis, Charles A.
LaGuardia, Francesca – Barrett, Warren Edward
Laing, Katherine – Elkins, George William
Lambert, Michelle Denise – Whitney, Donald Allen
Lampert, Jean Marie – Way, John Richard
Lampron, Annette W. – Evans, Kenneth G.
Lampron, Jamie Lynn – Vittum, James M.
Lampron, Karen A. – Haeger, Michael D.
LaPoint, Blanche J. (Goss) – Corrow, Eric Daniel
Lauder, Winnifred L. – Bernard, Paul L., Jr.
Lawless, Rosalie Elaine – Gates, Charles Patterson, Jr.
Lawless, Doreen M. – Murner, Lawrence
Lawless, Marion Frances – Skorupski, Frank Baltas
Lawrence, Hazel Lillian – Provan, Walter Fairfield
Lawrence, Bernice Wellesly – Williams, Roger Lester
Lawson, Jane – Bonaccorso, Robert Francis

Leach, Isabel W. (Walker) – Wilson, Philip C.
Leach, Janet H. – Willard, Robert L.
Leighton, Apryl Marie – Ames, Arthur Alan
Lemoyne, Anne-Marie J. – Wood, William H., III
Leroux, Judy – Reed, James Michael
Lester, Marjorie (Wood) – Stickle, William W.
Letoile, Lisa A. – George, Jeffrey L.
Letteney, Martha Elaine – Paige, Thomas Howe
Levy, Marla – Jalbert, Roland M.
Lewis, Pearle Mae – Gerstl, Ernest
Libbey, Etta A. – Allen, George W.
Libby, Sharon L. – Libby, Robert C.
Libby, Carol Jean (Smith) – Atwood, Hubert Loring
Libby, Lizzie A. – Wiggin, Everett D.
Librandi, Kerry L. - Hunt, Alexander C.
Lincoln, Marjorie L. – Towle, Francis S.
Lind, Dorothy G. – Costonis, Anthony F.
Lindquist, Joyce M. – Libby, Alan B.
Linnell, Barbara Joan – Stacy, Martin Hartly
Littlefield, Edith Frances – Chamberlain, John Adams
Locke, Jessica Y. – Shaffer, Aaron K.
Locke, Sandra N. – Eaton, Brian N.
Lomas, Barbara L. - Parsons, Douglas B.
Long, Viola M. – Lynch, Andrew P.
Lord, Blanche V. (Elliot) – Lassell, Francis M.
Lord, Esther Belinda – Page, Lincoln Ridler
Lord, Sarah Cecelia – Lamb, William Herbert
Lorenz, Brenda C. – Quinby, Kenneth A.
Lucas, Muriel V. – Hooper, Ellsworth W.
Lucia, Dorothy – Allen, Wilfred Joseph
Lund, Grace E. – Watson, Reginald M.
Lynn, Darlene A. – Day, Robert M.
Lyon, Victoria Davis – Downing, Daniel Frederick
Lyon, Pamela Byrd – Saballa, David Lineses

Mack, Doris Hazel – Sargent, Clarence Harold
Mack, Dora E. – Haley, Charles E.
MacWilliams, Muriel – Stockman, Frank, Jr.
Maddock, Sonya R. – Lapar, William H. R.
Maddock, Mary Grace – DeWitt, William Collins
Magrath, Ruth A. – DeLuca, Vincent J.

Maine, Elsie – Howe, Robert D.
Mandigo, Rhonda Lynn – Thompson, Adam L.
Marcotte, Liana M. – Dufton, William M.
Margeson, Dorcas A. – Damon, Christopher S.
Marion, Irene A. – Porter, David R.
Markell, Susan Marie – Leary, Richard Michael
Marlatt, Joan W. – Carlson, Ronald E.
Marsh, Cheryl Ann – Hudson, Harmon Paul
Marshall, Jane A. – Ennis, Barry T.
Martin, Jamie L. – Pierce, Donald H.
Martin, Joan D. – White, Lewis B.
Martino, Susan – Ivester, Kenneth R., Jr.
Martins, Janice – Greenwood, Kenneth A.
Marzerka, Lee Ellen – Hall, Roy Michael
Matson, Sharon L. – Johnson, Burton L.
Matthews, Ann Mary (Jarites) – Hodgdon, Nathaniel W.
May, Greta E. – Dow, Roland D.
McAllister, Vicki A. – Callender, Donald E., II
McGlaflin, Calista Anne – Meehan, Robert Michael
McGloin, Marilyn L. – Dow, Wayne A.
McGrath, Kerry L. – Steinbach, Gary T.
McIntire, Winnie M. – Stitt, Albert T.
McIntyre, Luella B. – Bain, Frederick William
McKenzie, Dianne M. - Porter, Scott W.
McLaughlin, Lynn Anne – Harrison, Kevin Kreutzer
McLaughlin, Nancy A. – Taylor, Louis A.
McLaughlin, Cheryl A. – Williams, Bruce A.
McLeod, Diane N. – Menlove, Mark Leo
McMullin, Lara C. – Crane, Nathaniel S.
McNair, Ann – Page, Norman J.
McNamara, Cynthia Ann – Bearse, Lawrence Thomas
McNamara, Helen J. (Hendrickson) – Mabbett, George
Meadows, Gail M. - Tuohig, Barry A.
Meiklejohn, Samantha J. – O'Brien, Mark J.
Melloon, Annice C. (Horne) – Welch, George
Merrifield, Velma A. – Hodgdon, Forest W.
Merrifield, Sandra J. – Gormley, Matthew M.
Merrifield, Amy M. – Keenan, Henry E.
Merrifield, Dorothy R. – Bailey, Clarence L.
Merritt, Deborah F. - Colburn, Everett E.
Metcalfe, Christine M. – Emert, Jason E.

Metz, Marjorie A. – Falk, George M.
Metzger, Evelyn M. – Schait, Harold P.
Meyer, Carla J. – Paige, Thomas H.
Michaud, Tracy Leigh – Eldridge, Ronald Robert
Michaud, Julie S. – Paul, Brian D.
Miles, Natalie T. – Miles, Robert K., Jr.
Milligan, Karen A. – Wiley, David C.
Milligan, Patricia A. – Taylor, Timothy A.
Milligan, Patricia A. – Taylor, Timothy A.
Misiaszek, Linda L. – Camire, Robert R.
Mitchell, Joleen May – Kendall, Luke Jonathan
Mixer, Mardy Gale – Bogar, John D.
Mixer, Judy M. – Stockman, Brian A.
Moody, Lula – Stillings, Charles H.
Moody, Dawn S. – Evans, Lane W.
Moore, Gloria Elaine – Bennett, David Lister
Moore, Nellie V. (Shattuck) – Sawyer, George W.
Moran, Stacey Lynn – Ames, John R.
Morgan, Judith P. – Morgan, Daniel S.
Morgan, Judith P. – Whiting, Robert C.
Morris, Cecil – Thompson, Simon T.
Morris, Jane M. – Hardie, John W., Jr.
Morris, Alice R. – Wilkinson, Melvin R.
Morris, Eleanor Josephine – Piper, Ivan Charles
Morrison, Susan E. – Williams, Lance A.
Morrison, Susan Elizabeth – Rogers, Keith Tryon
Morrison, Jodi Lynn – Johnson, Craig Robert
Morrison, Lizzie B. – Lord, Milton A.
Morton, Gloria (Spaulding) – Bullock, Charles Edwin, II
Moulton, Nancy J. – Heath, Richard H.
Moulton, Lorraine Bertwell (Andrews) – Nelson, Paul Williard
Mugridge, Carlina – French, Norman A.
Muir, Sally F. G. – Johnson, Andrew A.
Muldoon, Virginia M. – Schou, George Dewey
Murphy, Esther L. – Chapman, Walter F.
Murray, Meagan Joy – Daley, Jon Peter
Murray, Darilyn D. – Kenneally, Thomas G.
Musacchio, Andrea – Barnhill, Paul M.
Myers, Christina Theresa – Smith, Brett Allen

Neilson, Barbara H. - Shafto, Donald B.

Nelson, Cheryl A. – Hoover, Keith
Nickerson, Judith E. – Williams, Ward B.
Nickerson, Barbara (Sharp) – Gould, Lebias R.
Nickerson, Jean D. – Mixer, John M.
Nicol, Muriel Jocelyne – Greene, Francois Robert
Nisbet, Patricia Ruth – Owen, Derek
Noble, Cheryl L. – Montrose, Joseph F.
Novotny, Barbara E. – Duncan, James H. S.
Noyes, Linda R. – Holmes, Bruce E.
Nudd, Josephine M. – Ayers, Charles H.
Nudd, Edna M. – Thompson, Lester
Nunez, Angela M. – Jewett, Jameson H.
Nutter, Perlina (Ellis) – Freese, George C.

O'Connell, Alida Alma (DuPont) – Whittier, Randall A., Jr.
O'Grady, Eva J. – Madden, Leonard D.
O'Grady, Eva M. – Haney, Keith D.
O'Neil, Mary Jane – Blake, Joseph C.
O'Neil, Gertrude E. – Christian, William H., Jr.
O'Neil-Lord, Hester M. – Bushman, Richard J.
O'Neill, Rita V. (Enos) – Raulins, John D.
Olsen, Kathleen – Fulginiti, Dominick
Olson, Lori Beth – Redmond, Edward O.
Ordway, Edna I. – Strobridge, Edward P.
Osgood, Lillian C. – Brooks, Donald K.
Oulton, Ruth E. (Dunn) – Allen, Newton J.

Packard, Judith A. (Austin) – Keith, Rowland D. H.
Packard, Suzanne L. – Hertzwig, Kevin S.
Page, Inez Evelyn – Garland, Chester A.
Page, Kimberly B. – Haley, Richard A.
Paige, Eva H. (Howe) – Paige, Robert K.
Paige, Eva H. - March, Donald M.
Paige, Geraldine – Mahoney, Donald E.
Palmer, Frances (Harriman) – Lamprey, Wilbur H.
Palmieri, Tina L. – Sherman, Steven M.
Parizo, Glenda E. – Hardie, John W., III
Parker, Joy G. – Erickson, Robert E.
Parker, Leilani K. – O'Shaughnessy, Timothy E.
Parkhurst, Dorothea B. (Brummitt) – Hayes, Carl Dewey
Parris, Jeannette Marie – Moulton, Robert C.

Parsons, Sandra L. – Austin, Dale A.
Paterno, Dorothy S. – Colbert, Eugene T.
Patterson, Gladys Marion (Page) – Proverb, Leon Gladstone
Peake, Margaret Hannum – Stack, Arthur Edward
Pearson, Jessie Ella – Cook, James Herbert
Peaslee, Jean C. – Stockman, Philip A.
Perkins, Jean A. – Hormell, Robert S.
Perry, Hazel Bernice – Bennett, James William
Perry, Lena E. (Eaton) – Adjutant, Charles L.
Person, Cynthia Ann – Pollini, William Sherm
Person, Beverly Annette (Bean) – Willard, Emery Durgin
Peterson, Verna - O'Brien, Gordon A.
Phelps, Donna E. – Dolloff, Frederick J.
Phelps, Carolyn – Pennell, Dwight W.
Philippe, Alice (Mitchell) – Cheney, William Joseph
Picard, Andrea Lee – Brousseau, Andrew A.
Pike, Judith M. – Gates, Kenneth F., Jr.
Pike, Mary Ellen – Dorais, Philip E.
Pinard, Anita Ruth (Osgood) – Smith, Richard James
Pinard, Claudia Ann – Lewis, Harold Drury
Pinkham, Addie A. – West, Charles W.
Piper, Ina F. – Staples, Frank
Piper, Jane Elizabeth – Sanborn, Richard Willis
Piper, Addie (Geto) – Cordeau, Peter
Pitt, Heather R. – McLellan, Jacob M.
Plamondon, Nichole M. – Bevilaqua, Ralph J.
Plummer, Ella E. – Thompson, Moses
Poleman, Grace H. – Arsenault, Marshall
Porter, Brandie L. – Huot, Jean-Paul M.
Post, Valerie Linn – Aspinwall, John Francis
Potenza, Lisa M. – Greenwood, Kenneth A.
Potenza, Lisa M. – White, Ronald E.
Pouliot, Susan A. – Coggeshall, Robert M.
Powers, Anna Estelle – Ridlon, Arnold LeRoy
Pratt, Elizabeth – Barnett, Richard G.
Pratt, Marietta Joy – Whitten, Edward Russell
Prouty, Lillian M. (Wentworth) – Douglass, Oliver S.
Purcell, Kristina Kay – Pedone, William Anton
Purtell, Pamela Ann – Knapp, Richard Charles, Jr.

Rabzak, Theresa L. – Myers, Robert D.

Ramsbotham, Susan H. – Weeks, Charles E.
Raymond, Marion Jerusha – Noble, Leslie C.
Reade-Howell, Sylvia - Rollins, Richard A.
Redding, Joanne E. – Lawson, Duward A.
Reed, Marion Claire – Pike, Chester H.
Reed, Thelma Louise – Diltz, Melvin Arthur
Reed, Shirley A. – Ames, Rolland D.
Reed, Virginia D. – Richardson, Bruce D.
Reed, Barbara Jane – Frederick, C. Leslie
Reed, Lisa Robin – Moody, Scot Macdonald
Reed, Evelyn Rebecca – Clough, Robert William
Reed, Joyce Lorraine – Bean, Clyde Leroy, Jr.
Repucci, Angela Ruth – White, Ronald Ernest
Reynolds, Ellen – Vincenti, Edward Charles
Reynolds, Ellen C. – Hall, Thomas B.
Rice, Leonora P. – Quilliam, Francis P.
Rice, Sharlene Ann – Van Rooy, Frank
Rich, Nancy Nelson – Starrett, Raymond Eugene
Richardson, Lillian May (O'Brien) – Wilson, Philip Clark
Richardson, Virginia – Conrad, Thomas M.
Richardson, Maude (Betts) – Moore, Walter
Richardson, Marcia J. – Severance, Brian
Rico, Patricia A. – Stockman, John L.
Riddle, Emma C. – Riddle, Hollis L.
Ridlon, Bonnie L. - Gagne, Ernest A.
Ridlon, Sandra June – Cheney, Gilbert Frederick
Ridnour, Olivia Alice – Bushman, Richard John
Riley, Cheryl A. – Halepis, Andrew M.
Riley, Bertha May – Smith, Clifton Edward
Robinson, Ann – Snow, Stephen D.
Rodgers, Laura K. – Oldham, Nile Michael
Roebarge, Muriel Cecil – Haley, Delbert Clarence
Rogers, Melissa L. – Jenkins, Mark S.
Rollins, Andrea – Capron, David A.
Roome, Anne B. – Hardy, Warren R.
Rosell, Sally I. - Fiske, Charles W., Jr.
Rouleau, Marguerite Bertha – Kurth, John Edward
Rudolph, Sandra Lee – Newman, Theodore C., Jr.
Runey, Ann Ruth – Kohl, Waldemar Roy
Russell, Deborah M. – Scott, Richard C.
Ryan, Kelly Ann – Hollis, Bruce William

Sampson, Marion A. – Drouin, Wilfred E.
Santoro, Elizabeth A. – George, Richard W.
Sargent, Doris H. (Mack) – Smith, Walter R.
Sargent, Constance – Bean, Milton L. H.
Sargent, Lura P. – Bean, Ralph L.
Sargent, Theresa L. – Hlushuk, Wade A.
Saulnier, Cheryl A. – Lesnik, Roger H.
Sawyer, Kate M. – Hoyt, Charles S.
Sawyer, Patricia – Brown, John M.
Sayce, Carol Ann – Barratt, Stephen D.
Schaefer, Barbara L. – O'Grady, John P.
Schmidt, Alice – Glidden, Nelson R.
Schou, Mary Kathryn – Mendenhall, John Dean
Scudder, Shannon M. - Libby, Jeffrey A.
Seaman, Elizabeth Anderson – Davis, John McQuiston
Seegar, Barbara J. – Haley, Delbert C., III
Senecal, Elizabeth L. – Daly, Michael J.
Senecal, Janet J. - Sweeney, Thomas W., Jr.
Senior, Mary Grace – Foss, Guy Leslie
Senior, Gretchen Whitney – Bursaw, Burton Bechard
Severance, Molly – Grezatti, Stephen A.
Severance, Glenda M. – Eldridge, John C.
Seymour, Barbara H. – Wilson, Gale Sevey
Shaffer, Nancy M. – Massi, Ildo F.
Shaheen, Julia M. – Glidden, Troy S.
Shaw, Irene C. – Gray, Burton R.
Sheaff, Estelle – Panno, Harry Frederick
Sheahan, Lauren Kristen – Zelko, Darrell Patrick
Sheahan, Diana M. – Burbank, Paul H.
Sheen, Lugene M. – Duso, David A.
Sheridan, Kelly Jean – Hallam, Timothy Driesner, Jr.
Sherwood, Patricia J. – Foust, Howard W.
Shure, Joanne M. – Dunn, Kenneth G.
Shure, Dana L. – Bernier, Michael T.
Signoretti, Cynthia Diane – Bullis, Russell Hathaway, Jr.
Simick, Mary Ann – Flint, Stanley Reed
Simpson, Vina – Corson, Woodbury
Skinner, Patricia Ann – Lupo, Franklin Roosevelt
Sleeper, Virginia Margaret – Dunn, Robert Joseph, Jr.
Sleeper, Beatrice M. – Stillings, George E.
Sleeper, Ann G. (Hayes) – Edgerly, Albert L.

Sleeper, Virginia M. – McLeman, Scott D.
Sloane, Janet L. – Bushman, Robert J.
Smith, Carol Jean – Libby, Robert Carleton, Jr.
Smith, Nancy L. – French, Donald R.
Smith, Ruth E. (Adjutant) – Wakefield, George H.
Smith, JoAnn E. (Hill) – Thompson, Richard B.
Smith, Donna L. – Page, Lincoln A.
Smith, Peggy Joan – Ames, Rolland D.
Smith, Luella – Whitehouse, Maurice French
Smith, Nellie M. – Blake, Joseph C.
Smith, Cora A. (Beaulieu) – Nelson, Harry C. H.
Smith, Madalyn May – Panno, Harry Frederick
Smith, Mona Ellen – Elliot, Eugene Waldo
Smith, Rachel M. – Plodzik, Benjamin J.
Smith, Barbara J. – Swain, Robert W.
Smith, April Lynn – Bussiere, Thomas Jeffrey
Smith, Sandra E. – Straw, David G., Jr.
Smith, Elsie L. – McIntire, Delma L., Jr.
Smith, Marylin E. – Colby, Reginald C.
Smith, Kathleen A. – Stockman, William L.
Snyder, Louise W. (Thompson) – Motley, Harry G.
Southard, Jeri Lynn – White, Duane R.
Southard, Pamela Jean – Lohman, Andrew Davies
Southworth, Nellie N. (Lane) – Deal, Edward L.
Sparks, Deborah L. – Haley, Delbert C., III
Spaulding, Frances E. – Edwards, Judson F.
Spencer, Jean W. – Scott, John R.
Spencer, Cathy Marie – Danielson, Paul S.
Sprague, Florence D. – Ferguson, Levi D.
Springer, Muriel Agnes – Reed, Robert Arnold
Springer, Hattie B. – Hersey, Edwin C.
Stacey, Brenda J. – Lundquist, Courtney J.
Stacey, Kathie M. – Lamprey, Carroll A.
Stacy, Ruth C. (Dunn) – Oulton, Fred R.
Staples, Nellie F. – Piper, John F.
Staples, Ora B. – Robinson, Walter B.
Staples, Ora B. – Graham, John E.
Steadman, Linda G. – LeBlanc, Douglas P.
Stetson, Pamela – Comtois, Gerard J., Jr.
Stevens, Ramona Averill – Cantwell, Bruce David
Stevens, Penelope – Garrett, Edwin R.

Stevenson, Rebecca Lacy – Hlidek, Brian Drake
Stillings, Cora Emma – Smith, Walter Roy
Stockman, Mary Ann – Urquhart, Kenneth N.
Stockman, Nancy J. – Moulton, Robert C., Jr.
Stockman, C. Jean – Whitten, Charles F.
Stockman, Patricia A. – Bushman, Richard J.
Stokes, Mattie L. – Cheney, Wyatt D.
Stowe, Eliza G. – Martin, Ronald L.
Stowe, Marilyn L. – Tomb, William C.
Straw, Elizabeth J. – Haartz, Luther W.
Strickland, Sadie F. (Horne) – Moody, George A.
Sullivan, Shannon Lee – Mitchell, Kevin Maurice
Sullivan, Mary A. – Davis, Foster E.
Sullivan, Susan Anne – Croteau, Arthur J., III
Sullivan, Marjorie M. - McGorty, Peter F., Jr.
Sutherland, Edith R. – Chandler, Perry R.
Svenson, Kristen Ellen – Pike, Caleb Everett
Swain, Karin L. – Lovering, Jefferson S.
Swan, Nancy M. – Malette, Brian T.
Swanick, Anne C. – Vilders, Neil R.
Swanson, Regina M. (Larmay) – Johnson, Warren A.
Sweetman, Melanie E. – Buel, Anthony S.

Tallman, Debora Jane – McIntire, James Arthur
Tarbell, Shirley G. – Page, Lincoln R.
Taylor, Valerie A. - Veld, Richard P.
Taylor, Desira Lee – Hunter, Philip N.
Taylor, Carrie – Britton, Harry
Teger, Jean Ellaine (Oliver) – Jones, William Richardson
Tervo, Michele A. – Patterson, Robert J.
Thibault, Marlene M. – Kent, Roger
Thibedeau, Frances – Haley, Lawrence Ervin
Thomas, Heidi Margrit – Kennell, James S.
Thomas, Wendy Fox – Ingram, James Andrew
Thomas, Janet L. – Theriault, David A.
Thomas, Effie A. – Thomas, Chester I.
Thomas, Doris Louise – Bottomley, Bruce MacL.
Thompson, Fannie E. – Lamprey, Wilbur
Thompson, Eleanor May – Woodmancy, Charles Wesley
Thompson, Nellie M. – Merrifield, Perley
Thompson, Kathaleen M. - Ferland, Andrew M.

Thompson, Elaine E. - Shannon, Guy E.
Thompson, Doris Elizabeth – Davis, Roger Valentine
Thompson, Eleanor May – Davis, Willis Paige
Thornburg, Mary A. – Potter, Wilmer M.
Thurley, Annie P. (Hanson) – Ladd, John A.
Todaro, Christina L. – Reynolds, Mark Morgan
Todesco, Linda J. – Jamieson, Robert F.
Toms, Carolyn L. – Craigue, James E.
Towle, Maud Evelyn – Bennett, Ralph Vaughn
Treat, Mary Esther C. - Stetson, Frederick W., II
Tripp, Stephanie – Tupeck, Stephen C.
Tupeck, Hazel F. – Stock, James S.
Tupeck, Bernadette M. – Greenwood, Kenneth A.
Turner, Winnifred – McDougal, C. B.
Tutt, Dorothy Mae – Bennett, Donald Chase
Tweedell, Marjorie M. – Webster, Steven W.

Unander-Scharin, Catharine W. – Chiapetta, Michael L.
Upjohn, Mary E. – Stevens, Raymond L.

Van Tassel, LauraLee – Ames, James Ronald
Vappi, Rebecca A. - Morgan, Ricky M.
Veilleux, Cindy P. – O'Brien, James R.
Vieira, Ana Rosa T. – Thompson, Douglas R.
Vinnicombe, Anne T. – Goldschmidt, Steven O.
Vittum, Vanessa – Libby, Scott B.
Vittum, Vanessa – Ruggiero, Michael J.

Waddell, Kathryn I. – O'Connell, Richard P.
Wager, Frances (Arnold) – Bickford, John H., Jr.
Wakefield, Ruth C. - Cheney, Earl L.
Wakefield, Allura (Burrows) – Wilkins, Elmer L.
Wakefield, Linda L. – Lessard, William D.
Waldie, Deborah A. - Block, Andrew R.
Waldron, Emma E. – Moulton, James W.
Wallace, Eda M. – Davis, Albert E.
Walsh, Anna Laurie – Murray, Harrison Slade
Walton, Natalie M. – Kelloway, Wayne J.
Walton, Ruth Mildred (Ostmark) – Bennett, Douglas L.
Ward, Dorothy E. – Ran, Albert C.
Ward, Alice I. – Richard, James A.

Warner, Lisa Ann – Irvine, Michael Francis
Warner, Katharine L. - Charles, Richard H., Jr.
Warren, Wendy Lynn – Berry, Steven Dean
Watson, Beatrice Boyden – Whitten, Walter Francis
Webber, Susan J. – Heintze, Larry E.
Welch, Lisa Ann – Parkhurst, Walter R.
Welch, Ethel – Elliott, George W.
Welch, Mabel P. – Hayes, Henry F.
Welch, Sharon R. – Moreau, Ronald A.
Weller, Phyllis (Stacey) – Lamprey, Carroll A.
Wendell, Lenora A. – Lewis, Rainsford W.
Wendell, Mary E. (Lougee) – Meader, Charles
Wentworth, Carolyn Andersen – Riley, Adam Tracy
Wentworth, Carrie L. – Walker, Horace A.
West, Priscilla – Baxter, George P.
Wetherbee, Carol Ann – Bense, Theodore Charles
Whempner, Joy S. – Mitchell, Kenneth L.
White, Shelley Lee – Katwick, James Peter
White, Monica Soonie – Dwyer, Paul Richard
White, Martha J. – Baxter, Harry W.
White, Deanna L. – Richardson, Harold E., Jr.
Whitehead, Beth – Baker, Harold H.
Whiting, Mildred Frances – Reed, Frank Eugene
Whittemore, Madeline Elizabeth (Foster) – Shannon, Carroll Leroy
Whitten, Phoebe Carrie – Dore, Jesse James
Whitton, Mamie G. – Whitton, Joseph W.
Wiesner, Margaret B. – Sargent, David W.
Wiggin, Arlene Gertrude (Stillings) – Bennett, Ralph Vaughn
Wiggin, Evelyn M. – Cole, Irving C.
Wiggin, Marie L. – Shannon, Guy E.
Wiggin, Mina E. – Burleigh, Will C.
Wilber, Vicky Marie – Arcouette, Ronald James, III
Wilkin, Jean C. – Chandler, Norman P.
Willard, Virginia D. – Staples, Charles F.
Willard, Elsie M. – Dunn, Kenneth G.
Williams, Deborah L. – Eldridge, Bradley W.
Williams, Ann Celeste – Pike, Curtis A.
Williams, Susie C. – Mitchell, Thomas O., Jr.
Williams, Judith N. – LaBranche, Ronald E.
Williams, Mary Patricia – Hodgdon, Raeburn W.
Williams, Katherine E. – Hoffer, Frederic S., III

Williamson, Frances (Dow) – Hooper, Ernest L.
Wilson, Nancy A. – Stockman, Philip A.
Wingate, Sarah J. – Copplestone, Steven A.
Wistedt, Lisa Christine (Nelson) – Graham, John E.
Witham, Billie-Sue – Hale, Scott Joseph
Wood, Doris – Peterson, Lawrence B.
Wood, Barbara – Hunter, Bradbury E.
Wood, Michelle Y. – Bean, Benjamin A.
Wood, Barbara Jane – Garabedian, Martin Sarkis
Wood, Marjorie – Lester, Richard H.
Wood, Michelle Y. – Craigue, Scott B.
Woodbury, Linda H. – Perkins, Maurice L.
Worster, June B. (Kenneson) – Piper, Norman H.
Worthley, Katherine L. – Brown, Edmond M., Jr.
Wright, Sarah E. – Masterton, Kenneth R.
Wright, Mary A. – Hensley, Francis W.
Wright, Kathleen Stuart – Lochhead, Thomas John
Wright, Wendy – Cao, Ramiro
Wright, Noel Stuart – Cantwell, William J., Jr.

Yablonka, Candace A. (Hull) – Copp, Stuart O., Jr.
Yanez, Judith – Hall, Lindley H.
Yerden, Carol Ann – Chellman, Chester Eric, III
Young, Yvonne H. - Butler, Wendell R.
Young, Edna S. – Cheney, John G.

Zaborowski, Lois Ann – Pond, Jonathan D.
Zenk, Doris – Janes, Clarence W., Jr.

TUFTONBORO
DEATHS

ABRUZZI,
Peter F., d. 8/5/1940 at 39/11/23 at Sandy Is.; physician; married;
   b. Italy; Modesto Ferrini (Italy) and Carmela Ferrini (Italy)

ACKROYD,
John Franklin, d. 7/27/1905 at 22/6/7 in Tuftonboro; tuberculosis;
   single; b. Durham; John J. Ackroyd and Ella D. M. Goodall

ADJUTANT,
Blanche E., d. 11/13/1955 at 54 in Tuftonboro; at home; married; b.
   NH; Hiram Perkins and Henrietta Clough
Helen Phyllis, d. 2/20/1994 in Wolfeboro; Charles Dougherty and
   Estella Pleasanton
Lester, d. 5/5/1901 at 35/5/21 in Tuftonboro; osteo sarcoma of neck;
   single; b. Tuftonboro; Parkman D. Adjutant and Priscilla
   Thompson
Parkman D., d. 3/3/1903 at 77/0/10 in Tuftonboro; disease of
   prostrate glands; widower; Samuel Adjutant and Nancy Dore
Priscilla, d. 11/14/1894 at 66/1/8; housewife; married; b. Ossipee;
   Samuel Thompson and Betsy Kenny
Roscoe V., d. 7/1/1978 at 80 in Wolfeboro; b. Tuftonboro
Willie, d. 5/17/1944 at 84 in Wolfeboro; carpenter; widower;
   Parkman Adjutant (Tuftonboro) and Priscilla Thompson
   (Ossipee)

ALLARD,
John W., d. 1/3/1905 at 73/6 in Tuftonboro; heart disease; widower;
   b. Dover; William Allard and Elizabeth Hussy

ALLEN,
Blanche May, d. 12/21/1950 at 69 in Wolfeboro; at home; widow; b.
   E. Boston, MA; Noah William Sewall and Elizabeth A.
   Thompson
Charles B., d. 4/24/1969 at 63 in Wolfeboro; plant manager; single;
   b. MA; John Allen and Blanche M. Sewall
Edith L., d. 6/6/1985 in Tuftonboro; Frank E. Authur and Mary
   Chattaway
Edward M., d. 12/21/1975 at 68 in Wolfeboro; b. E. Boston, MA
Etta Ernestine, d. 12/27/1938 at 63/9/6 in Wolfeboro; post mistress;
   married; b. Tuftonboro; Levi W. Libbey (Tuftonboro) and Laura
   J. Staples (Effingham)

George W., d. 1/7/1944 at 76/5/24 in Tuftonboro; farmer; widower; b. Albany; Smith Allen (Tuftonboro) and Louisa Roberts (Albany)

Herbert, d. 8/1/1894 at 38; laborer; married; b. Canada; Alonzo Allen and Melissa Glidden

Howard Samuel, Sr., d. 3/4/1995 in Wolfeboro; Ernest Allen and Susie Sweet

John, d. 2/28/1937 at 65/5/26 in Melvin Village; married; b. NS; John Allen

Joseph H., d. 1/10/1980 in Wolfeboro; Walter Allen and Udella Steel

Lena H., d. 3/3/1977 at 85 in Wolfeboro; b. Salem, MA

ALLSTRIN,

Emma C., d. 4/6/1954 at 84 in Tuftonboro; at home; widow; b. Sweden; John Nelson and Anna Lisa

ALTEMUS,

Bill D., d. 6/22/2003 in Laconia; Lemon Altemus and Gladys Grimm

AMADON,

Irene M., d. 8/26/1975 at 49 in Rochester; b. Wolfeboro

AMBROSE,

David, d. 4/26/1905 at 81/8/1 in Melvin Village; old age; widower; b. Moultonboro; Nathaniel Ambrose and Irene Brown

Lucinda B., d. 3/25/1895 at 65/1/3 in Tuftonboro; pneumonia; married; b. Tuftonboro; Nathaniel Hodgdon and Lydia Caverly

AMES,

Douglas B., d. 5/15/1990 in Tuftonboro; Richard Ames and Barbara Bushman

Richard Wayne, d. 10/7/1994 in Tuftonboro; James Ames and Ada Eldridge

AMIRAULT,

Frank E., d. 10/16/2000 in Manchester; Frank Amirault and Eleanor McClusky

Frank E., d. 6/7/2001 in Laconia; George Amirault and Levinan Surrette

AMUNDSEN,

Otto Edvin, d. 9/22/1993 in Wolfeboro; Otto Amundsen and Helene

Andresen

ANDERSON,
Jessie L., d. 10/6/1901 at 30/10/18 in Tuftonboro; phthisis
pulmonalis; married; b. Kittery Point, ME; Franklin H. Bond and
Lizzie J. Todd

ANGULAT,
John Joseph, d. 12/31/1999 in Tuftonboro; John Matthew Angulat
and Marie Aaronson

APPLETON,
Carol Johnson, d. 6/16/1997 in Wolfeboro; Carl B. Johnson and
Louise P. Michle

ARSENEAU,
Andrew C., d. 8/28/2003 in Wolfeboro; Bernard Arseneau and Pearl
Mudge

ARSNEAULT,
Frank, d. 12/16/1926 at 36/4/11 in Tuftonboro; automobile painter;
married; Marshall Arsneault (Canada) and Jane Collet
(Canada)

AUSTIN,
Charles R., d. 5/13/2000 in Laconia; Jasper Austin and Nellie
MacCreighton
Jasper D., d. 1/16/1989 in Wolfeboro; Albert Austin and Hattie
Tucker
Nellie, d. 11/4/2004 in Tuftonboro; Charles MacCreighton and
Florence Kimball

AVERY,
Fred A., d. 4/21/1917 at 60/5/17 in Tuftonboro; married; b.
Wolfeboro; John Avery and Susan Horn

AYERS,
son, d. 10/11/1909 at 0/2/2; marasmus; b. Tuftonboro; Herbert Ayers
and Ina M. Adjutant
daughter, d. 4/30/1913 at 0/0/1; premature birth; b. Tuftonboro;
Herbert Ayers and Mabel Adjutant

Alfred, d. 6/11/1929 at 89/6/22 in Tuftonboro; retired; widower; b.
Tuftonboro; Levi Ayers and Sally Welch (Tuftonboro)
Carl Raymond, d. 1/18/1911 at 2/7/28; pneumonia; b. Tuftonboro;
Herbert Ayers and Ina M. Adjutant
Carrie B., d. 3/28/1933 at 56/5/22 in Ctr. Tuftonboro; housewife;
married; b. Woodsford, ME; Joseph J. Burleigh (Ctr.
Tuftonboro) and Sarah H. Shannon (Barnstead)
Charles, d. 9/23/1900 at 54/7/1 in Tuftonboro; valvular disease of the
heart; married; b. Tuftonboro; Levi Ayers and Sally Welch
Edmund L., d. 7/24/1922 at 72/6/12 in Tuftonboro; farmer; widower;
b. Tuftonboro; Levi Ayers and Sally Welch
Ella M., d. 3/27/1900 at 42/10/26 in Tuftonboro; diabetes; married; b.
Tuftonboro; John L. Canney and Beulah Mains
Ellerton F., d. 3/7/1906 at 0/10/20; capillary bronchitis; b. Tuftonboro;
Herbert Ayers and Ina Adjutant
Hannah, d. 2/28/1904 at 65/0/21 in Tuftonboro; heart failure;
married; b. Tuftonboro; Chandler Drew and Claracy Norris
Herbert, d. 7/8/1942 at 65/5/9 in Tuftonboro; farmer; married; b.
Tuftonboro; Edmond B. Ayers (Tuftonboro) and Ella M. Canney
(Tuftonboro)
Ina Mabel, d. 11/7/1973 at 86 in Wolfeboro; b. NH
James, d. 1/21/1911 at 67/10/7; pneumonia; widower; b. Tuftonboro;
Levi W. Ayers and Sally Welch
John, d. 5/27/1954 at 88 in Wolfeboro; farmer; widower; b.
Tuftonboro; James Ayers and Hannah Drew
Julia A., d. 5/11/1905 at 62/1/11 in Melvin Village; heart disease;
married; b. Tuftonboro; Josiah Tate and Annah Hull
Levi Langdon, d. 10/4/1961 at 70/1/24 in Wolfeboro; married; b.
Tuftonboro; Charles Ayers and Sarah Jane Kenney

AYLWARD,
Ruth Wilhelmina, d. 4/8/1995 in Wolfeboro; Ralph Hunt and Addie
Brown

BACON,
Albert H., d. 9/7/1916 at 71/6/7 in Tuftonboro; b. Southboro, MA;
Aaron Bacon and Mary Brooks
Myra A., d. 8/21/1949 at 72 in Laconia; at home; widow; b. Thornton;
George Gilman and Elizabeth J. Plummera

BAIN,
Frederick W., d. 7/5/1985 in Ossipee; James D. Bain and Augusta
   Bell
Luella M., d. 11/3/1989 in Tuftonboro; Lewis McIntire and Sadie Doe

BAIRD,
Lewis, d. 5/11/1894 at 82; farmer; married; b. Tuftonboro

BAISLEY,
Madeleine L., d. 4/20/1992 in Tuftonboro; Arthur A. Libby and
   Florence Hunt

BAKER,
Marou, d. 4/10/1985 in Wolfeboro; ----- and Maude -----

BALES,
Lawrence C., d. 12/25/1986 in Wolfeboro; Harold C. Bales and Edith
   Lawrence

BANFILL,
Willie, d. 1/28/1954 at 81 in Moultonboro; laborer; single; b.
   Madison; Andrew Banfill and Eliza Roberts

BARBA,
Raymond, d. 5/27/2001 in Wolfeboro; Erasmo Barba and Rachel
   Salamon

BARNARD,
Richard, d. 8/7/1976 at 69 in Tuftonboro; b. MA

BARNETT,
Anthony A., d. 9/25/2003 in Lebanon; Irving Barnett and Esther
   Davis

BARR,
Allen C., d. 1/3/1946 at 83/6/0 in Wolfeboro; farmer; widower; b. NS
Dora L., d. 9/29/1942 at 78/3/17 in Wolfeboro; housewife; married; b.
   Tuftonboro; William Thompson (Tuftonboro) and Eliza Jones
   (Tuftonboro)

BARTLETT,
Richard H., d. 10/11/1971 at 65 in Wolfeboro; b. MA

BASHE,
Charles J., d. 10/4/2002 in Wolfeboro; Edwin Bashe and Basilia
 Hauser

BATTERSBY,
Cowan W., d. 9/20/1978 at 85 in Tuftonboro; b. PEI

BAXTER,
George P., d. 3/7/1986 in Tuftonboro; Harry T. Baxter and Cristina
 Pringle
Priscilla, d. 7/16/1971 at 66 in Wolfeboro; b. NH

BAYER,
Margaret L., d. 2/24/2001 in Wolfeboro; John Lockwood and Pauline
 Deiesi
Robert K., d. 3/27/1967 at 50 in Wolfeboro; US Air Force; married; b.
 New York, NY; Frederick Bayer and Mary Connor

BEAN,
Alger L., d. 10/7/1892 at 9/0/24 in Tuftonboro; croup and pneumonia;
 b. Tuftonboro; Silas W. Bean (Tuftonboro) and Cora Bean
 (Saco, ME)
Arthur, d. 12/1/1943 at 75/3/2 in Wolfeboro; farmer; widower; b.
 Moultonboro; Agustan Bean (VT) and Lucy Libby
Augustin, d. 3/11/1916 at 89/9/29 in Tuftonboro; farmer; widower; b.
 VT; James B. Bean and Sally Bean
Blanche L., d. 11/20/1906 at 12/8/7; acute diabetes; b. Tuftonboro;
 Willie L. Bean and Ula D. Foss
Clara A., d. 8/21/1906 at 40/9/27; pulmonary tuberculosis; married;
 b. Lawrence, MA; Isaac R. Horne and Clarinda S. Neal
Constance F., d. 5/9/1989 in N. Conway; Jess Sargent and Leonora
 Potter
Cora A., d. 9/1/1915 at 54/4/9 in Tuftonboro; housewife; married; b.
 Saco, ME; Simon Bean (Tuftonboro) and Achsah Chase
 (Tuftonboro)
Cordelia A., d. 11/15/1936 at 65/11/11 in Wolfeboro; at home;
 married; b. Birmingham, England
Delia M., d. 12/15/1899 at 0/4/28 in Tuftonboro; b. Tuftonboro; Willie

L. Bean and Ula D. Foss
Dorothy A., d. 8/23/1906 at 3/3/12; tuberculosis of brain; b.
    Tuftonboro; John W. Bean and Clara A. Horne
Foster A., d. 9/9/1907 at 4/9; diabetes mellitus; b. Tuftonboro; Willie
    L. Bean and Ula D. Foss
Frank A., d. 8/30/1912 at 53/2/11; diabetes mellitus; single; b.
    Tuftonboro; Augustine Bean and Lucy A. Libby
Frank J., d. 11/29/2000 in Ossipee; John Bean and Claire Horne
George F., d. 2/19/1900 at 71/7/15 in Tuftonboro; cystitis; married; b.
    Tuftonboro; James Bean
James F., d. 4/29/1895 at 42/1 in Tuftonboro; disease of heart;
    married; b. Tuftonboro; Simon B. Bean and Axa M. Chase
John William, d. 4/22/1946 at 79/11/14 in Wolfeboro; caretaker;
    widower; b. Tuftonboro; Simon B. Bean (Tuftonboro) and Ascha
    A. Chase (Tuftonboro)
Lizzie, d. 3/15/1920 at 36/11/12 in Tuftonboro; housewife; married;
    b. Ireland; Cornelius Riley and Bridget Kelley
Lucy A., d. 6/8/1900 at 74/5 in Tuftonboro; heart disease; married; b.
    Scarboro, ME; Reuben Libby
Mark O., d. 1/20/1925 at 69/0/0 in Concord; steam fitter; single;
    Simon B. Bean and Ashsa Chase
Mary A., d. 9/14/1902 at 74/2/18 in Tuftonboro; valvular disease of
    heart; widow; b. Ossipee; Solomon Abbott and Dorcas Hanson
Mary Frances, d. 11/5/1939 at 83/11/27 in Wolfeboro; retired
    dressmaker and housewife; widow; b. Tuftonboro; Augustin
    Bean (VT) and Lucy Libbey (Spurwick, ME)
Ralph S., d. 11/25/1944 at 62 in Wolfeboro; farmer; married; b.
    Tuftonboro; Willie S. Beane (Moultonboro) and Nea D. Foss
    (Tuftonboro)
Sarah F., d. 10/23/1903 at 70/6/16 in Tuftonboro; chronic sastutic;
    widow; Grafton Abbott and Catherine Frye
Silas W., d. 1/8/1917 at 61/11/28 in Laconia; farmer; widower; b.
    Tuftonboro; Silas F. Bean and Mary A. Abbott
Ula Diana, d. 12/26/1939 at 77/2/8 in Wolfeboro; housewife; widow;
    b. Tuftonboro; Thomas Foss and Laura Blaisdell
Willie L., d. 7/23/1937 at 76/3/21 in Tuftonboro; farmer; married; b.
    Tuftonboro; Augustus Bean (Tuftonboro) and Lucy Libby
    (Scarboro, ME)

BEARCE,
Ellen B., d. 6/19/1972 at 96 in Wolfeboro; b. ME

BECK,
Albert Howard, d. 6/7/1962 at 91 in Wolfeboro; banker; widower; b.
    S. Boston, MA; James H. Beck and Elizabeth Proctor

BELANGER,
Lula Alice, d. 4/7/1996 in Wolfeboro; Charles Davis and Lula -----

BELL,
Kenneth E., d. 12/16/1970 at 76 in Wolfeboro; chem. engineer;
    married; b. MA; Alfred M. Bell and Mertie Rice

BELLEMEUR,
Eleanor, d. 11/2/1998 in Tuftonboro; Austin Hersey and Helen Piper
Raymond E., d. 9/2/2000 in Tuftonboro; William Bellemeur and Alta
    Jenness

BELMONT,
Augustus F., d. 10/3/2001 in Wolfeboro; Augustive Belmont and
    Minnie Payne

BENNETT,
Brian D., d. 7/27/1989 in Weirs Beach; Paul W. Bennett, Sr. and
    Edna Hersey
Charles, d. 3/31/1940 at 89/2/28 in FL; merchant; widower; b. NH;
    Albert Bennett (NH) and Hannah Pike (NH)
Edwena E., d. 2/13/1925 at 71/5/11 in Tuftonboro; at home; married;
    b. Tuftonboro; Mark F. Piper (Tuftonboro) and Susan Lovering
    (Freedom)
Eleanor G., d. 1/31/1965 at 74 in Ossipee; widow; b. Boston, MA;
    Alfred J. Dawes and Nellie Collins
Elizabeth M., d. 7/9/1956 at 82 in Tuftonboro; housewife; widow; b.
    NY
Frances E., d. 7/15/1926 at 77/5/20 in Tuftonboro; at home; widow;
    Calvin Fernald (S. Berwick, ME) and Belinda Caverly
    (Tuftonboro)
Frank Ernest, d. 4/27/1927 at 4/3/9 in Tuftonboro; b. Wolfeboro;
    Frank S. Bennett (Tuftonboro) and Eleanor G. Dawes (MA)
Frank S., d. 2/28/1957 at 73 in Tuftonboro; carpenter; married; b.
    Tuftonboro; James W. Bennett and Frances Fernald
Grace, d. 6/17/1963 at 77 in Wolfeboro; housewife; married; b.
    Worcester, MA; George Dewey and Helen Ryan

Hannah, d. 9/8/1899 at 77/9/17 in Tuftonboro; married; b. Tuftonboro; Aderial Welch and Dorcha Wadley
James A., d. 12/6/1910 at 63/3/3; apoplectic shock; married; b. Tuftonboro; John E. Bennett and Hannah Welch
John E., d. 4/6/1900 at 76/2/7 in Tuftonboro; heart disease; widower; b. Wolfeboro; John Bennett and Ruth Elkins
John E., d. 3/1/1965 at 76 in Wolfeboro; farmer; single; b. Tuftonboro; John Bennett and Lizzie Smith
John W., d. 7/31/1929 at 73/8/1 in Tuftonboro; farmer; widower; b. Tuftonboro; John E. Bennett (New Durham) and Hannah Welch (Tuftonboro)
M. Ethel, d. 4/27/1957 at 73 in Boston, MA; office worker; single; b. Tuftonboro; John W. Bennett and Sarah L. Smith
Orsino V., d. 6/6/1945 at 81/7/3 in Tuftonboro; farmer; married; b. Tuftonboro; John E. Bennett (New Durham) and Hannah Welch (Tuftonboro)
Ralph V., d. 6/30/1971 at 76 in Tuftonboro; b. NH
Ruth F., d. 9/2/1980 in Laconia; James A. Bennett and Frances Fernald
Sara Lizzie, d. 12/4/1925 at 69/8/4 in Tuftonboro; at home; married; b. Moultonboro; Ezekiel Eastman Smith (Newburyport, MA) and Mary Davis (New Durham)

BENSE,
Ella Louise, d. 4/20/1962 at 71 in Wolfeboro; housewife; married; b. Allston, MA; Charles N. Roberts, Sr. and Jennie M. Prentice
Theodore Alfred, d. 10/24/1966 at 72 in Tuftonboro; retired; widower; b. Boston, MA; Charles Bense and Ida H. Fernald

BENSON,
son, d. 1/26/1953 at 0/0/1 in Wolfeboro; b. Wolfeboro; Ronald Keith Benson and Norma E. Malloy
son, d. 2/27/1956 at – in Wolfeboro; Ronald K. Benson and Norma V. Malloy

BERG,
Clarence M., d. 7/13/2000 in Wolfeboro; Edward Berg and Mae Mannion
John, d. 10/13/2004 in Ossipee; Edward Berg and Mary Manning
Robert O., d. 10/24/1933 at 21/7/27 in Mirror Lake; recent college graduate; single; b. Brooklyn, NY; Robert C. Berg (Germany)

and Louise Mock (Brooklyn, NY)

BERNARD,
Albert, d. 5/23/1920 at 60 in Tuftonboro; leather merchant; Bernard Bernard and Lillian Kane
Paul Leslie, Jr., d. 2/22/1995 in Wolfeboro; Paul L. Bernard, Sr. and Helene O'Meally

BERRY,
Elizabeth B., d. 9/5/1990 in Wolfeboro; Ernest E. Gray and Clara Thomas
Harry O., d. 10/23/1976 at 87 in Wolfeboro; b. NH
Leander S., d. 8/3/1908 at 86/10/12; cerebral hemorrhage; widower; Nathaniel Berry and Olivia Cushman
Silas H., d. 8/3/1941 at 85/8/4 in Tuftonboro; retired sec.; widower; b. OH; James Berry and ----- Bingham

BEYERSTEDT,
Dorothy A., d. 9/9/2003 in Wolfeboro; Arthur Akins and Florence Holman

BIBEAULT,
Michael A., d. 11/13/2003 in Wolfeboro; Henry Bibeault and HeideMarie Becker

BICKFORD,
Deborah C., d. 4/2/1909 at 84/7/20; apoplectic shock; widow; b. Tuftonboro; James Bean
Helen J., d. 2/20/1964 at 64 in Wolfeboro; owner (smr. lodge); married; b. W. Newbury, MA; Patric J. Higgins and Mary Godfrey
Isaac C., d. 4/30/1896 at 74/11/27 in Tuftonboro; apoplexy; farmer; married; b. Tuftonboro; Nat Bickford (Dover) and Mary Bean (Moultonboro)
Isabella M., d. 5/18/1957 at 95 in Tuftonboro; artist; widow; b. Belmont, MA; Daniel T. French and Louise I. L. Woodman
Jackson S., d. 6/22/1969 at 46 in Wolfeboro; mechanic; married; b. MA; John Bickford and Helen J. Higgins
James, d. 5/19/1891 at 80/3/14 in Tuftonboro; softening of brain; farmer; widower; b. Somersworth; John Bickford (Somersworth)
John Hansen, Jr., d. 6/22/1965 at 62 in Tuftonboro; acrh. eng.;

married; b. Salem, MA; John H. Bickford, Sr. and Isabella M.
French
John W., d. 7/10/1891 at 88/3/6 in Tuftonboro; old age; farmer;
widower; b. Wolfeboro; W. Bickford (Dover) and Dolly Willand
(Dover)

BIGELOW,
Frances L., d. 9/5/1995 in Concord; Lars Emil Landin and Julia
Backstrom

BING,
Herbert A., d. 3/21/1990 in Manchester; Alfred Bing and Hannah
Andreason

BISBEE,
Addie M., d. 5/2/1953 at 75 in Wolfeboro; at home; married; b.
Tuftonboro; Levi W. Libby and Laura J. Staples
Arthur H., d. 1/30/1984 in Wolfeboro; Archer Clifton Bisbee and
Addie Staples
Maude Emery, d. 5/15/1966 at 80 in Laconia; housewife; married; b.
Tuftonboro; Charles Emery

BISHOP,
Dorothy M., d. 8/25/1991 in Wolfeboro; John Allen and Mary Driscoll
Elliott Foster, d. 4/22/1964 at 71 in Wolfeboro; hotel mgr.; married; b.
Long Island, NY; Jeremiah Bishop and Harriett Emmons
Greta B., d. 8/16/1976 at 81 in Wolfeboro; b. MA

BLACK,
Edmund A., d. 1/16/1894 at 64/2/9; shoemaker; married; b. Palermo,
ME; Edmund Black (Meredith) and Comfort Wiggin (Stratham)

BLAISDELL,
Alta May, d. 5/24/1955 at 68 in Wolfeboro; at home; widow; b. ME;
Charles H. Bryant and Ada M. Shortridge
Israel, d. 11/27/1892 at 76/11/29 in Tuftonboro; hemorrhage; farmer;
widower; b. Tuftonboro; Thomas Blaisdell (Pittsfield) and Polly
Hersey (Wolfeboro)
Richard C., d. 10/2/1903 at 84/1/17 in Tuftonboro; chronic nephritis;
widower; Thomas Blaisdell and Polly Hersey
Ruth M., d. 1/10/1903 at 63/3/26 in Tuftonboro; apoplexy; married; b.

Center Harbor; Jeremiah Brown and Abigail Noyes
Thomas Herbert, d. 7/31/1964 at 97 in Wolfeboro; farmer; widower;
b. Tuftonboro; Richard Blaisdell and Ruth Brown
Una M., d. 4/10/1944 at 65/5/8 in Tuftonboro; housewife; married; b.
Tuftonboro; Alonzo A. Moody and Viola J. Kenny (Tuftonboro)

BLAKE,
Emma F., d. 9/3/1918 at 67/0/7 in Tuftonboro; single; b. Center
Harbor; Charles Blake (Rochester)
James A., d. 6/2/1901 at 48/2/21 in Tuftonboro; accidental drowning;
single; b. Wolfeboro; David Blake and Martha A. Hayes
Joseph Clarence, d. 2/12/1951 at 91 in Tuftonboro; farmer; married;
b. NH; Charles Blake and Sara Welch
Mary Jane, d. 4/20/1963 at 85 in Tuftonboro; housewife; widow; b.
County Dowis, Ireland; James O'Neil and Sarah Balnur
Sadie E., d. 8/5/1900 at 41/6/9 in Tuftonboro; phthisis pulmonalis;
married; b. Tuftonboro; Stephen Piper and Emma P. Young

BLANCHARD,
Arthur, d. 10/14/2004 in Wolfeboro; Arthur Blanchard and Esther
Reynolds
Arthur Lord, Sr., d. 5/14/1998 in Tuftonboro; A. Starr Blanchard and
Irene Coogan

BLANEY,
Warren M., d. 9/26/2000 in Tuftonboro; Lester Blaney and Mildred
Mahew

BLAZO,
James Henry, d. 12/5/1926 at 82/5/19 in Tuftonboro; farmer;
widower; John Blazo (N. Parsonsfield, ME) and Nancy Towle
Lorenzo D., d. 12/4/1903 at 66/5/25 in Tuftonboro; renal calculi;
married; John Blazo and Nancy Towle

BLOUNT,
Eugene I., d. 10/17/1932 at 77/10/24 in Tuftonboro; manufacturer;
married; b. Stanstead, PQ; Gardner Blount (Stanstead, PQ)
and Mary Bragg (Stanstead, PQ)

BOARDMAN,
Forrest C., d. 9/3/1971 at 85 in Wolfeboro

BODGE,
Betsey H., d. 1/9/1892 at 60 in Tuftonboro; pneumonia and heart disease; housewife; widow; b. Kennebunk, ME; Oliver Woodwin (Kennebunk) and Betsy H. Gilprick
Elwood Lester, d. 1/5/1910 at 0/6/11; congestion of lungs; b. Ossipee; Walter C. Bodge and Maude F. Hanson

BODWELL,
Charles, d. 7/6/2004 in Mirror Lake; Charles Bodwell and Victoria Miner

BOLTON,
Corinne A., d. 7/22/2003 in Lebanon; Anthony Carreiro and Regina LaPlante

BOODY,
Forrest, d. 11/18/1960 at 88 in Hallowell, ME; retired; single; b. Moultonboro; John Boody and Lizzie Boody

BOSCHEN,
Virginia Mae, d. 12/19/1991 in Tuftonboro; Walter Jones and Ann Sass

BOSHER,
Joseph W., d. 8/29/1929 at 60/9/24 in Tuftonboro; real estate; married; b. Hafield, England; William Bosher (Hafield, England) and Frances Peck (England)

BOTTOMLEY,
Bruce M., d. 1/3/2002 in FL; Frank Bottomley and Helen Maclargen
Frank N., d. 12/15/1967 at 69 in Wolfeboro; Vice-Pres., mfg.; married; b. Yorkshire, England; Ernest Bottomley and Laura Rayner
Helen M., d. 9/4/1975 at 70 in Wolfeboro; b. Saugus, MA

BOTTS,
Sarah, d. 10/4/1955 at 84 in Tuftonboro; at home; widow; b. IL; Wyatt Botts and Rebecca J. Johns

BOULET,
daughter, d. 10/10/1941 at 0/0/2 in Wolfeboro; Howard F. Boulet

(Beebe Plains, VT) and Martha E. Malourn (Canada)

BOWKER,
Mary G., d. 8/2/1940 at 77/10/8 in Tuftonboro; at home; widow; b.
Mendon, MA; Lysander Grow (VT) and Priscilla Marsh
(Mendon, MA)

BOWLER,
Frederic E., d. 7/2/1985 in Tuftonboro; LeRoy Bowler and Maude ----

BOWMAN,
Charles Horsfall, d. 6/16/1963 at 88 in Wolfeboro; salesman;
married; b. New Haven, CT; Charles F. Bowman and Sarah L.
Horsfall
Mabel, d. 6/4/1972 at 92 in Wolfeboro; b. CT

BOXELL,
Thelma A., d. 2/17/1955 at 58 in ME; rest home operator; married; b.
Melvin Village; Victor Monroe Morse and Mary Elizabeth French

BOYD,
Hannah, d. 12/16/1939 at 90/3/26 in Mirror Lake; housewife; widow;
b. Gotland, Sweden; ----- Bohn (Sweden)

BOYDEN,
Lewis H., d. 9/17/1931 at 70/0/17 in Wolfeboro; upholsterer; married;
b. Boston, MA; Merrill N. Boyden (Rutland, MA) and Mary Lock
(Cambridge, MA)

BRACKETT,
Sarah, d. 10/24/1908 at 66/4/8; heart failure; married; James Small
and Eliza Raines

BRADBURN,
James R., d. 7/4/1977 at 66 in Tuftonboro; b. Los Angeles, CA

BRADEAU,
Joseph C., d. 4/2/1922 at 0/9/17 in Tuftonboro; b. Tuftonboro;
Joseph S. Bradeau and Mary Emery

BRADLEY,
Annie, d. 9/27/1914 at 80/1; widow; b. Gilmanton; Joseph P. Lougee and Mary H. Marsh
Ephraim H., d. 6/12/1909 at 78/3/17; apoplexy; married
Nathaniel, d. 2/21/1891 at 86/8 in Tuftonboro; paralysis; carpenter; widower; b. Wakefield; Nathaniel Bradley (Kingston) and Joan Howard (Strafford)

BRAMAN,
Louis A., d. 7/27/1913 at 26; accidental drowning; single; b. Boston, MA; Morris Braman and Celia Albertston

BRAWN,
Bernadette A., d. 9/7/1999 in Wolfeboro; ----- St. Louis and Anna Donahue
James Kenneth, Sr., d. 4/5/1993 in Wolfeboro; Kenneth A. Brawn and Rhoda M. Banks

BREWSTER,
Adelade L., d. 4/5/1911 at 58/5/1; Bright's disease; widow; b. Tuftonboro; Silas F. Bean and Mary A. Abbott
Dana W., d. 7/31/1896 at 49/2/13 in Tuftonboro; spinal apoplexy; painter; married; b. Tuftonboro

BRIGGS,
Maurice T., d. 3/28/1983 in Wolfeboro; George Briggs and Mary Elizabeth C.N.B.L.

BRIGHAM,
Linda, d. 9/6/2005 in Wolfeboro; Paul Brigham and Violet Ellis

BRITTON,
Ruth, d. 10/22/1986 in Laconia; George Simms and Harriet Goto

BRODMAN,
Russell, d. 6/20/1942 at 35/2/26 in Tuftonboro; physician; married; b. Philadelphia; Morris Brodman (NY City) and Frances Jacob (England)

BROWER,
Robert C., d. 7/13/1952 at 60 in Tuftonboro; co. sec.-treas.; married;

b. E. Orange, NJ; William L. Brower and Helen Swanson

BROWN,
daughter, d. 2/15/1892 at – in Tuftonboro; premature birth; b.
Tuftonboro; Charles H. Brown (Tuftonboro) and Katie E. Abbott
(Ossipee)
daughter, d. 2/16/1892 at – in Tuftonboro; premature birth; b.
Tuftonboro; Charles H. Brown (Tuftonboro) and Katie E. Abbott
(Ossipee)
Andrew J., d. 8/31/1903 at 74/7 in Tuftonboro; exposure; married;
Avery Brown and Sarah Brown
Bradley M., d. 9/9/1900 at 69/4/21 in Tuftonboro; married; b.
Wolfeboro; Moses Brown
Charles H., d. 10/21/1951 at 88 in Wolfeboro; farmer; married; b.
Tuftonboro; Andrew J. Brown and Martha Fox
Christopher Richard, d. 5/13/1998 in Laconia; Richard Sargent
Brown and June Varney
Frank P., d. 6/1/1941 at 87/1/6 in Wolfeboro; farmer; widower; b.
Wolfeboro; George W. Brown (Wolfeboro) and Judith Morrison
(Tuftonboro)
Lydia A., d. 6/27/1893 at 73/1/15 in Tuftonboro; heart failure;
housewife; widow; b. Salem, MA; Joshua Dodge and M. H.
Hubbard (Sandwich)
Morrill H., d. 5/31/1988 in Wolfeboro; George Brown and Mary Lee
Nancy J., d. 8/3/1978 at 22 in Hanover; b. Concord
Rachel P., d. 3/23/1897 at 80/7/16 in Tuftonboro; pneumonia;
married; b. Shapleigh, ME; Stephen Webber and Betsey
Roberts
Richard S., d. 1/29/1989 in Tuftonboro; Bernard N. Brown and Leslie
Sargent
Susan Hilton, d. 4/12/1927 at 79/8/16 in Tuftonboro; at home;
widow; b. Ossipee; Moses C. Nutter and Louisa Chick
(Ossipee)

BRYANT,
Nabby T., d. 12/21/1898 at 96/10/29 in Tuftonboro; pneumonia;
widow; b. Tuftonboro; Israel Piper

BULLOCK,
Phillis C., d. 11/6/1975 at 76 in Moultonboro; b. Haverhill, MA

BUNCE,
Vincent, d. 12/3/1999 in Wolfeboro; Wesley Johnson and Bertha -----

BUNNEY,
Cyrus, d. 5/31/1974 at 66 in Wolfeboro; b. MA
Isabelle Marie, d. 8/10/1995 in Ossipee; Peter Nadeau and Corrine
Boisvert

BURCHSTEAD,
Mary E., d. 2/26/1929 at 80/1/0 in Tuftonboro; at home; widow; b.
Moultonboro; Charles Brown (Somersworth) and Margaret
Rernby (Gloucester, MA)

BURKE,
Celia, d. 4/29/1956 at 59 in Franklin; housekeeper; single; b. MA;
William Burke and Nora W. Burke

BURLEIGH,
Caroline, d. 10/21/1905 at 86/1/24 in Tuftonboro; old age; widow; b.
Wolfeboro; Benjamin Tibbetts and Abigail Doe
Henry S., d. 7/15/1924 at 76/9/9 in Tuftonboro; farmer; single; b.
Tuftonboro; Jonathan H. Burleigh and Caroline Tibbetts
Jane M., d. 4/8/1936 at 51/4/27 in Ctr. Tuftonboro; housekeeper;
married; b. Moose Creek, ON; John McRae (Moose Creek, ON)
and Ellen McLean (NY)
Jonathan H., d. 6/7/1901 at 87/1/20 in Tuftonboro; hemorrhage of
brain; married; b. Tuftonboro; Jacob Burleigh and Susan
Dearborn
Joseph J., d. 2/23/1911 at 79/4/4; mitral insufficiency; married; b.
Tuftonboro; Samuel Burleigh and Lydia Kennard
Sarah H., d. 10/6/1911 at 70/5/6; senile debility; widow; b.
Gilmanton; Ephraim Shannon and Mary E. Hurd
Wilmer Ruth, d. 2/16/1920 at 3/5/24 in Tuftonboro; b. Tuftonboro;
William C. Burleigh and Jane E. McRae

BURWELL,
Elliot N., d. 6/20/1947 at 73/9/3 in Tuftonboro; ret. naval arch.;
widower; b. Montreal, Canada; George Burwell and -----
Edwards (London, England)

BUSHMAN,
Faye, d. 4/30/1971 at 51 in Laconia; b. NH
Robert J., d. 8/5/1989 in Wolfeboro; Hershal Bushman and Amanda
-----

BUTLER,
Richard T., d. 12/25/1909 at 34/7/9; pulmonary hemorrhage;
   married; b. England; Richard Butler and Cathelene -----
Waldo L., d. 1/29/1947 at 77/5/4 in Oakland, ME; contractor;
   widower; b. Moultonboro; William Butler (NH) and Mary
   Thompson (NH)
William Oscar, d. 5/14/1951 at 77 in Wolfeboro; shoemaker; married;
   b. Moultonboro; William Butler and Mary Thompson

BUTTERFIELD,
Nellie Bradley, d. 7/17/1966 at 92 in Wolfeboro; housewife; widow;
   b. Tuftonboro; Ephriam Bradley and Alarissa Lougee

BUZZELL,
Grace, d. 7/28/1892 at 21/3/14 in Tuftonboro; consumption;
   housework; single; b. Glasgow, Scotland; James Buzzell
   (Scotland)

BYERS,
Ronald G., d. 10/28/1989 in Tuftonboro; Eldon L. Byers and Sylvia
   A. Pluff

BYRON,
Gilbert Luke, d. 7/21/1967 at 67 in Tuftonboro; musician; married; b.
   Boston, MA; Edward J. Byron and Bertha A. Williams

CADIGAN,
Johannah E., d. 11/30/1953 at 81 in Tuftonboro; at home; single; b.
   Boston, MA; Michael Cadigan and Julia Donahue

CAHILL,
Sarah V., a/k/a Vernon S., d. 8/16/1981 in Wolfeboro; Warren Green
   and Catherine McMahon

CALLENDER,
Wynnefred A., d. 9/28/1999 in Tuftonboro; Edward Wadewitz and

Nettie Joselyn

CALNAN,
Robert C., d. 1/26/2001 in Rochester; Laurence Calnan and May Hammond

CAMPBELL,
Raymond Potter, Jr., d. 2/9/1997 in Lebanon; Raymond Potter Campbell and Katherine Browning

CANNEY,
Lizzie A., d. 4/13/1921 at 70/11/24 in Tuftonboro; housewife; married; b. Lebanon, ME
Nellie J., d. 2/26/1909 at 75/5; consumption; married; b. Wolfeboro; Walter N. Cotton
Wesley, d. 5/17/1909 at 83; influenza; widower; b. Tuftonboro; John Canney and Keziah Horne

CAPIZZI,
Saverio, d. 8/20/1977 at 80 in Tuftonboro; b. NY

CARDER,
Inez M., d. 11/7/1992 in Wolfeboro; Scott Misener and Olive Glass

CARNES,
James A., d. 7/2/1921 at 54/10/20 in Tuftonboro; carpenter; married; b. Ireland; John Carnes and Annie Armstrong

CARTER,
David, d. 3/31/2004 in Laconia; David Carter and Elizabeth Whiting

CAVANAUGH,
Donna Lynn, d. 12/4/1988 in Tuftonboro; Joseph T. Cavanaugh and Janet A. Killiam

CAVERLY,
Beatrice L., d. 2/26/1909 at 0/7/26; meningitis; b. Tuftonboro; Arthur L. Caverly and Emma L. Lamprey
Clara A., d. 2/5/1912 at 77/2/26; heart and kidney disease; widow; b. Moultonboro; Samuel Vickery and Elizabeth Morse
Daniel E., d. 10/2/1921 at 82 in Tewksbury, MA; married; b.

Moultonboro; Richard Caverly and Sally Gilman
Elizabeth R., d. 9/24/1907 at 83; apoplectic shock; single; b.
Moultonboro; Richard Caverly and Sally Gilman
Mary E., d. 1/6/1925 at 86/4/21 in Tuftonboro; housewife; widow; b.
Tuftonboro; Jefferson Sanborn and Martha Leavitt
Mary E., d. 6/5/1942 at 78 in Brookline, MA; at home; single; b.
Tuftonboro; George Caverly (Tuftonboro) and Nancy Smith
Samuel V., d. 8/2/1924 at 71/0/29 in Tuftonboro; farmer; single; b.
Tuftonboro; Jeremiah Caverly and Clara A. Vickery
Sarah H., d. 12/27/1906 at 36/4/19; pernicious anemia; single; b.
Tuftonboro; George N. Caverly and Nancy Smith
Walter H., d. 4/13/1945 at 76/1/19 in Tuftonboro; farmer; single; b.
Tuftonboro; Jeremiah Caverly and Clara A. Vickery

CELLARIUS,
Kenneth E., d. 6/18/1989 in Wolfeboro; Theodore Cellarius and
Edna Hersey
Theodore Walter, d. 4/13/1954 at 75 in Wolfeboro; ret. bookbinder;
married; b. Boston, MA; Edward Cellarius and Louisa Baldner

CHAFFEE,
Robert H., d. 5/6/1988 in Wolfeboro; Herman L. Chaffee and Violet
Forde

CHALMERS,
Robert, d. 5/23/2005 in Mirror Lake; Robert Chalmers and Lillie
Dunn
Susan A., d. 2/25/2002 in Tuftonboro; Eugene Chalmers and
Gertrude Bohack

CHAMBERLIN,
Hannah C., d. 12/30/1917 at 87/4/20 in Tuftonboro; single; b.
Tuftonboro; William Chamberlin

CHAMPAIGNE,
Jean W., d. 7/3/1954 at 23 in Nashua; moulder plastic co.; married;
b. NH; Francis Morton Lassell and Mary Helen Bessom

CHANDLER,
Florence M., d. 11/14/1971 at 80 in Rochester; b. MA
Henry P., Sr., d. 4/26/1976 at 89 in Laconia; b. MA

CHANNEL,
Cora E., d. 8/30/1925 at 63/6/14 in Tuftonboro; at home; single

CHAREST,
Maurice Charles, d. 2/3/1997 in Tuftonboro; Charles B. Charest and
Lillian Morin

CHASE,
Albert G., d. 8/28/1893 at 64/9/2 in Tuftonboro; Bright's disease;
farmer; married; b. Hamilton, MA; Green Chase (Gilmanton)
and Mary Patch (MA)
Horatio J., d. 1/27/1983 in Concord; George S. Chase and Florence
Geer
Paul B., d. 12/12/1978 at 54 in Hanover; b. New London, CT

CHENEY,
daughter, d. 5/7/1938 at 12 hrs. in Wolfeboro; b. Wolfeboro; Earl
Lorenzo Cheney (Tuftonboro) and Isabel Moore (Skowhegan,
ME)
Earl Lorenzo, d. 10/13/1997 in Tuftonboro; Wyatt D. Cheney and
Martha Stokes
George M., d. 12/10/1936 at 76/7/10 in Wolfeboro; farmer; married;
b. Dickinson Center, NY; Lorenzo Cheney (Washington Flats,
VT) and ----- Morfett (VT)
Gladys L., d. 7/25/1920 at 3/11/24 in Tuftonboro; b. Rochester;
Wyatt D. Cheney and Mattie L. Stokes
Gordon Warren, d. 1/14/1961 at 49/5/13 in Wolfeboro; married; b.
Tuftonboro; Wyatt D. Cheney and Martha Stokes
Isabelle M., d. 8/28/1972 at 52 in Moultonboro
John G., d. 5/25/1990 in Wolfeboro; George Cheney and Ella
Stevens
Margaret E., d. 10/29/1986 in Tuftonboro; Elmer Chamberlin and
Lottie Chamberlin
Martha L., d. 6/21/1967 at 79 in Concord; housewife; married; b.
Tuftonboro; Benjamin Stokes
Sidney E., d. 7/29/1988 in Wolfeboro; Lyle G. Cheney and Margaret
L. Chamberlin
Wyatt D., d. 8/28/1967 at 75 in Pittsfield; teamster; widower; b.
Dickerson Ctr., NY; George M. Cheney and Lottie Haskell

CHESLEY,
Russell E., d. 11/25/1980 in Wolfeboro; John P. Chesley and Addie M. Davis

CHIAPPISI,
Tracey E., d. 4/3/2000 in Tuftonboro; Harry Prendergast and Francois Porte

CHICK,
Charles D., d. 7/17/1942 at 86 in Boston, MA; Amsie Chick

CHITTENDEN,
Wentworth A., d. 2/22/1985 in Tuftonboro; Wentworth N. Chittenden and Anna G. Tatro

CHRISTIAN,
William H., d. 11/1/1982 in Wolfeboro; George S. Christian and Henrietta Canfield

CLAPP,
Edna B., d. 10/20/1979 in Wolfeboro; Robert J. Boyd and Isabelle Bears

CLARK,
Emeline H., d. 10/23/1955 at 70 in Wolfeboro; at home; married; b. RI; Robert B. Hawkins and Lotilla Mowry
Frederick B., d. 2/1/1939 at 69/4/21 in Wolfeboro; caretaker; widower; b. Conclville, VT; Abigail Clark (VT)
Hiram, d. 10/19/1898 at 88 in Tuftonboro; old age; married; Solomon Clark and Lydia Kenison
Lawrence, d. 9/29/2004 in Wolfeboro; George Clark and Marcia Nevills
William Francis, d. 1/3/1997 in Exeter; William R. Clark and Katherine R. Bates

CLARKE,
Howard Earl, d. 6/29/1978 at 73 in Tuftonboro; b. Providence, RI

CLAUSEN,
Sigrid, d. 5/18/1973 at 76 in Wolfeboro; b. Denmark

CLINTON,
Wills, d. 10/9/1985 in Wolfeboro; Earl Clinton and Florence McFarland

CLOUGH,
Russell E., d. 9/14/2001 in Tuftonboro; Harold Clough and Doris York

CLOW,
Fred E., d. 1/4/1941 at 59/2/9 in Tuftonboro; physician; married; b. Wolfeboro; Stephen W. Clow (Wolfeboro) and Carrie W. Canney (Wolfeboro)

COFFEY,
Stephen D., d. 7/29/1986 in Wolfeboro; Barry Coffey and Claire Hanley

COLBERT,
Eugene T., Jr., d. 8/29/2002 in Tuftonboro; Eugene Colbert and Madeline Connors

COLBY,
Allen K., d. 9/17/1973 at 67 in Wolfeboro; b. ME
Howard C., d. 7/14/1974 at 64 in Wolfeboro; b. NH
Ralph Melvin, d. 7/1/1959 at 79 in Wolfeboro; mill wkr.; married; b. NH; ----- and Sarah Knox
Robert S., d. 6/7/1945 at 4/4/19 in Tuftonboro; b. Wolfeboro; Royal Colby (Ctr. Ossipee) and Florence Littlefield (Oakland, ME)
Thelma E., d. 8/12/1981 in Leeds, ME; Ralph W. Drucker and Lela M. Staniels

COLEMAN,
Dorothy T., d. 2/9/1990 in Wolfeboro; Sverre Thorvaldson and Olga Groskopf
Roger Bray, d. 10/24/1996 in Wolfeboro; H. Roger Coleman and Virginia Bray

COMMONS,
Helen T., d. 6/15/2000 in Tuftonboro; Richard Timmermann and Mary Schmidt

CONANT,
son, d. 8/6/1914 at 0/0/2; b. Tuftonboro; Edward B. Conant and
   Eleanor H. Worth
Hilda Landon, d. 3/6/1990 in Tuftonboro; Archer Landon and Emma
   Gross
Jane M., d. 8/15/1992 in Wolfeboro; William R. Mitchell and Justine
   Brayton
Roger, d. 12/18/2004 in Wolfeboro; Roger Conant and Hilda Landon

CONNOR,
Lydia O., d. 6/17/1924 at 65/2/18 in Tuftonboro; housewife; widow;
   b. Tuftonboro; Daniel D. Wingate and Mary M. Wood
Priscilla T., d. 9/29/1984 in Wolfeboro; Thomas N. Tolar and Rachel
   Seavey

CONRAD,
Everett G., Sr., d. 4/27/1990 in Laconia; Charles Conrad and Annie
   Poole

CONWAY,
Grace E., d. 6/20/1975 at 82 in Tuftonboro; b. Vinal Haven, ME

COPP,
Charles H., d. 7/3/1891 at 74/10/28 in Tuftonboro; softening of brain;
   farmer; married; b. Tuftonboro; Moses Copp (Lebanon, ME)
   and Elizabeth Wiggin (Newmarket)
Clara A., d. 3/23/1954 at 97 in Wolfeboro; at home; widow; b. NH;
   Isiah Wiggin and Maria Elizabeth Piper
George W., d. 12/8/1933 at 79/1/5 in Melvin Village; retired; married;
   b. Tuftonboro; Charles H. Copp (Tuftonboro) and Arvilla
   Fernald (Tuftonboro)
Henry D., d. 5/4/1918 at 59/10/23 in Tuftonboro; foreman painter;
   married; b. Tuftonboro; Charles H. Copp (Tuftonboro) and
   Arvilla Fernald (Tuftonboro)

CORBETT,
Matthew Mark, d. 8/9/1974 at 51 in Tuftonboro; b. MA

CORDEAU,
Addie, d. 10/3/1937 at 62/6/13 in Wolfeboro; housewife; married; b.
   Tuftonboro; Louis Geto (France) and Hattie Parsons (Alton)

Mary E., d. 12/6/1926 at 67/10/12 in Tuftonboro; at home; married;
    Eben F. Pope (Marblehead, MA) and Eunice Cahoon (NS)
Peter, d. 9/1/1939 at 82/2/15 in Concord; shoemaker; widower; b.
    Canada; Peter Cordeau (Canada) and Hedwidge ----- (Canada)

CORR,
Robert James, d. 2/4/1969 at 53 in Manchester; salesman; divorced;
    b. WI; Dominic Corr and Anna Louise Rice

CORSON,
son, d. 12/1/1904 at – in Tuftonboro; premature birth; b. Tuftonboro;
    R. Corson and Lulu Horn

COTTON,
Adrienne Briggs, d. 12/16/1996 in Tuftonboro; Walter Briggs and
    Elsie Kirby
Frederick P., d. 6/4/2001 in Laconia; Frederick Cotton and Alice
    Audette

CRAIG,
Edith Merriam, d. 11/26/1956 at 72 in Wolfeboro; housewife; widow;
    b. Boston, MA; Dana W. Brewster and Adelaide B. Brewster

CRAIGUE,
Ellen Hayes, d. 3/23/1998 in Wolfeboro; Henry F. Hayes and Mabel
    P. Welch

CRANE,
Mildred B., d. 7/14/1974 at 69 in Tuftonboro; b. KY

CRAWFORD,
Andrew, d. 10/19/1977 at 80 in Wolfeboro; b. London, England

CRIMBLE,
Richard G., d. 11/10/1969 at 76 in Wolfeboro; machinist; married; b.
    England; George Crimble

CRISPINO,
Mary Jane, d. 5/23/1994 in Tuftonboro; George Roth and Florence --

CROOK,
Charles, d. 10/11/1967 at 80 in Concord; married; b. England
Emily Harriet, d. 6/13/1931 at 44/5/18 in Wolfeboro; at home;
married; b. Pontasdaive, S. Wales; James Wilcox (Devonshire, England)

CROSBY,
Louise Willard, d. 8/27/1996 in Wolfeboro; William Floyd Crosby and Louise Rogers

CROSSMAN,
Frances W., d. 11/30/1952 at 70 in Wolfeboro; at home; divorced; b. Providence, RI; George P. Crossman and Grace -----
Rhoda E., d. 2/12/1902 at 3/7/25 in Tuftonboro; tuberculosis meningitis; John S. Crossman and Mary A. Whyte

CROUSE,
Bruce, d. 10/19/2005 in Wolfeboro; Mervin Crouse and Frances Webb

CROWLEY,
Cynthia H., d. 4/2/2003 in Melvin Village; Adelbert Delano and Margaret Burke

CRUSIUS,
Carolyn W., d. 8/11/2003 in Melvin Village; Irving Wells and Mary Parker

CULLEN,
Alice A., d. 11/2/1905 at 32/5/22 in Tuftonboro; phthisis, pulmonary consumption; married; b. Passaic, NJ; Patrick Ash

CURRELL,
Gertrude M., d. 8/17/1996 in Meredith; Paul Downing and Elma F. Cross

CURRIER,
Angie V., d. 12/26/1974 at 65 in Tuftonboro; b. MA

CURRIER [or CURRY],
John, d. 3/3/1926 at 71 in Tuftonboro; laborer; single

CURTIS,
Jacquelin, d. 8/27/1964 at 49 in Chelsea, MA; housewife; married; b.
　　Lee; F. Morton Lassell and Mary Helen Bessom
Kenneth G., d. 9/18/1999 in Tuftonboro; Charles Curtis and Effie
　　Osborne

CUSUMANO,
William Worthington, Jr., d. 8/15/1959 at 16 in Tuftonboro; student;
　　single; b. MA; William W. Cusumano, Sr. and Dorothy Ellis

DAGNINO,
Gertrude M., d. 2/20/1975 at 67 in Wolfeboro; b. Malden, MA

DAHILL,
Leo Richard, d. 9/18/1980 in White River Jct., VT; Thomas Dahill
　　and Zebea Russell

DALTON,
Arvilla, d. 11/22/1919 at 88/8/20 in Tuftonboro; housewife; widow; b.
　　Tuftonboro; Thomas Blaisdell and Polly Hersey

DARLING,
Stanley A., Jr., d. 9/6/1996 in Rochester; Stanley A. Darling and Lola
　　Stratmen

DAVIS,
Albert E., d. 11/17/1969 at 74 in Tuftonboro; farmer; widower; b. NH;
　　Harry Davis and Sadie Gilman
Annie L., d. 12/6/1922 at 74/8/20 in Tuftonboro; housewife; widow;
　　b. Franklin; Joseph Brown and Mary D. Lehman
Arthur B., d. 1/19/1999 in Wolfeboro; Harry Davis and Sarah Gilman
Charles A., d. 1/2/1901 at 42/5/19 in Tuftonboro; anaemia
　　complicated; married; b. Moultonboro; William H. Davis and
　　Elizabeth A. Caverly
Charles W., d. 6/9/1939 at 97/5 in Wolfeboro; widower; b. New
　　Durham; George W. Davis
Eda M., d. 2/17/1967 at 67 in Tuftonboro; housewife; married; b.
　　Ossipee; Charles P. Wallace and Harriett Hurd
Eleanor M., d. 3/15/2003 in Wolfeboro; Simon Thompson and
　　Evelyn Bean
Ernest E., d. 8/15/1948 at 73/8/11 in Laconia; farmer; married; b.

Moultonboro; John P. Davis and Elizabeth Smith
Flora Belle, d. 4/27/1963 at 77 in Wolfeboro; housewife; married; b.
Moultonboro; Wiliam K. MacDonald and Clara Belle Prime
Grace M., d. 2/14/1968 at 75 in Meredith; housewife; married; b. NH;
Frank Horne and Jennie George
Harold L., d. 4/7/1971 at 79 in Laconia; b. NH
Harry A., d. 11/12/1941 at 68/10/21 in Tuftonboro; carpenter;
widower; b. Gilmanton; Jefferson T. Davis (Unity) and Annie L.
Brown (Franklin)
Harry L., d. 9/7/1975 at 93 in Wolfeboro; b. NH
Howard C., d. 9/22/1971 at 73 in Tuftonboro; b. CT
Jefferson T., d. 7/9/1896 at 54/9/14 in Tuftonboro; cancer; married;
b. Lempster; Oliver Davis (Unity) and Harriet Moore
John J., d. 6/23/1978 at 70 in Wolfeboro; b. Savannah, GA
Lena F., d. 7/6/1940 at 82/7/19 in Wolfeboro; housewife; widow; b.
Stillwater, ME; Freeman Gove and Ameda Smith
Leon, d. 9/2/1962 at 73 in Laconia; farmer; widower; b. Moultonboro;
Charles W. Davis and Cora Morrison
Mary Agnes, d. 3/9/1998 in Tuftonboro; John A. Sullivan and Mary
Emma McKenna
Mildred Loving, d. 8/21/1974 at 56 in Tuftonboro; b. Texas
Nancy L., d. 8/4/1912 at 84/3/17; epithelial carcinoma; widow; b.
Moultonboro; Eliphalet Smith and Mary Leavitt
Richard L., d. 4/9/1949 at 32 in Holderness; clerk; married; b.
Moultonboro; H. Lisle Davis and Grace M. Horne
Roger V., d. 12/24/1974 at 63 in Wolfeboro; b. Manchester
Russell E., d. 10/25/2001 in Tuftonboro; Lester Davis and Olivia
Blanchette
Ruth, d. 6/23/1941 at 53/7/8 in Concord; housewife; married; b.
Tuftonboro; Silas W. Bean (Tuftonboro) and Cora A. Bean
(Tuftonboro)
Sarah B., d. 1/30/1936 at 58/7/13 in Wolfeboro; housewife; married;
b. Tuftonboro; Aaron W. Gilman (Tamworth) and Emma F.
Quimby (Moultonboro)
Sarah Saphronia, d. 6/14/1926 at 82/5/20 in Tuftonboro; at home;
married; Calvin Fernald (S. Berwick, ME) and Belinda Caverly
(Tuftonboro)
William H., d. 5/22/1891 at 59/3/17 in Tuftonboro; mesenteric
disease; merchant; married; b. New Durham; Eleazer Davis
(Durham) and Martha Davis (New Durham)
Willis P., d. 6/14/1983 in Wolfeboro; Harry L. Davis and Flora Belle

MacDonald

DAWSON,
John W., Sr., d. 7/6/1988 in Wolfeboro; William J. Dawson and Gertrude Bakewell

DEARBORN,
Bessie, d. 4/16/1892 at 0/11/28 in Tuftonboro; tubercular meningitis; b. S. Boston, MA; G. E. S. Dearborn (Tuftonboro) and Mamie McKenna (E. Boston)
Elizabeth S., d. 9/7/1909 at 83/4/11; old age; widow; b. Tuftonboro; Nathan Jenkins
Estella E., d. 1/30/1954 at 93 in Wolfeboro; ret. dressmaker; single; b. NH; George E. Dearborn and Elizabeth Jenkins
George E., d. 12/18/1907 at 82/2/6; chronic nephritis; married; b. Boston, MA; Jonathan Dearborn and Sophia A. Fernald
George E. S., d. 7/5/1895 at 33/6/5 in Tuftonboro; consumption; married; b. Tuftonboro; George E. Dearborn and Elizabeth Jenkins
Louie W., Sr., d. 11/3/1980 in Wolfeboro; Howard Dearborn and Nellie F. Weeman
Lula J., d. 10/24/1993 in Ossipee; Frederick Douglas and Bertha Pike-Sawtelle

DECOSTA,
John S., d. 2/7/1980 in Tuftonboro; ----- DeCosta and Annie Blake

de RAMER,
Eva, d. 3/5/1990 in Wolfeboro; Trygve Briseid and Eva Scheen

DEROSE,
Carol L., d. 6/2/1987 in Wolfeboro; Arthur Lunch, Sr. and Catherine Henneberry

DEVERE,
Peter F., d. 9/18/2002 in Sandwich; Frederick Devere and Dorothy Daland

DEVORK,
Grace Dale, d. 11/23/1994 in Tuftonboro; Harold Dale and Lottie Marsden

DEWITT,
Helena S., d. 4/17/1987 in Wolfeboro; Wentworth N. Chittenden and
Anna Tatro
Walter A., d. 9/27/1985 in Wolfeboro; Newton DeWitt and Minnie ----

DICKEY,
Lillian M., d. 2/20/1964 at 78 in Wolfeboro; housewife; married; b.
Merrimac, MA; Uriah H. Trull and Emma Sands

DIGHT,
Oreatta McKinney, d. 8/3/1993 in Wolfeboro; A. Henry Mathes and
Etta Ross

DOE,
Andrew W., d. 4/24/1894 at 80/6/26; farmer; widower; b. Tuftonboro;
James S. Doe (Newmarket) and Dolly Foss
Jennie B., d. 7/16/1925 at 73/8/12 in Tuftonboro; housewife;
married; b. Tuftonboro; Calvin Fernald (Tuftonboro) and Belinda
Caverly (Tuftonboro)

DOEBSAM,
Emma Florence, d. 7/2/1959 at 78 in Wolfeboro; at home; widow; b.
MA; Edward H. Abele and Annie M. Stott

DONAHUE,
Richard F., d. 9/22/1984 in Wolfeboro; John Donahue and Mary
Burke

DONOVAN,
Joseph Lewis, d. 2/18/1990 in Tuftonboro; Joseph M. Donovan and
Gertrude Sturtevant

DORE,
Christopher, d. 10/22/2004 in Lebanon; Larry Dore and Sheila
Fountaine
Mildred Frances, d. 8/11/1996 in Wolfeboro; Harry Davis and Sarah
Gilman
Richard, d. 5/2/2005 in Wolfeboro; Leon Dore and Mildred Davis

DOTEN,
Clarence A., d. 12/28/1966 at 76 in Wolfeboro; retired; married; b.

Dorchester, MA; Scott T. Doten and Addie A. Whittaker

DOW,
Albert Henry, d. 6/5/1962 at 75 in Tuftonboro; architect; married; b.
   Tuftonboro; Alva E. Dow and Anna Nutter
Anna N., d. 8/27/1922 at 67/7/23 in Wolfeboro; housewife; married;
   b. Tuftonboro; Jacob Nutter and Nancy Young
Ausbrey N., d. 10/1/1971 at 80 in Wolfeboro
Bernice Ham, d. 3/31/1963 at 66 in Wolfeboro; housewife; married;
   b. Ossipee; Alpheus Judson and Mary Wentworth
Brenda Joyce, d. 8/18/1960 at 15 in Tuftonboro; student; single; b.
   Wolfeboro; Leroy E. Dow and Lucy I. Clark
Darias J., d. 11/3/1893 at 82/9/20 in Tuftonboro; old age; farmer;
   married; b. Gilmanton; Jonathan Dow (Epping) and Joanna
   Dow (Gilmanton)
Edith, d. 9/27/1892 at 3 in Tuftonboro; cholera infantum; b.
   Tuftonboro; Alvah Dow and Anna M. Nutter (Tuftonboro)
Ellis M., d. 1/3/1944 at 42/7/14 in Wolfeboro; mech., garage;
   married; b. Moultonboro; James Dow and Elizabeth Garland
   (ME)
Ernest H., d. 8/17/1968 at 69 in Wolfeboro; carpenter; married; b.
   NH; James Dow and Elizabeth Garland
Fannie F., d. 9/19/1897 at 76/5 in Tuftonboro; old age and cholera
   morbus; married; b. Walden, VT; Ammi C. Ransom and Betsey
   Corson
Harrison, d. 12/22/1901 at 82/0/14 in Tuftonboro; supperative
   hepatitis; married; b. Gilmanton; Jonathan Dow and Johanna
   Gilman
James A., d. 10/12/1930 at 81/7/11 in Tuftonboro; farmer; widower;
   b. Tuftonboro; Andrew Dow (Tuftonboro) and Mary Hersey
   (Tuftonboro)
Leroy E., d. 9/26/1980 in Franklin; Ernest H. Dow and Eva Mae
   Drew
Ludy I., d. 6/22/2003 in Wolfeboro; Enos Clark and Avis Gray
Meredith J., d. 1/2/1944 at 10/9/26 in Ossipee; b. Ossipee; Ellis Dow
   and Agnes Phinney
Rodney Nutter, d. 7/18/1963 at 14 in Ossipee; student; b. Rochester;
   Roland Dow and Greta May

DROUIN,
Marion, d. 11/4/2004 in Dover; Charles Govey and Louise Lyons

DROWNE,

Bradford C., d. 12/27/1970 at 21 in Wolfeboro; student; single; b.
MA; Edwin S. Drowne, Jr. and Lois Winslow

Doris T., d. 11/9/1982 in Wolfeboro; Samuel Thayer and Elizabeth
Hartitz

Edwin S., Jr., d. 3/9/1990 in Wolfeboro; Edwin Drowne, Sr. and Ethel
Hasbrouck

DRUCKER,

Edith A., d. 5/1/1942 at 89/0/15 in Tuftonboro; at home; widow; b.
Nashua; Cyrus Cross and Edith Ann Ober

June E., d. 10/23/1941 at 29/4/3 in Laconia; at home; single; b.
Londonderry; Ralph W. Drucker (Londonderry) and Lela M.
Staniels (Hillsboro Bridge)

Lela May, d. 12/26/1966 at 78 in Wolfeboro; tea rm. mgr.; married; b.
Hillsboro; George Staniels and Belle Kimball

Ralph W., d. 8/26/1971 at 84 in Tuftonboro; b. MA

DUBEL,

Charles Paul, d. 6/19/1996 in Wolfeboro; Martin Dubiel and
Elizabeth Macek

Marian S., d. 4/23/2002 in Wolfeboro; Henry Savage and Corrine
Rhinehart

DUBOIS,

Mary, d. 5/29/1938 at 66/11/22 in Tuftonboro; housewife; married; b.
Margeree, Cape Breton, Canada; Martin Muise (Canada)

DUCHARME,

Donald L., d. 5/25/2003 in Mirror Lake; Wilfrid Ducharme and
Eugenie Dussault

DUNN,

Elsie W., d. 2/14/1971 at 54 in Tuftonboro; b. MA

DUNSHEE,

Robert J., d. 8/11/1985 in Wolfeboro; Fred Dunshee and Edith Lind

DURGIN,

Dana B., d. 2/23/1930 at 83/10/3 in Wolfeboro; retired engineer;
married; b. Sandwich; James H. Durgin (Parsonsfield, ME) and

Jane Varney (Wolfeboro)
Georgianna, d. 1/30/1935 at 78/9/29 in Concord; at home; widow; b. Tuftonboro; Ira Canney (Tuftonboro) and Betsy Thompson (Gilford)

EATON,
Charles M., d. 11/12/1936 at 67/0/5 in Mirror Lake; retired police officer; married; b. Gilford; Martin V. B. Eaton (Gilford) and Melissa P. Rollins (Alton)
Martin V. B., d. 10/6/1929 at 93/9/14 in Tuftonboro; retired farmer; widower; b. Gilford; Elisha Eaton (Pittsfield) and Betsy Brown (Gilford)
Melissa P., d. 3/11/1926 at 88/6/20 in Tuftonboro; at home; married; Frederick B. Rollins (Alton) and Abigail Miller (Acton, ME)

EDGERLY,
Achsa M., d. 9/3/1912 at 87/11/18; cerebral hemorrhage; widow; b. Tuftonboro; John Chace and Ruth Burbank
Albert L., d. 1/29/1903 at 77/7/19 in Tuftonboro; intestinal obstruction; married; b. Wolfeboro; John Edgerly and Nancy Locke
Caroline Crossman, d. 11/2/1929 at 45/7/24 in Wolfeboro; at home; married; b. Providence, RI; George P. Crossman (Boston, MA) and Grace A. White
Charles G., d. 10/17/1901 at 88/2/23 in Tuftonboro; valvular disease of the heart; widower; b. Farmington; John Edgerly and Nancy Watson
Edwin B., d. 5/25/1971 at 87 in Tuftonboro; b. NH
John, d. 4/6/1895 at 79/6/17 in Tuftonboro; general debility; married
John Albert, d. 10/12/1937 at 81/1/1 in Wolfeboro; retired; married; b. Tuftonboro; Charles G. Edgerly (New Durham) and Mary E. Doe
John I., d. 8/10/2003 in Wolfeboro; Edwin Edgerly and Caroline Crossman
Mary C., d. 1/8/1917 at 57/8/25 in Tuftonboro; housewife; married; b. Center Harbor; Charles H. Blake and Mary C. Webster
Nancy, d. 5/26/1891 at 63/1/16 in Tuftonboro; consumption; housewife; married; b. Tuftonboro; James Hersey (Wolfeboro) and Nancy Lucas (Wolfeboro)

EDWARDS,
John Thomas, d. 2/1/1953 at 71 in Tuftonboro; ret. police officer; married; b. Roxbury, MA; James Edwards and Bridget Murphy

ELDRIDGE,
Dana N., d. 11/30/1968 at 86 in Wolfeboro; caretaker; married; b. NH; Daniel Eldridge and Lizzie Templeton
Esther M., d. 1/1/1967 at 61 in Tuftonboro; housewife; married; b. Tuftonboro; George Haley and Edith C. Ayers
Susie, d. 11/2/1972 at – in Ossipee; b. NH

ELLIOTT,
George Daniel, d. 12/1/1959 at 76 in Wolfeboro; lumber dealer; married; b. NH; William D. Elliott and Lucy Willoughby
Mehitable V., d. 1/24/1901 at 76/8 in Tuftonboro; abscess of liver; widow; b. Tuftonboro; John V. Caverly and Susan Elliott

EMERY,
Cora A., d. 2/18/1923 at 54 in Tuftonboro; housewife; married; b. Tuftonboro; Peter B. Hersey and Mary E. Weeks
Emma S., d. 5/15/1922 at 57/10/1 in Tuftonboro; housewife; married; b. Ossipee; Allan Swasey and Emma Thompson
George Harrison, d. 1/8/1938 at 55/8/8 in Tuftonboro; watchman; married; b. Tuftonboro; Charles Edwin Emery (Tuftonboro) and Lucy Ann Haley (Moultonboro)
Hiram, d. 12/24/1904 at 0/8/14 in Tuftonboro; innutrition; b. Ossipee; A. P. Emery and Ina M. Drew
Wendel Gotlon, d. 8/8/1961 at 80/1/25 in Wolfeboro; married; b. Tuftonboro; Charles Emery and Lucy Haley

ENGLE,
Carl R., d. 8/3/1990 in Tuftonboro; Ralph Engle and Dorothy Schneider

ENGLUND,
Carl Robert, Jr., d. 4/26/1996 in Wolfeboro; Carl Robert Englund, Sr. and Ethel Isabel Groat

ESTABROOK,
George C., d. 2/28/1956 at 74 in Tuftonboro; single; b. MA; Theodore A. Estabrook and Elizabeth Clark

EVANS,

Evelyn D., d. 6/25/1948 at 52/8/24 in Wolfeboro; at home; married; b. Tuftonboro; Alvah E. Dow (Hardwick, VT) and Anna Nutter (Tuftonboro)

Frank Edward, d. 3/19/1962 at 69 in Wolfeboro; engineer; widower; b. Martins Ferry, OH

Freeman Stephen, d. 7/19/1963 at 87 in Wolfeboro; salesman; widower; b. Norwood, MA; Frank Henry Evans and Julia Jones

Jessie Williams, d. 12/17/1958 at 81 in Wolfeboro; secretary; married; b. Newton, MA; John C. Williams and Rhoda Cotting

Priscilla M., d. 10/1/1931 at 2/4/0 in Wolfeboro; b. Wolfeboro; Frank G. Evans (Erie, PA) and Evelyn Dow

Urban, d. 3/7/1966 at 67 in Wolfeboro; woodsman; b. Rumney; Elmer Evans and Annie Wescott

FALL,

child, d. 7/31/1924 at –; stillborn; b. Tuftonboro; Ausbrey C. Fall and Mertie B. Thompson

Ann E., d. 12/17/1903 at 64/5/21 in Tuftonboro; heart disease; married; Ebenezer G. Gary and Hannah J. Wiggin

Edward Everett, d. 8/11/1906 at 73/1/1; chronic nephritis; widower; b. Alton; John Fall and Nancy Evans

Ella A.,d . 2/19/1914 at 45/11; single; b. Tuftonboro; Edward E. Fall and Martha Welch

FARR,

Arthur, d. 12/26/1991 in Wolfeboro; William S. Farr and Estelle Welch

FARRINGTON,

William M., d. 10/4/1937 at – in Wolfeboro; retired real estate agent; married; b. Allston, MA; John Farrington (Allston, MA) and Sophia Goodell (Paris, ME)

FARWELL,

Mary C., d. 1/3/1976 at 67 in Wolfeboro; b. Brattleboro, VT

Theodore A., Sr., d. 9/9/1984 in Wolfeboro; Norman P. Farwell and Elizabeth Austin

FERGUSON,

Levi D., d. 3/19/1942 at 90/7/11 in Wolfeboro; minister; divorced; b.

NS; Alexander Ferguson (NS) and Mary E. ----- (NS)
Lora Hunt, d. 8/6/1927 at 64/11/16 in Tuftonboro; at home; married;
    b. IN; David Hunt (IN) and Martha Hunt (IN)
Robert B., d. 1/5/1983 in Wolfeboro; Irving B. Ferguson and Marian
    Severance

FERNALD,
A. Maria, d. 9/20/1905 at 61/7/1 in Melvin Village; tuberculosis;
    married; b. Tuftonboro; Thomas J. Hersey and Sybel P. Hersey
Alzada M., d. 11/30/1911 at 55/4/9; pneumonia; married; b.
    Meredith; Edmund A. Black and Melissa A. Drew
Belinda, d. 10/30/1898 at 80/2/21 in Tuftonboro; old age; married; b.
    Tuftonboro; Samuel Caverly and Hannah Davis
Calvin, d. 7/1/1902 at 84/11/18 in Tuftonboro; old age; widower; b.
    Tuftonboro; Daniel Fernald and Lydia Perkins
Charles E., d. 10/3/1930 at 85/11/6 in Tuftonboro; retired farmer;
    widower; b. N. Wolfeboro; Mark Fernald (N. Wolfeboro) and
    Mary Furbish (S. Berwick, ME)
Daniel, Jr., d. 10/5/1905 at 82/10/23 in Melvin Village; bronchitis, old
    age; widower; b. Tuftonboro; Daniel Fernald and Lydia Perkins
Emily, d. 10/11/1940 at 64/0/6 in Wolfeboro; at home; married; b.
    Providence, RI; Harry Campbell (Leominster, MA) and Sarah
    Sahlstwon (Philadelphia, PA)
Hollis C., d. 3/4/1945 at 56 in Lynn, MA; retired; married; b.
    Tuftonboro; Hollis E. Fernald (Tuftonboro) and Alzada Black
    (Meredith)
James Frank, d. 5/17/1926 at 77/3/22 in Tuftonboro; retired;
    divorced; Calvin Fernald (S. Berwick, ME) and Belinda Caverly
    (Tuftonboro)
Joel, d. 3/17/1896 at 76/0/5 in Tuftonboro; heart disease; farmer;
    married; b. Tuftonboro; Daniel Fernald (Berwick, ME) and Lydia
    Perkins (Berwick, ME)
Mahala, d. 6/20/1901 at 84/10 in Tuftonboro; heart failure; widow;
    Samuel Caverly
Samuel E., d. 11/12/1892 at 51/2/14 in Tuftonboro; typhoid fever;
    farmer; married; b. Tuftonboro; Calvin Fernald (Tuftonboro) and
    Belinda Caverly (Tuftonboro)

FIELDS,
George H., d. 10/13/1911 at 56/3/27; angina pectoris; divorced; b.
    Newton, MA; John L. Fields and Mary D. Jones

Mary D., d. 1/23/1892 at 64/11/12 in Tuftonboro; heart failure;
housewife; married; b. Tuftonboro; Joseph Jones and Susan
Ayers

FLAHERTY,
Gertrude F., d. 2/9/1988 in Wolfeboro; Edward J. Flaherty and Elvira
Cabeceira

FLANAGAN,
Marlene A., d. 6/11/1972 at 21 in Tuftonboro; b. NH

FLANDERS,
Phoebe A., d. 2/14/1905 at 77/6/8 in Tuftonboro; valvular disease of
heart; widow; b. Sandwich; Tufton Witham and Phoebe
Bradbury

FLICKINGER,
William H., d. 10/7/1975 at 68 in Wolfeboro; b. KS

FLINT,
Harley A., Jr., d. 2/4/1993 in Wolfeboro; Harley A. Flint, Sr. and
Maude Fay
Marion R., d. 2/2/1979 in Tuftonboro; Clifford J. Reed and Grace
Framm

FOLSOM,
Allen Paul, Sr., d. 12/20/1998 in Tuftonboro; Leon Elmer Folsom and
Katherine Grace Shannon
Katherine, d. 8/9/2004 in Wolfeboro; Leando Shannon and Gladys
Kimball
Leon E., d. 7/21/1985 in Wolfeboro; Elmer E. Folsom and Bernice
LaFlame

FORSTER,
Howard W., d. 5/19/1985 in Wolfeboro

FORSYTH,
Cecile Martha, d. 1/23/1990 in Wolfeboro; Arthur Sanborn and Mary
Chase

FORSYTHE,
Frank F., d. 3/24/1969 at 66 in Rochester; laborer; married; b. MA;
Frank Forsythe

FORTUNE,
Peter John, d. 4/25/1953 at 0/1/15 in Tuftonboro; b. Watertown, MA;
Mark Fortune and Mary Sutherland

FOSS,
Anastasia, d. 8/28/1967 at 57 in Wolfeboro; housewife; married; b.
Hallowell, ME; Edward Crockett and Anastasia Burns
Laura A., d. 7/8/1910 at 69/10/23; cancer of uterus; widow; b.
Whitefield, ME; Israel Blaisdell and Diana Trask

FOWLER,
Robin Mortimor, d. 10/13/1994 in Wolfeboro; Thompson Ernest
Fowler and Agusta Johnson

FOX,
Asa D., d. 5/23/1893 at 54/5 in Tuftonboro; tumor; farmer; married;
b. Tuftonboro; George Fox (Wolfeboro) and Drusilla Hersey
(Wolfeboro)

FREESE,
Olive M., d. 6/26/1901 at 68/8/19 in Tuftonboro; apoplexy; Gilman
Lougee
Polina, d. 1/27/1908 at 79/9; pneumonia; widow

FREEZE,
George C., d. 3/11/1907 at 79; old age; married; b. Moultonboro;
William C. Freeze and Irene Brown
Margaret, d. 2/11/1893 at 80/9 in Tuftonboro; cancer; housewife;
married; b. Tuftonboro; William Watson (Pittsfield) and Hannah
Garland (New Durham)

FRENCH,
Annie M., d. 6/12/1914 at 96; widow; b. Great Britain; Daniel Larkin
and Mary Manning
Norman A., d. 9/7/1975 at 36 in Wolfeboro; b. Boston, MA
Thomas, d. 9/19/1897 at 68/6/2 in Tuftonboro; heart failure; married;
b. Tuftonboro; Thomas French and Elizabeth Foss

FRIEDMAN,
Helen L., d. 6/23/2002 in Tuftonboro; Leonard Loeser and Florence Markson

FRISBIE,
Ernest E., d. 6/10/1904 at 23/10/16 in Tuftonboro; pulmonary tuberculosis; married; b. Tuftonboro; Louis N. Frisbie and Addie A. Morrison

FROST,
Herbert W., d. 1/2/1931 at 76/8/18 in Tuftonboro; retired; married; b. Wolfeboro; John Curtis Frost (Wolfeboro) and Lucinda Adelaide Chamberlain (Wolfeboro)

FRYE,
Hazel D., d. 1/9/1944 at 20/7/27 in Wolfeboro; at home; single; b. Moultonboro; Louis W. Frye (Moultonboro) and Jennie F. Hoyt (Tuftonboro)

FULTON,
Caroline G., d. 9/29/1924 at 79/11/24 in Tuftonboro; widow; b. PA; John N. Gibbons and Maria Oliphant

FURMAN,
Silas H., d. 9/5/1908 at 44/9; peritonitis and appendicitis; married; John Furman and Virginia V. Holman

GALVIN,
Katherine, d. 8/8/1926 at 38 in Tuftonboro; saleslady; single

GARIEPY,
Cecile Mary, d. 4/3/1997 in Tuftonboro; James Homan and Addace Fournier

GARRARAD,
Robert William, d. 7/10/1960 at 2 in Tuftonboro; b. Melrose, MA; Arnold F. Garrarad and Mary Louise Wooten

GATELY,
Russell E., Sr., d. 8/14/1954 at 67 in Tuftonboro; tax auditor; married; b. MA; Peter Gately and Mary Russell

GAY,

Abner, d. 3/23/1894 at 84; blacksmith; married; b. Chelsea, MA; Abner Gay (Chelsea, MA) and Lydia -----

GENDRO,

Amelia I., d. 7/26/1927 at 73/3/14 in Tuftonboro; at home; married; Abraham Downing (Ellsworth, ME) and Parnelia Innis (Holderness)

Clement, d. 8/29/1937 at 87 in Plymouth; retired; married; b. Canada

Ida F., d. 1/31/1915 at 50/10/5 in Tuftonboro; housewife; married; b. Tuftonboro; Albert Elliott (Sandwich) and Mehitable Caverly (Tuftonboro)

GERRISH,

Grenville B., d. 9/25/1989 in Wolfeboro; Elmer Gerrish and Amy Fernald

Madeline M., d. 5/19/1992 in Wolfeboro; Orren H. Smith and Ethel M. Ford

Winslow Fernald, d. 7/21/1978 at 63 in Tuftonboro; b. Melrose, MA

GETO,

Hattie, d. 12/18/1893 at 42/9 in Tuftonboro; heart failure; housewife; widow; b. Alton; Fannie Doe

GEYER,

Albert E., d. 9/12/1967 at 69 in Tuftonboro; checker; married; b. Melrose, MA; ----- Geyer and Adaline May

Bertha Farr, d. 1/10/1993 in Ossipee; William S. Farr and Catherine A. McKenna

GILLOOLY,

Glenn Durgin, d. 6/22/1960 at 17 in Tuftonboro; policeman USAF; single; b. Wolfeboro; George F. Gillooly and Mrs. George F. Gillooly

GILMAN,

daughter, d. 1/30/1893 at – in Tuftonboro; stillborn; b. Tuftonboro; Charles L. Gilman (Moultonboro) and Georgie Buzzell (Moultonboro)

Aaron W., d. 3/30/1935 at 83/4/28 in Ctr. Tuftonboro; farmer; widower; b. Tamworth; George W. Gilman and Ellen Bickford

(Tuftonboro)
Charles H., d. 11/27/1895 at 0/0/21 in Tuftonboro; heart failure; b.
    Tuftonboro; Charles L. Gilman and Georgianna Buzzell
Chester H., d. 1/29/1968 at 79 in Wolfeboro; patrolman; married; b.
    NH; Aaron W. Gilman and Emma Quimby
Donald, d. 6/24/1944 at – in Wolfeboro; b. Wolfeboro; Roy G. Miller
    (E. Longmeadow, MA) and Louise Gilman (Tuftonboro)
Edith B., d. 10/24/1975 at 93 in Wolfeboro; b. Chelsea, MA
Emma F., d. 3/3/1923 at 66/10/17 in Tuftonboro; housewife; married;
    b. Moultonboro; John Quimby and Sarah Jacobs

GLIDDEN,
James R., d. 4/16/1896 at 81/9/19 in Tuftonboro; apoplexy; farmer;
    married; b. Tuftonboro; Peter Glidden (Topsfield, MA) and Anna
    Reynolds (New Durham)
Marie A., d. 12/18/2003 in Mirror Lake; Henry Champagne and Alice
    Lampron
Marjery, d. 5/8/1906 at 74/8/17; apoplexy; widow; b. Tuftonboro;
    John Sullivan and Nancy Grant

GOFF,
Derborn, d. 3/4/1896 at 84/11/29 in Chicago, IL; old age; farmer;
    widower

GOODHUE,
Mary, d. 2/14/1971 at – in Wolfeboro
Mona M., d. 4/27/1975 at 86 in Beverly, MA; b. Salem, MA

GOODRICH,
Alice R., d. 8/21/1971 at 80 in Wolfeboro; b. NH
Arthur E., d. 12/7/1946 at 50/9/5 in Tuftonboro; carpenter; single; b.
    Moultonboro; J. Fred Goodrich (Somersworth) and Ella Dow
    (Moultonboro)

GOODWIN,
Hiram A., d. 6/29/1984 in Wolfeboro; Guy A. Goodwin and Agnes J.
    Jones

GORDON,
Estella D., d. 6/4/1941 at 83/7/1 in Wolfeboro; at home; widow; b.
    Canada, NS

Ethel Gertrude, d. 11/15/1975 at 83 in Laconia; b. NS

Ruth M., d. 2/8/1913 at 80/7/18; apoplexy; widow; b. Tuftonboro; Eben Morrison and Nancy Ladd

Samuel L., d. 3/11/1891 at 65/0/8 in Tuftonboro; Bright's disease; farmer; married; b. Tuftonboro; Ebenezer C. Gordon (Brentwood) and Ruth Ladd (N. Hampton)

Willis P., d. 10/29/1911 at 53/3/5; uraemia; married; b. Tuftonboro; Jonathan L. Gordon and Eliza J. Hoytt

GORE,

Arthur J., d. 9/29/1986 in Wolfeboro; William Gore and Margaret Collins

Mildred E., d. 1/25/1998 in Wolfeboro; Edward J. Flaherty and Elvira Cabeceira

GOTT,

Bertha C., d. 8/21/1985 in Wolfeboro; Frank Reynolds and Eva Bell Gilman

John W., d. 3/2/1990 in Wolfeboro; John W. Gott, Sr. and Elizabeth Waterhouse

GOUIN,

Thornton X., d. 5/19/1967 at 56 in Tuftonboro; woodsman; married; b. Wolfeboro; Frank X. Gouin and Ethel Sawyer

GOULD,

Lebias Richardson, d. 12/25/1960 at 70 in Wolfeboro; wool carder; married; b. Canada; James Gould and Sarah Huntley

Lottie Bell, d. 2/3/1949 at 57/5/1 in Tuftonboro; housewife; married; b. Peabody, MA; William H. H. Gould and Sarah E. Walker

Robert, d. 2/13/2005 in Wolfeboro; Harold Gould and Roberta Porter

GOVE,

Almeda L., d. 3/9/1917 at 78 in Tuftonboro; housewife; married; b. Bucksport, ME; James Smith and Sophronia Ames

Freeman D., d. 10/7/1917 at 85/4/24 in Tuftonboro; farmer; widower; b. E. Corinth, ME; Samuel A. Gove and Elizabeth Ingalls

GRAHAM,

Mabel, d. 4/25/1914 at 27/8/14; married; b. Bethlehem; Fred Liberty and Rose Vermett

William, d. 9/29/2004 in Wolfeboro; Emery Graham and Blanche London

GRANGER,
Rachel, d. 6/5/2004 in Wolfeboro; Roland Levesque and Theresa Legasse

GRANT,
Ethel M., d. 3/31/1922 at 24/3/16 in Tuftonboro; saleslady; single; b. Berwick, ME; Orrin C. Grant and Mercy Joy

GRAY,
Arthur M., d. 11/2/1976 at 28 in Tuftonboro; b. Rochester
Ethel L., d. 1/23/1977 at 83 in Tuftonboro; b. Cambridge, MA
Jonathan, d. 1/6/1898 at 73 in Tuftonboro; cirrhosis of liver; widower; b. S. Berwick, ME

GREBENSTEIN,
Harold A., d. 7/18/1976 at 85 in Wolfeboro; b. Cambridge, MA

GREEN,
Blanche M., d. 10/27/1937 at 70 in Ctr. Tuftonboro; at home; single; b. Canada; Thomas P. Green (St. John, NB) and Eliza A. Warren (PEI)

GREENBANK,
Benjamin M., d. 8/25/1972 at 90 in St. Johnsbury, VT; b. VT

GREENWOOD,
Lionel Junior, d. 10/12/1993 in Wolfeboro; George L. Greenwood and Hellie A. Tripp

GRIFFIN,
Betsey J., d. 5/11/2002 in Tuftonboro; Eugene Hand and Marsha ----

GRISWOLD,
Florence A., d. 6/12/1913 at 33/0/3; tuberculosis; married; b. Tuftonboro; Oscar Goldsmith and Mary A. Bean

GROTT,
Alice C., d. 12/18/1999 in Wolfeboro; Andrew Doe and Esther

Appleton

GUARINO,
Donald Jay, d. 7/10/1996 in Tuftonboro; Caesar Guarino and Flora
Schultz

GUERRIERE,
Marilyn, d. 12/26/1998 in Tuftonboro; Dennis E. Mernin and Helen
Rita Bickman

GUILD,
Nelson H., d. 6/6/1937 at 42 in Pembroke; RR fireman; married; b.
Plainville, MA; Thomas Guild (Wrentham, MA) and Ida
Donavon (Taunton, MA)

GUILFOYLE,
Thomas M., d. 8/19/1969 at 45 in Tuftonboro; plant manager;
married; b. IA; William Guilfoyle and Irene Cavanaugh

GUPPY,
Annie M., d. 11/28/1909 at 59/1/6; widow; b. Tuftonboro; George E.
Dearborn and Elizabeth S. Jenkins
Elvin O., d. 9/9/1963 at 86 in Wolfeboro; farmer; widower; b.
Cambridge, MA; John Guppy and Annie Dearborn

GUTHRIE,
Charles Parks, d. 11/28/1979 in Ossipee; Thomas C. Guthrie and
Rue Wilson

HACKETT,
Abbie E., d. 4/7/1912 at 63/6/8; cerebral embolism; single; b.
Andover, MA; John Hackett and Abbie Stevenson

HALE,
Norman A., d. 5/17/1980 in Wolfeboro; Walter L. Hale and Adah F.
Carter

HALEPIS,
James M., d. 1/22/1981 in Concord; Manuel Halepis and Harriet
Mastis

HALEY,
son, d. 10/9/1902 at 0/1/15 in Tuftonboro; heart failure; b.
Tuftonboro; George H. Haley and Edith C. Ayers
Ann M., d. 1/7/1906 at 80/11; Bright's disease; widow; b. London;
Silas Whitney and Susan Lovering
Bernard E., d. 1/15/1988 in Wolfeboro; Willis Haley and Bernece
Dow
Berniece Ethel, d. 5/8/1960 at 72 in Wolfeboro; housewife; widow; b.
Moultonboro; James Dow and Elizabeth Garland
Bertha, d. 1/14/1951 at 81 in Manchester; housewife; widow; b. ME;
Albert A. Dean and Almira Bridges
Charles Edward, d. 12/26/1959 at 77 in Wolfeboro; carpenter;
married; b. Tuftonboro; Samuel Haley and Hattie Buzzell
Delbert C., Sr., d. 7/18/1969 at 61 in Laconia; carpenter; married; b.
NH; Irving Haley and Bernice Dow
Dora E., d. 10/4/1973 at 78 in Wolfeboro; b. NH
Edith C., d. 7/25/1936 at 62/9/7 in Tuftonboro; housewife; married; b.
Tuftonboro; James Ayers (Tuftonboro) and Hannah Drew
Frances Addie, d. 12/25/1997 in Wolfeboro; Maurice Thibodeau and
Addie Trainer
Frank E., d. 11/2/1895 at 0/0/16 in Tuftonboro; croup; b. Tuftonboro;
George H. Haley and Edith C. Ayers
George H., d. 4/2/1933 at 75/11/16 in Wolfeboro; retired; married; b.
Moultonboro; Samuel Haley (Moultonboro) and Nancy Cotton
(Moultonboro)
J. Makenzie, d. 12/31/1924 at 81/4/26 in Tuftonboro; farmer; single;
b. Tuftonboro; John Smith Haley and Mary Neal Piper
John Q., d. 3/4/1913 at 65/3/9; cerebral softening; married; b.
Tuftonboro; Samuel R. Haley and Nancy Cotton
Lawrence Ervin, d. 3/30/1995 in Wolfeboro; Ervin Haley and
Bernece Dow
Madeline E., d. 3/6/1911 at 1/1/1; ptomaine poisoning; b.
Tuftonboro; Willie I. Haley and Bernice E. Dow
Samuel R., d. 9/28/1896 at 78/0/25 in Tuftonboro; chronic nephritis;
laborer; married; b. Lee
William E., d. 11/7/1929 at 61/2/12 in Tuftonboro; carpenter;
married; b. Tuftonboro; Elijah Haley (Saco, ME) and Fannie
Dore (N. Berwick, ME)

HALL,
Marion Libby, d. 4/3/1995 in Wolfeboro; Scott D. Libby and Stella

Russell

HAM,
Adeline E., d. 4/22/1937 at 82/10/14 in Dover; at home; widow; b.
   Andover, MA; John E. Hackett (Brookfield) and Abigail
   Stevenson (Wolfeboro)
Ann Z., d. 3/6/1902 at 79/11/6 in Tuftonboro; cerebral hemorrhage;
   single; b. Newington; Ephraim Ham and Lydia Miller
Benjamin, d. 5/10/1899 at 83/2/12 in Tuftonboro; married; b.
   Newington; Ephraim Ham and Lydia Miller
Leroy E., d. 11/8/1981 in Tuftonboro; Porter Ham and Nancy
   Pillsbury
Sarah D., d. 5/29/1907 at 83/5; old age; widow; b. Tuftonboro; John
   Hall and Lydia Drew

HAMM,
Hiram O., d. 4/24/1938 at 85/11/19 in Tuftonboro; carpenter;
   widower; b. Lowell, MA; Hiram Hamm (Strafford) and -----
   Caverly (Strafford)

HANINGTON,
Gudrun, d. 4/27/2004 in Wolfeboro; Al McFadden and Joan McCabe

HANSCOM,
George Ed., d. 11/26/1928 at 55 in Rochester; shoemaker; divorced;
   ----- Hanscom (Ossipee) and Belle Moore (Ossipee)

HANSEN,
Carl Irvin, d. 3/28/1998 in Tuftonboro; Linus Hansen and Mathilda B.
   Larsen
Pearl A., d. 10/2/1995 in Lebanon; Nicholas Gulliford and Mildred C.

HARDIE,
Irene Bessie, d. 7/22/1961 at 70/1/19 in Wolfeboro; married; b. New
   York City; Peter M. Stagg and Cora Armstrong
John Warden, Sr., d. 12/18/1974 at 83 in Tuftonboro; b. NY, NY
Mary M., d. 10/18/1936 at 71/4/3 in Mirror Lake; widow; b. Scotland;
   William S. MacDonald (Scotland) and Mary Swanson
   (Scotland)

HARDING,
Lucille, d. 8/31/1984 in Wolfeboro; George W. Coffin and Minnie
Boyd

HARDON,
Corrinne T., d. 12/13/1962 at 87 in Wolfeboro; housewife; widow; b.
Boston, MA; William Thompson and Frances Keniston

HARDY,
Muriel A., d. 10/3/1984 in Wolfeboro; Cornelius Hayes and May
Griffith
Thomas, d. 11/26/2004 in Wolfeboro; Etney Hardy and Adele
Paulukonis

HARMON,
Ella M., d. 4/29/1937 at 72/9/13 in Tuftonboro; housekeeper; single;
b. Freedom; Ransom Harmon (Madison) and Elizabeth Durgin
(Freedom)

HASKELL,
William Freeman, d. 3/14/1996 in Tuftonboro; Raymond I. Haskell
and Christine Daggett

HATCH,
Albert C., d. 2/1/1902 at 34/9/14 in Tuftonboro; drowning; married; b.
Wolfeboro; George O. Hatch and Hattie Horne

HAYDEN,
Mary E., d. 1/9/1941 at 81/0/23 in Tuftonboro; housewife; widow; b.
Enfield; Timothy E. Fernald (Enfield) and Sarah Washburn
(Springfield)

HAYES,
Ann M., d. 5/13/1976 at 66 in Wolfeboro; b. Lawrence, MA
Edward Joseph, d. 5/16/1953 at 77 in Tuftonboro; ret. policeman;
widower; b. Co. Waterford, Ireland; Thomas Hayes and
Catherine A. Horan
Flora Belle, d. 3/31/1962 at 65 in Wolfeboro; sales & dressmaker;
married; b. Winchester; Charles Pickett and Idela Doolittle
Hannah, d. 8/3/1908 at 4/5/19; appendicitis; Charles W. Hayes and
Rosa E. Page

Henry E. F., d. 3/14/1945 at 64/1/13 in Tuftonboro; electrician; married; b. Center Harbor; Joshua Hayes (Somersworth) and Ida Steavens (Lakeport)

Mabel Pearl, d. 5/3/1960 at 74 in Wolfeboro; housewife; widow; b. Meredith; George Welch and Ellen Horne

HAYNES,
Louise Hoyt, d. 5/21/1958 at 50 in Wolfeboro; clerk; divorced; b. Sandwich; Louis Frye and Jennie Hoyt

HEALY,
Daniel C., d. 8/26/1980 in Wolfeboro; Daniel F. Healy and Carlie Clark

HEARN,
Ernest E., d. 7/18/1925 at 53/11/2 in Tuftonboro; accountant; married; John Hearn (England) and ----- (Bridgewater, NS)

HENDRICKS,
Elois, d. 5/25/1951 at 77 in Ossipee; housewife; widow; b. NY; Joseph LeRock and Mary Brown

HENDRY,
George D., d. 10/27/1978 at 76 in Wolfeboro; b. Scotland

HERBERT,
Ralph J., d. 12/15/1978 at 72 in Wolfeboro; b. Wolfeboro

HERSEY,
Ada Arvilla, d. 5/16/1950 at 84/10/24 in Wolfeboro; housewife; widow; b. Tuftonboro; Richard Blaisdell and Ruth Brown

Alonzo Jacob, d. 3/29/1927 at 79/0/11 in Tuftonboro; retired; widower; b. Tuftonboro; Thomas J. Hersey (Tuftonboro) and Sybel Colby (Bow)

Andrew L., d. 1/2/1895 at 82/10/1 in Tuftonboro; chronic diarrhea; married; b. Tuftonboro; James Hersey and Nancy Lucas

Caroline E., d. 9/22/1937 at 85/1/22 in Wolfeboro; housewife; widow; b. Norwood, MA; Jonathan Shapleigh and Rebecca -----

Charles, d. 3/18/1943 at 87/10/20 in Tuftonboro; farmer; married; b. Tuftonboro; Franklin S. Hersey (Tuftonboro) and Elizabeth Whitney (Tuftonboro)

Daniel Jefferson, d. 2/22/1931 at 88/8/23 in Tuftonboro; gas worker; married; b. Melvin Village; Thomas Jefferson Hersey (Wolfeboro) and Sebel B. Colby (Goffstown)

Edwin Charles, d. 11/2/1951 at 74 in Tuftonboro; farmer; married; b. Tuftonboro; John L. Hersey and Orianna Flanders

Elizabeth Jane, d. 3/4/1978 at 37 in Tuftonboro; b. Wolfeboro

Emeline S., d. 1/23/1896 at 62/8/22 in Tuftonboro; val. disease of heart; housekeeper; married; b. Tuftonboro; James B. Gilman (Ossipee) and Clarissa Hersey (Tuftonboro)

Emma E., d. 9/10/1918 at 64/5/18 in Tuftonboro; housewife; married; b. Boston, MA; James McCrillis (Rumford, ME) and Hulda Rowell (Augusta, ME)

Everett U., d. 4/25/1933 at 86/5/13 in Ctr. Tuftonboro; farmer; married; b. Tuftonboro; Jonathan B. Hersey (Tuftonboro) and Elizabeth Wiggin (Tuftonboro)

Forest W., d. 10/24/1956 at 69 in Wolfeboro; poultry farmer; married; b. NH; Charles E. Hersey and Ada M. Blaisdell

Frank A., d. 3/20/1916 at 60/7/8 in Tuftonboro; merchant; married; b. Tuftonboro; Andrew L. Hersey and Sarah L. Burleigh

Frank E., d. 9/15/1915 at 62/8/24 in Carroll; farming; single; b. Tuftonboro; Thomas J. Hersey (Tuftonboro) and Sibel Colby (Goffstown)

Franklin L., d. 7/9/1900 at 71/8 in Tuftonboro; disease of brain; widower; b. Tuftonboro; Jacob Hersey and Nancy Blaisdell

Harold George, Sr., d. 6/16/1975 at 68 in Tuftonboro; b. Tuftonboro

Hattie B., d. 12/29/1969 at 84 in Wolfeboro; housewife; widow; b. VT; Levi Springer and Hollis Farrar

James H., d. 1/20/1921 at 72/10/12 in Tuftonboro; farmer; married; b. Tuftonboro; James G. Hersey and Frances A. Hersey

John L., d. 7/24/1912 at 82/8/17; sclerosis of arteries; married; b. Tuftonboro; Peter Hersey and Eunice Bowen

Lizzie M., d. 7/3/1907 at 41/3; heart prostration; married; b. Tuftonboro; Nathaniel Hodgdon and Martha Straw

Margaret, d. 4/8/1944 at 65/3/2 in Tuftonboro; housewife; married; b. Chelsea, MA; John L. Bishop (NS) and Sarah Bigelow (Boston, MA)

Mary Chase, d. 3/4/1951 at 101/11/22 in Tuftonboro; at home; widow; b. Tuftonboro; Greene Chase and Mary Patch

Mary E., d. 8/14/1894 at 94/8/16; housewife; married; b. Canterbury; Woodbury L. Wiggin (Canterbury) and Susan Lovering (Loudon)

Mary E., d. 2/24/1905 at 57/7/28 in Tuftonboro; heart disease; widow; b. Ossipee; Levi Weeks and Hepzibah Goodwin

Orianna, d. 3/3/1938 at 84/5/3 in Tuftonboro; housewife; widow; b. Sandwich; Charles Flanders (Sandwich) and Phebe Vittum (Sandwich)

Otis A., d. 1/15/1969 at 85 in Wolfeboro; farmer; widower; b. NH; John L. Hersey and Oleander Flanders

Raymond F., d. 10/21/1918 at 29/8/29 in Tuftonboro; merchant; single; b. Tuftonboro; Frank A. Hersey (Tuftonboro) and Minnie A. E. Neal (Tuftonboro)

Sebel P., d. 5/1/1905 at 90/4/1 in Melvin Village; old age; widow; b. Bow; Enoch Colby and Polly Bamford

Sheryl Denise, d. 2/19/1996 in Tuftonboro; Richard Hersey and Betty Hamilin

Velzora V., d. 8/19/1932 at 72/9/8 in Tuftonboro; widow; b. Tuftonboro; Josiah Tate and Arner Hull

HESLOR,
Harry W., d. 1/5/1941 at 68/5/9 in Tuftonboro; retired; married; b. Worcester, MA; Birney J. Heslor (Marion, NY) and Emma L. Dayton (Worcester, MA)

HESS,
William R., d. 5/29/1999 in Lebanon; Herman Hess and Rose Wolfe

HILLIARD,
Frank, d. 12/25/1936 at 86/1/22 in Melvin Village; retired; widower; b. Kensington; Rufus K. Hilliard (Kensington) and Nancy Poore (Kensington)

Laura Jane, d. 9/12/1932 at 84/11/12 in Tuftonboro; at home; married; b. Kingston; Clark P. Smith (Kingston) and Henrietta L. DeRochemont (Portsmouth)

Louis Everett, d. 1/12/1961 at 82/8/11 in Wolfeboro; married; b. Brockton, MA; Frank Hilliard and Laura Jane Smith

Margaret E., d. 10/28/1974 at 90 in Ossipee; b. NB

HILTON,
Lydia B., d. 3/2/1903 at 84/9/17 in Tuftonboro; old age; widow; b. Pittston, ME; Thomas Cass and Lydia Barker

HLUSHUK,
Alvin Richard, d. 11/13/1950 at 16/9/26 in Wolfeboro; chopper;
single; b. Tuftonboro; Jack Hlushuk and Leora Adjutant
Harold, d. 5/13/1927 at 0/4/4 in Tuftonboro; b. Tuftonboro; Jack
Hlushuk (Russia) and Leora Adjutant (Tuftonboro)
Jack Steven, d. 3/6/1956 at 60 in Wolfeboro; lumberman; married; b.
Moscow, Russia; Stephan Hlushuk and Pauline F. Dugnaka
Leora E., d. 6/29/1985 in Ossipee; Willie Adjutant and Liza J. Piper

HOBART,
Earl W., d. 3/6/2001 in Tuftonboro; Earl Hobart and Bertha Griffith

HODGDON,
Ann M., d. 12/19/1982 in Wolfeboro; John Jarvis and Ursala -----
Charles H., d. 8/5/1945 at 74/7/26 in Tuftonboro; painter; married; b.
Tuftonboro; Nathaniel Hodgdon (Tuftonboro) and Martha Straw
(Tuftonboro)
Charles T., d. 1/12/1892 at 30/7/3 in Tuftonboro; consumption;
laborer; married; b. S. Berwick, ME; Thomas F. Hodgdon
(Ossipee) and ----- Russell (Ossipee)
Edwin J., d. 3/28/1970 at 59 in Wolfeboro; architect; married; b. NH;
Herman Hodgdon and Nora K. Burke
Florence, d. 4/9/1899 at 25/9 in Tuftonboro; married; b. Tuftonboro;
Lewis Geto and Hattie Parsons
Frances Canning, d. 7/15/1994 in Wolfeboro; Hinman Canning and
Fannie Mackay
Franklin H., d. 6/1/1956 at 88 in Wolfeboro; farmer; married; b.
Tuftonboro; Nathaniel D. Hodgdon and ----- Straw
George F., d. 11/14/1899 at 75/2/11 in Laconia; widower; b.
Tuftonboro; Samuel Hodgdon and Sobrina Stevens
Glenn F., d. 3/6/2002 in Lake Eustis, FL; Forrest Hodgdon and
Velma Merrifield
Herbert Freeman, d. 7/27/1938 at 78/10/26 in Wolfeboro; farmer;
widower; b. Berwick, ME; Thomas Freeman Hodgdon and Mary
Lois Buzzell
Jacob, d. 5/15/1915 at 78/8/8 in Tuftonboro; farming; widower; b.
Tuftonboro; Bardbury Hodgdon (Moultonboro) and Harriett
Hodgdon (Tuftonboro)
Joseph, d. 2/24/1902 at 70 in Tuftonboro; valvular disease of the
heart; widower; b. Tuftonboro; Samuel Hodgdon and Sabrina
Stevens

Lewis E., d. 10/22/1892 at 10/0/19 in Tuftonboro; diphtheria; b.
    Tuftonboro; A. D. Hodgdon (Tuftonboro) and Martha Straw
    (Tuftonboro)
Lillian E., d. 10/20/1929 at 71/5/11 in Tuftonboro; at home; married;
    b. Ossipee; Ivory Milliken (Effingham) and Lois Rogers
    (Hartland, VT)
Lizzie Emma, d. 5/9/1960 at 90 in Wolfeboro; housewife; widow; b.
    Presque Isle, ME; Woodbury Ladd and Meranda Mills
Luella P., d. 11/28/1954 at 69 in Wolfeboro; at home; married; b.
    MA; George L. Richardson and Ella Perigray
Lydia S., d. 2/1/1894 at 87/1/29; housekeeper; widow; b. Tuftonboro;
    Moses Copp (Lebanon, ME) and Elizabeth Wiggin (Lebanon,
    ME)
Maria F., d. 9/2/1912 at 76/6/23; old age; married; b. Parsonsfield,
    ME; John Blazo and Nancy Towle
Martha A., d. 4/7/1916 at 70/3/21 in Tuftonboro; housewife; married;
    b. Tuftonboro; William Straw and Mary Rogers
Nancy A., d. 2/4/1900 at 81/11 in Tuftonboro; blood poisoning;
    widow; b. Tuftonboro; Robert Sargent and Betsey Libby
Nathaniel D., d. 7/17/1925 at 82/1/0 in Tuftonboro; farmer; widower;
    b. Tuftonboro; Samuel Hodgdon (Tuftonboro)
Natt Leslie, d. 2/17/1982 in Wolfeboro; Natt W. Hodgdon and Annie
    Nicholson
Natt W., d. 11/11/1968 at 88 in Wolfeboro; storekeeper; married; b.
    NH; William Hodgdon and Ella F. Whitehouse
Ralph, d. 11/6/1921 at 14/3/8 in Tuftonboro; single; b. Tuftonboro;
    Franklin H. Hodgdon and Kate Burke
Ralph H., d. 2/28/1899 at 17/3/22 in Chelsea, MA; single; b.
    Tuftonboro; Jacob Hodgdon and Maria F. Blazo
Samuel Durbin, d. 1/1/1949 at 73 in Wolfeboro; gardener; single; b.
    Tuftonboro; Nathaniel D. Hodgdon and Martha Straw
Velma A., d. 11/15/1926 at 27/8/7 in Tuftonboro; at home; married;
    Perley E. Merrifield (ME) and Nellie M. Thompson (Tuftonboro)
Willie H., d. 1/19/1909 at 47/1/27; osteo sarcoma; single; b.
    Tuftonboro; Franklin Hodgdon and Nancy A. Sargent
William O. S., d. 4/4/1926 at 79/10/3 in Tuftonboro; salesman;
    widower; Thomas F. Hodgdon (Ossipee) and Mary E. -----
    (Ossipee)

HODGES,
Burgess G., d. 5/14/1971 at 56 in MA

Elisabeth F., d. 2/14/1971 at 71 in Wolfeboro; b. CT
Milton E., d. 10/29/1977 at 75 in Wolfeboro; b. Waterbury, CT

HODSDON,
Jonathan W., d. 4/29/1918 at 73/9/26 in Tuftonboro; farmer; married;
  b. Tuftonboro; Bradbury Hodsdon and Harriet Hodsdon
  (Tuftonboro)
Mira F., d. 8/18/1932 at 86/7/20 in Tuftonboro; at home; widow; b.
  Moultonboro; Frasier Moulton (Moultonboro) and ----- Brown
  (Moultonboro)

HOGAN,
Florence Lillian, d. 11/4/1953 at 82 in Wolfeboro; housewife; widow;
  b. Hopkinton, MA; Charles Harris and Rebecca Stone

HOLMES,
Beatrice D., d. 11/26/1988 in Wolfeboro; Joseph Decatur and Agnes
  Noel
Edwin A., d. 12/14/1966 at 85 in Wolfeboro; retired; married; b.
  Salem, MA; William Holmes and Elizabeth Hazelton
Ernest W., d. 7/25/1898 at 0/2/2 in Tuftonboro; enteritis; Wilbur F.
  Holmes and Minnie Woodman
Jeanne P., d. 10/18/2002 in Manchester; Edmund Parker and Ivy
  Wright
Nathan H., d. 7/15/1896 at 80/5 in Holland, VT; heart disease;
  farmer

HOLMQUIST,
Harold H., d. 12/9/1999 in Wolfeboro; Fritz Holmquist and Berth
  Anderson

HOOGHKIRK,
Norman F., d. 6/12/1973 at 81 in Wolfeboro; b. CT

HOOKWAY,
Ralph O., d. 7/21/1987 in Wolfeboro; Raymond H. Hookway and
  Georgette Dambach

HOOPER,
Edna J., d. 3/11/1905 at 55/4 in Melvin Village; tuberculosis;
  married; b. Surry, ME; Ellis Young and Mary Kimball

Harry E., d. 10/12/1948 at 61/7/16 in Tuftonboro; painter; single; b. Boston, MA; John Hooper and Edna -----
Lucy Jane, d. 1/6/1899 at 77/4/3 in Tuftonboro; gastritis; widow; b. Tuftonboro; Ezra Shepherd and Lydia French

HOPKINSON,
son, d. 3/31/1923 at 0/0/0 in Tuftonboro; b. Tuftonboro; Thomas Hopkinson and Sarah E. Jose
Richard H., d. 7/13/1925 at 0/0/2 in Tuftonboro; b. Tuftonboro; Thomas Hopkinson (England) and Sara E. Jose (Saco, ME)

HORLE,
Martha E., d. 11/3/1979 in Wolfeboro; Anthony J. Philpott and Georgianna S. Miles

HORMELL,
Jean A., d. 4/10/2000 in Tuftonboro; Reece Ashton and Jane Ross

HORNE,
son, d. 11/6/1900 at 0/1/12 in Tuftonboro; malnutrition; b. Tuftonboro; Charles A. Horne and Nellie Hersey
Charles H., d. 1/21/1906 at 68; cerebral hemorrhage; married; Noah Horne
Elmer E., d. 11/9/1944 at 84/4/10 in Groton; farmer; widower; b. Moultonboro; John S. Horne (Moultonboro) and Mary A. Bickford (Belfast, ME)
Estella, d. 7/25/1904 at 3/9/27 in Tuftonboro; obstruction of the bile duct; b. Tuftonboro; Charles A. Horne and Nellie L. Hersey
Gretchen, d. 1/23/1941 at 65/8 in Foxboro, MA; Robert Hill (England) and Myra ----- (England)
Lydia C., d. 2/14/1899 at 93 in Tuftonboro; widow; b. Beverly, MA; Joseph Eaton and Sarah Mack
Robert Steven, d. 6/25/1959 at 64 in Mansfield, MA; textiles; widower; b. Moultonboro; Frank E. Horne and Gretchen G. Hill
Rose, d. 9/25/1899 at 55/2/23 in Tuftonboro; married; b. Wakefield; James Perkins and Phebe Nute

HORNER,
Annie M., d. 3/20/1930 at 89/9/22 in Tuftonboro; at home; married; b. Pictou County, NS; Murdock Stuart (NS) and Jeannett Stuart (NS)

Daniel W., d. 6/9/1899 at 69/7/18 in Tuftonboro; married; b. Granby, Canada; John Horner and Mary Dore

Elizabeth A., d. 5/1/1913 at 84/7/8; old age; widow; b. Alexandria; Walter Cotton and Ellen C. Critcherson

George Sumner, d. 11/25/1938 at 76/9/0 in Concord; store keeper; widower; b. Tuftonboro; Daniel W. Horner (Granby, PQ) and Elizabeth A. Cotton (Alexandria)

Grace A., d. 10/4/1929 at 67/9/15 in Tuftonboro; at home; married; b. Tuftonboro; Jacob Hodgdon (Tuftonboro) and Maria F. Blazo (Parsonsfield, ME)

James, d. 5/27/1930 at 86/6/9 in Tuftonboro; retired; widower; b. Milford, MA; James Horner (Edinburg, Scotland) and Sarah Maxwell (Edinburg, Scotland)

HOWE,

Andrew D., d. 1/25/1972 at 60 in Wolfeboro; b. MA

David F., d. 12/7/1932 at 78/3/16 in Tuftonboro; carpenter; widower; b. Southboro, MA; Israel G. Howe (Westboro, MA) and Louisa Flagg

Dorothy R., d. 4/24/1989 in Wolfeboro; Manton Hull and Laura Anderson

Edward R., d. 11/24/1976 at 69 in Ossipee; b. Jamaica Plains, MA

Elsie M., d. 7/17/1942 at 52/11/3 in Brookline, MA; at home; married; b. Stonington, CT; William J. Main (WI) and Annie Bentley (Stonington, CT)

Robert D., d. 4/1/1977 at 80 in Tuftonboro; b. Southboro, MA

Sarah D., d. 6/10/1930 at 73/6/10 in Tuftonboro; at home; married; b. Troy, NY; Charles S. Davis (MA) and Mary Owen Brown (Cork, Ireland)

HOYT,

son, d. 4/1/1907 at 0/0/2; congenital heart disease; b. Tuftonboro; Herbert C. Hoyt and Mary M. Donahue

son, d. 4/3/1907 at 0/0/4; inanition; b. Tuftonboro; Herbert C. Hoyt and Mary M. Donahue

Calvin, d. 9/25/1896 at 65/8/6 in Tuftonboro; inflammation of stomach; farmer; married; b. Meredith

Charles S., d. 11/11/1952 at 82 in Wolfeboro; laborer; widower; Calvin Hoyt and Sarah Varney

Charles W., d. 6/22/1931 at 89/4/21 in Tuftonboro; retired; widower; b. Wolfeboro; Nathaniel Hoyt (Tuftonboro) and Eliza Dyer (New

Durham)

Frank E., d. 10/1/1954 at 85 in Center Harbor; medical doctor; widower; b. NH; Charles William Hoyt and Mary Hoyt

Harland, d. 10/15/1906 at 2/11/26; cholera infantum; b. Wolfeboro; Herbert C. Hoyt and Nora Donahue

Herbert C., d. 5/15/1943 at 88/5/4 in Wolfeboro; ret. market man; widower; b. Tuftonboro; Nathaniel C. Hoyt (Tuftonboro) and Eliza Dyer (Dover)

Nellie D., d. 5/5/1952 at 85 in Wolfeboro; at home; married; b. Salem; Nathaniel Paul and Jane Taylor

Nora, d. 9/28/1960 at 89 in Concord; housewife; widow; b. Ireland

HUBBARD,
Nellie E., d. 12/4/1922 at 50/6/1 in Tuftonboro; housewife; married; b. Sandwich; Reuben F. Abbott and Abbie Tappan

HUDSON,
Alice R., d. 8/2/1970 at 41 in Tuftonboro; housewife; married; b. MA; Johnson Buckley, Sr. and Catherine Glassley

HULL,
Clara Burchell, d. 5/3/1939 at 77/9/13 in Mirror Lake; housewife; widow; b. Boston, MA; John Evans (Cardiff, Wales) and Ellen E. Gallagher

Fred A., d. 3/12/1948 at 66/5/6 in Wolfeboro; painter; single; b. S. Boston, MA; Charles E. Hull (Tuftonboro) and Clara B. Evans (Boston, MA)

Herbert J., d. 8/13/1999 in York, ME; Charles Hull and Margaret Kent

Laura W., d. 12/2/1948 at 64/5/19 in Tuftonboro; at home; married; b. Pawtucket, RI; Joseph Anderton (Pawtucket, RI) and Mary LaFarge (Dobbs Ferry, NY)

Manton R., d. 5/18/1963 at 83 in Wolfeboro; farmer; widower; b. Providence, RI; Andrew Hull and Ida Greene

HUMPHREY,
Gorham B., d. 6/1/1932 at 72/8/26 in Wolfeboro; retired; married; b. San Francisco, CA; Leavitt Humphrey (Moultonboro) and Sarah Blanchard (Boston, MA)

HUNT,
daughter, d. 8/3/1893 at 0/0/1 in Tuftonboro; inanition; b. Tuftonboro; Christopher Hunt and Eva N. Bean (Tuftonboro)
Dorothy L., d. 10/9/1977 at 70 in Tuftonboro; b. Saugus, MA
Horace H., d. 10/5/1915 at 59/10/13 in Tuftonboro; mail carrier; married; b. Dallis Co., IA; David W. Hunt (NC) and Martha Elliott (IN)
Philip C., d. 11/3/1971 at 72 in Tuftonboro; b. NH

HUNTER,
Annie Cora, d. 4/26/1950 at 90/5/17 in Tuftonboro; housewife; widow; b. Tuftonboro; Jacob Hodgdon and Maria E. Blazo
Arthur C., d. 12/30/1927 at 69/6/14 in Tuftonboro; retired; married; Arthur Hunter (Topsham, ME) and Helen M. Atkins
Barbara Wood, d. 11/29/1997 in Wolfeboro; William Harry Wood and Inez Patterson
Bradbury Ellis, d. 3/23/1988 in Tuftonboro; Ernest M. Hunter and Margaret Ellis
Ernest M., d. 12/1/1971 at 80 in Wolfeboro; b. MA
Margaret Ellis, d. 12/13/1982 in Meredith; Fred Ellis and Gertrude Furber
Thomas W., d. 8/11/1990 in Wolfeboro; Ernest Hunter and Margaret Ellis

HUNTING,
Georgiana P., d. 8/2/1932 at 95/0/27 in Tuftonboro; at home; widow; b. Portland, ME; Charles Bradford (Auburn, ME)

HUOT,
Richard Allen, d. 9/7/1995 in Tuftonboro; Walter Huot and Ruth Andrews

HURLBURT,
Blanche Beatrice, d. 7/7/1962 at 77 in Wolfeboro; housewife; widow; b. Lunenburg, NS; ----- Celdert and Latisha -----
Blanche C., d. 8/16/1973 at 70 in Wolfeboro; b. MA
Fannie, d. 6/20/1943 at 85/6/26 in Tuftonboro; at home; widow; William Thompson (Wolfeboro) and Frances Kenniston (Wolfeboro)
H. F., Jr., d. 6/4/1948 at 68/4/10 in Wolfeboro; ret. lawyer; married; b. Lynn, MA; Henry F. Hurlburt (Hudson, MA) and Fannie E.

Thompson (Hudson, MA)
Henry F., 3rd, d. 1/27/1968 at 59 in Wolfeboro; banks; married; b.
    MA; Henry F. Hurlburt, Jr. and Blanche Goldert
John R., d. 1/5/1967 at 73 in Wolfeboro; secretary; married; b. Lynn,
    MA; Henry Hurlburt and Frances Thompson

IDE,
William S., Jr., d. 8/29/1940 at 28/0/9 at Sandy Is.; ins. underwriter;
    single; b. Detroit, MI; William S. Ide (E. Providence, RI) and
    Jessie E. Gray (Providence, RI)

INGALLS,
Joseph E., d. 10/27/1976 at 51 in Wolfeboro; b. MA

JACKSON,
George H., d. 10/22/1937 at 87/10/4 in Ctr. Tuftonboro; shoemaker;
    married; b. Rochester; Asa M. Jackson (Lee) and Sarah J.
    Pearl (Rochester)
Lydia J., d. 1/21/1894 at 76/8/28; housekeeper; widow; b. Sandown;
    ----- Carlton and ----- French
Mary, d. 5/18/1892 at 72/10/28 in Tuftonboro; gastritis; housewife;
    married; b. Eaton; Jonathan Jackson (Sandwich) and Mary
Jackson (Lebanon, ME)
Matthew, d. 2/2/1897 at 89/6/12 in Tuftonboro; old age; widower; b.
    Eaton, now Madison; James Jackson and Sally Perkins
Weymouth H., d. 10/23/1980 in Tuftonboro; John Jackson and Annie
    Fernald

JALBERT,
Joseph Hilaire, d. 9/4/1949 at 39/5/25 in Tuftonboro; shoeworker;
    married; b. St. Honere, Canada; Augustine Jalbert

JOHNSON,
Ada F., d. 7/27/1928 at 71/8/11 in Nashua; at home; widow; b.
    Moultonboro; George Brown and Sally Caverly
Bertha Mae, d. 12/1/1964 at 84 in Wolfeboro; housewife; widow; b.
    Tuftonboro; James A. Doe and Jennie B. Fernald
Charles, d. 5/5/1904 at 49 in Tuftonboro; pulmonary tuberculosis;
    married; b. Wolfeboro; Phineas Johnson
Charles Wesley, d. 6/23/1951 at 69 in Laconia; mail carrier; married;
    b. NH; Charles E. Johnson and Elizabeth Wiggin

Edwin W., d. 7/29/1951 at 65 in Wolfeboro; Navy Yd. emp.; married; b. Tuftonboro; Charles E. Johnson and Elizabeth Wiggin

Elizabeth Gould, d. 6/23/1961 at 73/5/20 in Tuftonboro; widow; b. Salem, MA; William H. Gould and Sarah E. Walker

Elizabeth W., d. 5/1/1936 at 75/6/13 in Wolfeboro; at home; widow; b. Tuftonboro; William Wiggin (Tuftonboro) and Ann Wiggin (Tuftonboro)

Eugene Henry, d. 5/28/1951 at 75 in Wolfeboro; fireman; married; b. MA; Edward C. Johnson and Vera Onianna

Grace S., d. 11/20/1971 at 87 in Wolfeboro

Louise P., d. 5/9/1985 in Wolfeboro; Edward Maichle and Louisa C. Rothfuss

Marshal, d. 8/24/2004 in Tuftonboro; Uno Johnson and Margaret Marshall

JOHNSTONE,
William George, d. 8/20/1966 at 63 in Tuftonboro; teacher; married; b. Glasgow, Scotland; John C. Johnstone and Isabel Newport

JONES,
Suzanne Taft, d. 8/4/2000 in Tuftonboro; Frank William Taft and Villo Latcher

JOWETT,
Raynold Irving, d. 8/26/1962 at 51 in Tuftonboro; lab. technician; married; b. Belmont, MA; Fred Jowett and Ludivine Custeau

KANE,
daughter, d. 10/23/1920 at – in Tuftonboro; b. Tuftonboro; Edward Kane and Angie M. Hersey

KELLEY,
Evelyn S., d. 5/18/1976 at 72 in Wolfeboro; b. MA

KELLY,
Charles Joseph, d. 5/10/1997 in Wolfeboro; William Kelly and Jenny Reidy

KENDAL,
Angela, d. 9/30/1976 at 2 ½ hrs. in Wolfeboro; b. Wolfeboro
Herbert G., d. 5/22/1991 in Tuftonboro; Herbert B. Kendal and

Charlotte Gouin

KENNARD,
Carrie E., d. 7/6/1892 at 36/0/14 in Tuftonboro; tum. & Bright's
disease; shoe vamper; married; b. Meredith; Nathan H. Holmes
(Jefferson) and Lucinda B. Bryant (Tuftonboro)

KENNEY,
Hiram, d. 6/16/1904 at 79/10 in Tuftonboro; old age; widower; b.
Wolfeboro; Elijah B. Kenney and Hannah H. Cook

KENNINGTON,
Edith Barrett, d. 10/10/1958 at 82 in Wolfeboro; housewife; widow; b.
Cambridge, MA; Edward G. Barrett and Mary C. Bulfinch

KENNISON,
Leona M., d. 9/19/1945 at 78/11/8 in Wolfeboro; cook; widow; b.
Newmarket; John Young (Ossipee) and Betsy Wiggin (Ossipee)

KESLER,
Hazel J., d. 7/30/1975 at 62 in Wolfeboro; b. MD

KIDD,
Peter L., d. 4/1/1959 at 74 in Wolfeboro; engraver; single; b.
Scotland; James Kidd and Elizabeth McMillan

KIMBALL,
Alston E., d. 2/23/1909 at 14/4/24; double pneumonia; single; b.
Tuftonboro; Amos W. Kimball and Fannie E. Kimball
Amos W., d. 4/5/1917 at 54/7/13 in Tuftonboro; mail carrier; married;
b. Tuftonboro; Charles S. Kimball and Frances Brown

KING,
Kenneth B., d. 9/9/1977 at 82 in Wolfeboro; b. GA

KIRKLAND,
Hugh M., d. 11/16/1970 at 75 in Wolfeboro; bus driver; widower; b.
VT; Theodore W. Kirkland and Isabelle Smith

KISH,
Michael, d. 3/3/1975 at 65 in Wolfeboro; b. Hungary

KLING,
Fred Madsen, d. 12/11/1926 at 44/2/8 in Tuftonboro; accountant; married; Peter M. Kling (Denmark) and Minnie Casper (St. Louis, MO)

KLUGE,
Theodora T., d. 6/24/1976 at 68 in Tuftonboro; b. MS

KNAPP,
Arline J., d. 2/15/1992 in Wolfeboro; Walter Dagy and Alice Frazier

KNIGHTS,
John Franklin, d. 1/16/1980 in Exeter; Frank A. Knights and Edith E. Kimball

KNIVILLE,
Dorothy, d. 9/26/1999 in Tuftonboro; Nelson Edmands and Alice Blaney

KREY,
Arthur William, d. 2/22/1964 at 93 in Natick, MA; real estate; widower; b. Boston, MA; Henry Krey and Katherine Oakley
Minnie E., d. 9/5/1944 at 67/10/18 in Natick, MA; housewife; married; b. Hampton; John Kee (Hampton, NB) and Katherine Fitzgerald (Hampton, NB)

KRIPPENDORF,
Dorothy S., d. 4/6/1975 at 56 in Tuftonboro; b. MA
Ernst P., d. 12/31/1999 in Wolfeboro; Paul Krippendorf and Amelia Wremlin
Maryse B., d. 3/3/2002 in Tuftonboro; ----- Brunteau

KURTH,
Charles F., d. 8/11/1903 at 16/5/4 in Tuftonboro; valvular disease of heart; single; Richard Kurth and Jennie T. McKennea

LADD,
Bertha, d. 11/14/1896 at 11/7/11 in Tuftonboro; congestion of brain; single; b. Tuftonboro; George M. Ladd (Tuftonboro) and Juliett Bickford (Tamworth)
Byron A., d. 12/2/1974 at 82 in Ossipee; b. MA

Eliza, d. 12/1/1898 at 76/5/4 in Tuftonboro; bronchial pneumonia; married; Jacob Moulton and Eunice Bean

Elsie E., d. 11/28/1899 at 0/8 in Tuftonboro; b. Tuftonboro; George M. Ladd and Juliet Bickford

George, d. 7/28/1937 at 81/9/18 in Concord; farmer and carpenter; widower; b. Melvin Village; Gordon B. Ladd (NH) and Eliza Moulton (NH)

Gordon, d. 6/13/1900 at 86/10/10 in Tuftonboro; old age; widower; b. New Hampton; Samuel Ladd and Comfort Dow

Harvey A., d. 3/26/1913 at 55; pneumonia; married; b. Tuftonboro; Gordon Ladd and Eliza Moulton

Irvetta S., d. 11/4/1976 at 86 in Ossipee; b. Mediapolis, IA

John A., d. 8/30/1907 at 74/11/29; old age and arterial sclerosis; married; b. Tuftonboro; Samuel Ladd and Nancy Young

Jonathan D., d. 1/9/1891 at 81/8/5 in Tuftonboro; paralytic shock; farmer; married; b. N. Hampton

Juliette, d. 12/11/1934 at 77/11/10 in Laconia; housewife; married; b. Tamworth; James Bickford (Madbury) and Sarah J. Tilton (Tamworth)

Levi W., d. 4/26/1931 at 87/9/15 in Tuftonboro; master mechanic; widower; b. Tuftonboro; Gordon Ladd (NH) and Dolly Ladd (Tuftonboro)

Maranda S., d. 10/31/1922 at 79/8/19 in Tuftonboro; housewife; married; b. Hudson, MA; George Mills and Elizabeth Stickney

Mary, d. 11/2/1940 at 76 in Malden, MA; at home; widow; b. Quebec; Roger Hopper (Quebec) and Sarah Rhinehart (Canada)

Susan, d. 4/15/1898 at 88/1/9 in Tuftonboro; apoplexy; widow; b. Tuftonboro; John Young and Hannah Ham

LAFLASH,
Hosea, d. 10/7/1928 at 64/3/28 in Tuftonboro; weaver; married; b. Westford, VT; Peter LaFlash and Amanda -----

LAGUARDIA,
Lionel G., d. 1/9/1981 in Wolfeboro; Garibaldi LaGuardia and Francesca Scicigliani

LAING,
George, d. 11/14/1987 in Wolfeboro; James Laing and Agnes Williamson

LAKEY,
Charles D., d. 8/24/1919 at 87/8 in Tuftonboro; journalist; widower;
  b. Palmira, NY; Thomas Lakey and ----- Durfee

LAMPREY,
Carroll A., d. 5/7/1965 at 66 in Tuftonboro; self-employed; married;
  b. Tuftonboro; Robert Lamprey and Mary McKenna
Fannie R., d. 9/20/1919 at 42/3/17 in Wolfeboro; housewife; married;
  b. Tuftonboro; Theodore Thompson and Rosie Tibbetts
Gertrude A., d. 11/26/1963 at 61 in Wolfeboro; housewife; married;
  b. Dorchester, MA; Gustaf A. Olsson and Segne Olsson
Kathie Stacy, d. 8/9/1960 at 63 in Wolfeboro; housewife; married; b.
  Cornish, ME; Charles O. Stacy and C. Maud Watson
Mary F., d. 6/22/1921 at 53 in Tuftonboro; housewife; married; b.
  Boston, MA; C. McKenna and E. Earley
Robert, d. 4/12/1922 at 75/5/17 in Tuftonboro; farmer; widower; b.
  Moultonboro; Robert Lamprey and Almira Moulton
Theodore B., d. 11/28/1970 at 67 in Tuftonboro; gardener; widower;
  b. NH; Wilbur H. Lamprey and Fannie Thompson
Wilbur Henry, d. 2/2/1938 at 66/0/9 in Tuftonboro; laborer; married;
  b. Moultonboro; George Riley Lamprey (Moultonboro) and
  Emma Gowen (Dover)

LANGLEY,
Guy, d. 4/27/1974 at 70 in Manchester; b. NH

LASSELL,
Francis Morton, d. 4/30/1966 at 79 in Tuftonboro; farmer; married; b.
  Lynn, MA; Bernard Lassell and Carie Hughes
Mary H. B., d. 6/18/1945 at 55/1/26 in Concord; housewife; married;
  b. Lynn, MA; John F. Bessom (Lynn, MA) and Mary T.
Simmons (N. Ellsworth, ME)

LAURA,
Bruno, d. 11/6/1991 in Tuftonboro; Alfred Laura and Theresa
  DeFalchi

LAVENDER,
John R., d. 9/7/2003 in Wolfeboro; John Lavender and Katherine
  Rand

LAWLER,
Anna, d. 1/12/1984 in Wolfeboro; Hugo Hendricks and Eleanor Shabatka

LAWRENCE,
Muriel Reed Bessom, d. 7/17/1959 at 77 in Tuftonboro; housewife; divorced; b. MA; John F. Bessom and Mary T. Simmons

LAWTON,
Lewis, d. 9/29/1994 in Tuftonboro; Lewis Lawton and Mercedes Horton

LAZENBY,
Francis J., d. 5/13/2002 in Wolfeboro; Francis Lazenby and Evelyn Abbott

LEARY,
John N., d. 8/9/1952 at 96 in Meredith; laborer; married; b. Tuftonboro; Daniel Leary and Helen Swanson
Martha, d. 11/5/1917 at 65/0/2 in Concord; housewife; single; b. Tuftonboro; Daniel Leary and Mary Swett
Mary A., d. 4/7/1918 at 97/8/17 in Tuftonboro; housewife; widow; b. Stewartstown; Samuel Swett and Mehitable Neal (Greenland)

LEAVITT,
Harold J., d. 1/14/2002 in Wolfeboro; Fred Leavitt and Elsie Wahlen
Louise, d. 2/6/2004 in Wolfeboro; Chester Gilman and Edith Fernald

LEFAVRE,
William O., d. 11/12/1972 at 90 in Wolfeboro; b. IL

LEHNER,
Eugene W., d. 8/31/1930 at 55/2/24 in Tuftonboro; packer; married; b. Germany; Christian Lehner (Germany)

LEONARD,
Parker Franklin, d. 10/3/1997 in Wolfeboro; Stanley T. Leonard and Helen Parker

LEROUX,
Aura M., d. 1/25/2003 in Ossipee; Percy Beattie and Lola Owen

Edward Guy, Sr., d. 9/14/1997 in Wolfeboro; Benjamin LeRoux and Elizabeth Butt

LESLIE,
Herbert H., d. 6/20/2002 in Tuftonboro; Herbert Leslie and Louise Reed

LESTER,
Alice E., d. 12/26/1977 at 53 in Wolfeboro; b. NC
Richard H., d. 7/23/1990 in Wolfeboro; Thomas J. Lester and Leora Bacon

LEVESQUE,
Roland J., d. 6/10/1994 in Wolfeboro; Donat Levesque and Alma Boutin

LEVITCH,
Alexander, d. 10/30/1960 at 89 in Wolfeboro; cabinet maker; married; b. Grouno, Poland; Vincient Levitch and Victoria Skoush
Emmie L., d. 10/27/1976 at 89 in Concord; b. NY

LEVY,
Mabel Deland, d. 4/10/1946 at 71/4/21 in Wolfeboro; housewife; widow; b. Lynn, MA; Alfred N. Deland (MA) and Hulda Perkins (MA)
Maurice Eugene, d. 7/23/1960 at 58 in Whitefield; Maurice Levy and Mabel Deland

LEWIS,
James L., d. 10/13/2001 in Wolfeboro; George Lewis and Margaret -
Lenore Alma, d. 8/24/1950 at 70/4/14 in Rochester; housewife; widow; b. Tuftonboro; Isaiah A. Wendall and Alma Horne

LIBBY,
son, d. 4/28/1892 at 0/0/29 in Tuftonboro; lung fever; b. Tuftonboro; Fred C. Libby (Tuftonboro) and Gusta M. Thomas (Tuftonboro)
Ethelda, d. 3/9/1925 at 0/0/1 in Tuftonboro; b. Tuftonboro; Frank Libby (Tuftonboro) and Bernice Canney (Ossipee)
Frank, d. 10/9/1919 at 69/11/25 in Tuftonboro; farmer; married; b. Tuftonboro; James C. Libby and Susan Briar

Hazel V., d. 1/12/1980 in Tuftonboro; Norris McKenney and Jeanette
    Sables
Helen S., d. 2/4/1976 at 79 in Tuftonboro; b. Ossipee
Laura J., d. 5/3/1931 at 75/9/16 in Tuftonboro; at home; widow; b.
    Effingham; Christopher Staples and Basherfer Edwards
Levi W., d. 2/10/1927 at 77/7/5 in Tuftonboro; farmer; married; b.
    Tuftonboro; William Libby (Tuftonboro) and Nancy Colbath
    (Farmington)
Lucy E., d. 12/20/1927 at 73/0/20 in Tuftonboro; housewife; widow;
    b. Tuftonboro; Samuel Haley (Tuftonboro) and Nancy Cotton
    (Moultonboro)
Robert M., d. 4/1/1978 at 82 in Hanover; b. Tuftonboro
Susan, d. 1/13/1893 at 64/5/18 in Tuftonboro; heart failure;
    housewife; widow; b. Tuftonboro; Samuel Briard (Portsmouth)
    and Lydia Moulton (Moultonboro)
William, d. 5/14/1906 at 83/5/22; progressive muscular atrophy;
    widower; b. Tuftonboro; Levi M. Libby

LILLIS,
daughter, d. 9/22/1946 at 0/0/0 in Wolfeboro; b. Wolfeboro; John P.
    Lillis (Malden, MA) and Glenna Seafield (Rock Springs, WY)

LINCOLN,
Fanny M., d. 7/13/1896 at 48 in Tuftonboro; abscess on liver;
    housekeeper; married; b. Boston, MA; Thad Gould and Francis
    Ober (Boston, MA)

LINNELL,
Donald Jay, d. 11/17/1987 in Wolfeboro; Clifton Linnell and Delma
    Lyford
Virginia T., d. 6/25/1979 in Wolfeboro; John Hart Taylor and Maude
    S. Goodwin

LITCHFIELD,
Joshua I., d. 2/22/1957 at 88 in Rockland, MA; teacher; widower; b.
    Cohasset, MA; Anson B. Litchfield and Eliza Jane Whittcomb
Mabel B., d. 2/27/1948 at 71/1/28 in Laconia; housewife; married; b.
    Rockland, MA; Anson F. Bicknell (Weymouth, MA) and Olive
    Puttilow (Weymouth, MA)

LITTLEFIELD,
Stilson W., d. 9/23/1966 at 70 in Wolfeboro; laund. mgr.; married; b. Woburn, MA; Warren Littlefield and Catherine O'Brien

LOCKWOOD,
John A., d. 1/15/1971 at 82 in Ossipee
Pauline M., d. 3/28/1961 at 80/9/19 in Tuftonboro; married; b. Pittsburgh, PA; Mario L. deLesi and Margaret Forest Mazurie

LOETHER,
Alycemae, d. 11/17/1996 in Wolfeboro; Walter H. Demmler and Vera Werner

LOPAUS,
Roy Chester, d. 5/15/1988 in Wolfeboro; Roy Clark Lopaus and Amy S. Lynch

LORD,
Charles Sumner, d. 1/10/1957 at 75 in Wolfeboro; caretaker; married; b. Effingham; Andrew Lord and Ida Cousins
Elizabeth, d. 7/18/1942 at 68/11/26 in Wolfeboro; at home; married; b. Tuftonboro; John L. Morrison (Tuftonboro) and Sarah Brown (Moultonboro)
Milton A., d. 12/6/1951 at 73 in CO; widower; Andrew A. Lord and Ida C. Richardson

LORING,
George Anderson, d. 7/12/1934 at 77/1/5 in Mirror Lake; retired; married; b. Hingham, MA; Enos Loring (Hingham, MA)

LOVEDAY,
Barbara, d. 11/12/2005 in Wolfeboro; William Braumann and Hope Transeaux
Henry Albert, d. 1/27/1995 in Tuftonboro; James A. Loveday and Pauline Bowley

LOW,
Charles, d. 2/17/1907 at 84; double pneumonia; widower; b. Moultonboro
Livonia, d. 2/9/1907 at 76/11/9; pneumonia; married; b. Alton; James Langley

Lucy Viola, d. 11/18/1968 at 76 in Wolfeboro; dressmaker; married; b. NH; Hiram Corson and Ellen Furbush

LUCAS,
Benjamin G., d. 1/7/1921 at 87/1/29 in Tuftonboro; farmer; widower; b. Tuftonboro; James Lucas
Carroll Franklin, d. 10/10/1963 at 66 in Wolfeboro; retired; married; b. Wolfeboro; Alfred Ernest Lucas and Harriette Lucas
Delia, d. 2/24/1918 at 76/1/0 in Tuftonboro; housewife; married; b. Bangor, ME; Patrick Tracey (Ireland) and Eliza Mullen (Ireland)
Ervin Alfred, d. 1/22/1949 at 21 in Wolfeboro; waiter; single; b. N. Brookfield, MA; Carroll F. Lucas and Flora E. Charron
Henry, d. 8/17/1899 at 70/4/19 in Tuftonboro; b. Wolfeboro; Hannah Lucas

LUGG,
Eva Ruth, d. 4/12/1958 at 68 in Tuftonboro; housewife; married; b. Lowell, MA; William Davis and Mary Ann Marshall
John J., d. 2/11/1963 at 73 in Tuftonboro; stone mason; widower; b. Concord; John Lugg and Sarah A. Williams

LUNDIN,
Oscar H., d. 5/16/1985 in Tuftonboro; Hans Lundin and Anna -----

LUTTRELL,
Arthur J., d. 9/3/1928 at 21/8/6 in Tuftonboro; clerk; single; b. Boston, MA; P. J. Luttrell (Boston, MA) and Helen F. Donovan (Boston, MA)

MACK,
George F., d. 10/27/1916 at 26/8/2 in Tuftonboro; laborer; married; b. Sandwich; Fred Mack and Nellie Abbott

MACLEAN,
Priscilla, d. 1/23/1966 at 50 in Tuftonboro; nursing; divorced; b. Somerville, MA; Herbert A. Dodge and Beatrice A. Leseur

MACMILLAN,
Carter C., d. 9/3/1979 in Tuftonboro; Edward P. MacMillan and Ida May Brokaw
Hazel K., d. 9/10/1969 at 72 in Wolfeboro; librarian; married; b. PA;

James Kallett and Mary A. Platts

MADDEN,
Ashley V., d. 10/16/1986 in Newton, MA; Steven Madden and Linda Rivers
Barbara P., d. 6/11/1980 in Wolfeboro; Horace J. Perry and Helen Baker

MALMGREN,
Barbara, d. 6/20/2005 in Ossipee; Albert Chamberlin and Eleanor Bowker

MANSFIELD,
Lindsey E., d. 12/20/1983 in Tuftonboro; David C. Mansfield and Lorraine Stafford

MARCH,
Helen G., d. 8/13/1974 at 67 in Wolfeboro; b. VA

MARGESON,
Edward A., d. 10/17/1980 in Concord; William H. Margeson and Gertrude M. Lowd

MARKLEY,
Elizabeth, d. 10/27/1986 in Wolfeboro; Herman N. Verbick and Petronella -----

MARLATT,
Wilmot R., d. 10/1/1990 in Laconia; Herbert Marlatt and Edna Schenck

MARRIMORE,
Ella A., d. 1/24/1974 at 86 in Wolfeboro; b. IN

MARRIOTT,
John Willard, Sr., d. 8/13/1985 in Wolfeboro; Hyrum W. Marriott and Ellen Morris

MARSH,
Dexter Henry, d. 2/28/1962 at 64 in Wolfeboro; broker; married; b. Springfield, MA; Oliver Marsh and Cynthia E. Ricker

Ruth B., d. 11/23/1978 at 76 in Wolfeboro; b. Keene

MARTIN,
Albert H., d. 1/19/1895 at 71/9 in Tuftonboro; cancer; married
    Ethel A., d. 10/19/1962 at 87 in Dover; housewife; widow; b.
    Tuftonboro; Charles E. Ham and Adeline -----
Marcia Susie, d. 1/10/1963 at 81 in Wolfeboro; housewife; married;
    b. Ossipee; George Willand and Grace Fay
Walter F., d. 3/16/1965 at 86 in Wolfeboro; fireman; widower; b.
    Lynn, MA; James Martin and Sarah E. Bessom

MASSEY,
Clifford W., d. 6/17/1971 at 64 in Wolfeboro; b. CT

MATTHEWS,
Eleanor Troop, d. 9/26/1958 at 70 in Melvin Village; housewife;
    widow; b. NS; John Lockwood and Harriet DeWolf Lockwood
Leroy Allen, d. 4/15/1958 at 69 in Tuftonboro; biologist; married; b.
    Malden, MA; ----- Matthews and ----- Whitmarsh

MAYO,
Orran A., d. 5/19/1921 at 84 in Tuftonboro; nurse; widower; b.
    Belfast, ME

McDONALD,
George H., d. 12/6/1952 at 69 in Moultonboro; carpenter; single; b.
    Tuftonboro; Harry McDonald and Marguerite C. Prime

McDUFFEE,
Donald, d. 3/16/1916 at 0/0/1 in Tuftonboro; b. Tuftonboro; Irving
    McDuffee and Minnie Templeton
Henry D., d. 5/10/1913 at 81/3/12; arteriosclerosis; widower; b.
    Rochester
Irving, d. 10/2/1940 at 70/10/14 in Tuftonboro; carpenter; divorced;
    b. Tuftonboro; Henry McDuffee (Rochester) and Sarah Cotton
    (Ossipee)
Marcus D., d. 12/26/1923 at 90/1/2 in Tuftonboro; retired; b. Alton;
    Jacob McDuffee and Hannah Piper
Sarah G., d. 5/3/1904 at 71/7/2 in Tuftonboro; apoplexy; married; b.
    Ossipee; Smith Cotton and Hannah Hilton

McGALL,
Robert, d. 4/4/2004 in Mirror Lake; Ernest McGall and Alberta Mach

McGORTY,
Marjorie Marie, d. 8/31/1997 in Tuftonboro; John Victor and Jessie
    Graham
Peter F., d. 7/6/1974 at 75 in Wolfeboro; b. MA
Peter F., Jr., d. 4/2/1988 in Wolfeboro; Peter F. McGorty and
    Florence Moreau

McGOWEN,
Brian K., d. 4/22/1993 in Manchester; Carl McGowen and Elsie G.
    Morang

McINNIS,
Mary E., d. 7/23/1934 at 68/0/19 in Ctr. Tuftonboro; widow; George
    Chase (Portsmouth)

McINTIRE,
daughter, d. 4/14/1891 at 30 mins. in Tuftonboro; heart failure; b.
    Tuftonboro; Lewis McIntire (Tuftonboro) and Nettie C. Libby
    (Tuftonboro)
son, d. 4/11/1892 at 0/0/7 in Tuftonboro; inanition; b. Tuftonboro;
    Lewis McIntire (Tuftonboro) and Nettie C. Libby (Tuftonboro)
son, d. 1/19/1930 at 20 hrs. in Tuftonboro; b. Tuftonboro; Delma
    McIntire (Tuftonboro) and Eunice Frye (Plymouth)
Charles A., d. 2/16/1917 at 87/1/5 in Tuftonboro; farmer; married; b.
    Tuftonboro; Isaiah McIntire and Sarah A. Stevens
Charles W., d. 12/24/1893 at 52/1/1 in Tuftonboro; heart disease;
    farmer; married; b. Tuftonboro; Stephen McIntire and Parmelia
    Welch
Delmar L., d. 7/14/1971 at 66 in Wolfeboro; b. NH
Eunice E., d. 8/26/1973 at 67 in Wolfeboro; b. NH
Harriet, d. 3/30/1941 at 89/10/9 in Tuftonboro; housewife; widow; b.
    Wolfeboro; Phineas Johnson (Brookfield) and Hannah C.
    Young (Wolfeboro)
Horace F., d. 1/2/1922 at 73/8/1 in Tuftonboro; farmer; married; b.
    Tuftonboro; Peletiah McIntire and Hannah Welch
Nellie C., d. 5/27/1903 at 33/10/19; pneumonia; married; Daniel
    Libbey and Ann E. Canney
Sadie Belinda, d. 11/23/1958 at 72 in Tuftonboro; housewife; widow;

b. Tuftonboro; James A. Doe and Jennie B. Fernald
Selden, d. 7/4/1946 at 82/4/18 in Wolfeboro; farmer; single; b.
Tuftonboro; Charles A. McIntire (Tuftonboro) and Emily C.
Wiggin (Tuftonboro)

McINTOSH,

Mary A., d. 4/18/1971 at 63 in Wolfeboro; b. NY

McINTYRE,

Lewis, d. 2/1/1945 at 77/0/10 in Tuftonboro; carpenter; married; b.
Tuftonboro; Charles A. McIntyre (Tuftonboro) and Emily Wiggin
(Tuftonboro)

McIVER,

Eugene J., d. 12/14/1981 in Wolfeboro; Michael J. McIver and
Catherine Hughes
Frances J., d. 1/28/1988 in Tuftonboro; Henry Gallant and Judith
Doucet

McKEAN,

Annie, d. 12/22/1930 at 54/4/21 in Tuftonboro; at home; married; b.
Ctr. Tuftonboro; Augustus McIntyre (Mirror Lake) and Emily
Wiggin (Mirror Lake)

McKEE,

Donald C., d. 12/22/1980 in Tuftonboro; Charles A. McKee and
Melvina Rakestraw

McKINLEY,

Hannah L., d. 12/10/1920 at 72/9/28 in Boston, MA; widow; b.
Bucksport, ME; Henry S. Lampher and Abby Ames

McLAUGHLIN,

Charles W., d. 11/12/1933 at 65/8/3 in Wolfeboro; widower; b.
Boston, MA; William W. McLaughlin (Ireland)
Laura S., d. 4/22/1916 at 47/4/4 in Tuftonboro; housewife; married;
b. Boston, MA; John Evans and Ellen E. Galager

McLEAN,

Jane A., d. 2/12/1944 at 0/0/1 in Wolfeboro; b. Wolfeboro; Forrest
McLean (Waltham, MA) and Helen M. Hodges (Somerville, MA)

McMANUIS,
George Joseph, d. 3/31/1982 in Tuftonboro; George McManuis and
 Catherine Foley

McNEIL,
John P., d. 3/24/1914 at 39/5/24; married; b. Picton, NS; John
 McNeil

McPHERSON,
Robert A., d. 8/20/1966 at 75 in Tuftonboro; own ser. sta.; widower;
 b. Haverhill, MA; James McPherson

MEADER,
Charles, d. 9/26/1928 at 76/5/26 in Tuftonboro; retired; married; b.
 Somersworth; Daniel Meader
Mary Ellen, d. 2/9/1930 at 81/4/9 in Tuftonboro; at home; widow; b.
 Gilmanton; Joseph P. Lougee (Gilmanton) and Mary H. Marsh
 (Gilmanton)

MEALS,
Gertrude, d. 8/22/1943 at 69/9/29 in Wolfeboro; at home; widow; b.
 Corry, PA; William Whittier (Canada) and Hattie Judson
 (Cleveland, OH)

MEGEE,
William J., d. 8/13/1922 at 57/7/21 in Tuftonboro; salesman; married;
 b. Cambridge, MA; Morris Magee and Annie James

MERENA,
John H., d. 9/5/1931 at 79/8/11 in Tuftonboro; retired; married; b.
 Pensacola, FL; John H. Merena (Spain)

MERRIFIELD,
Gladys V., d. 8/8/1912 at 17/0/15; tubercular meningitis; single; b.
 Tuftonboro; Perley Merrifield and Nellie M. Thompson
Lyndon E., d. 2/7/1919 at 12/7/24 in Tuftonboro; student; b.
 Tuftonboro; Perley Merrifield and Nellie May Thompson
Nellie May, d. 9/15/1949 at 73 in Laconia; retired; widow; b.
 Tuftonboro; W. Thompson, Jr. and Mary Ambrose

MERRITT,
Rosey E. E., d. 1/15/1937 at 84/0/15 in Ctr. Tuftonboro; at home; widow; b. Tuftonboro; George E. Dearborn (Boston, MA) and Elizabeth Jenkins (Tuftonboro)

MERROW,
Oscar E., d. 12/14/1962 at 67 in Tuftonboro; manager; married; b. Peabody, MA; Herbert E. Merrow and Mary Cremer

MEWA,
Leokadia L., d. 10/21/1991 in Tuftonboro; ----- Bochacki

MICHAUD,
Rodney E., d. 3/7/1983 in Tuftonboro; Zenon Michaud and Beulah Michaud

MILKE,
Minnie E., d. 7/26/1976 at 79 in Wolfeboro; b. Turners Falls, MA

MILLER,
Ellis Field, d. 7/21/1943 at 74/2/13 in Tuftonboro; retired clerk; married; b. Somerville, MA; Ellis F. Miller (Boston, MA) and Harriet S. Field (Boston, MA)
Glenna A., d. 6/10/1945 at 64/11/3 in Lexington, MA; housewife; widow; b. Lowell, MA; Huston ----- (Derry) and Carrie V. Cotton (Lowell, MA)
Harold Borden, d. 6/21/1979 in Wolfeboro; Frank Miller and Minnie R. Lockhart

MILLIKEN,
Lois, d. 3/3/1907 at 83/6/23; bronchitis; widow; b. Hartland, VT; Silas Rodgers and Betsey Shattuck

MILLS,
George A., d. 8/28/1944 at 57/5/5 in Tuftonboro; board saywer; married; b. Hopkinton; Fred W. Mills (Boscawen) and Maria I. Brown (Hopkinton)

MINOT,
John, d. 4/24/1940 at 77/9/13 in Tuftonboro; tinsmith; married; b. Boston, MA; Joel M. Minot (Portugal) and Marie M. Lynch

(Canada)
Mary A., d. 8/7/1941 at 70/5/12 in Tuftonboro; at home; widow; b.
Boston, MA; Michael Cadigan (Capecleare, Ireland) and Julia
Donahue (Capecleare, Ireland)

MITCHELL,
Bernard W., d. 11/27/1982 in Wolfeboro; Samuel Mitchell and
Caroline Cate
John Charles, d. 10/7/1958 at 85 in Wolfeboro; carpenter; married;
b. Wakefield, MA; David Mitchell and Catherine Cummings
June B., d. 3/18/1940 at 0/0/1 in Wolfeboro; b. Wolfeboro; Thomas
O. Mitchell (Canada) and Marion E. Hersey (Tuftonboro)
Marian Hersey, d. 8/22/1996 in Tuftonboro; Edwin C. Hersey and
Hattie B. Springer
Minnie Louise, d. 11/9/1959 at 83 in Wolfeboro; housewife; widow;
b. PEI; Thomas L. Green and Ann Warren
Thomas Osborne, d. 8/30/1995 in Tuftonboro; J. Charles Mitchell
and Minnie L. Greene

MIXER,
Clarence M., d. 8/28/1954 at 63 in Tuftonboro; realtor ret.; married;
b. MA; J. Frank Mixer and Gertrude Maxwell
Julia A. M., d. 5/5/1957 at 73 in Tuftonboro; housewife; widow; b.
Somerville, MA; Frank W. Mardan and Jennie Ayer

MONROE,
Henry W., d. 4/4/1961 at 74/3/3 in Wolfeboro; widower; b.
Somerville, MA; James A. Monroe and Mary J. Trask

MOODY,
Chester E., d. 7/23/1966 at 58 in Wolfeboro; laborer; married; b.
Parsonsfield, ME; Frank Moody and Hattie Marston
Evelyn Edith, d. 6/28/1959 at 83 in Wolfeboro; housewife; married;
b. Ottawa, Canada; Joseph A. Vallieu
George A., d. 7/7/1919 at 73 in Tuftonboro; farmer; widower; b.
Ossipee; Amasa Moody
Lydia, d. 7/16/1904 at 67 in Tuftonboro; paralysis of heart; married;
b. Tuftonboro; Hiram Clark and Adah Clark
Sarah F., d. 7/1/1919 at 72/10/5 in Tuftonboro; housewife; married;
b. Lowell, MA; Thomas Horne and Sally York
Verna Natalie, d. 3/2/1960 at 68 in Wolfeboro; housewife; married; b.

Wolfeboro; Frank P. Brown and Hattie Brown

Viola, d. 6/5/1931 at 78/1/27 in Tuftonboro; at home; widow; b.
Tuftonboro; Simon Kenney (Wolfeboro) and Rhoda Goodwin
(New Durham)

MOORE,

Elta H., d. 6/27/1954 at 64 in Wolfeboro; at home; married; b. MA;
Isaac B. Harrington and Angie B. -----

Paul A., d. 9/24/2000 in Moultonboro; Paul Moore and Shirley Mellor

Walter, d. 2/6/1965 at 77 in Newton, MA; hdwe. mer.; married; b.
Belchertown, MA; Louis E. Moore and Addie Howard

William A., d. 4/24/1984 in Wolfeboro; John A. Moore and Muriel
Hatt

MORGAN,

Laura A., d. 12/15/1976 at 24 in Wolfeboro; b. Glen Cove, NY

Lloyd C., d. 6/7/1984 in Wolfeboro; Harry D. Morgan and Eleanor
Wentworth

MORRILL,

Fred, d. 11/2/1937 at 80/7/26 in Wolfeboro; farmer; married; b.
Moultonboro; William H. Morrill (Moultonboro) and Susan E.
Brown (Tuftonboro)

Susan E., d. 8/23/1919 at 83 in Tuftonboro; widow; b. Moultonboro;
John L. Brown and Syrena Walker

MORRIS,

Hattie Josephine, d. 5/4/1950 at 83/7/4 in Wolfeboro; housewife;
widow; b. Meredith; ----- Buzzell and Eliza -----

Robert G., d. 1/6/1999 in Wolfeboro; Alfred Morris and Hattie Buzzell

MORRISON,

Charles I., d. 5/1/1900 at 67/11/9 in Tuftonboro; heart disease;
married; b. Tuftonboro; Jonathan Morrison and Belinda Libby

George L., d. 4/3/1932 at 77/4/14 in Tuftonboro; farmer; widower; b.
NY City

John D., d. 11/1/1906 at 64/7/12; disease of liver, due to malaria;
widower; b. Tuftonboro; Jonathan Morrison and Belinda Libby

Jonathan L., d. 12/29/1911 at 81/7/19; incinerated in a burning
building; widower; b. Tuftonboro; Eben Morrison and Nancy
Ladd

Julia C., d. 9/5/1903 at 70/5 in Tuftonboro; pulmonary phthisis; married; Mark Wiggin and Hulda Swett
Julia N., d. 12/30/1921 at 72/5/1 in Tuftonboro; housewife; married; b. Newton, MA; Charles A. Wiggin and Hannah Piper

MOULTON,
Arvilla, d. 3/25/1911 at 85/3/24; delayed shock; widow; b. Tuftonboro; Daniel Fernald and Lydia Perkins
Frances E., d. 6/18/1964 at 62 in Concord; housewife; widow; b. Center Harbor; Royal Cook and Rose M. Brown
Frederic, d. 7/7/1941 at 80/10/25 in Tuftonboro; farmer; widower; Levi Moulton (Bartlett, ME) and Esther Andrews
John S., d. 3/6/1902 at 82/5/21 in Tuftonboro; complication of diseases; married; b. Sandwich; John Moulton
Lucy J., d. 5/5/1891 at 70/2/20 in Tuftonboro; old age; housewife; married; b. Lowell, VT; Robert Allen and Lucy Smith (Gilmanton)
Lyman, d. 6/9/1943 at 26/1/24 in Easton, ME; mechanic; married; b. Meredith; Edward Moulton (Meredith) and Mabel Hoyt (Malden, MA)
Mabel, d. 1/11/1948 at 69/4/16 in Concord; housewife; married; b. Malden, MA; Herbert Hoyt (Tuftonboro) and Harriet Prime (Moultonboro)

MUGRIDGE,
Donald J., d. 12/11/1986 in Wolfeboro; Thomas Mugridge and Anna Gillis

MUNROE,
Bertha Willoughby, d. 12/22/1959 at 71 in Wolfeboro; housewife; married; b. MA; George T. Willoughby and Ann M. Sprague

MURCH,
Thomas H., d. 9/13/1955 at 71 in Tuftonboro; sheet metal worker; married; b. MA; John Edward Murch

MURRAY,
Robert Edward, d. 8/18/1962 at 47 in Tuftonboro; shipping clerk; married; b. Adamsdale, MA; Robert E. Murray and Loretta Buffin

MYERS,

Ada Gilbert, d. 10/28/1960 at 77 in Wolfeboro; housewife; widow; b. Auburn, NY; ----- Gilbert and ----- Hustead

Louis A., d. 12/8/1951 at 69 in Wolfeboro; retired; married; b. Montezuma, NY; George A. Myers and Flora M. Kearns

NASH,

Donald M., d. 8/8/1987 in Wolfeboro; Ernest R. Nash and Anna R. Moore

NASS,

Karl W., d. 9/30/1988 in Wolfeboro; Olaf Nass and Alma Olson

NEAL,

Isaac N., d. 7/19/1933 at 67/4/10 in Ctr. Tuftonboro; farmer; widower; b. Tuftonboro; James H. Neal (Tuftonboro) and Adeliza J. Copp (Tuftonboro)

James H., d. 11/12/1906 at 72; heart disease; married; b. Tuftonboro; David Neal

John, d. 9/17/1929 at 66/6/11 in Tuftonboro; farmer; single; b. Tuftonboro; James H. Neal (Tuftonboro) and Adeliza J. Copp (Tuftonboro)

Mary E., d. 11/25/1893 at 80/3/25 in Tuftonboro; pneumonia; housewife; widow; b. Portsmouth; Jonathan Folsom (Portsmouth) and Lycho Folsom

Mary M., d. 8/26/1891 at 66/3/7 in Tuftonboro; neuralgia of heart; housewife; widow; b. Lowell, VT; Robert Allen and Lucy J. Smith (Gilmanton)

Nathaniel, d. 1/5/1892 at 81/5/10 in Tuftonboro; heart disease; farmer; married; b. Brownfield, ME; Enoch Neal and Nancy Towle

NEDEAU,

Ernest Henry, d. 10/14/1996 in Wolfeboro; Augustus J. Nedeau and Emma M. LaFlam

NEWCOMB,

Everett W., d. 2/26/1974 at 79 in Wolfeboro; b. NJ

Marion F., d. 3/25/1986 in Wolfeboro; Nelson W. Faulks and Adel Servis

NICHOLLS,
William Hord, d. 8/4/1978 at 64 in Tuftonboro; b. Lexington, KY

NIELSEN,
Harry William Frederick, d. 6/22/1979 in Wolfeboro; William Nielsen
and Augusta Bott
William, d. 1/19/1965 at 75 in Wolfeboro; butcher; widower; b.
Portland, ME; William Nielsen and Laura Hansen

NORDEN,
Carl A., d. 6/18/1975 at 62 in Tuftonboro; b. Woburn, MA

NOYES,
Violet Bowen, d. 7/4/1992 in Wolfeboro; Azro Bowen and Verna
Pember

NUTE,
Amelia Ake, d. 9/22/1964 at 77 in Tuftonboro; housewife; married; b.
Newark, NJ; Adolphus M. Ake and Amelia Stout

NUTTER,
Addie S., d. 4/12/1935 at 76/8/22 in Ctr. Tuftonboro; housewife;
widow; b. Ossipee; Moses C. Nutter (Ossipee) and Louise
Chick (Ossipee)
Llewellyn, d. 7/22/1955 at 72 in Tuftonboro; laborer; single; b. ME;
Henry Nutter and Elizabeth Edgecomb
Mercy, d. 4/23/1892 at 86/6/23 in Tuftonboro; old age; housewife;
widow; b. Ossipee

O'CONNELL,
Homer J., d. 12/23/1973 at 65 in Wolfeboro; b. NV

O'GRADY,
John L., d. 7/14/1976 at 53 in Wolfeboro; b. NY, NY

O'KEEFE,
Anna, d. 10/13/1969 at 69 in Tuftonboro; shoe worker; widow; b.
Holland; ----- and Theadora Freidoff

O'NEIL,
Oceana Hester, d. 9/5/1992 in Wolfeboro; Edwin Signer and Mary

Wohlleber

OLIVOLO,
Louis, d. 10/14/1978 at 61 in Wolfeboro; b. Revere, MA

OLSEN,
John L., Jr., d. 1/15/1997 in Wolfeboro; John L. Olsen, Sr. and Inga Johannessen

ONUFRAK,
Michael, Jr., d. 9/16/2002 in Wolfeboro; Michael Onufrak and Amelia Ruchniak

ORRELL,
Charles S., d. 10/16/1920 at 76/4/29 in Tuftonboro; farmer; b. Somersworth; Samuel R. Orrell and Adeline S. Curry

OSGOOD,
Alfred Earle, d. 9/23/1961 at 60/9/18 in Hooksett; married; b. Freeport, ME; David Earle Osgood and Mary Ward

OULTON,
Fred Russell, d. 1/8/1966 at 77 in Wolfeboro; grinder; married; b. Cambridge, MA; James Oulton and Carlotta -----

OWEN,
Milton H., d. 1/26/1991 in Wolfeboro; Edward H. Owen and Gertrude Mann

PACKARD,
Lucius E., d. 12/5/1976 at 62 in Tuftonboro; b. Somerville, MA

PAGE,
Esther L., d. 3/22/1975 at 67 in Wolfeboro; b. Tuftonboro
Lincoln Ridler, d. 1/14/1996 in Wolfeboro; Norman Page and Helen White

PAIGE,
Robert K., d. 10/11/1971 at 66 in Littleton; b. VT

PALMER,
Dana, d. 5/10/1899 at 46/9/12 in Tuftonboro; married; b. Tuftonboro;
William Palmer and Huldah Swett
Daniel B., d. 6/11/1948 at 85/11/9 in Wolfeboro; farmer; single; b.
Tuftonboro; Ellen Palmer (Tuftonboro)
Huldah S., d. 9/18/1902 at 84/10/27 in Tuftonboro; chronic enteritis;
widow; b. Stewartstown; Samuel Sweatt and Sarah M. Neal
Linda A., d. 9/14/2003 in Wolfeboro; Carl Peterson and Marie
O'Leary
William, d. 7/21/1899 at 84/11/17 in Tuftonboro; married; b.
Tuftonboro; Joseph Palmer and Lydia Evans

PARKER,
Alexander, d. 10/20/1999 in Wolfeboro; John Parker and Antoinette
Davidson
Catherine, d. 9/8/2004 in Bedford; Horace Otis and Ivy Smith
Lena B., d. 11/29/1977 at 89 in Tuftonboro; b. Townsend, MA
Mabel A., d. 8/1/1985 in Ossipee; Daniel Quimby and Agnes Foster

PARKHURST,
Maggie, d. 9/16/1926 at 77/5/9 in Tuftonboro; retired; widow
Oscar, d. 10/28/1925 at 84/0/8 in Tuftonboro; painter; married; b.
Woodstock, VT; John Parkhurst (Thetford, VT) and Mary A.
Parkhurst (Thetford, VT)
Wayne L., d. 1/25/1963 at 59 in Tuftonboro; ins. adjustor; married; b.
Columbia; George Parkhurst and Jeanette Merrill

PARMENTER,
Grace M., d. 2/5/1968 at 85 in Tuftonboro; housewife; widow; b.
Canada; Ira Gould and Clara -----

PARSONS,
Charles, d. 5/11/1942 at 70/0/16 in Tuftonboro; retired broker;
married; b. Malden, MA; Charles Parsons (Concord) and
Elizabeth Dyer (Ellsworth, ME)

PASSANISI,
Dominic, d. 8/29/1944 at 31/0/19 in Tuftonboro; warehouseman;
married; b. Boston, MA; Salvatore Passanisi (Italy) and Rose
Caruso (Italy)

PATTERSON,

Henry S., d. 9/24/1957 at 80 in VT; mechanic; widower; b. Gloucester, MA; Frank Patterson and Sarah Geren

PATTON,

Gertrude L., d. 10/7/1987 in Ossipee; John Lind and Hedvig Winnergren

James P., d. 3/23/1990 in Wolfeboro; James W. Patton and Esther Perry

PEASE,

Jeanne F., d. 3/10/1990 in Wolfeboro; James M. Fradd and Agnes Woodbury

PEAVEY,

Benjamin F., d. 2/27/1911 at 80/7/4; valvular heart disease; married; b. Tuftonboro; Eben Peavey

Edwin A., d. 8/24/1907 at 49/8/17; diabetes; widower; b. Tuftonboro; Albert Peavey and Sarah Bryant

PERRY,

Arthur Harry, d. 12/2/1960 at 76 in Wolfeboro; painter; divorced; b. Brookfield; John Perry and Priscilla Crowdis

Donald B., d. 11/16/1981 in Wolfeboro; John Perry and Dinah Carnell

PETERSON,

Clifford Otto, d. 9/19/1997 in Wolfeboro; Carl P. Peterson and Agnes Harding

Doris W., d. 1/15/1990 in Manchester; W. Harry Wood and Inez Peterson

Lawrence B., d. 12/12/1974 at 87 in Wolfeboro; b. MA

Neale Lawrence, d. 7/30/1994 in Wolfeboro; Lawrence Joy Peterson and Ethel May Demont

Phyllis D., d. 2/21/1988 in Tuftonboro; William A. Danner and Hazel G. Dwyer

Theodore L., d. 8/3/1956 at 96 in Wolfeboro; ret. church organ and cabinet builder; widower; b. MA; Ludwig Peterson and Charlotte Johnson

PHELPS,
Dorothy V., d. 9/3/2002 in Wolfeboro; Henry Crusius and Dorothy
    Wilkins
Leo E., d. 2/14/2002 in Wolfeboro; Hugh Phelps and Irene Frye

PHILBRICK,
daughter, d. 4/17/1913 at – in Tuftonboro; stillborn; b. Tuftonboro;
    Alfred Philbrick and Elsie Drown
Elsie C., d. 4/17/1913 at 31; childbirth; married; b. Waterboro, ME
Eugenie S., d. 7/31/1987 in Wolfeboro; John Schutt and Blanche
    Colbath
Hiram, d. 4/1/1894 at 79/11; farmer; married; b. Rye; Joseph
    Philbrick and Sarah Pitman
Ralph Nelson, d. 1/26/1990 in Wolfeboro; Nelson P. Philbrick and
    Jennie Mae Kelsey

PHILLIPS,
Norma Prentis, d. 7/21/1994 in Wolfeboro; James Prentis and
    Norma Joyce

PICKEN,
Jeannette, d. 12/29/2003 in Wolfeboro; Joseph Young and Lillian
    Livermore

PICKETT,
Idella H., d. 1/16/1940 at 77/6/11 in Tuftonboro; housewife; widow;
    b. Winchester; Charles Dolittle (Winchester) and Susan Hayes
    (VT)

PIGOTT,
Eva Martha, d. 4/25/1963 at 76 in Wolfeboro; housewife; widow; b.
    Cambridgeport, MA; William H. Dam and Elizabeth Wilson
Thomas E., d. 10/22/1952 at 66 in Tuftonboro; retired banker;
    married; b. Boston, MA; Thomas E. Pigott and Katharine
    Mustagh
Thomas E., d. 10/19/1997 in Wolfeboro; Thomas Pigott and Eva
    Dam

PIKE,
Eva Bell, d. 11/27/1953 at 81 in Wakefield; housewife; widow; b.
    Effingham Falls; Joshua W. Thurston and Arvilla Chick

Marion C., d. 12/29/2000 in Wolfeboro; Mildred Whiting

PINKHAM,
Charles W., d. 7/23/1926 at 76/11/11 in Tuftonboro; merchant;
  married; William R. Pinkham (London, England) and Mary Doe
  (Tuftonboro)
Hattie M., d. 7/18/1937 at 62/5/17 in Ctr. Tuftonboro; retired
  merchant; single; b. Tuftonboro; Charles Pinkham (Newmarket)
  and Sarah Moulton (Moultonboro)
Sarah E., d. 2/2/41929 at 82/3/9 in Tuftonboro; at home; widow; b.
  Moultonboro; Nathan Moulton (Moultonboro) and Priscilla
Senter (Tuftonboro)

PIPER,
son, d. 9/25/1902 at – in Tuftonboro; premature birth; b. Tuftonboro;
  Frank E. Piper and Carrie Low
son, d. 10/19/1916 at – in Tuftonboro; b. Tuftonboro; John F. Piper
  and Nellie Staples
Alonzo D., d. 5/24/1915 at 66/2/8 in Tuftonboro; farming; single; b.
  Tuftonboro; Richard Piper (Tuftonboro) and Sarah J. Griffin
Annie E., d. 3/26/1899 at 10/6/25 in Tuftonboro; b. Tuftonboro; Frank
  E. Piper and Carrie Low
Benjamin Y., d. 8/28/1985 in Wolfeboro; Benjamin B. Piper and Ruth
  Martin
Carrie Susan, d. 11/20/1939 at 75/2/28 in Wolfeboro; housewife;
  widow; b. Tuftonboro; Charles Low (Moultonboro) and Livonia
  Langley (Alton)
Charles G., d. 5/30/1927 at 76/0/23 in Tuftonboro; farmer; married;
  b. Tuftonboro; Richard Piper (Tuftonboro)
Clara H., d. 7/1/1904 at 44/10/28 in Tuftonboro; intestinal
  obstruction; married; b. Wolfeboro; Samuel Eaton and Mary E.
  Berry
David E., d. 5/24/1901 at 62/5/21 in Tuftonboro; valvular disease of
  the heart; widower; b. Tuftonboro; David Piper and Sally Haley
Edward C., d. 2/28/1905 at 0/7 in Tuftonboro; pneumonia; b.
  Tuftonboro; Frank E. Piper and Carrie Low
Elsie, d. 5/4/1895 at 97/11/12 in Tuftonboro; old age; widow
Emerline P., d. 3/24/1914; widow; b. Wolfeboro; Joseph Young and
  Patience Chase
Ernest B., d. 11/1/1976 at 63 in Wolfeboro; b. NH
Forrest E., d. 9/20/1967 at 63 in Rochester; Navy Yard; married; b.

Wolfeboro; John Piper and Nellie Staples

Frank E., d. 4/3/1929 at 63/2/27 in Tuftonboro; farmer; married; b. Tuftonboro; John G. Piper (Tuftonboro) and Rhoda Piper (Tuftonboro)

Frank F., d. 3/26/1986 in Wolfeboro; John H. Piper and Susie Fernald

Fred L., d. 7/7/1940 at 82/5/7 in Wolfeboro; minister; widower; b. Tuftonboro; Thatcher Piper (Tuftonboro) and Nancy Allen (Tuftonboro)

George G., d. 3/18/1932 at 75/11/9 in Farmington; farmer; widower; b. Tuftonboro; George W. Piper (Alton) and Mary E. Burke (Alton)

George W., d. 3/7/1942 at 83 in Boston, MA; retired police; widower; b. Boston, MA; William Piper

Greenleaf, d. 2/7/1892 at 84/10/26 in Tuftonboro; general debility; farmer; widower; b. Tuftonboro; Francis Piper (Lee) and Abigail Wiggin

Howard F., d. 12/8/1914 at 18/10/3; single; b. Tuftonboro; Frank E. Piper and Carrie S. Low

James, d. 12/22/1893 at 86/8/9 in Tuftonboro; old age; farmer; married; b. Brookfield; Stephen Piper and Hannah Widden

John F., d. 6/17/1967 at 86 in Wolfeboro; farmer laborer; married; b. Tuftonboro; David Piper and Ann E. Piper

Lester M., d. 10/28/1936 at 31/1/17in Ctr. Tuftonboro; single; b. Tuftonboro; John F. Piper (Tuftonboro) and Nellie F. Staples (Parsonsfield, ME)

Mark F., d. 9/23/1905 at 80/8/6 in Laconia; nephritis; widower; b. Tuftonboro; Timothy Piper and Hannah Neal

Mary E., d. 6/21/1909 at 80/6; old age; widow; b. Alton; James Burk

Nancy M., d. 8/1/1915 at 87/1 in Tuftonboro; housewife; widow; b. Cabot, VT; Robert Allen and Lucy Smith

Nellie F., d. 4/9/1978 at 92 in Tuftonboro; b. Parsonsfield, ME

Preston H., d. 12/18/1985 in Tuftonboro; John Piper and Nellie Staples

Ralph G., d. 9/24/1975 at 89 in Rochester; b. Tuftonboro

Richard V., d. 1/25/1892 at 72/11/21 in Tuftonboro; heart failure; farmer; widower; b. Tuftonboro; Gilman Piper

Rose Markl, d. 9/12/1995 in Franklin; Louis Markl and Victoria Huber

Sally, d. 6/16/1898 at 88/8/23 in Tuftonboro; old age; widow; b. Wolfeboro; Isaac Wiggin and Nancy Thurston

Samuel J., d. 2/25/1895 at 78 in Tuftonboro; disease of heart;

married; b. Tuftonboro
Sarah J., d. 12/22/1900 at 78/5/19 in Tuftonboro; apoplexy; widow;
    b. Barton, VT; Samuel Smith and Sally Stafford
Thatcher W., d. 11/22/1893 at 69/6/13 in Tuftonboro; appendicitis;
    clergyman; married; b. Tuftonboro; Samuel Piper (Tuftonboro)
    and Elsie Haley (Alfred, ME)
Thomas F., d. 5/27/1918 at 55/8/27 in Tuftonboro; merchant;
    married; b. Tuftonboro; Joseph B. Piper (Tuftonboro)

PLUMER,
Helen G., d. 8/17/1895 at 24/7 in Tuftonboro; apoplectic fit; married;
    b. Salem, MA; P. W. Phillips
Sarah, d. 8/10/1933 at 83/8/1 in Mirror Lake; retired; widow; b.
    Rocky Hill, CT; Lubin Rockwood (Wilton) and Abby Abbott
    (Wilton)

POOR,
Rebecca M., d. 1/18/1924 at 71/11/3 in Tuftonboro; housewife;
    married; b. Waterville, ME; Jedediah Morrill

POORE,
Edwin S., d. 8/31/1941 at 86/10/23 in Wolfeboro; retired; widower; b.
    Raymond; Westley Poore (Raymond)

POPE,
Eben R., d. 9/23/1908 at 71/4; pulmonary embolism; widower
Grace Hall, d. 10/16/1967 at 87 in Hingham, MA; housewife; widow;
    b. Boston, MA; Levi Fernald and ----- Hall
Samuel Downes, d. 11/10/1954 at 78 in Tuftonboro; broker; married;
    b. MA; Alexander Pope and Alice Downes

POSSON,
Myral Jean, d. 10/30/1993 in Wolfeboro; Ralph M. Towle and Harriet
    Sutherland

POWERS,
Paul P., d. 11/11/1983 in Wolfeboro; Harris E. Powers and Anna J.
    Pollock

PRATT,
Chester J., d. 8/3/1976 at 79 in Wolfeboro; b. NY, NY

Lisette D., d. 9/12/1979 in Wolfeboro; Harmon Droge and Rebecca von Dohlin

PRESTON,
Emma Elizabeth, d. 8/1/1979 in Ossipee; Frederick Gerkensmeyer
Leonard Frederick, d. 3/24/1994 in Rochester; Herbert Preston and Emma Gerkensmeyer

PRIEST,
Warren A., d. 5/17/1964 at 87 in Wolfeboro; retired; widower; b. Charlestown, MA; John Priest

PROKEY,
Larrie Pedro, d. 3/1/1939 at 40 in Tuftonboro; laborer; married; b. Russia; Pedro Prokey (Russia) and Irona Prokey (Russia)

PROUTY,
Gardner Edward, Jr., d. 1/2/1992 in Wolfeboro; Gardner E. Prouty and Ethel Brown

PUFFER,
Luther W., III, d. 8/8/1954 at 45 in Tuftonboro; insurance broker; married; b. MA; Luther W. Puffer and Annie A. -----

PYBURN,
Harold W. R., d. 1/18/1991 in Tuftonboro; James Pyburn and Jane Fuller
Thelma Johnson, d. 5/30/1990 in Wolfeboro; Charles Williams and Judith Johnson

QUICK,
Matthew Ryan, d. 5/20/1996 in Tuftonboro; William J. Quick and Lesley Shriver

RAMSBOTHAM,
Annette, d. 2/19/2004 in Wolfeboro; Marcus Offers and Evelyn Fellows

RAYNER,
Artemus W., d. 8/8/1923 at 67/6/27 in Tuftonboro; builder; married; b. PEI; Joseph Rayner

READY,
William E., d. 7/13/1987 in Hanover; John Ready and Etta Donegan

REED,
Anna B., d. 6/24/1945 at 80/3/21 in Wolfeboro; retired housewife; widow; b. Moultonboro; Augustin Beane (Tuftonboro) and Susie A. Libby (Portland, ME)
Frank Eugene, d. 11/22/1963 at 63 in Tuftonboro; lumberman; married; b. Houlton, ME; Addison Reed and Florence Hanson
Marjorie Florence, d. 9/26/1962 at 34 in Tuftonboro; housewife; married; b. Woodman; George E. Chick and Kathleen Ringer
Mildred, d. 6/5/1970 at 60 in Hanover; widow; b. NH; Leon Whiting and Mary Francis
Norman Elsmore, d. 11/2/1994 in Wolfeboro; Ausltin Reed and Rosamond Levette
Roberta Ellen, d. 12/11/1996 in Wolfeboro; Harold Drew and Marion Robie

REHBERG,
Edward, d. 5/30/1952 at 81/9/8 in Effingham; retired sea capt.; widower; b. Sandusky, OH

REID,
James, d. 7/2/1913 at 56/1/2; chronic myocarditis; married; b. NS; James Reid and Jerusia Hingley

REINHARD,
Margaret E., d. 11/3/2002 in Wolfeboro; Joseph McLaughlin and Della Gerrity

RENNIE,
Wallace, d. 10/26/1985 in Ossipee; George Rennie and Margaret Thompson

RENZONI,
Anthony A., d. 3/16/2003 in Wolfeboro; Antonio Renzoni and Guistina Boggio

REPETTA,
Arthur D., d. 5/2/1991 in Tuftonboro; John J. Repetta and Catherine Norton

Evelyn, d. 2/23/1991 in Wolfeboro; Arthur Day and Alice Whittier

RICHARDS,
Catherine M., d. 10/17/1897 at 57/4/21 in Tuftonboro; valvular
disease of heart; widow; b. Shelburne, NS; Joseph Holden and
Maria Spinney

RICHARDSON,
Albertha Rebecca, d. 10/23/1982 in Tuftonboro; Henry A. Lantz and
Margaret Grey
Anna A., d. 11/23/1945 at 81/11/4 in Somerville, MA; housewife;
widow; b. Charlestown, MA; ----- Berry (Sweden) and Charlotte
Johnson (Sweden)
Claribel, d. 5/24/1898 at 38/9/9 in Tuftonboro; pneumonia; married;
b. Tuftonboro; Gordon Ladd and Eliza Moulton
Eugene A., d. 5/23/1935 at 84/8/29 in Ctr. Tuftonboro; retired;
widower; Charles Richardson (Limington, ME) and Olive T. Dorr
(Sutton, MA)
Florence M., d. 10/16/1960 at 86 in Wrentham, MA; housewife;
widow; b. Tuftonboro; Daniel Libby and Ann E. Canney
Fred A., d. 10/21/1907 at 66/3/15; apoplectic shock and acute
perclantis; widower; b. Moultonboro; John W. Richardson and
Mary D. Wainwright
George, d. 9/20/1944 at 73/7/5 in Moultonboro; mechanic; married;
b. Tuftonboro; Orlando Richardson (Moultonboro) and Abba L.
Trafton (Biddeford, ME)
George L., d. 2/19/1952 at 55 in Wolfeboro; poultry farm; married; b.
Needham, MA; Joseph L. Richardson and Alice L. Wilcox
Mary D. W., d. 1/16/1902 at 97/5/5 in Tuftonboro; heart disease and
old age; widow; b. Gloucester, MA; Thomas Wainwright and
Lydia Levere
Orlando, d. 5/21/1912 at 68/8/3; general tuberculosis; married; b.
Moultonboro; Luciern Richardson and Joanna F. Doe

RICKER,
Arthur W., d. 10/26/1974 at 65 in Tuftonboro; b. NH
Eliza A., d. 12/9/1912 at 74/8; senile pneumonia; single; b. Ossipee;
Hiram Ricker and Irene Chick
Irene, d. 1/11/1899 at 87 in Tuftonboro; acute bronchitis; widow; b.
Ossipee; Samuel Chick

RIDDLE,
Emma C., d. 6/29/1981 in Wolfeboro; Clarence P. Woodbury and
Anna M. Riley

RIDLON,
Arnold L., d. 3/13/2000 in Wolfeboro; Arthur Ridlon and Lena
Shannon
Arthur L., d. 10/18/1969 at 75 in Wolfeboro; carpenter; married; b.
MA; Charles F. Ridlon and Della Walker
Lena G., d. 10/25/1972 at 90 in Wolfeboro; b. NH

ROBBINS,
Aimee Stocker, d. 9/26/1960 at 83 in Tuftonboro; housewife; widow;
b. Saugus, MA; Frederic Stocker and Ida Peabody

ROBBLEE,
John W., d. 2/14/1916 at 30/3/10 in Tuftonboro; mec. engineer;
single; b. W. Newton, MA; James R. Robblee and Barbara
Marchback

ROBERTS,
Arthur F., d. 7/27/1893 at 5/9/3 in Tuftonboro; diphtheria; b.
Tuftonboro; Andrew R. Roberts (Tuftonboro) and Clara E.
Glines (Eaton)
Clara Estelle, d. 10/11/1931 at 74/9/27 in Tuftonboro; at home;
widow; b. Ossipee; Truman Glines (NH) and Mary Kenison
(NH)
George Andrew, d. 12/20/1961 at 81 in Wolfeboro; carpenter; single;
b. Tuftonboro; Andrew K. Roberts and Clara Glines
Lydia, d. 3/10/1919 at 81 in Tuftonboro; widow; b. Moultonboro

ROBICHAUD,
Fred, d. 7/2/1943 at 70/11/4 in Tuftonboro; board sawyer; married; b.
Canada; Jean Robichaud (Canada) and Julie Maillet (Canada)

ROBIE,
George William, d. 9/25/1963 at 85 in Wolfeboro; school teacher;
married; b. Londonderry; Samuel Robie and Adeline Rowell
Marion Horner, d. 8/18/1990 in Wolfeboro; G. Sumner Horner and
Grace Hodgdon

ROBINSON,
Edward Ainslee, d. 2/12/1964 at 65 in Wolfeboro; engineer; married;
    b. Mt. Vernon, NY; Edward A. Robinson and Martha W. Hecker
Mark Frederick, d. 8/13/1993 in Wolfeboro; Frederick J. Robinson
    and Olive M. Moody

ROGERS,
Charles William, Jr., d. 9/21/1996 in Wolfeboro; Charles William
    Rogers, Sr. and Evelyn E. Riley
Myra C., d. 9/12/1991 in Wolfeboro; Malcolm Campbell and Marion
    Turner

ROGHAAR,
Edward N., d. 12/23/1945 at 65/9/2 in Wolfeboro; caretaker;
    widower; b. Boston, MA; Gertrude Appleman (Holland)
Ida M., d. 4/2/1944 at 62/4/5 in Tuftonboro; housewife; married; b.
    Poughkeepsie, NY; George E. Ogden (Poughkeepsie, NY) and
    Martha Basnett (Poughkeepsie, NY)

ROLLINS,
Carolyn, d. 10/9/2004 in Tuftonboro; James Todd and Clara Sauer
Howard A., d. 2/24/1976 at 77 in Wolfeboro; b. Salem, MA
Nana Bickford, d. 5/24/1959 at 72 in Wolfeboro; artist; married; b.
    MA; John A. Bickford and Isabella M. French

ROOME,
William J., II, d. 6/12/1983 in Wolfeboro; Reginald Roome and
    Gabrielle McQuide

ROSELL,
Charles Ferdinand, d. 6/26/1998 in Wolfeboro; Charles Theodore
    Rosell and Anna Marie Stronbeck
Grace I., d. 3/27/2003 in Mirror Lake; Magnus Sundbye and Hannah
    Olsen

ROSS,
Elizabeth, d. 7/5/2004 in Wolfeboro; Frederick Bates and Elizabeth
    Barker
John, d. 4/12/2004 in Tuftonboro; John Ross and Genevieve Dodge

RUDOLPH,

Ada S., d. 12/4/1989 in Wolfeboro; George Speight and Martha Parker

Gerald F., d. 8/19/1999 in Manchester; Bryson Rudolph and Ada Speight

Mary Alice, d. 8/19/1998 in Wolfeboro; Robert M. Libby and Helen Eldridge

RUTOLO,

Claire A., d. 7/19/1986 in Tuftonboro; Robert E. Bouchard and Pauline Paquin

SABA,

Rosalene K., d. 1/29/1991 in Wolfeboro; Benjamin F. Kerns and Eliza Sutphin

SAMBATARO,

Andree M., d. 5/8/1999 in Tuftonboro; Yvon Gelinas and Camilliene Deschenes

SANBORN,

Martha E., d. 6/20/1902 at 54/7/23 in Tuftonboro; fatty degeneration of heart; single; b. Moultonboro; Thomas J. Sanborn and Martha A. Leavitt

SANDERS,

Carl J., d. 8/8/1978 at 82 in Tuftonboro; b. Indianapolis, IN

SARGENT,

Clarence Harold, d. 9/19/1960 at 55 in Wolfeboro; woodsman; divorced; b. Moultonboro; Jesse Sargent and Ida Rogers

Etta M., d. 9/22/1948 at 80/7/6 in Tuftonboro; housewife; married; b. Presque Isle, ME; Levi W. Ladd (Melvin Village) and Maranda Mills (Hudson, MA)

Ida Ellen, d. 3/2/1936 at 54/4/11 in Tuftonboro; housewife; married; b. Moultonboro; George W. Rogers (Moultonboro) and Ellen B. Denny (Moultonboro)

Jesse, d. 5/5/1936 at 64/10/5 in Tuftonboro; farmer; widower; b. Porter, ME; Jesse Sargent (Porter, ME) and Martha Varney (Porter, ME)

SASS,
Guy V., d. 8/1/1944 at 53/9/17 in Tuftonboro; mfg. elec. sup.; married; b. Quincy, MA; William H. Sass (Germany) and Pauline Gilliat (NS)

SAUNDERS,
Priscilla H., d. 5/12/1986 in Concord; Peter Gray 3rd and Ethel Crawford

SAVAGE,
Corrine M., d. 2/23/1985 in Wolfeboro; Charles Reichardt and Mary - ----

SAWYER,
Barbara B., d. 3/7/1984 in Wolfeboro; Dwight Braley and Doris Higgins
Christie C., d. 6/14/1908 at 66/0/12; pneumonia; married; William T. Cate and Betsy Cate
Florence Gill, d. 1/12/1990 in Wolfeboro; Edward L. Gill and Annie Dawson
George W., d. 6/15/1913 at 75/7/23; accidental injury; married; b. Porter, ME; Lemuel Sawyer and Mary Berry
Hannah Barret-Brown, d. 12/7/1996 in Tuftonboro; Michael P. Sawyer and Chris Barrett

SCHMERMOND,
Frances M., d. 4/17/2003 in Tuftonboro; Adam Siwakoski and Stelly Bryk

SCHMUCK,
Harriet W., d. 5/17/1990 in Tuftonboro; Albert Wheeler and Gladys Tucker

SCHULTZ,
Arnold R., d. 8/11/1983 in Laconia; Ralph H. Schultz and Matilda Felsentrager

SCLIRIS,
Louis, d. 11/11/1957 at 44 in Tuftonboro; salesman; married; b. Haverhill, MA; Constantinou E. Scliris and Laura A. Welch

SCOTT,
Clarence. d. 1/19/1977 at 75 in Tuftonboro; b. Newfoundland
Ernest R., d. 7/25/1980 in Wolfeboro; T. Henry Scott and Nina
    Stewart
Ethel K., d. 10/9/1974 at 63 in Tuftonboro; b. WV
Florence D., d. 6/4/1980 in Wolfeboro; Leonhard Doersam and E.
    Florence Abele
Marjorie Evelyn, d. 8/4/1994 in Tuftonboro; William Anderson and
    Elizabeth Harris

SCRIGGINS,
Annie, d. 7/4/1940 at 76/2/5 in Concord; needlemaker; widow; b. Ctr.
    Sandwich; Charles Mudgett and Mary Wallingford

SEAVEY,
James C., d. 1/6/1892 at 75 in Tuftonboro; paralysis and congestion
    of lungs; farmer; widower; b. Pittsfield; Joseph Seavey

SELESKY,
Edna L., d. 6/2/1992 in Wolfeboro; Edward J. Lurcott and Lillian
    Anderson

SENECAL,
Elizabeth E., d. 7/4/1987 in Tuftonboro; William B. Earle and Willie
    Wicker

SEVERANCE,
Grace C., d. 6/11/1978 at 86 in Laconia; b. Wolfeboro
Katherine M., d. 5/4/1990 in Wolfeboro; Thomas F. Mackey and
    Ruth Church
Roland T., Sr., d. 7/26/1988 in Wolfeboro; William R. Severance and
    Edna Tyler

SEWELL,
Bernard J., d. 6/15/1985 in Wolfeboro; Aaron Sewell and Helen T.
    Casey

SHANNON,
Augusta E., d. 4/13/1935 at 76/5/8 in Mirror Lake; housewife; widow;
    b. Tuftonboro; Charles Wiggin (Tuftonboro) and Hannah Quint
    (Ossipee)

Carroll L., d. 8/14/1979 in Wolfeboro; Edward A. Shannon and
    Marion Hannah Haley
Charles E., d. 6/17/1893 at 15/11/7 in Lake Winnipesaukee;
    drowning; single; b. Tuftonboro; Frank Shannon (Moultonboro)
    and Augusta E. Wiggin (Tuftonboro)
Edwin A., d. 12/2/1962 at 82 in Wolfeboro; lumberman; married; b.
    Alton; Steven Shannon and Sarah Rollins
Frank, d. 7/25/1920 at 62/10/13 in Tuftonboro; painter; married; b.
    Moultonboro; George Shannon and Lucinda Horne
Guy E., d. 3/6/2000 in Manchester; Edward Shannon and Marion
    Hamm
Marion H., d. 7/26/1999 in Wolfeboro; ----- Haley
Mattie M., d. 6/3/1922 at 1/5/22 in Tuftonboro; b. Tuftonboro; Edwin
    A. Shannon and Marion Haley

SHAW,
Daniel W., d. 7/4/1910 at 84; old age; married; b. Eaton

SHAY,
Franklin T., d. 11/9/1992 in Laconia; Thomas W. Shay and Ethel M.
    Lezzette

SHEPHERD,
Bertha L., d. 12/29/1972 at 92 in Wolfeboro; b. NH
Carrie F., d. 9/24/1900 at 61/3/15 in Tuftonboro; apoplexy; married;
    b. Tuftonboro; Silas F. Bean and Usula A. Seavey
Charles H., d. 8/20/1919 at 82/6/21 in Tuftonboro; retired; widower;
    b. Dover; Ezra Shepherd and Lydia French
Fannie C., d. 5/2/1914 at 65/1/29; married; Samuel P. Dore and
    Betsey Thompson
Leon Franklin, d. 4/29/1954 at 72 in Laconia; ret. salesman; married;
    b. MA; Charles Shepherd and Carrie Bean

SHIPPEE,
Elsa N., d. 2/8/1973 at 76 in Rochester; b. MA
John Willard, d. 5/7/1961 at 68/7/4 in Wolfeboro; married; b.
    Greenwich, RI; Benjamin Shippee and Amanda Fecteau

SHOESMITH,
Emma I., d. 4/12/1974 at 87 in Rochester; b. PA
Thomas, d. 9/27/1974 at 89 in Rochester; b. CT

335

SIMMONS,
Edward, d. 7/4/1915 at 21/0/5 in Tuftonboro; machinist; single; b. Canton, MA

SINCLAIR,
Sabatina, d. 3/23/2004 in Wolfeboro; Louis DePalma and Louise Casiello

SINGLETON,
Kenneth, d. 6/29/2004 in Wolfeboro; Berthrim Singleton and Carrie Aker

SKINNER,
Blanche A., d. 4/20/1985 in Wolfeboro; Sebastian Schifferdecker and Amelia Beska
Herbert I., d. 3/15/1972 at 72 in Tuftonboro; b. MA
Isabell Cora, d. 2/14/1953 at 80 in Tuftonboro; at home; widow; b. Quincy, MA; Peter Thomas
Walter W., d. 7/7/1945 at 73/7/1 in Tuftonboro; caretaker; married; b. Biddeford, ME; Eliza Skinner (Biddeford, ME) and Rosela Mayo (Bangor, ME)

SLEEPER,
Theresa R., d. 11/5/1999 in Portsmouth; Louis O'Leary and Nora Toomey

SMEDAL,
Eunice A., d. 9/11/1983 in Tuftonboro; Albert Whitmore and Isabelle Ostrom
Magnus I., d. 7/23/1981 in Tuftonboro; Harald Smedal and Anna Evans

SMIRLES,
George, d. 8/29/1995 in Tuftonboro; Niketas Smirles and Mary Scouros

SMITH,
Abbie L., d. 10/20/1963 at 86 in Wolfeboro; housewife; widow; b. Barrington, NS; Warren Smith and Emily Knowles
Arthur Burton, d. 7/30/1966 at 53 in Tuftonboro; laborer; married; b. Effingham; James W. Smith and Abbie Smith

Bertha, d. 11/4/2004 in Wolfeboro; Henry Riley and Abbie Brown
Carrie, d. 6/26/1926 at 45 in Tuftonboro; cook; widow; ----- Tower
Charles M. W., d. 9/24/1915 at 40/9 in Tuftonboro; retired; married;
    b. Cortland, NY; R. A. Smith and Maria Wordrup (Cortland, NY)
Clifton E., d. 11/16/1970 at 60 in Wolfeboro; machinist; married; b.
    MA; James Smith and Abbie Smith
Cora E., d. 4/14/1972 at 63 in Wolfeboro; b. NH
Doris, d. 9/8/2004 in Wolfeboro; George Mack and Dora Bragg
Frederick L., d. 4/12/1977 at 79 in Tuftonboro; b. MA
Harold F., d. 10/26/1987 in Wolfeboro; Walter N. Smith and Eleanor
    -----
James W., d. 3/3/1925 at 51/0/1 in Tuftonboro; farmer; married; b.
    Lowell, MA
Jean Adele, d. 5/21/1997 in Wolfeboro; William P. McIntosh and
    Alice W. Kenison
Judith, d. 11/20/2005 in Tuftonboro; Leon Bean and Arlene Henry
Matthew E., d. 1/1/5/1972 at 75 in Wolfeboro; b. MN
Philip Charlesworth, d. 3/15/1996 in Wolfeboro; Fred A. Smith and
    Bertha Maude Charlesworth
Robert, d. 9/9/1911 at 70/4/8; heart failure; widower; b. Newmarket;
    Nathaniel Smith and Laura Mills
Walter R., d. 5/28/1986 in Tuftonboro; James W. Smith and Abby L.

SNOW,
Elizabeth, d. 7/3/1914 at 4/10/11; b. Chicago, IL; Arthur C. Snow and
    Laura D. Harris
Marion Evans, d. 3/23/1998 in Wolfeboro; Walter W. Evans and
    Alice B. -----

SNYDER,
George Edward, d. 1/7/1979 in Wolfeboro; Stephen Snyder and
    Alma E. -----

SPENCER,
Thomas D., d. 6/6/1971 at 56 in Tuftonboro; b. MA
William P., d. 9/20/1953 at 62 in Beverly, MA; mechanic; married; b.
    Beverly, MA; Thomas P. Spencer and Ida Lovett

SPYCHER,
Peter Christian, d. 7/14/1998 in Tuftonboro; Carl Spycher and Rosa

Fischer

STACEY,
Charles O., d. 4/9/1923 at 57/7/4 in Tuftonboro; carpenter; married; b. Porter, ME; Oliver Stacey and Ann M. McDonald

STACK,
Elmer S., d. 9/28/1952 at 81 in Tuftonboro; hot water eng.; married; b. Canada; William Stack and Mary A. Irving

STACKPOLE,
Amanda A., d. 6/10/1931 at 82/2/15 in Tuftonboro; at home; widow; b. Tuftonboro; Stephen Fernald (Ossipee) and Elizabeth Hodgdon (Tuftonboro)
Mary D., d. 5/3/1915 at 105/5/19 in Wolfeboro; housewife; widow; b. Tuftonboro; John Canney (Salmon Falls) and Sally French (New Durham)

STACY,
Maud C., d. 10/15/1955 at 88 in Tuftonboro; at home; widow; b. ME; Charles W. Watson and Josephine Pugsley

STAMMERS,
Herman, d. 3/29/1975 at 62 in Wolfeboro; b. VT

STANLEY,
Donald C., d. 7/18/1967 at 35 in Alton; construction; married; b. New York, NY; Donald C. Stanley and Sara Hixon

STAPLES,
Frank George, d. 9/28/1954 at 88 in Wakefield; laborer; widower; b. NH; William Staples
John W., d. 9/4/1907 at 0/1/18; inanition; b. Tuftonboro; John W. Staples and Lizzie A. Nichols
William G., d. 8/13/1959 at 29 in Milton; lumbering; b. Wolfeboro; Christopher W. Staples and Ada F. Keniston

STEADMAN,
Kenton E., Jr., d. 9/1/1984 in Wolfeboro; Kenton E. Steadman and Ethel W. MacFadvean
Kenton E., Sr., d. 6/3/1974 at 73 in Tuftonboro; b. MA

STEVENS,
Esther M., d. 1/25/1965 at 67 in Wolfeboro; housewife; married; b. Tuftonboro; Wilbur S. Bean and Cora A. Bean
John B., d. 11/3/1913 at 57/1/14; aortic regurgitation; widower; b. Tuftonboro; Daniel Stevens and Elizabeth Hoyt
Sarah P., d. 8/8/1906 at 56/8/26; arsenical poisoning; married; b. Tuftonboro; William Narey and Mary Trask
Weston G., d. 3/22/1986 in Tuftonboro; Warren Stevens and Phebe Redden

STICKLE,
Marjorie W., d. 3/16/2003 in Tuftonboro; William Wood and Ethel Patterson

STILLINGS,
Agnes M., d. 7/1/1954 at 45/8/3 in Ossipee; hotel; married; b. NH; David Whitton and Nellie Hoyt
Charles, d. 8/18/1935 at 81/11/9 in Ctr. Tuftonboro; invalid; married; b. Ossipee; Ivry Stillings (Ossipee) and Lydia Wentworth (Ossipee)
Luella, d. 10/23/1944 at 61/4/14 in Wolfeboro; housewife; widow; b. Wolfeboro; Charles Moody (Wolfeboro) and Belle Berry (New Durham)
Rufus, d. 12/3/1979 in Tuftonboro; Charles Stillings

STOCKMAN,
Andrew J., d. 9/--/1986 in Tuftonboro; John Stockman and Patricia Rico
Doris Lucas, d. 1/31/1998 in Wolfeboro; Anthony W. Lucas and Elizabeth Clarkson
Frank, d. 12/14/2001 in Lebanon; Frank Stockman and Doris Lucas
Frank L., Sr., d. 7/9/1985 in Wolfeboro; Frank L. Stockman and Mabel Munroe
John Lawrence, d. 11/13/1994 in Wolfeboro; Frank Leland Stockman, Jr. and Muriel Williams
Muriel W., d. 10/1/1985 in Wolfeboro; Roger Williams and Berenice Lawrence

STOKES,
Benjamin F., d. 1/5/1932 at 87/2/20 in Wolfeboro; retired; widower; b. Lawrence, MA

Lydia B., d. 5/16/1927 at 75/5/25 in Tuftonboro; at home; married; b. S. Eliot, ME; Samuel Remick (Eliot, ME) and Susan Burleigh

STONE,
Ernest Alfred, Jr., d. 1/11/1992 in Tuftonboro; Ernest A. Stone, Sr. and Rita Jones

STORMONT,
James Emery, d. 10/29/1988 in Wolfeboro; James T. Stormont and Edith MacDougal

STRAW,
Barbara E., d. 7/9/2000 in Wolfeboro; Ralph Drucker and Lela Staniels
Francis, d. 12/4/1915 at 76/6/29 in Tuftonboro; farming; married; b. Tuftonboro; William Straw and Mary Rogers
George Daniel, d. 6/15/1956 at 81 in Union; mail carrier; widower; b. Tuftonboro; Frank Straw and Elizabeth -----
Harriet Florence, d. 11/16/1963 at 80 in Wolfeboro; housewife; widow; b. Tuftonboro; James Frank Bean and Mary F. Bean
Robert W., d. 2/11/2003 in Wolfeboro; Harry Straw and Harriet Bean
William, d. 3/3/1896 at 85/8/2 in Tuftonboro; phthisis; farmer; widower; b. Thornton; John Straw (Alton) and Mary Rogers (Alton)

STREETER,
Albert W., d. 9/5/1908 at 68/6/4; tuberculosis; married; William W. Streeter and Christianna Crouch
Christiana, d. 3/2/1902 at 84/1/25 in Tuftonboro; old age; widow; b. Truxton, NY; Daniel Crouch and Celinda Crouch
Ruth A., d. 2/24/1915 at 81/4/22 in Tuftonboro; housewife; widow; b. Tuftonboro; John Chace (Tuftonboro) and Ruth G. Burbank (Tuftonboro)

STRICKLAND,
Richard B., d. 4/29/1978 at 65 in Wolfeboro; b. Westfield, MA

STROUT,
Clarence, d. 9/1/1935 at 56/8/25 in Mirror Lake; farmer; widower; b. Danville, ME; Joseph Strout (ME) and Clara Mulvin (MA)

STUART,
Betsy, d. 12/2/1908 at 59/3/22; cancer of tongue; married; Newell
Cook and Mary A. Thompson

STURTEVANT,
Araminta, d. 10/10/1924 at 83/8/17 in Tuftonboro; housewife; widow;
----- and Asenath Hawkins

SULLIVAN,
Mary Augusta, d. 5/9/1931 at 95/4/9 in Wolfeboro; retired; widow; b.
Moultonboro; John W. Richardson (Moultonboro) and Mary D.
Wainwright (Rockport, MA)

SVENSON,
Agnes E., d. 1/28/1986 in Tuftonboro; Carl Gustavson and Helen
Bergquist
Carl Norman, d. 11/18/1996 in Tuftonboro; Carl Alfred Svenson and
Carolina Wilhelmina Gustafson

SWETT,
Albert H., d. 12/29/1933 at 82/0/25 in Mirror Lake; retired farmer;
widower; b. Tuftonboro; William Swett (Tuftonboro) and Ellen ---
Asa, d. 1/16/1892 at 73 in Tuftonboro; cong. of lungs; foundryman;
married; b. Parsonsfield, ME; Stephen Swett (Parsonsfield) and
Rachel Colcord (Parsonsfield)
Dana F., d. 1/12/1973 at 73 in Wolfeboro; b. MA
Ruth E., d. 8/23/1894 at 42/2/17; housewife; married; b. Tuftonboro;
Silas Whitney (Tuftonboro) and Mary W. Hersey (Wolfeboro)
William, d. 10/27/1908 at 88/6/5; old age; widower; Robert Swett and
Mary Wiggin

SWIFT,
Paul, d. 11/8/1981 in Tuftonboro; Ralph Swift and Fannie Whittle

TARBOX,
Eliza C., d. 10/24/1923 at 74/5/25 in Tuftonboro; retired; widow; b.
Berwick, NS; William A. Davidson and Catherine C. Norwood

THAYER,
Ann Campbell, d. 7/27/1993 in Wolfeboro; Eugene Campbell and
Harriet Caulkins

Gordon O., d. 9/3/1988 in Wolfeboro; William Thayer and Mary Jackson

THIBODEAU,
Myrtle M., d. 5/14/1920 at 18/11/1 in Concord; housewife; married; b. Tuftonboro; William W. Adjutant and Eliza Piper
Wayne, d. 3/26/1940 at 0/1/5 in Wolfeboro; b. Ossipee; Fred Thibodeau (St. Albans, VT) and Ellen Delorier (Lowell, MA)

THIELKER,
Alvin H., d. 5/13/1971 at 67 in Hanover; b. MO

THOMAS,
son, d. 4/29/1891 at 0/0/4 in Tuftonboro; convulsions; b. Tuftonboro; Edgar M. Thomas (Tuftonboro) and Myra G. Welch (Springvale)
Andrew, d. 3/7/1899 at 76/5/2 in Tuftonboro; married; b. Tuftonboro; Greenlief Thomas and Hannah Wiggin
Donald E., d. 9/19/1987 in Wolfeboro; Clayton Thomas and Mabel Weatherbee
Donald E., 2nd, d. 4/17/1963 at 0/0/29 in Tuftonboro; b. Wolfeboro; Edwin D. Thomas and June E. Meyer
Dorothy Jane, d. 4/23/1993 in Wolfeboro; David Botts and Sarah Botts
Ella L., d. 1/16/1936 at 82/11/11 in Mirror Lake; housekeeper; widow; b. Hubbardston, MA; ----- Hatstack
Frank M., d. 1/14/1902 at 51/0/12 in Tuftonboro; tuberculosis; married; b. Tuftonboro; William E. Thomas and Nancy Libby
Lillian E., d. 7/5/1897 at 26/6 in Tuftonboro; tuberculosis; married; b. Tuftonboro; Horace McIntire and Hattie E. Johnson
Mabel I., d. 11/9/1926 at 43/5/14 in Tuftonboro; housewife; married; Charles Hodgdon and Emma Swasey (Ossipee)
Martha A., d. 2/15/1900 at 65/2/15 in Rochester; pneumonia; widow; b. Tuftonboro
Myra Gertrude, d. 12/23/1949 at 81 in Wolfeboro; housewife; widow; b. Springvale, ME; John Welch and Mary Dame
Nancy J., d. 3/7/1895 at 66/1/5 in Tuftonboro; disease of heart; married; b. Tuftonboro; Daniel Libbey and Ada Clough
Walter Harold, d. 8/26/1949 at 49/2/15 in Wolfeboro; auto sales; widower; b. Wolfeboro; Edgar M. Thomas and Myra G. Welch
William E., d. 10/29/1897 at 71/6/28 in Tuftonboro; peritonitis; widower; b. Tuftonboro; Enoch Thomas and Hannah Horne

Willie W., d. 5/4/1941 at 80/4/9 in Wolfeboro; farmer; widower; b. Tuftonboro; Willie E. Thomas (Tuftonboro) and Nancy Libbey (Alton)

THOMPSON,
Albert, d. 9/4/1935 at 80/8/17 in Mirror Lake; laborer; b. Ossipee; John Thompson (Ossipee) and Mary Wilkinson (Eaton)
Alice, d. 8/26/1976 at 67 in Wolfeboro; b. NH
Annie F., d. 10/4/1920 at 61/4/10 in Tuftonboro; housewife; married; b. Tuftonboro; Washington Thompson and Joanna Beacham
Annie M., d. 6/8/1909 at 37/10/26; pneumonia; widow; b. Moultonboro; Charles W. Pinkham and Sarah E. Moulton
Asa B., d. 2/25/1925 at 72/2/20 in Tuftonboro; farmer; married; b. Tuftonboro; Washington Thompson (Tuftonboro) and Joanna Beacham (Ossipee)
Barbara, d. 11/17/1931 at 1/6/0 in Wolfeboro; b. Tuftonboro; Simon Thompson (Melvin Village) and Alice Clough (Wolfeboro)
Chester E., d. 8/28/1921 at 7/1/24 in Tuftonboro; b. Tuftonboro; Simon T. Thompson and Evelyn L. Bean
Edna Mae, d. 10/12/1997 in Laconia; Wallace E. Nudd and Blanche Leclair
Evelyn L., d. 5/16/1924 at 32/11/15 in Tuftonboro; housewife; married; b. Tuftonboro; Willie L. Bean and Ula D. Foss
Frances S., d. 12/18/1934 at 100/0/4 in Tuftonboro; at home; widow; b. Somersworth; George Kenison (Newton) and Lizia N. Peavey (Farmington)
Frank, d. 1/26/1944 at 71/0/21 in Ctr. Ossipee; carpenter; married; b. Cambridge, MA; Freeman Thompson (Ossipee) and Sarah Bacon
Fred, d. 12/18/1904 at 26 in Tuftonboro; hemorrhage of lungs; married; b. Tuftonboro; Charles Thompson and Emma Fernald
Hannah P., d. 2/12/1901 at 87/9/29 in Tuftonboro; old age; widow; b. Ossipee; Richard Beacham and Hannah Pitman
Irving D., d. 4/29/1910 at 15/3/12; ruptured blood vessel in lungs; single; b. Conway; Lafayette Thompson (by adoption)
James, d. 7/11/1940 at 0/0/3 in Wolfeboro; b. Wolfeboro; Percy Thompson (Conway) and Pauline M. Chute (NY City)
Joanna, d. 9/6/1902 at 85/4/5 in Tuftonboro; valvular disease of heart; widow; b. Ossipee; Richard Beacham and Hannah Pitman
John Theodore, d. 2/21/1938 at 62/8/27 in Wolfeboro; carpenter;

married; b. Tuftonboro; Theodore Thompson (Tuftonboro) and Rose Tibbetts (Ossipee)

Lafayette, d. 4/18/1918 at 60/7/0 in Tuftonboro; farmer; married; b. Tuftonboro; Theodore Thompson (Tuftonboro) and Hannah Beacham (Ossipee)

Leona L., d. 6/13/1986 in Wolfeboro; Robert Libby and Helen Eldridge

Lester W., d. 7/23/1999 in Wolfeboro; Simon Thompson and Evelyn Bean

Lizzie, d. 4/10/1923 at 63/10/28 in Tuftonboro; housewife; married; b. NS; Jacob Browning

Madeline A., d. 11/27/1927 at 0/3/27 in Tuftonboro; b. Tuftonboro; Simon T. Thompson (Tuftonboro) and Cecil Morris (Tuftonboro)

Mary E., d. 6/29/1892 at 47/8/1 in Tuftonboro; h. fail. & gastritis; housewife; married; b. Moultonboro; Albert Ambrose (Moultonboro) and Almina Piper (Tuftonboro)

Moses, d. 1/2/1895 at 67/6/28 in Tuftonboro; apoplexy; married; b. Tuftonboro; Theodore Thompson and Mary Briard

Roy E., d. 2/26/1937 at 29/10/19 in Melvin Village; carpenter; single; b. Tuftonboro; Simon Thompson (Tuftonboro) and Evelyn Bean (Tuftonboro)

Simon B., d. 12/7/1933 at 79/0/22 in Melvin Village; farmer; widower; b. Tuftonboro; Theodore Thompson (Tuftonboro) and Hannah Beacham (Ossipee)

Simon T., d. 7/8/1979 in Meredith; Simon B. Thompson and Lizzie Browning

Theodore, d. 12/30/1922 at 75/3 in Tuftonboro; farmer; married; b. Tuftonboro; Theodore Thompson and Hannah Beacham

Washington, d. 1/9/1892 at 80/2/5 in Tuftonboro; la grippe; farmer; married; b. Tuftonboro; Theodore Thompson and Mary Bryer

Washington, d. 1/21/1894 at 46/11/29; farmer; widower; b. Tuftonboro; Washington Thompson (Tuftonboro) and Joanna Beacham (Ossipee)

TILTON,

Bessie F., d. 5/2/1940 at 67/2/7 in Wolfeboro; housewife; married; b. Bridgewater, MA; Elijah S. Haley (Somersworth) and Fannie E. Dore (Somersworth)

TISDALE,

Grace S., d. 1/9/1981 in Wolfeboro; Hugh Stewart and Mary A.

Connor

Harden V., d. 1/10/1981 in Wolfeboro; George W. Tisdale and Agnes M. Findlay

TOMB,

Ethel F., d. 11/5/1979 in Meredith; Jacob Frick Frantz and Gertrude Osborne

TORREY,

David E., d. 8/23/1915 at 0/11/3 in Tuftonboro; b. Tuftonboro; Roy Torrey (Ferrisburg, VT) and Olive Carr (Waybridge, VT)

TOTMAN,

Helen Durfee, d. 9/12/1996 in Wolfeboro; Robert Durfee and Effie Robinson

TREAT,

Arthur W., d. 9/26/1914 at 39/0/4; married; b. Watertown, MA; William W. Treat and Lucy B. Bean

TRUMAN,

Diana, d. 8/22/2004 in Lebanon; Albert Lewis and Iris Cook

TUCKER,

Carroll M., d. 3/28/1984 in Wolfeboro; Everett Tucker and Lizzie Farin

Daniel B., d. 6/11/1898 at 70/10/6 in Tuftonboro; cancer of liver; married; Benjamin Tucker and Abagail Wheeler

Ethelyn S., d. 12/3/1946 at 48/1/11 in Wolfeboro; at home; married; b. Tuftonboro; Fred L. Osborn (Rochester) and Lena Shannon (Tuftonboro)

Madeleine Collidge, d. 11/7/1993 in Ossipee; Eugene L. Collidge and Lenora M. Stevens

TUPECK,

son, d. 6/10/1936 at 0/0/0 in Wolfeboro; b. Wolfeboro; Steve Tupeck (Russia) and Bernece E. Ayers (Tuftonboro)

Bernice, d. 4/12/1964 at 56 in Tuftonboro; housewife; married; b. Tuftonboro; Herbert Ayers and Mabel Adjutant

Caroline Tappan, d. 12/5/2002 in Tuftonboro; Wallace Nudd and Blanche LeClair

Henry S., d. 7/29/2000 in Tuftonboro; Steve Tupeck and Bernice
Ayers

Stephan, d. 9/28/1978 at 84 in Manchester; b. Russia

TURNER,
Bertha Wright, d. 1/14/1964 at 85 in Stoneham, MA; at home;
widow; b. Charlestown, MA; Henry E. Wright and Sarah J. Hall

Harry C., d. 7/29/1963 at 85 in Wakefield, MA; retired Pres.; married;
b. Barnard, VT; Obed C. Turner and Harriett Stanton

TUTTLE,
Elizabeth S., d. 1/31/1968 at 1/31/1968 at 82 in Needham, MA;
housewife; widow; b. NH; Thomas Spooner and Clara Prescott

Eugene, d. 1/20/1965 at 82 in Tuftonboro; educator; married; b.
Brewer, ME; Allison E. Tuttle and Katherine Starbird

VALENTINE,
Hildur Marie, d. 8/1/1983 in Tuftonboro; Anders Carlsen and Bertha
Krogenas

VAN WAGNER,
Clifford, d. 6/18/1978 at 78 in Wolfeboro; b. Brooklyn, NY

VARNEY,
Fenton W., d. 9/1/2001 in Wolfeboro; George Varney and Olive
Blake

VARSON,
Dorothea K., d. 4/24/1986 in Wolfeboro; Adam Krauth and Mary
Brown

VEDRANI,
Robert, d. 11/26/2004 in Mirror Lake; Robert Vedrani and Helen
Coffey

VERY,
Albert, d. 7/28/1910 at 74/8/5; osteo sarcoma; widower; b. Danvers,
MA

VIANELLO,
George Leslie, d. 1/12/1959 at 78 in Arlington, MA; engineer;

346

married; b. Lewiston, ME; George G. Vianello and Alice
Dunham
Reba Annie, d. 1/15/1965 at 78 in Concord; telephone co.; married;
b. Lynn, MA; Thomas Speirs and Jeannette Speirs

VICKERY,
Nancy L., d. 10/2/1929 at 87/3/21 in Rochester; widow; b.
Tuftonboro; Samuel Ladd (Tuftonboro) and Mary Moulton
(Tuftonboro)

WAKEFIELD,
Annie F., d. 8/10/1928 at 69/1/13 in Tuftonboro; retired; divorced; b.
Lowell, MA; Warren S. Foote (Lowell, MA) and Mattie Swain
(Clarkesville, MO)
Edna C., d. 10/25/1972 at 79 in Meredith; b. NH
George Henry, d. 12/16/1959 at 60 in Wolfeboro; contractor;
married; b. NH; William Wakefield and Bessie Conning
William Henry, d. 10/12/1951 at 78 in Moultonboro; blacksmith;
married; b. Canada; Henry Wakefield and Elvira Horne

WALDRON,
John B., d. 2/18/1897 at 69/4/22 in Tuftonboro; pneumonia and
disease of liver; married; John Waldron and Lizzie Gray

WALKER,
Abbie, d. 8/19/1900 at 90/3/4; arterial degeneration; widow; b.
Tuftonboro; Timothy Piper and Hannah Neal
Arabine W., d. 8/9/1894 at 51/2; housewife; married; b. Durham, ME;
Horace Wright (Durham) and Mary A. Lincoln (Durham)
Carrie L., d. 5/16/1913 at 43/9/24; mitral insufficiency; married; b.
Moultonboro; Clark Wentworth and Elizabeth Allard
Ernest T., d. 7/5/1976 at 88 in Wolfeboro; b. Biddeford, ME
Horace Albert, d. 1/7/1950 at 79 in Henniker; retired; married; b.
Richmond, ME

WALLACE,
Charles Parker, d. 5/5/1927 at 68/7/22 in Tuftonboro; farmer;
married; b. Ossipee; Simon P. Wallace (Ossipee) and
Mehitable Welch (Ossipee)
Harriet G., d. 1/23/1959 at 95 in Concord; housewife; widow; b.
Boston, MA; Ivery A. Hurd and Josephine L. Runly

Mary E., d. 3/20/1911 at 69/0/4; osteo sarcoma; widow; b. Tuftonboro; William Canney and Pamelia Edgerly

WALLMANN,
Janet H., d. 3/1/2003 in Manchester; James Hughes and Alma Jediney

WALSH,
Catherine J., d. 11/29/1987 in Tuftonboro; Charles Armour and Mary Shoemaker

WALTER,
Esther V., d. 10/24/1979 in Wolfeboro; John Minot and Mary -----
Otto Charles, d. 3/15/1962 at 71 in Tuftonboro; tel. worker; married; b. E. Boston, MA; Otto Walter and Emma Scheidegger

WARD,
Albra Samuel, d. 6/18/1956 at 64 in Wolfeboro; caretaker, estate; married; b. NH; Asa Ward and Annie Garland
Lillian M., d. 2/9/1963 at 82 in Rochester; housewife; widow; b. Effingham; Josiah Thurston and Arvilla Clark

WARDROP,
David A., d. 7/15/1902 at 0/5/19 in Tuftonboro; meningitis; b. Dorchester, MA; George W. Wardrop and Helen Page

WARREN,
John Stephen, d. 2/1/1979 in Wolfeboro; Stephen John Warren and Florence Garland

WATANABE,
Roy, d. 6/9/2004 in Alton; Roy Watanabe and Deanna Wong-Yan

WATERBURY,
Frank, d. 8/16/1917 at 62/1/1 in Tuftonboro; merchant; married; b. Noroton, CT; Frances N. Waterbury and Sarah Fitch

WATERS,
Herbert B., d. 9/5/1957 at 86 in Tuftonboro; publisher; married; b. Somerville, MA; Rueul Waters and Emily Hall

WATSON,
Alfred O., d. 7/3/1971 at 84 in Wolfeboro; b. NH
Cecile M., d. 4/12/1975 at 81 in Wolfeboro; b. Tuftonboro
Edna, d. 1/19/1968 at 78 in Laconia; housewife; married; b. NH;
    James Canney and Lydia Adjutant
Edward M., d. 2/10/1966 at 71 in Hanover; auto dealer; married; b.
    Rochester; Charles Watson and Latitia McDuffee
Ermina G., d. 7/29/1951 at 82/5/23 in Meredith; housewife; widow; b.
    Tuftonboro; Albert Elliott and Mehetible Caverly
Nathaniel Russell, d. 2/28/1937 at 72/5/23 in Wolfeboro; farmer;
    married; b. Center Harbor

WATT,
Frederick Ellsworth, d. 9/7/1951 at 41 in Tuftonboro; teacher;
    married; Frederick Watt and Jennie Baker

WEISS,
Ted, d. 6/18/2000 in Tuftonboro; Albert Weiss and Rose Hermer

WELCH,
daughter, d. 10/18/1971 at 0/0/2 in Wolfeboro; b. NH
Andrew, d. 12/31/1909 at 78/0/2; senility; widower; b. Tuftonboro;
    Adriel Welch and Dosia Wadleigh
Ann B., d. 5/10/1904 at 84/9/23 in Tuftonboro; old age; widow; b.
    Tuftonboro; Mark Wiggin and Hulda Swett
Blanche E., d. 8/2/1959 at 60 in Ossipee; prac. nurse; married; b.
    Tuftonboro; Howard Emery and Emma Swasey
George, d. 10/19/1893 at 78/6/14 in Tuftonboro; angina pectoris;
    farmer; married; b. Tuftonboro; Jonathan Welch and Parnelia
    Wilson
George, d. 12/11/1945 at 85/6/19 in Tuftonboro; farmer; married; b.
    Tuftonboro; Andrew Welch (Tuftonboro) and Jane Thompson
    (Tuftonboro)
James W., d. 1/28/1911 at 71/9/16; heart disease; married; b.
    Tuftonboro; Joseph Welch and Mary McIntire
John J., d. 4/27/2003 in Wolfeboro; Wade Welch and Annie Boston
Maurice C., d. 6/11/1966 at 63 in Tuftonboro; laborer; widower; b.
    Ossipee; Orin Welch and Jennie Bean
Orrin E., d. 6/30/1940 at 78/0/2 in Wolfeboro; farmer; married; b.
    Ossipee; John Welch (Ossipee) and Lydia Elliott (Ossipee)
Sarah F., d. 10/23/1918 at 73/4/24 in Tuftonboro; housewife; widow;

b. Ossipee; John Thompson (Ossipee) and Mary Williams
(Eaton)

WELSH,
Anice Cordelia, d. 2/25/1960 at 97 in Ossipee; housewife; widow; b.
Moultonboro; Henry Horn and Ann Wallace

WENDELL,
Alma H., d. 12/22/1915 at 73/5/12 in Tuftonboro; housewife; widow;
Nathan Holmes and Lucinda Bryant
George, d. 12/31/1899 at 87/4/19 in Tuftonboro; widower; b.
Thornton; John Straw and Abagail Piper
Isaiah, d. 11/23/1907 at 69/1/3; cancer of stomach; married; b.
Tuftonboro; George Wendell and Sally Horne
John R., d. 1/6/1909 at 63/11/4; uraemia; married; b. Tuftonboro;
George Wendell and Sally Horne
Sally, d. 1/20/1893 at 87/10 in Tuftonboro; old age; housewife;
married; b. Wolfeboro; John Horne and Jane Rust (Portsmouth)
Sara J., d. 9/24/1922 at 71/9/9 in Wolfeboro; housewife; widow; b.
Tuftonboro; John L. Canney and Beulah Mains

WENTWORTH,
Anna, d. 10/12/1937 at 81 in Concord; housewife; b. NH; Albert
Pavey
Jessie L., d. 10/24/1967 at 84 in Center Harbor; housewife; widow;
b. Hebron; Andrew Morgan and Fidelia -----
John, d. 6/11/1950 at 73 in Wolfeboro; retired; married; b. Hudson;
Nathaniel Wentworth and Martha E. Greeley

WEST,
Addie A., d. 10/18/1942 at 70/1/23 in Tuftonboro; housewife; widow;
b. Tuftonboro; Charles Pinkham (Newmarket) and Sarah E.
Moulton (Moultonboro)
Charles W., d. 1/6/1932 at 57/8/8 in Tuftonboro; farmer; married; b.
London, England; William West (London, England) and
Charlotte Smith (London, England)
Harold P., d. 3/21/1905 at 3/0/6 in rx; choked to death; b.
Tuftonboro; Charles W. West and Addie R. Pinkham

WHEDON,
Oscar Allen, d. 3/30/1938 at 70/4/2 in Tuftonboro; gardner; married;

b. Sandgate, VT; John M. Whedon and Mary E. Parker

WHEELER,
Clara H., d. 8/15/1988 in Wolfeboro; Frank Hayden and Henrietta
   Holt
Francis Q., d. 3/26/1952 at 58 in Wolfeboro; banker; widower; b.
   Yonkers, NY; Frank E. Wheeler and Lucy Quick

WHITE,
Donald H., d. 10/16/1980 in Hanover; Charles D. White and Esther
   L. Horne
Lois, d. 10/2/1988 in Tuftonboro; Emery Thompson and Arah Davis

WHITEHEAD,
May C., d. 5/10/1967 at 81 in Wolfeboro; antique dealer; widow; b.
   Providence, RI; Andrew Ross and Mary E. Glodding

WHITEHOUSE,
Aaron, d. 7/25/1895 at 84 in Tuftonboro; Bright's disease; widower;
   b. Tuftonboro
Dorothy E., d. 3/12/1998 in Manatee, FL; Dwight Woodford and
   Laura Holt
Frank, d. 2/20/1923 at 87/11/20 in Tuftonboro; widower; b.
   Tuftonboro; Aaron Whitehouse and Sally Copp
Matilda, d. 6/8/1910 at 79; bronchitis; widow; b. Ossipee; Samuel
   Thompson and Betsey Canney

WHITING,
Craigue A., d. 2/12/1983 in Wolfeboro; Robert Whiting and Judith
   Morgan
Fred M., d. 5/12/1971 at 82 in Wolfeboro; b. NH
Irma M., d. 3/29/1980 in Wolfeboro; Samuel B. Osgood and Helen
   Marr
Mary Frances, d. 1/13/1953 at 65 in Tuftonboro; at home; widow; b.
   Cambridge, MA; Joseph Frances and Rose Gomez

WHITNEY,
Arlene Virginia, d. 9/29/1996 in Tuftonboro; Jacob Hlushuk and
   Leora Adjutant
John, d. 9/20/1962 at 89 in Wolfeboro; laborer; married; b. Boston,
   MA; Enoch Whitney and Susan -----

WHITTEN,

son, d. 9/11/1896 at 0/0/1 in Tuftonboro; heart disease; b. Tuftonboro; Edmund Whitten (Winchester, MA) and Teresa Robinson (England)

Carrie G., d. 3/30/1949 at 79/7 in Tuftonboro; at home; widow; b. Tuftonboro; John A. Wiggin and Abbie Bickford

Charles Frank, d. 6/3/1998 in Wolfeboro; Joseph Whitten and Mamie Whitten

Evie G., d. 5/17/1946 at 60/2/4 in Concord; housewife; married; b. Porter, ME; Martha J. Sargent (ME)

Frank E., d. 5/27/1935 at 79/1/12 in Ctr. Tuftonboro; farmer; married; b. Moultonboro; Joseph Whitten (Limerick, ME) and Sally Wallace (Limerick, ME)

John R., d. 1/31/1976 at 77 in Wolfeboro; b. Tuftonboro

Joseph B., d. 3/15/1898 at 65/0/9 in Tuftonboro; disease of heart and liver; married; b. Tamworth; Samuel Whitten and Sally Hawkins

Joseph Wiggin, d. 1/20/1961 at 73 in Tuftonboro; farmer; b. Wolfeboro; Joseph W. Whitten and Katie Gove

Mamie G., d. 1/1/1974 at 84 in Wolfeboro; b. NH

Martha, d. 11/16/1904 at 80/1/17 in Tuftonboro; heart disease; widow; b. Tuftonboro; Aaron Wiggin and Mary Horn

Oscar L., d. 11/9/1909 at 6/4/12; heart disease; b. Tuftonboro; David V. Whitten and Nellie J. Hoyt

Theodora H., d. 3/24/1969 at 70 in Tuftonboro; tourist home; divorced; b. NH; Frank Hayes and Alice Martin

William Joseph, d. 1/30/1960 at 80 in Moultonboro; laborer; widower; b. Moultonboro; Joseph Whitten and Jane Roberts

WHITTIER,

Randall A., d. 4/9/2002 in Wolfeboro; Randall Whittier and Jane Blakney

WHITTLE,

Milton H., d. 6/14/1971 at 84 in Wolfeboro; b. MA

WIGGIN,

son, d. 3/3/1894 at –; b. Tuftonboro; John W. Wiggin (Acton, ME) and Mary A. Elliott (Tuftonboro)

son, d. 3/24/1894 at 0/0/20; b. Tuftonboro; John W. Wiggin (Acton, ME) and Mary A. Elliott (Tuftonboro)

son, d. 1/17/1910 at 0/0/8; inanition; b. Tuftonboro; Lewis C. Wiggin
and Ella M. Clark
Abbie, d. 5/1/1919 at 78/3/17 in Tuftonboro; housewife; widow; b.
Tuftonboro; Stephen Bickford and Hannah Young
Augustus, d. 5/25/1898 at 71/10/4 in Tuftonboro; bilious fever and
disease of lungs; married; b. Tuftonboro; Richard Wiggin and
Eleanor Chamberlin
Bennie, d. 8/20/1948 at 73/10/8 in Tuftonboro; farmer; single; b.
Ossipee; John A. Wiggin (Tuftonboro) and Abbie Bickford
(Ossipee)
Blanche H., d. 3/6/1999 in Wolfeboro; Minot Bickford and Etta Dow
Charles, d. 2/10/1898 at 69/3 in Tuftonboro; disease of stomach;
married; b. Tuftonboro; John A. Wiggin and Susan P. Wiggin
Charles A., d. 9/19/1913 at 91/2/24; old age; married; b. Tuftonboro;
Mark Wiggin and Hulda Swett
Clara A., d. 5/17/1971 at 88 in Wolfeboro; b. NH
Ella J., d. 9/24/1914 at 60; married; b. Somersworth; George Holmes
and Jane Hoyt
Everett D., d. 1/14/1917 at 53/1/11 in Tuftonboro; merchant; married;
b. Tuftonboro; Isaiah S. Wiggin and Maria Piper
Frank, d. 3/7/1965 at 81 in Wolfeboro; gardener; married; b.
Tuftonboro; John Wiggin and Abbie Bickford
Frederick, d. 7/26/1940 at 82/0/15 in Tuftonboro; clergyman;
married; b. Tuftonboro; William H. Wiggin (Tuftonboro) and Ann
Swett (Tuftonboro)
Hannah, d. 2/19/1917 at 95/11/12 in Tuftonboro; housewife; widow;
b. Parsonsfield, ME; Amri R. Quint and Anna Sargent
Harold I., d. 10/16/1969 at 67 in Wolfeboro; proprietor; married; b.
MA; Lewis C. Wiggin and Ella Clark
Harry R., d. 4/4/1922 at 19/0/21 in Tuftonboro; single; b. Wakefield;
Harry L. Wiggin and Mabel Drowns
Isaiah S., d. 11/18/1915 at 87/11/28 in Tuftonboro; farming; married;
b. Tuftonboro; William Wiggin and Dolly Snell
John A., d. 3/21/1905 at 67/0/27 in rx; necrosis of the shoulder joint;
married; b. Tuftonboro; Thomas J. Wiggin and Susan P. Wiggin
Lewis C., d. 6/19/1925 at 72/5/15 in Tuftonboro; cabinet worker;
widower; b. Tamworth; Alonzo Wiggin (Wakefield) and Hannah
Emery (Ashland)
Louvisa M., d. 12/17/1911 at 92/7/11; apoplexy; widow; b. Palermo,
ME; Edmund Black and Comfort Wiggin
Mabel, d. 10/17/1948 at 68/5 in Laconia; retired; widow; b.

Tuftonboro; James A. Bennett (Tuftonboro) and Frances
Fernald (Tuftonboro)
Maria, d. 1/20/1896 at 76/8/8 in Tuftonboro; dropsy; married
Maria, d. 2/10/1929 at 93/0/17 in Tuftonboro; at home; widow; b.
Tuftonboro; George Piper (Tuftonboro) and Arvilla Copp
(Tuftonboro)
Mehitable, d. 5/10/1891 at 64/9/19 in Tuftonboro; congestion of
lungs; housewife; widow; b. Tuftonboro; Richard Wiggin
(Tuftonboro) and Eleanor Chamberlain (Tuftonboro)
Minnie, d. 11/16/1898 at 25/4/26 in Tuftonboro; pneumonia; single;
b. Tuftonboro; Arthur Wiggin and Ella Holmes
Woodbury L., d. 1/2/1892 at 76 in Tuftonboro; paralysis and
softening of brain; carpenter; married; b. Tuftonboro

WILCIN,
Arvid, d. 11/13/2000 in Wolfeboro; John Wilcin and Matilda Gale

WILCOX,
Nell H., d. 7/1/1957 at 92 in Wolfeboro; housewife; widow; b. Ft.
Byron, NY; William Hayden and Martha Carter
Norman T., d. 12/31/1937 at 75/2/7 in Wolfeboro; married; b.
Meriden, CT; Edmund Wilcox and ----- Tryon (Meriden, CT)

WILEY,
Joan Theresa, d. 8/23/1995 in Wolfeboro; Joseph E. Forgette and
Leona R. Normandin

WILKIN,
Elizabeth C., d. 10/31/1972 at 74 in Tuftonboro; b. PA
Hugh, d. 12/4/1980 in Wolfeboro; Robert H. Wilkin and Fannie
Louise -----

WILKINSON,
Alvin Thomas, d. 11/4/1958 at 74 in Newton, MA; Ret. CPA; married;
b. Providence, RI; Thomas Wilkinson and Ann Higgins

WILLAND,
John F., d. 4/7/1891 at 81/7/14 in Tuftonboro; paralysis and old age;
married; b. Tuftonboro; John Willand and Sally Kenniston
Woodbury, d. 3/22/1941 at 88/1/21 in Tuftonboro; farmer; married; b.
Ossipee; John Willand (Ossipee) and Lydia Jenkins (Ossipee)

WILLARD,
Emery D., d. 5/29/1976 at 57 in Wolfeboro; b. Lynn, MA
Iva M., d. 6/6/1985 in Wolfeboro; Henry C. Durgin and Mary Ella
  Chapman
Mary F., d. 3/3/1945 at 83/10/12 in Tuftonboro; housewife; widow; b.
  Tuftonboro; Charles W. Dame (Tuftonboro) and Elizabeth
  Bickford (Tuftonboro)

WILLIAMS,
Berenice L., d. 7/8/1981 in Tuftonboro; Wellesley Lawrence and
  Muriel Bessom
Frank V., d. 8/10/1908 at 0/0/4; inanition; George V. Williams and
  Nellie M. Haley
George V., d. 11/28/1927 at 74/8/4 in Tuftonboro; carpenter;
  married; b. Taunton, MA; Bildad Williams and Angeline White
Nathaniel, d. 8/25/2005 in Lebanon; Charles Williams and Dorothy
  Hyde
Nellie May, d. 1/7/1938 at 62/8/3 in Tuftonboro; housewife; widow; b.
  Tuftonboro; Elijah Sylvester Haley (Tuftonboro) and Calista
  Frances Dore (S. Berwick, ME)
Richard Bessom, d. 3/9/1936 at 5 hrs. in Wolfeboro; b. Wolfeboro;
  Roger Lester Williams (Brockton, MA) and Berenece Welsley
  (Lawrence, Lynn, MA)
Richmond Bessom, d. 3/9/1936 at 6 hrs. in Wolfeboro; b. Wolfeboro;
  Roger Lester Williams (Brockton, MA) and Berenece Welsley
  (Lawrence, Lynn, MA)
Roger Lester, d. 3/25/1988 in Wolfeboro; George V. Williams and
  Nellie Haley
Ward T., d. 8/27/1986 in Tamworth; Ward B. Williams and Judith
  Nicherson

WILSON,
Philip C., d. 9/1/1961 at 55/5/29 in Wolfeboro; married; b. Nahant,
  MA; Fred A. Wilson and Alice Campbell
Susan Inez, d. 2/2/1979 in Tuftonboro; Clifford J. Reed and Grace
  Framm

WINGATE,
Amos W., d. 11/29/1894 at 59/1; farmer; married; Jeremy B.
  Wingate (Middleton) and Nancy H. ----- (New Durham)
Daniel D., d. 9/5/1924 at 98/4/7 in Tuftonboro; farmer; widower; b.

Alton

Mary W., d. 1/7/1900 at 66/8/15 in Tuftonboro; apoplexy; married; b. Newmarket; John Wood and Lydia Doe

Ruth, d. 6/23/2002 in Wolfeboro; Harry Turner and Bertha Wright

WOOD,

son, d. 3/7/1950 at 16 hrs. in Wolfeboro; b. Wolfeboro; William Harry Wood, Jr. and Carolyn Phillips

Carl Adams, d. 1/23/1969 at 83 in Tuftonboro; exec. VP; married; b. MA; George O. Wood and Grace Adams

William Harry, d. 10/19/1953 at 71 in Laconia; factory agent laundry sup.; married; b. MA; William B. Wood and Mary Emma Day

WOODBURY,

Anna F., d. 8/17/1951 at 72 in Wolfeboro; housework; widow; b. MA; James Riely and Anna Foley

Clarence P., d. 9/6/1936 at 57/7/24 in Ctr. Tuftonboro; contractor and builder; married; b. Allston, MA; Isaac F. Woodbury (Salem, MA) and Emma F. Woodbury (Concord)

WOODMANCY,

Florence I., d. 2/14/1952 at 78 in Wolfeboro; at home; married; b. Boston, MA; John Evans and Ellen Elizabeth

Henry, d. 2/1/1943 at – in Portsmouth; b. Portsmouth; Henry Woodmancy (Boston, MA) and Elsie G. Stewart (Concord)

Henry A., d. 2/24/1957 at 80 in Portsmouth; retired fireman; widower; b. Boston, MA; Henry Woodmancy and Louise -----

WOODWORTH,

Amanda M., d. 3/24/1909 at 60/9/18; pneumonia; married; b. Tuftonboro; Jonathan Ladd and Susan Young

Clarence E., d. 7/28/1898 at 28/10/3 in Tuftonboro; tuberculosis; married; b. Greenland; Elisha E. Woodworth and Amanda D. Ladd

Elisha E., d. 12/19/1912 at 70/2/19; pneumonia; widower; b. Little Compton, RI; Elisha Woodworth and Lydia Brownell

Mary E., d. 12/17/1892 at 22/7 in Tuftonboro; lungs and heart; housewife; married; b. St. James, NB; Moses L. Hovey (Northumberland) and Elizabeth Lang (Northumberland)

Ralph E., d. 6/24/1894 at 2; b. Tuftonboro; C. E. Woodworth (Greenland) and Mary E. Hovey (Oak Hill, NB)

WORRICK,
Roberta Smith, d. 6/27/1996 in Wolfeboro; Adelbert W. Smith and
Roberta Baker

WORTHEN,
Jane E., d. 3/11/2002 in Lawrence, MA; Harold H. Holmquist and
Bessie Bishop

WRIGHT,
David M., d. 10/13/2003 in Wolfeboro; E. Wright and Alice Morris
Donald C., d. 10/6/1999 in Wolfeboro; Edwin Wright and Lillian Dyer
E. Stanley, d. 9/6/1959 at 66 in Tuftonboro; Pres. Wright; married; b.
MA; Morris S. Wright and Alice Morris
Mary A., d. 2/17/1891 at 69/7/3 in Tuftonboro; general debility;
housekeeper; widow; b. Durham; Nathaniel Lincoln (Durham,
ME) and Mary A. Lincoln (Durham)

WRYE,
George E., d. 6/14/1975 at 67 in Tuftonboro; b. Boston, MA
Jean Charlton, d. 4/24/1997 in Wolfeboro; Blair Charlton and Edith
Gallupe

WYMAN,
Marius Coipel, d. 5/7/1954 at 75/8/22 in Somerville, MA; restaurant
prop.; married; b. NS; George B. Wyman and Rebecca Eldridge

YEATON,
Josephine, d. 4/14/1904 at 42 in Tuftonboro; heart disease; married;
b. Alton

YOUNG,
Howard E., d. 4/7/1955 at 82 in Wolfeboro; farmer; widower; b.
Ossipee; Arthur P. Young and Emma F. Kenniston
Joseph B., d. 7/28/1972 at 74 in Tuftonboro; b. MA
Josephine E., d. 4/12/1911 at 57/4/18; cancer of liver; married; b.
Tuftonboro; Richard B. Neal and Nancy Piper
Lillian P., d. 12/2/1966 at 61 in Wolfeboro; married; b. Sanbornville;
Edwin Livermore and Ellen McDonald
Lura M., d. 9/4/1938 at 68/7/1 in Tuftonboro; housewife; married; b.
Tuftonboro; George A. Hilton (Ossipee) and Susan A. Nutter
(Ossipee)

Mary A., d. 1/28/1894 at 81/6/18; housekeeper; widow; b.
Holderness; Solomon Jackson and ----- Morrill
Mary Ann, d. 1/16/1902 at 80/11/11 in Tuftonboro; apoplexy;
married; b. New Hampton; Ebenezer C. Gordon and Ruth Ladd
Royal Pierce, d. 7/6/1950 at 76/11/29 in Newton, MA; book dealer;
widower; b. Wolfeboro; George Young and ----- Tibbetts

ZINSER,
Mabel R., d. 8/10/1984 in Ossipee; William Heinze and Mary Ann
Baker

BROOKFIELD BIRTHS

ADJUTANT,
son, b. 7/17/1887; first; George E. Adjutant (farmer, 22, Tuftonboro) and Clara E. Eaton (27, Wolfeboro)

ALLEN,
daughter, b. 7/23/1888 in Brookfield; seventh; Samuel M. Allen (farmer & mason, Brookfield) and Emma F. Cummings (Brookfield)
son, b. 12/12/1890 in Brookfield; eighth; Samuel M. Allen (farmer and mason, 48, Brookfield) and Emma F. Cummings (38, Brookfield)
Samuel Mortimer, b. 3/23/1894 in Brookfield; eighth; Samuel M. Allen (mason, Brookfield) and Emma F. Cummings (Brookfield)

BAKER,
Marjorie Louise, b. 7/29/1915 in Brookfield; first; Christopher W. Baker (farmer, 38, NS) and Elaine Smith (26, Brookfield); residence - Westford, MA

BALSOR,
Esther M., b. 12/1/1924; fifth; Christopher Balsor (farmer) and Elaine F. Smith

BARNARD,
Emerson Scott, b. 5/6/2002; Bruce Barnard and Sandra Barnard

BARNES,
Katherine Vesta, b. 2/23/1926 in Brookfield; first; George W. Barnes (farmer, Raymond) and Nellie J. Stacy (Raymond)

BECKWITH,
Sarah Louise, b. 7/1/1980; William Henry Beckwith and Dawn Marie Hanson

BELKNAP,
Debra Ann, b. 9/6/1955 in Wolfeboro; second; James Lyman Belknap (farmer, 43, Boston, MA) and Mary Frances Witham (34, Brookfield)
Marsha J., b. 4/11/1953 in Wolfeboro; first; James L. Belknap (farmer, MA) and Frances Witham (Brookfield)

BLAIR,

Rebecca Sue, b. 8/12/1981; Christopher S. Blair and Susan Ann
 Nordberg

Scott Robert, b. 3/22/1983; Christopher S. Blair and Susan Ann
 Nordberg

Shawn Christopher, b. 1/1/1980; Christopher Seeking Blair and
 Susan Ann Nordberg

BOSTON,

son, b. 12/14/1888 in Brookfield; sixth; Henry Boston (farmer,
 Littleton, VT) and Susan A. Drew (Brookfield)

daughter, b. 8/10/1893 in Brookfield; Henry Boston (farmer, Littleton)
 and Susan Drew (Brookfield)

BRADY,

Earl Winfield, b. 9/17/1992; Christopher Michael Brady and Joyce
 Allison DeBow

BROOKS,

Caitlyn Elizabeth Negent, b. 9/17/1993; John Arthur Brooks and
 Janice E. N. Newgent

BROWN,

daughter, b. 9/7/1887; third; Langdon D. Brown (clerk, 35,
 Northwood) and Effie Drew (33, Brookfield)

daughter, b. 11/2/1891; fourth; Langdon D. Brown (clerk,
 Northwood) and Alfaretta Drew (Brookfield)

daughter, b. 5/27/1893 in Brookfield; Langdon D. Brown (clerk,
 Northwood) and Alfacetia Drew (Brookfield)

stillborn son, b. 1/4/1900 in Brookfield; Langdon D. Brown (farmer,
 48, Northwood) and Alfretta Drew (45, Brookfield)

Dana Lauren, b. 6/10/1974; Peter G. Brown and Lauren Ann
 Cormier

Mary Ellen, b. 5/15/1897 in Brookfield; Langdon Brown (laborer, 47,
 Northwood) and Alfretta Drew (43, Brookfield)

Peter Gudmund, Jr., b. 8/27/1975; Peter Gudmund Brown, Sr. and
 Lauren Ann Cormier

BURROUGHS,

Alice Gertrude, b. 7/18/1918 in Brookfield; fourth; Howard W.
 Burroughs (farmer, Brookfield) and Mercy Kimball (Wolfeboro)

Wilbur, b. 4/23/1915 in Brookfield; fifth; Howard W. Burroughs
   (farmer, 57, Brookfield) and Mercy Kimball (32, Wolfeboro)

BURROWS,
son, b. 7/14/1905 in Brookfield; fifth; Howard B. Burrows (farmer, 45,
   Brookfield) and Mercy M. Kimball (29, Wolfeboro)
Benjamin Steven, b. 2/4/1995; Steven Richard Burrows and Karen
   Taatjes
Kalee Elizabeth, b. 4/8/1991; Steven Richard Burrows and Karen
   Taatjes

CADDELL,
Ashley Christine, b. 11/1/1991; Mark Edwin Caddell and Beth Ann
   Foster
Courtney Elizabeth, b. 6/27/1995; Mark Edwin Caddell and Beth Ann
   Foster

CAMPBELL,
daughter, b. 2/25/1903 in Brookfield; Walter Campbell (laborer, 20,
   Wolfeboro) and Carrie M. Ellis (17, Strafford)
daughter, b. 6/10/1906 in Brookfield; third; Walter F. Campbell
   (farmer, 23, Wolfeboro) and Carrie M. Ellis (20, Strafford)
Forest F., b. 4/7/1904 in Brookfield; second; Walter F. Campbell
   (laborer, 21, Wolfeboro) and Carrie M. Ellis (18, Strafford)
Ivory Ruthven, b. 5/12/1899 in Brookfield; Elbert R. Campbell
   (carpenter, 37, Milan, VT) and Luella M. Davis (35, Lyman, ME)

CAPPELL,
stillborn daughter, b. 8/22/1908 in Brookfield; first; Frank Cappell
   (broker, 36, Keene) and Caroline Hill (27, Brookline); residence
   - Keene

CATE,
son, b. 7/2/1891; first; Harry W. Cate (farmer, Brookfield) and -----
   (LA)
daughter, b. 10/6/1892; second; Harry W. Cate (farmer, Brookfield)
   and Amy Bagniz (LA)
daughter, b. 4/7/1894 in Brookfield; third; Harry W. Cate (farmer,
   Brookfield) and Amy Beaugez (Bayou La Fourche, LA)
son, b. 7/27/1895 in Brookfield; fourth; Harry W. Cate (farmer, 35,
   Brookfield) and Amy Beauyez (25, Bayou La Fourche, LA)

son, b. 6/15/1898 in Brookfield; Harry W. Cate (farmer, 38, Brookfield) and Annie Beangez (38, LA)
daughter, b. 11/17/1900 in Brookfield; seventh; Harry W. Cate (farmer, 41, Brookfield) and Annie Beaugez (41, LA)
stillborn daughter, b. 1/16/1932 in Brookfield; first; Norris E. Cate (carpenter, Brookfield) and Irene L. Cotton (Wolfeboro)
Claire Elaine, b. 1/2/1940 in Wolfeboro; third; Herbert H. Cate (agent, Gonic) and M. Olive Fogg (Ossipee)
Mary Louise, b. 10/12/1934 in Wolfeboro; first; Herbert H. Cate (painter, Gonic) and Mabelle O. Fogg (Ossipee)
Roberta Evelyn, b. 5/27/1927 in Brookfield; fifth; Raymond M. Cate (farmer, Brookfield) and Myrtie D. Libby (Gray, ME)

CEFALO,
Alexander James, b. 1/27/1986; Gregory Norman Cefalo and Carolyn Elizabeth Cossette

CERRONE,
Elijah Matthew, b. 11/13/2005; Bernard Cerrone and Zina Bernard
Rebecca Ann, b. 10/10/2001; Bernard Cerrone and Zina Cerrone

CHAMBERLAIN,
son, b. 7/24/1890 in Brookfield; third; Robert L. Chamberlain (farmer, 29, New Bedford, MA) and Gertrude L. Hanson (30, Brookfield)
Ashton B., b. 4/2/1888 in Brookfield; second; Robert L. Chamberlain (farmer, New Bedford, MA) and Gertrude L. Hanson (Brookfield)
Hazel Mary, b. 12/16/1893 in Brookfield; Robert L. Chamberlain (farmer, New Bedford, MA) and Gertrude L. Hanson (Brookfield)

CHRYSAFIDIS,
Mark Paul, b. 8/15/1998; Paul Chrysafidis and Debrah Janet Farmer

CHURCHILL,
daughter, b. 10/21/1893 in Brookfield; Charles I. Churchill (farmer, Brookfield) and Amanas E. Place (Middleton)
stillborn son, b. 6/6/1895 in Brookfield; second; Charles I. Churchill (meat merchant, 26, Brookfield) and Amanda E. Place (21, Middleton)

stillborn son, b. 3/3/1902 in Brookfield; Lester L. Churchill (meat
    dealer, 42, Brookfield) and Hattie B. Ferguson (45, Brookfield)
daughter, b. 6/10/1906 in Brookfield; second; Charles I. Churchill
    (horse trainer, 37, Brookfield) and Ethel G. Burhoe (21,
    Marlboro, MA)
Amey Lynn, b. 8/25/1943 in Brookfield; fifth; Frederick W. Churchill
    (farmer, 38, Marlboro, MA) and Amey T. Spencer (40,
    Providence, RI)
Freeman Richard, b. 8/5/1940 in Brookfield; fourth; Frederick W.
    Churchill (farmer, Marlboro, MA) and Amey Tucker Spencer
    (Providence, RI)
James Wilton, b. 4/2/1938 in Brookfield; third; Frederick W. Churchill
    (farmer, Marlborough, MA) and Amey Tucker Spencer
    (Providence, RI)
Judith Lindsey, b. 10/25/1936 in Brookfield; second; Frederick Wills
    Churchill (farmer, Marlboro, MA) and Amey Spencer
    (Providence, RI)
Randolph E., b. 11/9/1907 in Brookfield; first; Guy L. Churchill
    (laborer, 22, Brookfield) and Alice M. Emerson (28, Stowe, ME)
Ruth V., b. 5/19/1924; third; Charles L. Churchill (farmer) and Ethel
    G. Burhoe

CILLEY,
Elsie M., b. 3/19/1901 in Brookfield; Anthony Cilley (farmer, 62,
    Plymouth) and Rosetta Foss (36, Stowe, ME)
James Anthony, b. 12/14/1892; second; Anthony Cilley (farmer,
    Plymouth) and Rosetta Foss (Stowe, ME)
Mattie A., b. 4/28/1896 in Brookfield; third; Anthony Cilley (farmer,
    57, Plymouth) and Rozetta Foss (32, Stowe, ME)

CLARK,
Doris Agnes, b. 11/16/1912 in Brookfield; third; James Edward Clark
    (farmer, 43, Tuftonboro) and Martha N. Hoyt (22, Rochester)
Edith Lillian, b. 11/15/1909 in Brookfield; first; James E. Clark
    (farmer, 39, Tuftonboro) and Martha A. Hoyt (19, Rochester)
Ella Fay, b. 10/16/1920; sixth; James E. Clark (farmer, 52,
    Tuftonboro) and Martha A. Hoyt (30, Rochester)
James Edwin, b. 6/6/1914 in Brookfield; fourth; James E. Clark
    (farmer, 44, Brookfield) and Martha A. Hoyt (23, Rochester)
Katherine, b. 1/7/1924; seventh; James E. Clark (farmer) and
    Martha Hoyt

Nellie Marcia, b. 4/1/1911 in Brookfield; second; James E. Clark
(farmer, 42, Tuftonboro) and Martha N. Hoyt (21, Rochester)
Wilbur Arthur, b. 10/21/1917 in Brookfield; fifth; James E. Clark
(farmer, 48, Tuftonboro) and Maith A. Hoyt (27, Rochester)

CLINE,
Bryce Anthony, b. 9/9/2002; James Cline and Danielle Cline
James Gordon, b. 6/7/2001; James Cline and Danielle Cline

COLE,
Tarah Laurence, b. 2/26/1988; Bradley Alan Cole and Melody Lynn
Green
Tyler Daniel, b. 6/14/1986; Bradley Alan Cole and Melody Lynn
Green

COLLIGAN,
Cortney Ann, b. 5/3/1988; Terrance Michael Colligan and Diane
Marie Fay

COLMAN,
Charles Wilson, b. 9/22/1909 in Brookfield; first; Wilson Colman
(farmer, 37, Brookfield) and Helen P. Chamberlain (23,
Brookfield)
Dorothy Gertrude, b. 6/2/1912 in Brookfield; second; Wilson Colman
(farmer, 39, Brookfield) and Helen Chamberlain (26, Brookfield)
Frances Margaret, b. 4/18/1920; third; Wilson Colman (cattle dealer,
47, Brookfield) and Helene P. Chamberlain (35, Brookfield)

CONSTANTINE,
Benjamin Robert, b. 3/6/1989; Robert Lewis Constantine and Valerie
Jean Hensel
Brady Lewis, b. 12/5/1994; Robert Lewis Constantine and Valerie
Jean Hensel

COOK,
daughter, b. 9/13/1887; first; Frank E. Cook (shoemaker, 22, Milton)
and Ida C. Hatch (16, Wolfeboro)
Joseph Lincoln, b. 9/10/1911 in Brookfield; first; James L. Cook
(farmer, 44, Brookfield) and Ida F. Richards (38, Wakefield)

COONS,
Bradley Daniel, b. 2/26/1987; Daniel Edgar Coons and Melinda June
Clay

COPP,
Gerald LeRoy, b. 3/5/1914 in Brookfield; second; Roy Copp (laborer,
23, Bangor, ME) and Rena B. Bean (21, Ossipee)

COTTON,
son, b. 7/19/1908 in Brookfield; fourth; Charles S. Cotton (farmer,
47, Wolfeboro) and Emma S. Nute (36, Wolfeboro)
Hazel Hattie, b. 7/21/1913 in Brookfield; fourth; John Cotton
(carpenter, 32, Wolfeboro) and Leona Neal (27, Brookfield)
Henry J., b. 5/31/1921 in Brookfield; fifth; John A. Cotton (farmer,
Wolfeboro) and May Neal (Brookfield)
James Almond, b. 12/9/1946 in Brookfield; second; Charles A.
Cotton (carpenter, Brookfield) and Mary A. Borsey (Stamford,
CT)
M. H. [male], b. 11/25/1948 in Wolfeboro; third; Charles A. Cotton
(carpenter, Brookfield) and Mary A. Borsey (Stanford, CT)

CROOK,
Robert Arthur, b. 7/31/1986; Lawrence Edward Crook, Jr. and
Pamela Marie Jones

CURTS,
daughter, b. 7/26/1890 in Brookfield; second; Joseph S. Curts
(farmer, 33, Brookfield) and Fannie E. Butler (28, Milton)

DAGGETT,
Andrea Hope, b. 10/16/2005; Andrew Daggett and Erin Daggett
Audrey Faith, b. 2/15/2004; Andrew Dagget and Erin Dagget
Autumn Grace, b. 9/2/1999; Andrew Daggett and Erin Daggett

DAMBERG-MAUSER,
Caitland Elizabeth, b. 6/20/1983; Richard A. Mauser and Susan N.
Damberg
Rebecca Anne, b. 5/6/1986; Richard Arthur Mauser and Susan
Marcia Damberg

DANSEREAU,

Jesse Alan, b. 10/10/1996; John Douglas Dansereau and Susan Marie Guilmette

Jordan Douglas, b. 12/21/1994; John Douglas Dansereau and Susan Marie Guilmette

Sabrina Marie, b. 7/31/1999; John Dansereau and Susan Dansereau

DAVIS,

Jessica, b. 9/24/1982; Kenneth William Davis and Carolyn Elizabeth Cossette

DAY,

Frances May, b. 6/1/1911 in Brookfield; second; Alden B. Day (laborer, 23, Newfield, ME) and Sarah Allen (23, Brookfield)

Marion Louisa, b. 11/8/1912 in Brookfield; third; Alden P. Day (teamster, 25, Newfield, ME) and Sarah Allen (24, Brookfield); residence - Keene

DEBOW,

Brenda Doreen, b. 9/27/1971; Currie L. M. DeBow and Eleanor Sandra Linton

Christopher Anderson, b. 7/22/1965; Lawrence Wilmot DeBow and Rena Jo-Ann Stetson

Dwight Edward, b. 1/21/1967; Currie Lyndon Morley DeBow, Jr. and Eleanor Sandra Linton

Joyce Allison, b. 12/13/1969; Currie Lyndon M. DeBow, Jr. and Eleanor Sandra Linton

Pamela Jo-Ann, b. 9/27/1966; Lawrence Wilmot DeBow and Rena Jo-Ann Stetson

Paul Wesley, b. 10/20/1965; Currie L. M. DeBow, Jr. and Eleanor Sandra Linton

DENVER,

Jason Richard, b. 1/9/1981; Richard L. Denver and Cynthia Jean Crowe

Sara Jean, b. 9/18/1983; Richard L. Denver and Cynthia Jean Crowe

DEVRIES,
Carrie Elizabeth, b. 3/21/1985; Jack DeVries and Susan Elizabeth
  Long
Catharina Adele, b. 5/15/1989; Jack Devries and Susan Elizabeth
  Long
Nicole Christine, b. 12/22/1986; Jack DeVries and Susan Elizabeth
  Long

DIPRIZIO,
Curt Charles, b. 3/25/2001; Curt DiPrizio and Jamie DiPrizio

DODIER,
Earleen S., b. 4/28/1947 in Wolfeboro; first; Earl S. Dodier (laborer,
  Somerville, MA) and Mary E. Hannigan (Providence, RI)
Lenard Frank, b. 9/28/1951 in Wolfeboro; fourth; Frank R. Dodier
  (carpenter, Somerville, MA) and Ruth V. Churchill (Brookfield)
Pamela A., b. 6/2/1947 in Wolfeboro; second; Frank R. Dodier (road
  agent, Somerville, MA) and Ruth V. Churchill (Brookfield)
Terry Edith, b. 6/18/1949 in Wolfeboro; third; Frank R. Dodier
  (machinist, Somerville, MA) and Ruth V. Churchill (Brookfield)

DOE,
Steven Edwin, Jr., b. 1/29/1995; Steven Edwin Doe and Cindy Lou
  Holmes

DONNELLY,
Owen Joseph, b. 3/30/1990; Edward Charles Donnelly and Karen
  Ann Deluca
Samantha Capen, b. 1/18/1992; Edward C. Donnelly and Karen Ann
  Deluca

DOWNING,
son, b. 8/9/1893 in Brookfield; Henry E. Downing (painter, Eliot, ME)
  and Maude Etta Moran (Portsmouth)

DRAPEAU,
Marie, b. 3/6/1916 in Brookfield; sixth; George J. Drapeau (laborer,
  27, Wakefield) and Lucy Houde (31, Wakefield)

DREW,

son, b. 5/17/1888 in Brookfield; seventh; Henry Drew (farmer, Brookfield) and Emeline Dyer (Brownfield, ME)

son, b. 2/29/1896 in Brookfield; ninth; Henry W. Drew (farmer, 60, Brookfield) and Emeline Dyer (46, Brownfield, ME)

Christine Elizabeth, b. 2/17/1919; fifth; John E. Drew (laborer, 34, Brookfield) and Elizabeth E. Foss (33, Farmington)

Corrine Elizabeth, b. 8/12/1938 in Wolfeboro; second; Arthur F. Wilkins (truck driver, Acton, ME) and Christine E. Drew (Brookfield)

Florence Ellen, b. 11/22/1915 in Brookfield; fourth; John E. Drew (laborer, 32, Wakefield) and Lizzie E. Foss (29, Farmington)

Forrest Warren, b. 3/3/1936 in Brookfield; first; Harold Barratt and Christina E. Drew (Brookfield)

Fred Lloyd, b. 1/17/1908 in Brookfield; first; John E. Drew (laborer, 23, Wakefield) and Lizzie E. Foss (21, Farmington)

Madeline Luella, b. 7/25/1910 in Brookfield; second; John E. Drew (laborer, 25, Wakefield) and Lizzie E. Foss (24, Farmington)

Mary Louisa, b. 8/4/1912 in Brookfield; third; John Edward Drew (laborer, 27, Wakefield) and Lizzie E. Foss (26, Farmington)

Maurice Warren, b. 2/11/1921 in Brookfield; sixth; John E. Drew (laborer, Wakefield) and Elizabeth E. Drew (Farmington)

DRUGG,

Meghan Eileen, b. 10/26/1985; Charles Scott Drugg and Patricia Ann Hogan

EAGLE,

Jonathan K., b. 4/4/1959; Thomas Eagle, Jr. and Joanne Richter

EASTMAN,

daughter, b. 11/19/1887; first; J. Frank Eastman (shoemaker, 35, Dover) and Marcia L. Brown (25, Conway); residence - Dover

EATON,

Forest M., b. 11/25/1903 in Brookfield; Martin H. Eaton (farmer, 25, Brookfield) and Florence L. Elkins (23, Stowe, ME)

EISCHEN,

Joseph William, b. 3/25/2003; Joseph Eischen and Rebecca Eischen

ELDRIDGE,
Ernest Roy, b. 8/10/1946 in Wolfeboro; first; Roy E. Eldridge
(lumberjack, Effingham) and Lillian A. Dore (Wolfeboro)

ELLIOTT,
Catherine Jannette, b. 3/16/1955 in Wolfeboro; second; Edward R.
Elliott, Jr. (asst. elec. eng'r, 29, MA) and Gertrude W. Murdock
(30, MA)
Charles Henry, b. 7/12/1922 in Brookfield; first; Henry F. Smith
(alleged) (teamster, Rollinsford) and Ruth May Elliott (Exeter);
residence of alleged father - Dover
Elizabeth Ann, b. 3/19/1965; Edward Roland Elliott and Gertrude
Weir Murdock
Pamela May, b. 6/18/1956; Edward Roland Elliott and Gertrude
Murdock

ERNEST,
Benjamin Stanley, b. 8/18/2003; Brian Ernest and Brandy Ernest

FENTON,
Michael Richards, b. 10/13/1997; Kyle Dixon Fenton and Theresa
Lyn Care

FERGUSON,
Anne Greenleaf, b. 3/25/1951 in Wolfeboro; fourth; Malcolm M.
Ferguson (book salesman, Arlington, MA) and Priscilla L.
Taylor (Boston, MA)
Elizabeth L., b. 2/18/1950 in Wolfeboro; second; Malcolm M.
Ferguson (book seller, Arlington, MA) and Priscilla L. Taylor
(Boston, MA)
Grace T., b. 2/18/1950 in Wolfeboro; first; Malcolm M. Ferguson
(book seller, Arlington, MA) and Priscilla L. Taylor (Boston, MA)
S. T. [male], b. 2/19/1948 in Wolfeboro; first; M. M. Ferguson (book
seller, Arlington, MA) and Priscilla L. Taylor (Boston, MA)

FIFIELD,
Austin Timothy, b. 7/17/1997; Jason Alan Fifield and Sarah Jean
Wilkins
Lillian May, b. 2/26/1909 in Brookfield; first; Charles H. Fifield
(laborer, 30, Conway) and Agnes E. Pelton (35, Boston, MA)

FLETCHER,
Lauree, b. 4/29/1967; Melvin Ernest Fletcher and June Adams Tutt

FOGG,
Carolyn Phyllis, b. 5/6/1925; fourth; Austin F. Fogg (farmer) and
Ellen W. Sceggell
Harvey, b. 4/19/1906 in Brookfield; first; Leroy Harvey (shoemaker,
21, Dover) and Gertrude Fogg (17); residence of father - Dover

FOSTER,
Gregory David, b. 5/4/1992; David Arthur Foster and Lauren
Elizabeth Flood

FOTHERGILL,
Cory James, b. 5/22/1991; William James Fothergill and Chris Ann
Haley
Ryan William, b. 8/26/1992; William James Fothergill and Chris Ann
Haley

FREDERICKS,
Victoria Blair, b. 8/14/1985; William David Fredericks and Carol Lynn
Kirby

GANEM,
Jennifer Mary, b. 10/25/1967; Philip Joseph Ganem and Shirley
Helen Essa
Lawrence Philip, b. 1/7/1964; Philip Joseph Ganem and Shirley
Helen Essa

GARLAND,
daughter, b. 10/11/1902 in Brookfield; Fred Garland (laborer, 24,
Brookfield) and Hattie M. West (24, Brookfield)
daughter, b. 12/15/1903 in Brookfield; Fred Garland (laborer, 25,
Brookfield) and Hattie M. West (26, Brookfield)

GRIFFIN,
Matthew Michael, b. 10/6/1973; Michael Allen Griffin and Jane
Louise Hooper

HABRIAL,
Nathaniel Reece, b. 8/30/1999; Jansen Habriel and Debra Habriel

HACKETT,
Harry C., b. 9/5/1902 in Brookfield; Arthur S. Hackett (farmer, 31, Brookfield) and Florence M. Penty (30, Dartmouth, NS)
Phyllis Sophia, b. 9/6/1916 in Brookfield; first; Bert S. Hackett (farmer, 39, Brookfield) and Anna Schmidt (22, Kennebunkport, ME)

HAINES,
Benjamin Frank, b. 5/6/2003; Paul Haines and Patrice Haines
Joshua Emerson, b. 4/10/2001; Paul Haines and Patrice Haines

HALL,
James H., III, b. 3/4/1962; James H. Hall, Jr. and Joan M. Walsh
Jayme A., b. 3/4/1962; James H. Hall, Jr. and Joan M. Walsh

HANSEN,
Mary Ann, b. 8/8/1937 in Wolfeboro; first; Otto Hansen (laborer, Denmark) and Dorothy Bryant (Amesbury, MA)
Peter Christian, b. 11/9/1957; William Hansen and Fanny E. Fletcher

HANSON,
daughter, b. 1/3/1887; second; John F. Hanson (farmer, 25, Newburyport, MA) and Abbie M. Eaton (19, Wolfeboro)
daughter, b. 1/12/1890 in Brookfield; first; Sidney I. Hanson (brakeman, 25, Brookfield) and Mary F. Hanson (19, Brookfield)

HARDMAN,
Laurie Jean, b. 9/16/1967; Ross Martin Hardman and Edythe May Foley
Ross Martain, Jr., b. 12/19/1963; Ross Martain Hardman, Sr. and Edythe May Foley

HARMON,
son, b. 9/30/1888 in Brookfield; first; John M. Harmon (farmer, Freedom) and Sarah M. Eaton (Wolfeboro)
daughter, b. 10/27/1890 in Brookfield; second; John M. Harmon (farm laborer, 21, Freedom) and Sarah M. Eaton (26, Wolfeboro)
son, b. 7/27/1893 in Brookfield; John M. Harmon (farmer, Freedom) and Sarah M. Eaton (Wolfeboro)

daughter, b. 5/5/1896 in Brookfield; fourth; John M. Harmon (farmer, 26, Freedom) and Sarah M. Eaton (31, Wolfeboro)

HARTFORD,
son, b. 6/4/1908 in Brookfield; sixth; Clarence W. Hartford (farmer, 38, Deerfield) and Ardelia Thompson (35, Plaistow)

HAYNES,
daughter, b. 4/5/1918 in Brookfield; first; George R. Haynes (laborer, England) and Elsie M. Browne (England)

HEALD,
Robert Michael, b. 1/13/1967; James Albion Heald and Priscilla Drayton Lawrence

HELGERSON,
Meredith Brittany, b. 2/25/1987; Daniel Sangser Helgerson and Karen Jean Gaudet

HERBERT,
Cheyenne Nichole, b. 6/1/1987; Mark Stephen Herbert and Kimberly Robin McStay

HERRICK,
stillborn son, b. 1/20/1930 in Wolfeboro; first; George S. Herrick (farmer, Newfield, ME) and Nellie M. Clark (Brookfield)

HILL,
Josephine, b. 12/11/1912 in Brookfield; first; Herschel E. Hill (farmer, 26, Halifax, VT) and Florence Bell (30, Boston, MA)

HILTON,
Ora J., b. 3/22/1904 in Brookfield; first; John A. Hilton (electrician, 48, Newfields) and Grace M. Witham (30, Brookfield); residence - Plaistow

HODGDON,
Brett David, b. 11/12/1980; David Glenn Hodgdon and Janice Ann Copplestone

HOOPER,
Barbara May, b. 10/1/1932 in Brookfield; fifth; Jesse Hooper (farmer, Wakefield) and Annie May Clow (Wolfeboro)
Charles Rodney, b. 11/15/1956; Ralph E. Hooper and Arlene D. Haines
Doris Irene, b. 7/25/1925; second; Jesse Hooper (farmer) and Annie May Clow
Thomas M., b. 1/2/1947 in Wolfeboro; first; Ralph E. Hooper (mason's tender, Wolfeboro) and A. Dorothy Haines (Wolfeboro)
William Jesse, b. 3/16/1951 in Wolfeboro; second; Ralph E. Hooper (woodsman, Wolfeboro) and Arlene D. Haines (Wolfeboro)

HORNE,
Charles Hayden, b. 5/6/1895 in Brookfield; first; Rufus Horne (painter, 27, Wakefield) and Mary A. Cunniff (22, Chester, England)

HOWARD,
Syd James, b. 10/1/1982; Michael Lewis Howard and Cynthia Mae Rouleau

HOYT,
Barbara Frances, b. 10/7/1925; fourth; Percy Hoyt (farmer) and Frances Staniford

HUBBARD,
son, b. 5/18/1892; first; William H. Hubbard (mfg. lumber, Derry) and Ellen A. Goodhue (Brookfield)

HUGHES,
Ryan Scott, b. 7/10/1993; Raymond Scott Hughes and Holly Anne Climo
Stephen Vincent, IV, b. 8/7/1980; Stephen V. Hughes III and Linda Ann Therese Jasley
William Robert, b. 7/2/1991; Raymond Scott Hughes and Holly Ann Climo

HUTCHINS,
daughter, b. 8/9/1889; second; Stephen H. Hutchins (farmer, Wakefield) and Lizzie M. Wentworth (Wakefield)

son, b. 2/4/1896 in Brookfield; third; Stephen H. Hutchins (farmer, 44, Wakefield) and Lizzie M. Wentworth (32, Brookfield)
Caroline Betsey, b. 4/17/1922 in Brookfield; first; John L. Hutchins (farmer, Brookfield) and Alice A. Lyford (Cincinnati, OH)
John Baltimore, b. 3/5/1928 in Baltimore, MD; second; John L. Hutchins (farmer, Brookfield) and Alice A. Lyford (Cincinnati, OH)

IRVINE,
Joseph Michael, b. 9/2/1993; Joseph M. Irvine and Deborah R. Tanner

JACKMAN,
R. P. [male], b. 7/10/1948 in Wolfeboro; first; R. C. Jackman (salesman, Arlington, MA) and Norma E. Boyce (Cambridge, MA)

JACOBSON,
Laura Jane, b. 3/21/1989; Anders Shaw Jacobson and Nancy Erikson

KATWICK,
James Peter, b. 11/21/1964; Robert Tilden Katwick, Jr. and Gloria Doris Adjutant
Linda Jean, b. 3/7/1962; R. T. Katwick, Jr. and Gloria D. Adjutant

KELLY,
Tarynn Elizabeth, b. 7/1/2005; William Kelly and Elizabeth Johnson

KINVILLE,
Caleb Reed, b. 5/24/2000; Christopher Kinville and Kate Kinville
Calvin Rie, b. 8/29/2002; Christopher Kinville and Kate Kinville
Jennifer Lee, b. 12/12/1982; Richard Nelson Kinville and Gloria Carol Stephens

KNAPP,
Beverly Vaugh, b. 6/9/1922 in Wolfeboro; third; Arthur Knapp (farmer, Orange, MA) and Delsie Van Horne (KS)

KRAINCHICH,
Elizabeth Diane, b. 8/6/1989; Vladimir D. Krainchich and Elizabeth
  Hope Glum

LAMPSON,
Joseph Alcide, b. 1/4/1910 in Brookfield; tenth; Severance Lampson
  (laborer, 44, Canada) and Marie Tutras (38, Canada)

LANG,
son, b. 5/11/1888 in Brookfield; first; John E. Lang (farmer,
  Brookfield) and Lizzie Palmer (Stoneham, MA)
Gordon Wheeler, b. 8/19/1935 in Wolfeboro; first; Joseph W. Lang
  (machinist, Brookfield) and Katherine E. Wheeler (Parsonsfield,
  ME)
Joseph Wallace, b. 11/18/1909 in Brookfield; first; Wallace F. Lang
  (farmer, 21, Brookfield) and Abbie Cotton (23, Wolfeboro)
Reuben Payson, b. 7/2/1893 in Brookfield; John E. Lang (farmer,
  Brookfield) and Lizzie Palmer (Stoneham, MA)

LEE,
Sarah Lynne, b. 9/10/1977; Robert Edward Lee, Jr. and Judith
  Elaine Glidden

LEIGHTON,
daughter, b. 9/14/1896 in Brookfield; first; George Leighton (laborer,
  30, Dover) and Ethel Churchill (17, NS)
Una Catherine, b. 7/10/1902 in Brookfield; E. F. Leighton (laborer,
  28, Salem, MA) and Mary Field (26, Houlton, ME); residence -
  Salem, MA

LEONARD,
Amanda Marylyn, b. 5/2/1999; William Leonard and Lisa Leonard
Robert Harlan, b. 11/11/1990; William Earle Leonard and Lisa Lynn
  Sewall

LEVINE,
Daniel Richard, b. 4/11/1982; Robert Charles Levine and Kristine
  Elizabeth Johnson
Kathryn Grace, b. 7/3/1984; Robert Charles Levine and Kristine
  Elizabeth Johnson

LINEHAM,
David Edward, b. 9/20/1988; David Alan Lineham and Helen
    Elizabeth Duchano
Haley D., b. 8/16/1993; John Robert Lineham and Kimberly Osborne
Morgan Datson, b. 10/25/1991; John Robert Lineham and Kimberly
    Rae Osborne

LOUGEE,
Jacqueline Ann, b. 10/26/1969; Philip Winslow Lougee and Marjorie
    Fessie Labor

LYON,
Victoria Davis, b. 4/15/1971; Peter Byrd Lyon and Sandra Davis

LYONS,
Pamela Judith, b. 7/23/1952 in Wolfeboro; first; Edward P. Lyons
    (student, LI, NY) and Nancy S. Churchill (Salem, VA)

MACBRIEN,
Bruce A., Jr., b. 7/21/1963; Bruce A. MacBrien and Cynthia H.
    Adjutant
Wayne Neal, b. 9/19/1964; Bruce A. MacBrien and Cynthia H.
    Adjutant

MACDONALD,
Sara Lucille, b. 7/15/1983; Russell T. MacDonald, Jr. and Jo Anne
    Marie Ricci
Suzanne Marie, b. 7/15/1983; Russell T. MacDonald, Jr. and Jo
    Anne Marie Ricci

MACE,
Pamela G., b. 10/9/1958; Donald Mace and Jane Keating
Richard Charles, b. 8/23/1956; Donald H. Mace and Jane E. Keating

MAGGY,
Jacob Edmund, b. 7/9/1997; Darrin William Maggy and Melissa Ann
    Young

MARSH,
Elizabeth Joanna, b. 8/30/2002; William Marsh and Stefanie Marsh
Samual Alfred, b. 9/17/1999; William Marsh and Stefanie Marsh

MARTIKKE,
Erika Jean, b. 2/13/1977; Erwin John Martikke, Jr. and Vera Louise
Bouffard
Lauren Jean, b. 3/12/1975; Erwin John Martikke, Jr. and Vera
Louise Bouffard

MARTIN,
son, b. 2/6/1905 in Brookfield; first; Frank Martin (laborer, 24, N.
Wakefield) and Charlotte Fogg (17, Worcester, MA); residence
- N. Wakefield
Aiden Rhys, b. 5/3/2003; David Martin and Nicole Martin

McBRIEN,
Robert Wayne, b. 12/4/1946 in Brookfield; fourth; Philip J. McBrien
(wood chopper, Lynn, MA) and Mabel F. Harmon (Ossipee)

McGEE,
Hudson Riley, b. 12/14/2004; Michael McGee and Teresa McGee

MEADER,
son, b. 9/21/1908 in Brookfield; third; Lyman Meader (farmer) and
Meda Hall

MELANSON,
daughter, b. 7/13/1929 in Brookfield; fourth; Carroll Melanson
(chauffeur, Canaan) and Hazel Sibley (Lynn, MA)
Carroll Omar, b. 3/10/1926 in Brookfield; second; Carroll T.
Melanson (laborer, Canaan) and Hazel R. Sibley (Lynn, MA)
Jeane E., b. 12/20/1924; first; Carroll T. Melanson (teamster) and
Hazel R. Sibley
Lawrence Ernest, b. 5/21/1927 in Brookfield; third; Carroll T.
Melanson (farmer, Canaan) and Hazel Sibley (Lynn, MA)

MEROSKI,
Natasha Lynn, b. 9/17/1980; Robert Stanley Meroski and Charlene
Ann Cotton

MOORE,
Daniel Gary, b. 1/2/2001; Michael Moore and Judith Moore

MORRILL,

son, b. 8/13/1932 in Brookfield; sixth; Harry W. Morrill (laborer, N. Windham, ME) and Phyllis M. Grant (Acton, ME)

Colleen Jane, b. 12/6/1933 in Brookfield; seventh; Harry W. Morrill (farmer, N. Windham, ME) and Phyllis Grant (Acton, ME)

Miriam Louise, b. 5/4/1936 in Brookfield; eighth; Harry Morrill (farmer, N. Windham, ME) and Phyllis Grant (Acton, ME)

NASON,

daughter, b. 5/28/1905 in Brookfield; second; Almon L. Nason (laborer, 26, Bridgeton, ME) and Nancy J. Streader (20, Sanbornville)

Deborah Lee, b. 8/28/1957; Robert F. Nason and Loraine E. Wilson

Gabriel Joseph, b. 12/9/2000; Edward Nason and Tina Nason

Katherine Elizabeth, b. 2/10/2003; Edward Nason and Tina Nason

Madeline Faith, b. 7/26/2004; Edward Nason and Tina Nason

NEAL,

son, b. 10/9/1888 in Brookfield; second; Charles H. Neal (farmer, Brookfield) and Ida F. Rankin (Lewiston, ME)

NELSON,

Laura Ann, b. 9/15/1959; Rufus Nelson, Jr. and Cynthia Knight

O'NEILL,

Shelley Francis, b. 4/6/1990; Daniel Ramsdell O'Neill and Louise Ann LaPrise

OSBORNE,

Abigail Patricia Lewis, b. 4/6/1995; Kenneth Bruce Osborne and Molly Patricia Lewis

OTIS,

Lindsey Erin, b. 3/18/2005; Michael Otis and Jana Otis

OUELLETTE,

Janet Martha, b. 1/24/1936 in Rochester; first; Roland Ouellette (caretaker, Sanbornville) and Winona Karcher (Effingham)

PAPPAS,
David Andrew, Jr., b. 5/20/1991; David Andrew Pappas and Gwen Marie Lancey

PATRIQUIN,
Christopher Neil, b. 10/20/1984; Stephen Charles Patriquin and Gail Ann Parsons
Hillary Maxwell, b. 3/16/1982; Stephen Charles Patriquin and Gail Parsons

PEAVEY,
daughter, b. 2/8/1905 in Brookfield; second; Henry W. Peavey (farmer, 58, Strafford) and A. Mary Walton (32, NS)

PENNELL,
Reginald Elden, b. 3/22/1938 in Brookfield; Edward A. Pennell (trackman, Tamworth) and Dora L. Williams (Tamworth); residence - Tamworth

PERREAULT,
Ryan Richard, b. 5/25/1978; Richard George Perreault and Diane Marie Leclerc

PERRY,
Everett G., b. 7/31/1896 in Brookfield; first; John Perry (farmer, 21, Wolfeboro) and Lena Eaton (19, Dover)
Katelyn Ann, b. 3/26/1986; Francis Frederick Perry, Jr. and Cheryl Ann Conner

PETTIT,
Dustin Wayne, b. 5/13/1978; Russell W. Pettit and Kathy J. Buttrick
Irena Marie, b. 9/9/2003; Dustin Pettit and Jacqueline Pettit

PHINNEY,
Ashley Rose, b. 1/5/1987; Charles Douglas Phinney and Tammy Lynn Nason
Charles Douglas, Jr., b. 3/7/1990; Charles Douglas Phinney and Tammy Lynn Nason

PIKE,
stillborn son, b. 7/21/1892; fourth; Caleb H. Pike (laborer, Ossipee) and Lydia E. Clow (Wolfeboro)
son, b. 10/2/1902 in Brookfield; Caleb H. Pike (farmer, 46, Ossipee) and Lydia E. Clow (41, Wolfeboro)
Arthur G., b. 1/13/1894 in Brookfield; Caleb H. Pike (farmer, Ossipee) and Lydia E. Clow (Wolfeboro)

PLACE,
Kyle Derek, b. 10/21/2004; Derek Place and Karon Place

PLUMMER,
Bernard F., b. 2/29/1924; second; John C. Plummer (farmer) and Mary A. Woodman

PULSIVER,
stillborn daughter, b. 8/13/1908 in Brookfield; first; William Pulsiver (farmer, 42, Milton) and Cora E. Boston (32, Farmington); residence - Milton

RAWSKI,
Harley Anna, b. 8/13/2004; Dereck Rawski and Michelle Rawski

REMICK,
daughter, b. 2/24/1898 in Brookfield; Henry J. Remick (stone mason, 30, Brookfield) and Sarah M. Moore (21, Berwick, ME)

RINES,
son, b. 8/22/1888 in Brookfield; fifth; Elihu Rines (farmer, New Durham) and Mary E. Stevens (Middleton)
daughter, b. 5/29/1901 in Brookfield; Elisha M. Rines (farmer, 49, New Durham) and Mary E. Dearborn (40)
Philip Henry, b. 2/16/1920; first; Walter F. Rines (farmer, Brookfield) and Grace N. Spiller (Ossipee)

RINGER,
Kenneth C., III, b. 6/22/1960; Kenneth C. Ringer and Jeanne A. Morgan

ROULEAU,
Amy Yvonne, b. 4/26/1975; Samuel Joseph Rouleau, Jr. and
Barbara Mae Herrick
Cy Matthew, b. 3/8/1973; Samuel J. Rouleau, Jr. and Barbara Mae
Herrick
Cynthia Mae, b. 8/6/1957; Samuel J. Rouleau and Barbara Herrick
Linda E., b. 8/13/1958; Samuel Rouleau and Barbara Herrick
Syd J., b. 9/8/1959; Samuel Rouleau, Jr. and Barbara Herrick

ROUSSEAU,
Brent Eric, b. 9/11/1977; Charles John Rousseau and Paula Tressie
Walker
Brian Marc, b. 9/11/1977; Charles John Rousseau and Paula
Tressie Walker

SANBORN,
daughter, b. 8/29/1890 in Brookfield; third; Charles H. Sanborn
(farmer, 33, Newfield, ME) and Ada Brackett (21, Wakefield)

SAUJON,
Crystal Lee, b. 3/27/1981; Royce Saujon II and Frances Weinroth

SCEGGEL,
Ellen Wentworth, b. 9/2/1899 in Brookfield; Arthur L. Sceggel
(farmer, 30, Wolfeboro) and Emma O. Wentworth (28,
Brookfield)
Roland Joseph, b. 9/13/1905 in Brookfield; second; Arthur L.
Sceggel (farmer, 36, Wolfeboro) and Emma O. Wentworth (34,
Brookfield)

SEAMAN,
Mary Katharine, b. 7/28/1988; Robert Anthony Seaman and
Kathleen Mary Polchowski

SHORTRIDGE,
daughter, b. 1/16/1898 in Brookfield; Albert S. Shortridge (farmer,
21, Brookfield) and Grace M. Stevens (21, Dover)
Albert Richard, b. 9/25/1931 in Portsmouth; first; Ralph S. Shortridge
(carpenter, Brookfield) and Ella Gillespie (Portsmouth)
James Robert, b. 7/7/1935 in Rochester; second; Ralph Shortridge
(painter, Brookfield) and Ella Gillespie (Portsmouth)

Ralph Stevens, b. 7/4/1904 in Brookfield; second; Albert S. Shortridge (farmer, 28, Dover) and Grace M. Stevens (28, Dover)

SKEHAN,
Timothy Michael, b. 1/21/1976; James Peter Skehan and Ann Isabel Popolski

SMITH,
daughter, b. 6/29/1889; first; Charles R. Smith (laborer, Bigby, NS) and Ida Foss (Stowe, ME)
daughter, b. 2/19/1895 in Brookfield; third; Charles R. Smith (farmer, NS) and Ida Foss (Stowe, ME)
daughter, b. 12/10/1896 in Brookfield; fourth; Charles R. Smith (laborer, 37, NS) and Ida Foss (35, Stowe, ME)
Marion Pinkham, b. 11/8/1946 in Wolfeboro; second; Pinkham Smith (Lt. Col., USAAC, Pelham, NY) and Cornelia Hoge (Norfolk, VA)

SONRICKER,
Kelly Nicole, b. 6/22/1998; Robert Laverne Sonricker and Jennifer Ann Jackson

SOUCY,
Anne Elizabeth, b. 4/1/1952 in Wolfeboro; first; Armand J. Soucy (blacksmith, Wakefield) and Louise L. Swinerton (Wakefield)
David Richard, b. 6/8/1954 in Wolfeboro; fourth; Armond J. Soucy (sandblaster, Rochester) and Louise L. Swinerton (Sanbornville)
Gloria Marie, b. 9/28/1956; Armond J. Soucy and Louise Swinerton
James C., b. 1/17/1962; Armond J. Soucy and Louise Swinerton
John Michael, b. 5/19/1955 in Wolfeboro; fifth; Armand Joseph Soucy (sandblaster, 26, Rochester) and Louise Laura Swinerton (23, Sanbornville)
Joseph A., b. 4/11/1953 in Wolfeboro; third; Armand J. Soucy (blacksmith, Wakefield) and Louise L. Swinerton (Wakefield)
Mark F., b. 3/3/1958; Armond Soucy and Louise Swinerton
Mary A. E., b. 10/21/1924; second; Alfonse J. Soucy (laborer) and Rossanna Lavertu; residence - Sanbornville
Therese C., b. 3/20/1960; Armond J. Soucy and Louise Swinerton
Thomas S., b. 3/12/1959; Armand Soucy and Louise Swinerton

SPINNEY,
Nathalie Ann, b. 8/13/1934 in Rochester; third; Ernest Spinney (poultryman, Kittery, ME) and Ida L. Cotton (Wolfeboro)

STEVENS,
daughter, b. 1/10/1887; third; Warren J. Stevens (farmer, 30, Waterville, ME) and Laura E. Eaton (25, Wolfeboro)
daughter, b. 11/18/1890 in Brookfield; fifth; Warren J. Stevens (farm laborer, 34, Waterville, ME) and Laura J. Stevens (29, Wolfeboro)

STEVENSON,
Pauline L., b. 6/26/1918 in Brookfield; first; Robert L. Stevenson (shoe maker, Glasgow, MA) and Gertrude V. Fogg (Ossipee)

STURTEVANT,
Dorothy Anita, b. 2/18/1931 in Brookfield; third; Leon H. Sturtevant (farmer, Hardwich, MA) and Jessie F. MacIntosh (S. Boston, MA)

TAATJES,
Tristan Scott, b. 5/10/2005; Brian Taatjes and Stacy Taatjes

TASKER,
Dale Howard, b. 6/1/1956; F. Bruce Tasker and Gladys E. Farris

THOMES,
Annie M., b. 1/8/1895 in Brookfield; Horace L. Thomes (farmer, Denmark, ME) and Hattie M. Goodhue (Brookfield)
Lawrence G., b. 7/5/1896 in Brookfield; second; Horace L. Thomes (farmer, 32, Denmark, ME) and Hattie M. Goodhue (26, Brookfield)

THOMPSON,
Evan Robert, b. 11/12/1975; Denis Ross Thompson and Monika Martini

TIBBETTS,
Dorothy Louise, b. 8/7/1901 in Brookfield; Everett J. Tibbetts (farmer, 30, Brookfield) and Susie L. Weeks (25, Wakefield)

Lewis E., b. 10/25/1903 in Brookfield; Everett J. Tibbetts (farmer, 32, Brookfield) and Susie L. Weeks (27, Wakefield)

TOWLE,
son, b. 4/23/1905 in Brookfield; fourth; Milton S. Towle (farmer, 36, Eaton) and Mary L. Wentworth (26, Ossipee); residence - Eaton
Daniel M., b. 8/15/1900 in Brookfield; second; Milton Towle (laborer, 31, Eaton) and Mary L. Wentworth (25, Ossipee)
Hattie M., b. 11/22/1898 in Brookfield; Milton Towle (farmer, 30, Eaton) and Mary L. Wentworth (19, Ossipee)
Levi, b. 7/11/1903 in Brookfield; Milton S. Towle (farmer, 34, Eaton) and Mary L. Wentworth (24, Eaton); residence - Eaton
Mary-Elizabeth, b. 8/7/1968; David Q. Towle and Martha Jane Filgate
Michael David, b. 5/12/1971; David Quimby Towle and Martha Jane Filgate

TRAINOR,
Cary Richardson, b. 4/18/1985; Thomas Edward Trainor and Cary Randolph Anderson

TUCKER,
Katherine Virginia, b. 11/2/1922 in Brookfield; fourth; Orin Tucker (saw mill fireman, Ware) and Marion L. Fogg (Deerfield); residence of father - Lebanon

TULLY,
Alexander Clayton, b. 6/27/1986; Hugh Michael Tully and Leslie Carol Holmes
Andrea Clare, b. 6/5/1980; Hugh Michael Tully and Leslie Carol Holmes

VACHON,
Ammie Marie, b. 11/12/1977; Robert Alan Vachon and Joan Marie Hall

VELEZ,
Cristina Maria, b. 11/29/1989; Alejandro Velez and Leeanne Leonard
David Antonio, b. 10/27/1992; Alejandro Velez and Lee Anne Leonard

VENO,
daughter, b. 6/29/1891; Samuel Veno (lumbering, Canada) and Alice
    Cameau (NS)
Samuel, b. 5/23/1892; fourth; Samuel Veno (laborer, Canada) and
    Alice Como (NS)

WALSH,
Alexandra Brittany, b. 7/13/1986; Christopher Fulton Walsh and
    Joan Marie Fraga

WARD,
Harold P., b. 12/18/1902 in Brookfield; Asa Ward (fireman, 32,
    Madison) and Annie B. Garland (34, Conway)

WARREN,
Brooke Marie, b. 3/23/1987; Lawrence Joseph Warren and Susan
    Kathleen O'Shaughnessy
Samuel Richard, b. 8/26/1989; Lawrence Joseph Warren and Susan
    O'Shaughnessy

WEEKS,
Hillary May, b. 5/4/1977; Nathan Osgood Weeks and Sandra Louise
    Jones

WENTWORTH,
Cecil Edmund, b. 3/1/1918 in Brookfield; third; William R. Wentworth
    (farmer, Brookfield) and Myrtle Nute (Rollinsford, ME)

WEST,
daughter, b. 4/9/1907 in Brookfield; first; George E. West (farmer,
    23, Brookfield) and Lillian M. Brown (20, Brookfield)

WHITE,
Kara Michelle, b. 1/19/1973; Robert Heaton White, Jr. and Cheryl
    Jean Combs
Kristin Patricia, b. 3/11/1975; Robert Heaton White, Jr. and Cheryl
    Jean Combs

WHITKENS,
Garrick Victor James, b. 9/27/2000; David Whitkens and Loriann
    Whitkens

WHITNEY,
daughter, b. 5/11/1907 in Brookfield; first; Frank Whitney (actor, 20, Old Orchard, ME) and Jennie LaFrance (19, Canada)

WHITTEMORE,
Dawna Georgina, b. 2/24/1979; James E. Whittemore and Linda Jane Tsoukalas
Kelsey Ann, b. 2/17/1988; James Edwin Whittemore and Laurie Mae Gallagher
Kristopher James, b. 2/10/1986; James Edwin Whittemore and Laurie Mae Gallagher

WHITTEN,
Bethany Ann, b. 4/3/1995; Joseph Dean Whitten, Jr. and Cheryl Ann Cornellier
Brandon Dean, b. 4/3/1995; Joseph Dean Whitten, Jr. and Cheryl Ann Cornellier
Joseph Roger, b. 4/3/1991; Joseph Dean Whitten, Jr. and Cheryl Ann Cornellier

WIGGIN,
Alvah Taylor, b. 1/25/1893 in Brookfield; Alvah A. Wiggin (farmer, Wakefield) and Etta M. Taylor (Kezar Falls, ME)
Catherine Amy, b. 9/4/1914 in Brookfield; fourth; Frank H. Wiggin (farmer, 38, Brookfield) and Mabel Pike (28, Harrison, ME)
Donald Ellis, b. 2/20/1917 in Wolfeboro; fifth; Frank H. Wiggin (farmer, 40, Brookfield) and Mabel A. Pike (30, Harrison, ME)
George Reginald, b. 7/12/1912 in Brookfield; third; Frank H. Wiggin (farmer, 36, Brookfield) and Mabel A. Pike (25, Harrison, ME)
Hazel Endora, b. 9/22/1908 in Brookfield; first; Frank H. Wiggin (farmer, 32, Brookfield) and Mabel A. Pike (21, Harrison, ME)
Herbert Adna, b. 5/13/1910 in Brookfield; second; Frank H. Wiggin (farmer, 34, Brookfield) and Mabel A. Pike (23, Harrison, ME)

WILKINS,
Sarah Jean, b. 6/6/1980; Kevin Lee Wilkins and Rosalie Ann Sirois

WILLET,
Mackenzie Paige, b. 2/12/2003; James Willett and Karen Willett

WILLEY,
son, b. 7/6/1895 in Brookfield; fourth; Charles Willey (farmer, 35, Brookfield) and Martha A. Willey (33, Acton, ME)
Tracy, b. 3/2/1892; third; Charles Willey (farmer, Brookfield) and Mattie A. Willey (Acton, ME)

WILSON,
Cynthia Lorraine, b. 10/10/1968; Kenneth H. Wilson and DonnaLee Drew
Kenneth Hall, b. 10/16/1938 in Wakefield; third; Daniel H. Wilson (laborer, Union) and Florence E. Drew (Brookfield); residence - Union
Kenneth Hall, Jr., b. 5/27/1971; Kenneth Hall Wilson and Donnalee Drew
Lorraine Ellen, b. 10/11/1933 in Brookfield; first; Daniel H. Wilson (laborer, Union) and Florence E. Drew (Brookfield); residence - Union
Nathan Gregory, b. 3/29/1976; Richard Eastwood Wilson and Harriet Ann Keene
Rachel Marie, b. 1/9/1979; Richard E. Wilson and Harriet Ann Keene

WITHAM,
Mary Frances, b. 6/24/1921 in Wolfeboro; second; Charlie Witham (farmer, Wolfeboro) and Mary E. Woodsome (Limerick, ME)

WOOD,
Edward C., b. 8/17/1924; second; Milton E. Wood (carpenter) and Grace M. Cate; residence - Rochester

WYATT,
Joshua Jonathan, b. 3/21/1979; Jonathan G. Wyatt and Martha-Anne Basel
Rebecca Jamie, b. 4/3/1976; Jonathan George Wyatt and Martha-Anne Basel

ZIEGLER,
Emma Storm, b. 8/6/2002; Scott Ziegler and Cheryl Ziegler

BROOKFIELD MARRIAGES

ADJUTANT,
Geoffrey N. m. Susan L. **Wright** 6/10/2000 in Wolfeboro

ALIBRANDI,
Joseph Anthony m. Katherine Louise **Fowler** 11/3/1973 in
Wolfeboro

ALLEN,
Chester A. of Brookfield m. Alice E. **York** of Wolfeboro 4/30/1905 in
Wakefield; H - 21, mill hand, b. Brookfield, s/o Samuel M. Allen
and Emma F. Cummings; W - 18, weaver, b. Wolfeboro, d/o
Frank H. York and Hattie E. Reid
Harry G. m. Maud E. **Stevens** 3/8/1903 in Dedham, MA; H - 24,
mason, b. Brookfield, s/o Samuel M. Allen and Emma F.
Cummings; W - 19, housework, b. Laconia, d/o Elmer F.
Dearborn and Lillia J. Robinson
Herbert A. of Brookfield m. Frances A. **Webster** of Berwick, ME
7/18/1906 in Dover; H - 29, mason, b. Brookfield, s/o Samuel
M. Allen and Emma A. Cummings; W - 18, housekeeper, b.
Berwick, ME, d/o Joseph E. Webster and Eudora F. Archer
Phillip M. of Brookfield m. Eliza J. **Gosselin** of Rochester 4/27/1913
in Chocorua; H - 22, brick mason, b. Brookfield, s/o Samuel M.
Allen and Emma F. Cummings; W - 25, housework, 2nd, b.
Canada, d/o Frank Cooley and Mary Preston

ARNER,
Robert m. Charlotte **Hahn** 7/25/1956 in Brookfield

BARRETT,
Walter William, III m. Susan Elizabeth **Dwyer** 3/1/1988 in Tamworth

BATTEN,
James A. m. Barbara M. **Hooper** 1/20/1957 in Portsmouth

BELKNAP,
James Lyman of Brookfield m. Mary Frances **Witham** of Brookfield
10/26/1941 in Wakefield; H - 29, farmer, b. Boston, MA, s/o
James Lyman Belknap (Dorchester, MA, doctor) and Maude
Ausborne (Arlington, MA, at home); W - 20, at home, b.
Wolfeboro, d/o Charles Asa Witham (Brookfield, farmer) and
Mary Ellen Woodsome (Limerick, ME, housewife)

BERRY,

Stephen L. m. Cynthia **Towle** 7/14/2001 in Brookfield

BIXBY,

William A. of Brookfield m. Sara W. **Cate** of Wolfeboro 12/25/1899 in Wolfeboro; H - 41, farmer, b. Hopkinton, MA, s/o Oliver C. Bixby and Waty A. Ranlet; W - 33, school teacher, b. Wolfeboro, d/o Daniel P. Cate and Caroline Whitaker

BOSTON,

Arthur of Brookfield m. Bernice M. **Perkins** of Acton, ME 12/19/1934 in Rochester; H - 45, laborer, b. Brookfield, s/o Henry Boston (Littleton, VT) and Susan A. Drew (Brookfield); W - 50, housekeeper, 2nd, b. Acton, ME, d/o Moses D. Willey (Salem, MA, farmer) and Abbie Goodwin (Acton, ME, housewife)

BRADLEY,

Earl M. of Milton m. Lillian M. **West** of Brookfield 5/18/1930 in N. Salem; H - 23, farmer, b. Lynn, MA, s/o Joseph H. Bradley (Haverhill, MA, shoe worker) and Myrtle V. Carter (W. Pembroke, ME, heel worker); W - 23, at home, b. Brookfield, d/o George E. West (Brookfield, farmer) and Lillian M. Brown (Brookfield, housewife)

BRADY,

Christopher Michael m. Joyce Allison **DeBow** 5/16/1992 in Brookfield

BREARY,

George J. of Lewiston, ME m. M. Pauline **Moulton** of Sanford, ME 6/13/1936 in Brookfield; H - 25, die maker, b. Sanford, ME, s/o Arthur H. Breary (Yorkshire, England, block printer) and Delia M. Cloutier (Canada); W - 23, nurse, b. Sanford, ME, d/o Albert S. Moulton (Sanford, ME, lumberman) and Paulina E. Calef (Rochester, teacher)

BRODERICK,

Charles W. of Brookfield m. Jean F. **Marks** of Fairhaven, MA 2/3/1952 in Fairhaven, MA; H - 31, student, 2nd, b. MA, s/o Charles H. Broderick (MA) and Elsie L. Haron (MA); W - 31, admin., b. MA, d/o Tracy W. Marks (PA) and Maude E. Kenyon (MA)

BROOKS,
Vincent Edward m. Cynthia Lorraine **Wilson** 9/16/1989 in Wakefield

BROWN,
Dana Eugene m. Charlotte Dee **Hicks** 7/5/1971 in Wakefield
Douglas Martin m. Marie Elizabeth **Nason** 7/22/1990 in Brookfield
Grover C. of Brookfield m. Emma **Huntress** of Wakefield 4/1/1906 in Wakefield; H - 21, farmer, b. Brookfield, s/o Edwin L. Brown and Susan E. Willey; W - 39, housework, 2nd, b. Harmony, ME, d/o William C. Richards and Eunice D. Dyer
Kenneth R. m. Carolyn E. **Dubuc** 8/27/2005 in Wolfeboro
Langdon D. of Brookfield m. Lucy A. **Rollins** of Brookfield 4/27/1901 in Somersworth; H - 49, miller, 2nd, b. Northwood, s/o John F. Brown and Eleanor H. Carter; W - 44, housekeeper, 2nd, b. Brookfield, d/o Charles F. West and Syrene Ricker

BURHOE,
Horace G. of New York City m. Margaret E. **Muller** of Peabody, MA 8/12/1911 in Wakefield; H - 28, steam fitter, b. Charlottetown, PEI, s/o Richard W. Burhoe and Eliza J. Emmon; W - 25, domestic, b. Newark, NJ, d/o John Muller and Elizabeth Messon

BURKHART,
Roger m. Ellen **Lankhorst** 7/4/2004 in Wakefield

BURROUGHS,
Howard of Brookfield m. Ida B. **York** of Dover 8/4/1891 in Middleton; H - 32, engineer, 2nd, b. Brookfield, s/o Warren Burroughs (Middleton, farmer) and Abbie M. Willey (Brookfield, housework); W - 18, housework, b. S. Berwick, d/o David P. York (shoemaker) and Susan M. Smart (housework)
Roy of Brookfield m. Marion **Chamberlain** of Milton 10/11/1924 in Dover; H - 21, b. Brookfield; W - 17, b. Chelsea, MA
Warren of Brookfield m. Madeline G. **White** of Milton 10/9/1924 in Lebanon, ME; H - 24, b. Wolfeboro; W - 18, b. Rochester

BUTLER,
Charles E. of Melrose m. Joan I. **Feist** of Brookfield 1/22/1955 in Sanbornville; H - 24, testman, b. MA, s/o Edgar J. Butler (MA) and Margaret E. Barnes (MA); W - 19, at home, b. Brookfield, d/o Harold Feist (MA) and Adeline Boucher (MA)

BYE,
David F. m. Janet E. **Plant** 6/26/1982 in Wolfeboro

BYRNE,
Robert Gregg, Jr. m. Sandra Mae **Noonan** 8/14/1971 in Brookfield

CADDELL,
Mark E. m. Beth A. **Foster** 6/16/1987 in Wakefield

CARLL,
Robert Lenwood m. Sonja Louise **Anderson** 12/15/1966 in Brookfield

CARPENTER,
Stephen Alan m. Leslie Ann **Hardman** 6/26/1971 in Sanbornville

CARVILLE,
Joseph W. of Biddeford, ME m. Carrie A. **Stevens** of Brookfield 10/13/1916 in Brookfield; H - 32, locomotive fireman, b. Saco, ME, d/o Willard Carville and Elizabeth Taylor; W - 23, housekeeper, b. Middleton, d/o Warren J. Stevens and Laura E. Eaton

CASE,
James Powell, Jr. m. Jessica Ann **Haskin** 2/28/1999 in Tuftonboro

CASWELL,
Norman E. of Newfield m. Inez L. **Cotton** of Brookfield 1/1/1953 in Wakefield; H - 36, farmer, 2nd, b. Greenland, s/o Austin W. Caswell (Nottingham) and Bella A. Caswell (Hillsboro); W - 40, egg grader, b. Wolfeboro, d/o John A. Cotton (Wolfeboro) and Mary L. Cotton (Brookfield)

CATE,

Herbert H. of Brookfield m. Mabelle O. **Fogg** of Sanbornville 4/14/1934 in Rochester; H - 52, painter, b. Gonic, s/o Joseph A. Cate (Brookfield, painter) and Adelia S. Foss (Barrington, housewife); W - 25, telephone op., b. Ossipee, d/o George W. Fogg (Ossipee, laborer) and Carrie B. Garland (Sanbornville, housewife)

Norris E. of Brookfield m. Irene L. **Cotton** of Brookfield 9/27/1930 in Brookfield; H - 33, carpenter, b. Brookfield, s/o Harry W. Cate (Brookfield, farmer) and Aimee Beaugez (Byon Laurfaurch, LA, housewife); W - 21, at home, b. Wolfeboro, d/o John A. Cotton (Wolfeboro, carpenter) and May L. Neal (Brookfield, housewife)

Raymond M. of Brookfield m. Mertie **Libby** of Gray, ME 3/21/1916 in Ossipee; H - 24, fireman, b. Brookfield, s/o Harry W. Cate and Amy Beaugez; W - 16, housework, b. Gray, ME, d/o Leroy Reed and Minnie Libby

CEFALO,

Gregory N. m. Carolyn E. **Cossette** 5/4/1985 in Brookfield

CHAMBERLAIN,

Frank H. of Revere, MA m. Marion J. **Carroll** of Lynn, MA 6/8/1935 in Sanbornville; H - 31, contracting, b. Somerville, MA, s/o Thomas W. Chamberlain (Lynn, MA, supt.) and Anne Quinland (Charleston, MA, at home); W - 30, at home, b. Lynn, MA, d/o David F. Carroll (Ireland, foremaster) and Margaret McEncoe (Rockland, MA, at home)

CHASE,

Bernard C. of Concord m. Doris A. **Clark** of Brookfield 6/3/1929 in Sanbornville; H - 25, RR section man, b. Winchendon, MA, s/o George P. Chase (New London, RR man) and Ellen L. Chase (New London, housewife); W - 16, housework, b. Brookfield, d/o James E. Clark (Tuftonboro, farmer) and Mattie A. Hoyt (Rochester)

CHELLMAN,

Chester Eric, Sr. of Brookfield m. Christine B. **Wiseman** of Jamaica Plains, MA 12/17/1941 in Sanbornville; H - 53, retired, 2nd, b. Boston, MA, s/o John Chellman (Sweden, tailor) and Betty Ericson (Sweden); W - 38, nurse, b. Springdale, Newfoundland, d/o Walter Wiseman (Newfoundland, accountant) and Bessie Hull (Newfoundland)

CHICK,
Mark A. m. Susan R. **Plant** 10/26/1985 in Wolfeboro

CHURCHILL,
Charles I. of Brookfield m. Jennie M. **Wentworth** of Wakefield 6/27/1889 in Wakefield; H - 20, butcher, b. Brookfield, s/o T. L. Churchill (Brookfield, farming) and N. M. Churchill (Barnstead); W - 17, housekeeper, b. Farmington, d/o G. Wentworth (Farmington, farming) and N. M. Wentworth (Alton)

Charles I. of Brookfield m. Amanda E. **Place** of Middleton 11/24/1892 in Wakefield; H - 24, farmer, 2nd, b. Brookfield, s/o Thomas L. Churchill (Brookfield, farmer) and Nancy Seward (Barnstead, housework); W - 18, housework, b. Middleton, d/o William Place (Middleton, farmer) and Lydia Whitehouse (Middleton, housework)

Frederick W. of Wolfeboro m. Thelma E. **York** of Brookfield 8/27/1949 in Wolfeboro; H - 44, automobile dealer, 3rd, b. MA, s/o Charles I. Churchill (NH); W - 30, secretary, b. NH, d/o Ethel Burhoe (NH)

Guy L. of Brookfield m. Alice M. **Emerson** of Stowe, ME 1/19/1907 in Brookfield; H - 21, fireman, b. Brookfield, s/o Lester L. Churchill and Hattie B. Ferguson; W - 26, school teacher, b. Stowe, ME, d/o Leonard Emerson and Marilla Charles

Lester L. of Brookfield m. Anna S. **Downs** of Haverhill 10/15/1922 in N. Haverhill; H - 62, farmer, 3rd, b. Brookfield, s/o Thomas L. Churchill and Sarah A. Stackpole; W - 53, cook, 2nd, b. E. Haverhill, d/o William Spooner and Susan Tibbetts

Lester L. of Brookfield m. Ada **Dickson** of Wolfeboro 1/1/1927 in Sanbornville; H - 67, farmer, 4th, b. Brookfield, s/o Thomas L. Churchill (Brookfield) and Sarah E. Stackpole (Limerick, ME); W - 67, housewife, 2nd, b. Wolfeboro, d/o Joshua Stackpole (Wolfeboro) and Mary Stackpole (Wolfeboro)

Randolph m. Harriet **Clap** 1/14/1956 in Brookfield

CLARK,
James E. of Brookfield m. Mattie **Hoyt** of Tuftonboro 12/10/1908 in Brookfield; H - 38, farmer, b. Brookfield, s/o Charles E. Clark

and Emma M. Willand; W - 18, housekeeping, b. Rochester, d/o Alonzo Hoyt and Lillian Edgerly
Raymond G. of Brookfield m. Anna E. **Brown** of Brookfield 10/27/1921 in White River Jct., VT; H - 28, farmer, b. Barnard, VT, s/o Henry S. Clark and Iva B. Rogers; W - 28, housekeeper, b. Brookfield, d/o Langdon D. Brown and Alfretta Drew

COLBATH,
Dale R. m. Jennifer Ann **Murphy** 10/10/1992 in Brookfield

COLMAN,
Henry m. Harriet Selena **Ford** 6/22/1903 in Cambridge, MA; H - 33, postal clerk, b. Brookfield, s/o Charles Colman and Salome Cotton; W - 33, typewriter, b. Boston, MA, d/o Thomas B. Ford and Amanda E. Rundlet
Wilson m. Helene P. **Chamberlain** 5/10/1903 in Brookfield; H - 29, farmer, b. Brookfield, s/o Charles Colman and Salome A. Cotton; W - 17, housework, b. Brookfield, d/o Robert L. Chamberlain and Gertrude Hanson

COOK,
Gilbert H. of Brookfield m. Harriet H. **Hanson** of Brookfield 5/7/1899 in Brookfield; H - 27, farmer, b. Brookfield, s/o Peter Cook and Sarah Gage; W - 26, housekeeper, b. Brookfield, d/o Charles Hanson and Mary C. H. Buzzell
James L. of Brookfield m. Ida F. **Richards** of Wakefield 12/11/1907 in Berwick, ME; H - 40, farmer, b. Brookfield, s/o Peter Cook and Sarah Gage; W - 34, housework, b. Wakefield, d/o Charles Richards and Keziah Quimby

CORMIER,
Raymond E. m. Norma **Cate** 12/6/1956 in Rochester

CORROW,
Eric D. of Claremont m. J. Doris **Prescott** of Brookfield 8/9/1952 in Wakefield; H - 21, mill oper., b. Milan, s/o Eric Corrow (VT) and Blanche Lavelle (VT); W - 17, waitress, b. Derry, d/o George Prescott (Merrimack) and Louise Prindall (Lynn, MA)

COTTON,

Henry J. of Brookfield m. Irene **Champaigne** of Wolfeboro 9/29/1945 in Wolfeboro; H - 24, mechanic, b. Brookfield, s/o John A. Cotton (Wolfeboro, carpenter) and M. Leona Neal (Brookfield, housewife); W - 19, shop, b. Wolfeboro, d/o Theo. Champaigne (Rochester, woodsman) and Albena M. Valley (Plymouth, housewife)

Henry John m. Erika K. A. **Garland** 5/5/1965 in Brookfield

COY,

William R. m. Geraldine G. **Gosselin** 9/1/1991 in Brookfield

CROTEAU,

Joseph S. m. Lisa F. **Hastings** 12/1/1984 in Brookfield

DAVIS,

Kenneth W. m. Carolyn E. **Cossette** 9/7/1980 in Wakefield

William G. of Canada m. Lilla M. **Rines** of Brookfield 8/9/1894 in Brookfield; H - 21, laborer, b. Canada; W - 22, housekeeper, 2nd, b. New Durham, d/o Frank Whitehouse and Rhoda McDaniels

DELAND,

Thomas T. of Brookfield m. Julia **Fletcher** of New Durham 4/6/1889 in Brookfield; H - 65, farmer, 2nd, b. Brookfield, s/o J. Deland (Brookfield, farming) and Betsy Deland; W - 50, housekeeper, 2nd, b. New Durham, d/o J. Willey (New Durham) and Lucy Willey

DENISON,

Steven K. m. Barbara E. **Bannon** 6/24/2005 in Meredith

DOUGLAS,

Fred S. of Arlington, MA m. Maude A. **Foster** of Arlington, MA 4/29/1945 in Brookfield; H - 56, salesman, 2nd, b. Somerville, MA, s/o John A. Douglas (Scotland, contractor) and Salome C. Craig (Scotland, housewife); W - 56, shopkeeper, 2nd, b. Pawtucket, RI, d/o Frederick McMally (Pawtucket, RI, livery) and Catherine Jones (England, housewife)

DOYAL,
Timothy E. m. Robin C. **Martikke** 9/28/1985 in Sanbornville

DOYLE,
Michael Curtis m. Jennifer **Weeks** 3/21/1970 in Durham

DREW,
Clarence L. of Milton m. Ida L. Coffin **Russell** of Milton 11/16/1936
in W. Milton; H - 49, laborer, 2nd, b. Wakefield, s/o John W.
Drew (Brookfield, laborer) and Addie Thibbedaux (Oldtown,
ME, housewife); W - 49, practical nurse, 3rd, b. Belleville, ON,
d/o Richard N. Cornell (Belleville, ON, laborer) and Isabelle
Brown (PEI, housewife)
Fred L. of Brookfield m. Helen E. **Luscomb** of E. Lynn, MA
1/24/1934 in Rochester; H - 25, laborer, b. Brookfield, s/o John
E. Drew (Brookfield, laborer) and Lizzie E. Foss (Farmington,
housewife); W - 27, housekeeper, 2nd, b. Concord, d/o Harry
Thompson (Concord, storekeeper) and Alice Caulder
(housewife)
Henry W. of Brookfield m. Addie L. **Cilley** of Brookfield 8/28/1897 in
Wakefield; H - 27, farmer, b. Brookfield, s/o Henry Drew and
Emeline Drew; W - 15, housekeeper, b. E. Hebron, ME, d/o
Anthony Cilley and Arvilla Twombly
John E. of Brookfield m. Lizzie E. **Foss** of Milton 4/22/1904 in
Wakefield; H - 19, laborer, b. Brookfield, s/o John Drew and
Abbie Thibodeaux; W - 18, housekeeper, b. Farmington, d/o
Henry Foss and Mattie Foss

DUBUC,
Paul E m. Andrea C. **Tully** 9/6/2003 in Moultonboro

EATON,
Martin H. of Brookfield m. Florence Leach **Elkins** of Brookfield
11/27/1902 in Stowe, ME; H - 23, b. Brookfield, s/o John C.
Eaton and Lois H. Martin; W - 21, b. Stowe, ME, d/o Albert C.
Elkins and Ella Wentworth

EDWARDS,
Harvey L. of Long Beach, NY m. Charlotte A. **Hahn** of Brookfield
12/27/1950 in Ossipee; H - 21, student, b. Germany, s/o Louis
F. Edwards (PA) and Claire Reiner (NY); W - 24, student, b.

Long Beach, NY, d/o Franz Hahn (Germany) and Lotte Jastrow (Germany)

EICHEN,
Joseph E. m. Rebecca A. **Zirpolo** 4/14/2001 in Wolfeboro

ELLIOTT,
Charles H. of Brookfield m. Luna E. **Drew** of Ossipee 11/21/1921 in N. Wakefield; H - 70, farmer, 3rd, b. Lisbon, s/o Henry P. Elliott and Mary Bennett; W - 45, housekeeper, 3rd, b. Ossipee, d/o Alpheus Eldridge and Dorothy Jenness

ERSKINE,
Alan R. L. m. Margaret **Erskine** 10/19/1977 in Brookfield

FAIR,
William M. m. Sonja M. **Pulkinen** 6/6/1981 in Wolfeboro

FALLON,
Paul Andrew m. Cathleen Ann **McGinley** 6/5/1999 in Sanbornville

FLETCHER,
Melvin E. m. June A. **Tutt** 9/8/1956 in Wolfeboro

FLOYD,
John D. of Brookfield m. Edith M. **Nason** of Wakefield 7/3/1930 in Wakefield; H - 16, laborer, b. Roxbury, MA, s/o John M. Floyd (Worcester, MA, laborer) and Ella C. Loud (W. Newfield, ME, housewife); W - 16, at home, b. Wakefield, d/o Almon D. Nason (Wakefield, laborer) and Nancy J. Streader (Wakefield, housewife)

FOGG,
Simon E. of Brookfield m. Sylvina A. **Higgins** of Newton, MA 6/10/1909 in Brookfield; H - 25, laborer, b. Ossipee, s/o Daniel Fogg and Julia Collins; W - 28, housekeeper, b. Galway, Ireland, d/o Martin Higgins and Sylvina Reddington

FOTHERGILL,
William James m. Chris Ann **Haley** 5/19/1990 in Sanbornville

FRENCH,
Charles L. m. Orilla May **Edmisten** 8/4/1990 in Wolfeboro
Lawrence of Brookfield m. Rosa **Dodier** of Sanbornville 1/19/1927 in
Rochester; H - 21, laborer, b. New Durham, s/o Leander
French (Farmington) and Nettie Tufts (Alton); W - 15,
housekeeper, b. Sanbornville, d/o Joseph Dodier (Quebec) and
Edith Dodier (Quebec)

GLIDDEN,
David Allen m. Amy Yvonne **Rouleau** 5/26/1996 in Brookfield

GOODRICH,
Kenneth J. m. Luanne F. **Hume** 4/25/2001 in rx

GRANT,
Clarence of Wells, ME m. Anna M. **Farley** of York, ME 5/28/1944 in
Wakefield; H - 48, machinist, 2nd, b. Wells, ME, s/o Silas M.
Grant (NS, farmer) and Margie Donald (Wells, ME, housewife);
W - 36, stenographer, 2nd, b. York, ME, d/o Winthrop Wade
(Brockton, MA) and Ida M. Cooks (PEI)

HACKETT,
Bert S. of Brookfield m. Anna **Schmidt** of Wakefield 10/19/1915 in
Saco, ME; H - 38, blacksmith, b. Brookfield, s/o John F.
Hackett and Nellie M. Bennett; W - 21, housekeeper, b.
Kennebunkport, ME, d/o Henry N. Schmidt and Nellie F. Towny

HAINES,
Paul Lawrence m. Patrice Jay Healy 10/23/1999 in Dover
Samuel E. of Philadelphia, PA m. Elizabeth L. **Sawyer** of Brookfield
7/3/1948 in Wolfeboro; H - 24, civil engineer, b. Philadelphia,
PA, s/o Samuel E. Haines (Philadelphia, PA, merchant) and
Elsie B. Pinkham (Lynn, MA, housewife); W - 21, student, b.
Fall River, MA, d/o Howard P. Sawyer (Concord, physician) and
Mary G. Willard (Concord, housewife)

HANSEN,
Carl C. of Brookfield m. Marie Ada L. **Sanborn** of Newfield, ME
1/30/1937 in Rochester; H - 43, laborer, b. Denmark, s/o
Morten Hansen (Denmark, laborer) and Karen M. Johansen
(Denmark, housewife); W - 26, at home, b. Newfield, ME, d/o

Harry Sanborn (Newfield, ME, laborer) and Alice Shepard (Brockton, MA, housewife)

Otto J. of Brookfield m. Dorothy M. **Bryant** of Wakefield 1/1/1936 in Sanbornville; H - 40, laborer, b. Denmark, s/o Morton Hansen (Denmark) and K. Marie Johnson (Denmark); W - 18, at home, b. Amesbury, MA, d/o Almon H. Bryant (Eaton, laborer) and Nellie M. Ellis (Eaton, housewife)

HANSON,

Joseph H. of Brookfield m. Lucretia **Weeks** of Brookfield 6/11/1889 in Wakefield; H - 23, RR fireman, b. Brookfield, s/o C. H. Hanson (Brookfield, farming) and M. C. Hanson; W - 23, housekeeper, b. Brookfield, d/o N. C. Weeks (Brookfield, farming) and A. J. Weeks (Brookfield)

Sydney Q. of Brookfield m. Mary T. **Johnson** of Brookfield 12/22/1888 in Wakefield; H - 24, farmer, b. Brookfield, s/o Charles H. Hanson (Brookfield, farming) and Mary C. Hanson (Brookfield, housekeeping); W - 18, housekeeper, b. Wakefield, d/o Thomas H. Johnson (Wolfeboro, farming) and Mary E. Johnson (Wolfeboro, housekeeping)

HARDIN,

Charles W. of Brookfield m. Ruth **Wilkinson** of Wakefield 6/20/1893 in Wakefield; H - 61, farmer, 3rd, b. Burlington, VT, s/o James Hardin and Betsey Allen; W - 46, housekeeper, 2nd, b. Brownfield, ME, d/o Simeon Dyer and Nancy Day

HASTINGS,

Brian C. m. Jennifer L. Beattie **Rose** 8/4/1984 in Brookfield

HERRICK,

George S. of Wakefield m. Nellie M. **Clark** of Brookfield 4/8/1929 in Union; H - 25, teamster, b. Newfield, ME, s/o George S. Herrick (Portland, ME, clerk) and Lena V. Patch (W. Newfield, ME, housewife); W - 18, housework, b. Brookfield, d/o James E. Clark (Tuftonboro, farmer) and Mattie A. Hoyt (Rochester)

HICKEY,

S. Michael m. Josephine Sanborn **Cossette** 9/19/1964 in Brookfield

HILL,
Alfred J. m. Marybeth **Towle** 5/1/1987 in Brookfield
Harry L. of Brookfield m. Etta L. **Sanborn** of Brookfield 6/11/1904 in
    Wakefield; H - 29, teamster, b. Brookline, s/o David Hill and
    Caroline Weatherbee; W - 36, housekeeper, 2nd, b. Ossipee,
    d/o Thatcher M. Thompson and Frances Tibbetts
Herschel E. of Brookfield m. Florence **Bell** of Brookfield 7/5/1911 in
    Wakefield; H - 24, farmer, b. Halifax, VT, s/o Frank O. Hill and
    Ellen P. Rose; W - 29, music teacher, b. Boston, MA, d/o
    William E. Bell and Sarah E. Chapman

HOBBS,
Neal Clayton m. Christine Ellen **Alexander** 10/10/1970 in Newport

HODGDON,
David Glenn m. Janice Anne **Copplestone** 12/28/1974 in Wakefield

HOOPER,
Sidney E. of Sanbornville m. Bernice E. **Cate** of Brookfield 3/8/1933
    in Rochester; H - 49, merchant, b. Wakefield, s/o Charles E.
    Hooper (Wakefield, deceased) and Nellie Downs (Wakefield,
    deceased); W - 40, housewife, b. Brookfield, d/o Harry W. Cate
    (Brookfield, deceased) and Aimee Beaugez (Bayou LaFourche,
    LA, deceased)
Thomas Martin m. Judith Alma **Lord** 9/3/1966 in Wolfeboro

HOWARD,
Jed M. m. Mariellen **Macpherson** 9/24/2005 in Manchester

HUBBARD,
Henry C. of Boston, MA m. M. R. **King** of Westford, VT 8/13/1894 in
    Brookfield; H - 43, attorney-at-law, 2nd, b. Boston, MA, s/o J. G.
    Hubbard and Emily C. Farrington; W - 34, dressmaker, 2nd, b.
    Fairfax, VT, d/o Charles King and Phebe Minor

HUGHES,
Raymond S. m. Holly Anne **Climo** 6/17/1989 in rx
Roland S. of Quincy, MA m. Adelaide **Robinson** of Brookfield
    6/15/1935 in Brookfield; H - 30, salesman, b. Quincy, MA, s/o
    Samuel Hughes (Wales, custodian) and Annie Morris (Wales,
    at home); W - 26, at home, b. Portland, ME, d/o Wallace

Robinson (Portland, ME, M.D.) and Addie Bowden (Chicago, IL, at home)

HUTCHINS,
John L. of Brookfield m. Alice A. **Lyford** of Brookfield 5/13/1921 in Union; H - 25, farmer, b. Brookfield, s/o Stephen H. Hutchins and Lizzie M. Wentworth; W - 31, 2nd, b. Cincinnati, OH, d/o George H. A. Lyford and Alice Williams
Joseph H. of Wakefield m. Marguerite O. **Grant** of Brookfield 11/4/1933 in Auburn, ME; H - 36, laborer, b. Wakefield, s/o Edwin Hutchins (Dover, deceased) and Ina Emma Linscott (Newfield, ME, deceased); W - 31, housewife, b. Rochester, d/o Orrin Grant (Acton, ME, farmer) and Jennie V. Emerson (Northwood, housewife)

INGEMI,
Riccardo Paul, Jr. m. Elizabeth Piper **Arthur** 7/4/1991 in Ossipee

INGRAHAM,
William H. of Brookfield m. Minerva W. **McLane** of Brookfield 2/8/1955 in Brookfield; H - 79, retired, b. MA, s/o Henry Ingraham (MA) and Catherine Harrison (MA); W - 60, at home, b. Canada, d/o Ausbrey McLane (Canada) and Rebecca Richie (Canada)

JACOBSON,
Paul A. m. Eliza J. **Marr** 7/8/2000 in Wakefield

JOSLIN,
Richard Arthur m. Fenneke Ge' **ter Weele** 6/21/1964 in Wolfeboro

KATWICK,
Arthur David m. Catherine Mary **Martell** 9/15/1973 in Wakefield
Robert Tilden m. Gloria Doris **Adjutant** 8/12/1961 in Wolfeboro

KERR,
John J. H. of Brookfield m. Elizabeth K. **Reed** of Brookfield 8/4/1948 in Wolfeboro; H - 46, retired, 2nd, b. Pueblo, CO, s/o Guy M. Kerr (Cape Girard, MO, retired) and Bertha Thompson (Little Compton, RI); W - 46, at home, 2nd, b. Boston, MA, d/o Wendell

P. Keene (Boston, MA, at home) and Lulu G. Greenleaf
(Boston, MA)

KINVILLE,
Theodore Scott m. Catherine Mary **Jarnot** 8/9/1997 in Sanbornville

KNIGHT,
Gary m. Carol **Delaurier** 7/2/2004 in Brookfield

LAMB,
Peter Henshaw m. Susan Davis **Thorne** 9/10/1994 in Brookfield

LANG,
Daniel of Brookfield m. Carrie V. **Johnson** of Wolfeboro 11/3/1888
   in Wolfeboro; H - 19, brakeman, b. Brookfield, s/o Daniel W.
   Lang (Brookfield, farming) and Mary A. Lang (Ossipee,
   housekeeping); W - 20, shoe stitcher, b. Wolfeboro, d/o
   Phineas Johnson and Ursula Johnson
John E. of Brookfield m. Francena K. **Drew** of Wakefield 10/7/1914
   in Wakefield; H - 56, butcher, 2nd, b. Brookfield, s/o John W.
   Lang and Johana Drew; W - 55, housekeeper, 2nd, b. Madison,
   d/o Ami Kennett and Sally Chick
John H. of Brookfield m. Mabel A. **Hanson** of Brookfield 10/15/1889
   in Brookfield; H - 23, clerk, b. Brookfield, s/o D. W. Lang
   (Brookfield, farming) and M. A. Lang (Ossipee); W - 25,
   housekeeper, b. Brookfield, d/o C. H. Hanson (Brookfield,
   farming) and M. C. Hanson
Joseph W. of Brookfield m. Katherine **Wheeler** of N. Abington, MA
   6/20/1933 in Rochester; H - 23, machinist, b. Brookfield, s/o
   Wallace F. Lang (Brookfield, farmer) and Abbie C. Lang
   (Wolfeboro, housewife); W - 24, stenographer, b. Parsonsfield,
   ME, d/o Leon C. Wheeler (Rockland, MA, chauffeur) and Mae
   L. Wheeler (Effingham, housewife)
Reuben of Brookfield m. Idella L. **Wiggin** of Wakefield 8/18/1888 in
   Brookfield; H - 28, merchant, b. Brookfield, s/o John W. Lang
   (Brookfield, farmer) and Joanna Lang (Brookfield,
   housekeeping); W - 23, housekeeper, b. Wakefield, d/o Josiah
   W. Wiggin (Wakefield, farmer) and Mary E. Wiggin (Wakefield,
   housekeeping)
Reuben P. of Brookfield m. Bernice H. **Pike** of Wakefield 4/30/1913
   in Nashua; H - 19, grocer, b. Brookfield, s/o John E. Lang and

Lizzie Palmer; W - 23, school teacher, b. Wakefield, d/o William
W. Pike and Sarah A. Tibbetts
Wallace F. of Brookfield m. Abbie H. **Cotton** of Wolfeboro
6/10/1908 in Brookfield; H - 20, butcher, b. Brookfield, s/o John
E. Lang and Lizzie Palmer; W - 22, millinery, b. Wolfeboro, d/o
Daniel J. Cotton and Hattie S. Hurd

LAVENDER,
Thomas E. m. Dulcie Lee **Helm** 9/7/2002 in Brookfield

LAWRENCE,
Charles R. of Brookfield m. Harietta F. **Crowley** of Boston, MA
11/29/1899 in Boston, MA; H - 21, farmer, b. Charlestown, ME,
s/o Joseph K. Lawrence and Hannah A. Jenness; W - 34,
school teacher, b. Lowell, MA, d/o Timothy A. Crowley and
Harriet F. Crowley

LEBLANC,
Patrick E. m. Ellen R. **Bozner** 10/25/2003 in Ossipee

LEE,
Robert Edward, Jr. m. Judith Elaine **Glidden** 3/17/1977 in
Wolfeboro

LEEPER,
Verne Pembleton m. Maxine Virginia **Richards** 5/13/1989 in
Wolfeboro

LEWIS,
Mark m. Nicole **Comtois** 5/4/2005 in Wolfeboro
Philip Virgil, Jr. m. Penny Candy **Tirrell** 8/9/1980 in Union

LIMBARGER,
Luther E. of Hopie, RI m. Madeleine L. **Drew** of Brookfield 4/10/1926
in Sanbornville; H - 36, electrician, 2nd, b. Trundles Cross
Roads, TN, s/o M. William Limbarger (Knoxville, TN) and Mollie
Limbarger (Knoxville, TN); W - 15, at home, b. Brookfield, d/o
John E. Drew (Brookfield) and Elizabeth E. Foss (Farmington)

LINEMAN,
John R. m. Kimberly Rae **Osborne** 10/3/1987 in Wolfeboro

LOW,
Edgar of Wolfeboro m. Marjorie G. **Shortridge** of Brookfield
7/15/1917 in Brookfield; H - 20, chauffeur, b. Sanford, ME, s/o
Edward Low and Blanche Carpenter; W - 19, housekeeper, b.
Brookfield, d/o Albert S. Shortridge and Grace Stevens

LUND,
Forrest C. m. Barbara A. **Baczkiel** 4/1/2000 in Wolfeboro

LUSCOMB,
Kenneth K. of Brookfield. m. Juanita **Clough** of Milton Mills
4/22/1949 in Sanbornville; H - 19, lumberjack, b. MA, s/o Arthur
A. Luscomb (MA) and Helen Thompson (MA); W - 15,
housekeeper, b. NH, d/o Warren Clough (NH) and Marguerite
Weeks (NH)

LYON,
Peter Byrd m. Sandra **Davis** 9/14/1965 in Wakefield

LYONS,
Edward P. of Wakefield m. Nancy S. **Churchill** of Brookfield
12/24/1950 in Sanbornville; H - 19, student, b. NY, s/o Henry E.
Lyons (MA) and Almira B. Palmer (MA); W - 15, student, b. VA,
d/o Fred. W. Churchill (MA) and Amey T. Spencer (RI)

MACBRIEN,
Bruce A. m. Cynthia H. **Adjutant** 10/6/1962 in Wakefield
Luther Andrew of Brookfield m. Hazel Octavia **Ayer** of Winchester,
MA 5/29/1937 in Winchester, MA; H - 25, truck driver, b. Lynn,
MA, s/o W. J. Luther MacBrien and Louise N. Prindall; W - 28,
clerk, b. Winchester, MA, d/o William A. Ayer and Octavia T.
Knowlton
Philip James of Brookfield m. Mabel Francis **Harmon** of Ossipee
7/31/1938 in Effingham; H - 21, laborer, b. Lynn, MA, s/o Luther
MacBrien (Lynn, MA, fireman) and Louise M. Prindall (Lynn,
MA, housewife); W - 18, waitress, b. Ossipee, d/o John
Harmon (Brookfield, laborer) and Georgie I. Frost (Madison,
housewife)

MACKIE,
Millard F. of Wakefield m. Ida B. **Eaton** of Brookfield 6/5/1893 in
Brookfield; H - 18, mill hand, b. Limington, ME, s/o George F.
Mackie and Ellen Burnham; W - 20, housekeeper, b.
Brookfield, d/o Samuel S. Eaton and Lizzie Smith

MAGNUSON,
Richard Axel m. Edna Louise **Manzer** 5/23/1969 in Durham

MATTSON,
Godfrey of Brookfield m. Ethel M. **Woodus** of Brookfield 4/1/1925 in
Sanbornville; H - 28, caretaker, b. Angola, NY; W - 26, at home,
b. Haverhill, MA

MAY,
Rolf G. of Washington, DC m. Cornelia A. **Hahn** of Brookfield
6/25/1949 in Wolfeboro; H - 30, lawyer, b. Germany, s/o
George F. May (Germany) and Hiadgerde Brie (Silesia); W -
28, landscape architect, b. Germany, d/o Franz T. Hahn
(Germany) and Lotte B. Jastrow (Germany)

McGEE,
Michael S. m. Teresa A. **Russo** 1/5/2002 in Wolfeboro

McROBBIE,
James Arthur m. Bonilynn **Hofmann** 6/3/1972 in Sanbornville

MOORE,
George J. m. Kathryn J. **DePree** 5/23/1992 in Alton Bay
Russell Raymond, Jr. m. June Katherine **Brown** 8/11/1974 in
Brookfield

MORAN,
John Michael m. June E. **Reed** 10/21/1995 in Rochester

NASON,
Edward Bruce m. Arline Mabel **Zalenski** 2/24/1961 in Sanbornville
Ernest E. of Sanbornville m. Dorothy M. **Cate** of Brookfield
9/18/1937 in Wakefield; H - 21, laborer, b. Sanbornville, s/o
Almon L. Nason (Bridgton, ME, laborer) and Nancy J. Streader
(Sanbornville, housewife); W - 19, at home, b. Gray, ME, d/o

Raymond Cate (Brookfield, laborer) and Myrtie Libbey (Gray, ME, housewife)
Michael Wayne m. Nancy Naomia **Eldridge** 5/21/1989 in Brookfield

NEAL,
Charles H. of Brookfield m. Edna B. **Richards** of Wakefield
8/26/1913 in Wakefield; H - 24, farmer, b. Brookfield, s/o
Charles H. Neal and Ida F. Rankins; W - 23, housework, b.
Wakefield, d/o Charles C. Richards and Kisiah F. Quimby

NICHOLS,
Kezar Guild, Jr. m. Diane Leslie **Burnham** 7/3/1965 in Brookfield

NOBLE,
Edwin Jerome m. Nancy Joan **Hobbs** 6/9/1973 in Brookfield

NUTTER,
Llewellyn of Brookfield m. Mary D. **Wakefield** of Brookfield
11/29/1921 in Brookfield; H - 36, teamster, b. Fryeburg, ME, s/o
Henry Nutter and Elizabeth Edgecomb; W - 38, housekeeper,
2nd, b. Pine Point, ME, d/o David L. Frye and Eunice Braisher
William H. of Brookfield m. Flora E. **Clow** of Wolfeboro 9/4/1920 in
Sanbornville; H - 28, fireman, b. Fryeburg, ME, s/o Henry Nutter
and Elizabeth Edgecome; W - 19, weaver, 2nd, b. Maplewood,
ME, d/o Aleck Martin and Ruth McGill

PALMER,
John Frederick m. Anne Elizabeth **Pizey** 8/19/1989 in Brookfield

PEAVEY,
Henry W. of Brookfield m. Albina May **Walton** of Brookfield
11/6/1894 in Brookfield; H - 47, blacksmith, 2nd, b. Strafford, s/o
John C. Peavey and Mary A. Caverly; W - 22, housekeeper,
2nd, b. NS, d/o Hibbard Robar and Rebecca Robar

PENNIMAN,
William Frederick, III m. Judith **Milne** 8/1/970 in Manchester

PHINNEY,
Charles D. m. Tammy L. **Nason** 11/24/1984 in Sanbornville

PIKE,
Christopher Charles m. Erin Michelle **Saunders** 3/8/1997 in Weare
John Raymond m. Martha Atwood **Niewenhous** 8/6/1991 in
Brookfield
Loring Robert m. Georgia Sue **Promise** 9/15/1964 in Wakefield

PINKHAM,
Christopher Choate m. Alice-Ann Bailey **Johnston** 10/26/1974 in
Wakefield

PLANT,
Darrell E. m. Paula A. **Sabol** 10/30/1985 in Brookfield

PLASMATI,
Richard B. m. Mary E. **Buckland** 8/18/1984 in Brookfield

REMICK,
Samuel A. m. Cora **Nason** 9/19/1903 in Brookfield; H - 21, laborer,
b. Brookfield, s/o Mark Remick and Eleanor E. Young; W - 21,
housework, b. Wakefield, d/o Hardy Nason and Lucinda Nason

RICHARDS,
Walter of Wakefield m. Lena **Leavitt** of Brookfield 7/16/1927 in
Milton; H - 40, farmer, 2nd, b. Wakefield, s/o Charles Richards
(Wakefield) and Keziah Quimby (Newfield, ME); W - 46,
housekeeper, 3rd, b. Parsonsfield, ME, d/o Leonard Hill
(Parsonsfield, ME) and Gertrude Varney (Lebanon, ME)

RICKER,
John David m. Jean **Adams** 4/10/1965 in Derry

RINES,
George W. of Brookfield m. Emma **Hodgdon** of Brookfield 8/1/1889
in Brookfield; H - 25, farmer, b. New Durham, s/o C. H. Rines
(New Durham, farming) and S. M. Rines; W - 25, housekeeper,
b. Boston, MA, d/o M. Hodgdon (farming) and L. Hodgdon
Philip H. of Brookfield m. Frances M. **Colman** of Wakefield 3/6/1942
in Concord; H - 22, student, b. Brookfield, s/o Walter F. Rines
(Brookfield, farmer) and Grace Nichols (Ossipee, at home); W -
21, student, b. Brookfield, d/o Wilson Colman (Cotton Valley,
farmer) and Helen Chamberlain (Brookfield, at home)

RINGER,
Kenneth C. m. Jeanne A. **Riley** 9/25/1959 in Farmington

ROBERTS,
Reed Turney m. Mary Palmer **Rockwell** 7/30/1970 in Wakefield

ROBINSON,
John F. of Brookfield m. Rose **Witham** of Brookfield 8/7/1897 in
    Wakefield; H - 47, farmer, 2nd, b. Brookfield, s/o Noah Robinson
    and Judith Cook; W - 41, housekeeper, 2nd, b. Newport, VT, d/o
    Ezra Hardy and Eliza Hardy
Walter L. of Brookfield m. Daisy M. **Davis** of Effingham 6/30/1906 in
    Wakefield; H - 30, farmer, b. Brookfield, s/o John F. Robinson
    and Ruth F. Lindsay; W - 25, housework, 2nd, b. Effingham, d/o
    Thatcher M. Thompson and Fanny H. Tibbetts

ROGERS,
Thomas Wilson m. Thelma Flinn **Wigglesworth** 9/1/1977 in
    Brookfield

ROSS,
Ovila of Providence, RI m. Christina E. **Drew** of Brookfield
    12/30/1939 in Lebanon, ME; H - 21, truck driver, b. Providence,
    RI, s/o Louis R. Ross (Providence, RI, general work) and
    Gladys W. Adams (Providence, RI, housewife); W - 20,
    housework, b. Brookfield, d/o John E. Drew (Brookfield, saw
    mill worker) and Elizabeth E. Foss (Farmington, housewife)

ROULEAU,
Cy Matthew m. Jennifer Kelly **Mann** 8/23/1997 in Sanbornville

ROYLE,
Norman Harold m. Margaret **Thompson** 12/22/1973 in Wakefield

RUFUS,
Lewis H. of Brookfield m. Amy B. **Burnell** of Naples, ME 12/17/1917
    in Rochester; H - 45, laborer, b. Lebanon, ME; W - 30,
    housekeeper, b. Sebago, ME, d/o Leonard S. Burnell and
    Jennie P. McKinney

RUSSO,
Robert Francis m. Adeline Morris **Hughes** 5/6/1973 in Wolfeboro

SANDERSON,
Charles Henry of Roxbury, MA m. Helen Elizabeth **Martel** of
Somerville, MA 7/7/1932 in Brookfield; H - 21, draftsman, b.
Hamilton, ON, s/o Charles H. Sanderson (London, England,
carpenter) and Mary Bella Dyer (Oldham, England, housewife);
W - 26, factory worker, b. Cambridge, MA, d/o James Clarence
Martel (S. Boston, MA, laborer) and Clara Sophia Camel
(Holyoke, MA, housewife)

SAUJON,
Royce A., II m. Frances H. **Weinroth** 11/8/1980 in Brookfield

SCEGGEL,
Arthur L. of Wolfeboro m. Emma O. **Wentworth** of Brookfield
6/2/1890 in Wakefield; H - 21, farmer, b. Wolfeboro, s/o James
Sceggel (Wolfeboro) and Sarah Batchelor; W - 21,
housekeeper, b. Brookfield, d/o Joseph S. Wentworth
(Wakefield, farmer) and Mary E. Weeks (Brookfield,
housekeeper)

SCHLAGETER,
Mark Stephen m. Michele Marie **Moon** 9/21/1991 in Brookfield

SCHRIETER,
Augustus of Brookfield m. Alice N. **Piper** of Berwick, ME 11/23/1945
in New Durham; H - 42, mechanic, b. Kittery, ME, s/o Augustus
Schrieter (Dresden, Germany, Navy) and Jennie McLane (C.
Breton, PI, housewife); W - 23, at home, b. Wolfeboro, d/o
John Piper (Ctr. Tuftonboro, laborer) and Nellie Staples (W.
Parsonsfield, ME, housewife)

SHEFFER,
Daniel J. m. Kristan N. **Perry** 4/2/2005 in Ctr. Ossipee

SHORTRIDGE,
Albert S. of Brookfield m. Grace M. **Stevens** of Dover 4/21/1897 in
Dover; H - 21, farmer, b. Brookfield, s/o Sylvester Shortridge

and Emma F. Clark; W - 21, housekeeper, b. Dover, d/o James N. Stevens and Sarah A. Emery

SINAPIUS,
Gerald Thomas m. Diane Elaine **Bridges** 11/22/1991 in Brookfield

SMITH,
Albert Webster of Dover m. Leon Mary **McDonald** of Brookfield 1/13/1954 in Milton; H - 68, janitor, 2nd, b. MA, s/o J. Albert Smith (MA) and Ida Cook (MA); W - 69, housewife, 2nd, b. NH, d/o Edward Hall (Canada) and Ora May Hall (Canada)

James R. of Brookfield m. Audrey E. **Moody** of Effingham 10/15/1955 in Ctr. Effingham; H - 19, in service, b. MA, s/o Arthur E. Smith (MA) and Verna B. McDonald (MA); W - 19, at home, b. NH, d/o Eugene H. Moody (NH) and Blanche L. Moody (ME)

Robert Andrew, Jr. m. Rita Mary **Phelan** 9/25/1976 in Wakefield

SOUCY,
David Richard m. Sandi Jo **Knowles** 4/29/1978 in Wolfeboro

STEBBINS,
Richard H. of Brookfield m. Sadie E. **Garside** of Brookfield 4/17/1917 in Rochester; H - 40, steam mill, 2nd, b. Newbury, VT, s/o Edward H. Stebbins and Martha Townsend; W - 37, housekeeper, 2nd, b. New Durham, d/o Remey Daphney and Sarah Elizabeth

STEVENS,
Reginald m. Priscilla **Heald** 4/13/1973 in Springvale, ME

SYER,
William A. m. Helen Eva **Lineham** 6/25/1988 in Ossipee

TASKER,
B. Dean m. Elinor L. **Buswell** 9/30/1967 in Ossipee

TAYLOR,
Peter Haywood m. Brigette Elizabeth **Sarde** 8/16/1997 in Brookfield

THOMES,
Horace L. of Brookfield m. Hattie M. **Goodhue** of Brookfield 10/28/1891 in Brookfield; H - 31, farmer, b. Denmark, ME, s/o George Thomes (Denmark, farmer) and Elvira L. Newcomb (Denmark, housewife); W - 21, teacher, b. Brookfield, d/o Thomas Goodhue (Brookfield, farmer) and Sarah Witham (Milton, housework)

TIBBETTS,
Everett J. of Brookfield m. Annie E. **Trott** of Ossipee 12/11/1892 in Brookfield; H - 22, farmer, b. Brookfield, s/o James H. Tibbetts (Brookfield, farmer) and Eliza A. Avery (Wolfeboro, housework); W - 18, housework, b. Portland, ME, d/o Thayer S. Trott (Portland, ME, farmer) and Emma I. Mathews (Wakefield, housework)
Everett J. of Brookfield m. Susie L. **Weeks** of Wakefield 6/21/1896 in Brookfield; H - 25, farmer, 2nd, b. Brookfield, s/o James H. Tibbetts and Eliza Avery; W - 20, housekeeper, b. Wakefield, d/o Brackett M. Weeks and Matilda Allen

TRIPP,
Edward Arnold m. Beverly Ann **Swaine** 5/28/1966 in Newton, MA

VALLEY,
Arthur of Brookfield m. Bertha **Demeritt** of Rochester 7/27/1894 in Brookfield; H - 21, laborer, b. Canada, s/o James Valley; H - 17, housekeeper, b. Rochester, d/o Charles A. Demeritt

VAN DYKE,
Bruce Edwin m. Velma Jean **Hobbs** 1/20/1973 in Wakefield

VANDERPOOL,
Douglas Warren m. Dorothy Ellen **Locke** 8/31/1991 in rx

VELEZ,
Alejandro m. Lee Anne **Leonard** 3/30/1985 in Dover

WALPOLE,
Jonathon Mathew m. Sally Ann **Cornwell** 9/14/1996 in Brookfield

WALTERS,
Donald E., Jr. of Wolfeboro m. Roberta F. **Nason** of Brookfield
4/29/1950 in Wolfeboro; H - 21, farming, b. Wolfeboro, s/o
Donald E. Walters (NH) and Bernice Piper (NH); W - 16, at
home, b. ME, d/o Raymond Nason (NH) and Ada M. Baker
(ME)

WENTWORTH,
Henry E. of Brookfield m. Mabel **Heath** of Wakefield 10/24/1891 in
Wakefield; H - 27, painter, b. Wakefield, s/o Stephen
Wentworth (Wakefield, farmer) and Ann Smith (Newry, ME,
housework); W - 28, housework, b. Newfield, ME, d/o Simon
Heath (Newfield, ME, farmer)
Reginald E. of Brookfield m. Virginia A. **Cole** of Woburn, MA
9/19/1943 in E. Wolfeboro; H - 42, insurance, b. Brookfield, s/o
William R. Wentworth (Brookfield, farmer) and Myrtle B. Nute
(Salmon Falls, at home); W - 29, secretary, b. Milo, ME, d/o A.
Russell C. Cole (W. Gardiner, ME, inspector) and Bessie L.
Elliott (Litchfield, ME)
Stephen S. of Brookfield m. Lucy **Appleton** of Brookfield 12/8/1893
in Brookfield; H - 65, farmer, 2nd, b. Parsonsfield, ME, s/o
Spencer Wentworth and Lydia Wentworth; W - 47,
housekeeper, 2nd, b. Boston, MA, d/o John Welch and Margaret
Welch

WEST,
George E. of Brookfield m. Lillian M. **Brown** of Brookfield 6/6/1906
in Brookfield; H - 22, farmer, b. Wakefield, s/o Charles F. West
and Betsey J. Whitehouse; W - 20, seamstress, b. Brookfield,
d/o Edwin L. Brown and Susan E. Willey

WHITE,
Bernard L. of Ctr. Ossipee m. Agnes M. **Ponkop** of Ctr. Ossipee
11/15/1952 in Conway; H - 26, truck driver, b. Ossipee, s/o
Belmont White (Ossipee) and Grace Eldridge (Ossipee); W -
33, at home, 2nd, b. Ossipee, d/o Wilbur Eldridge (Ossipee) and
Myrtle Templeton (Ossipee)
Robert Heaton, Jr. m. Cheryl Jean **White** 10/25/1997 in Brookfield

WHITTEMORE,
James E. m. Laurie M. **Gallagher** 10/4/1980 in Wolfeboro

James Edward m. Sandra Louise **Hooper** 9/5/1971 in Tuftonboro

WHOLLEY,
William Ernest m. Brenda **Ford** 4/16/1978 in Brookfield

WICKBOLDT,
Richard m. Marie DelCarmen **Arellano** 12/13/1987 in Manchester

WIGGIN,
Frank H. of Brookfield m. Mabel A. **Pike** of Harrison, ME 11/24/1907
in Brookfield; H - 31, farmer, b. Brookfield, s/o George A.
Wiggin and Amy F. Ordway; W - 21, school teacher, b.
Harrison, ME, d/o Adna D. Pike and Dora B. Dunham
Harry F. of Brookfield m. Alice R. **Woodward** of York, ME 4/18/1904
in Dover; H - 25, motorman, b. Brookfield, s/o George A.
Wiggin and Amy F. Ordway; W - 21, housekeeper, b. York, ME,
d/o Frank P. Woodward and Abbie H. Chase
William P. of Brookfield m. Jennie E. **Peterson** of Brighton, MA
5/19/1915 in Wakefield; H - 33, merchant, b. Brookfield, s/o
George A. Wiggin and Amy F. Ordway; W - 24, waitress, b.
Roxbury, MA, d/o Axel N. Peterson and Christina Danielson

WILLEY,
Charles Tracy of Brookfield m. Eva **Calef** of Rochester 8/27/1919 in
Sanford, ME; H - 27, farmer, b. Brookfield, s/o Charles Willey
and Mattie A. Willey; W - 23, teacher, b. Rochester, d/o Frank
Calef and Grace Roberts
Leon M. of Brookfield m. Flora W. **Downs** of Milton 4/21/1917 in
Rochester; H - 21, manufacturing, b. Brookfield, s/o Charles
Willey and Mattie A. Willey; W - 19, housekeeper, b. Milton, d/o
John A. Downs and May Thompson

WILSON,
Daniel H. of Union m. Florence E. **Drew** of Brookfield 6/24/1933 in
Rochester; H - 18, laborer, b. Union, s/o William J. Wilson (NB,
carpenter) and Edith M. Hall (Union, housewife); W - 17, at
home, b. Brookfield, d/o John E. Drew (Sanbornville, laborer)
and Elizabeth E. Foss (Farmington, housewife)
James E. of Acton, ME m. Edna **Greenfield** of Ware, MA 10/6/1945
in Sanbornville; H - 30, farmer, b. Acton, ME, s/o Edward
Wilson (Providence, RI, farmer) and Agnes Young (Acton, ME,

414

housewife); W - 22, sch. teacher, b. Fitchburg, MA, d/o Melvin Greenfield (Durhanville, NY, sch. supt.) and Blanche Doe (Fitchburg, MA, housewife)

WITHAM,
Charles A. of Brookfield m. Mary E. **Woodsome** of Limerick, ME 11/25/1914 in Limerick, ME; H - 35, farmer, 2nd, b. Brookfield, s/o Charles H. Witham and Rosa Hardy; W - 24, housekeeper, b. Limerick, ME, d/o John H. Woodsome and Mary L. Chadburn

WRIGHT,
Donald Burton m. Gladys Editha **Tasker** 1/30/1968 in Brookfield

WYATT,
Donald Louis m. Virginia Roberts **Snow** 11/23/1991 in Wolfeboro

WYMAN,
Robert W. m. Elaine B. **Simpson** 7/6/2001 in Wolfeboro

ZEIGLER,
Michael L. m. Rachel M. **Nichols** 6/25/2000 in Wolfeboro

ZIEGLER,
Scott Paul m. Cheryl Kaukuk **Allen** 12/16/1990 in Brookfield

Adams, Jean - Ricker, John David
Adjutant, Gloria Doris - Katwick, Robert Tilden
Adjutant, Cynthia H. - MacBrien, Bruce A.
Alexander, Christine Ellen - Hobbs, Neal Clayton
Allen, Cheryl Kaukuk - Ziegler, Scott Paul
Anderson, Sonja Louise - Carll, Robert Lenwood
Appleton, Lucy (Welch) - Wentworth, Stephen S.
Arellano, Marie DelCarmen - Wickboldt, Richard
Arthur, Elizabeth Piper - Ingemi, Riccardo Paul, Jr.
Ayer, Hazel Octavia - MacBrien, Luther Andrew

Baczkiel, Barbara A. - Lund, Forrest C.
Bannon, Barbara E. - Denison, Steven K.
Bell, Florence - Hill, Herschel E.
Bozner, Ellen R. - Leblanc, Patrick E.
Bridges, Diane Elaine - Sinapius, Gerald Thomas
Brown, Anna E. - Clark, Raymond G.
Brown, Lillian M. - West, George E.
Brown, June Katherine - Moore, Russell Raymond, Jr.
Bryant, Dorothy M. - Hansen, Otto J.
Buckland, Mary E. - Plasmati, Richard B.
Burnell, Amy B. - Rufus, Lewis H.
Burnham, Diane Leslie - Nichols, Kezar Guild, Jr.
Buswell, Elinor L. - Tasker, B. Dean

Calef, Eva - Willey, Charles Tracy
Carroll, Marion J. - Chamberlain, Frank H.
Cate, Norma - Cormier, Raymond E.
Cate, Dorothy M. - Nason, Ernest E.
Cate, Bernice E. - Hooper, Sidney E.
Cate, Sara W. - Bixby, William A.
Chamberlain, Helene P. - Colman, Wilson
Chamberlain, Marion - Burroughs, Roy
Champaigne, Irene - Cotton, Henry J.
Churchill, Nancy S. - Lyons, Edward P.
Cilley, Addie L. - Drew, Henry W.
Clap, Harriet - Churchill, Randolph
Clark, Doris A. - Chase, Bernard C.
Clark, Nellie M. - Herrick, George S.
Climo, Holly Anne - Hughes, Raymond S.
Clough, Juanita - Luscomb, Kenneth K.

Clow, Flora E. (Martin) - Nutter, William H.
Cole, Virginia A. - Wentworth, Reginald E.
Colman, Frances M. - Rines, Philip H.
Comtois, Nicole - Lewis, Mark
Copplestone, Janice Anne - Hodgdon, David Glenn
Cornwell, Sally Ann - Walpole, Jonathon Mathew
Cossette, Josephine Sanborn - Hickey, S. Michael
Cossette, Carolyn E. - Davis, Kenneth W.
Cossette, Carolyn E. - Cefalo, Gregory N.
Cotton, Abbie H. - Lang, Wallace F.
Cotton, Inez L. - Caswell, Norman E.
Cotton, Irene L. - Cate, Norris E.
Crowley, Harietta F. - Lawrence, Charles R.

Davis, Daisy M. (Thompson) - Robinson, Walter L.
Davis, Sandra - Lyon, Peter Byrd
DeBow, Joyce Allison - Brady, Christopher Michael
Delaurier, Carol - Knight, Gary
Demeritt, Bertha - Valley, Arthur
DePree, Kathryn J. - Moore, George J.
Dickson, Ada (Stackpole) - Churchill, Lester L.
Dodier, Rosa - French, Lawrence
Downs, Flora W. - Willey, Leon M.
Downs, Anna S. (Spooner) - Churchill, Lester L.
Drew, Francena K. - Lang, John E.
Drew, Madeleine L. - Limbarger, Luther E.
Drew, Florence E. - Wilson, Daniel H.
Drew, Luna E. (Eldridge) - Elliott, Charles H.
Drew, Christina E. - Ross, Ovila
Dubuc, Carolyn E. - Brown, Kenneth R.
Dwyer, Susan Elizabeth - Barrett, Walter William, III

Eaton, Ida B. - Mackie, Millard F.
Edmisten, Orilla May - French, Charles L.
Eldridge, Nancy Naomia - Nason, Michael Wayne
Elkins, Florence Leach - Eaton, Martin H.
Emerson, Alice M. - Churchill, Guy L.
Erskine, Margaret - Erskine, Alan R. L.

Farley, Anna M. (Wade) - Grant, Clarence
Feist, Joan I. - Butler, Charles E.

Fletcher, Julia (Willey) - Deland, Thomas T.
Fogg, Mabelle O. - Cate, Herbert H.
Ford, Brenda - Wholley, William Ernest
Ford, Harriet Selena - Colman, Henry
Foss, Lizzie E. - Drew, John E.
Foster, Beth A. - Caddell, Mark E.
Foster, Maude A. (McMally) - Douglas, Fred S.
Fowler, Katherine Louise - Alibrandi, Joseph Anthony

Gallagher, Laurie M. - Whittemore, James E.
Garland, Erika K. A. - Cotton, Henry John
Garside, Sadie E. (Daphney) - Stebbins, Richard E.
Glidden, Judith Elaine - Lee, Robert Edward, Jr.
Goodhue, Hattie M. - Thomes, Horace L.
Gosselin, Geraldine G. - Coy, William R.
Gosselin, Eliza J. (Cooley) - Allen, Phillip M.
Grant, Marguerite O. - Hutchins, Joseph H.
Greenfield, Edna - Wilson, James E.

Hahn, Charlotte - Arner, Robert
Hahn, Cornelia A. - May, Rolf G.
Hahn, Charlotte A. - Edwards, Harvey L.
Haley, Chris Ann - Fothergill, William James
Hanson, Harriet H. - Cook, Gilbert H.
Hanson, Mabel A. - Lang, John H.
Hardman, Leslie Ann - Carpenter, Stephen Alan
Harmon, Mabel Francis - MacBrien, Philip James
Haskin, Jessica Ann - Case, James Powell, Jr.
Hastings, Lisa F. - Croteau, Joseph S.
Heald, Priscilla - Stevens, Reginald
Healy, Patrice Jay - Haines, Paul Lawrence
Heath, Mabel - Wentworth, Henry E.
Helm, Dulcie Lee - Lavender, Thomas E.
Hicks, Charlotte Dee - Brown, Dana Eugene
Higgins, Sylvina A. - Fogg, Simon E.
Hobbs, Nancy Joan - Noble, Edwin Jerome
Hobbs, Velma Jean - Van Dyke, Bruce Edwin
Hodgdon, Emma - Rines, George W.
Hofmann, Bonilynn - McRobbie, James Arthur
Hooper, Sandra Louise - Whittemore, James Edwin
Hooper, Barbara M. - Batten, James A.

Hoyt, Mattie - Clark, James E.
Hughes, Adeline Morris - Russo, Robert Francis
Hume, Luanne F. - Goodrich, Kenneth J.
Huntress, Emma (Richards) - Brown, Grover C.

Jarnot, Catherine Mary - Kinville, Theodore Scott
Johnson, Carrie V. - Lang, Daniel
Johnson, Mary T. - Hanson, Sydney Q.
Johnston, Alice-Ann Bailey - Pinkham, Christopher Choate

King, M. R. - Hubbard, Henry C.
Knowles, Sandi Jo - Soucy, David Richard

Lankhorst, Ellen - Burkhart, Roger
Leavitt, Lena (Hill) - Richards, Walter
Leonard, Lee Anne - Velez, Alejandro
Libby, Mertie - Cate, Raymond M.
Locke, Dorothy Ellen - Vanderpool, Douglas Warren
Lord, Judith Alma - Hooper, Thomas Martin
Luscomb, Helen E. (Thompson) - Drew, Fred L.
Lyford, Alice A. - Hutchins, John L.

MacDonald, Leon Mary (Hall) - Smith, Albert Webster
Macpherson, Mariellen - Howard, Jed M.
Mann, Jennifer Kelly - Rouleau, Cy Matthew
Manzer, Edna Louise - Magnuson, Richard Axel
Marks, Jean F. - Broderick, Charles W.
Marr, Eliza J. - Jacobson, Paul A.
Martel, Helen Elizabeth - Sanderson, Charles Henry
Martell, Catherine Mary - Katwick, Arthur David
Martikke, Robin C. - Doyal, Timothy E.
McGinley, Cathleen Ann - Fallon, Paul Andrew
McLane, Minerva W. - Ingraham, William H.
Milne, Judith - Penniman, William Frederick, III
Moody, Audrey E. - Smith, James R.
Moon, Michele Marie - Schlageter, Mark Stephen
Moulton, M. Pauline - Breary, George J.
Muller, Margaret E. - Burhoe, Horace G.
Murphy, Jennifer Ann - Colbath, Dale R.

Nason, Cora - Remick, Samuel A.

420

Nason, Roberta F. - Walters, Donald E., Jr.
Nason, Mary Elizabeth - Brown, Douglas Martin
Nason, Tammy L. - Phinney, Charles D.
Nason, Edith M. - Floyd, John D.
Nichols, Rachel M. - Zeigler, Michael L.
Niewenhous, Martha Atwood - Pike, John Raymond
Noonan, Sandra Mae - Byrne, Robert Gregg, Jr.

Osborne, Kimberly Rae - Lineman, John R.

Perkins, Bernice M. (Willey) - Boston, Arthur
Perry, Kristan N. - Sheffer, Daniel J.
Peterson, Jennie E. - Wiggin, William P.
Phelan, Rita Mary - Smith, Robert Andrew, Jr.
Pike, Bernice H. - Lang, Reuben P.
Pike, Mabel A. - Wiggin, Frank H.
Piper, Alice N. - Schrieter, Augustus
Pizey, Anne Elizabeth - Palmer, John Frederick
Place, Amanda E. - Churchill, Charles I.
Plant, Janet E. - Bye, David F.
Plant, Susan R. - Chick, Mark A.
Ponkop (Eldridge) - White, Bernard L.
Prescott, J. Doris - Corrow, Eric D.
Promise, Georgia Sue - Pike, Loring Robinson
Pulkinen, Sonja M. - Fair, William M.

Reed, Elizabeth K. (Keene) - Kerr, John J. H.
Reed, June E. - Moran, John Michael
Richards, Maxine Virginia - Leeper, Verne Pembleton
Richards, Edna B. - Neal, Charles H.
Richards, Ida F. - Cook, James L.
Riley, Jeanne A. - Ringer, Kenneth C.
Rines, Lilla M. (Whitehouse) - Davis, William G.
Robinson, Adelaide - Hughes, Roland S.
Rockwell, Mary Palmer - Roberts, Reed Turney
Rollins, Lucy A. (West) - Brown, Langdon D.
Rose, Jennifer L. Beattie - Hastings, Brian C.
Rouleau, Amy Yvonne - Glidden, David Allen
Russell, Ida L. Coffin (Cornell) - Drew, Clarence L.
Russo, Teresa A. - McGee, Michael S.

Sabol, Paula A. - Plant, Darrell E.
Sanborn, Etta L. (Thompson) - Hill, Harry L.
Sanborn, Marie Ada L. - Hansen, Carl C.
Sarde, Brigette Elizabeth - Taylor, Peter Haywood
Saunders, Erin Michelle - Pike, Christopher Charles
Sawyer, Elizabeth L. - Haines, Samuel E.
Schmidt, Anna - Hackett, Bert S.
Shortridge, Marjorie G. - Low, Edgar
Simpson, Elaine B. - Wyman, Robert W.
Snow, Virginia Roberts - Wyatt, Donald Louis
Stevens, Maud E. - Allen, Harry G.
Stevens, Grace M. - Shortridge, Albert S.
Stevens, Carrie A. - Carville, Joseph W.
Swaine, Beverly Ann - Trimm, Edward Arnold

Tasker, Gladys Editha - Wright, Donald Burton
ter Weele, Fenneke Ge' - Joslin, Richard Arthur
Thompson, Margaret - Royle, Norman Harold
Thorne, Susan Davis - Lamb, Peter Henshaw
Tirrell, Penny Candy - Lewis, Philip Virgil, Jr.
Towle, Cynthia - Berry, Stephen L.
Towle, Marybeth - Hill, Alfred J.
Trott, Annie E. - Tibbetts, Everett J.
Tully, Andrea C. - Dubuc, Paul E.
Tutt, June A. - Fletcher, Melvin E.

Wakefield, Mary D. (Frye) - Nutter, Llewellyn
Walton, Albina May (Robar) - Peavey, Henry W.
Webster, Frances A. - Allen, Herbert A.
Weeks, Lucretia - Hanson, Joseph H.
Weeks, Susie L. - Tibbetts, Everett J.
Weeks, Jennifer - Doyle, Michael Curtis
Weinroth, Frances H. - Saujon, Royce A., II
Wentworth, Emma O. - Sceggel, Arthur L.
Wentworth, Jennie M. - Churchill, Charles I.
West, Lillian M. - Bradley, Earl M.
Wheeler, Katherine - Lang, Joseph W.
White, Cheryl Jean - White, Robert Heaton, Jr.
White, Madeline G. - Burroughs, Warren
Wiggin, Idella L. - Lang, Reuben
Wigglesworth, Thelma Flinn - Rogers, Thomas Wilson

Wilkinson, Ruth (Dyer) - Hardin, Charles W.
Wilson, Cynthia Lorraine - Brooks, Vincent Edward
Wiseman, Christine B. - Chellman, Chester Eric, Sr.
Witham, Rose (Hardy) - Robinson, John F.
Witham, Mary Frances - Belknap, Charles Lyman
Woodsome, Mary E. - Witham, Charles A.
Woodus, Ethel M. - Mattson, Godfrey
Woodward, Alice R. - Wiggin, Harry F.
Wright, Susan L. - Adjutant, Geoffrey N.

York, Alice E. - Allen, Chester A.
York, Ida B. - Burroughs, Howard
York, Thelma E. - Churchill, Frederick W.

Zalenski, Arline Mabel - Nason, Edward Bruce
Zirpolo, Rebecca A. - Eichen, Joseph E.

BROOKFIELD
DEATHS

ABEL,
Mildred Ridge, d. 3/19/1996 at 69; b. NC

ADJUTANT,
Ann A., d. 2/15/1887 at 37/5/12; housekeeper; married; b. Ossipee;
William F. Garland (Ossipee) and Olive Kennerson (Ossipee)
Celia M., d. 5/8/1928 at 23/11 in Danvers, MA; waitress; single; b.
Sanbornville; Leonard E. Adjutant (Wolfeboro) and Selina
Eaton (Brookfield)
Everett, d. 11/19/1889 at 2/4/2; b. Brookfield; George E. Adjutant
(Wolfeboro) and Clara E. Eaton (Wolfeboro)

ALBRO,
Elinor, d. 12/2/1999 at 96; b. Quincy, MA
Harry R., d. 4/9/1987 at 83; b. MA

ALIBRANDI,
Joseph Francis, d. 3/27/1994 at 71; b. Boston, MA

ALLEN,
Deborah, d. 10/27/1895 at 83 in Brookfield; housekeeper; widow; b.
Brookfield; John Weeks (Wakefield) and Abigail Colomy (New
Durham)
Edna Mason, d. 2/1/1993 at 77; b. MA
Ernest, d. 7/19/1887 at 1/3/14; b. Brookfield; Samuel M. Allen
(Brookfield) and Emma F. Cummings (Brookfield)
Garland, d. 10/22/1888 at 78/6/23; farmer; married; b. Wakefield;
Mark Allen (Wakefield) and Mary Locke (Wakefield)
Lloyd E., d. 3/1/1987 at 67; b. MA
Roderick T., d. 11/17/1986 at 35; b. MA

ANDERSON,
Earl A., d. 5/10/1995 at 63; b. MA

ATKINS,
Joseph R., d. 3/30/1911 at 84/8/10 in Brookfield; sea captain;
widower; b. Provincetown, MA

AVERY,
Roberta Shailer, d. 3/9/1976 at 82; b. IL
Shailer, d. 8/7/1994 at 73; b. MA

BAKER,
Freeman, d. 10/16/1895 at 83 in Brookfield; builder; married

BARNARD,
Jacqueline H., d. 3/5/1980 at 40; b. MO

BEHAN,
Anna A., d. 12/24/1977 at 81; b. MA

BELKNAP,
Maude A., d. 10/28/1959 at 81; b. Arlington, MA

BERRY,
Lincoln H., d. 3/11/2000 at 86; b. Lemington, VT

BJORKROTH,
Eric C. W., d. 10/16/1978 at 88; b. Sweden
Gunhild M., d. 4/7/1983 at 85; b. Sweden

BLAKE,
Eliza W., d. 4/30/1896 at 79/0/22 in Brookfield; housekeeper; widow;
    b. Brookfield; Thomas W. Wentworth (Berwick, ME) and Mary
    Hanson (Brookfield)
Frances, d. 2/24/1896 at – in Brookfield
William, d. 9/30/1899 at 81/2/14; apoplexy; widower; William Blake
    and Abagail Cook

BLODGETT,
Albert W., d. 5/10/1934 at 68/7/24 in Rochester; retired; married; b.
    Danvers, MA; William Blodgett (Danvers, MA) and Susan
Andrews (Danvers, MA)
S. E., d. 5/16/1948 at 70/1/15 in Dover; none; widow; b. Brookfield;
    Samuel Eaton (Brookfield) and Mary E. Berry

BOSTON,
Arthur, d. 7/3/1964 at 75; b. Brookfield
Cora, d. 8/7/1961 at 85; b. Farmington
Eva M., d. 6/20/1966 at 73
George H., d. 12/22/1952 at 70 in Union; single; b. Brookfield; Henry
    Boston and Susan Drew

Henry, d. 4/1/1901 at 61/5/14 in Brookfield; pulmonary consumption; married; b. Lunenburg, ME; Joseph Boston and Eleanor Miller
John W., d. 3/19/1916 at 70/6/28 in Brookfield; laborer; single; b. New Durham; Joseph Boston and Ellen Miller (Alton)
Nathan, d. 3/26/1945 at 64/8/16 in Brookfield; farming; single; b. Brookfield; Henry Boston (Littleton, VT) and Susan Drew (Brookfield)
Susan A., d. 11/24/1922 at 70/2/13 in Brookfield; at home; widow; b. Brookfield; Ivory Drew (Brookfield) and Abbie Ricker (Ossipee)
Will F., d. 10/23/1959 at 75

BOWDEN,
Alexine P., d. 2/19/1918 at 65 in Portland, ME; retired; widow; b. Portsmouth; John Ferguson and M. A. L. Pike

BRAM,
Edward, d. 6/21/1903 at 75 in Brookfield

BREWSTER,
Glenn, d. 2/13/1987 at 39; b. NH

BROWN,
stillborn son, d. 1/4/1900 at –; Langdon D. Brown and Alfretta Drew
Alfretta, d. 1/4/1900 at 45/6/19; acute Bright's disease; married; Elizabeth Drew
Dorothy L., d. 11/18/1972 at 57; b. ME
Edwin L., d. 7/21/1921 at 75/7/28 in Brookfield; farmer; married; b. Ossipee; James L. Brown and Hannah T. Hussey
Elsie J., d. 11/3/1979 at 93; b. ME
Ernest Haywood, d. 7/18/1989 at 76; b. ME
Grover C., d. 12/5/1959 at 76; b. Brookfield
John F., d. 3/2/1896 at 76/11 in Brookfield; farmer; married; b. Nottingham; Samuel Brown and Betsey Brown
Langdon D., d. 5/26/1924 at 72/7/5; b. Northwood; John F. Brown and Ellen Carter
Lucy D., d. 5/23/1916 at 58/7/25 in Brookfield; housewife; married; b. Brookfield; Charles E. West and Cyrena Ricker
Mary E., d. 1/7/1914 at 16/7/22 in Brookfield; single; b. Brookfield; Langdon D. Brown (Northwood) and Alfreda Drew (Brookfield)

Susan E., d. 6/26/1928 at 79/4/8 in Brookfield; at home; widow; b. Brookfield; William Willey (Brookfield) and Susan R. Henderson (Rochester)

BUCKLAND,
Charles, d. 4/19/2003 in MA

BULLARD,
Walter Gould, d. 8/7/1957 at 69; b. N. Bellingham, MA

BURLEIGH,
Angeline, d. 4/8/1915 at 68/7 in Brookfield; housekeeper; single; b. Ossipee; James Burleigh (Ossipee) and Nancy Burleigh (Ossipee)

BURNHAM,
Alice, d. 7/20/1929 at 77/10/12 in Brookfield; at home; widow; b. Middleboro, MA; Sidney Eaton

BURROUGHS,
Abigail M., d. 7/26/1895 at 54/6/26 in Brookfield; housekeeper; widow; b. Brookfield; William Willey (Brookfield) and Susan Henderson (Rochester)
Howard W., d. 10/1/1928 at 69/6/18 in Brookfield; farmer; married; b. Brookfield; Warren M. Burroughs (Brookfield) and Abbie M. Willey (Brookfield)

BYRNE,
Valerie B., d. 2/22/1983 at 76; b. MA

CALEF,
Frank, d. 6/25/1938 at 84/0/25 in Brookfield; retired; widower; b. Farmington; James Calef (Farmington) and Emily Ricker (Sandwich)

CAMPBELL,
Edith S., d. 12/7/1906 at 0/5/27 in Brookfield; b. Brookfield; Walter Campbell (Wolfeboro) and Carrie M. Ellis (Strafford)

CASWELL,
Inez, d. 4/25/2003 in Wolfeboro

CATE,
daughter, d. 1/16/1932 at – in Brookfield; b. Brookfield; Norris E.
  Cate (Brookfield) and Irene Cotton (Wolfeboro)
Adelia S., d. 1/7/1943 at 87/5 in Brookfield; housewife; widow; b.
  Gonic; John Foss and Priscilla Foss
Aimee B., d. 2/28/1933 at 73/6/20 in Brookfield; at home; widow; b.
  Bayou LaFouche, LA; Gauchette Beaugee (Paris, France) and
  Ernestine LeBlanc (Bayou LaFouche, LA)
Almira, d. 1/3/1899 at 84/0/27 in Brookfield; senile gangrene; widow;
  Thomas Burley and Nancy Smith
Charles F., d. 2/21/1909 at 59/10/1 in Brookfield; married; b.
  Brookfield; Isaac W. Cate (Barrington) and Almira Burleigh
  (Brookfield)
George Albert, d. 2/21/1921 at 74/11/10 in Brookfield; none; single;
  b. Brookfield; Isaac W. Cate and Elmira Burley
Harry W., d. 7/4/1931 at 71/7/4 in Brookfield; farmer; married; b.
  Brookfield; Moses C. Cate (Brookfield) and Susan Wentworth
  (Wakefield)
Herbert H., d. 10/17/1946 at 65/3/11 in Brookfield; painter; married;
  b. Gonic; Amasa Cate (Brookfield) and Adelia Foss (Gonic)
Irene L., d. 3/7/1991 at 81; b. NH
Isaac F., d. 12/20/1898 at 55/7/12 in Brookfield; carcinoma of
  bowels; single; Isaac W. Cate and Almira Burley
Joseph A., d. 11/1/1944 at 92/1/3 in Wolfeboro; painter; widower; b.
  Brookfield; Isaac Cate and Elmira Burleigh
Lauretta A., d. 5/25/1909 at 51/8/21 in Brookfield; housewife; widow;
  b. Provincetown; Joseph Russell Atkins (Provincetown) and
  Martha Willis Cook (Provincetown, MA)
Myrtie D., d. 3/19/1943 at 43/8/26 in Rochester; housewife; married;
  b. Gray, ME; Wendell Small (Gray, ME) and Minnie Libby
  (Gray, ME)
Norris E., d. 10/23/1976 at 79; b. NH

CHAMBERLAIN,
Howard A., d. 9/12/1967 at 20; b. Wolfeboro

CHAPIN,
Sarah E., d. 12/14/1952 at 93 in Brookfield; at home; widow; b.
  Boston, MA; Luther P. Wiggin and Margaret McCully

CHAPMAN,
Catharine W., d. 5/5/1915 at 92/2/9 in Brookfield; widow; b. Boston, MA; James Bell (Leyden, MA) and Sarah Shepardson (Guilford, VT)

CHURCHILL,
Alice Maude, d. 5/27/1967 at 89; b. Stowe, ME
Charles, d. 2/13/1918 at 72/1/13 in Brookfield; retired; single; b. Brookfield; Joseph Churchill and Martha Wiggin
George A., d. 7/16/1897 at 47/3/3 in Brookfield; inflammation of liver and exhaustion; single; b. Brookfield; Joseph T. Churchill and Martha M. Wiggin
Gladys Ferguson, d. 5/8/1978 at 78
Guy L., d. 3/9/1946 at 59/9/4 in Wolfeboro; dairy farmer; married; b. Brookfield; Lester Churchill (Brookfield) and Harriet Ferguson (Portsmouth)
Harriet M., d. 12/10/1970 at 52; b. NJ
Hattie F., d. 12/26/1920 at 59/10/27 in Portsmouth; housewife; married; b. Brookfield; John H. Ferguson (Brookfield) and M. A. Loraine Pike (Brookfield)
James W., d. 3/4/1939 at 0/11/2 in Dover; b. Brookfield; Frederick W. Churchill (Marlboro, MA) and Amey Spencer (Providence, RI)
Joseph, d. 12/3/1933 at 90/5/3 in Brookfield; retired; widower; b. Brookfield; Joseph Churchill (Newmarket) and Martha Wiggin
Lester L., d. 2/16/1933 at 72/2/14 in Wolfeboro; farmer; widower; b. Brookfield; Thomas L. Churchill (Brookfield) and Sara Stackpole (Limerick, ME)
Nancy M., d. 12/14/1918 at 86/11/14 in Brookfield; housewife; widow; b. Barnstead; Nicholas G. Seward and Nancy Marilla
Randolph E., d. 7/23/1972 at 64; b. NH
Thomas L., d. 4/8/1913 at 90/11/22 in Brookfield; clergyman; married; b. Brookfield; John T. Churchill (Brookfield) and Mahitable Willey (Brookfield)

CILLEY,
Andrew, d. 7/14/1895 at 87/3/27 in Brookfield; farmer; widower; b. Hebron; Job Cilley (Hebron) and Susanna Seavey (Andover)

CLARK,

Barbara E., d. 2/11/1919 at 1/7/7 in Brookfield; b. Wakefield; J. Frank Clark and Gladys M. Pickering

Betsey M., d. 3/3/1895 at 81/4 in Brookfield; housekeeper; married; b. Middleton; Jacob Horne (Middleton) and Polly French (Farmington)

Charles E., d. 4/25/1916 at 73/8/25 in Brookfield; farmer; married; b. Middleton; James C. Clark (Lebanon, ME) and Betsey I. Horn (Middleton)

Ella M., d. 5/20/1916 at 65/10/6 in Brookfield; housewife; widow; b. Tuftonboro; John Willand

Frank E., d. 12/24/1889 at 18/8; farmer; single; b. Berwick, ME; James F. Clark (Brookfield) and Sarah Abbott (Berwick, ME)

James C., d. 1/27/1909 at 88/8/7 in Brookfield; farmer; widower; b. Lebanon, ME; Solomon Clark (Lebanon, ME) and Lydia Kennerson (Ossipee)

James E., d. 1/31/1942 at 71/6/4 in Wolfeboro; farmer; widower; b. Tuftonboro; Charles E. Clark (Middleton) and Ella M. Willand (Ossipee)

Mattie A., d. 1/19/1924 at 33/10/2; b. Rochester; Alonzo Hoyt and Gertrude Edgerly

Priscilla W., d. 7/3/1894 at 81/9/27 in Brookfield; housekeeper; single; b. Eaton; Solomon Clark (Lebanon, ME) and Lydia Kennison (Ossipee)

CLARKE,

Anna E., d. 12/1/1984 at 91

CLEMENTS,

Amelia, d. 2/22/2004 in Ossipee

CLIMO,

William C., d. 7/4/1997 at 59; b. Stoneham, MA

COLMAN,

Charles, d. 1/19/1917 at 82/9/19 in Brookfield; minister; widower; b. Brookfield; Charles Colman (Boston, MA) and Eliza Neal (Brookfield)

Charles D., d. 4/22/1912 at 0/2/15 in Brookfield; b. Boston, MA; Charles Colman (Boston, MA) and Jennie Setterland (Boston, MA)

Cordelia C., d. 9/1/1890 at 72/11 in Brookfield; dropsy; single
Dudley C., d. 2/9/1911 at 82/4/22 in Wolfeboro; retired; single; b.
   Brookfield; Charles Colman and Eliza Neal (Portsmouth)
Harriet, d. 5/31/1945 at 75/7/17 in Brookfield; housewife; married; b.
   Boston, MA; Thomas Ford and Amanda Runlet
Mary E., d. 6/21/1938 at 71/1/22 in Brookfield; retired; single; b.
   Brookfield; Charles Coleman (Brookfield) and Salome A.
   Cotton (Wolfeboro)
Salome A., d. 6/11/1905 at 63/5/18 in Brookfield; housekeeper;
   married; b. Wolfeboro; Daniel Cotton and Eliza Lang

COMER,
Chester W., d. 10/21/1973 at 78; b. MA

COOK,
Frank E., d. 1/23/1923 at 57/10/29 in Brookfield; shoe worker;
   married; b. Milton; Jeremiah Cook (Middleton) and Emily
   Whitehouse (Tuftonboro)
Harriet H., d. 11/29/1918 at 45/9/25 in Brookfield; housewife;
   married; b. Brookfield; Charles H. Hanson and Mary C. Buzzell
Ida R., d. 10/3/1922 at 49/9/14 in Rochester; housewife; married; b.
   Wakefield; Charles Richards (Wakefield) and Keziah Quimby
   (Newfield, ME)
James L., d. 4/7/1926 at 58/7/15 in Brookfield; farmer; widower; b.
   Brookfield; Peter Cook (Wakefield) and Sarah J. Gage
   (Wakefield)
Peter, d. 3/10/1903 at 79/2/11 in Brookfield; married; Thomas Cook
   and Mary Safford

COPPLESTONE,
Miriam L., d. 1/24/1983 at 62; b. NY

CORBETT,
Andrew James Leo, d. 11/12/1956 at 57

COSSETTE,
Aurore L., d. 12/27/1995 at 95; b. NH
Ludger J., d. 10/17/1987 at 92; b. NH
Paul J., d. 2/15/1999 at 69; b. Rochester

COTTLE,
Mary L., d. 3/8/1899 at 80/11/5; apoplexy; widow; Jonathan Ranlett and Nancy Pettigrew

COTTON,
John A., d. 12/25/1951 at 70 in Brookfield; contractor; married; b. Wolfeboro; John Q. Cotton and Idella Adjutant
Mary Leona, d. 7/17/1960 at 74; b. Brookfield
Sherman H., d. 10/–/1918 at 21/3/17 in Brookfield; laborer; single; b. Wolfeboro; Charles S. Cotton and Emma S. Nute

COWAN,
Nellie E., d. 3/9/1955 at 66 in Brookfield; homemaker; widow; b. Wolfeboro; Albert Libby and Lillian Clow

COX,
Mary E., d. 8/17/1983 at 65; b. MA

CRITCHERSON,
Ethel Markland, d. 3/28/1968 at 53; b. Lynn, MA
George W., d. 3/12/1976 at 67; b. MA

CROWLEY,
Alonzo F., d. 5/28/1950 at 81 in Wolfeboro; auto., retired; married; b. G. Lake, NB; Dennis Crowley and Abbie Foster

CURTIS,
Abigail, d. 10/7/1890 at 73/4/7 in Brookfield; dyspepsia, disease of heart, typhoid fever; housekeeper; married; b. Acton, ME; Joseph Sanborn (Acton, ME) and Sally Farnham (Wakefield)

DAY,
Maude E., d. 11/28/1977 at 77; b. NY

DEARBORN,
Leroy S., d. 3/4/1894 at 54/7 in Brookfield; laborer; single; b. Wakefield; Frances Dearborn (Wakefield)

DEBOW,
Currie, d. 11/8/2005 in Brookfield

DEL DEO,
Almerinda, d. 1/5/1984 at 85; b. RI

DELAND,
Mary E., d. 9/27/1887 at 60/2/18; housekeeper; married; b.
Marblehead, MA; William Beals (Marblehead, MA) and Mary
James (Marblehead, MA)

DIMICK,
Carroll D., d. 7/5/1912 at 70/3 in Brookfield; watchman; married; b.
Lyme; Daniel B. Dimick (Lyme) and Diadema P. Wales (Lyme)

DINSMORE,
Emma, d. 3/17/1943 at 83/5/19 in Ossipee; housewife; widow; b.
Milo, ME; Stephen Millett (Milo, ME) and Abbie Perriga (Milo,
ME)

DONOVAN,
Martin J., d. 4/11/1973 (about) at 81; b. MA (1978)

DREW,
Abbie Ann, d. 5/1/1921 at 94/11/25 in Brookfield; at home; single; b.
Brookfield; William Drew and Betsy Brown
Addie, d. 10/26/1920 at 71/10/17 in Brookfield; housewife; widow; b.
Brookfield; John Tibideau
Addie L., d. 1/16/1902 at 18/10/27 in Brookfield; tuberculosis
consumption; married; b. Hebron; Anthony Cilley and Arvilla
Twombly
Charles, d. 8/28/1908 at 62/6/8 in Brookfield; single; b. Brookfield;
William Drew (Brookfield) and Sarah Leavitt
Elizabeth E., d. 5/21/1946 at 60/2/14 in Wolfeboro; housewife;
married; b. Farmington; Henry Foss
Freddie, d. 9/21/1889 at 1/4/3; b. Brookfield; Henry Drew
(Brookfield) and Emeline Dyer (Brownfield, ME)
Hannah, d. 1/29/1889 at 73/10/26; housekeeper; widow; b. Dover;
Eben Dame (Dover) and Martha Davis (Kittery, ME)
Henry W., d. 2/1/1912 at 75/8/23 in Milton; married; b. Brookfield;
Benjamin Drew (Milton) and Hannah Drew (Dover)
John W., d. 4/6/1915 at 55/4/17 in Brookfield; farmer; married; b.
Brookfield; Ivory C. Drew and Elizabeth Drew

Jonas, d. 1/31/1892 at 5/6/3 in Brookfield; b. Brookfield; Henry Drew (Brookfield) and Emeline Dyer (Porter, ME)
Mary E., d. 5/29/1888 at 57/7/12; housekeeper; single; b. Brookfield; William Drew (Milton) and Betsey E. Brown (Strafford)
Maurice Warren, d. 3/2/1921 at 0/0/20 in Brookfield; b. Brookfield; John E. Drew and Elizabeth Foss

DUCHANO,
Marjorie W., d. 3/29/1988 at 61; b. MA

DUFFY,
Gloria, d. 1/20/2005 in Wolfeboro

DUNN,
Edwin J., d. 5/27/1987 at 69; b. NY

EATON,
Samuel S., d. 6/21/1912 at 75/11/21 in Brookfield; farmer; married; b. Wolfeboro; Chandler Eaton and Mary J. Cottle

EDGERLY,
Perley, d. 6/15/1957 at 84; b. Durham

ELLIOTT,
Betsey E., d. 12/13/1910 at 68 in Brookfield; housework; married; b. Ossipee; Upton Hammond and Lydia Gellison

FERGUSON,
Donald G., d. 6/16/1977 at 84; b. MA
John H., d. 12/2/1910 at 87/9/29 at "Maine Hospital"; retired; widower; b. Portsmouth; Stephen Ferguson (Portsmouth) and Maria Seward (Portsmouth)
Mary A. L., d. 2/7/1906 at 77/6/18 in Brookfield; housewife; married; b. Brookfield; Dudley Pike (Middleton) and Adeline Chamberlain (Brookfield)

FETTER,
Nora M., d. 6/2/1979 at 89; b. Ireland

FLETCHER,
Ruth C., d. 6/24/1983 at 83; b. MA

FLOYD,
Frederick L., d. 3/2/1934 at 14/1/12 in Brookfield; school; b. Dracut, MA; John M. Floyd (Worcester, MA) and Ella Lowd (W. Newfield, ME)

FOGG,
Daniel, d. 10/16/1932 at 76/2/17 in Brookfield; farmer; divorced; b. Ossipee; Simon Fogg (Ossipee) and Mary A. Seward (Wakefield)
Neil Sterling, d. 10/26/1986 at 54; b. MA
Steven Mark, d. 4/22/1985 at 26; b. NH

FOLSOM,
Joanie M., d. 6/20/2003 in Brookfield

FORD,
Lillian A., d. 9/13/1972 at 93; b. USA

FOSS,
Abigail B., d. 11/7/1895 at 66/5/13 in Brookfield; housekeeper; married; b. Stowe, ME; Andrew Johnson (Stowe, ME) and Charity Johnson (Stowe, ME)
Eliza A., d. 12/16/1937 at 87/6/3 in Brookfield; retired; widow; b. Wakefield; John Davis (Wakefield) and L. Gilman (Wakefield)

FRANGES,
Ivan, d. 3/8/1972 at 72; b. Yugoslavia
Justine C., d. 8/29/1973 at 65; b. Washington, DC
Mira D., d. 11/3/1953 at 53 in Brookfield; housewife; married; b. Zagret, Yugoslavia; Anthony Sharer and Della Kalaminec
Nicholas O., d. 2/27/1990 at 87; b. Yugoslavia

FRENCH,
Charles Lewis, Jr., d. 12/5/1998 at 75; b. Boston, MA
Gilbert E., d. 9/15/2002 in Wolfeboro

GARLAND,
Guy West, d. 8/14/1957 at 59; b. Sanbornville
Hattie E., d. 12/21/1891 at 1/3/29 in Brookfield; b. Wakefield; Charles H. Garland (Tuftonboro) and Sophia S. Drisko (Addison, ME)

John F., d. 5/6/1978 at 80

GARNEY,
Amos Franklin, d. 3/6/1967 at 90; b. Lynn, MA
Grace E., d. 5/26/1944 at 73/4/2 in Brookfield; housewife; married;
    b. Maynard, MA; Henry Haynes (Maynard, MA) and Fanny
    Lovering (Maynard, MA)

GILMAN,
Martha C., d. 7/20/1914 at 73/10/4 in vx; widow; b. Brookfield;
    Joseph T. Churchill (Newmarket) and Martha M. Wiggin
    (Brookfield)

GOODHUE,
Sarah E., d. 4/9/1939 at 90/5/4 in Rochester; at home; widow; b.
    Milton; Asa H. Witham (Milton) and Harriet Fellows (Wakefield)
Thomas, d. 5/5/1896 at 51/3/22 in Brookfield; farmer; married; b.
    Brookfield; Joseph Goodhue (Nottingham) and Hannah
    Stevenson (Wolfeboro)

GOODRICH,
Christine A., d. 9/4/1986 at 39; b. ME

GOVE,
Frank D., d. 11/12/1922 at 70/8/2 in Brookfield; shoemaker;
    widower; b. Barrington; Edward S. Grove (Pittsfield) and
    Caroline Foss (Barrington)

GRANT,
Lucy D., d. 3/30/1978 at 75; b. MA

GRIFFIN,
Joseph A., d. 4/8/1966 at 69; b. Lynn, MA
Susan D., d. 2/26/1983 at 88; b. MA

HACKETT,
John F., d. 9/8/1914 at 72/11/27 in Brookfield; blacksmith; widower;
    b. Wolfeboro; Samuel Hackett and Mary Jane Lang
Nellie Maria, d. 5/9/1904 at 59/10/6 in Brookfield; housekeeper;
    married; b. Freedom; Sylvester Bennett and Olive Lang

HAHN,
L. Beate, d. 6/3/1970 at 76; b. Germany

HALL,
Annie Lucy, d. 4/16/1970 at 67; b. England
James H., Sr., d. 1/2/1979 at 76; b. RI

HAMILTON,
Betsey G., d. 11/22/1907 at 77/6/18 in Brookfield; housewife; widow;
    b. Eaton; John Hart (England) and Hannah Cottle (Eaton)

HAMMOND,
May E., d. 4/14/1977 at 100; b. Great Britain

HANSEN,
Carl C., d. 2/1/1988 at 94; b. Denmark
Karen Marie, d. 3/4/1932 at 79/5/14 in Brookfield; widow; b.
    Denmark; Johan Resmussen (Denmark) and Maren Johnson
    (Denmark)
Ludwig, d. 1/5/1940 at 63/11 in Boston, MA; machinist; married; b.
    Sweden; Morton Hansen (Sweden) and Karen Johnson
    (Sweden)
Marie Ada, d. 10/19/1998 at 88
Otto J., d. 8/19/1974 at 79

HANSON,
Charles H., d. 6/14/1913 at 81/5/1 in Brookfield; farmer; married; b.
    Wakefield; Reuben Hanson, Jr. (Brookfield) and Mary Watson
    (Wolfeboro)
Christine, d. 4/9/1958 at 74
Laura Etta, d. 11/26/1893 at 10/1/28 in Brookfield; acute Bright's
    disease and meningitis; b. Brookfield; Frank A. Hanson and
    Lizzie R. Laskey
Maria A., d. 4/18/1991 at 83; b. Canada
Sarah A., d. 2/5/1887 at 68/6/8; housekeeper; married; b.
    Nottingham; Thomas Ford (Nottingham) and Hannah Bean
    (Nottingham)

HART,
Claire Patricia, d. 2/3/1997 at 72; b. Lynn, MA

HEINLEIN,
Robert, d. 8/24/2005 in Brookfield

HERRICK,
Edith M., d. 10/26/1983 at 69; b. NH

HILL,
Josephine, d. 12/11/1912 at 0/0/1 in Brookfield; b. Brookfield;
    Herschel E. Hill (Halifax, VT) and Florence Bell (Boston, MA)
Leonard, d. 10/2/1929 at 74/3/12 in Brookfield; farmer; married; b.
    Parsonsfield, ME; Johnson Hill (ME) and Almyra Berry
    (Cornish, ME)
Virginia, d. 8/22/1973 at 61; b. MA

HOOPER,
Annie M., d. 5/18/1963 at 72; b. Wolfeboro
Arlene Dorothy, d. 5/17/1998 at 70; b. Wolfeboro
Ralph, d. 6/12/2001

HORNE,
John, d. 5/17/1995 at 93; b. MA
Octavia Pearl, d. 12/4/1993 at 94; b. Newfoundland

HOWES,
Edward L., d. 1/29/1978 at 74; b. CT
Ruth L., d. 1/25/1974 at 70; b. Washington, DC

HUBBARD,
Harold T., d. 8/29/1923 at 0/0/4 in Rochester; b. Rochester; Philip
    Hubbard (Brookfield) and Margaret Young (Rochester)

HUGHES,
Adelaide R., d. 10/27/1992 at 84; b. ME
Roland S., d. 10/22/1980 at 75; b. MA

HUTCHINS,
Abbie G., d. 3/27/1888 at 56/6/23; housekeeper; single; b.
    Wakefield; Stephen D. Hutchins (Wakefield) and Nancy P.
    Sanborn (Wakefield)
Amanda Arden, d. 5/22/1982 at 6

Betsy, d. 10/20/1911 at 87/2/4 in Brookfield; housewife; widow; b. Brookfield; Theopholus W. Lyford (Brookfield) and Mary Goodhue (Milton)

Elizabeth W., d. 12/6/1953 at 91 in Wolfeboro; housewife; widow; b. N. Wakefield; Joseph S. Wentworth and Mary E. Weeks

Florence, d. 1/28/1958 at 68; b. Brookfield

Frank, d. 12/22/1910 at 56/4/3 in Brookfield; manufacturer; widower; b. Brookfield; John Hutchins (Wakefield) and Betsey Lyford (Brookfield)

Frank, d. 11/22/1959 at 57; b. Wolfeboro

John Lyford, d. 11/14/1932 at 36/9/10 in Rochester; lumber operator and surveyor; married; b. Brookfield; Stephen H. Hutchins (Wakefield) and Lizzie A. Wentworth (Wakefield)

Sadie M., d. 5/25/1966 at 62

Stephen, d. 3/6/1929 at 78/6/14 in Brookfield; farmer; married; b. Wakefield; John S. Hutchins (Wakefield) and Betsey Lyford (Brookfield)

Susan A., d. 1/23/1895 at 73/0/4 in Brookfield; housekeeper; single; b. Wakefield; Stephen D. Hutchins (Wakefield) and Nancy P. Sanborn (Wakefield)

INGRAHAM,
William Hector, d. 2/9/1955 at 79 in Brookfield; retired; married; b. Framingham; Henry Ingraham and Catherine Harrison

JACKSON,
Earle W., d. 12/20/1900 at 5/6/12 in Brookfield; burned in dwelling house; b. N. Beverly, MA; Edward L. Jackson and Grace M. Tufft

JAHN,
George H., d. 3/15/2003 in Brookfield

JOACHIM,
Anna Johanna Eleanora, d. 9/21/1980 at 74; b. Germany

JOUBERT,
Clement Francis, d. 11/30/1991 at 72; b. MA

KATWICK,
Peter James, d. 7/31/1963 at 18; b. Brockton, MA

Robert T., Sr., d. 9/11/1972 at 51; b. MA

KEENE,
Wendall P., d. 10/4/1966 at 90; b. Boston, MA

KNIGHT,
Albert P., d. 7/9/1972 at 80; b. PA
Charlotte Ahbe, d. 4/29/1969 at 69; b. MN

KODA,
Philip, d. 11/27/1992 at 83; b. CT

LANDERS,
Charles, d. 10/10/1928 at 50 in Brookfield; merchant; married

LANG,
Almira P., d. 7/25/1976 at 79; b. MA
Caroline A., d. 2/19/1901 at 82/11/16 in Brookfield; paralysis; widow;
    b. Brookfield; Francis Drew and Olive Dearborn
Daniel W., d. 9/4/1905 at 78/5/18 in Brookfield; farmer; widower; b.
    Brookfield; Reuben Lang (Brookfield)
Frank P., d. 7/10/1919 at 34/1/2 in Concord; single; b. Brookfield;
    Frank P. Lang and Ida F. Rankin
Harry L., d. 5/13/1944 at 85/7/24 in Brookfield; farmer; single; b.
    Brookfield; Henry Lang (Portsmouth) and Caroline A. Drew
Henry, d. 4/23/1893 at 77/4/9 in Brookfield; softening of the brain,
    acute complications; farmer; married; b. Portsmouth; Samuel
    Lang and Lydia Thurber
Herbert, d. 4/24/2004 in Wolfeboro
Joanna, d. 5/29/1903 at 82/5/6 in Brookfield; widow; Joseph Drew
    and Bethiah York
John W., d. 11/19/1893 at 78/1/18 in Brookfield; general debility and
    old age; farmer; married; b. Brookfield; Reuben Lang and Mary
    Whitehouse
Lizzie, d. 5/8/1914 at 54/7/20 in Brookfield; housewife; married; b.
    Stoneham, MA; Isaiah Palmer and Mary Baker
Mary A., d. 10/24/1901 at 68/2/28 in Newfield, ME; diabetes;
    married; b. Ossipee; Mark Glidden and Nancy Roles
Mary A., d. 12/9/1903 at 58/2/11 in Brookfield; single; Henry Lang
    and Caroline Drew

Wallace F., d. 4/11/1941 at 52/11 in Wolfeboro; farmer; married; b. Brookfield; John E. Lang (Brookfield) and Lizzie Palmer (Stoneham, MA)

LANGLAIS,
Joseph Remi, d. 3/16/1991 at 67; b. MA

LANKHORST,
Jan, d. 2/14/1991 at 54; b. Holland

LARUE,
Margaret Hansen, d. 3/17/1972 at 82

LEE,
Anne, d. 7/2/1974 at 73
Helen C., d. 2/2/1958 at 59
John H., d. 8/1/1970 at 70; b. MA

LEEPER,
Mary Louise, d. 12/23/1984 at 84; b. CT

LEONARD,
Robert, d. 9/25/2005 in Brookfield

LILLY,
Charles Edwin, d. 11/14/1998 at 80; b. Lynn, MA

LIVELY,
Jennifer, d. 2/26/1986 at 18; b. NH

LORD,
Fred, d. 2/8/1889 at 17/10/1; single; b. Brookfield; John B. Lord (Effingham) and Elvira E. Stevens (Middleton)
John B., d. 5/21/1892 at 44/3 in Brookfield; farmer; married; b. Effingham; Samuel Lord (Effingham) and Marian Boothby (Parsonsfield)

LOVERING,
Plumer G., d. 9/20/1891 at 75/11/18 in Brookfield; farmer; married; b. MA; Jesse Lovering and Polly Taylor (Goffsfield, MA)

Susan A., d. 11/14/1917 at 95/7/12 in Wakefield; widow; b. Wakefield; Joseph Wentworth (Somersworth) and Elizabeth Plummer (Rochester)

LYNCH,
Daniel J., d. 4/3/2002 in Wolfeboro

MACKIE,
Perley Augustus, d. 11/1/1897 at 0/1/21 in Brookfield; loss of vitality; b. Wakefield; Millard Mackie and Ida Eaton

MAGOUN,
Richard, d. 10/20/1979 at 77; b. MA

MALEHAM,
Frank, d. 10/26/1910 at 63/4 in Brookfield; laborer; single; b. Wolfeboro; John Maleham (Wolfeboro) and Jane Key

MANTON,
Frank Stead, d. 9/19/1909 at 71/5/22 in Brookfield; retired; married; b. Providence, RI; Saluro Manton (Providence, RI) and Anstriss Dyer (England)

MANZER,
Arthur Lloyd, d. 2/25/1972 at 60; b. NY
Edna L., d. 12/16/1979 at 65; b. IN

MARCOUE,
Lester Joseph, d. 9/27/1971 at 61; b. MA
Mary A., d. 1/22/1986 at 74; b. MA

MARSH,
Frank M., Sr., d. 7/9/1972 at 85; b. MA

MATLOCK,
Frances S., d. 10/6/1999 at 73; b. Waterloo, NY

MATLOCKE,
George J., d. 7/16/1988 at 68; b. NY

MATTSON,
Jennie Louise, d. 4/26/1983 at 84
Johanne M., d. 10/11/1953 at 79 in Brookfield; housewife; married;
    b. Karleby, Denmark; Morten Hansen and Karen Johansen
M. Godfrey, d. 3/26/1959 at 62; b. Angola, NY
Otto, d. 5/11/1957 at 94; b. Halmstadt, Sweden

MAUSER,
Robert J., d. 3/5/1951 at 29 in Brookfield; invalid; single; b.
Cambridge, MA; George W. Mauser and Florence Scherber

McCAULEY,
Lillian A., d. 1/5/1986 at 70; b. MA

McDONALD,
Robert, d. 9/26/1980 at 75; b. MA
Rose R., d. 2/25/2000

MEAD,
William C., d. 5/18/1982 at 60; b. NJ

MEADE,
Juanice J., d. 8/2/1999 at 69; b. Portland, ME

MEADER,
son, d. 10/1/1908 at 0/0/10 in Brookfield; b. Brookfield; Lyman
    Meader and Meda Hall

MELANSON,
Delose Thomas, d. 5/29/1927 at 53/2/26 in Brookfield; teamster;
    married; b. Manchester; Joseph Melanson (Canada) and Delia
    Groves (Canada)

MEROSKI,
Charlene A., d. 1/29/1995 at 39; b. NH

MILLS,
Clara A., d. 2/12/1918 at 54/4/10 in Brookfield; single; b. Canada;
    John Mills and Sarah Tyler

MIX,
Ella M., d. 11/3/1988 at 98; b. MA

MONAHAN,
John J., d. 6/20/1960 at 67; b. Boston, MA

MORRILL,
Howard Earle, d. 4/25/1934 at 5/8/18 in Brookfield; child; b. E.
    Rochester; Harry W. Morrill (N. Windham, ME) and Phyllis L.
    Grant (Acton, ME)
Miriam Louise, d. 6/25/1936 at 0/0/46 in Brookfield; single; b.
    Brookfield; Harry W. Morrill (N. Windham, ME) and Phyllis L.
    Grant (Acton, ME)

MOULTON,
Herbert, d. 11/30/1947 at 47/1/29 in Brookfield; shoeworker;
    married; b. Acton, ME; Justine Moulton (Farmington) and Edith
    Ham (Farmington)

MOWREY,
Rena C., d. 2/17/1974 at 76; b. MA

MULLER,
Joseph P., d. 12/12/1951 at 65 in Brookfield; signal eng.; married; b.
    Ft. Presidio, CA; Richard Muller and ----- Fleuren

MURRAY,
Arlene, d. 8/3/2005 in Wolfeboro

NASON,
Raymond L., d. 5/23/1997 at 88; b. Sanbornville

NEAL,
Charles H., d. 3/31/1911 at 73/8/3 in Brookfield; farmer; married; b.
    Brookfield; Enoch Neal (Brookfield) and Elizabeth Roles
    (Ossipee)
Charles H., d. 7/19/1930 at 41/9/10 in Brookfield; farmer; married; b.
    Brookfield; Charles H. Neal (Brookfield) and Ida Rankins
    (Lewiston, ME)
Elizabeth E., d. 6/27/1921 at 7/6/20 in Brookfield; student; b.
    Brookfield; Charles Neal and Edna B. Richards

445

Ida F., d. 4/23/1919 at 64/7/23 in Brookfield; retired; widow; b. Lewiston, ME; Abel Rankin and Abbie D. Rankin

NELSON,
Cora A., d. 11/9/1980 at 76
Howard C., d. 12/16/1978 at 67

NICHOLS,
Bertha Alice, d. 6/12/1994 at 75; b. NH
Ernest Charles, d. 6/6/1994 at 84; b. NH

NUTE,
Eli W., d. 8/21/1939 at 74/11/12 in Wolfeboro; retired; married; b. Dover; Hopley Nute (Dover) and Sarah Hayes (Ossipee)
Elvira A., d. 2/15/1940 at 78/7/29 in Brookfield; housekeeper; widow; b. Rollinsford; Amos E. Johnson (Saranac Lake, NY) and Louisa M. Johnson (Saranac Lake, NY)

NUTT,
Lizzie, d. 3/10/1942 at 98/0/2 in Brookfield; housewife; widow; b. Chatham; Orin Edgecomb

PALM,
Carl Henry, Jr., d. 7/2/1966 at 49; b. Portsmouth

PALMER,
Albert Tresnon, d. 8/8/1961 at 59
Bertha W., d. 9/11/1979 at 95; b. NH
Isaiah W., d. 7/25/1899 at 74/1/25; general debility; married; Trueworthy Palmer and Betsy Emerson
Jasper T., d. 5/5/1959 at 76; b. Brookfield
Nathaniel P., d. 8/4/1893 at 0/2/7 in Brookfield; spina bifida; b. Manchester, MA; Aaron B. Palmer and Lyle P. Connell
Robert T., d. 7/5/1986 at 70
Susan T., d. 9/26/1944 at 78/5/22 in Wolfeboro; housewife; widow; b. England; John Tresnon (England) and Margaret Marshall (Everett, MA)

PARKER,
Joseph Edwin, d. 6/1/1960 at 61; b. Kittery, ME

PEARL,

Ellsworth, d. 9/14/1949 at 88/1/2 in Brookfield; retired; widower; b. Derby Line, VT; Gilman Pearl and Nancy Yeldin

Gertrude C., d. 10/8/1948 at 81/5/2 in Wakefield; housewife; married; b. Rochester; John E. Chesley and Elizabeth Horne (Rochester)

PEAVEY,

Abbie F., d. 7/19/1893 at 41/10 in Brookfield; consumption; housekeeper; married; b. Brookfield; Ezekiel Prescott and Alzira Fernald

Albina M., d. 3/18/1920 at 46/11/1 in Brookfield; housewife; married; b. New Germany, NS; Hibbard Robar and Rebecca Whorton

Carrie R., d. 3/1/1911 at 18/4/16 in Brookfield; single; b. Boston, MA; A. May Robar (N. Germany, NS)

George A., d. 5/20/1910 at 60/9/25 in Brookfield; laborer; single; b. Strafford; John Peavey (Strafford) and Mary Caverly (Strafford)

Shirley A., d. 12/23/1916 at 11/10/15 in Brookfield; b. Brookfield; Henry W. Peavey and Albena Robar

PERRY,

William F., d. 3/5/1923 at 0/4/28 in Brookfield; b. Wakefield; Perley D. Perry (Brookfield) and Gladys Fogg (Deerfield)

PETERSON,

Clarence A., d. 2/27/1969 at 69

Maren Hansen, d. 12/31/1955 at 78

Ruth M., d. 6/21/1973 at 71; b. NH

PIKE,

daughter, d. 1/11/1887 at 0/0/13; b. Brookfield; Caleb H. Pike (Ossipee) and Lydia E. Clow (Wolfeboro)

Anna, d. 7/17/1955 at 93 in NH State Hospital; housewife; widow; Thomas Johnson and Mary Webster

Augusta M., d. 12/12/1895 at 78/1/18 in Brookfield; housekeeper; married; b. Wakefield; William Sawyer (Westminster, MA) and Mary Yeaton (Portsmouth)

Elizabeth, d. 2/5/1899 at 82/0/5 in Brookfield; senility and congestion of lungs; widow; Timothy Johnson and Bethiah York

John C., d. 8/11/1923 at 67/2/23 in Brookfield; retired; married; b.
   Brookfield; Robert Pike (Brookfield) and Elizabeth Johnson
   (Brookfield)
John R., d. 8/7/2003 in Wolfeboro
Joseph, d. 2/11/1901 at 88/10/2 in Brookfield; pneumonia; widower;
   b. Brookfield; Robert Pike and Rosanna Hanson
Mary Ellen, d. 12/8/1939 at 86/8/19 in Brookfield; housekeeper;
   divorced; b. Middleton; Ebenezer S. Pike (Middleton) and
   Drusilla Hodge (Brookfield)
Robert H., d. 7/20/1889 at 34/6/4; single; b. Brookfield; Robert Pike
   (Brookfield) and Elizabeth Johnson (Brookfield)

PINKHAM,
Alice-Ann, d. 5/25/2005 in Brookfield

PITMAN,
Nancy H., d. 8/6/1887 at 86/5/22; housekeeper; widow; b. Brookfield

PLUMMER,
Almon R., d. 3/9/1889 at 33/6/16; farmer; single; b. Brookfield;
   Samuel H. Plummer (Wolfeboro) and Jane Rankins
   (Monmouth, ME)
Samuel H., d. 3/30/1915 at 86/3/10 in Brookfield; carpenter;
   widower; b. Brookfield; Reuben Plummer
Thomas E., d. 12/12/1896 at 39/4 in Brookfield; farmer; married; b.
   Brookfield; Samuel M. Plummer and Jane Rankins (Monmouth,
   ME)

PODRASNIK,
Addie E., d. 11/5/1954 at 78 in Brookfield; homemaker; widow; b.
   Chicago, IL; Thomas A. Bowden and Alexine Ferguson
Joseph N., d. 12/23/1940 at 63/2/7 in Portland, ME; retired; married;
   b. Chicago, IL; Alois Podrasnik (Austria) and Anna Klapperick
   (Chicago, IL)

POLLARD,
Addie I., d. 7/20/1948 at 92/8/28 in Brookfield; housewife; widow; b.
   Lincoln; Stephen Russell and Unice Hanson

PORTER,
Frances M., d. 10/12/1986 at 90; b. MA

George W., d. 1/10/1989 at 91; b. ME
Hattie L., d. 1.8/1919 at 36/3/15 in Wakefield; housework; divorced; b. Wakefield; Frank P. Lane and Ida F. Rankin

PRESCOTT,
Ezekiel, d. 4/4/1893 at 85 in Brookfield; old age; farmer; widower

PRINDALL,
John L., d. 4/4/1961 at 87; b. Wolfeboro
M. M., d. 6/27/1948 at 75/1/13 in Brookfield; housewife; married; b. Marblehead, MA; Andrew Knowloud (Marblehead, MA)

PRIZER,
H. A., Jr., d. 6/30/1949 at 57 in Brookfield; retired; married; b. Haddonfield, NJ; Harry A. Prizer and Dolly Mann

PURBY,
Thomas F., d. 12/24/1889 at 18/1; farmer; single; b. Worcester, MA; Michael J. Purby and Mary Gray

QUARNSTROM,
Ralph H., d. 7/19/1990 at 86; b. MA

RACINE,
Cora Mae, d. 10/5/1909 at 0/5/25 in Brookfield; b. Middleton; Cyrus Racine (Hudson, MA) and Mary Brownell (Vanceboro, ME)

REMICK,
Henry J., d. 2/20/1898 at 30/6/22 in Brookfield; phthisis pulmonalis; married; Mark Remick and Ellen S. Young
Mark, d. 9/25/1900 at 62/3/3 in Brookfield; paralysis due to injury; married; James Remick

RHOADES,
Eleanor A., d. 9/19/2003 in Brookfield

RICHARDS,
Keziah F., d. 11/15/1916 at 69/11/1 in Brookfield; housekeeper; widow; b. Newfield, ME; Daniel Quimby and Filene Doe

RICHTER,
Florence W., d. 10/27/1969 at 67; b. CT
Horace F., d. 8/3/1975 at 77; b. NJ

RIDEOUT,
Ida W., d. 10/2/1954 at 82 in Brookfield; none; widow; b. ME;
George F. Whelpley and Elizabeth A. Belyea

RILEY,
David W., II, d. 11/20/1984 at 63; b. MA

RINES,
Elihu M., d. 1/22/1930 at 77/1/17 in Brookfield; farmer; married; b.
New Durham; Charles Rines and Sarah Boston
Emma M., d. 4/16/1917 at 56/7/16 in Brookfield; housewife; married;
b. Middleton; Drake Dearborn and Hannah Whitehouse
Grace N., d. 8/24/1969 at 84; b. NH
Herbert, d. 9/17/1947 at 59/0/21 in Hartford, VT; painter; single; b.
Brookfield; Elihu M. Rines (New Durham) and Emma Dearborn
(Middleton)
Walter, d. 4/28/1973 at 87; b. NH
Zaphina M., d. 5/17/1924 at 71/3/21; b. Middleton; Loren Colbath
and Elmira Willey

ROBBINS,
Vernon E., d. 1/13/2000

ROBERTS,
Noah H., d. 5/31/1917 at 85/3/20 in Brookfield; farmer; married; b.
Rochester; Lon Roberts (Rochester)
Reed T., d. 5/19/1980 at 78; b. IL

ROBINSON,
Judith C., d. 9/19/1899 at 84/7/16; apoplexy; widow; Thomas Cook
and Mary Safford
Rosa, d. 5/31/1921 at 67/11 in Brookfield; housewife; married; b.
Wolfeboro; Ezra Hardy and Eliza Hardy

ROCKWELL,
George H., d. 9/6/1967 at 76
Mary P., d. 1/19/1988 at 84; b. NY

Maude H., d. 11/10/1954 at 93 in Brookline, MA; at home; widow; b. Peru, IN; John H. Helm and Margaret Ridenom

ROSE,
Robert W., d. 8/7/1986 at 65; b. MA

ROSS,
John E., d. 1/31/1918 at 62/1/9 in Brookfield; married
Mary Ann, d. 4/21/1945 at 82/2/19 in Brookfield; housewife; widow; b. Pembroke, ME; William Hillas (England) and Mary A. Croft (England)

ROURKE,
Anne F., d. 9/2/1972 at 88; b. NH

ROYLE,
Josephine B., d. 11/22/1972 at 66; b. Chile
Norman, d. 8/5/2000 at 94; b. Waltham, MA

RUFF,
Helen, d. 10/13/1980 at 53; b. CT

RUSSELL,
Mabel J., d. 8/27/1957 at 84; b. Ashburnham, MA

RYER,
Robert P., d. 1/8/1930 at 73/4/1 in Brookfield; farmer, retired; married; b. Shelbourne, NS; Martin Ryer (NS) and Margaret McKay (Clyde, NS)

SANBORN,
Caroline M., d. 12/6/1935 at 71/6/4 in Wolfeboro; retired; single; b. Brookfield; John W. Sanborn (Brookfield) and Lizzie Buzzell (Brookfield)
Elizabeth A., d. 4/28/1911 at 78/3/20 in Brookfield; housewife; widow; b. Rochester; Joseph Buzzell (Madbury) and Hannah Stoddard (Brookfield)
Harry E., d. 4/16/1901 at 31/10/8 in Brookfield; consumption; married; b. Brookfield; Luther M. Sanborn and Nellie C. Blake

Jonathan W., d. 6/17/1894 at 76/11/5 in Brookfield; farmer; married; b. Brookfield; Ezekiel Sanborn (Brookfield) and Abigail Chamberlain (Brookfield)

Mary, d. 12/25/1936 at 63/6/9 in Wakefield; retired; single; b. Brookfield; John W. Sanborn (Brookfield) and Elizabeth Buzzell (Brookfield)

Mary Jane, d. 11/20/1905 at 51/3/20 in Brookfield; housewife; married; George K. Whitaker (Conway) and Levina Kenniston (Conway)

Nellie C., d. 4/12/1904 at 52/4/16 in Brookfield; housekeeper; married; b. Brookfield; William Blake, Jr. (Brookfield) and Frances P. D. Kelley (Gilmanton)

Truman R., d. 1/17/1894 at 82/10/17 in Brookfield; apoplexy; carpenter; widower; b. Brookfield; Ezekiel Sanborn and Abigail Chamberlain

Walter, d. 1/10/1939 at 74/4/21 in Wolfeboro; miner; single; b. Brookfield; John W. Sanborn (Brookfield) and Lizzie Buzzell (Brookfield)

Walter, d. 10/16/1952 at 78 in Concord; woodsman; single; b. S. Conway; Sylvester Sanborn and Lizzie Edgecomb

SAWYER,

Martin Herber, d. 9/20/1940 at 72/10/17 in Salem, MA; retired; widower; b. Wolfeboro; George W. Sawyer (Portland, ME) and Christie Cate (Brookfield)

Mary A., d. 1/9/1897 at 53/1/13 in Brookfield; housekeeper; divorced; b. Wakefield; William Sawyer, Jr. and Mehitable Yeaton

Mary G., d. 10/13/1959 at 66; b. Concord

SCEGGELL,

Arthur, d. 10/20/1943 at 78/8/3 in Wakefield; carpenter; widower; b. Wolfeboro

Ellen O., d. 4/4/1915 at 43/6/27 in Brookfield; housewife; married; b. Brookfield; Joseph S. Wentworth (Wakefield) and Mary E. Weeks (Brookfield)

SCHULTZ,

Leonard, d. 7/8/2005 in Brookfield

Peter B., d. 7/2/1987 at 90; b. Holland

SCOTT,
Natt Harlan, Rev., d. 7/3/1968 at 75; b. Wolfeboro

SEIBERLICH,
Joseph, d. 6/12/1981 at 84; b. Germany

SEIBERT,
Julien C., d. 9/29/2002 in Wolfeboro

SHAW,
Ruth I., d. 2/25/2003 in Wolfeboro

SHORTRIDGE,
Asa A., d. 8/26/1930 at 72/3/14 in Brookfield; farmer; single; b.
    Wolfeboro; Leonard Shortridge (Wolfeboro) and Mary J.
    Tibbetts (Wolfeboro)
Ella, d. 11/23/1980 at 73; b. NH
Emma F., d. 12/29/1919 at 65/5/1 in Brookfield; married; b. Dover;
    John Clark and Lucinda Gilman
Grace, d. 8/19/1947 at 71/11/1 in Wolfeboro; housewife; married; b.
    Dover; James Stevens (Middleton) and Sarah A. Emery
Leonard, d. 11/24/1892 at 71/8/3 in Brookfield; farmer; married; b.
    Wolfeboro; James N. Shortridge (Brookfield) and Mary Nutt
    (Wolfeboro)
Mary J., d. 3/16/1895 at 71/10 in Brookfield; housekeeper; widow; b.
    Wolfeboro; Ichabod Tibbetts (Wolfeboro) and Anna Nute
    (Wolfeboro)
Mary T., d. 1/3/1888 at 87/0/10; housekeeper; widow; b. Wolfeboro;
    Samuel Nutt (Manchester) and Martha Tibbetts (Brookfield)
Ralph S., d. 5/20/1991 at 86; b. NH
Sylvester, d. 8/20/1924 at 72/0/27; b. Wolfeboro; Leonard Shortridge
    and Mary Tibbetts

SMITH,
Charles Howard, d. 6/3/1957 at 74; b. S. Abington, MA
Franklin W., d. 10/9/1911 at 85/1/25 in Brookfield; retired; married;
    b. Boston, MA; Benjamin Smith (Rowley, MA) and Mary O.
    Lany (Provincetown)
Grant, d. 3/30/1995 at 80; b. VT
Ida, d. 7/10/1903 at 42/2/27 in Brookfield; married; Nathaniel Foss
    and Abagail B. Johnson

Marion Pinkham, d. 3/1/1966 at 80; b. Lynn, MA
Ruhama, d. 5/22/1902 at 73 in Brookfield; cancer of the liver and
    bowels; married; b. Wolfeboro; James Shortridge and Mary
    Nutt
Virginia M., d. 3/20/1984 at 63; b. MA

SOUCY,
Armand J., d. 11/28/1999

SPENCER,
Elizabeth, d. 12/31/1962 at 92; b. Stoneham, MA
George A., d. 1/24/1995 at 80; b. MA
Kathleen R., d. 10/14/1995 at 77; b. Canada

SPILLER,
Jennie, d. 6/22/1944 at 71/11/17 in Brookfield; housewife; divorced

SPINNEY,
William R., d. 6/17/1944 at 71/7/14 in Brookfield; farmer; single;
    Joseph Spinney (Wakefield) and Helen Wentworth (Rochester)

STANTON,
Jacob P., d. 2/2/1887 at 72/7; none; single; b. Brookfield; Jacob
    Stanton (Brookfield) and ----- Fernald (Wolfeboro)

STAPLES,
Nell E., d. 3/11/1905 at 0/6/27 in Brookfield; b. Milton; Isabel Staples

STERLING,
Norman L., d. 11/1/1997 at 81; b. Manchester, CT

STEVENS,
Charles A., d. 7/4/1910 at 64/0/11 in Derry; widower; b. Ossipee;
    James Stevens (Ossipee) and Hannah Small
James M., d. 1/4/1917 at 69/4/10 in Brookfield; belt maker; widower;
    b. Middleton; George Stevens
Priscilla, d. 11/2/1975 at 35; b. Boston, MA

STRASBAUGH,
Susan Marie, d. 5/9/1997 at 51; b. New York, NY

SWETT,
George, d. 9/30/1958 at 77
William, d. 12/22/1914 at 66/1/3 in Brookfield; carpenter; married; b.
   Standish, ME; Burnece P. Swett and Lydia J. Thorn

SYER,
Harriet C., d. 1/3/1987 at 69; b. MA

TAPPAN,
Hannah, d. 2/26/1896 at 89/0/23 in Brookfield; housekeeper; widow;
   b. E. Kingston; Barnard Eastman (Salisbury) and Elizabeth Hoyt
   (Newton)

TARLETON,
Harriet Clifford, d. 6/18/1965 at 82; b. Salem, MA
William W. D., d. 7/13/1966 at 85; b. Gloucester, MA

TASKER,
F. Bruce, d. 5/12/1964 at 37; b. Brighton, MA

ter WEETE,
Carl, d. 11/17/1976 at 73; b. Holland

TEWKSBURY,
Robert L., d. 1/10/1995 at 59; b. RI

THOMES,
Hattie N. Goodhue, d. 5/1/1898 at 28/0/12 in Brookfield;
   consumption; married; Thomas Goodhue and Sarah Witham
Horace L., d. 2/26/1905 at 44/11/18 in Brookfield; farmer; widower;
   b. Denmark, ME; George Thomes (Denmark, ME) and Elvira
   Newcomb (Denmark, ME)
Lawrence G., d. 8/9/1896 at 0/1/4 in Brookfield; b. Brookfield;
   Horace L. Thomes (Denmark, ME) and Hattie M. Goodhue
   (Brookfield)

THOMPSON,
Hugh, d. 1/27/1972 at 69; b. Ireland

THORNE,
Ivan Jerome, d. 4/16/1970 at 70; b. Canada

THORNTON,
Lillian G., d. 6/9/1892 at 1/7/4 in Brookfield; b. Boston, MA; Maggie Thornton (England)

TIBBETTS,
Daniel D., d. 3/10/1889 at 50/6/23; farmer; single; b. Brookfield; John Tibbetts, Jr. (Brookfield) and Nancy Dow (Tuftonboro)
Edward F., d. 10/30/1899 at 65/2/19; apoplexy; married; John Tibbetts and Nancy Dow
Eliza D., d. 10/19/1889 at 64/7/29; housekeeper; single; b. Brookfield; Henry Tibbetts (Brookfield) and Sally Dearborn (Effingham)
James H., d. 4/1/1895 at 64/3/17 in Brookfield; farmer; married; b. Brookfield; Henry Tibbetts (Brookfield) and Sarah Dearborn (Effingham)
Nancy, d. 3/1/1889 at 80/7/6; housekeeper; widow; b. Tuftonboro; Ebenezer Dow (Tuftonboro) and Lydia Drew (Hollis, ME)
Nathan W., d. 4/23/1896 at 63/2/1 in Brookfield; farmer; single; b. Brookfield; John Tibbetts, Jr. (Brookfield) and Nancy Dow (Tuftonboro)

TOBIN,
Margaret Sarah, d. 7/13/1940 at 64/11/7 in Wolfeboro; housekeeper; widow; b. Greenwich, PA; James Grenair (Ireland) and ----- Gilchrist

TOWLE,
Raymond Dudley, d. 8/24/1957 at 71; b. Dover
Ritta Effie, d. 10/30/1968 at 81

TRABER,
Julia V., d. 5/2/1982 at 88; b. NH

TSOUKALAS,
Spyros, d. 11/8/2005 in Brookfield

TUCKER,
James Carroll, d. 7/14/1967 at 75; b. Sanbornville
Morris A., d. 11/10/1976 at 79; b. NH
Thomas R., d. 12/29/2000 at 58; b. Lynn, MA

TULLY,
Carol A., d. 10/4/1999

TURNER,
Mary E., d. 8/4/1904 at 61/3/13 in Brookfield; single; b. Barnstable, England; George Rice Turner (Barnstable, England) and Sally Bulton (Barnstable, England)

TUTT,
Charles H., d. 10/24/1926 at 76/9/18 in Brookfield; retired printer; widower; b. Lynn, MA; Benjamin Tutt (Marblehead) and Mary A. Chase (Newburyport, MA)
Louisa M., d. 11/24/1920 at 67/1/3 in Brookfield; housewife; married; b. Brookfield; James Estes and Louisa Roberts

WALKER,
Arthur Thomas, d. 9/24/1994 at 63; b. MA

WARREN,
Barbara, d. 2/11/1981 at 89; b. NH
George E., d. 9/1/1930 at 69/10 in Brookfield; mechanical engineer; married; b. Exeter
Helen, d. 2/4/1983 at 87; b. RI

WATERHOUSE,
Lilliam E., d. 2/27/1955 at 99 at Homestead; homemaker; widow; Joseph Emerson and Mary Charles

WEEKS,
Anna J., d. 8/3/1897 at 76/8/20 in Brookfield; chronic bronchitis; widow; b. Wakefield; Spencer Wentworth and Lydia Dow
Dolores O., d. 7/19/2003 in Wolfeboro
Elizabeth, d. 4/22/1899 at 80/4/23; la grippe; widow; Nathaniel Sanders and Sarah Chatman
Jennifer, d. 9/24/2002 in Rochester
John S., d. 3/12/1916 at 64/5/18 in Derry; married; b. Brookfield
John W., d. 3/23/1902 at 73/11/23 in Malden, MA; Bright's disease; married
Lyman, d. 12/5/1889 at 24/11/30; pressman; single; b. Brookfield; J. Wesley Weeks (Brookfield) and Nancy Quimby (Wakefield)

Nathan C., d. 8/21/1894 at 76/1/27 in Brookfield; farmer; married; b. Brookfield; John Weeks (Wakefield) and Abigail Colomy (New Durham)

WELCH,

Benjamin F., d. 7/17/1955 at 61 in Brookfield; teamster; married; b. Ossipee; Paul Welch and Sarah Goodwin

Louis, d. 5/6/1968 at 74; b. ME

WENTWORTH,

Ann B., d. 8/9/1891 at 69 in Brookfield; widow; b. Newry, ME; David Smith

David L., d. 9/5/1899 at 71/11/19; valvular disease of heart; married; Edmund Wentworth and Eliza Lang

Joseph S., d. 7/20/1916 at 84/3/5 in Brookfield; farmer; married; b. Wakefield; Edmond Wentworth and Eliza Lang

Lydia M., d. 5/25/1918 at 68/1/12 in Wakefield; housewife; married; b. Milton; John Corson and Levina Ellis

Mary, d. 7/2/1904 at 84/10/25 in Brookfield; housekeeper; widow; b. Wakefield; Mark Wentworth and Mary Locke

Mary E., d. 3/27/1918 at 77/11/17 in Brookfield; housewife; widow; b. Brookfield; William Weeks and Elizabeth Sanders

Myrtle B., d. 4/8/1982 at 99; b. NH

Reginald E., d. 8/6/1994 at 93; b. NH

Sherman, d. 10/4/1912 at 51 in Concord; farmer; single; b. Brookfield; Joseph S. Wentworth and Mary Weeks

W. R., d. 7/20/1949 at 71 in Brookfield; insurance; married; b. NH; J. S. Wentworth and Mary E. Weeks

WEST,

George Everett, d. 5/4/1960 at 76; b. Wakefield

Lillian, d. 2/24/1989 at 81; b. NH

Lillian M., Sr., d. 4/15/1979 at 92; b. NH

WETHEBY,

James, d. 12/13/1904 at 0/4 in Brookfield; James Wetheby and Alice Wetheby

WEYMOUTH,

Sarah, d. 4/15/1910 at 49/8/7 in Brookfield; housewife; married; b. Lewiston, ME; Reuben Brown and Betsey Evans

WHEELER,
Leon C., d. 11/5/1958 at 78
Mae Lizzie, d. 6/19/1961 at 75; b. Effingham

WHELPLEY,
Elizabeth A., d. 5/6/1939 at 95/1/21 in Brookfield; at home; widow; b.
St. John, NB; Solomon Belzea (St. John, NB) and Mary
Whitney (NB)

WHITE,
Edward E., d. 2/6/1987 at 84; b. MA
Iola F., d. 2/24/1987 at 84; b. MA

WHITEHOUSE,
Orinda F., d. 4/17/1887 at 43/7; housekeeper; married; b. Ossipee;
Daniel Berry (Corinth, VT) and Nancy Fall (Ossipee)

WHITTAKER,
Albert E., d. 2/10/1968 at 76; b. MA
Winifred, d. 3/20/1974 at 76; b. NH

WHITTEMORE,
Edwin C., d. 7/19/1983 at 84; b. MA
Georgina Yates, d. 12/7/1993 at 92; b. CT
Jessica Mae, d. 12/29/1982 at 0; stillborn; b. NH

WHITTIER,
Scott W., d. 9/3/1919 at 23/9/3 in Wakefield; farmer; married; b.
Wolfeboro; James N. Whittier and Cora Morgan

WICKBOLDT,
Steven, d. 3/6/1982 at 24; b. NY

WIGGIN,
Frank Herbert, d. 1/1/1975 at 98
George A., d. 7/18/1916 at 78/5 in Brookfield; farmer; married; b.
Durham; Oliver T. Wiggin and Lydia A. Drew
Harry F., d. 7/22/1955 at 76 in Rochester; carpenter; widower; b.
Brookfield; Andrew Wiggin and Amy F. Ordray

Jennie E., d. 10/11/1918 at 28/4/11 in Winchester, MA; housewife; married; b. Roxbury, MA; Axel Peterson and Christina Danielson

John F., d. 5/6/1913 at 73/4/23 in Brookfield; farmer; widower; b. Durham; Oliver T. Wiggin and Lydia J. Drew (Durham)

Lydia J., d. 3/18/1889 at 91/5/5; housekeeper; widow; b. Brookfield; Andrew Drew (Dover) and Joanna Hodgdon (Limerick, ME)

Mary E., d. 4/25/1905 at 19/11/21 in Brookfield; housework; single; b. Brookfield; George A. Wiggin (Durham) and May F. Ordway (Lincoln, ME)

William P., d. 6/17/1975 at 93; b. NH

Winifred R., d. 12/3/1968 at 84; b. MA

WILLAND,

Lydia E., d. 12/22/1902 at 80/3 in Brookfield; old age; widow; Nathan Jenkins and Rose Horn

WILLEY,

C. Tracy, d. 6/22/1966 at 74; b. Brookfield

Charles, d. 10/1/1923 at 64/2/4 in Brookfield; farmer; married; b. Brookfield; James H. Willey (Brookfield) and Elmira Shortridge (Brookfield)

Elmira F., d. 10/10/1921 at 80/9/7 in Brookfield; none; widow; b. Wolfeboro; Leonard Shortridge and Rosella Fernald

Eva D., d. 6/6/1952 at 56 in York, ME; school teacher; married; b. Rochester; Frank Calef and Grace D. Roberts

James H., d. 11/2/1917 at 79/7/13 in Brookfield; farmer; married; b. Brookfield; William Willey (Brookfield) and Susan R. Henderson (Brookfield)

Mattie A., d. 9/11/1945 at 84/0/13 in Brookfield; housewife; widow; b. Acton, ME; James L. Willey (Acton, ME) and Mary Applebee (Milton Mills)

WILSON,

Nella F., d. 10/29/1927 at 72/3/0 in Brookfield; housewife; widow; b. Portsmouth; John H. Ferguson (Portsmouth) and Marie A. L. Pike (Brookfield)

WINSLADE,

Leonard A., d. 7/22/1997 at 89; b. England

WITHAM,
Asa H., d. 5/26/1899 at 82/1/2; apoplexy; married; Obediah Witham
    and Nancy Hanson
Charles H., d. 3/23/1892 at 44/1/18 in Wolfeboro; farmer; married; b.
    Milton; Asa H. Witham (Milton) and Harriet Fellows (Wakefield)
Charlie Asa, d. 5/15/1962 at 83; b. Brookfield
Frank A., d. 4/13/1934 at 52/0/6 in Rochester; retired; single; b.
    Brookfield; Asa Witham (Wakefield) and Betsy J. Bedell (N.
    Berwick, ME)
Mary Elizabeth, d. 1/10/1968 at 77; b. ME

WITTERWELL,
Louise Carolina, d. 3/22/1962 at 84; b. Germany

WOODUS,
John F., d. 6/4/1949 at 83 in Brookfield; farmer - carpenter; widower;
    b. Madbury or Dover; John F. Woodus and Elizabeth Church

WRIGHT,
Wallace, d. 6/4/1947 at 62/3/16 in Brookfield; corp. pres.; married; b.
    Lynn, MA; Frank E. Wright (Lynn, MA) and Alberta Clark (Lynn,
    MA)

WYATT,
Donald Louis, d. 10/13/1995 at 75; b. MT
Katherine Louise, d. 12/22/1990 at 69; b. PA

YOUNG,
Gertrude K., d. 5/22/1961 at 83; b. Boston, MA
Richard Tolman, d. 7/1/1996 at 83; b. ME

UNIDENTIFIED,
baby girl, found dead 6/29/1968

Other books by Richard P. Roberts:

Alton, New Hampshire Vital Records, 1890-1997

Barnstead, New Hampshire Vital Records, 1887-2000

Barrington, New Hampshire Vital Records

Dover, New Hampshire Death Records, 1887-1937

Gilmanton, New Hampshire Vital Records, 1887-2001

Marriage Records of Dover, New Hampshire, 1835-1909

Marriage Records of Dover, New Hampshire, 1910-1937

Milton, New Hampshire Vital Records, 1888-1999

Moultonborough, New Hampshire Vital Records

New Castle, New Hampshire Vital Records, 1891-1997

New Hampshire Name Changes, 1768-1923

New Hampshire Name Changes, 1923-1947

Ossipee, New Hampshire Vital Records, 1887-2001

Rochester, New Hampshire Death Records, 1887-1951

Vital Records of Durham, New Hampshire, 1887-2002

Vital Records of Effingham and Freedom, New Hampshire, 1888-2001

Vital Records of Farmington, New Hampshire, 1887-1938

Vital Records of Lyme and Dorchester, New Hampshire, 1887-2004

Vital Records of New Durham and Middleton, New Hampshire, 1887-1998

Vital Records of North Berwick, Maine, 1892-2002

Vital Records of Orford and Piermont, New Hampshire, 1887-2004

Vital Records of Tamworth and Albany, New Hampshire, 1887-2003

Vital Records of Wakefield, New Hampshire, 1887-1998

Vital Records of Warren, New Hampshire, 1887-2005

Wolfeboro, New Hampshire Vital Records, 1887-1999